MANAGING CASINOS

MANAGING CASINOS

A GUIDE FOR ENTREPRENEURS,

MANAGEMENT PERSONNEL

AND ASPIRING MANAGERS

RUBEN MARTINEZ

BARRICADE BOOKS

New York

Published by Barricade Books Inc.
150 Fifth Avenue
New York, NY 10011

Printed in the United States of America.

Library of Congress Cataloging-in-Publication Data

Martinez, Ruben, 1951–
        Managing casinos: a guide for entrpreneurs, management personnel and aspiring managers / Ruben Martinez.
        p.   cm.
        Includes bibliographical references.
        ISBN 1-56980-045-6 (cloth)
        1. Casinos—United States—Management. I. Title.
        HV6711.M37 1995
        795'.068—dc20   95-31449
                                                             CIP

First printing

CONTENTS

PART II   MANAGEMENT THEORY

PART IV OTHER DEPARTMENTS

PART V GAMING-RELATED SUBJECTS

ACKNOWLEDGMENTS

Above all those who helped me and made contributions to this book, I would like to thank my wife Judi, who stood by me every inch of the way and through every tedious hour. She not only inspired and kept me going, at times she was the only one who was there. She worked just as hard as I did.

I would also like to thank all the many individuals in the different government organizations who helped me with statistical and logistical data. This was greatly helpful.

Finally, I would like to dedicate this book to the memory of my father, who taught me I could do anything I put my mind to. He was always proud of me, as I was of him.

INTRODUCTION

The face and nature of the casino gaming business drastically changed in the 1980s. Almost gone is the image of plush hotel resorts, and *in* is the image of gambling saloons, small slot establishments, card rooms, Indian casinos, and riverboat gambling. It is because of this new wave of gambling that I have decided to revise and update the casino management views expressed in the 1982 version of *Casino Management* by Bill Friedman.

The dramatic growth of casino gambling in the United States and other countries has sent a multitude of investors and would-be entrepreneurs scrambling in search of answers to tough questions that can only be answered by experts in the industry. The problem is that the *so-called* experts have varying opinions on the nature of the business. This has added to the confusion of those who would like to become a part of this fast-building, major-growth industry, with over 200 billion dollars wagered annually in this country.

It is not my intention to provide guidance to these people, but to offer information helpful in decision-making, whether this involves pre-development, development, or operational decisions of a casino. This book will include sources of information for this decision-making process plus a structured view of each casino department. Everything will be presented from the perspective of a manager, who is the catalyst that makes it all happen.

The primary purpose of *Casino Management* is to provide a useful view of the mechanics of a casino operation. Basically whether you are an entrepreneur, an investor, a casino manager or aspire to be one, you need to know how the operation works and how its potential can be maximized.

I will explore the many faces the gaming business has taken throughout the United States and how these differences affect management of the operation. At this writing there are eight states that offer casino gambling. Contrast this with a decade or so ago when Las Vegas and Atlantic City were the only two legal gaming outlets in this country. Each new region has introduced its own color and flavor, and this has made the gaming business a very interesting phenomenon.

In the following pages I will take you on a journey through the different operations to see if there are, in fact, noticeable differences or if these differences are just legal stratagems of interested parties to entice constituents and politicians to promote a lucrative industry. I will also examine a fast-growing business within the gaming industry which is positively related to the main subject of this book, i.e., *casino management companies*, and their by-product, the gaming consultant. Are they the *real thing* or are they charlatans masquerading as experts?

I have divided this book into four parts. One gives an overview of casino operations, management companies, and the evolution of gambling and these institutions. A second examines the different components of management and how they relate to casino gambling. A third describes the functions and operations of the different casino departments. The fourth sums up other gaming-related subjects such as casino mathematics, governmental considerations, the differences in geographical areas, and statistical information that is pertinent to the decision-making process.

PART I

OVERVIEW OF CASINO OPERATIONS

CHAPTER 1

INTRODUCTION TO CASINO ORGANIZATIONS

It used to be very simple. There was Vegas gambling. Period. But then came Atlantic City and the face of casino operations changed. In contrast to the loose, seemingly lawless gaming environment of Las Vegas, which had gradually formalized, Atlantic City brought the concept of strict regulation to its maximum expression. It also brought a new standard to gaming, where plush hotels, restaurants, and facilities were mandatory. These standards forced Las Vegas mega-resorts to get face-lifts.

Then, just when it seemed that the industry had established a new character, savvy Indians on their reservations demanded a piece of the pie.

With the emergence of Indian Gaming, some state governments realized that, if they didn't move quickly, not only would they lose potential tax revenues but they'd also lose the opportunity to improve their failing economies. This philosophy has given rise to what seems poised to be one the biggest industry expansions in United States history. Eight states have approved casino gaming, six states have approved card games, and others are discussing future possibilities.

This gaming expansion has been promoted under different guises such as Low-Limit Gaming, Indian Gaming, Riverboat Gaming, Video Lottery, and Card Rooms. It has prompted discussion on the possibility of implementation in every state. This gaming wave isn't only a national trend. Around the world more and more countries have introduced casino gaming. Will casino gaming continue triumphantly into the twenty-first century? Or will it bottom out, as some analysts predict?

The following topics categorize casino organizations.

LOW-LIMIT CASINOS

The phenomenon of low-limit gaming began in 1989 in Deadwood, South Dakota in the guise of harmless gaming because of the maximum five-dollar bets. In a political move geared to facilitate passage of the gaming bill, state legislators argued this type of gambling could not do financial harm to local residents or, for that matter, anyone else. What they failed to realize, either purposely or not, was that most of the revenues generated in a casino operation come from slot machines of one dollar or less. An example is Colorado, which produced total gross revenues from all gambling sources of $325,685,641 and, of this, in 1994 slot machines accounted for $298,811,102, or 92 percent. In the one-year period ending December 31, 1994, New Jersey had gaming revenues of $3,419,750,000 of which 67 percent came from slots. Nevada had gaming revenues of $7,007,586,000, of which 61.5 percent came from slots. Since slot machines of over $1 get comparatively little action, one must assume that most of that income came from slot machines of $1 or less. So it doesn't take a genius to understand that low-limit gaming isn't without a social risk and that it can generate wealth and a steady stream of income through various sources to the governments.

In effect, had the governments of states offering low-limit-stakes gaming been more realistic and less political, they would have allowed greater limits on the table games and presented a type of gaming that is fairer to patrons and more labor intensive. This would have offered patrons more fun for their money while creating new and better jobs. However, this doesn't necessarily mean more revenues for the state, and that could have had a bearing on these political decisions. Later on in this book I will detail how government and gaming interact and how the different games and wagers affect the purses of the patrons and the revenues of the casinos.

As for low-limit casinos, their success has been evident, although not enjoyed by all those involved. The states, of course, have done well. Deadwood, South Dakota, had collected almost $15 million dollars in tax revenues from gaming alone by January of 1995. That figure doesn't include the related industries that got a solid boost from the gaming industry or the taxes paid by gaming industry employees. Colorado took in over $107 million in gaming tax revenues up until February of 1995. Such figures omit fees separate from the gaming tax. Notable among these are device fees. The state of Colorado charges $150 per gaming device. Central City charges $1,000, Black Hawk charges $800, and Cripple Creek charges $1,200. If we multiply this by the cumulative number of devices as of December of 1994 (32,010), the state of Colorado took in $4,801,500, Central City took in $10,634,000, Black Hawk $8,551,200 and Cripple Creek $12,956,400.

That paints a pretty picture, and such a tax take would be considered excellent for most industries. However, gaming seems to be a quite different phenomenon because, in spite of its apparent success, the state of Colorado then increased taxes on all gaming revenues above one million dollars to 20 percent shortly after it started. One fifth! No wonder casinos in that state fell like flies doused with Raid. It seems obvious that someone was sending a message loud and clear, and trying to choke the goose that lays the golden egg. Colorado changed the tax structure, yet the state still has to go a long way to repair the damage to its gaming industry.

Iowa almost missed the boat when, across the river in Illinois, that state announced plans to promote unlimited gambling on their riverboats. Iowa didn't get the message and two of the five boats that were initially stationed at Bettendorf drifted downstream in search of better scenery and better fishing for dollars. Others threatened to pull out, and would have, if Iowa hadn't finally reacted and amended their gaming law. Unlimited and dockside gaming is now allowed in Iowa.

Other experiments in low-limit gambling have occurred in states like Montana; and Indian Tribes like the Mountain Ute and the Southern Ute in Colorado have also reached Compact agreements with the state. The Indians, of course, didn't have much choice in the matter of limits. The Indian Gaming Act of 1988 forces the Indian tribes to negotiate a Compact with their respective states in order to allow Indian gaming. Although the states are obliged to negotiate in good faith, the truth of the matter is that an unavoidable rivalry exists between the tribes and the states and good faith hardly ever exists in these negotiations.

Another variation of low-limit gaming exists in different states in regard to Indian Gaming. For example, at this writing, Washington State Indians are only allowed $25 maximum bets, some table games, but no slot machines. Arizona Indians are allowed slot machines and bingo, but no table games! It is hard to imagine the rationale behind all these variations, but I'll try to make some sense of them when I go into more detail regarding government regulation.

RIVERBOAT CASINOS

In April of 1991, the *Casino Belle*, the *President* and the *Diamond Lady* set sail or, better said, paddled their way down the Mississippi hoping to recreate and exploit a colorful way of life from our past. People flocked into the tight quarters seeking to relive the glitter of the nineteenth century. Besides, like most gamblers, they wanted a chance at the *big one*. But they didn't find the *big one* because the state made sure the people were *protected*. They were only allowed to buy in for $200 per trip, and they couldn't bet more than $5 a wager. They had to pay to get aboard, and they had to pay high prices for food and drink. (Obviously, you can't blame the casinos for those charges because, somehow, they have to make up the difference for the limited wagers.)

For about a year, limited gaming on the Iowa riverboats prospered. But then the gambling fever spread down the Mississippi and to other rivers where better opportunities were being offered. This was the case in Illinois and Mississippi, where successful gambling operations have succeeded those of Iowa. Louisiana and Missouri have also joined the riverboat states. The Mississippi and other rivers are coming alive and promise to return to some of the splendor they enjoyed in the past century. Riverboat gambling has two different faces. First, there are the free-flowing riverboats that cruise the Mississippi or the Missouri or other nav-

igable rivers where the law allows. These take off on scheduled cruises and afford patrons a true riverboat experience. People can come on deck and enjoy the changing scenery. More than just a gambling spree, they get entertainment that had disappeared until now.

Secondly, there's the barge-type riverboat that is docked all year long. On this boat the customer is going nowhere except maybe broke! The states would be wiser to allow inland gaming, for the barge is as stationary as any other land-based building, with the added advantage (and disadvantage to the state) that if things aren't going well, or the fishing is better in another port, the barge can be towed up or down river and taken to another destination. It's a win-win situation for the operator, a very risky one for the state.

Riverboat gambling can't offer the comfort of Nevada and New Jersey casinos. The space allocation for tables and slots within the boat is limited, making it hard to get around when crowds are peaking. There's no room for fancy showrooms and classy support systems such as pool decks, shops, and banquet rooms. Comfortable rooms and suites are not possible, again robbing the state and its constituents of another good source of income and trade.

Everything considered, however, riverboat gambling does provide a good boost to a state's economy and a great tourist attraction and source of entertainment. As an industry, riverboat gambling is bound to enjoy success, at least for most of what remains of this century.

INDIAN GAMING

On October 17, 1988, Congress approved Public Law 100-497, the Indian Gaming Regulatory Act. This was in response to mounting pressure both from the Indian tribes themselves and the states where Indian gaming was either established, or in the process of being established. Ever since, Indian nations have been trying to find a way to provide a steady and reliable source of income for their tribal members. The economic situation of most tribes has been one of deep need. Poverty is widespread, and social problems such as unemployment and alcoholism plague many of the Reservations. In an effort to combat these problems, Indian nations have looked upon gambling as a divine inspiration and a quick-fix solution to these ills. So far, Indian gaming has provided many tribes with rich profits and has enabled many of their members to escape welfare and unemployment lines. Minnesota offers an example of how this has worked successfully.

However, the road to gaming success has not been a smooth one for the Indian nations. Much friction has existed between Indian tribes trying to exert their sovereign rights and the states trying to establish their government's laws and regulations. These confrontations have ranged from armed opposition in Arizona to a multitude of court and legislative battles, one of which prompted the United States Congress to approve the Gaming Act of 1988, which is still under fire to this day. It will be interesting to see how the appointment of Bruce Babbitt as Secretary of the Interior will affect Indian Affairs in the long run. Babbitt had promised to champion Indian causes, and gaming has been among the most pressing of all their concerns in recent years. Mr. Babbitt and the Congress contend with the inordinate amount of pressure that is being exerted by the Nevada Hotel Association and state governments across the nation. Those entities are concerned by the lack of regulation and taxation on tribal reservations. The state governments are losing millions of dollars in tax revenues because they're unable to tax casinos on tribal lands. They're also afraid they will not be able to stop the infiltration of crime figures into reservation gaming. Although this concern is legitimate, it is a tribal concern as well, and most Indian tribes are being very careful with whom they associate. Also alert to this possibility are the Bureau of Indian Affairs and the Department of the Interior, both of which must approve gaming contracts, directly or indirectly. It is, therefore, unlikely that crime figures will infiltrate Indian gaming, although there have been some isolated incidents in the past.

The Nevada Hotel Association, however, has been forthrightly opposed. The Association spent hundreds of thousands of dollars in campaign contributions and advertising to halt the expansion and proliferation of Indian gaming. Their concern is competition. Indian tribes will be able to purchase or reclaim land in or near major metropolitan areas and erect major resorts that will compete with Nevada casinos and could compete unfairly because of their proximity to the tourist populations that support Nevada. The Indians would have the hometown advantage and would enjoy tax advantages.

GRIND OPERATIONS

The term *grind* is a pejorative used by the gaming industry to refer to operations that make a living milling morsels of cash from what are perceived to be insignificant players. These are the patrons who don't qualify for steep credit lines and can't make substantial cash deposits and wagers. However, the huge success that some *so-called* grind joints have enjoyed has challenged the concept of the insignificance of these minor players. Circus Circus in Las Vegas is an example of what a bountiful resource these *insignificants* can be. Circus Circus is one of the strongest gaming corporations.

Grind in reference to these operations is a misnomer; yet the term does differentiate the mega-resorts such as the Mirage, Caesars Palace, the Hiltons, Tropicana, Bally, and the Atlantic City casinos from other operations that don't have the luxury facilities or the patronage of the high-end players commonly known as *high rollers*. But even then, some of these operations that are forced to market strongly to a lower-end clientele are tagged with the label *grind joint*. Operations such as the Claridge in Atlantic City, the Sands in Las Vegas, the Aladdin, and the downtown casinos on Fremont Street would fall under this category.

So which is the true grind operation? It's hard to tell. Those operations that can't provide hotel accommodations and credit lines would rate this label. Yet such an interpretation would include operations that rarely get the action associated with premium operations and exclude operations such as luxury riverboats and some Indian reservation casinos that cater to both high- and low-end patrons. Still, when casino analysts and operators refer to grind operations, they generally refer to operations that cater to a low-end clientele.

A better idea of what grind used to refer to can be seen mostly in casinos spread throughout Nevada where the main emphasis is on slot machines. Many of these can be found in Downtown Las Vegas, Reno, Railroad Pass, State Line, and in other small towns in Nevada. In the emerging gaming industry they can also be found in all of Colorado and South Dakota and, basically, wherever low limits exist.

MEGA-RESORTS

I said before that there can be a substantial difference between casino operations that offer hotel accommodations and those that are considered mega-resorts, such as the distinction between Circus Circus in Las Vegas and luxury resorts like the Mirage and Caesars Palace. When I use the name Circus Circus, I refer to the parent company and not to the actual facility. This allows me to use as an example the Excalibur hotel which, if size were the only gauge, would qualify as a mega-resort. Actually, depending upon where I drew the line, Circus Circus could qualify also. *Mega*, of course, by definition refers to largeness, to greatness, to powerfulness.

Generally speaking, most industry analysts use the term mega-resort in a large sense. That would be semantically correct since mega usually means one million. However, this conceptualization would pair resorts such as the Mirage and the Las Vegas Hilton with Circus Circus and the Riviera and, possibly, relegate to a lower level a grand resort such as Caesars Palace. To the reader this may seem a misconception of greatness, yet it isn't my intention to belittle operations such as the Circus Circus and the Riviera, which may be great in their own right.

This may be the reason Bill Friedman in *Casino Management* used the term *premium* to refer to the great luxury resorts. Although it would seem a logical choice to make this distinction clear, the term *premium* is rarely used today to refer to any resort. Since the term *mega* is so used, I have decided to apply it to those operations that truly embody all the word is intended to express—casinos that exhibit largeness, greatness in every sense, and powerfulness by their presence and all they represent. Mainly I am speaking of operations such as the Mirage, the Las Vegas Hilton, and the Tropicana, and I will include Caesars Palace even though it has fewer than 1,000 rooms because it makes up for it in facilities, greatness, and power.

The MGM promises to rise to the top of this already exclusive group, and one more operation deserves to be in this company, again, for greatness and power: The Taj Mahal.

It isn't coincidental that these properties would also be considered *premium* operations. Yet there are other operations that qualify as *premium* operations that don't have the grandiose quality that these operations do. As a matter of fact, if I accepted the definition of *premium* operations used by Bill Friedman ($2,500 and up credit line patrons), I would place a large number of resorts into this category. To allow for inflation, I would probably be looking more at $5,000 credit lines. Of course, these are nothing compared to some of the credit lines seen lately at the Mirage, which hover around $5,000,000!

You can find many distinctions in attempts to classify casino operations. Yet categorizing and labeling aren't really functional when you are making managerial decisions. Each situation is unique, and each situation has to be addressed as such. A dissection of the components of a premium operation or a grind operation isn't going to help the manager confronted with the task of managing a hybrid operation. What's critical is targeting a market and building the operation around the target.

INTERNATIONAL GAMING

The move for gaming expansion may seem to be an American phenomenon. It isn't. Casino gaming is spreading through the world. Canada is experimenting with gaming in different provinces and the tribes there are also fighting for the right to start their own industries. Even Russia is setting in motion a gaming industry, as is Bulgaria. There's speculation about Cuba and Mexico, both countries prime candidates for such a move. Argentina and Chile have moved toward privatizing casinos. Panama and Peru are revitalizing their industries. In the Pacific, the Tinian Islands have approved gambling. Brazil approved gambling legislation but at this writing has been unable to enact it. The world is bustling with gambling fever. These are but a few examples of what is happening in terms of growth.

There are serious concerns as to where all this casino development will lead. Las Vegas felt the impact of a downturn in the Japanese market previously, the result of a sluggish economy in Japan. It meant the loss of premium players who accounted for at least a hundred million dollars in annual revenue. What will happen when other areas closer to Japan provide the services these mega-gamblers require? The Orient is full of gambling expansion plans and these can have a serious impact on the American gaming industry because Taiwan, Taipei, and Hong Kong are *high roller* powerhouses.

In the last decade, the American gaming industry has become increasingly tied to trade from the Orient, and a whole infrastructure has been erected to promote this trade so successfully. But, if the international expansion of gaming continues, this profit source will be destroyed.

Though gaming is expanding at an accelerated pace, this expansion may come to a halt because everyone is thinking along the same lines. There are going to be many casinos in Europe, Asia, Africa, Central America, South America, Australia and, of course, North America. This increased competition will force casino management to seek creative and disciplined minds to guide them through mine-infested terrain. In these circumstances, one bad decision can be the very last decision a management team may make. *Sound management principles must be applied in order to succeed in a competitive environment.*

CHAPTER 2

MANAGEMENT COMPANIES

Casino management companies have been around for quite some time now although they have been mainly associated with major operations such as Caesars and Hilton. With the increasing popularity of casino gaming across the United States, new hotel casino management companies have sprung up lately, like the floral display in the desert after strong spring rains. Like the flowers in the desert, too, each variety exhibits its own particularities, some of which can be so diametrically opposed that their effects can be equally diverse.

WHAT THEY ARE AND WHAT THEY DO

A casino management company contracts with the owners to operate the casino. Operational decisions such as hiring and firing are made by the managing company with very little intervention by the owners. In some instances the owners participate in managerial decisions, and this is sometimes a source of conflict. Usually this happens when projections fail to reach goals.

Management changes occur most frequently when the owners contract their own management team, starting with a general manager. This individual then brings in his or her own people to fill key managerial spots. In today's market, the management company does much more than manage everyday operations. With many companies starting from scratch and without experience, casino management companies also function as investment advisers and project developers. Obviously, the chances of an operation succeeding depend on the market in which it will compete.

After the prospective casino's site has been selected, the task of developing the property begins. The casino management or consulting company usually takes an active role from the ground up, since casino design and construction vary from traditional projects. You must have or hire expertise to insure that the building conforms to the needs of a very specific clientele and business. There are unique structural, layout, and design specifications inherent in a casino operation. Paying careful attention to them can make the difference between success and failure.

The casino management team should have experience in dealing with similar projects and can guide the owner in choosing the right development company and negotiating the best possible contract with them.

MAJOR MANAGEMENT COMPANIES AND THEIR STRUCTURE

In recent years major companies have scrambled to be among the first to enter new lucrative markets like Illinois, Connecticut, and Louisiana. Because of the political clout and financial resources required, this has been a race among the casino giants. Even these titans sometimes have had to team up with each other for financial backing in order to do business.

As a rule, casino management companies keep 10 to 40 percent of net revenues for their role as operators and managers. More recently, companies have gone for the more secure percentage of gross revenues. Sometimes, fixed monthly management fees are set in addition to net revenue percentages or as the sole basis of the management fee. For example, Donald Trump charges steep management fees that net him millions of dollars annually. This may have been one of the reasons his properties went bankrupt and why the poor, unsuspecting bondholders were crushed. Of course, this is the exception and not the rule. Management fees are usually much more modest. The more financial risk

the management company assumes, the greater the net revenue percentage it will require. Conversely, if the management company decides to minimize its financial risk by requiring a large fixed payment, then its net revenue percentage will be lower.

It seems fitting that, since management companies are in a gaming business, they are required to gamble on their financial future. Conservative companies, like conservative gamblers, often choose the safer route of a higher fixed payment even though it will cost them a lot of revenue if the operation turns out to be highly successful. On the other hand, aggressive companies can go broke, just like most gamblers do when they shoot for the moon in search of the pot of gold. This truism gives an insight into the behavior of casino management personnel around the world. What may seem irrational to the observer becomes more meaningful when poor gambles by management companies are compared to the aberrant behavior of some casino gamblers who, also, have a lot at stake.

To understand the mechanics of how casino management companies work and how their policies are disseminated, it is important to know how they're structured. Unlike a business person or sales representative, the casino management firm can't rely on marked-up sales items for revenue and cost control. It is subject to chance fluctuations and the financial decisions made at contract signing. It is these influences that motivate management and dictate managerial decisions. These are the forces at play in every casino operation that present a confusing picture to outsiders. One employee may seem careless and unconcerned, while another will seem obsessed and irrationally irritated with losses. To understand this phenomenon, you must first know the chain of command and how it works.

I previously mentioned the upper hierarchy of the management company. Usually, in the casino operation, department heads answer to the general manager or chief executive officer. The casino department itself is highly structured. In ranking order are the vice president, the manager, the assistant manager, various shift managers, their assistants, pit bosses, and floor supervisors and boxpersons. Most customers usually deal only with boxpersons and floor supervisors. Sometimes they see pit bosses. In most corporations, these latter employees don't receive bonuses and stock. The higher an employee is in the company's hierarchy, the greater the probability of participating in some kind of profit-sharing or bonus, and the more precarious the job becomes. This may motivate the profit-sharers to make unreasonable demands on subordinates, who may then fear for their job safety.

LEVELS OF MANAGEMENT

In casino management companies there can be a sole proprietor, different partnerships, or different corporations. The type of entity will determine the structure of management. At the highest level there will be a sole owner, a president or a chairman. As more properties come into play, there's room for more than one president, who in turn must answer to the chairman or owner. All of these, of course, can be the same person. Usually such a high-level executive has little to do with the operation of the casino itself. This level of administration concerns itself with broader goals, long-term projections, image planning, and the general outlook of the business.

From this level, casino operations are closely monitored to insure smooth operation and avoidance of future problems. It is usually where the entrepreneurial spirit lies and where future ventures are planned and examined. This is the final decision level where the proverbial buck ends.

Below this level, casino management truly begins. This is where the property managers reside. At the top of this level is the general manager, who oversees the entire operation. The general manager must coordinate all departments so that their functions compliment each other, much as a watch's synchronized movement is made possible by integrating parts that connect with each other. Although all departments are important to the casino operation, by definition the casino department is of the utmost importance. It is here where most of the revenue is generated and the main reason other departments enjoy greater revenue, so it would seem only fair that salaries and benefits would be greater here. Yet that isn't always the case.

The general manager oversees a series of department heads usually titled vice president or director. Among the most important are vice president of casino operations, vice president of marketing, and vice president of finance. There can exist other vice presidential titles of importance such as a senior executive vice president, but the above three are the most essential.

The vice president of casino operations is, of course, in charge of the casino operation. In many instances, the vice president of casino operations is the casino manager, eliminating the need for an additional large salary. Where both positions are separate, the vice president of casino operations assumes an executive role and is hardly ever seen on the casino floor. That role is mostly of leadership at the upper level, dealing mainly with the right-hand person—the casino manager—and, of course, with the general manager and other upper-level managers. The vice president of casino operations writes reports and makes recommendations, and is usually involved in endless meetings. When special events are held, such as those at major casino resorts, this executive takes on a public relations role, and mingles with and, to a certain extent, entertains highly regarded patrons. That function, although loathed by some, lends variety to an otherwise monotonous job. In some casinos, however, vice presidents distance themselves from the patrons.

The casino manager's position, in most places, is a hands-on job. This individual is in charge of the general operation of all shifts. It is a job that concerns itself with many status reports, which are constantly and closely monitored. Any radical changes in the normal course of operation will generally send the casino manager out onto the casino floor. This could be a patron or patrons enjoying a large winning streak, or it could be the opposite, where great losses are being suffered by patrons. Suspicions of misconduct, illegal activity, etc., will also bring the casino manager onto the casino floor, usually after conferring with shift managers and the surveillance department.

The casino manager has a versatile role including responsibility for long-term projections, development and analysis of programs, personnel status and changes within the casino floor, promotions, demotions, hirings and firings. The casino manager also plays a role in public relations, especially where premium players are involved, and is expected to participate in major promotional activities such as parties, golf tournaments, and sporting events. The casino manager also conducts staff meetings to discuss rules and regulations, special events, operating procedures, and training programs.

Below the casino manager are the field officers or shift managers. These employees are in charge of the casino operations of their respective shifts. Each shift has a shift manager and one or two assistant shift managers. There are also relief shift managers who are in charge of the respective shifts on the off days of the shift managers. These individuals can be a relief shift manager or assistant shift manager on the same shift.

The shift managers are an extension of the casino manager. Their role is to implement the policies of the casino manager or casino operation and to insure that the operation runs smoothly. They make certain those under their supervision are doing their jobs and that patron needs are being met. They also serve a public relations role. Special requests and certain types of complimentaries can only be granted from the shift manager level up. These would include airfare reimbursement, gourmet dinner complimentaries, extensions of credit, cash-back requests, special transportation needs such as helicopters, Lear jets, limousines, room and suite complimentaries, and show complimentaries. In some casinos, if not most, major jackpots and payouts must be authorized by a shift manager.

The assistant shift managers serve the same role as the shift managers, but they're subordinate to the shift managers and must sometimes refer certain special requests to the shift manager. However, they must exercise good judgment here. In the casino business, all individuals are held accountable for their decisions, and there are gray areas for which there are no hard and fast rules. It is precisely these gray areas that account for most of the dismissals and firings and the subsequent need to *pass the buck* at this level of management.

At the next level of middle management is the pit manager or pit boss. This person is in charge of the operation of the respective gambling pits. The gambling pit is usually composed of a cluster of similar games, but it can have an assortment of games sectioned off or roped in together. In Atlantic City and Las Vegas, for example, it is customary to see sections of craps tables or sections of blackjack tables. Sometimes combinations of roulette and blackjack tables along with less popular games such as paigow, big six, red dog, etc., will be seen in the same fashion. The baccarat pit is usually a separate entity on the casino floor, mostly because it is geared toward a special type of clientele.

These game sections or pits are the domain of the pit boss or pit manager. In these sections the pit boss supervises the floor supervisors and the dealers, issues certain types of complimentaries to patrons, maintains a record of customer activity and table activity within the pit, and generates a report at the end of the shift after reconciling the opening inventory, fills, credits, and closing inventory against the cash drop and markers. This is the main role of the pit boss.

At the bottom end of casino management is the floor supervisor or floorperson. This is the person with whom the general public comes into contact when there is conflict or when they have a request they wish granted from the casino. In this role, the floor supervisor is both arbitrator and public relations representative for the casino. In some casinos, the floor supervisor is allowed to issue certain complimentaries such as drinks and parking fees. In others, the authority may include issuance of buffet, coffee shop, and show complimentaries. For the most part, however, the floorperson's authority to issue complimentaries is increasingly rare.

Depending upon the business philosophy of the casino, the main function of the floor supervisor will vary tremendously. In one casino it may be public relations. In another, it may be strict vigilance, which can completely eliminate the public relations role. Somewhere between these philosophical extremes is the right answer.

The slot department falls under the aegis of the casino department although it is a separate entity. However, as a separate entity, it has its own hierarchy of supervision. It begins with the slot manager, who manages the slot operations but for the most part responds directly to the vice president of the casino operation. This person constantly monitors the slot reports, verifies the authenticity of major payouts, looks for unusual variations in operations, examines the efficiency of different programs and promotions, and works on future promotional activities and programs.

Below the slot manager are the slot shift managers. Like their counterparts in table games, these casino officers are in charge of their respective shifts. Depending on the size of the operation there can be assistant shift managers and/or slot supervisors. Although the slot department configuration differs from that of the table games, the slot supervisor carries functions similar to those of the pit bosses and supervisors. The slot supervisor oversees the slot floorpersons, the cashiers, and the change persons. They have to verify major slot payoffs and must sign major jackpot slips.

The next level of slot management is the slot floorperson. Some casinos classify slot floorpersons as senior and junior floorpersons. They're also called slot attendants. Slot floorpersons supervise their assigned area of slot machines, take care of any problems with the machines, insure the safety of their operations, and attend to customer needs. Making hopper fills and paying out jackpots are also their responsibilities.

THE NEW BREED OF MANAGEMENT COMPANIES

With the explosion of casino gambling across the United States has come a new breed of casino management companies. This new group has been the product of a major financial opportunity that has arisen from the expansion of casino gaming. Financially stable entrepreneurs have teamed up to form management companies for which they have hired experienced casino personnel. Some of these have been extremely successful, taking advantage of exploding markets at an opportune time. Others have lagged behind, weighed down by financial difficulties, lack of vision and, in some instances, too much planning.

For the prospective owner of a casino establishment it is important to distinguish between truly qualified and experienced individuals and those who are just presenting a facade of qualifications.

THE FLY BY NIGHT MANAGEMENT TEAM

The pejorative term *fly by night* refers not only to management companies, but also to the management teams that are put together by individuals to manage specific casino operations. *Fly by night* is actually quite appropriate for casino operations where management teams come and go with astonishing regularity. And if it weren't for contractual obligations, they would be moving even faster. In the first two years of operation, the Claridge in Atlantic City went through six casino managers. From 1989 to 1991 the Dunes in Las Vegas turned over six casino managers. Some places experience an even faster turnover.

The question here is *Why?* It's not an easy question to answer but the term *fly by night* in reference to the qualifications of some of the individuals and companies that are put in these positions has something to

do with it. To do justice to those individuals who are wrongly dismissed, I must say that a lack of qualifications isn't always the reason management changes occur. In fact, many management changes occur regardless of the individual's or the group's qualifications. Part of the problem seems to be that the gaming business is still a mystery to most people, including company owners and corporations. Lack of true gaming knowledge is commonplace on the part of the owners and of those individuals and groups who pretend to be highly qualified in these matters.

The problem here stems from a tradition of equating experience and connections with gaming knowledge or, better yet, gaming administration knowledge. It also stems from the concept that there's nothing new in gaming and that what worked for the old-school mentality still works today. Not true. The gaming world has been constantly evolving and becoming more and more sophisticated. Computers are now an integral part of gaming, and information systems have become more and more complex, requiring lots of study and updating. I believe that when the giant wave of gaming settles and the gaming waters level, those individuals and companies that have done their homework and have kept up to date will rise in the gaming world, and those that have not will be weeded out.

MANAGERS: ARE THEY THE KEY TO SUCCESS?

Casino managers carry a great responsibility on their shoulders. They're held responsible and accountable for the success of a casino operation. Whether this is a fair judgment must be answered in light of the total concept of casino gaming. Gaming is riddled with inconsistencies and fluctuations. Is the casino manager going to be made responsible for these occurrences? Can the casino manager predict them and make workable plans in spite of them? Is there a right way of managing a casino and a wrong way? If the casino has a losing week, month, or year, is it the casino manager's fault? These and many other appropriate questions need to be addressed not only by owners and scholars, but by those of us who must determine what really is *casino management*.

For now, it is important to realize that casino managers are not the only variable responsible for the success of a casino operation. However, they're an important part of that equation. Equally important are the owner's foresight, financial and emotional commitment, long-term goals, and a well-conceived plan. If all these things are put together appropriately, the casino operation can withstand any inconsistency and fluctuation in the gaming environment. If owners have done their parts to insure success, then it is easy to evaluate performances of casino managers, who are integral to the equation for success.

Casino managers are important because they're responsible for putting together and maintaining the parts of the gaming machinery that insure production. Their job begins with the selection of key personnel to faithfully carry out the game plan and the mandates. Although not always involved in the selection of all casino personnel, casino managers are responsible for these selections and must make sure they will accomplish the tasks set forth in the game plan.

The casino manager is also responsible for issuing clear mandates inspired by a well-defined business philosophy. If that manager is unable to communicate with clarity, the system falls apart, and chance rules the operation. The casino manager can be the key to success, yet not necessarily the only one.

IS THE MANAGER EXPECTED TO BE AN ENTREPRENEUR?

The casino manager, as an employee, isn't expected to be an entrepreneur although this person may be required to evaluate certain entrepreneurial prospects. This function may be expanded to the point where a clear definition of an entrepreneur is pushed into a gray area. For example, when the owner empowers the casino manager to search for other gaming opportunities, to evaluate other gaming environments, and to design improvement and expansion projects, the casino manager can then be considered, to a certain extent, an entrepreneur.

In today's evolving gaming market, more casino managers are being asked to take on the perilous and complicated task of being an entrepreneur. A lot of experience, knowledge, and research must serve this function. Any manager taking on that task should be well aware of this, especially when the blame for an unsuccessful venture will likely fall into that manager's lap. The fact that nine out of ten businesses fail in this country indicates that the job of the entrepreneur is among the most difficult. This enterprise should not be entered upon without an intricate plan and the necessary resources to accomplish the job.

The casino management firm, as manager, is a different matter altogether. By definition the firm is a business, which is an entrepreneurial venture. In this instance, the casino management firm is an entrepreneur for itself and serves many entrepreneurial functions for its clients, the owners of casino properties.

COMMON FACTORS IN CASINO MANAGEMENT ORGANIZATIONS

Although the business philosophies of casino management organizations may vary tremendously, they do share common areas. These common areas help explain why management companies exist and why it is necessary to have someone coordinate all these factors. When evaluating common characteristics, one of the first factors to remember is *resources*. These resources may include people (employees), necessary capital or funding, equipment and materials, and information. Of course, the major resource in a service business such as the gaming industry is people. Without people the materials can't be used, the equipment can't be operated, the information can't be disseminated, and the capital can't be obtained.

Another factor common to all casino management firms is the *environment*. We must remember that environment includes economic conditions, social attitudes and values, politics, government regulations, international events, natural resources, climate, customers, employees, the competition, etc. Whether we like it or not we are all dependent upon the environment. We must all establish a relationship with the outside world, which is ever changing and beyond our control. We can make predictions, we can respond effectively to changes in the environment, but we can't control it. Caesars Palace had no control over Steve Wynn's decision to place the Mirage next to it and entice a large number of its premium customers. Casinos in Colorado were powerless to prevent the state from raising the cap on gaming taxes from 12 to 20 percent. The riverboat casinos in Iowa were powerless to stop Illinois from allowing their riverboats to have unlimited gambling. These are just a few examples of how dependent all casinos and casino management firms are on the environment that surrounds them.

Another area of commonness among management firms is the *horizontal division of labor*. If the same person had to deal the cards, make out the markers, issue the comps, do the accounting, and get the fills and put them on the tables, few hands would be dealt. Perhaps a better example of horizontal division of labor is seen on the crap table. If every game had a stick-person who had to call the dice, retrieve them, collect and make the payouts on the layout, then return and collect the center bets and pay them, the game would not move along. But as the labor is divided into specialized and meaningful jobs, patrons are serviced faster and have a more enjoyable time.

In contrast to the horizontal division of labor is the vertical division of labor. The vertical division of labor is the coordination of tasks, the essence of what managing is. If everyone performed a task in the casino like dealing, writing markers, fills, and credits and no one coordinated these tasks so that they became interrelated, the tables would soon empty out and the games would be over. In order to keep the games going and to keep the casino open, someone must define and coordinate the tasks. It then becomes evident that there are two inherent forms of division of labor: one that performs the tasks and one that coordinates the tasks.

All casinos and casino management companies must be divided into smaller operating units to increase effectiveness. These are the departments. In the casino you have the finance department, the food and beverage department, the hotel department (if it is a hotel casino), the security department, the surveillance department, the marketing department, the entertainment department, and the table games and slot department. These are all sub-units of the whole operation, although in some, two or more departments may be integrated due to the size of the operation. Sub-units within the sub-units may also exist, as seen on the casino floor where craps, blackjack, roulette, and baccarat are usually considered separate departments or sections. Although these subdivisions may be considered separate organizations, they're consciously coordinated toward the common objectives of the casino operation itself.

Finally, *the need for management* is common to all casino management firms and casinos in general. If employees were constantly taking orders from different persons without a clear understanding of who was in charge, chaos would reign and the employees would find it very hard to perform their tasks effectively. Customers would also be confused, unable to remember what rules and regulations applied when. To avoid this, casinos must appoint a manager to direct all employees and clearly define what the tasks will entail.

SUCCESSFUL MANAGING

The Elements of Success

How to evaluate or measure success in managing is sometimes difficult to determine without a clear understanding of what successful management entails. When a casino organization or a casino management firm is formed, it establishes goals. The *establishment of goals* is the main element of success. The firm's goals may differ from those of the entity it represents. A duality of goals that may conflict then exists. To measure success in this instance requires specificity.

For example, let's assume that the goal of a casino management firm is to generate a million dollars in revenue for itself. It contracts with a property owner to manage the casino for 30 percent of the net revenue. The casino in question generates four million dollars in net revenue, producing $1,200,000 in revenue for the management firm and $2,800,000 for the owner. In appearance this has been a successful venture. However, the owner, who was counting on $20,000,000 (which would make at least 10 percent on the $200,000,000 investment), was lucky to break 1 percent. Was this managerial approach successful? Yes and no. It was successful for the management firm that surpassed its revenue goals, but it wasn't successful from the operation's point of view because it failed to meet the owner's goals. Part of the problem is that there are all types of contractual agreements, and sometimes expectations and goals are unrealistic and impossible to meet although the results may be viewed as successful by a detached analyst. Yet, as a rule, a successful managerial approach is one that achieves the goals it sets out to meet.

Other elements of success are *effectiveness* and *efficiency*. Peter Drucker, an expert in managerial affairs, says that effectiveness is *doing the right things* and efficiency is *doing things right*. Traditionally, successful companies have done the right thing by meeting needs in the environment. The Excalibur did the right thing by developing a resort that was both inexpensive and entertaining. The Mirage did the right thing by developing a resort that was both attractive and entertaining. The Taj Mahal did the right thing by developing a resort that is luxurious and grandiose, yet didn't do things right when it underestimated the impact of operational costs. This proves a very important point: In order to succeed, effectiveness and efficiency are equally important. This is the difference between the Taj Mahal and the Mirage and the Excalibur. The latter resorts were well aware of their bottom line, and because of it they have been very profitable.

Another important aspect of success is *productivity*. Generally speaking, the more efficient an organization is, the higher its productivity will be. Different indicators in gaming determine productivity: gross revenue, net revenue, total win figure, total drop figure, and the hold figure. Gross revenues are a good indicator of effectiveness but not necessarily efficiency. Total net revenue is usually a good indicator of efficiency and productivity because operating costs have been deducted and profits can be compared to investment. However, when evaluating managerial efficiency, it is questionable whether a management company that produces more income and retains a larger percentage of the action in a casino is being more efficient than a management company that produces less and retains a smaller percentage, just because the latter happens to be faced with insurmountable odds.

That brings us to the inner workings of casino revenue, which are *the drop, the win* and *the hold*. The drop is the amount of money that is deposited in the *drop boxes* in the casino tables or that flows down to the drop buckets in the slot machines. In one case it is the total cash out of the customer's pocket, in the other it's the overflow of coins and tokens the customer puts into the machine after the drop level of the hopper has been filled. Assuming that all machines are full when played, the coins the customer puts in will be diverted to the drop bucket. The money deposited into bill validators would also be considered drop.

The drop can be misleading as a measure of efficiency and productivity. Casino programs and special events are sometimes measured for efficiency by this concept and casino personnel are blamed when a program turns out to be unprofitable in spite of a large drop. The fault usually lies in the program itself, which attracts customers who have been coached to inflate

drop in an effort to make themselves, junket representatives, and casino hosts look better than they really are. Basically, what is being done is money recycling. The customers repetitively purchase chips and cash them out shortly after. This is called *false drop* and is one of the reasons drop figures are not always a good indication of productivity and efficiency. The same hold true for excessive markers or markers which exceed what would be appropriate according to the player's action.

The *win* figure is probably one of the best indicators of efficiency and productivity. A large win figure, such as that seen at the MGM, Caesars, and the Mirage, leaves no doubt that something was done right. But since drop and win are interrelated, do we still assume that the organization was efficient if it only retained a small percentage of the drop? Is another organization more efficient if it retained a much higher percentage of the drop? Is the small percentage retained the price we have to pay to obtain this otherwise unattainable heavy win? These are questions that are difficult to answer and the main reason some inefficient managers and management groups survive in this business. Events that are ruled by probability by definition are not going to be accurate.

Efficiency in casino management can only be measured by a thorough analysis of all systems. This analysis should measure consistency and congruency with the owner's business philosophy and should be equal in all departments. In gaming, this is the only thing that can be measured objectively.

In general terms, *productivity and efficiency* are going to be determined by income because that is the bottom line of any business venture. And it will be up to the manager to decide on productivity objectives, methods to achieve these objectives, and incentives to motivate workers to improve their productivity.

Another element of success is *implementation*. Managerial decisions can only be as far reaching as the actions that follow them. In other words, a manager can have a clear understanding of what has to be done to make things happen, yet if this mandate isn't implemented, nothing will happen. So a successful decision is one that is implemented, and implemented the way it was intended. This conversion of idea into action must be done effectively and efficiently. In the casino environment, this isn't a simple task. Knowing how to develop a successful operation and getting the job done are skills a manager must master.

The first thing is to understand how complex casinos are. There are many departments that move independently and usually don't communicate very well with each other. Researchers who have studied complex systems like this have devised general processes to aid managers in planning, organizing, motivating, controlling, communicating and making decisions. After studying the general environment and methodology, managers have to study their particular situations to see what similarities and differences exist between their operations and research findings. That is called the situational approach. These situational variables fall into two categories: *internal* and *external variables*.

Internal variables are those that are contained within the organization itself. Among them are the company's objectives, the resources it possesses, its size, the way the tasks are distributed, and the way it uses its resources and people. Because these are internal, they're under the manager's control. In most instances, these variables are the result of the manager's decisions on how the company should operate and who should carry out what function. These decisions will determine how effective and efficient the company is going to be in regard to the competition. However, in the complex world of gaming, company objectives may be defined by the owners and become something the management team has to live up to rather than something it proposes. In this instance, as I mentioned earlier, management objectives and company objectives may be in conflict.

The *determination of key resources* is another element of successful management. For management to fulfill company objectives, it must determine what its key resources are. For example, when the Mirage Hotel opened on the Las Vegas Strip, it managed to attract a great number of premium players from other local operations because it understood that the key resource of these operations was key employees with a large premium customer base. The Mirage acquired these key employees, motivated them with incentive programs, and provided an attractive environment for their customer base. Subsequently, revenues declined somewhat at the Mirage, and Caesars regained most of the ground it had lost because Caesars understood that its key resource was its employees. By treating its employees and customers well, Caesars gradually won back its old customers.

Contrary to the internal environment where managers can exercise control, the external environment can present even the best of managers with insurmountable obstacles beyond their control. All managers can do in this instance is try to predict and react quickly when unexpected changes in the external environment occur. Examples of major external variables are: added competition, technological breakthroughs, social changes, economic changes, and government regulation. In order to succeed, management must be aware of its external environment, respond appropriately to any changes, and realize that changes in the environment, which affect everyone differently, must be approached differently. What works in one instance isn't necessarily going to work in another. In this respect, the manager must be a leader and not a follower.

When Masao Nangaku bought the Dunes Hotel & Country Club in 1988 he thought he could benefit, as other operators have, by leasing the casino. He leased it to Dennis Gomes and quickly found out that he had underestimated his mortgage payments and expenses and wasn't doing as well as he expected. Noting Gomes's success, he had thought he could achieve the same by appointing his own management team to operate the casino. What he failed to realize was that success for Gomes resulted from his connections and from inflated credit lines that drew the high-level action. This is a dangerous strategy that can be very successful but can also backfire, as Gomes later found out at the Golden Nugget. However, it had nothing to do with what happened to Nangaku, who seemed to think that what works for one will work for the other—an assumption that may have driven the historic Dunes to extinction.

The Integrated Approach

I have identified casino management success and pointed out certain elements of it. However, this knowledge alone isn't going to let you know what decisions will help you achieve the goals you have set. The fact is that all the managerial functions are interrelated, and a decision that affects one will affect the others. So when visualizing the operation and its particular situations, you must look at the whole rather than its parts.

The management process is begun by establishing and implementing a set of internal variables, which is basically the company. These variables, added to the external environment, will give the manager the needed framework to begin the planning process. During this stage, management determines what the company's objectives will be and how they will be best served based on a conscientious appraisal of what the market demands are at the time and what the external conditions are. The planning process is then followed by an organizational process which develops and defines tasks and the departments that will handle them. Among other things, this process will consider the size of the operation, the number, size, and quality of the available equipment and information sources, and the qualifications and composition of the available human resources.

Once the operation has been planned and organized, the manager must implement the motivational process, which allows for influencing people to work productively to attain company objectives. This is a very important process that few companies handle well. Nationwide surveys have verified that many people are not satisfied with their employment. In the gaming business, which has a very high turnover rate, this is even more evident.

Finally, the controlling process will tell managers if their approach has allowed them to carry out their plans. If so, it would mean they have met the needs of their market. If this has been done, the manager is successful.

Because of internal and external variables constantly interacting and changing, the manager will never be certain that any decision made or any given method employed was, in fact, the *right one* until success is evident. Circus Circus Corporation has consistently catered to the masses or low-end gamblers and has been successful in doing so. Caesars, the Mirage, and the Hilton have catered more to the high-end gamblers and have been successful in doing so. These are examples of two radically different approaches, yet both of them proved to be successful. But there are many other casino operations that employed one or the other of these strategies and failed.

Changes in the environment require managerial decisions that, similarly, have no predetermined right answer, yet will be judged by their results. Possibly in anticipation of difficulties with the Asian markets, some Las Vegas casinos shifted gears to attract families and tourists. The Mirage developed Treasure Island, Circus Circus developed an indoor water recreation facility, and the MGM spent an astronomical amount of money to develop a resort that is both casino and amusement park. Only time will tell if these moves are successful. In this context, they would prove to be the right decision. However, there are too many variables involved to ascribe success to a singular concept.

In dealing with the above limitation, a manager must think in terms of decisions that carry positive or negative consequences. It would be nice if you could always hire the best people possible, have the best resources at your disposition, and have luck on your side. But it doesn't happen that way and, because you have to deal with the limitations before you, management becomes a balancing act. You must make sacrifices in order to compensate for deficiencies that are inherent in all operations. Because you are forced to hire individuals of whom you know very little, you must realize that some of them are going to be inefficient. This is one of the reasons the turnover rate is so high in the gaming business. Yet you know this, so you must develop a strategy to use this resource as effectively as possible. You must develop standardized procedures that simplify tasks and allow for easier supervision. You must also develop training programs and provide incentives for productive behavior. By implementing strategies such as these, you turn the balance of positive consequences so that they outweigh the negative ones.

The main thing to keep in mind is that, as a manager, you must be able to recognize what the major tradeoffs are by visualizing things as a whole and by implementing an integrated approach. By keeping in view the company's objectives and the particular circumstances of its situation, you can achieve success by managing according to them.

CHAPTER 3

THE EVOLUTION OF CASINO GAMBLING AND MANAGEMENT

HISTORICAL OVERVIEW OF CASINO GAMBLING

No one really knows when gambling began. Even before Christ, bones were thrown to predict events. Bones became the first source of dice, and they're still referred to by that nickname. *"Pass me the bones"* is a common expression in the game of craps. Roman soldiers were shooting dice as Jesus Christ was nailed to the cross. Spaniards were shooting dice as they collected the riches from the New World. However, it wasn't until the early 1800s in New Orleans that Black Americans simplified the playing rules of the English game of hazzard, which the French sometimes called craps, and made it into a totally different game, which was later referred to as private craps.

Baccarat, which was first called *baccara,* meaning zero, was first played in Italy in 1490 during the reign of Charles VIII. It quickly became Europe's favorite gambling pastime, especially among France's nobility. Around the year 1500, baccarat began in France, the country that eventually took the game to its peak in popularity. Two variations of the game that developed in France—*baccarat en banque* and *chemin de fer*—are the most popular in Europe today.

The game of blackjack may have originated in sixteenth-century Spain. The earliest reference to the Spanish game one and thirty is made in the *Comical History of Rinconete and Cortadillo* (1570). The translation of the game, as referenced in John Scarne's *Guide to Casino Gambling*, may be incorrect since a private game called thirty-one still exists in Spanish-speaking countries. The object of the game is to get as close to thirty-one as possible without going over, much in the same way as blackjack with the count of twenty-one. In any event, the Spanish claim responsibility for the origin of the game, as do the Italians because of their game *baccara* and seven and a half.

Scarne believed that the Italians had greater merit to their claim since seven and a half is a draw game where going over seven and a half produces a losing or *bust* hand. The French claim blackjack has its origin in vingt-un and trente et quarante. In Crockford's, a London casino dating back to 1827, such personalities as the Duke of Wellington, the Marquis of Queensberry, Talleyrand, and Prince Esterhazy played a game called quinze. The objective of this game was to reach a count of fifteen.

Regardless of blackjack's origin, in 1875 the *American Hoyle* called blackjack vingt-un, *Foster's Hoyle* called it vingt-et-un, the English called it Van John and the Australians called it pontoon, yet they all played it the same way. The objective of the game was to reach the count of twenty-one. It wasn't until 1910 that twenty-one, as it was first called, was introduced as a banking game in the United States at Evansville, Indiana. The game became popular so quickly that it replaced the game of baccarat in the United States.

The name blackjack came from a bonus payoff that no longer exists today. In the course of playing twenty-one, if the player held an ace of spades and a jack of spades or clubs on the first two cards, he received a bonus of five dollars for every fifty cents wagered in addition to a three to two payoff. Shortly after this bonus was introduced, players of twenty-one began to differentiate two card twenty-one from three or more card twenty-one by calling it *blackjack*.

Gambling in the United States preceded the European explorers who introduced the European games of chance. American Indians were avid gamblers, although their games of chance apparently have not survived the test of time. As early as 1624 the Virginia Assembly passed a law that discouraged ministers from excessive drinking and playing dice, cards, or any other unlawful game. This seems to indicate that there was already some type of casino activity shortly after the *Mayflower* landed.

In 1674, Charles Cotton in his *Complete Gamester* stated that the most popular game in England at the time was hazzard, the precursor of modern craps. English casinos from the seventeenth to the nineteenth century featured the games of hazzard, faro, macao, quinze, trente et quarante, and rouge et noir. During the same period French casinos fancied roulette and trente et un, since baccarat was mainly a noble pastime. The English nobility were the members of White and Brooks' in the eighteenth century and of Crockford's in the nineteenth century.

The first luxuriously decorated casino in the United States appeared in New Orleans in 1827. John Davis, the owner of the Theatre d'Orleans, built the casino and imported all furnishings and gambling tables from Europe. He is also credited with introducing the complimentary meal, offering a buffet supper at his casino. Just like Las Vegas casinos, Davis's casino was open twenty-four hours a day and was frequented by the wealthy plantation owners of Louisiana. In 1835, he closed his casino down and returned to the theater business after the Louisiana legislature passed a law making the operation of a gaming establishment a felony. By that time, Davis had already set the precedent for other operators to establish lavishly decorated casinos such as the Palace of Fortune that Edward Pendleton founded in Washington, D.C., in 1832, where certain legislators, cabinet members, federal officials and the President himself, became regular visitors. Pendleton operated the casino until his death in 1858. Now, a century and a half later, the Louisiana legislature has reopened the door to gambling.

By the mid-1800s gambling was rampant across the United States. Mining towns became prime locations because of the availability of gold, and riverboats flourished on the Mississippi, attracting card cheats and amateurs alike. Faro was the game of choice back then, yet it failed the test of time. It is a game that was so advantageous to the house that it gave the public little chance to win.

After the closing of the Palace of Fortune, a casino that would become legendary opened its doors. It all began when Prince Charles of Monaco, desperate for funds for his ailing principality, issued a gambling concession to a French combine. However, residents of Monaco were not allowed to gamble and, after various ownerships, the casino was about to fail when Francois Blanc, a convicted stock con artist who owned a gambling concession in Homburg, Bavaria, purchased the ailing casino for 1.7 million francs.

Blanc spent millions of dollars in renovations and turned the casino into a showplace that attracted many people from Nice (only a short distance away). In 1870, when his Homburg casino closed, Blanc transferred his headquarters to Monte Carlo and eventually invested all of his fortune in the operation, plus a steady stream of borrowed funds. Under Blanc's personal management, the Monte Carlo casino flourished so tremendously that by the time of his death in 1877, he had accumulated a fortune of two hundred million francs. The Blanc family turned this Monte Carlo casino into the most famous casino in the world and in history.

Many people believe Bugsy Siegel is the most renowned casino operator in American history. To a certain extent, that statement is true. But of all American operators, the name that stands out is Richard Canfield. His enterprises in New York City and Saratoga were renowned from 1890 to 1905. Most of his clientele were distinguished personalities, unequaled in any other part of the country. He operated three famous casinos: the Madison Square Club, Number Five East Forty-Fourth Street, and the Saratoga Club House (operated only during the racing season).

After its inception around the year 1800, the game of private craps moved up and beyond the Mississippi in steamboats, river wharfs, cotton fields, and saloons. Then in 1890 it was introduced in casinos in the form of bank craps. Its development was slow because of the one-way action, but in 1907 John H. Winn, a dice-maker from New York, booked the first crap game with two-way action. He allowed players to bet for or against him and charged them a 5 percent commission. Winn began to make a lot of money with his new style of gambling, and players began to realize how strong the 5 percent commission really was. It was this strength that coined the name *vigorish,* from the word *vigor*, that is still used today to refer to all commissions on casino games.

Around 1915, two games new to the casino circuit made their debut. One was fading craps and the other was blackjack. In fading craps, players could wager among themselves and bet with the bank, a practice that isn't allowed in regulated modern-day casinos. A couple of years later a variation of fading craps was introduced called bank craps. In this game all bets had to be made against the bank. Although unpopular at first, it later replaced faro as the main casino game.

Faro continued to lose popularity as more games, with much better odds, began to appear in the gaming panorama. In fact, more games were established early in the twentieth century than at any other time in American history. Games such as blackjack, chuck-a-luck, under and over seven, slot machines, bank craps, money craps, klondike, and keno were all introduced then. Some of these games offered such a distinct advantage over their predecessors that gaming began to flourish enormously during this period. It was the prelude to the casino explosion and large, organized casino operations.

Nevada gambling became legal in 1931 even though gambling had existed there long before. Its growth through Depression years was slow and did not compare to the luxurious illegal casinos that existed on the East Coast. But after Christmas of 1946, Bugsy Siegel opened the first luxurious casino in Nevada. His Flamingo on the Las Vegas Strip marked the beginning of a different concept in gaming. The idea was that a luxurious entertainment center in the middle of the desert would hold a captive audience. Where else could these high-end players go in this desert town?

Siegel didn't live to see his idea work, but his death may have contributed to the fulfillment of his prophecy that Las Vegas would become a gambling mecca. Three years after his death, the Las Vegas Strip began a frenzied development that hasn't stopped to this day. Now, Circus Circus has developed its Luxor casino, Mirage Resorts has developed Treasure Island, and MGM has developed the largest hotel resort in the world. These developments have certified what everybody already knew, that Las Vegas is the gambling capital of the world.

The next occurrence of legalized gambling in the United States took place outside of the North American continent in the Commonwealth of Puerto Rico in 1948. Since then, gambling has become a major tourist attraction there. From its inception, Puerto Rican gambling has been a model for government regulation and supervision. Many of the regulations effected in Atlantic City were inspired by Puerto Rico's strict supervision of its gambling. A trained government inspector is assigned to every casino from the beginning to the end of the operation. All gaming equipment is methodically checked by the gaming inspectors to ensure fairness to all concerned.

In 1973, the government of Puerto Rico followed the lead of the Panamanian and pre-Castro Cuban government and became a slot operator. Sixty percent of the revenues produced by the slot machines of Puerto Rico goes to the government, which in turn uses the money to support the University of Puerto Rico and other social programs. The hold percentage on these slot machines is an exorbitant 13 percent, yet the government figures that, if it has to live with a socially disruptive practice, it might as well fund social programs with it.

In 1976 by a majority vote of three-to-two, the state of New Jersey approved casino gambling in Atlantic City. Inspired in part by Puerto Rico gaming regulations that required the gambling establishment to provide a certain number of hotel rooms and facilities, New Jersey legislation required that casino operators provide at least 500 hotel rooms, 25,000 square feet of meeting hall, and a 40,000-square-foot entertainment center. The idea was to improve the Atlantic City skyline and create many jobs.

These and many other stringent regulations forced a slow growth pace in Atlantic City at first and allowed Resorts International, who had refurbished a landmark brick building, to monopolize gambling and break all kinds of income records for a time. In its first complete year of operation, Resorts International won a record-setting $220,000,000.

In its first decade, Atlantic City grew to what it is today, with the exception of the Taj Mahal. It is important to note that, in spite of having only twelve casinos, Atlantic City produces more than half as much income as all of the casinos in the whole state of Nevada.

In October of 1988, gaming reached another milestone. The Indian Gaming Act was approved, allowing Native Americans to have Class III gaming on their lands with the approval of the state government. Class III gaming includes all banking card games such as blackjack, poker, and baccarat. Although craps and roulette are not mentioned, they also fall into the Class III category. It also includes slot machines.

This law was strongly opposed by the state of Nevada, and it is still controversial. Actually, neither side in this disputed issue is satisfied with the law as it is written. The Indian Nations claim the right to sovereignty over their lands, and casino operators and regulators fear the competition and the proliferation of organized crime on Indian lands. In the meantime, gaming compacts between Indian tribes and state governments continue to proliferate, and Indian gaming is expanding across the nation even faster than gaming in general. At this writing, Washington, Oregon, California, Nevada, Arizona, Montana, Colorado, South Dakota, Minnesota, Wisconsin, Iowa, Mississippi, New York, Connecticut, and Florida have all approved Indian Gaming of one type or another, and many other states are in the process of negotiating Compacts. I believe that new legislatures are going to have to deal with this controversy again.

In 1989 the advent of yet another milestone in gambling was seen. South Dakota approved what has come to be known as limited stakes casino gambling. The main objective is to allow casino gambling revenues to stimulate the local economy without putting an unnecessary burden on the communities surrounding the casinos. It is a sort of trade-off for allowing something that is viewed as morally wrong. Since the limit on all wagers is only five dollars, the reasoning is that no one will be financially ruined by frequenting these casinos. This isn't necessarily the case.

Because of South Dakota's success, other limited stakes movements began. Iowa was the next to follow, launching the first riverboat gambling operation this century in April of 1991. In a way, this also marks a milestone in gambling because of the return of riverboat gambling to this nation. At first Iowa enjoyed great success, yet it failed to respond to the competition of other markets and evidently went through difficult times. Riverboat gambling, however, is thriving. It has moved on to the states of Illinois, Mississippi, Missouri and Louisiana, with others soon to follow.

Colorado was next to follow South Dakota's land-based limited stakes gambling lead by approving gambling in three impoverished historic mining towns:

Central City, Cripple Creek, and Black Hawk. From a general point of view, gambling has been an economic success in Colorado although many growing pains have been experienced in all three towns. Fortunately, Colorado voters decided in November of 1992 that they would not allow any other city in the state to have gaming operations, at least not for another four years. That should give Colorado enough time to better understand its gambling industry.

Legislatures all across the nation are dealing with various gaming propositions and it is evident that the gaming boom is far from over. And although I have taken gaming from its Old World origins and focused on the United States, I don't want to lose sight of what is happening elsewhere. Most countries in the world either have gambling, are proposing expansions, or are proposing the establishment of gaming operations. The gaming boom is more than a national phenomenon, it is an international one as well.

THE CONCEPT OF HOUSE ADVANTAGE

Since the inception of casino gaming and even before, people have attempted to predict chance events in such a way that a profit could be derived. By doing so, certain events have become business propositions. This was one of the first ways in which unsuspecting people were taken advantage of, aside from cheating, of course. Sly bookmakers made their living this way. Aware of the true odds of chance events such as the roll of the dice, bookmakers would offer odds that were far below the true odds. However, people eventually realized they were being ripped off, and that's one of the reasons institutions such as church and government interceded to curtail the development of gambling.

By understanding that rule changes in the game affect the outcome of gaming events, bookmakers, and later casino owners, realized they could create games that were fairer to the customers and would nibble at their fortunes instead of swallowing them whole in one night. This realization allowed for the creation of craps, blackjack, baccarat, and roulette as we know them today and is credited with increasing the popularity of casino games.

These rule changes that I have mentioned affect the house advantage, which is the percentage the house has in its favor over the player. The house needs an advantage over the player because the house is offering a costly service. As in any other service business, entrepreneurs deserve to charge a commission for their services. So, not only must the house charge for the cost of the service, it must also mark it up in order to profit. Since the product or service the house provides is intangible, the house must rely on chance events and its advantage at the games to profit.

Now that you know what the house advantage is and understand the need for it, let me explain how it works. The pass line bet at the game of craps carries a house advantage of 1.4 percent, blackjack fluctuates between .5 percent to 4 percent on average depending on the skill of the player, American roulette has a house advantage of 5.26 percent, and bank bets in baccarat have a house advantage of 1.19 percent. What does it all mean? Well, for one thing it means that, if you are a perfect strategy player in blackjack and you are playing against Las Vegas Strip rules, your chances of winning are better than at the other games I mentioned. It also means that, since the house has an advantage of .5 percent, you will have to place that bet 200 times before the house can win that wager.

To players who lose their money quickly, that statement may seem unreal. But it isn't. What may seem even more unrealistic is that on a full blackjack table it would take about four hours for the house to win one bet from a player. In other words, if that player were to bet five dollars a hand on that table, the five-dollar chip would be traded back and forth until, at the end of a four-hour period, the casino would finally win it. Fortunately, not everybody plays perfect blackjack, and not everybody plays a few dollars a hand; otherwise, most casinos would go out of business.

This is one of the reasons casinos provide a variety of games and a variety of bets within those games. If craps only had pass and don't pass bets, this would be a difficult proposition for the casino, especially since the house allows crap bettors to take odds on these bets and doesn't charge them a vigorish to do so. By adding full double odds to a pass or don't pass bet, the player reduces the house's advantage to about .5 percent. And even though craps can be a faster game than blackjack, it wouldn't be fast enough to make a considerable difference. But craps has many other bets, ranging from 1.5 percent to almost 17 percent. Also, crap players are there to try to make a score and they realize the only way to do it is to put more money into action. And that's how the house pays for its high cost of operation.

This explanation illustrates how the house advantage works in theory and not in practice. In the actual game environment, some people will lose, some will win, and some will break even. The sum of all this action over a long period of time will come close, although it will not be exactly the same as in theory. That's because, as I mentioned earlier, probability presupposes a lack of precision, and chance events are ruled by probability. What is certain, however, is that the house is going to win most of the time.

When explaining house advantage, I was dealing with actual small percentages of the main house games. This may have made the process look more complicated than it is. An illustration of a slot machine set at 10 percent might be an easier example to follow. As you can see, 10 percent fits into 100 percent ten times. Therefore, theoretically, if a customer puts ten $1 coins into a slot machine set at 10 percent, the machine would keep one and return nine. In other words, it would keep 10 percent and return 90 percent. In reality, you may find that the machine keeps all of them. That is because the reels are set for randomness, and the jackpots they pay vary from two coins for cherries up to thousands and possibly millions of dollars for progressive jackpots. The cash jackpots have been figured into the randomness equation and, therefore, most people will end up broke while others will hit the big one, or one of the big ones.

If you look at the slot win figures from Iowa, South Dakota, and Colorado, where slot machines were mostly set at 10 percent, you will see how close the win figures come to that 10 percent at the end of the month. The percentages will fluctuate between 8 and 12 percent but will mostly be close to 10 percent. By the way, competition has changed the 10 percent take.

One last thing to keep in mind when picturing the effect of the house advantage is that it is directly related to the number of decisions on each game. A decision is the resolution of the game—when the bet that was placed is either taken, paid, or left because the resolution of the game was a tie. When the dealer completes the hand and begins to take and pay on the blackjack table, that is a decision. When the dice on a crap table land on a winning or losing combination and the dealers proceed to take and pay, that is a decision.

The number of decisions per hour in every game varies. In blackjack, on average, there are about 60 decisions per hour. In craps there are about 50, in roulette about 40, and in baccarat about 60. These will vary with the number of patrons in the game, the number of bets on the game, and the speed of the dealer. These decisions are multiplied by the house advantage of the respective game to determine what percentage of the bets will be won in one hour. If you multiply 5.26 times 40, you'll find out that in one hour's time you will have won 210 percent of the player's bet in roulette. Assuming a 2 percent advantage in blackjack times 60 decisions per hour, you'll win 120 percent of the player's bet. But how can you take 210 percent of a bet? You can't. The player will have lost two bets and 10 percent of the next in that one-hour period. Remember, these are theoretical losses!

HOUSE ADVANTAGE AS THE BASIS FOR FINANCIAL SUCCESS

Obviously, it is necessary for the casino operation to have an advantage on all bets in order to realize a profit and cover operational expenses. It is also necessary for the operation to have a good mix of games and bets. Understanding this, it is easy to realize how important it is to have the "right" mix of games and bets and to have the "right" set of rules for those games and bets. If you tilt the scales heavily either way, by having a small house advantage or by having a strong one, financial ruin is certain to come. A small house advantage will not cover costs, and a strong house advantage will pummel the clientele, and they will not return nor will anyone else visit after the word gets out.

The above conceptualization of house advantage gives the impression that the solution to this equation is very simple: Keep your house advantages somewhere between small and strong, and you've got it made. In theory it is simple, but unless you understand exactly how the statistical background of the games work, you're not going to be able to do the mix appropriately nor will you know what the returns on your games and programs are supposed to be. A couple of examples may give a clearer picture of this problem.

In 1978 when Resorts International opened in Atlantic City, playing rules in the game of blackjack gave the player the advantage over the house. Of course, this privilege was only available to expert players who knew how to use the rules in their favor, and many did. These players flocked to Atlantic City, considering it the land of milk and honey. This wasn't necessarily the plan of the casino operator since it was the Casino Control Commission of New Jersey who prescribed these rules. Yet had the operators been more aware of the implications of these rules they could have made a better case to have them changed. It wasn't until the casino got swamped with card counters taking in great profits that they finally exerted enough pressure to have the rules changed.

The interesting thing here is that the casino operator should have been aware of its house advantage in the game of blackjack, but apparently it wasn't. What's even more interesting is that so-called experts, John Scarne among them, were unaware of this also. In his book *Scarne's Guide To Casino Gambling,* Scarne criticizes the Casino Control Commission for implementing what he believes to be ridiculous rules. He says that the surrender bet is unfavorable to the player, with a monstrous 22.5 percent house advantage. Contrary to what Scarne says, the early surrender bet that was implemented in Atlantic City and later eliminated carried a whopping .624 percent advantage for the player. And although it may seem exaggerated to say whopping to less than 1 percent, it isn't if compared to other blackjack rules such as doubling down on three cards or more (.20 percent), drawing on split aces (.14 percent), and doubling down on split pairs (.13 percent). Most of all, it isn't exaggerated when compared to the house advantage on a six-deck shoe with strip rules that carry a house advantage of from .55 percent to .60 percent, depending on whether or not the casino allows the player to double down on split pairs. It certainly wasn't exaggerated in Atlantic City where the rule gave the player a .20 percent advantage on a four-deck shoe and a .11 percent advantage on a six-deck shoe.

Casinos aren't in the nonprofit category of business and will not survive without strict attention to the house-advantage concept. However, it is easy to criticize from a distance and make cold decisions based on facts and figures, but not as easy to react effectively when the competition uses rule changes and other gimmicks to attract customers. That is why a clear understanding of the concept of house advantage is so important to the casino's financial success. When responding to changes in the gaming environment such as competition, we must be able to make educated and calculated decisions, and be well aware of the costs and consequences of every action.

THE OLD SCHOOL OF GAMING

In gaming, as in many other businesses, some people believe old ways are the best ways. The people who cling to these old precepts in gaming are said to have an *old-school mentality* or to be coming from the old school. Unfortunately, many of the people who think this way have worked themselves into different management levels. Their antiquated ideas have miraculously survived and have become the subject of written and unwritten gaming procedures. Here are just a few examples of these old-school beliefs. Fortunately, they're not being practiced everywhere.

Women don't belong in the gaming business. This concept probably stemmed from the banning of women in early casinos. Gaming was viewed as masculine entertainment; therefore, women were not allowed to gamble or even be employed by a casino. This thinking has gradually disappeared, mainly because women's groups have fought hard for equality in the workplace. However, up until a quarter of a century ago, women were not allowed to be dealers or supervisors in a casino. Today, most managements have learned that female employees can be just as efficient as male employees. However, some from the old school still dispute the fact that women can perform as competently as male managerial employees. There's no justification for people who base hiring, game assignments, and promotion decisions on irrational and biased ideas such as those that suggest gender inferiority.

Women don't belong in the crap pit. Of all casino games, craps was the last one to welcome women players and employees. Traditionally, it has been regarded as the hardest of all games to learn and has mainly attracted aggressive male players who frequently use foul language when excited. Because of this view of the game, many thought it wasn't the best place for a woman. This view of women presumed that they were not as smart as men and couldn't handle themselves in an abusive situation. Time has proven otherwise. Today in the crap pit women are both players and very efficient employees. They not only deal the game as well as men; they have also handled abusive patrons well and have forced management to do something about abusive behavior in general.

Employees should never ask questions, they should do as they're told. Some employees have lost their jobs because of adherence to this message. For example, at the Golden Nugget in Atlantic City, Frank Sinatra used his influence to force the casino employees to violate a state regulation by dealing blackjack to him out of the hand. Management forced the reluctant dealer to comply with Sinatra's request, a violation that made national news and cost various employees their jobs and the casino a hefty fine. Quite often, casino employees are asked to violate rules and regulations to favor the house or to accommodate some influential customer's request. Employees, fearful of being fired for insubordination, usually comply with these requests. Such compliance may lead to criminal charges against them.

These practices are prevalent in the gaming business, and they have to stop. State regulatory agencies should try harder to uncover these violations so that employees don't have to be at risk of the consequences. I realize that if no one comes forth (and employees may be afraid to) it will be hard for regulatory agencies to act, but something has to be done. Employees should be encouraged to report such problems; and managers should be aware that they may be reported so that they don't fall into this trap.

The customer is always right. This is one of business's greatest mottoes. Customer satisfaction must be at the forefront of any business if it is to succeed. The main idea behind the concept is that a business should be structured to satisfy customers. However, the attempt to satisfy should not include violating rules and regulations that must be adhered to, nor should it include violations of moral and human decency codes. Many times customer requests are inappropriate and should not be honored.

Every day in casinos all over the world, premium customers make unreasonable requests, and they are accommodated because management fears loss of the customer's business to the competition. At Caesars in Atlantic City, a customer requested that a female employee be taken off the game he was playing and that no female employee be put on the game. Management complied with the customer's request and removed the employee from the game. This action resulted in a large fine to the casino and later made headline news. It

prompted various female employees to sue the casino. In this instance, the employees fought back, but usually employees get caught in the middle of management's unfair business demands and are forced to do inappropriate things that they would not do if they didn't fear retaliation. It is time these practices cease!

Never take things out of the pit. This is similar to saying you don't air your dirty laundry in public, except that in this case you are hiding the dirty laundry from the head of the household, which is the casino. If an employee is wronged or witnesses a violation that he or she is obliged to report to a higher authority within the same casino, it would be obvious to assume that it should be reported. However, old school hard-liners don't see it that way. They believe it to be a violation of the sanctity of their domain, of some kind of secret oath that can't be violated—right or wrong. Casinos are intolerant of this managerial style and have mechanisms in place to deal with it. In practice, though, the employee still has to work with the person who issues such an order and the casinos are slow, if not ineffective, in dealing with harassment due to violations of this code.

Fear of job loss is a weapon for productivity. Many people in the gaming business believe that, in order for employees to do their jobs well, they should be constantly reminded that their jobs are a privilege and can be taken away at any time. The message is usually conveyed in a stern manner. Even if this principle isn't spoken, managerial attitudes that trickle down the chain of command are a constant reminder of it. Many times when supervisors communicate discontent with casino win figures, employee complacency will be blamed as the cause of the downswing, and one supervisor after another will be blamed for allowing this complacency. These attitudes don't make for a healthy working environment. Furthermore, they tend to decrease productivity rather than increase it.

Employees must sweat games in order to show they care. The term *sweat* in gaming means to express extreme concern about the outcome of a game. This is the attitude of the employee who stands behind the game, is very concerned about the possibility of a great loss, and is afraid the loss will be blamed on him or her. This employee feels personally responsible for the outcome of the game. It is an attitude that stems from the old belief that supervisors and dealers could exercise some sort of control over the games and that there's such a thing as lucky and unlucky dealers. It further extends to the belief that, if you don't show concern, you are being disloyal to the company. Both of these beliefs are irrational. This type of employee is a public relations nightmare and has no business on the casino floor. Employees like these, and there are many, should find employment elsewhere.

Some employees are inherently unlucky and shouldn't be placed on certain games. Supervisors who assign employees to games will many times place dealers, and sometimes other supervisors, on games according to their perceived luck or unluckiness. Some will even take this a step further, changing dealers perceived to be unlucky when a game takes a turn for the worse. This is an irrational attitude that has its basis in superstition. Dealers and supervisors who are subjected to these labels become offended, especially when dealers are said to have poor dealing skills because they lose. These attitudes are unprofitable as well as illogical and must be stopped.

Dice and cards must be changed when the house is suffering heavy losses on a game. Fortunately, this practice doesn't happen often, but it does still happen. Dice and cards are inspected before they're placed on casino games and shouldn't be the object of concern once this function has been performed adequately, and measures are being taken to ensure their safety.

Players will take offense when cards, dice, or dealers are changed on them just because they're winning, and rightfully so. This action shows an antagonistic attitude toward the players, making them feel like enemies or criminals rather than patrons. In addition, sometimes this action is an act of robbery such as the case in blackjack where percentage variations occur as the deck is depleted. If a player has been sitting through bad decks with percentages highly in favor of the house and all of a sudden the percentages change in favor of the player, to reshuffle or change the deck is a cheating act. The house would only be justified in taking such an action if the decks have been switched or if the cards have been marked.

If someone is counting cards on the game, the house is justified in reshuffling the deck if a sizable bet is made, but not in replacing the decks. By the way, this action is unfair to the other patrons on the game, but the house would be justified in protecting its inter-

ests. The house should exercise caution, however, when taking such an action, because of the injustice to other players and because the chances of the card counter winning the bet are almost even with the house. Rarely does a card counter have an advantage greater than 3 percent, which means that he or she will seldom have better than a 51.5 percent chance of winning any given bet. The reverse of this equation is that the house has a 48.5 percent chance of winning the same bet.

With these kinds of odds, you have to ask yourself if it's truly worth cheating the other players out of the opportunity that is rightfully theirs. A real assessment of the possible damage the bet can do is in order at this time, and it should also be viewed in terms of the proximity of the end of the shoe when the house can protect itself by cutting the deck in half for the next shoe. Just to give an example of the true risk of a card counter, imagine a count of true plus five with four decks remaining and playing to strip rules. For those of you who are unfamiliar with card counting, true plus five is considered an extremely favorable situation, and it rarely occurs. A bet placed in these circumstances would have an advantage of 1.30 percent. In other words, the card counter would have a 50.65 percent chance of winning, and the house would have a 49.35 percent chance of winning. Almost a fifty-fifty shot, isn't it? As we get closer to the end of the shoe, that same true plus five count with two decks remaining translates to a 1.40 percent advantage or a 50.70 percent chance of winning. With one deck remaining, the card counter's advantage jumps to 1.70 percent or a 50.85 percent chance of winning.

So why all the hype about card counters? Because organized and heavily bankrolled card counters can beat the casino out of a substantial amount of money over a long period of time and because no one likes to lose. Yet confidential records kept on known card counters do prove three things: Most of them are losers, they eventually become gamblers, and they're basically no major threat. Ex-card counter and crooked gambling authority, Darwin Ortiz, will be the first to admit that he stopped counting cards because it became unprofitable and that most card counters do lose. So the next time you see Dustin Hoffman in *Rain Man,* remember, it's Hollywood!

To increase the PC or house hold, more rolls, more spins, and more hands have to be dealt. This precept is partly based on fact. It is a fact that, if a dealer puts out 70 hands on a blackjack table as opposed to 50, the house hold is going to increase. Hypothetically, if this activity continued through a 24-hour period, the dealers putting out 70 hands would put out 1,680 hands and the dealers putting out 50 hands would put out 1,200 hands. Assuming a 2 percent advantage on both sides, full tables of players betting five dollars a hand, the seventy-hand dealers would generate $1,170 per table, and the fifty-hand dealers would generate $840 per table. If you further assume that the buy-ins or chip purchases at these tables amounted equally to $5,800, then the seventy-hand dealers retained 20 percent of the cash and the fifty-hand dealers retained 14.48 percent. So you can conclude that, by increasing the amount of hands, you did increase the house hold or PC.

The problem with the above conclusion is that there are other variables that come into play. One of them is customer service and satisfaction. If customers feel the dealers and supervisors are bloodthirsty and want to suck the cash right out of their pockets, they will take their business elsewhere and the casino will lose that revenue. Other problems resulting from this attitude are that dealers will make more mistakes, they won't allow players enough time to bet, and they won't allow players enough time to make decisions. This will lead to arguments that will hold up the game and lose the time gained and leave ill feelings among players. Moreover, these problems will decrease the amount of action the casino will get because of the inability of the players to place their bets. The result: The casino has made enemies out of customers and doesn't have an additional dime to show for it.

And what's even worse, a gag rule usually follows an order to pick up the pace. This places a chill on the game that makes the players very uncomfortable. It's bad enough to be a stranger, but to be certified as one by the silence and unfriendliness of the dealer is even worse. Sometimes even if the gag rule isn't in effect, the fast pace that is forced upon the dealers won't allow them to be friendly.

Probably the longest gag rule of present time was enacted in 1988 at Trump Castle in Atlantic City. For months, the vice president of casino operations did not allow dealers or supervisors to speak to customers except to take requests and place bets. This cost the company many customers who took their business else-

where. Whether Donald Trump was aware of this or not is uncertain. I do know that employees did complain and that a letter sent to Donald Trump's office elicited no reply. Eventually, the gag rule and the vice president of casino operations were replaced.

The computer doesn't know anything about issuing comps. The advent of the computer put a dent into the style of the old-time gamesters who were used to playing the big shot and issuing comps to whomever they pleased. To this day, some will argue that the computer's assessment of a player's action is inaccurate. It is true that computer data bases and evaluation programs are only as good as the people who feed them information, as it is also true that the computer can't reason and weigh factors such as the other business that is generated by a given customer. But the computer data base's memory is much better than that of most human beings, its calculations are more accurate, and it doesn't have to be present when the action occurs. Therefore, the computer is invaluable as a source of information. It is also better equipped to make an unemotional and unbiased assessment of a player's worth. There's always room to take into account other situations that warrant extra consideration. That's part of the decision-making process key employees are paid for.

Bettors that hedge their wagers betting on both sides of an event shouldn't be comped. This is a controversial issue that has been the subject of many arguments and for the most part is accepted by most managers in the gaming industry. It is a complicated issue to explain, and you will understand it better once you have acquired a clearer understanding of the framework of casino management and all the elements that affect the managing process. But in the meantime, let me just say that, theoretically, if a player places a two hundred dollar bet on the pass line and another player places a one hundred dollar bet both on the pass line and on the don't pass within a certain period of time, be it one hour, two hours, or twenty-four, at the end of that time both players will have lost approximately the same amount of money. If the amount of action and the potential loss are the criteria that are used to evaluate the player's comp value—and they are—then the necessary conclusion is that both players have the same amount of comp value. The issue is more complex than that; this is a simplified assessment of it. A system comparison can be found in Chapter 17.

SEXUAL HARASSMENT AND DISCRIMINATION

For many years, women in the gaming business have been the object of sexual discrimination and sexual harassment, although few cases have been reported. The main reason for women's reluctance to report these cases, as it probably is in any other work environment, is that women fear retaliation or being labeled troublemakers.

Since women are generally paid lower wages than men, to lose the opportunity of above-average paying jobs such as the ones available in the gaming business does serve to deter complaints. But the fact remains that this abuse does exist, and it shouldn't be tolerated in any form. No human being, male or female, should have to compromise his or her morals to further a career or to ensure job security. No human being should be subjected to unwanted insinuations, language, or gestures that are in bad taste or offensive. These practices must stop and should be a major concern of all managers, especially if they want harmony and productivity in the workplace. So far management hasn't done enough to eradicate this issue.

This isn't only a problem that stems from management toward subordinate employees; it goes deeper than that. Female employees are sometimes pressured into attending parties and events to serve as a source of entertainment to premium customers. They're also requested at gaming tables by premium players and are many times subjected to insinuations and abusive behavior. Management will, most of the time, overlook this unwarranted behavior for fear of offending the valuable customer or because the supervisors hold to an old way of thinking that, if a woman doesn't want to be subjected to this behavior, she shouldn't be in the gaming business. I believe that the people who don't belong in the gaming business, or in management in general, are the people who think this way.

DISCRIMINATION OF CUSTOMERS

Until the late sixties, in Nevada black employees and entertainers were not allowed to enter the front doors of the casinos, and black patrons were not allowed to drink out of glasses in some casinos. And even today, people of certain ethnicities, nationalities, and religious backgrounds are many times the victims of rude and unfriendly attitudes on the casino floor. Included in this group of discriminated-against patrons are those who make small wagers and those who bet in unorthodox ways. Discrimination of any kind is not only unlawful, it is also unacceptable to most people and to management as a whole, but there may be exceptions among managers.

Some people still reminisce about the way things used to be, and perhaps hold high-ranking positions in the casino hierarchy. Management should screen employees well and should not hesitate to reprimand or terminate any employee who exhibits discriminatory behavior. Management should strive to promote good attitudes and customer relations. Every patron, regardless of wagering style, is valuable to the operation and should be treated accordingly. Circus Circus has proven that customers of modest means can be an invaluable resource to a casino operation. Circus Circus has made itself one of the most successful gaming corporations in the world, and it has done it by catering to tourists, families, and individuals with limited gambling budgets. Patrons are out to have fun and don't deserve the common pejorative used to exemplify them, i.e., *fleas*. This concept is even taken to the extreme when some refer to one-hundred-dollar-a-hand bettors in some baccarat pits as *fleas*.

Another discriminatory act occurs when patrons who make certain unorthodox bets are treated disdainfully because the employees feel inconvenienced by the additional work these bets entail. Management and casino employees should realize that all bets on casino layouts carry a house advantage, except for odds bets in craps. So whatever betting system a player uses will result in the house taking in its commission and making a profit on the play. No player should be harassed in any way because of the way he or she bets. All customers should be treated with respect, dignity, and appreciation. Managers and other employees should be happy that anyone, in any betting category, frequents their casinos and allows them to make a profit or draw a salary.

IMPROPER VALUATION OF SLOT PLAYERS

Slot machines were popular in the late seventies, but they weren't the revenue giant that they are today. Back then, casinos who catered to high-end customers derived most of their profits from the table game action and considered slot players unimportant. Yet even then, the considerable amount of revenue produced by the slot operation should have warranted much more attention than it did. Today, slot machines produce at least 60 percent of the income of most casinos and, in some cases, more than 90 percent. This makes the slot department the most important department of the casino. Despite this, the slot department is often subordinated by the casino manager, who in most instances knows little about slot machines. Even worse, slot payoffs over certain amounts of cash have to be approved by casino shift managers in most casinos. This is unreasonable and will probably change in the near future but, until then, more attention has to be given to the slot operation.

The same lack of respect that has been given to the slot department has been given to slot patrons. Until recently, no one bothered to track slot players, and they didn't invest anything close to what was invested on table game programs. That has gradually changed, to the point that many places now favor the slot department. Still, the importance of this department should be taken more seriously. Those operations that find a way to make slot players feel wanted and respected instead of like second-class citizens are going to succeed in drawing these patrons from other operations.

To a much greater extent than before, casinos are starting to realize the importance of slot machine players and have been competing for their patronage. This is going to continue to be the trend, and creativity is going to play an important role. Already, for the slot player's enjoyment, the Rio in Las Vegas has simulated a jungle environment in conjunction with television monitors in a section of slot machines. Other casinos have experimented with pleasing odors to increase the play time of slot players. The latter really doesn't qualify as catering to slot players, but it does show that the casino realizes the importance of the slot department. There are many other things that can be done to cater to slot players and it will be to the casino's benefit to explore them. Those who think slot players don't deserve the same respect as casino high rollers are wrong in my opinion.

SUPERSTITIONS AND HOW THEY AFFECT THE CASINO OPERATION

There's evidence that many casino employees govern themselves according to superstitious beliefs. This is especially true of the crap game. A stickperson who calls out many winning combinations for the players is said to be singing. Some dealers will be branded with the tag of singers and will be considered unlucky. The idea of making the stickperson responsible for the turns of the dice is a common superstition in gaming. Many times during long rolls in a crap game, boxpersons will be seen shaking the dice, turning them a certain way, flipping the drop box paddle, and making many other superstitious moves which they believe influence the events. One pit boss, who is at this writing the director of a casino, once said that it was a question of mind over matter, and because of that he would switch dealers with weak minds from a losing game.

As I mentioned earlier, some pit bosses will blame the dice—they'll change them for what they believe to be a better pair. Some pit bosses and shift managers will refrain from putting certain name brands on the tables because they believe them to be unlucky (Passing Paulsons). Hector Bird, a respected casino manager at the Cerromar Beach Hotel in Puerto Rico years back, used the same dice for weeks. When they had a losing day, he would use another pair. There was no way to tell if the game had lost because of chance variations or because the dice had lost their edges and corners and were almost as round as marbles. Unlike Mr. Bird, most people know that gaming events are based strictly on chance, and superstitions and luck have nothing to do with them. Those who still believe in these superstitions should wake up and open their eyes to the twentieth century.

THE MOVE TOWARD A SCIENTIFIC APPROACH

In business in general, beginning at the end of the nineteenth century, attempts were made to increase the efficiency of organizations by introducing scientific methods. The introduction of the computer, which was available to Dr. Edward O. Thorp in 1961 when he developed his blackjack strategy, brought a new dimension to the world of management. However, it didn't seem to spark the same interest in the gaming business, which didn't start to use this invaluable technological advance with any efficiency until the early 1980s.

In 1978, when Resorts International opened in Atlantic City, and even a few years later, complimentaries were issued based on a visual assessment of a player's action. Other casino programs were also evaluated without the aid of computer programming. Resorts, which quickly became the number one casino in the world, didn't take advantage of the incredibly useful computer technology that had existed for quite some time. Its failure to do so was symptomatic of the anti-modern attitudes that existed in the gaming business and still exist today, to a certain extent.

In Puerto Rico and many other countries, nobody really knew what a card counter was until Ken Uston popularized the technique in the 1980s. This, even though Dr. Edward Thorp had already published *Beat the Dealer* in 1962, Dr. Allan N. Wilson had published *The Casino Gambler's Guide* in 1965, and Lawrence Revere had published *Playing Blackjack as a Business* in 1969.

True, the blackjack rules were so unfavorable in Puerto Rico and other countries that they were practically immune to this assault. Nevertheless, casino operators should have been more aware. And card counting wasn't the only thing they were unaware of; for the most part there was very limited knowledge of player worth. Only one operator in Puerto Rico, Diego Sorroche, truly understood this concept and was the first to incorporate computer-aided assessments in his casino and monitored surveillance.

Today, most casinos are equipped with surveillance equipment capable of zooming in to determine the size of a player's bet, of recording the time and date an action occurs, and of keeping audiovisual records of all casino monetary transactions. Gaming aids such as automatic shufflers, hole card readers, roulette wheel win displays, and many other inventions and technological advances continue to pop up every year. Computer software that allows the casino to track the play of its customers is commonplace, and more casinos are using player-tracking systems for the slot machines. Change machines are also becoming part of the casino landscape, and the machines themselves are being constructed with the ability to read paper currency.

Technology is catering to the fast-growing casino industry, but where the industry seems to lag behind is in the use of modern management techniques. Most casinos still haven't been able to solve the problem of communication breakdowns and personnel management. Most casino operators don't require or encour-

age their managers and supervisors to further their education nor do they provide them with information sources to help them keep up to date. In fact, some casino supervisors frown upon employees who bring reading material to work and will not allow them to store books or magazines in the pits. This is just another example of the retrograde mentality that many display in the gaming industry. It's as if some supervisors fear that subordinates will learn something they don't know and advance to their position or beyond.

Until casino operators realize that, in an everchanging world, attitudes and practices must also change, some of them will be left behind with one foot in the Dark Ages. In the meantime, others who get the message may sail triumphantly into the future.

COMPUTERIZATION OF SYSTEMS

Most casinos employ software that keeps track of all business transactions, analyzes results, and aids them in making business decisions. There's a wide range of software available for this purpose that takes into account different casino functions. The EDT system from IGT is one such system that applies to slot machines. The LSI and the SDS systems are more comprehensive and take into account the whole operation. Among the functions these systems take care of are marketing, credit management, table games management, slot management, reservations and yield management, player visit and player tracking, cage functions, pit functions, manager's functions, auditing functions, accounts receivable functions, soft count and hard count, personnel management, business source functions, commissions management, office automation, and parameters. All these information systems make the manager's job a lot easier.

Computer systems don't only simplify the manager's job, they provide a ready source of information that can be scrutinized at any time by regulatory agencies, owners, and auditors. They're an invaluable tool of modern technology and are essential to the proper functioning of all departments.

THEORETICAL WIN

Theoretical win is a concept used in gaming to determine, by means of mathematical statistics, the amount of revenue the casino will generate from a given bet on a specific game or by a betting system a player uses.

I exemplified it somewhat in Chapter 2 when I discussed house advantage. House advantage and theoretical win are interrelated because, to determine the theoretical win, you must take into consideration the house advantage of the betting pattern the player uses. That can be simple, but sometimes it becomes a complicated issue, especially in the game of craps, where betting systems can be quite complex.

To keep an accurate assessment of a customer's play, a supervisor must record the player's action on a rating card. Once the play has been recorded, the information is transferred to the computer where, if properly programmed, a determination of what the player's action was worth to the casino will be given. For example, let's say that a player has been playing at a blackjack table for an hour and a half, betting a straight $25 bet, and that the supervisor judges the player's level of blackjack skill to give the house an advantage of 1 percent. The pit clerk will then feed this information into the computer which, when prompted, will give a theoretical win figure on the play or a comp value figure, depending on how it was programmed. The theoretical win figure in this case would be $22.50. The comp value will vary from casino to casino, and will depend upon how the casino views its cost of operation and the amount of profit it feels it should make for its investment. A commonly used figure is 30 percent, but it can vary both ways, usually on the high side.

In the example above, 30 percent of $22.50 would entitle this patron to a complimentary of $6.75. An old rule of thumb used to be that, if a player played for a $25 average for one hour, he could be issued a coffee shop complimentary that sometimes had a value of $50. Regardless of the cost of this comp to the casino, you should be able to see how myopic the eye of an old school thinker could be.

Yet returning to the subject of theoretical win, a step by step account of the process will help you understand how I arrived at $22.50. First, I assumed that the number of patrons on the game and the speed of the dealer allowed him to get out 60 hands per hour. Since each hand represents a decision, each hand accounted for 1 percent of the player's money. In one hour and a half, the dealer would have 90 decisions and, therefore, take in 90 percent of the player's money. Ninety percent of $25 is $22.50. Remember, this doesn't mean

that I made change of the player's $25 bet; it just represents what he loses in theory.

Many casino supervisors disagree with the way some computers calculate comp value and will override the computer's assessment and make their own judgment. In some instances they're justified because the system is only as good as its designer and the people who have been feeding it data.

RATING SYSTEMS

Rating systems are used to evaluate the play of casino patrons, junket groups, marketing programs, and special events. It begins at the pit level or on the slot floor, where casino supervisors record the raw data of player action on rating cards and sheets. As you saw in the previous section, some of the information gathered requires judgment on the part of the casino supervisor. You see then how from the very beginning, you are dealing with a questionable independent variable.

In blackjack, for example, the supervisor is asked to judge the average wager of a player during the entirety of his or her play (which can carry on for many hours). Since the floor supervisor isn't a computer, it is impossible to mentally record, add, and divide each wager to find out what the average bet is. The task is even more complicated since the floor supervisor is usually required to watch four games. So supervisors must devise techniques to accomplish this goal. Some supervisors watch the first ten bets the player makes, add them, divide them by ten, and come up with an average, or they use the most prevalent wager during those first ten bets. Other supervisors are instructed to use the first three bets, since they may be distracted between the time the player places the first bet up until the tenth. For example, the supervisor may be required to fill a game, issue a marker, or attend to a customer need.

The problem with these techniques is that players don't always play consistently. Some will increase their bets as they're losing and some will increase their bets as they're winning. Some play systems, and some just play hunches. The issue becomes even more complicated when some in the gaming business feel that, if players increase their wagers because they're winning, they shouldn't get credit for those actions because they're playing with the casino's money. Not so. The money in the dealer's rack belongs to the casino, and the money in front of the customers and in their pockets is theirs. They're not obliged to re-wager the money they won, and they can walk away with it.

You can see then that a fairer assessment of the player's action is needed, and it is going to take a conscientious effort on the part of the supervisor, together with proper training, to accomplish this important task. Yet averaging the player's bet is just the beginning since the supervisor will be required to make other rating judgments depending upon the game being supervised. Blackjack supervisors will also be required to evaluate the level of skill of the player. This is even more difficult because routine plays will occur more often than critical plays. Most people handle routine plays easily, yet fumble when confronted with critical plays such as doubling down on certain counts, splitting certain pairs, and hitting certain hands. How they fare in dealing with these critical hands determines their playing skill. In other words, the number of strategy mistakes and the percentage of advantage for a particular play are going to determine the percentage of disadvantage the player is going to have. Since supervisors don't possess computer brains, they will have to rely on generalized assumptions.

Such a determination varies from casino to casino. Some casinos don't evaluate the player's strategy at all and just apply a set percentage to all players. Some will use three levels of play and will determine those levels based on the quantity and not quality of strategy mistakes the player makes. Others will use up to five levels of play, based on the same principle. Each level of play will carry within itself a house advantage. For example, level one might carry a house advantage of 1 percent, level two, 2 percent, and level three, 3 percent. These assumptions are basically arbitrary, but they do have some basis in fact.

Craps presents wholly different rating problems. The crap layout allows a multitude of bets with at least nine different house advantages. This doesn't include place bets to lose, don't bets that bar the ace deuce, two other variations of field bets, the big six and eight, and the effect of adding single, double and triple odds. The number of possible combinations of these bets adds yet another dimension to this rating nightmare.

In spite of all this, rating systems have been devised to make crap ratings functional by grouping certain bets and by making time and other allowances. The problem is that the systems rely heavily on the ability and moti-

vation of supervisors to understand the system. Unfortunately, rating systems are not explained well enough to casino supervisors, and varying interpretations of the different betting systems and the significance of the rating itself do exist. Because of these differences of opinions, most casino rating systems are highly inaccurate.

Are they better off without the system, then? No. At least with the system they have some idea as to the nature and worth of a player's action. Furthermore, it is a step in the right direction that just needs some fine tuning to prove highly effective in the near future.

Now that you have a better understanding of some of the mechanics of the rating system, you can go through the entire process and see how it works. First, you have the floor supervisor who fills out a rating card with the name and account number of the player, the number and code of the game where the action is taking place, the date and times the action is taking place, the average wager being bet, the amount of cash, checks, and/or credit the player has bought-in for, and the amount the player won or lost. From the floor supervisor the rating card goes to the pit boss, who then checks its accuracy and retrieves whatever information is useful. The pit boss passes the rating card or a copy to the pit clerk, who then brings up the computer file with the customer's information and adds the new data into the system.

The system usually has a trip history of the player and a cumulative record of his or her win/loss, total chip purchases, total credit, total cash, and the average bet. Some, if not most, will have a cumulative comp value that aids key employees in making comp decisions such as food and beverage, rooms, shows, special events, and transportation. Some systems are defaulted to section out a certain amount of trips or a period of time where it will compute comp dollars. All other trips or action do not count. In other words: *What have you done for me lately?* That, encapsulated, is what a rating system does at an individual level. But it also serves other functions.

In order to draw more business into the casino, operators initiate special programs. One of the most common is a *junket*. A junket is a group of players who are put together by a *junketeer*. These junket players make a verbal contractual agreement to play in a certain way. These agreements vary depending upon the complimentaries that are being offered or requested and, also, depending upon the different casino's rules. Even though some of the requirements are standard, play time requirements and average bets will vary from casino to casino.

The junketeers receive a commission for the action they bring in and, because of this, accuracy in rating is very important both to the casino and the junketeers. The casino also wants to make sure that the investment to procure this play is worth it. Sometimes this expense can include chartering a plane, and that is extremely expensive. So you can imagine how important the rating system becomes.

Special events, such as golf tournaments with cash prizes, boxing matches, sporting events in general, and gala events, are going to cost the casino a lot of money to stage. The casino will make special invitations to these events, and they will have to evaluate the success of the event. One measurement of the success is obvious. How much money did we make? But many times special events result in heavy losses, and an assessment has to be made to see if the losses were due to a chance event or if the event itself was poorly staged or improperly marketed. The computer data base and the rating system can answer those questions.

TRAINING PROGRAMS

In 1980, Resorts International first implemented a casino employee training program in an effort to standardize procedures and improve employee performance on the games. Until then casinos were either satisfied with their employees' performance or they simply believed they couldn't improve. The instructors assigned to this task were not academically trained but were at least highly experienced and competent in their games. The program was successful for a while and had a lot of potential. However, it wasn't managed properly and fell into disuse.

Other casinos followed Resorts' lead, and these programs in varying degrees have existed since. Unfortunately, not enough of them exist, and not all trainers are qualified to do the job.

I don't mean to criticize the people who had enough vision to put these programs together. On the contrary, they deserve a lot of credit. But lack of control and supervision on the part of upper management allowed some of these programs to become ineffective and unproductive. I see this trend also in private train-

ing institutions, where lax conditions allow trainers to come unprepared to class and to interact with students as they see fit. An instructor in the Atlantic City Casino Career Institute used to leave his students practicing while he would go out to play golf. Another instructor in the same school would read magazines all day while her students practiced. At the Atlantic Casino Training Academy, one instructor would spend most of his time at the bar while another would bring his Walkman to class and listen to all the ball games. It's simply a shame that such a grand opportunity is wasted because some people don't care enough to make a difference.

In today's gaming world, with the rapid expansion it is experiencing, training will become of utmost importance, since the turnover of the work force is going to be outrageous. Those who are prepared for this challenge will succeed in maintaining their properly functioning operations, but those who are not will suffer the consequences for their lack of vision. In early 1994, a Mississippi casino was caught off guard and was unprepared to respond to a number of resignations in the casino department due to the opening of two properties who fiercely competed for their manpower. These resignations occurred in a two-week period, but all the indicators for what was to come were there. Only one person could clearly see what was coming and knew what had to be done. That manager eventually bailed the property out of the position they had allowed themselves to fall in, but it still cost the operation much revenue and grief. That experience taught the casino that training can't be overlooked.

Information sources and learning techniques have existed for a long time and will continue to improve. *Training* and *retraining* are going to become everyday words for the next few years as our country tries to reclaim the stature that it once held in the world. Expectations of us will be higher, and the gaming business had better be prepared to respond. No company can afford to live in the past or to deny itself the wealth of information that exists. Successful management entails making informed decisions.

STANDARDIZATION OF OPERATIONS AND GAMING PROCEDURES

For many years, some standards existed in gaming procedures, but for the most part dealers were allowed to develop their own style. These personal preferences were also part of managerial views on how operations and procedures on the casino floor should be conducted. Still today, operating procedures from one operation to another and even from one shift to the other will vary, sometimes considerably. State regulators have attempted to standardize those procedures that are liable to allow gross infractions and have enacted rules, regulations, and laws that cover them. So in this respect, the gaming business has come a long way, but it needs to make an extra effort to eradicate the inconsistencies that still exist.

Without standardization, too much time and effort are spent trying to figure out what went wrong and where. It is difficult to conclude that any given variable affected the results being analyzed. If one department is deviating from normal procedures in its relationship with another department, the latter department may be unfairly blamed for a fluctuation in the end result.

For example, assume that the casino department and the marketing department have been issued the same comp procedures. Together, these two departments plan a special event, for which a great number of high-end customers are invited. The event in question produces revenues of $100,000, but the cost of the event, complimentaries included, is $200,000. Obviously the casino manager isn't going to be satisfied with these results. He or she is going to blame someone else since, *most certainly*, it isn't the manager's fault. Nine times out of ten, casino personnel will become the scapegoats. In the case before us, marketing personnel overextended their comp privileges and accounted for most of the unwarranted complimentaries that inflated the cost of the operation. If the program analysis reveals this fact, the marketing department will probably point the finger at the casino department and say that the complimentaries were issued at their request. No one will take the blame. That's why standardization is so important and why it is also important to have competent and well-trained people working for you.

Another case in point is the standardization of gaming procedures. On the one hand, procedures can be put in place that minimize the risk of stealing, and on the other, clarity for easier supervision is insured. Dealers don't realize that by seeking individuality in their dealing style, they force the supervisor to take an extra look at what they're doing. If everyone is doing this, it puts an unwarranted burden on the supervisor. Supervisors' jobs are much easier when everyone is doing the same thing, and any deviation from that norm truthfully signifies caution.

A gross misconception of dealing procedures was part of the pride crap dealers in Puerto Rico felt. They had even managed to convince upper management that their dealing style was far more efficient than their counterparts in the mainland United States because it was faster. The logic was that because their payoffs were all-inclusive and because they drop-cut payoffs directly in front of the player, the game moved faster and smoother. But dealers with far less experience in Atlantic City quickly proved that this was a fallacy. Although it was true that the Puerto Rican dealing procedure did save some steps, mainland dealers proved they could deal just as fast, with a lot more clarity and more to the customer's satisfaction. Clarity and customer satisfaction more than compensated for any insignificant difference that may have existed between the two dealing styles.

MODERN CASINO MANAGEMENT

I have spent some time presenting a picture of how things were in the gaming business and, to a certain extent, where we are now. The term *modern* assumes the current or at least recent status. It is purposely intended as a deviation or a distinction from how it used to be in the gaming business. As I have stated, many things remain the same, but my intention is to focus on those things that are not the same, those things that make modern casino management a new philosophy and part of the movement toward mainstream management theory.

Idealism or realism? Modern casino management is really a little bit of both. Some industry analysts believe the casino business is so different from other business ventures that it can't be seen in the same light nor can it be subjected to the same principles that apply to business in general. Most casino managers are firm believers of this concept, especially since they're not required to have a business degree or a degree of any kind. It is a business whose managers rely on hands-on experience. There's nothing wrong with that concept, since firsthand knowledge of the inner workings of an organization does prove to be a valuable asset in understanding how the organization works. But there's something wrong with the attitude that all that is to be learned about the organization comes from the ranks.

Oil magnate John Paul Getty said that business is business and that business principles don't change; the fundamentals remain constant no matter what the field or industry involved. He exemplifies his statement by referring to his success as personnel manager of Spartan Aircraft Corporation and Spartan Aeronautical School during World War II, even though he knew nothing about airplane manufacturing. The point here is that there is such a field as management and that knowledge of this field and the research that has been done is an invaluable resource to all managers, including casino managers. Modern casino management should include study and adequate use of information sources.

It is true that some corporations have attempted to use management principles in the casino business without a clear understanding of the business, and they have failed. But these isolated incidents should not discourage aspiring managers, it should serve as an example of the mistakes that need to be avoided. These were not mistakes that can be ascribed to the management field, but to the managers who used the management principles inadequately. It is there where the *art* of managing comes into play, in taking the scientific and academic principles and molding them into something that works to a particular situation. Ignorance should not be an excuse for failure.

Having said all this, I now take the position that modern management principles can apply to modern casino management, and that the only implicit idealism stems from those who believe the future will change the way casino management is perceived in general.

Already changes have taken place to adapt to the rapid expansion of gaming and the fierce competition that exists. State regulators are taking a careful look at what other states have done in the way of regulation, the problems they have faced, and possible ways of correcting them. These changes have a ripple effect that forces changes upon the casino operations themselves. They also make the new operator stop and think about the possible motivation that inspired certain regulation, and sometimes there's a lesson to be learned.

Competition has also forced casino operators to be more creative in the way they manage their personnel.

The expanding markets have created a huge need for qualified personnel, leaving casino operators scrambling to acquire the best possible employees and the most experienced. This has forced them to put into place training and retraining programs. Also, operators have had to improvise and adapt to a new set of circumstances that in some instances greatly differs from the traditional setting of metropolitan land-based casinos. Today there are riverboat casinos that take on passengers and cruise inland waters, there are barge casinos that are set up on the river and gulf docks, there are Native American operations that are based on Indian lands and must conform to Indian and state laws, and there are many other possibilities that only the future can tell.

Modern casino management is, therefore, not just a different way of looking at casino management; it is also casino management as seen in the expanding market of today. Modern casino managers must look at the operation differently from their predecessors. The casino manager must understand the management process, must understand human behavior both at an individual and group level, must understand systems analysis, must utilize the best techniques for planning and controlling the operation, and must understand quantitative decision-making.

Casino managers must also understand that there are going to be trade-offs in the decision-making process, and they must have the ability to weigh the advantages and disadvantages in the applications of certain techniques and concepts. In this sense, they're like surgeons trying to predict the consequences of applying a surgical procedure. Will the patients be better off after the operations, or will they be worse? Is the trade-off of lost wages during the convalescence period going to be offset by the increased productivity after? Like surgeons, managers must be able to predict the probable consequences.

Another thing modern casino managers must do is recognize which factors are more important in any given situation and how their different alternatives in dealing with the situation are going to affect the outcome. Say, for example, revenues in the crap pit have diminished considerably in a one-month period. By chance, a casino executive passes by a crap table and notices a dealer making inappropriate change in a cashout while he tries to charm the player out of a tip. The casino executive becomes irate about this behavior and generalizes that all crap dealers are doing the same and, because of that, they're losing customers and casino revenues into the dealers' pockets. Based on this information that by now has probably been exaggerated ten times, the casino manager takes various actions. He enacts a gag rule, restricts the way dealers can thank customers for their tips, restricts the services a dealer can provide for the customer, puts into effect stiff disciplinary action for violators of these rules, and demands an increase in the speed of the game. This is what I call a myopic decision. Based on an isolated incident, a conclusion has been made, and action has been taken.

In the above case, revenues continued to fall drastically in the crap pit, some employees quit to go elsewhere where they could make a better living without the hassles, and those who stayed were miserable and performing a sloppy job. The dealer caught hustling a tip in this case was the only one in the whole pit who exhibited this behavior, and it wasn't even customary in his case. He should have been disciplined for his action, but his fellow employees shouldn't have had to pay for the consequences of his act. Customer service declined as a result of management's action and, in that respect, the customer paid for the dealer's mistake also. In reality, the downturn in revenues was due to economic conditions that were an indirect consequence of the Persian Gulf War. Some casinos quickly recovered, but this one did not. Management in this casino was near-sighted—couldn't see well enough to interpret the situation at hand.

Once modern casino managers have familiarized themselves with the tools of their profession, have interpreted all the particular situations that apply to their operation, and have weighed all the pros and cons of the alternatives to dealing with their particular situations, they will then be able to attain their operations objectives in the most effective way. This is what modern casino management is all about.

PART II

MANAGEMENT THEORY

CHAPTER 4

COMMUNICATION

P ossibly the biggest problem that casino operations experience is the breakdown of communication. This may occur between the different departments of the casino and between the different levels of management and employees. It is a problem that needs to be appropriately addressed.

Management theory considers communication and decision-making interrelated and part of a linking process that bridges the gap between other management functions like planning, organizing, motivating, and controlling. Without communication it isn't possible to obtain valuable information to make effective decisions, and without it decisions can't be conveyed effectively to other people. Effective communication, therefore, determines how well decisions will be implemented.

When we think of communication, we think of such communicating devices as telephone calls, formal reports, meetings, memorandums, and face-to-face discussion. These are the preferred methods of communication, but they're mostly the means we utilize to communicate within the operation.

Communication **59**

There's also a need to communicate with the outside world in order to make an operation successful. Advertising and other types of promotional programs are examples of this type of communication, as are written rules and regulations intended for regulatory agencies, additions and deletions submitted to these agencies, and financial and marketing reports for stockholders, potential investors, and prospective employees. Union negotiations, legislative efforts, and legal proceedings are just a few other possible communication interactions that are part of the interaction with the outside environment.

Communication flows two ways in the operation of a casino: from the higher levels of management down to the front-line employees through different levels of middle management, and from the front-line employees back to the higher levels of management, also following the chain of command. Let's say, for example, a dealer is constantly hearing customers praise a new nonsmoking policy that has been implemented on certain casino tables or certain sections of the casino, and also hears customers complain that not enough of these tables exist. The dealer is probably going to communicate this information to the floor supervisor who, hopefully, will pass it on to the pit boss who, hopefully, will pass it on to the shift manager and so on until it reaches the main decision center, whether at the office of the casino manager or the vice president of casino operations. The general manager will probably have something to say on the subject also.

You may have noticed I said *hopefully* in regard to passing this information. In the gaming business, as in all others, personalities and idiosyncrasies get in the way of effective communication. The floor supervisor in question may be a smoker who feels this action is a violation of smokers' rights and therefore decides to remain silent. Although there are other floor supervisors who can communicate this information, the pro-smoking judgment may be shared by someone up the chain of command, and the result will be the same— the communication line will be ruptured.

COMMUNICATION BREAKDOWN

Sometimes this type of upward communication meets immediate resistance for different causes. One reason could be the way it was communicated. A dealer may feel he or she is more competent than the supervisor and has been passed over for promotion. Aware that a customer on the game has been ripping off the casino for some time and the supervisor isn't doing anything about it (or at least it is perceived that way), the dealer might become angry or displeased with the supervisor and suggest that he or she had better do something about it. This type of communication is probably going to irritate the supervisor, who might then tell the dealer to shut up and do his job. The casino might lose a considerable amount of money because of this.

Also, this dealer might conclude no one really cares and not communicate any further infractions or make any suggestions at all. This can also happen above this level with floor supervisors and middle managers who could get shot down when making suggestions that might benefit the operation. These employees will think twice next time before making suggestions and recommendations that could profit the organization.

I believe that, in order for casino operations to achieve their maximum potential, managers have to find ways to facilitate effective communication up and down the organization. There should be training programs to teach communication skills, assistance to such programs should be recognized, effective communication should be rewarded, and employees found to be disrupting this process should be disciplined.

Trainers in these programs should be qualified individuals and effective communicators. Management should supervise these programs to ensure that trainers are in fact doing their jobs and that they're getting the employees to participate and learn. Follow-up supervision should occur at department levels to ensure that the lessons learned are being practiced, especially on the casino floor. Evaluation of communication skills should occur on a continuing basis, not only when it is time for evaluations. Supervisors should be evaluated by their subordinates and rated on communication skills. Of course, supervisor evaluations by subordinates must remain anonymous.

Improper communication, whether it is toward officers, subordinates, or customers, must be dealt with immediately. The employee or supervisor should be required to undergo retraining and, if communication continues to be ineffective, he or she should be disciplined. A supervisor who can't communicate effectively is in the wrong profession. The supervisor ought to be retrained for a new position and, if unable to adapt to the new circumstances, should face termination of employment.

In the gaming business it has become customary for supervisors to shout at subordinates, to threaten jobs, and even to use profanity when issuing orders or reprimanding unwanted behavior. This type of conduct may be effective on the battlefield or in situations where a certain behavior must cease immediately, but in the gaming business it is inappropriate and unnecessary. Better results are achieved by praising, rewarding, and instructing.

Management must make employees feel that, by learning effective communication skills, they're contributing to the organization in a way that is appreciated. It should show its appreciation to all employees who show true motivation and progress in communication training. Incentives of different types can be offered for successful completion of training and for progress made during the course. Handling communication well in addition to other positive traits should lead to advancement in the company hierarchy. Communication skills should be an important determinant of in-house promotions.

Another way in which the casino can promote communication skills is to provide an atmosphere conducive to this learning. This can be done in many different ways, but the main idea is to make the employee feel comfortable and at ease. Employees are not going to feel this way if they're tense or under stress because of harassment, lengthy hours, exhaustion, or boredom.

HORIZONTAL COMMUNICATION

Communication between the different departments is called horizontal communication, and it is important in order to coordinate activities and objectives. Say, for example, the marketing department invites one hundred premium Asian customers for a special event, and it forgets to tell the casino manager, making the assumption that the casino has enough personnel to handle the extra business. But what they don't realize is that these customers are mostly baccarat players and that as a habit they usually play together. When these players arrive, they immediately swarm into the baccarat pit, but find that there are only two baccarat games available and that no dealers speak their native tongue. This example is a bit exaggerated, but similar situations have occurred. At many major casinos, special events have

been modified or canceled, yet no one informed the scheduler who had made employees come in on their days off. The reverse has also been true at many major casinos where someone has planned special events without informing schedulers or pit managers, later causing conflict because the operation wasn't prepared for the additional play. Something like this should never happen. The baccarat and any other pit that may be targeted in any special event or program should have a calendar of special events, a list of invited guests, and any special requirements these guests may have.

You have seen one dimension of this communication problem, but there's yet another. When planning future programs and events, departmental input is necessary to determine costs, logistical problems that may exist such as physical size, available employees, available resources, and the cost effectiveness of the program or event. Without interdepartmental communication, assembling this information isn't possible.

COMMUNICATION BETWEEN SUPERIORS AND SUBORDINATES

Most of the communication in the organization, however, will be between managers and subordinates. Porter and Roberts in the *Handbook of Industrial and Organizational Psychology* say two-thirds of the communication in an organization occurs between superiors and subordinates. Communication between superiors and subordinates entails clarification of tasks, identifying priorities, discussing and clarifying performance expectations, instructing and training employees to improve upon their abilities, motivating employees through praise and by recognizing their efforts and abilities, discussing departmental objectives and performance problems, gathering information about problem areas and situations that are current and those that could occur in the future, informing employees of changes in effect and changes to come, and any other person-to-person information such as ideas and suggestions.

The manager also communicates with groups that help coordinate tasks and with groups such as the individual departments. This type of communication saves time since all of the members of the group are present and can participate by identifying problem areas, adding to suggestions and solutions, and discussing current and upcoming changes. The manager is able to establish priorities, give reports on the status of the operation, and listen to the concerns of the employees.

INFORMAL COMMUNICATION

Informal communication occurs in all casinos, usually in the form of rumors, although sometimes orders will be issued informally to avoid a paper trail. These would be sensitive directives that are in violation of rules and regulations or general codes of ethics. For example, in Puerto Rico, betting limits used to be comparatively low, with maximum bets established at two hundred dollars. This put an inordinate burden on casino operations, since most of their revenues were made during a short season. Because of this fact, some casino operators would allow certain premium players to exceed the regulated limits. In some cases, identities of select patrons were concealed in paperwork showing different names even though that practice might violate state and federal laws. Such an exception was made solely through informal communication with no written directive for the authorities to point to, but employees were very well aware of the consequences for noncompliance.

The grapevine provides a legitimate and very popular means of informal communication and rumors may sweep through a casino almost every day. According to the findings reported in Keith Davis's *Personnel Journal,* 80 to 99 percent of grapevine information for noncontroversial company information is accurate. I must clarify, however, that predictions of management changes account for a great number of these rumors, and with the short life expectancy of some casino management positions, this really isn't a meaningful revelation. However, it does seem odd sometimes that casino dealers are aware of radical changes to come before middle management knows about them. This happens so often you wonder through what channels this information flows.

THE COMMUNICATION PROCESS

In order to communicate effectively, the manager needs to understand the communication process. It involves the *sender* of the information, the *message* that is being sent, the *channel* that is chosen to transmit the information, and the *receiver* who interprets the information. Most of the time when there's a communication breakdown, it originates at the source. The message is doomed from the start because the sender did not take enough time to formulate the idea properly. In order for the sender to have any chance of communicating, he or she has to have thought out the idea or message to be conveyed.

EVALUATIONS

Before an idea is formulated, the sender has a notion of what needs to be communicated. This could be the need to appraise employee performance so as to improve work performance and provide a basis for employee promotions. Employee evaluations in the gaming business are this type of concept. Usually, the intention of the evaluation is to praise and reinforce appropriate and wanted behavior and to constructively criticize unwanted and inappropriate behavior. How this message is conveyed makes the difference between its intent and its actual interpretation.

Unfortunately, evaluations in the gaming business are a source of discord. The intended message is often not conveyed appropriately, and many employees' feelings are hurt. Employee morale declines and so does productivity. Employees who are doing a good job at customer relations may cease to give that extra effort if a superior has made a negative comment in their evaluations. Other employees *not* giving extra effort, who are unjustly favored by the superior doing the evaluation and praised and rewarded for something they weren't doing, interpret this to mean they're doing fine, so they don't give an extra effort.

I have yet to see a casino where a fair and effective evaluation system is put into practice. The main problem is that systems put in place don't account for the effect of personality conflicts, differences of opinion and interpretation, lack of standardization and clear specifications of accepted behavior patterns, and the motivation of the evaluator. Since the idea and the concept are in conflict, the casino would be better off not doing evaluations at all. Promotions in the gaming business are hardly ever done on the basis of evaluations anyway, so casinos might as well deal with the demoralization when promotions are announced instead of having to do it at evaluation time. Some might argue that the evaluations serve as a paper trail for disciplinary actions or as a guide if layoffs are necessary, but the paper trail can exist without the evaluations, and so can the selection of layoff candidates.

CONCEPT VS. IDEA

Another instance where inconsistency occurs between the concept and the idea expressed is when employees are told to do something that burdens them, yet they are not told why. This is because most casino supervisors don't want to be questioned about their decisions. A favored phrase in the gaming business is *dummy up and deal.* In other words, don't think, just do your job or else! But no human being likes to be treated like a puppet, a robot, or an animal. Such treatment will result in immediate compliance, but in the end the result will be the exact opposite of that intended. The dealer isn't going to forget the insult, and may retaliate by performing his or her job in a way that is costly to the casino. In contrast, the dealer will probably give an extra effort if we show our appreciation.

If you want to communicate a need for extra work and productivity that might disrupt the normal course of a person's life, such as an increase in work hours or workdays, make sure the employee is well informed of the reason for your request. Advise him or her of the necessity for the increased work load, explain the important role he or she will play in reaching the desired goal, and demonstrate your gratitude for the extra effort.

THE MESSAGE

The second part of the communication process is the message. The message is encoded into communication symbols such as words, body language, and tone of voice. A pair of darting eyes sends a message loud and clear: *Don't mess with me!* You don't even have to look at a person to know when the meaning of a word or phrase changes just by the rise in decibels and the inflection of the voice. This is quite common in American culture, where swear words are judged as friendly or unfriendly according to the tone of voice. Sometimes these gestures and tone fluctuations are intentional, and sometimes they're not. Either way they carry a message that is going to be interpreted by the receiver. It is, therefore, important to be aware of what you are saying and how you are saying it.

THE MEDIUM

The medium you choose to communicate a message is another important factor. Mediums include: verbal communications, letters, memos, bulletins, newspaper articles or any other information means, videotapes, television, telephones, telegraphs, and the FAX machine. Each medium will, depending upon the circumstance, carry a certain amount of effectiveness and efficiency. For example, it is better to relay the news of a lost loved one in person than it is to submit it to the newspaper. That's why the names of accident victims are withheld from the media until the next of kin can be informed. It is better to communicate a promotion face to face than to send it by letter, regardless of how eloquent the letter may be. It is better to deal with serious violations in a formal setting, possibly with other supervisors present and accompanied by a written notification for the employee's file, rather than by just patting the employee on the back and telling him or her to be more careful next time.

WRITE-UPS

A closer view of this medium, which is quite popular in the gaming business, would be appropriate. First of all, threats to write-up employees are quite prevalent, yet they're rarely carried out. This doesn't usually happen until management decides it is time to get rid of an employee and then they start a paper trail to justify the termination, or when a directive is issued for strict compliance with a certain procedure or procedures. An employee may receive a directive of this type when there has been a decline in revenue production, which in gaming doesn't necessarily mean something is being done wrong. In fact, a casino may have been producing way above expectancies, and the natural, inevitable decline might have this effect.

The issuance of this type of notice is confusing to employees who have become accustomed to doing things in a certain way and, all of a sudden, learn that what wasn't wrong before is now a major offense, punishable by written notification and suspension. This puts an element of stress into the job. It doesn't have a positive effect on revenues. It can have a negative one. This may seem absurd, but it does happen often. Here are two actual examples of such incidents:

At the Dunes in Las Vegas, a floor supervisor was written up and suspended for one week because a player with an average bet of $100 a hand pressed his bet $50 and the dealer didn't notice it. This occurred even though a directive was in place that all shuffles had to be watched in their entirety regardless of whatever else was happening on the games (the supervisor had three other busy games to watch). What is more ridiculous is that the dealer on the previous shift had made management aware that the customer had attempted to do it to her, continued to play with his wager money in spite of her warnings, and was being uncooperative in general. Management allowed the situation to continue and no one bothered to inform the supervisor on the next shift about what was happening. The supervisor lost $675 from his pay while the player beat the casino out of $50 and continued to play at the casino—probably until it was permanently shut down. Who was the real criminal here? And what was the message being communicated?

Another ridiculous write-up procedure still exists at this writing in one of the major casinos on the Las Vegas Strip. An employee who fails to punch the time clock once is issued a verbal (documented) warning, the second time he or she is issued a written warning, and the third time is suspended for three days. One employee was written up because he thought the machine had not clocked him in, so he ran his card through the machine again. His written notice read that he had attempted to get paid twice! And what makes this even worse, the casinos contend that supervisors are salaried employees and therefore don't deserve to get paid time and a half for overtime. So if they're salaried employees, why are they punching the clock? And why are they receiving infractions for their inability to do so?

Examples of this nature are plentiful. Casino operators must realize that the messages and the media being utilized in today's gaming business may not be the most efficient. They should evaluate their systems to make sure they're getting across the desired messages in order to accomplish their objectives.

DECODING

Once the message has been transmitted by whatever means chosen to be appropriate or most effective, the receiver must then decode it. In other words, the receiver must translate the symbols and interpret them. If the symbols employed by the sender of the message have the same meaning to the receiver, the message has been conveyed effectively.

FEEDBACK AND NOISE

Two other concepts of communication theory are feedback and noise. Feedback is the basis for two-way com-

munication. It is the receiver's response to the message of the sender. Through feedback, the manager can evaluate how effective the communication was, since communication is never perfect. The concept of noise, which is anything that distorts meaning, is the main impediment to perfect communication. Language barriers, both verbal and nonverbal, are examples of noise. Perceptual and status differences between managers and subordinates are also considered noise, since they distort meaning.

No two people see everything alike. The casino manager must bear in mind that people will oftentimes receive messages according to what they perceive to be happening in their environment. So in order to communicate effectively with them, you have to see things the way they see them. The casino manager may issue an order for all personnel to increase their efficiency levels because revenues have decreased. To the casino manager *efficiency* might mean to do the job faster, to the floor supervisor it might mean to increase the accuracy of the payoffs, and to the dealer it might mean to improve customer relations. How *efficiency* is perceived in this case isn't only a matter of semantics, but also of the personal framework of the individuals involved. The manager believes a job well done is a job that is done fast and increases the hold percentages (PC) of the house. The floorperson believes a job well done is one that is done accurately so costly monetary mistakes are avoided, and he or she doesn't have to intervene to make corrections or to request the return of unearned money. Dealers, on the other hand, may believe that being more friendly and outgoing with customers assures that people will stay longer in the casino and will frequent the casino more often, and this will increase the revenues of the casino. They also believe this attitude will enable them to make more money in tips, which in most cases is their main source of income.

Other factors that will cause people to perceive things differently are emotional states and environmental conditions. Previously we mentioned how a forceful attitude by a subordinate got in the way of an otherwise useful suggestion. Such attitudes cause friction between individuals and influence the way they perceive communication. The next time these two individuals communicate, they probably won't be listening carefully to each other, and they probably will be hearing words as they want to hear them.

This isn't just a limitation of attitude barriers, but also of people in general. We are prone to block out new information if this information conflicts with our preconceived ideas. Research conducted by Dearborn and Simon confirms the tendency of people to perceive problems from the frame of reference of their job functions. This makes communication between managers and subordinates very difficult.

Negative feelings will not only affect the frequency with which individuals communicate, but will also affect the way in which they communicate. A work environment that is permeated by negativity will foster discord and distrust and will restrict the flow of information. That is why a positive communication atmosphere is so important. Studies by J.D. Mellinger and others have concluded that trust increases the quantity and quality of information among people in an organization. Other studies have suggested that, when managers are more open in their conversations, employees will communicate with them with the same ease and will feel a greater sense of satisfaction. R.J. Burke and D.C. Wilcox confirm this in the *Academy of Management Journal*.

Casino managers and operators are sometimes overwhelmed by their circumstances, and they shut themselves out of the work environment. But if they want to be more in tune with what is happening in their organizations so they can make effective decisions, they have to find ways to increase the flow of information. A great beginning would be to remove the perceptual barriers between them and their employees. They have to learn to put themselves in the shoes of the employees and see through their eyes. They also have to make the employees feel that their communication and frankness are appreciated.

SEMANTIC BARRIERS

Communicators commonly experience semantic barriers. Language can be precise but, unfortunately, many words have varied meanings. A voyage through the dictionary will demonstrate that almost every word has more than one meaning. The word set tops the list with more than one hundred different meanings, and the word round with seventy-nine. Because of these varied meanings, communicators have to make sure they're using words in the right context so the intended receiver understands what is meant.

Another problem with word meanings is that they're ever-changing. The meaning of a word in the past isn't necessarily the meaning of that word today. Then there are cultural and social influences on words. The word *bad* to teenagers today means *real good*, although to most of us it continues to signify bad. So it is virtually impossible to keep up with all the semantic changes that occur. The best we can do is to keep the lines of communication open so meanings are clarified as much as possible and to make sure the context in which we are using our words conveys the message we want to communicate.

In the casino, words like *ace, action, bang up, bank, big six, bum move, bust, clock, count, cut, English, front money, going south, line bet, marker, move, point, stiff,* and *take,* all have more than one meaning. When using these words on the job, the manager or supervisor must be well aware of the context in which they're being used and to whom they refer. A comment like, "That's a bust if I ever saw one!" on a blackjack table where there's a female dealer who has large breasts can have serious implications, even if the supervisor was innocently referring to a major wager that went over the count of twenty-one. Vague words like *adequate, all right, average,* and *enough* can signify that a job was performed well, yet may leave the employee believing it was judged to be mediocre.

Although some semantic problems are beyond the control of the manager and supervisors, care should be taken in choosing words. Vague words should be avoided altogether or applied in conjunction with words that clarify their meaning.

NONVERBAL COMMUNICATION

Nonverbal communications such as darting eyes, a raised eyebrow, a tight lip, clenched teeth, crossed arms with a stern look, a raised fist, tight facial muscles, downcast eyes, a twisted mouth, a swinging motion, relay messages far better than words do. Mehrabian claims that 55 percent of a message is perceived through facial expression and posture, 38 percent from vocal intonation and inflection, and 7 percent through words. You see then that messages are transmitted mostly by the way you say them and not by the words you choose to express your ideas. Sometimes when you don't say anything at all, your body language has spoken loud and clear as if you had. That is why when dealing with people you must distance yourself from your personal situations. A personal problem at home, a heavy work load, job-related stress, etc., can move you to say things in a way you don't intend. This can stop an employee from relaying a message that may be important.

THE LISTENING PROBLEM

One of the biggest problems in communication is that people are not taught to listen properly. Studies have shown that the average manager listens to about 25 percent of capacity. If we block out 75 percent of what we hear, how can we expect to understand what is being said?

The casino manager has to be more receptive and listen carefully to subordinates. When there's a problem, the manager should stop talking and let them do the talking, and he or she should learn to listen beyond the words. I have already established that 93 percent of the message has nothing to do with words. So if you ask an employee how everything is going and the employee first sighs and then says *fine*, don't take the answer at face value just because you're in a hurry or that's the answer you want to hear. You may be circling a major problem that you will eventually have to deal with, and by then it may be too late. Say, for example, the person who answered *fine* was a female employee who is being sexually harassed by one of her supervisors. The man in question is a disturbed individual who later rapes and kills the female employee. Consequently, the woman's husband sues the corporation for millions of dollars and wins because, as it turns out, everyone in the pit knew the employee was being harassed and had complained to her pit supervisor, who had promised to handle it. But since the supervisor in question was a personal friend of the pit boss, the incident was never reported. You, the casino manager, end up being fired and sued, because you are held responsible for your operation. Had you only read through the word *fine*, you could have saved yourself, the woman, and the company a lot of grief. Far-fetched? Stalking laws are being enacted all over the country because women are being harassed and killed by unwanted suitors.

In 1983, the keno manager of the Horseshoe Casino, who was known to exhibit aberrant behavior and to sexually harass women, killed his wife and himself in a jealous rage. Today, more than ever, women are coming forward in the gaming business and complaining about sexual harassment. The next time you ask employees how they are and they say, "*Fine*," make sure they're smiling and they mean it. If they don't, ask what's bothering them.

And don't forget that personal problems are not the only ones that can escape scrutiny by your failure to listen between the lines. Cheating scams, false recording, comp violations, and many other serious infractions can go undetected because the manager doesn't have an ear to the ground and a hand on the pulse of the workplace. You have to keep your door open and, when someone enters, listen to the heartbeat. If you can do that, you can listen to anything else your employees have to say.

EFFECTIVE LISTENING

On the subject of effective listening, there's much that can be said. However, I believe no one has had a better handle on it than Professor Keith Davis, who established a ten-step guide.

The first step, Davis says, is to *stop talking!* When you are talking, you are producing noise that interferes with your hearing and concentration. Also, while you are thinking of what to say and how to say it, you are not concentrating on what the other person is saying. If you are a person of authority, your speech may force other people into passive roles and prevent them from expressing themselves. You may also intimidate these people and make them forget what they were about to say. So be quiet and listen.

The second step is to *put the talker at ease*. Make these people feel comfortable and relaxed enough to open up to you. Let them know they can trust you, that what they say will be used constructively. Make them feel as though they're talking to a friend, someone who cares.

The third step is to *show the talker that you want to listen*. Let people know that you are interested in what they're about to say and that you value whatever it is. Face these people and look them in the eyes with a look that clearly indicates that you are interested. Doing other work or looking bored or pressured for time sends the opposite message.

The fourth step is to *remove distractions*. Hand, feet, or any other kind of body movements can break the talker's concentration and place a barrier on communication. Music, television, loud machines, and open doors can also be very distracting. Avoid these nuisances whenever possible, and if you can't, keep them to a minimum or, better yet, find another time or place for the conversation.

The fifth step is to *empathize with talkers.* Empathy means putting yourself in the other person's place so you can better understand their thoughts and feelings—their point of view. This was a technique first made popular by the Client-Centered School of Psychology and Carl Rogers. The idea is that a therapist showing empathy toward clients or patients makes it easier for them to open up and trust the therapist.

The sixth step is to *be patient.* Some things take time to communicate, especially if they're delicate matters. Allow the talkers all the time they need to express themselves without interruption. A glance at your watch or a move to the door will indicate to the talkers that you wish them to leave. If you are too busy to talk or have other scheduled appointments, make the talkers aware of this. Unless their issues are matters of such immediate urgency that they must be dealt with at once, emphasize that what they have to say is important to you and you would like to schedule a later time to talk.

The seventh step is to *hold your temper.* Anger gets in the way of reasoning. Words and gestures are taken out of context and perceived differently from the way they were intended. If something is bothering you, whether it's part of the reason the talker is before you or not, take a few seconds to relax and clear your mind of all hostile thoughts.

The eighth step is to *go easy on argument and criticism.* When debating issues, regardless of what they are, put a hold on your passion and your pride. Assume the position of a reporter rather than a critic. A steady, even, matter-of-fact tone of voice will avoid a defensive and angry attitude from the talker. Argumentative conversation usually has no constructive outcome, and no one really benefits from it, even if someone considers himself or herself the winner.

The ninth step is to *ask questions.* By asking questions you show interest and you encourage the talker to elaborate and to continue to talk. It also gives the talker the satisfaction of knowing that you are listening to what is being said. Your questions also help jog the talker's memory and allow that person to develop ideas further and more accurately.

And finally, the tenth step is to *stop talking!* Yes, that's what I said. This isn't a typo. Davis ends his list the same way he started it because all of his other guides are dependent upon the fact that you can't do a good job of listening if you are talking.

CONCLUSIONS AND RECOMMENDATIONS

Make your ideas clear. This is another way to improve your communication skills. Take the time to analyze the ideas, issues, situations, and problems you wish to address. Understand the theme of your message, and make sure your communication elaborates on that theme. Be aware of semantic problems in communication. Use specific terms that identify precise times, places, and items. Instead of saying, *"Jack, whenever you get a chance, give me a report on the pit status,"* say something like, *"Jack, at three P.M. today, I want you to call my office with a total win/loss figure for every game in the pit, and I also want a total action report on anyone who is winning or losing five thousand dollars or more."* Specificity makes communication far more accurate.

Be conscious of your body movements. When talking to subordinates or vice versa, be conscious of your body movements, facial expressions, and the tone of your voice. Make sure that any inflection in your voice or any type of body language that you express reflects the message you want to relay. Remember, 93 percent of your message will be relayed this way, not with words. Don't send conflicting messages with your body that may make the other person frown, then stop and say, *"Oh, I get it,"* just before winking at you and nodding. If this happens, you know they're not taking you at face value.

Communicate at an understandable level. Make sure the message you are communicating to a person is packaged in a way understandable to that individual. If you are going to speak to a person of limited education, speak in terms that individual can understand. If you have doubts or read doubt through body language, be more explicit and repetitive until you are sure your intended message is received. In doing this, make sure your body language communicates respect and appreciation for the task this person performs so you don't leave the impression that your repetitiveness or explicitness was an attempt to belittle the person.

If you are dealing with someone who is methodical, approach that person in a methodical way. When dealing with people who are insecure, reassure them. Communicate so as to make them feel at ease. All this is called empathy; it means making a sincere effort to see the things the way your listeners see them, and by doing so, to be able to communicate at that level.

Be open-minded. Prejudice, preconceived ideas, and stereotypes are, unfortunately, inescapable in our world. These are barriers that restrict the natural flow of communication. We all have preconceived ideas of some sort, but those of us who are open-minded set these ideas aside and face the facts as they're presented to us. Judges are faced with this dilemma on an ongoing basis. Morally, they may feel something is wrong, yet legitimately, they know it is right, or at least not wrong. They must be able to differentiate between who they are as persons, and who they are as judges. The person can have an opinion, but the judge must interpret the facts in view of the law. Similarly, the manager must maintain an open mind to understand the person he or she is communicating with.

Obtain feedback. Without feedback you can never be sure your message is being understood. So you must get some kind of feedback unless you want to hope and pray that things will be done the way you want them. That might work for the clergy, but it doesn't work in the casino. One obvious form of feedback is to see if your order is being carried out. If you issue an order that floor supervisors must watch the shuffle in the blackjack pit, a stroll through the casino floor and by the blackjack pit should quickly verify compliance. Now, in one section you notice a floor supervisor is watching the shuffle, then is called over to another game for a fill, and stops watching it. In another section of the pit, the floor supervisor has two games held up because of watching and facing one particular game where the dealer is shuffling. You move to the next section where the floor supervisor is so positioned as to watch three shuffles at the same time, although not at close range. You realize then that part of your message got through, but not all of it. This could have been your fault because you weren't specific, or the message could have been diluted through the chain of command. Either way, this type of feedback has made you aware that the message, as you intended it, was only partly successful.

There are other types of feedback that could have helped you avoid this problem. If, when you told the shift managers that you wanted the shuffles to be watched, you noticed a certain hesitation on their part, or they were looking away from you after you said it, or they were looking down, or there was tension in their facial expressions, or they weren't paying much attention to you, you should have known then that there was a problem with the request. It could be that you intimidate the shift managers and they're afraid to ask you exactly how this is going to be implemented. It could be that the shift managers are afraid to look ignorant or stupid in your eyes, so they implement the order as they understand it. It may be that the shift managers disagree with the order and they have decided they will implement it the way they think best. And finally, it may be that the shift managers just don't like you or the order you gave, and they're going to attempt to sabotage it. All these situations occur in the gaming business, and the way to ensure you have been understood is to use another feedback technique called *questioning.*

If you feel the responses of your subordinates imply a lack of understanding, confusion, or whatever, ask them. The best way to ask is to have the subordinates tell you how they intend to ensure that your orders will be carried out. If they recite them the way you envision them, you know the message has gotten through, at least at that level. It is always good to phrase questions in a way that subordinates feel their cooperation is greatly appreciated. The manager could say something like, *"Jill, what do you think would be the best way to make sure everyone understands that I want them to pay close attention to the shuffles, but at the same time I want them to keep the games going?"* Jill now feels appreciated because you have asked for her input, and at the same time you are going to know if Jill understood what you wanted and if she has a problem with the implementation of this rule. With one question you have achieved more than one goal.

A follow-up memo clearly specifying the action to be taken is always a good idea. This, in addition to an open-door policy, will allow for another kind of feedback. If any doubts remain after the written communication, subordinates will come to you for clarification, input, and concerns. I realize this can present certain complications to casino managers who are very busy, but at the very least there should be certain time periods when the casino managers can make themselves available to their subordinates of any rank.

This provision will probably send a shock wave throughout the casino world because the chain of command seems to be writ in stone like the Ten Commandments. However, by being in touch with employees of all rank, the casino managers get a better feel for what is happening under their roof. This structure can sometimes be made of glass and can easily break and fall down on you.

It isn't that the chain of command is a bad idea in itself; it's that it doesn't work efficiently. Sure, it serves the role of delegation of authority, which is important in large organizations, but it also distorts communication. To begin with, up and down the chain of command are many individuals with varied points of view. This, added to all the other interpersonal communication barriers I have mentioned in this chapter, limits the flow of information. Diverse points of view not only serve as a barrier to how the information is understood, they also distort communication because someone up or down the line disagrees with the message being carried and purposely changes it to accommodate preconceived ideas or prejudices.

Filtering. Another necessary process of the communication system in the casino serves to restrict and distort the flow of information. *Filtering* is the process by which information is summarized and condensed to suit the needs of the different departments. This filtering sometimes results in loss of meaning and loss of important information in general. The different managers participate in this process and are subject to the barriers previously expressed. Also, the distribution process is subject to irregularities. Some departments will miss certain communications while others will receive some that are incomplete or distorted. A study conducted by Ralph Nichols and reported in *Nation's Business* found that vice presidents only received 63 percent of the information sent out by the board of directors, 40 percent was received by plant managers, and 20 percent was received by the workers. It's not surprising then that three different floor supervisors can be enforcing a shuffle rule in three different ways when the information in a casino sometimes must flow through nine different levels of management: the board of directors, the general manager, the vice president of casino operations, the casino manager, the assistant casino manager, the shift manager, the assistant shift manager, the pit boss, and the floor supervisor. That's

without including the position of games manager, which in many casinos doesn't exist. The information doesn't always travel straight down this line, but that is the chain of command.

Another reason for distortion of messages is status differences between employees in the casino. These status differences get in the way of effective communication in two ways: On the one hand they influence the information subordinates pass to their supervisor, and on the other they affect the way supervisors evaluate the information given them by the subordinates. In the first instance, an employee may fear unwanted news will not be well received by the superior because he or she only wants to receive good news. This point of view can allow problem situations to go on until their severity forces them out into the open, and by that time they may cost the operation in more ways than one. The other side of the coin is that supervisors have a tendency to listen more carefully to their superiors than they do to their subordinates. This lack of interest or disdain can also cost the casino precious resources both human and monetary. This is a serious problem that most casinos pretend not to have. But if there were ever an industry where this holds true, the gaming industry is one. A possible reason for this may be that, because there are so many supervisory positions available, everybody believes they are within their reach. This gives way to a strong, competitive spirit that in some instances becomes fierce and cutthroat. The people who manage to climb the ladder sometimes assume an attitude of superiority and those who are left behind resent that attitude. It is amazing that communication can flow at all.

Improving the communication flow. If the casino wants to increase the flow of information and improve communication in the workplace, a first place to start is through the chain of command. One way to accomplish this is to shorten the chain of command or management levels. Circus Circus, one of the most efficient gaming operations in the world, has managed to do this successfully. Another way to accomplish this is to regulate the communication flow.

Through meetings with subordinates, casino managers can exchange information and clarify areas that are vague. New plans, strategies, and objectives can be topics of discussion where employee participation is welcomed and rewarded. Employee input on plans is important because, eventually, employees will be the ones who will be carrying on the work. Employees can see the performance of a task from a perspective the manager can no longer see. As in the example given before, this type of exchange can serve to see how the manager's plan will be implemented and any possible difficulties can be tackled beforehand. Once everyone understands what has to be done, the manager can keep the communication lines open by scheduled progress checks and follow-up reports.

The communication flow between departments can be improved by regular meetings or discussions among representatives of those departments. Interaction between the marketing department and the table games and slot department is essential to successful implementation of programs. Communication between the food and beverage department and the casino department is important also because the casino issues a great number of food complimentaries. These are just two examples of interdepartmental communication that is vital to the proper operation of the casino.

One of the greatest feedback tools available is employee surveys. Employee surveys are becoming increasingly popular, although casinos in general have not availed themselves of this useful resource. There are so many issues that could be polled through this medium that it is really surprising that casinos haven't caught on. Managers could find out in a relatively short time if the casino objectives are understood, if there are any interpersonal or job-related problems, if new equipment facilitates tasks, if customers are responding to a certain approach, if supervisors are doing their jobs, if job descriptions are understood, etc. And the beauty of this system is that employees can express themselves freely without fear of exposure.

Suggestion boxes haven't been as effective as they could have been because employees rarely get feedback on what they suggest and because the reward systems in place haven't managed to attract enough attention. If a system were put in place that would answer all suggestions, explaining all the pros and cons and the reason the suggestion was not being used or why it was being used, employees would be more apt to offer them.

Enticing rewards would also increase participation. These rewards should vary so that many would have the opportunity to participate. Suggestions that save the company substantial sums of money or produce sub-

stantial amounts of money should be rewarded accordingly. Suggestions that just make for better morale or communication, facilitate a job procedure or increase customer satisfaction, etc., should be rewarded also with gifts the casino can afford to give without incurring a major company expense. Examples of these gifts would include a stay in a hotel suite at a time when it isn't busy, complimentary meals in different restaurants, the use of a limousine for one night, a party, or complimentary tickets to sporting events and shows. The possibilities are endless, and the boost to morale is unquestionable. It also makes good reading in the company newsletter, not only for the announcement of the gifts that were granted, but for all of the colorful suggestions that will be sure to arise.

An employee hot line is another way of facilitating communication. This could serve a dual purpose. On the one hand, employees can voice their opinion on varied company issues and, on the other, a counselor or counseling-inclined personnel can be on hand to help employees through difficult times and to serve as a sounding board. This would probably reduce employee absenteeism and turnover, and at the same time help with morale issues. Like *Dear Abby* letters, some of these conversations could be published in the employee newsletter and responses solicited and published. This can make management aware of possible serious problems. If nothing else, it serves a cathartic purpose, which in itself is very healthy.

Newsletters, if published with some degree of professionalism, can serve many important purposes. Up-to-date information on medical advances and health and nutrition issues can raise the awareness of employee health, not only providing a valuable service to the employee, but also to the company. Healthy employees are more productive and less prone to use sick time. General information that helps make life easier for employees can also become part of the employee newsletter. Employees can be polled to gather this material and any other information useful to the company. These services relay the message that the company and management really care about their employees. Employees who feel appreciated will do a better job for the company and complain less.

The financial status of the company, upcoming programs, products in development, etc., are all things employees are interested in knowing about. Since the information lines in the casino are so distorted, employees will never take at face value what supervisors communicate to them. An official communication from the company in the form of a report or printed in the newsletter gives more credence to facts that may seem hard to believe. Being informed of such aspects as hold percentages, win figures, the success of different programs, etc., employees are less apt to suspect that they're being misled when required to do something extra or to forfeit a cost of living raise or a bonus. This idea is controversial since some employers don't like to give out this type of information. However, since it is being released anyway, sometimes inaccurately, I believe this type of feedback has a positive effect.

Videotapes can also be a useful tool in the workplace. Company information can be disseminated this way, procedures can be demonstrated, training aids can be developed, employee activities can be recorded, employee talent can be displayed, employee commentary can be available to everyone. This is just another modern-day tool that is yet to be used as effectively as it could be in the workplace.

The employee discussion group also can facilitate communication today. Employees meet on a regular basis and discuss concerns and ideas for improving work tasks and the work environment. A representative or the group itself can then schedule meetings with management to discuss their concerns. Management can employ this same system with its middle management or between its middle management and the front-line employees.

CHAPTER 5

THE DECISION-MAKING PROCESS

When I think of a manager, I think of someone in control, someone who makes organizational decisions and implements them through other people. People make hundreds of decisions every day—some easier than others—and making them is an inevitable task.

Managers must make decisions that affect the organizations for whom they work and the employees who work for them. These decisions can have serious implications. People can lose jobs over them, companies can go bankrupt, cities can be impoverished, and countries can be devastated. America is paying today, and will continue to pay for many years, for the decision of the Savings and Loans to invest in junk bonds. History was changed by Harry Truman's decision to drop the bomb on Nagasaki and Hiroshima.

Because of their great responsibilities, managers can't afford to make hasty decisions. When a manager has to decide between letting an employee go and giving a second chance, as so often occurs in the gaming business, it is never simply a matter of whether or not the individual did wrong, but whether he or she really has to go. There are always consequences of the decision made and of the action taken. For one thing, the employee is going to lose livelihood and may be severely devastated. It not only has an economic impact on the person, it also has a psychological effect. These people might see their jobs as an extension of themselves. By losing the jobs, these people might feel a loss of a part of themselves and be unable to function. This is why some disgruntled employees have returned to their work environment and lashed out by killing everyone in sight or the persons responsible for their separation. Another consequence of the termination can be lack of support to their families.

Then there are the legal implications of termination. Today far more than in past years employees may fight back when they feel they have been unjustly terminated. And although Nevada recognizes the right of employers to terminate at will, even in Nevada cases have made it to the courts, costing thousands of dollars to defend against, with the possibility that the damages could amount to millions of dollars. In the case of the terminated Hilton employees, the court originally had granted the employees millions of dollars in damages, yet the Hilton prevailed on appeal. At the time of this writing, Hilton employees are still appealing the case. Given today's political climate, the future might not shine so brightly on the casinos. So it is time to measure these decisions.

On the other hand, it may be that the consequences of retaining an employee can be extremely detrimental to the operation and to the company. An employee who threatens the safety of the company or the employees within the company must be terminated, and so must an employee who is rude and costing the company revenues by the loss of many good customers. The point is that, regardless of the decision we make, something negative is going to come out of it.

TYPES OF DECISIONS

Organizational Decisions

Management theory distinguishes between two types of organizational decisions: Programmable decisions and nonprogrammable decisions. The term programmable decision was coined by Herbert Simon. It refers to reaching a decision by going through specific steps or actions. This resembles following the steps to resolve a mathematical equation. This is the type of

decision a scheduler makes when allocating personnel to games. In other words, if you need one floorperson for every four games in the blackjack pit and you need to open twenty games, how many floorpersons do you need? Simple mathematics answers that question and any other regarding the scheduling of employees to table games on the casino floor. Another programmable decision on the casino floor would be to allocate table games according to the house advantage from the casino entrance to the casino cage, if so requested by company officials. The manager would have to see what games he or she has available on the floor, what is the general PC of that game, and then design the layout of the pits accordingly. Comps issued to patrons are other examples of programmable decisions. Formulas are made or minimum guidelines are written to determine how these will be granted. By specifying how these decisions are to be made, management insures that errors are kept to a minimum. This makes the decision-making job of lower level managers and employees easier and less time-consuming. It is no surprise then that management tries to have as many programmable decisions as possible, especially for recurring situations.

Procedure manuals are full of programmable decisions that tell supervisors how to handle different situations. So frequently in casinos, new management takes over operations and immediately wants to change procedures. From the new management's point of view, this makes sense. But from the employees' point of view, it's an inconvenience they have had to endure many times and will probably have to endure many more. As they see it, they'll have to take the time to learn these new ways, only to have someone else in a few months come in and tell them to do something different. It is understandable that in these circumstances cooperation is difficult to attain. And it happens often that employees follow the new procedures for a while but then go back to their old ways. Studies have determined that it is usually desirable to communicate the rationale behind what is being implemented. If you don't do this, you risk encountering resistance that may force you to take further steps that may lead to a hostile and unproductive working environment. You have to understand that what you see clearly as beneficial to the company or your personal philosophy, someone else may find frustrating or insulting. It is, therefore, to your benefit and to the benefit of the company to explain the *why,* and if possible, to invite commentary and suggestions. You may learn something in the process.

Nonprogrammable decisions are required for situations that are new, inherently unstructured, or involve unknown factors. These decisions apply to objectives, improving the design of your games, improving upon supervisory functions, motivating your employees, etc. The causes of problems in these areas as well as the array of possible solutions can be many. To determine what the problem is and the best way to deal with it, you have to isolate the situation and analyze it closely.

INTUITIVE, JUDGMENTAL, AND RATIONAL DECISIONS

While there are two types of organizational decisions, there are three ways a decision can be made. One is by *intuition,* another is by *judgments,* and the final is by *rationality.* Rarely will a decision fit perfectly into any of these categories.

An *intuitive* decision is one that a person makes because it feels right. No reasoning is involved; it is just a matter of making a decision, period. Hunches and gut feelings are parts of this process. Intuitive decisions are unavoidable, especially at the top level of management, as pointed out by Peter Schoderbek and corroborated by Henry Mintzberg. Mintzberg states that top managers rely heavily on intuition. In fact, a study conducted by J. Mihalasky and H.C. Sherwood in *Nation's Business* indicates that there's a correlation between business success and extrasensory perception.

However, although intuition may be good in some cases, many corporate decisions are complicated and involve thousands of possible choices. The odds are heavily stacked against intuition in a situation like that.

A *judgmental* decision is one based on past experiences or knowledge. This experience or knowledge is used to approach situations that are similar to those in the manager's past. Common sense is then used to choose the alternative that worked before. Judgmental decisions can work well in organizational situations because they recur frequently, but sometimes they are faulty. For example, some people would discourage people over forty years of age, sometimes younger, from learning how to deal craps. Experience had told

these people that craps is a game better assimilated at a younger age. Like most judgmental decisions, this one isn't based on fact, but it may have some basis in common sense. However, it doesn't take other important factors into consideration, and it is a discriminatory act. For this reason, it is the wrong type of judgmental decision, and it shows the limitations of decisions made this way.

The advantage of a judgmental decision is that it is fast and economical. Research studies, expensive surveys, etc., are avoided. The down side is that it is ineffective when dealing with situations that are unique and complicated. It is very hard for most human beings to analyze many factors and come up with an effective decision without the aid of information systems or other devices. Plus, when managers make judgmental decisions frequently, it's probably because they're planted in the past and reluctant to learn new ways. Judgmental decisions have their place in time and depend on the circumstances, but they can't be relied upon when the stakes are high or when you're not stepping on common ground.

The advantage of the *rational* decision is that it isn't dependent on past experience, although that can be part of the process. The main advantage is that a rational decision is based on an objective and analytical process. This process is far more complicated and it involves making a series of choices that end only when the problem is solved. The first step in resolving a problem rationally is to define or diagnose the problem. There are two ways of doing this: One way is a reactive way, the other is a proactive way. The reactive way is for you to view a situation that should have happened but didn't. You then try to find out what went wrong and try to correct it. In gaming that would be like buying a large quantity of tickets for a special event, then sending out the invitations, only to find out that few people are interested. Now, after your program has failed, you have to try to find out why the people you sent the invitations to weren't interested.

In the proactive way of rational problem-solving, even though everything is going well with your program or programs, you take a closer look to see how you can improve. It may very well be that you have overlooked future trouble areas or that you neglected to consider a weakness that can be exploited by your competition. For example, let's say you start a $5 bettor junket program and it is doing very well. However, one of the groups you bring in doesn't have the same results as previous groups. When you take a closer look at the program, you realize that the drops and average bets of the group being questioned are far below the ones you had previously brought in. You do further research and you find that the results you enjoyed from the previous junkets were way above average and uncommon. In fact, you were very lucky. Based on the actual industry averages, you find that the amount of giveaways and promotions that went into this program far exceed the expected return on the program. Obviously, if you continue the program as it is, you are going to lose a lot of money. An adjustment to this program is in order, even though it has been successful heretofore.

Slot tournaments may also show the importance of a rational approach. A casino's slot program can be very successful for a while but then become repetitive at the same time the competition innovates new programs. If you continue with your program as it is, sooner or later the competition is going to draw customers away from you. So it is necessary for you to be innovative as well and make changes to maintain the interest of your customers. The old saying, *"If it ain't broke, don't fix it,"* doesn't apply here. Because if we don't fix it, it is going to get *"broke."* Peter Drucker expresses it best when he says, *"Results must come from the exploitation of opportunities."*

DIAGNOSING AND SOLVING PROBLEMS

Diagnosing a complex problem isn't an easy task and must be done in different stages. The first stage is to recognize and identify the symptoms of difficulty or opportunity. I use *symptom* here the same way a doctor does in relation to disease, although opportunity would be better related to prevention in order to reap future benefits. Some common symptoms of operational disease are low profits, low drop figures, low house hold percentages, excessive comping, poor customer relations, low morale, an abundance of hostility and conflict, and high employee turnover rate. Some of these will occur at the same time, such as hostility and conflict and a high turnover rate, or low drop figures and low profits.

Identifying these symptoms helps identify the problem and narrow down the possible factors that may be contributing to it. Just as in medicine or psychol-

ogy, managers should not be quick to react to symptoms, but treat them like what they are—an indication of something else that is going wrong. One of Freud's greatest contributions to psychology was to show us that apparent and sometimes obvious indications aren't always reality. With the use of hypnosis, he was able to cure paralysis in a young patient who evidently wasn't paralytic at all. Her paralysis was based in fear.

A Puerto Rican psychotherapist, Carlos Albizu, reports a woman who was brought to him blind and whom he cured with hypnosis, only to have her return months later, blind again. In essence, the woman was a very religious person who couldn't stand to look at the man whom she secretly loved and who was her sister's husband. Her blindness was a defense mechanism of her troubled mind—a symptom of her desperate fear. So like doctors and therapists, you as manager must dig deep to uncover the causes of what ails the operation. It is a common mistake in gaming to blame employees for low house holds, when in reality the fault may lie in the way the casino compensates its agents or the message it gives out directly or indirectly. It is a common belief among junket patrons and premium players that constant buy-ins indicate worthiness and value as a patron. They also believe, and it is sometimes true, that by hiding their chips (as if they lost them), they can fool the casino into giving them more perks, they can claim to have played more time and not been rated, and they can make no-interest loans from the casino by not paying back their markers immediately. All these maneuvers, in one way or another, affect drop figures and the house hold percentages. It is, therefore, no surprise that when casinos have major events, the drop is usually very high but the PC is very low. There seems to be a correlation between a very high drop volume and a low hold percentage.

I conclude then that to invest in incentive programs or to come down on the employees because of a low house hold percentage in these circumstances is a matter of reacting to a symptom in a way that isn't productive to the operation. It is better to invest those resources and energy into finding the true cause of the problem by collecting and analyzing information that is pertinent to the situation. Factors both within and outside the operation should be taken into consideration.

It is also important to realize that just collecting information isn't going to do the trick. You can end up being so overwhelmed by the data you collect, that in the end you're right back where you started. That's why the information you collect must be *relevant information*. Such information is data that is screened and applicable to a particular problem, person, goal, and time.

It is important to note that collecting complete and accurate information for an operational problem is very difficult. As I mentioned previously when discussing problems of communication, psychological factors come into play. These factors can distort the information you receive. In a casino, a shift manager's hostile approach may cause dealers to unite and decide to slow their pace on the games and give poor service. Their attitudes result in decreased hold percentages, decreased drop, and decreased win figures. The casino manager notices the trend, but when he asks the shift managers if anything is wrong, the shift managers don't want to communicate to him that there is a problem, so they just blame it on slow business. This explanation can hold for a few months, but after a while the casino manager should wise up and become aware of the problem. By then, however, irrevocable damage may have been done. It's possible that by then 25 percent of all dealers have been replaced due to resignations or terminations, and the casino is operating with demoralized help and with new dealers that aren't as productive. Even when the shift managers aren't at fault, they may conclude that they can be blamed for the situation, regardless. That's why you must be careful. The mere existence of a problem will cause stress and anxiety that will distort the information received. Managers many times are going to hear what workers think they want to hear because *there's no sense in upsetting the boss*.

CONSTRAINTS OF DECISION-MAKING

Sometimes the solutions to certain problems are beyond the control of the managers, and there isn't much they can do about them. These limiting factors are called constraints, and the gaming business is full of them. Because of the stigma associated with gambling, governments always impose a lot of constraints on casino operators. The perfect example for this lies in Colorado where casino speculation escalated to such a degree that property costs became prohibitive and those who invested were faced with a very difficult sell

because of government legislation that only allowed them to have five-dollar maximum bets on any game in the casino. It became aggravated even further when an anti-casino government imposed a higher tax structure that choked the major investors. At one time, any casino with over a million-dollar gross win had to pay 20 percent of all revenues thereafter to the state, in addition to escalating fees for gaming units, parking fees, etc. It is no wonder so many casinos went under during this period, one year after the state opened for legalized gambling. If you don't understand and identify the constraints you face, you risk wasting time, money, and energy in choosing a course of action that may be unrealistic and aggravating instead of helping solve the problem.

One investor in Colorado failed to see what most people already knew, that banks were not going to touch casino investments in that state. He decided to move forward, basing his judgment on his banking relationship and on informal confirmation of interest by the bank. Had he realized the true nature of the difficulties associated with Colorado gaming, he wouldn't have lost his three-million-dollar investment when the bank denied the financing he needed. This particular investor chose a course of action that was unrealistic.

DECISION CRITERIA

In addition to identifying constraints, the manager must also identify the decision criteria. These are the standards against which alternative choices must be measured. Let's say, for example, that a casino is experiencing diminishing revenues in the table game department and that in a meeting among managers it is decided that what is needed is an influx of new gaming on the casino floor to entice new customers. So the decision is made to bring in new games, but everyone has a different idea of what those games should be. The manager decides to establish criteria for the introduction of new games by determining exactly what qualities those games should possess. A consensus among managers comes up with the following: The new games should not cost more than $1,000 a month in licensing fees, should have a house advantage between 2 and 5 percent, should at least average forty-five decisions per hour, should allow at least six people to play at one time, should have a track record of at least a 17 percent hold, and a track record of at least a $4,000 drop, and should be fun and entertaining. These are the decision criteria.

ALTERNATIVES

The next step in rational problem-solving is to identify the available alternatives. It would be idealistic to expect managers to identify and evaluate every possible alternative, because they rarely have the time or the knowledge required for it. It is, therefore, best for the manager to limit the choices to those that seem most desirable. You must be careful here because all too often this limitation can lead to a judgmental decision and not enough choices are examined. Managers should have a good sample of the different choices available in order to make an educated decision.

Don't forget that there's always the alternative of inaction, which in some cases may seem wiser. This attitude usually leads to in-depth analysis of a problem or opportunity, rather than a reaction to a symptom. Most of the time inaction isn't the wisest course but, where the possibility of a future breakthrough or development is near, it may pay off to do nothing at the time. This situation can happen when, for example, an antiquated slot operation is lagging behind the competition and the obvious solution is to modernize the equipment. The slot director is anguishing over what equipment to buy when a subordinate hands him or her literature on promising slot technology that is going to be available in a month or so. The question then is, will it be worth it to invest in obsolescent equipment now so as to salvage this month, or will it be worth the wait for the new equipment that could outdo the competition?

Once you have identified a manageable number of desirable alternatives, you are faced with the task of evaluating them to see which one is the most viable. The manager must weigh the pros and cons of each and the possible consequences that choosing one would bring. To compare the solutions to each other, the manager needs a standard against which each alternative can be measured. These standards are the decision criteria.

Previously I established decision criteria for introducing new games onto the casino floor. Obviously, any game that didn't meet any one of the criteria would not be an alternative unless it was decided that a certain criterion was far more important than others and would qualify as an alternative by itself.

Nearly all of the criteria previously expressed had a quantitative value attached and could be easily measured. One, however, didn't. *Fun* and *entertaining* are qualitative terms that have to be rated in order to serve the purpose of evaluation. The managers can reach an agreement as to what exactly is fun and entertaining, then use a scale of say 1 to 3, or 1 to 5, where 3 or 5 is the highest ranking on the scale. You can then proceed to rate all the other criteria with the same scale and make a determination by point total of which is the most desirable game to introduce.

However, as is usually the case, some criteria will be perceived as being more important than others. For example, *fun* and *entertaining* might be viewed as twice as important as the other criteria. In the same way, the $4,000 drop criterion might be relegated to a lower status than the rest because you believe you can market such a game better and make it produce more. So you rate that criteria at half its value.

Another thing that has to be determined is what side of the PC spectrum is more important to you. You may judge that the ideal percentage is 3 percent, followed by 2 percent, then by 4 percent and finally by 5 percent. This would be a scale from 1 to 4 where 3 percent would be 4 (the highest rating) and 5 percent would be 1 (the lowest rating). If you wanted to keep the scale at 5, you could present it as 2.6 percent to 3.2 percent, 2.0 percent to 2.6 percent, 3.2 percent to 3.8 percent, 3.8 percent to 4.4 percent, and 4.4 percent to 5.0 percent. After rating each criterion, new games on the market would be given a point total for each category and multiplied by the factor of the criterion to determine a total number of points. The highest point total would then be the first choice.

Not all decisions can be measured this way since many factors can come into play. Environmental changes and the inability to implement the decision could prevent a solution from being put into effect as planned. Therefore, you must consider the probability of implementation of a solution to a problem. If one solution is more desirable than another but the chances of being implemented are far less, then it becomes a less desirable alternative. So, when evaluating alternatives, managers must consider the amount of certainty or risk associated with them.

Choosing alternatives when the problem is complicated and many tradeoffs are required or when much of the information you are dealing with is subjective is going to leave you with no clear winner. Basically, this is when the manager has to draw upon his or her experience and knowledge and make a judgment call. But at least here, the judgment isn't only based on that past experience and knowledge; it has other input to aid in the decision process. Although it is ideally expressed in those terms, this is where the decision process can get messy. Herbert Simon, author of *Administrative Behavior*, says his research indicates that managers make decisions that satisfy the need rather than pushing for the best decision to meet that need. In other words, managers choose alternatives that, even though acceptable, usually aren't the best alternatives. You can view these sorts of decisions as laziness in the decision-making process. But the truly effective managers do study the alternatives and they try to maximize rather than merely rationalize an earlier choice. This assertion is corroborated by Professor John B. Miner, who states that the body of evidence indicates this. But he also says that when the problem is very complex and there are too many possible choices of action, real maximizing may prove very difficult.

IMPLEMENTATION

However, whether you have the best possible solution or not, the problem-solving process doesn't end here. Now you have to put your solution into action, and doing so isn't an easy task either. Many managers have brilliant ideas that never get put into use because those who must carry out the solutions throw a monkey wrench into the system. So the manager must not only make a decision, but make sure it is implemented effectively. To do so, he or she must sell subordinates on the merit of the decision.

In the gaming business, many managers will frown upon the suggestion that they must sell the merits of their decisions to subordinates but, as Norman Maier has indicated, the degree to which decisions are effectively implemented can be increased if they're accepted by the people affected. If the objective is to have your well-thought-out solution implemented efficiently, then maybe it is worth having a chat with the troops, instead of firing a salvo over their heads, threatening to make them roll if anything goes wrong. This certainly doesn't work in today's world where so many educated people are part of the work force. It could be more of a problem in the gaming business where, many times, subordinates are better educated than their superiors. Implementation works out better when the people involved in the implementation have a say in the solution process and believe in what they're doing, or at least clearly understand the reasons why, even if they disagree.

In any event, the manager is going to have to monitor the situation closely regardless of the approach used, to make sure that things go according to plan and that no serious consequences follow the implementation of a solution. The process which facilitates this monitoring is called feedback.

Feedback is achieved by collecting data that is directly or indirectly related to the solution that was put into practice. With this information, the manager can compare the results achieved with what he or she expected to occur. If a negative deviation from the projections that were made occurs, the manager can take measures to correct the situation and avoid a harmful situation for the company.

RISK AND CERTAINTY

Previously I mentioned the concept of risk, which is the opposite of certainty. With certainty you know exactly what alternative is best, whereas when there's risk involved, an assessment of probability is needed. In the gaming business few things are without risk. Even the slot machines with their fixed percentages will deviate somewhat from results expected to be a certainty. However, with slot machines, the casino does know what to expect because, despite small variations, the differences are so minor they aren't significant. You can just about tell exactly how much money you are going to make if you can determine how much drop is going to be dumped into the machines. Table games, however, are heavily subject to risk. You can plan a promotion expecting to collect a certain amount of drop and to retain a certain amount of that money, but the result is always dependent on chance. You could even lose heavily, as so many times has occurred.

There are two ways to measure probability: objectively and subjectively. Probability is objective when we can determine it by statistical analysis of past experience. Table games themselves, for the most part, fall into this category. In other words, we know that the dice on a crap table are going to land on each of its six numbers one time in six, because they're perfect cubes. We also know that because there are two dice, the probability of any event occurring is going to be measured in terms of thirty-six trials, which is the number of possible combinations two six number dice (6 x 6) will produce. Likewise, in roulette we know that, since there are thirty-eight numbers, the probability of the ball landing on one of them is one in thirty-eight or 2.63 percent. Based on this information, the game is designed so that the casino wins more times than the player. This type of risk is easy to measure.

But when a casino makes decisions on what programs and ad campaigns to invest in and where to do expansion projects, other sources of information must be taken into consideration to determine risk, objectively. Relevant information can be obtained from governmental sources such as census, labor, and economic reports. These sources of information can make you aware of population density and composition in areas where you are contemplating gaming expansion. It also allows you to make income projections for viability studies. Income distribution, wages, unemployment figures, educational levels, etc., can also be found in these sources, helping us to not only make expansion decisions, but also decisions on marketing approaches. When pertinent information needed to make informed decisions isn't available in these sources, then private sources can be explored. If you still don't have the information you require, then make your own studies, provided they are cost effective for the goals you wish to attain.

One thing to keep in mind when using objective probability is that probability is only valid as an average and in the long run. If you determine that an action that you take is going to increase your hold percentage by at least two points, you can't expect to see this increase immediately. In gaming, a one-year trial period is ideal but, depending on your company's needs, you may not have that time available to prove a point. That's why game designers are forced to simulate play on computers, since it would be too time-consuming to do live trials. The problem with simulated play is that too many other variables aren't taken into consideration, yet there's very little the designer can do to compensate for this deficiency. As far as designers are concerned, their job ends when they successfully design a game that has a fair house advantage and is able to draw interest to

itself. From then on, it's up to the casino to make the people sit down and play.

Examples of objective probability gone wrong are the many gaming establishments that went wrong in the city of Cripple Creek, Colorado. Many inexperienced operators used statistical data to determine that building a gaming operation in this city would be cost effective and profitable because the national win averages on slot machines ranged from a low of $68 in Nevada to a high of $224 in New Jersey in 1990. In 1991, these averages went up to $69 in Nevada and $237 in New Jersey. Because of this statistical data, most projections in Cripple Creek were based on a win per unit that ranged from $85 to $125. Unfortunately, these estimates didn't hold up as the number of gaming units began to escalate quickly. The win per unit averaged out to around $60 for 1992, precipitated by a sudden drop at the peak of the season. The month of July saw the win per unit fall to $49 and it hasn't made a substantial recovery since. Not even those who were basically considered conservative at $85 came close in their estimates. The result—it was a cold winter in Cripple Creek. By January of 1993, seven casinos out of thirty-three had closed down, and quite of few others were struggling along. This indicates that statistical data alone can't be used to make decisions.

OTHER CONSIDERATIONS

Conditions of uncertainty leave the manager with two basic choices: One is to try to gather additional relevant information and do further analysis, and the other is to reach into archives of past experience, make judgment calls, use a little intuition, then assign subjective probabilities to the different outcomes. The first uses this added information to simplify the problem and then uses the second to infer probabilities. Of course, in this situation most people choose to skip right to the second and get it over with. However, truly effective managers don't do that.

But there are situations that force even the most effective manager to skip to the second choice. This occurs when time limitations or cost considerations don't allow for further collection of information. Timing is very important, as we all well know. Some people study things extensively, only to find that when they are ready to implement their findings, the window of opportunity has already slammed shut. This happened in Colorado when gaming was initially approved. There was a lot of hesitation and skepticism on the part of many investors, including the major names in gaming who could have capitalized on a potentially good situation.

This allowed some speculators to make a lot of money since at first very few people believed there was a future in Colorado gaming. One speculator, Carwin Bleidt, of Limited Gaming of America, placed options on properties with a total of $25,000 that he later converted into a sales agreement that netted his company $10,000,000 plus stock participation of a casino that was to be eventually erected on the property that he optioned. That casino is Harveys. Also, for a minimal investment, a couple who owned a small casino in Deadwood, South Dakota, put up an unpretentious building called the Gold Mine in forty-five days that began producing royally from the very first day it opened its doors.

ITT Sheraton is an example of a company that studied the casino market extensively while many opportunities passed them by. It finally decided to hire one of Nevada's most respected casino executives, John Giovenco, who was the gaming division president for Hilton Hotels. It has since begun to make gaming decisions, the foremost of which was to take over Caesars.

Other limitations to the decision process occur from a behavioral standpoint. Some of these occur when a manager perceives the existence and severity of problems differently from others. This will usually lead to disagreements and conflicts that hinder the decision-making process. Another limitation that affects managers in the decision-making process is the amount of work they have and the overwhelming amount of information before them. This will usually lead to a failure to perceive opportunities. That's why delegation and distribution of the work load are so important in management.

Finally, personal bias may influence the decision-making process. This may be the case where a manager has a pet program that is failing but, because it was the manager's baby, it is allowed to go on further than it should, costing a company a lot of money. It is also the case where the managers put down subordinates or fellow managers' ideas because they dislike them, or because those people failed to support these managers on one of their ideas. Anyone who has been in the gaming business for over a year is very much aware of behavioral constraints in the decision-making process. They certainly don't make for good management.

I have already noted that negative consequences of most major decisions are a given in the gaming business. That fact is so important in understanding the decision-making process that I must reiterate it. The problem here is one of comparing the disadvantages with the advantages in order to find the greatest overall gain in attaining the goals of the company, or those that we have set out to achieve. This will often require that the manager make subjective judgments as to what negative effects are actually acceptable in order to achieve the desired result. The manager should be aware, however, that there are some negative consequences that are totally unacceptable, and those are the ones that involve violations of laws, regulations, and moral and ethical standards. This is important to remember since the gaming business is notorious for these types of violations and the manager should be emphatically reminded that decisions such as these *are* totally unacceptable. No means justify the end, in this case. Period.

Finally, it is important to keep in mind that in gaming, as in other managerial endeavors, decisions don't exist in a vacuum. They are related to other decisions and will have an effect, one way or another, upon each other. One decision could, by necessity, spawn hundreds of other decisions in a complex organization. This is the case, for example, when the marketing or promotions department decides to put together a special event that is going to increase the number of guests in a hotel. The hotel department needs to decide how many rooms to allocate for the event, the food and beverage department has to decide on how to handle complimentaries and the increased traffic into the restaurants and lounges, the casino department has to decide how many employees to schedule and how many games of what kind to open, etc. Almost every department is affected by that decision.

As managers move up the casino ladder, their abilities to visualize the whole picture and to understand how all these decisions influence each other become of the utmost importance. Being able to see the total picture and to make decisions accordingly is the true mark of a good manager.

In most businesses, this perceptual ability is greatly appreciated and sought out because it is indeed a great asset. However, in gaming, the situation is so complex that true visionaries many times get overlooked. Maybe now that gaming is expanding so rapidly, these people will have an opportunity to shine.

CHAPTER 6

MOTIVATION

Possibly of all the areas covered so far, none strikes the interest of business as much as motivation does. If we can find a way to make our employees do the things we want them to do, the way we want them to do them, and make them feel good about doing them, we have found the key to successful business. This has been a concern of all business people since business became a concern of humankind. Social scientists and psychologists of this century have tried to make some sense out of the concept of motivation, yet to this day it remains somewhat of a mystery, and research is ongoing.

HISTORICAL BACKGROUND

Throughout history, people have believed that motivating is a simple matter of offering an economic reward. This was the view of Adam Smith's economic man in Wealth of Nations. However, as so many business people and casino operators have found out, this isn't always the case. In today's market, people are more educated and in better financial situations than they were when Smith wrote his book in the eighteenth century. They aren't the beggars who cherished the opportunity to work fourteen hours a day in an unhealthy environment for pennies. Today's worker usually has more than one skill, a supportive spouse or family, unemployment insurance, and a court system and government who are willing to back up the plaintiff in case of a legitimate dispute. With that kind of backing, you need something more than the offer of a job to motivate the worker.

THE CONTENT THEORIES

The content theories of motivation are based on inward drives that move people to action. These drives are called needs. Psychologists say a person has a need when a psychological or physiological deficiency is perceived by the individual. When a need arises, the individual's drive toward satisfaction of that need becomes the goal. Management should use this concept by aiming for working situations that cause employees to perceive that they can satisfy needs through behaviors that forward the company's goals.

For example, let's say the casino manager creates a program offering incentives for the winning teams in different table game departments for increases in decisions per hour. The rules of the program must be standardized to ensure equality. Of course, there should be some reward if increases are achieved, but even for the losers the need to belong has been satisfied. For the winners, the need to achieve has been satisfied. Depending upon how the casino handles those who increased productivity yet didn't win, the need for esteem may have been satisfied for both groups, and in the meantime, the company's objective—increased productivity—is also accomplished.

The above is a simplistic example. The cost of monitoring such a program could outweigh the results, and other variables could come into play. A similar program was once implemented at Fitzgerald's in Las Vegas.

If anything stands out in the study of motivation it's that there's no one best way to motivate people. Stephen Carroll and Henry Tosi concluded that the individual's need structure is determined by socialization, or early learning experiences. And what is more important, there are many ways in which a particular kind of need may be satisfied. One individual's ego needs could be satisfied by recognition as the fastest crap dealer, while another individual's need might be satisfied by being the smartest crap dealer.

Carroll and Tosi further state: *"The specific manner in which an individual satisfies a particular need is learned by reinforcement experiences early in life. We learn through experience that some situations are more desirable than others, and we seek these out. Other situations are the ones we seek to avoid."* So when you create jobs to motivate people, you must keep in mind that adjustments may have to be made to meet the needs of the people whom you are targeting.

REWARDS

The concept of reward is a very important one in motivation, and is also very tricky. In order for a reward to have the effect of reinforcing wanted behavior, the individuals who are being targeted by the reward must perceive it as such. That is precisely the definition of reward—something that is perceived to be valuable by the individual. A vacation in the Caribbean would be perceived by many as an incredibly valuable reward, while the same Caribbean vacation as a guardian to a younger pesky brother would be perceived as punishment. A million dollars in cash for most people is a chance of a lifetime, while the same reward to a primitive tribesman in Africa would just be a bad substitute for kindling wood.

Since money is the most obvious way in which companies reward individuals, it is important to see how effective it really is as a stimulus, at least from a research point of view. To the human relations movement, money is a secondary need. They contend that a person's social needs are of more importance. This view is opposed by the scientific management view that economic rewards always increase motivation. Somewhere between them is Frederic Herzberg, who recognizes the possibility of money as a need, just as long as it is linked to employee performance. However, since money isn't usually directly linked to performance, for the most part it isn't a need.

Behavioral scientists in their investigation of expectancy theory have found that money will serve as a need as long as a person places a high value on pay and believes there's a direct relationship between performance and pay. In other words, such persons need to feel their pay will increase if they increase their performance. But as William F. Glueck states in his book, *Personnel: A Diagnostic Approach*, although managers claim to pay on the basis of performance, in actuality they compensate primarily on the basis of seniority and attendance.

This is one of the biggest problems with motivation in the gaming industry. Gaming employees can't see (and there isn't) a direct relationship between performance and pay. A dealer who deals 80 hands an hour gets paid the same amount as a dealer who deals 50 hands an hour. And what aggravates the situation even further is that it might be the fifty-hands-an-hour dealer who gets the next promotion. Yet even if we could avoid this situation and actually determine that we are going to base pay on this type of production, quantification presents us with another big problem. Basically, in order to have a reasonable amount of accuracy, we would have to assign people to do nothing else but count the hands put out per hour per individual. Obviously, if we did that, we would need one person for each person, which would be inconceivable since the added production would be negated many times over by this investment in human resources. The alternative would be to review video tapes in fast forward. Yet even this approach would require a large amount of personnel, and the profitability of this program would be questionable. It is no wonder then that casinos don't want to invest in this type of approach, especially since there isn't an immediate link between increased decisions and revenue.

Of further consequence is the fact that more speed could add to the number of errors, making the extra production negligible. Finally, in gaming, production of revenues is determined by many factors aside from hands per hour, and it varies from department to department. So even if a computer program could be developed to accurately quantify production this way, the above definition of production would still be questionable.

Rewards are categorized as intrinsic and extrinsic. Intrinsic rewards are those that are derived from the work itself. In other words, our job gives us a sense of achievement, it presents us with a challenge, it increases our self-esteem, it promotes friendship, it allows us to interact with other people, and it makes us feel our work is meaningful. These rewards are taken into consideration when job descriptions, duties, and working conditions are designed.

Extrinsic rewards, on the other hand, are rewards provided by the company itself. These would include pay, awards, praise, company cars, vacations, health and insurance benefits, complimentary use of restaurants, promotions, private offices, etc. Since it is obvious that all these incentives work to a certain extent, to what extent and in what proportion they should be used as enticements was the task that content theories set out to resolve.

The most noted of all content theorists were Abraham Maslow, Frederick Herzberg, and David McClelland. I've already mentioned Maslow and Herzberg, but it is important to note that Maslow's need hierarchy begins with the more predominant and easier to satisfy primary needs (physiological needs, and the need for safety and security), up to the need that is never actually fulfilled, which is the need for self-actualization.

Primary needs are more concrete and easier to deal with. The employee's pay allows satisfaction of hunger, thirst, shelter and rest, and can even allow satisfying the sexual need. Pay and pension, to a certain extent, satisfy the need for security and safety.

But the secondary needs, which include social interaction, esteem, and self-actualization, present the employer with more of a challenge and require a good understanding of the work force and the individuals who represent it. The good news is that, since self-actualization can never be totally satisfied, there will always be a need that will keep a person going. The problem with the hierarchy theory is that it assumes an escalation of enticements up the ladder as the lower hierarchy needs are satisfied. When actually, basic needs are, for the most part, so easily attainable, they do usually factor at the organization's level. Also, what's an important need for one person isn't an important need for another.

Even cultural groups as a whole show noticeable differences, as evidenced by a study reported by Haire, Ghiselli, and Porter, pertaining to international groups of managers. This is important to keep in mind, since the United States is a melting pot of diverse cultural backgrounds. The gaming business is inundated with a great variety of minority groups given the international markets they cater to, and the ease with which underprivileged people can enter it.

MCCLELLAND'S CONCEPT OF NEEDS

McClelland, on the other hand, uses a different approach to motivation. He assumes that, since the lower-level needs are so easily satisfied, they aren't worth considering. By contrast, he categorizes needs as the need for power, the need for achievement, and the need for affiliation. People who are motivated by the need for power tend to show it by being outspoken, forceful, confrontational, and stubborn regarding their original position. They're very demanding people who expect a lot from others. Power-hungry people usually find their way into management positions, where they can exercise their need for power. Sometimes these power-crazed people can turn their need into positive energy that directs them to achieve not only their goals, but the goals of the company as well. Other times, the power craze feeds on others, and eats through employee relations like cancer spreading through lymph nodes. Operators must be aware of the symptoms of the negative side of this need, since, as I have said, many power-crazed people reach managerial positions. The effect of a power-crazed person bent on destruction can be devastating to a business, especially in the gaming business, where symptoms don't tend to appear until the damage is extensive.

The need for achievement isn't satisfied by perceived success, but by the process that involves taking work to a successful completion. Individuals motivated by the need to achieve are risk-takers. They strive on taking personal responsibility for problem situations that carry moderate risk, but expect to be credited with the solution in a concrete and clear way. McClelland says that these employees can be valuable to the organization, but if they aren't given opportunities to demonstrate their capabilities, they can't succeed. They need to take the initiative and to be rewarded for it. Otherwise they will be frustrated, and the company will lose out on an excellent resource.

Individuals with a need for affiliation are those who thrive on social interaction. These individuals are ideal for jobs such as hosting positions that bring them in close contact with people. Fortunately, in the gaming business there are many jobs that allow individuals to interact with people. This is something that must be kept in mind before enacting policies that restrict employees' social interaction. Often casino management will prohibit employees from socializing with customers or among themselves because they believe this to be the cause of decreased hold percentages or revenues. This is hardly ever the case, and to enact procedures that prevent employees from socializing *will* have a negative effect, not only on hold percentages, but also on revenues, eventually. This was the case at Trump Castle in 1989 when a form of gag order was issued prohibiting conversations between customers and employees. That may not have been the only factor contributing to the company's decreased revenues in 1990, but it sure was a contributing factor. The customers were made aware that their friendship wasn't welcome, and revenues dropped from $264,835,000 to $233,870,000, an 11.7 percent decrease.

HYGIENE FACTORS AND MOTIVATORS

Herzberg differentiates between what he calls hygiene factors and motivators. Hygiene factors are things like company policy and administration, working conditions, pay, interpersonal relations with superiors, co-workers and subordinates, and quality of supervision. Motivators are achievement, advancement, recognition, responsibility, and growth opportunities. Hygiene factors are mostly environmental, while motivators are related to the work itself. The important thing to remember about hygiene factors is that they cause dissatisfaction only if they aren't present or are inadequate. Adequacy in this case isn't a motivator. In others words, if the pay is average, it's not going to matter to the employee one way or another. However, if it's too low, you can take odds that the employee will be looking for another job or is going to leave at the first opportunity. The same holds true for company policy. If the rules are too restrictive or too lax, the employee isn't going to think much about it. But if the company starts to restrict the employee's freedom of movement or ability to perform tasks, or if no one is watching the store and supervisors can't be found when needed, the employee is going to feel frustrated, and there will be negative consequences.

Surprisingly, if motivators are inadequate or absent, they don't produce dissatisfaction. Yet when adequate, they do motivate employees and assure job satisfaction. So the lesson to managers is that both hygiene factors and motivators should be present in the working environment so that employees perform better and are more content. If management wants to increase productivity, then it should focus on designing tasks that provide the employees with challenging endeavors, freedom to act, individual responsibilities, diversity of tasks, and the feeling that they are somehow responsible for a project or task from beginning to end. It would work even better if the individuals had the opportunity to choose, from all these factors, the ones that motivate them best.

You can see that this theory has interesting implications and that to a certain extent it makes sense. However, studies conducted by Robert House and L.A. Wigdor indicate that a given factor can cause job satisfaction for one person and job dissatisfaction for another person. This goes back to what I said before, that different people have different needs, and that in that context, either factor, be it hygiene or motivator, can motivate people. Richard Darder, in a study conducted for his master's thesis at University of Nevada-Las Vegas, found that Clark County dealers' primary concern was pay. And for those of us who have worked in the gaming business, money does seem to be an important concern. But I also know of people who have stormed out of casinos and quit, even though their pay was considered high by most standards. So to attempt to generalize either way can prove to be a serious mistake that should be avoided if you want your program to be effective.

PROCESS THEORY

Irrational acts such as a shift manager storming out of a casino and quitting a job that paid $70,000 a year can't be explained easily by a theory based on needs. Because of the disparities between acts and motivation theory, process theories evolved. The intention of process theorists was not to dispute the existence of needs; it was to explain those actions that were inconsistent with the need theory. According to them, behavior is also a function of the individual's perceptions and expectations regarding a situation and the possible outcome of the actions taken to achieve goals.

EXPECTANCY THEORY

The expectancy theory contends that, in order for individuals to be motivated, they must expect the behavior to lead to satisfaction or getting what is desired. In this sense, expectancies can be viewed as an individual's estimate of the probability that a certain event will occur.

Regarding work performance, there are three factors: effort-performance expectancies, performance-outcome expectancies, and valence of the outcome. Effort-performance basically means that motivation is going to increase if people feel there's a direct relationship between their efforts and performance, and motivation will decrease if they feel there isn't. In a gaming situation, a floor supervisor might seek customer names aggressively and fill out many rating cards if it is believed that he or she will be praised for the extra effort. However, the reverse will also be true: The supervisor who believes nobody cares will most likely turn in as few rating cards as possible, depriving the casino of one of its best customer relations opportunities.

Performance-outcome expectancies means that a certain outcome will result from a given level of performance. This is usually viewed in terms of rewards. In the case of the floorpeople who are hustling to get customer names and rating cards done, it very well may be that they expect that this performance will give them the recognition needed to get a promotion or an increase in salary. But, as in the example above, if employees perceive this not to be the case, then they will not bother, and will do as little as possible.

There is, however, another situation that applies here. If the employees believe the performance will get them the reward but that they aren't capable of doing what is needed, then performance will also decrease. In other words, if the floorpeople are introverts and fear being ridiculed by customers or admonished for asking their names, then they aren't going to do it even though they believe they would earn a promotion or a salary increase. This is only one example, but there are other situations that would prompt employees to reason this way in other situations. It could be that the individual has low self-esteem, isn't qualified, is poorly trained, or the job description precludes seeking the outcome that would assure the promotion or salary increase.

That's why it's so important to recognize everyone's effort. Many times contests will be designed where only those who are victorious are rewarded, and performance evaluations greatly favor those who are doing exceptionally good jobs. But what we tend to forget is that many times there are individuals who are giving 110 percent of what they have to offer while remaining below the leaders due to limitations that they have. Yet the leaders may be working at 80 percent of their capacity and are simply gifted, or have been doing the task so long that it is second nature to them.

In the experiment at Fitzgerald's, those dealers who increased their output to 375 hands per hour in blackjack (approximately 94 decisions) for four months without mistakes were given a $300 bonus. The average was determined to be 324 hands per hour (approximately 81 decisions). Those who didn't make the average were counseled and given pointers on how to improve. Hypothetically, let's assume that the dealers who exceeded the 375 hands per hour were averaging 360 hands per hour and that the dealers who didn't make the average were doing 295 hands per hour and increased their output to 320. The net gain for the underachievers is 25 hands per hour for an increase of 8.5 percent. The net gain for the overachievers is 15 hands for an increase of 4.2 percent. In terms of improvement percentage, the underachievers performed twice as well as the overachievers yet ended up getting counseled for it, while the others were rewarded. If this were the case, then the operator failed to realize that the supposed underachiever produced more new income for the house—approximately two decisions per hour—than the overachievers. The marketers of multiple action blackjack have based a marketing campaign on the finding that their new game will achieve 2.1 more decisions per hour, so that shows us how strong the performance of the underachievers could be for the casino operation.

I don't intend to imply that these were the circumstances that were present when Fitzgerald's conducted its experiment. What I am saying is that there are many ways to measure performance, and that all of them should receive consideration if the operation wants to profit from motivating programs.

The last factor in the expectancy theory is the valence of the outcome. This refers to the perceived value of outcome or the reward being offered. It is the anticipated satisfaction or dissatisfaction that results from the outcome or the reward. Obviously, if the value associated with the reward or outcome is low, the motivation level of the individual will also be low and so will performance. If it is high, then the performance level will be high. This is important to note, not only from an employer's perspective, but also from a marketer's perspective. Many times programs are designed that have very little perceived value to our customers.

Obviously, if the valence is low, the turnout will be low. The message is: Know your customers, and know your employees. Otherwise you're not going to satisfy anyone. Computers can be a great aid in this respect. Data bases can be filled with information that is relevant to the needs of both your customers and your employees. It can tell you whether the majority of your employees don't like sports, so don't invest in a golf tournament for employees. Or it might tell you that they do like golf, so invest in a golf tournament.

What becomes obvious is that, if any of the expectancies above are low, performance is going to be low. Also obvious is the fact that the expectancy theory relates to individual needs and that these vary from person to person. Therefore, management should take individual needs into consideration when determining what rewards to offer to whom. This may seem like too much work, especially in the larger properties where thousands of people are employed, but the benefits that can be reaped from it will outweigh the inconvenience. Casinos are so stratified anyway that there are always supervisors in proximity to their workers who should have knowledge of their subordinates' needs and wants.

Another lesson to be learned from the expectancy theory is that there should be a strong relationship between performance and reward. Policies that reward attendance establish this type of relationship. This can be done either by giving a reward such as a day off with pay, complimentaries, or by assigning monetary value to sick pay. In other words, the operation can establish that, after a certain amount of accumulated sick days, the company will pay cash if they aren't used within the year. This gives the employee an incentive to come to work everyday because of anticipating getting the money as a bonus toward the end of the year.

Casinos are at a disadvantage with other industries when it comes to establishing direct relationships between performance and rewards because it is difficult to quantify production in most departments. Also, in a service business such as a casino, quality of service is many times preferred to quantity. A dealer can be very productive by putting out 80 hands an hour of blackjack, but may in the process bypass customer requests and fail to answer questions and important customer concerns. So the dealer achieves more hands per hour, but the customers leave the table early because they feel it is inhospitable. The casino loses because, even though it has more decisions per hour, it has fewer decisions per drop. The house hold is then reduced. The same is true of the speedy waitress. She may get more tables done, but will the customers she served want to return? Somewhere between these two positions is the ideal, where the work task is performed at adequate speed and the customer's need for affiliation, recognition, affection, friendship, and esteem is satisfied. Defining that in a measurable way is the challenge casino operators face and must respond to if they intend to compete effectively in markets that are becoming more and more restrictive.

Another lesson the expectancy theory teaches is that the expectations establishments have of their employees should be realistic, although there's nothing wrong with setting them high as long as they're attainable. If an extra effort allows all employees to achieve the goals set by the establishment, then it is high enough and realistic enough to increase performance. It should also be noted that, if management doesn't help employees see themselves as capable of attaining the performance goals management sets for them, the employees may not perceive themselves as capable, or may feel that management is treating them as machinery or possessions to be used and abused. The ideal conceptualization here is that of a team with common, mutually beneficial goals. If the employees can see that their extra effort is going to help the company succeed, and that by doing so, they're going to benefit by rewards that are meaningful to them, the program will succeed.

A statement by Sterling Livingston is something to keep in mind about managerial attitudes. *"The way managers treat their subordinates is subtly influenced by what they expect of them. If a manager's expectations are high, productivity is likely to be excellent. If his expectations are low, productivity is likely to be poor. It is as though there were a law that caused a subordinate's performance to rise and fall to meet his manager's expectations."* Keep this in mind as you counsel employees and prepare their evaluations. Your expectations are usually clearly expressed in these situations, and you may be fostering exactly what you are trying to avoid. It is very common in the gaming business for supervisors to linger on the negative and to make demeaning and derogatory remarks about their employees. It is also very common to believe that most people don't care about their work and, therefore, the only way to combat this attitude is to threaten their jobs and to verbally abuse them. For those of you who believe this way, a closer look at Livingston's statement may give you greater insight. Of course, you can assume the attitude that this is just a theory and you know better, but most research tends to support expectancy theory.

THE EQUITY THEORY

The equity theory has to do with how individuals subjectively determine the ratio of reward received to effort extended and compare their ratios to those of other employees doing similar work. In other words, if an employee sees that another person is putting out less effort at the same task for the same compensation, the other person is then perceived as receiving a greater reward for his or her effort. A situation of imbalance is noted here, and it results in psychological tension. The result will be that the individual will seek to reduce this tension and return to a state of balance. Exactly how the person does this will vary from individual to individual, but it will usually be through a reduction in work output. This situation is very common in the gaming business, where dealers can easily see that other dealers aren't putting out the same effort as they are, yet get compensated exactly the same. They can also see it in the distribution of breaks, where some people tend to be favored because of their relationship to the person who is doing the schedules. They may spot it in the distribution of early outs, a concept that refers to employees being allowed to catch an early start home. And they can also note it in the assignment of games, where some people end up with relative frequency on games where little effort is required or none at all, while others always seem to end up on the busy games. Ironically, it is the better dealers who end up on the busier games because management realizes they're more productive and can serve the situation better. This would be fine if such employees were compensated or rewarded in some way to make up for the difference in effort, but unfortunately this doesn't occur. What results is the imbalance I spoke of, and a lot of psychological tension, since almost everyone tries to see who is getting away with the least amount of work. The same holds true for the floor supervisors and many other employees throughout the casino.

Equity theory makes a strong point that can't be overlooked since it is so relevant to what happens in the gaming industry.

Equity theorists recommend to management that they make employees understand why some people are rewarded better than others. It should be made clear that the experience of some others allows them to produce more, therefore they're compensated more. If the difference is due to the effectiveness of the other person, then it should be pointed out that as soon as the employee becomes as effective as that other person, compensation will rise accordingly.

The problem in gaming is that this is very hard to demonstrate. A person may have more experience and yet be less knowledgeable and perform less adequately. The other problem is that, because of the relationships that are established in the gaming business, a person doesn't have to be effective to be compensated more. Evaluations are so subjective that they're easily influenced by the biases of the evaluators, and effective employees are many times passed over for less competent ones.

The mission in the gaming business seems to be to standardize well-defined effectiveness guidelines so that everyone can be equitably measured by them. Having done so, an ongoing record of employee performance should be kept by which the supervisor can derive information for monthly, trimestral, or semestral evaluations. These should be quantified and qualified to reach more valid conclusions than subjective and biased recollections after a long period of time has transpired. This forces the supervisors to pay true and careful attention to the performance of their employees, to be careful about their biases since their records will be compared to relief and substitute supervisors, and will make them cautious about their conclusions since there will be a paper record of their previous assessments and progress reports. So, if after a six-month period a supervisor says that an employee has bad customer relations, but there's no record on the employee log of counseling to that effect and a progress report maintained thereafter, the supervisor has a lot of explaining to do, especially of how he or she allowed the situation to go on for such a long time without taking action. If it were to come to your attention that in a six-month evaluation a pit boss judged a dealer to have bad customer relations and there's no record that

this dealer was counseled to that effect or that progress reports and the situation weren't monitored, you would have to consider terminating the pit boss because this is such a vital aspect of your business. The potential loss of revenue during this period due to the dealer's attitude and the supervisor's neglect could have equaled a purposeful error amounting to hundreds of thousands of dollars, for which any employee would have been fired. Obviously the pit boss has seriously compromised the job and deserves to be terminated.

THE PORTER-LAWLER MODEL

The Porter-Lawler Model makes a couple of great contributions to the study of motivation. One is that performance depends on an individual's effort, abilities, traits, and perceived role. The other is that performance leads to satisfaction, and not vice versa, as the early human relations theorists claimed. This model takes into consideration both expectancy theory and equity theory. Basically, the effort is going to be based on the perceived value of the reward and the perceived probability that the effort is going to result in attaining the reward. Performance is going to be based on the abilities and traits individuals possess, the role individuals believe themselves to have, and the effort they are willing to put forth. Attainment of a certain level of performance is going to earn the individual intrinsic rewards (feelings of competence, self-esteem, etc.) and may earn extrinsic rewards such as bonuses, raises, and promotion. It is understood that the latter possibility isn't necessarily true because the company may not recognize or appreciate the increased level of performance.

The parallel with the equity theory comes in the next step where the individual evaluates the perceived equability of the rewards attained. Satisfaction will result from the combination of the rewards attained and the equity perceived in them.

The most relevant contribution of this theory to management is that, contrary to what many managers believe, performance is a cause of satisfaction, not a result of it. The idea that happier workers work harder is questionable, and must be seen in relation to other variables within motivation theory. It is here that the Porter-Lawler Model makes its greatest contribution to motivation theory: It makes us aware that motivation isn't a simple matter of cause and effect. In fact, it is the Porter-Lawler contention that a sense of achievement leads to satisfaction and will probably result in increased performance. This explains why some people don't seem to need incentives to do their job efficiently and do their work with a high degree of productivity. All they need is the opportunity to perform and the right conditions in which to perform. This explains why we sometimes see contrasting attitudes toward the same job: While some employees are dissatisfied with the way things are run and show extreme concern about their jobs and how they perform them, we may see other employees who look happy yet don't seem to care much about what's happening around them. These individuals take a lot of pride in their work and are happy if they're proven to be more productive or effective than other workers. Sometimes this is the only satisfaction they can hope for since no one else, except maybe customers and subordinates, recognizes their talent or seems to care.

Of further importance is the fact that the satisfaction these individuals derive from performance of the work is going to be rated in terms of its perceived value to the individual, and this perception is going to affect the perception of this reward in future situations. This can affect the way employees perform their work in the future. As demonstrated by the Porter-Lawler model, most people feel this way even though the perception of their rewards may have changed the way they see their jobs, so it is important to take note.

CONCLUSIONS AND RECOMMENDATIONS

I hope at least a few aspects of motivation have become clearer through this discussion of motivation theory. One is that there are no easy answers to motivation problems. Two, many factors come into play and should be considered. Three, not once was there mention of negative reinforcement, a concept made popular by behavioral psychologists. The reason negative reinforcement was never considered by modern motivation theory is that from the beginning it was considered medieval and ineffective. It was a part of what early studies called the carrot-and-stick motivation because of its similarity with the classic method of getting the donkey to move. Even behavioral psychologists will admit that negative reinforcement by itself is ineffective and full of drawbacks, while they're quick to point out that positive reinforcement or rewards are far more effective. This is precisely the point that B.F. Skinner made.

However, it doesn't take long to realize that negative reinforcement or punishment is a widely used motivation practice in the gaming business. Supervisors constantly remind employees their jobs are on the line if they don't perform adequately, they shout orders at employees, they threaten them with write-ups, they verbally abuse employees, and they harass them to the point of forcing some to quit, to work under psychological tension, or to seek support from an internal or external source such as the employee relations department, the labor board, the civil rights department, or the Equal Employment Opportunity Commission.

The implications of this type of behavior to employers should be obvious, especially in today's working environment where so many people feel discriminated against. A *Psychology Today* survey showed that many minority, female, and handicapped people perceived themselves to be treated unfairly on the job. From an equity theory standpoint alone, this has serious implications for the employers. If on top of this perception you add a perceived abusive supervisor, you have a situation that isn't conducive to a good and productive work environment. Considering that well over 60 percent of the work force is comprised of females, minorities, and handicapped workers, it spells the possibility of a major volatile situation, that has already begun to manifest itself. This is another reason subordinates should be required to evaluate their superiors or at least be questioned as to specific situations that could be the source of operational problems. This would alert management to potential problem situations that could be highly detrimental to the company.

In 1991, five female employees of the Mirage filed suit against the company for failing to take measures to protect them against sexual harassment from one of the company's executives. The details of this situation are intricate, but suffice it to say that this abusive behavior went on for almost two years before the executive was terminated. Had the company used subordinate evaluations of superiors, they would have known of the situation long before the problem got out of hand and could have taken corrective measures.

I believe the preponderance of negative reinforcement in the gaming business has to be evaluated closer in terms of what it attempts to achieve. Then it should be compared to other forms of motivation and weighed to see which has the potential of accomplishing the company's goals more effectively. I don't advocate that employees should be handled with kid gloves, especially when their actions call for firm punishment. But there's no need to degrade employees or to deprive them of the dignity and respect that every human being deserves. Management should take an active role in insuring that everyone is treated with respect and equality. Less than that is unacceptable in today's world.

In general, management should provide equal pay for equal work and clarify in every way possible the relationship between increased performance and increased pay. They should give recognition to employees by tangible means for their extra efforts and for exceeding average job performance. They should create jobs that allow for social interaction and team spirit. They should show employees that they care for them by promoting outside activities to bring the team together. They should design tasks that challenge the skills of employees so they feel compelled to meet the challenge. Chances for advancement should be made available and, when not present, the possibility of lateral movement to other areas of interest should be explored together with exploration of other work possibilities that can sustain the interest of employees. Jobs should be designed to allow employees to develop their abilities. For those who have creative minds, situations that require creativity should be presented to them. Many situations or future projects lend themselves to a lot of planning and exploration; therefore, the company can benefit from the input of subordinates in goal-setting and decision-making. Don't be afraid to delegate authority. This raises the employee's self-esteem, and it takes a load off the superior, leaving more time to do other important things. Show that you care for the employee's welfare by providing a healthful work environment. Promote good and effective relationships between superiors and subordinates. Keep employees informed so they don't feel they're being used or that your secrecy is intended to conceal your real intentions. Don't make unreasonable demands of your employees. Don't support special privileges for managers that increase the status of the manager at the expense of the people who actually do the work.

Employees can sense when management has ulterior motives or is trying to make up for what it should have done but didn't do because the situation has changed against it. I see this quite often when a new, influential property is about to open, and management fears it is going to lose a good portion of its qualified help. That's not the time to think about satisfying your employees' needs; it needed to be done way before that.

The long list of things I presented that I feel will make employees respond better to management wishes aren't by any means the totality of what is possible. All of those things are mere guidelines to clarify the theories discussed. Before I end this discussion, I do want to present a few concrete examples of possible ways to motivate employees in the gaming business.

The first example is one that satisfies the need for recognition, esteem, social interaction, self-actualization, responsibility, and to a certain extent, the primary physiological needs. The idea here is to train employees to interact effectively with customers so they can serve a customer relations function such as a hosting or a position in customer services. The main targets of this policy are dealers, marketing clerks, and floor supervisors, although any other employee can be used as well. Every day, one or more employees will be selected to serve as a host on the casino floor or to aid people at the customer service desk. The more people selected, the better. This should be done on a rotating basis to give as many people as possible the opportunity to do it. If an employee's interest is in another department, he or she should be allowed to work in that department instead of hosting. In the same way, employees in other departments should be allowed to learn job tasks in the gaming department. This not only gives a better understanding as to how the operation works; it also gives a clearer picture of the service they provide for the company. And it also provides the company with substitute employees when shortages occur in the different departments. This is a great way to combat the inevitable employee boredom and rapid turnover experienced in the gaming department.

An even more effective variation of this policy is to have employees share higher responsibilities. Give all dealers the opportunity to be floor supervisors once in a while, and give all floor supervisors the chance to be assistants to the pit boss, and so forth up the ladder. If you want to make it even more interesting, you can have a casino manager for a day, given at random, every once in a while. The casino manager can supervise the person chosen and make sure that blunders aren't committed. Other than that, the person gets a feel for the job and a look at something to shoot for. This gives supervisors a little more to do, but it pays off in the long run because everyone is trained to assume a higher position. For even more participation, instead of whole working days, upper-level tasks can be assigned at various intervals of the day. Suggestions could also be accepted as to job designs that would make life easier and more productive for the casino, while increasing the interest and motivation level of the employees.

Probably one of the greatest challenges in casino management is to measure performance and to link it to rewards. In the marketing department, hosts can be measured by the number of new customers they bring in, by the amount of drop their customers bring into the casino, and by the amount of action they place in the casino. But even then, most of the new customers accredited to that host could be customers that walked in on their own and were given to the host by the pit boss. This really doesn't require much of an effort on the host's part except to walk over to the pit and offer his or her services to the customer. So even the position most likely to be measurable in the casino presents its own challenges.

Yet of all the casino positions, aside from casino hosts, the dealer seems to be the most sought-out target for increased productivity. The reason is that the dealer is the only person on the casino floor who handles drop and can affect the speed with which it is deposited. That is why when casinos are pressed to increase their win figures and hold figures, they come down strong on the dealer to make it happen. But what's in it for the dealer?

Most casino supervisors correlate speed with production when it comes to the dealer. This assumption, although theoretically correct, is realistically incorrect. Previously I mentioned the correlation between speed and errors. There's also a correlation between speed and diminished customer play time. Finally, a correlation exists between speed and employee burnout. All these negative factors negate whatever advantages could have been derived by the increased speed. Assuming that the dealer manages to increase output by ten decisions per hour, in an eight-hour period he or she will have increased output by eighty decisions. At 2 percent that means retention of 160 percent of the average bets. That times an average of four bets

per hand means retention of 640 percent of the average bet. If we assume the average bet to be $10, we end up with an added win of $64. That's great! But now let's factor in two extra mistakes in the eight-hour period. At a $10 average, and assuming these were bets that would have otherwise lost, the customers end up with an additional $40—the $10 they would have lost plus the extra $10 the dealer gives them, times two. Now our net revenue is reduced to $24. Still not bad. But, if you factor in the most likely possibility, which is that the dealer will be left with an average of three players or fewer instead of four, and the fact that this figure will decrease even further once the word gets out that you can't even blink in this casino without losing your chance to make a decision, plus the fact that many of these players will not return, plus the fact that the dealer will quit and you will have to replace him or her with someone less productive, by the time you add all that up, you're broke.

NINE-POINT PRODUCTIVITY SCALE

So you see speed isn't the solution to increased productivity, although it is a factor to be considered. The system I have in mind measures nine aspects of productivity. One is speed and dexterity, setting a good pace that doesn't require the dealer to fix cards on the layout, allows the players to place their wages, split, double down, insure their bets, and make a decision within a reasonable time frame.

Two is for accuracy, since mistakes negate the power of the house advantage. These first two aspects require visual inspection and some flexibility on the part of the observer. All dealers will make mistakes, so the supervisor should not assume that, just because one was caught, the dealer is inaccurate or careless. A record should be kept in a log, and if there seems to be an indication of diminished capacity in this area, the case should be referred to the pit boss, who can request the cooperation of surveillance to clock the errors this employee commits in a prescribed time frame. This visual inspection can then be compared to a similar sample of a few other dealers. If it turns out that this dealer commits more errors on the average than the sample dealers he or she is compared against, then the supervisor can mark that category as a negative for that rating period. The dealer can then be counseled to that effect and given advice on how to improve performance through concentration or any other aid that he or she may require.

The next aspect to be evaluated, number three, is the dealer's general disposition toward the customers. In other words, is he or she pleasant and smiling most of the time?

The fourth one is the social magnetism that dealers display. Do they attract people to the tables and make them want to sit and play at their tables? Do they welcome people to the game and make them feel welcome? It's not enough to say, *"How are you?"* or *"Welcome to the Mirage, home of Cirque Du Soleis, how may I help you?"* The customer actually has to believe the dealer means it.

The fifth one is the ability of the dealer to entertain. If people feel they're having fun at a gaming table, chances are they're going to stay much longer than they intended. This extra time spent at the tables translates into dollars for the casino. The sixth one is attendance, measured separately from any program that rewards for unused sick days. Just as in sports, the more a dealer plays the game, the more he or she can produce for the team. Attendance is, therefore, highly regarded.

The seventh one is supervisory relations. This isn't an area of productivity itself, but an area that can disrupt productivity when conflict exists.

The eighth one is employee relations, for the same reasons. The ninth and final aspect of productivity is game protection, because a slip in this area can negate all the ground gained through the other areas. However, what game protection actually entails must be clearly specified to the dealer to insure awareness of exactly what needs to be done to qualify in this area, and what will be considered violations.

I realize this looks and feels like an evaluation, and it is, but it will differ inasmuch as it will be quantified and qualified daily; some areas will be judged to be more productive than others and will be quantified higher, while others will be quantified lower. The minimum evaluation period should be one month, at which time those who produce to minimum standards should be rewarded accordingly, probably on a point system that would allow them to accumulate points to achieve awards that are meaningful to them. Points should be awarded on a scaled basis, ranging from minimum qualifying production to optimum and the highest production. Rewards should be varied to encompass the

spectrum of needs and wants and should be based on the motivation theory principles that I discussed. Examples of rewards the casino could offer are all the complimentaries casinos offer to patrons, in addition to parties, tickets for special events, dinner with a high-ranking officer of the company, invitations to special parties where celebrities are going to be present, cash awards, vacations, the chance to be present at a corporate meeting, desirable gifts from one of the hotel's shops, or the opportunity to solve a major casino concern or problem, the solution of which would earn the employee a greater reward. There should be something available to match up with any of the diverse interests.

This is just a general idea of how such a program would work; more details would be required to understand exactly what should be done. The point is: In order to increase performance in the casino, you need to send the message that you have a way of measuring performance, that you are willing to define it and consider suggestions to improve it, and that there will be a direct relationship between the way you evaluate increased performance and how you reward it and, finally, that the rewards will not be chosen by you, they will be chosen by the employees. And in this respect, you are also willing to consider suggestions on what rewards to include.

Just as was done with the dealers, a measurement system can be developed for each job description, with rewards that are meaningful to those employees. All you need to do is figure out what areas of the person's job performance increases productivity, directly or indirectly, and in what measure. You can then structure a value system that you can quantify.

One last suggestion that will probably be strongly opposed is that superiors and executives be required to perform lower-level jobs every so often. This isn't only a morale booster; it serves to remind higher executives where they came from, the difficulties associated with these jobs, and how important these jobs really are. This won't have the desired effect unless the executive is forced to put in a full day's work. *Good luck with this one!*

PART III

TABLE GAMES

CHAPTER 7

GAMES DEPARTMENT

STRUCTURE OF THE GAMES DEPARTMENT

The games department is divided both horizontally and vertically. Vertically, you see the structure of management and supervision. There's a chain of command that spans at least nine levels. When the distribution of the managerial functions reaches the games manager or pit manager level, you then begin to see the horizontal structure of the games department, which is divided into pits or casino sections.

UPPER MANAGEMENT

The vertical structure of the games department is a consequence of the vertical structure of the casino. The first two levels of management in the casino, assuming that the board of directors is one and the general manager is another, rarely have anything to do with the operation of the games department. The true responsibility for the games department begins with the vice president of casino operations, although that person is rarely seen on the casino floor. The casino manager and the assistant casino manager supervise the entire operation of the games department, all shifts included, but rarely intervene directly, except in smaller operations where middle management is very limited.

The true managers and most influential decision-makers on the casino floor are the shift managers. These are middle-management executives, who in some places are considered upper management. Because of their influence and power, other shift managers will rarely make a decision of any kind on that shift.

The power of the shift manager allows the bypassing of rules and regulations established by the casino manager. This is one indication of how strong the chain of command in the casino environment is. This also accounts for the variations that are seen in casino rules, regulations, and procedures on the different shifts. In some instances the casino manager is aware of these differences and allows the shift manager this latitude, but generally the casino manager is oblivious to these changes in rules and how they're being implemented or interpreted. The casino manager needs to be aware of these differences, but the chain of command places a barrier and prevents this from happening.

The assistant shift managers serve the same function except that they're subordinate to the shift managers and therefore will not usually take it upon themselves to make rule changes when they're in charge. This subordinate position will also make them hesitate on some critical decisions and seek the advice of the shift manager. In some casinos, assistant shift managers will split the supervision task of the casino according to their expertise and forte. One shift manager might be in charge of the blackjack and baccarat pits while the other one will be in charge of the craps and roulette pits. And even though these divisions exist, they'll cover each other and supervise each other's section when one is not available.

Few casinos employ games managers, and those that do usually have problems with the division of power and authority. The games manager is in charge of a particular table game on all shifts. It is easy to see where this can cause conflict, since the shift managers are in charge of the total operation of their shift, as are the assistant shift managers. Rules, regulations, and procedures are usually the domain of the games manager, while general operation and personnel are the domain of the shift managers. It is inevitable that these functions have areas in common, and this is where conflicts will arise. The casino manager can resolve the problem of authority, but the employee at the bottom doesn't know whose rules to follow.

LOWER-LEVEL MANAGEMENT

Up to this point, management has been seen in a vertical line and generally limited to the games operation. The next level of management, the pit manager, establishes the beginning of the horizontal structure of the table games. In large casinos, the pit manager manages and is responsible for what happens in his or her section of games. In smaller casinos, the pit manager can be in charge of as many sections or pits as is necessary.

To establish clarity in structure, let's look at the pit manager in Atlantic City gaming. This middle management employee, the last on the list of key employees as described by the New Jersey Casino Control Commission, manages the operation of a section of casino games limited to a total of twelve, depending on the type. Eight crap tables, and twelve blackjack games are the most allowed in a pit. When table games are mixed in a pit, the maximum allowed will vary, depending on the nature of the games. These tables are usually roped in a section and separated from the rest of the pits by aisles on the casino floor.

Each pit of the casino will be issued an identifying number to distinguish it from the rest. Even though the pit can be seen as a department in itself, the table games of which it is composed have assigned numbers also and will be grouped together with other games of the same type for accounting purposes. This will give the casino manager an idea of how specific game classes are performing, helping to determine and measure the effect of procedural and rule changes.

So you see that, structurally, the casino is divided not only in pit sections with their own pit managers, but also in game departments such as blackjack, roulette, craps, baccarat, and other available games. The pit sections are the responsibility of the pit manager, who must oversee floor supervisors and dealers. Here, a strange thing happens. The pit clerk, who is assigned to work in a given pit and does pit work, isn't under the supervision of the pit manager. This provision may be based on security, but in practice it doesn't serve that function, and at times it may cause unnecessary friction.

In laying down the building blocks of the table games department, you may have noticed that what keeps this structure together is the delegation of authority within the chain of command. You also saw that a couple of cracks in the structure, namely the overlapping functions of the shift managers and games managers and the lack of authority of the pit manager over the pit clerk, threatened to weaken the operation. If you add the other managerial communication barriers that I discussed in Chapter 4, you will realize that the delegation of authority, although necessary to ensure the smooth operation of an organization, presents many problems in the complex environment of a casino.

OBJECTIVES OF THE GAMES DEPARTMENT

The main goal of the games department is to ensure compliance with all rules, regulations, and procedures established by management and to do it as effectively as possible. The objectives of this department are necessarily subordinate to the objectives of the company. Yet contrary to the general operation where revenue goals can be established even if they're based on fantasy, the games department can only aspire to enforce rules, maintain controls, and serve a customer relations function. Sure, revenue goals can be established, but there's nothing that the table games department can do to produce more, because it doesn't produce anything. Revenues are a byproduct of their efforts, not a consequence of them.

There are some things the table games department can do to have a positive effect on revenue production. Most of these are pre-defined for them in procedure manuals, memorandums, and management directives. Strict adherence to these rules is one way to achieve this positive effect, provided, however, that the rules themselves have a positive effect on revenue production. A rule that prohibits friendly exchanges between employees and customers isn't going to have a positive effect on revenue production. On the other hand, where such a rule doesn't exist, dealers and supervisors who make customers feel comfortable make a big difference. The way they perform their jobs can also have a positive effect on the operation and can be part of the objectives of the department itself. The way employees and supervisors interact can also be a part of the objectives of the department.

At the final frontier, where customers and employees interact, additions and deletions to the department objectives will occur. The pit bosses will set their own goals and will manage their pits accordingly. These objectives can be based on reality, such as pit rules applicable to specific, acceptable work tasks and the determination of appropriate pit behavior, or they can be based on irrational assumptions and unrealistic ideas of production. Pit bosses are only kidding themselves when they set a goal of holding 30 percent of the drop. It's not that this can't happen, it's that there's nothing they can do to make it happen. Objectives in the games department and in the pit should then be based on what can be accomplished, and not on what might happen by accident.

Realistic objectives within the pit can be set that will make almost all customers great customers when they sit down on the game, make almost all employees smile and maintain a joyful attitude while performing their jobs, make almost all employees adhere to dealing procedures on the games, make almost all supervisors treat their subordinates with respect and appreciation, make almost all supervisors protective of their games and equipment at all times. These objectives, as the word *almost* indicates, are unrealistic in their own way. But at least they're within the control of the pit managers. Enforcement of these rules and directives will be directly influenced by the manager's effort.

MANAGEMENT OF THE TABLE GAMES

As you have seen, management of the table games occurs in different ways at different levels. At the level of the vice president and the casino manager, policy and procedures are established, programs are designed and planned, and results are analyzed. At the level of the shift managers, policy and procedures are enforced (interpreted by their own bias), programs are monitored, and reports and recommendations are made. In addition, the shift managers will be required to directly supervise the table games department and may be required to participate in meetings involving analysis of company programs. But pit managers are the true managers of the table games. They must enforce company policy and procedures and the directives they receive from the shift managers. They are also responsible for the smooth running of company programs and must compile valuable data for use in analyzing company programs.

THE SHIFT MANAGER

The shift manager manages the casino. This becomes clear when a customer requests to see the casino manager. Invariably, he or she will be directed to the shift manager. Since the casino manager, for the most part, rarely makes an appearance on the casino floor (except in small casinos), technically the shift manager is correct in assuming the role of the casino manager.

As manager of the casino operation on the shift, the shift manager will make routine stops into the different pits to check the data that the pit manager gathers and to ask about any unusual development in the pit. If any problem has developed, the shift manager will offer assistance in solving it. If there's any action in the pit that merits the shift manager's assessment, the pit manager will point it out and provide details regarding it.

From a distance, the shift manager will observe the total operation and look for things that are out of the norm. If something seems out of the ordinary, the shift manager needs to take a closer look. Things that would warrant a closer look are suspicious body language or communications between two or more customers, between customers and dealers, between customers and supervisors, and between dealers and supervisors. Other actions that would make the shift manager come to the pit would be employees' poor job performance. The shift manager might notice that a dealer isn't calling out the total points of each hand as required or that the dealer's back is turned on the game in a way that threatens the safety of the game. A new shuffle procedure might not be followed, a supervisor might not be paying attention to the games, or someone might be rude to a customer. All these and many more are problems that can be spotted from a distance. This is why the shift manager will often find a good vantage point on the casino floor and just observe for long periods of time.

The shift manager must also be aware of any special events, the arrival times of groups, the time that shows and parties conclude, convention and group meetings that might affect the operation. All these events will influence the occupancy of tables in the casino and must be prepared for. The proper number of tables should be ready to seat all these patrons. The reverse of this situation deserves care also. Too many tables open with dealers standing idle give the impression that (1) the casino isn't doing well and people aren't supporting it for some reason, and (2) that management doesn't know what it's doing. A better approach is to open games judiciously, as needed. This not only shows more efficiency; it earns the appreciation of the employees.

In their inevitable role as disciplinarians, shift managers should use caution, understanding, and incomparable judicial savvy. The latter characterizes the shift managers as judges, which they unavoidably become. They must be able to weigh the operation's cost against the negative act being punished and against the impact their decision will have on the operation both from an interpersonal standpoint and from a financial standpoint. This isn't easy to do. But like a judge, the shift managers need to put themselves in the position of the offender. They must explore the motivations that led to the offense and try to understand them from the offender's point of view. Once they understand why, it is easier to estimate the cost to the operation and come up with an equitable punishment. Clearly, a dealer's insubordination to a supervisor would seem wrong and unjustified. However, if after hearing the dealer's account of the incident with an open mind, the shift manager determines that there might be more to the situation than is obvious, the manager might find that the supervisor in question has a tendency to harass employees. And although this doesn't justify the dealer's action, it does present a mitigating circumstance that should be taken into consideration when determining punishment. It also has revealed the existence of another problem that may require disciplinary action, or at least a closer look.

That all people are created equal, that everyone is innocent until proven guilty, and that justice is blind shouldn't be words in the wind, but smart words to live by. Many times we have seen that when a subordinate and a superior are involved in a conflict, or both have been party to errors of judgment, managers will punish the subordinate because he or she is further from the seat of power. This type of judgment is flawed and biased.

The reverse side to the punisher or disciplinarian is the role of rewarder or promoter of good will. If strict discipline is absolutely necessary to get a point across, then it should be employed without hesitation. But cracking a whip all the time doesn't make for a healthy environment, so shift managers must balance their disciplinarian roles with the role of an appreciative leader. Don't just call people into the office to reprimand them, call them in to thank them for a job well done. Do a little something extra once in while so they know they're appreciated and that it's not their blood you're after. Show that you can differentiate between the people who are doing their jobs and the ones who aren't. Don't make the mistake of punishing everyone for the infraction that one or two people commit. Aim your disciplinary actions at the offenders. Reward those who are doing the right thing.

There's a false impression in some circles of the gaming business that, if you punish the entire group, the group will gang up on the actual offender. This, they believe, will deter others from trying the same in the future. This is an outdated concept. In today's world, the punisher becomes the enemy.

You have seen the shift managers in their roles as managers and in their relationship to subordinates. The next role they must play is the role of subordinate. In the course of a day, the casino manager will call the shift manager to ask how the operation is doing and if anything unusual is happening. The shift manager will also call the casino manager to speak of the status of the operation, the arrival of an important patron, the arrival of a special group, the status of the group's action, the status of the special player's action, and so forth. Now, you have seen how important the shift manager's job is, and I have indicated how important some shift managers view themselves. In this role of subordination, the shift managers are going to find themselves in a position that is somewhat tricky. Many of them believe that because of their stature they can handle anything the operation has to offer in the form of challenge. In many instances, they have been led to believe this. So it isn't surprising that a vague phrase such as *"Anything unusual?"* is going to be interpreted by each individual in a different way and cause conflicts.

A vice president of a casino operation in Las Vegas came onto the casino floor in a drunken rage, overturning chairs, breaking glasses, and shouting obscenities at a casino shift manager because he didn't inform him, at three o'clock in the morning, that a customer was winning $10,000. First of all, these aren't the usual working hours of a vice president of operations, and second, $10,000 in most places isn't considered an extraordinary win. This demonstrates a few things: One, there are some pretty unprofessional managers out there; two, vague terms do make for bad communication; and, three, the shift manager should have known for whom he was working, keeping in mind his place in the chain of command.

Aside from their role as on-site disseminators of information, the shift managers will be required to meet periodically with the manager or vice president to discuss operation issues. Work performance on the casino floor is discussed frequently at this level as are questions regarding fluctuations of game hold percentages, drop variations, complimentary issuance, customer relations, and usual and unusual treatment of special customers. The casino manager will also ask questions about different previous directives and the effect they have had on employees and customers. These are just a few examples of the exchanges that might occur at this level.

THE PIT MANAGER

As indicated before, true management of the table games takes place at the pit level. The pit manager is directly responsible for what happens in the pit, which is where table games are located. This company official supervises a group of table games, usually of the same kind, although a few different tables are also a possibility. Pit personnel consist of floor supervisors, dealers, and pit clerks although, as I have already mentioned, the pit clerk isn't under the pit manager's direct supervision. The pit manager makes his or her subordinates aware of pit procedure and of any particular rules of special importance.

Depending on the casino, the pit manager may or may not assign dealers and floor supervisors to their games. Where scheduling is part of assigned duties, the pit manager will assign floor supervisors to a group of tables according to their respective abilities and knowledge. If it is felt that all supervisors are qualified to handle all action and all games in the pit, the manager may opt to rotate them. Even in the case of rotation, the pit manager may make changes if it is felt that a certain supervisor isn't qualified to handle a particular situation on his or her assigned games. Regarding the dealer table assignments, the pit manager may choose to personally assign the dealers to the tables, or to assign a floor supervisor this task. Again, these assignments will probably be made according to the abilities of the dealers.

In addition to the scheduling function, the pit manager also serves an accounting function, a public relations function, a disciplinary function, and an administrative function. The pit accounting serves as an indicator of the financial status of the casino operation at any given time. Usually, the shift manager will require a status report from all the pit bosses at a scheduled time every day. Some shift managers don't have any specified time; they just ask whenever they're curious or when some unusual event could affect the status of the daily operation. To be ready for the shift manager's inquiry, some pit managers will have the floor supervisors take inventory of their assigned games at regular intervals, others will have them make a complete win/loss assessment, and yet others will just take a look at their player activity sheets. A mental record of the rating cards that have been handed in and the pit accounting sheet can provide a general idea of where the pit should be in terms of win/loss.

These procedures for estimating win/loss vary from casino to casino. Some casinos won't allow floor supervisors to make *rundowns* because they feel the time spent in determining the win/loss of the games takes away from the primary functions of the floor supervisor. Others are quite strict about them. They will not only question the supervisors and make them redo estimates thought to be inaccurate, but they will also hold supervisors accountable for this information. This latter attitude is ludicrous. To begin with, as Angel Rodriguez, a Puerto Rican casino manager, used to say, "It never adds up the next day, so why bother?"

Next, accounting skills aren't required for this job and aren't part of the job description. Furthermore, the time it takes to serve this function does take away from the protection of the games and can interfere with the public relations function that the supervisor should indubitably serve.

Too many casino supervisors have gotten needlessly into trouble trying to estimate win/loss figures that will be accurately available in less than twenty-four hours. Nothing this person can do will change anything, nor can the person who is receiving the infor-

mation change the amount of cash or credit that is going to end up in the box or the amount of chips that are going to be exchanged with the casino patrons. Some will argue that the *rundowns* can point to problem areas that can be dealt with immediately. But the truth is that shift managers will react only to major fluctuations in win/loss, which the pit manager would have made them aware of anyway, regardless of a rundown.

This isn't to say that the floor supervisor ought not to be aware of table game bankrolls or that he or she shouldn't know where the money is going. That's an integral part of the floor supervisor's job. But it isn't necessary to count tables down every two hours to know this.

Another accounting function that pit managers must carry out is the pit accounting function. When pit managers take over the pit, they have already participated in the inventory count, have verified its accuracy, and have a record of the pit status. This information is contained in the shift transfer sheet. Any other pertinent information such as the status of high-stakes players is also transferred at this time, together with information on cash buy-ins and credit used and available. The pit managers are required not only to keep an accounting of the pit itself, but also of high-stakes players who can have an impact on the pit status.

The public relations role of pit managers is very important. They must recognizes regular casino patrons, who look forward to being greeted by important figures in the casino. The pit manager is the highest ranking officer in the pit and, therefore, the person most patrons want to be recognized by. Yet, in spite of this, you rarely see outgoing pit managers. It is surprising that such an important function in a business that has nothing to offer but service is being disregarded. One problem may be that some people believe customers don't want to be bothered when they're playing; another may be that some believe socializing slows the games down and decreases casino revenues. I disagree with both of these perceptions.

Although there may be some customers who don't want to be bothered when they're playing, these are the exceptions to the rule. Furthermore, the idea that socializing slows down the game isn't necessarily true. For one thing, even if the pit manager doesn't interact with the customer, the customer is probably going to interact with other customers, the supervisor, or the dealer. Another thing to take into consideration is that the player usually decides beforehand how much money to win or lose before leaving the casino. This could take three hours in a fast-dealing situation or it could take four hours in a slow-dealing situation. Either way, the speed of the game isn't going to make a difference to the player, except in one instance. If the player feels you're trying too hard to take his or her money (and your lack of warmth will confirm this), the player may leave sooner than intended. On the other hand, a friendly pit manager, supervisor or dealer can encourage a customer to continue to play beyond the goal set because of feeling comfortable with the surroundings. Not only that, the customer will return more often to your casino because of the pleasure of your company.

In some busy casinos, the pit manager is swamped with paperwork and is unable to serve a public relations role. Managements should never put their pit managers in this position. Casino paperwork is so simple that it shouldn't require the services of an employee who makes from forty to sixty thousand dollars a year. That's why so many high-limit pits today have subordinates who do most of the paperwork for pit managers. The strange thing is that we still observe pit managers neglecting their public relations functions even though they have someone doing most of the paperwork for them. So if they aren't doing the paperwork and they aren't doing public relations, what are they doing?

That's a good question, and one that is repeated constantly throughout the casino floor. Dealers and floor supervisors always seem to be asking themselves the question: What is my superior doing? But before I answer it, I want to make clear that I think this is a good question because it is one that concerns subordinates and outside observers. There are two other important functions that the pit manager serves: One is the role of disciplinarian, and the other is the role of administrator. The pit manager is fulfilling these roles when not doing paperwork or public relations.

Although *administrator* really encompasses everything the pit manager does, these functions need to be clarified. As a disciplinarian, the pit manager serves another very important role. The pit manager is expected to oversee supervisory employees and dealers who have prescribed duties that may be carried out

with efficiency, as a boring everyday routine, or maybe not at all. The pit manager decides how those duties are carried out. The individual who functions as a disciplinarian and administrator is supposed to reward efficiency, is supposed to motivate those who find their duties boring, and is supposed to take disciplinary action against those who don't do their prescribed duties. How this is done makes a big difference in the efficiency of the pit. If the rewards for efficiency are nonexistent, scarce, or distributed by bias, they aren't going to have a positive effect. If they fail to make the employees feel appreciated, they aren't going to have a positive effect.

Finally, the real tough job is to discipline justly when required. When violations of problem behavior occur within the pit, all eyes and ears are centered upon the pit manager. Employees want to know that a justice system is in place that will take into consideration the efforts they're making and at the same time recognize the deviation from those efforts by other employees. In other words, they want to feel that equality does exist and that, when there is a violation of work ethics, it is treated the same regardless of the violator. Friends and lovers of the pit managers shouldn't be treated any differently than any other infractor is, and punishment should be equal to the infraction. If anything, management should show leniency when mitigating circumstances exist and when the consequences of the infraction lack financial or ethical importance. Obviously, if the infraction isn't purposeful, the financial importance has to go a long way before it can be measurable against the casino's resources. Visualizing discipline in this way makes for a good working relationship and raises the efficiency with which the pit operates.

Pit managers' roles as administrators are the sum of all of their functions. They oversee the operation of the pit. They supervise all employees and make sure that they're carrying out their duties as prescribed by the employee manual, that they're carrying out the pit and game procedures, and that they're following any other directives that the pit manager may have issued. The pit manager monitors employee appearance and customer relations to see if they're consistent with guidelines in the employee manual. The pit manager will also interact with the floor supervisor, remain aware of what is happening on the tables, and provide assistance to the floor supervisor whenever needed. This function is mostly served by providing fills and credits for the tables, and complimentaries for the customers who merit it. But it also includes giving the supervisor a hand when that person is too busy. Many pit managers won't serve this function because they believe it's a job for their subordinates and not for them. Yet an attitude like that only works against the pit manager because an important player might walk away due to the length of time it took to wait for a marker, to buy a marker back, for a complimentary, or just to speak to someone. Employees will also lose respect for a superior who won't assist in carrying out or easing the work load of an employee who is overworked at a given time. This definitely doesn't show appreciation for the employee.

Employee needs and customer needs within the pit are many times related, as shown in the example above. The manager may feel that carrying out the customer relations function is limited to issuing comps when requested and making reservations for shows and restaurants. But, as in the example above, the customer can see it entirely differently if there is a long wait time to be taken care of. A waiting period is sometimes inevitable because of the number of patrons involved, but measures can be taken to handle periods that will be busy. The manager should use all available resources to avoid lengthy waiting periods for customer requests. It can be done.

ESTABLISHING LIMITS ON THE TABLE GAMES

The issue of limits on the table games is directly related to the caliber of play being targeted, provided of course that government regulations allow the casino to make its own determination in this respect. Low-stakes gaming states don't provide this option. In some places, such as Puerto Rico, the state sets maximum limits that aren't low but that do restrict the casino's ability to set higher limits for high-stakes gamblers. (I should mention that in Puerto Rico the state did make some concessions to the gaming industry and raised the limits from $200 to $2,000 on regular games and $4,000 in baccarat.)

In states where limits are set by the casino operation, competition is sometimes a factor. This was the scene in Atlantic City when Steve Wynn raised the limits on all his table games to $5,000. Although the other

casinos were slow to react to the move that many thought to be ludicrous, eventually all of the casinos began to raise their table limits because of the competition and because of Steve Wynn's success. Another factor, as I said earlier, is the caliber of play you are targeting. The limits at the Aladdin and Circus Circus aren't the same as the limits at Caesars and the Mirage even though all four casinos are located on the Las Vegas Strip. Both of the reasons I have mentioned apply in this case. The first two casinos aren't trying to attract the same caliber of play that Caesars and the Mirage are and, although they're all on the Strip, these casinos aren't in direct competition with each other, for that same reason.

Individual Limits

Another way in which limits in a casino are established is by special requests from individual players. The players will request exceedingly high limits as a matter of stature to test their worth in the eyes of management, to assure themselves a quick way to recover from losses, or to make profits when games are excessively favorable to them. Competition will again dictate what these limits will be, and the players themselves will place the casinos against each other to see how far they can go. The technique of increasing individual limits and credit lines became increasingly popular during the 1980s when casino managers dared to take more risks in order to prove that they could turn operations around. This technique proved quite effective for a few casino executives who today enjoy great stature in the gaming business. It has been a matter of controversy and lawsuits for others.

It's hard to assess how effective this technique really is. From a strict business and management standpoint, high-stakes players shouldn't be allowed to exceed the normal range of their play. For these high-end players an acceptable range is 50 to 1, a better range would be 20 to 1. In other words, if a player is betting a minimum of $1,000, it would be best to let him or her go up to $20,000. However, it is acceptable, in some cases, to allow the player to go to $50,000, depending upon his or her bankroll. Actually, at this level of play, both cases would require a substantial bankroll or credit line. Ten percent is usually the rule of thumb guideline. In other words, if you have a credit line or deposit of $100,000, you can have a maximum bet of $10,000, provided the casino has the capability for such play. Very few casinos can allow players to exceed a $100,000 maximum bet.

Competition, of course, forces managers to make tough decisions in this regard. If a player with a credit line of $1,000,000 wants a $100,000 maximum bet but wants to bet a minimum of $50, the request is ridiculous but the casino would be hard pressed to deny it. The effort should be made to have this player agree to at least a $1,000 bet, but casino executives are so fearful of losing their jobs over a dispute with a customer of this stature, they don't even attempt to barter most of the time. An executive with good communication skills would probably manage to talk this player into the $1,000 bet and would be all the better for it.

Unfortunately, competition has prompted many exceptions to the rules. One of the dangers of this situation is that a player will have credit lines in more than one casino, usually exceeding the capability to pay back. In desperation, as has happened in the case of Leonard Tose and David Zarin, players will go for broke and casinos will get stuck with the debt and the costly expenses of collection. Sometimes casinos will have made enough off the play to cover all losses and expenses, but that isn't always the case. It's one of the reasons a casino owner in Las Vegas is suing a casino executive.

So when you think about drawing play by increasing credit lines and limits, this is one of the things that has to be kept in mind. You should ask yourself: Can I afford to do this? Or am I going for broke? Some management teams already have other jobs lined up and leave before any negative consequences begin to show up. It's a smart maneuver, but not necessarily an ethical one.

Normal Ratios

Casinos that don't cater to high-end customers approach limits in a different way, since their minimum wagers usually begin around the dollar mark. A 20 to 1 or 50 to 1 ratio doesn't work in this case. To accommodate most average play, a $500 maximum bet works well, even though many limited-budget casinos will use $200 as their average. Five-dollar tables will usually fluctuate between a $500 maximum and a $5,000 maximum. Most casinos won't go over $2,000 on a $5 minimum table.

In most casinos, upper management determines the limits of the tables. In some instances, the pit manager will be able to determine appropriate limits, subject to the scrutiny of the shift manager. However, regarding the maximum bet allowable or special limits for high-end customers, the pit manager won't be authorized to make those judgments. Decisions like that will be made, usually, at the casino manager level.

The advantage or disadvantage of a high limit on a table game will be directly related to the casino's bankroll and to the market it intends to capture. If the casino has $5,000 maximum limits, yet 99 percent of their clientele bets under $100, on the high end, it has become a gambler. The probability that it will be profitable with the sporadic play that it will attract at the high end is almost the same as if it were to flip a coin. Because of this it is possible that one player can come in one day and wipe out the entire revenues of a month or maybe even a year. This gamble doesn't make good business sense. Casinos can't afford to take risks on high-end players unless they're going to do marketing to maintain a steady stream of these players.

GAME RULES: HOW THEY AFFECT PC

In Blackjack

Blackjack, as I have already mentioned, is the most popular casino game in the United States. However, many different rules affect the game of blackjack. First of all, blackjack is a game of depleting resources. The resources, which are the cards, are pulled out of a shoe or from a hand until the resources are almost depleted and the cut card shows up. Early blackjack didn't have a cut card; therefore, the resource was totally depleted. As this resource is being depleted, the advantage of the house diminishes (if all other variables remain equal). This distinction shows that, if more tens and aces have come out, the game would then be favorable to the house. The reverse is also true. If more small cards have come out (2-6), then the player would have an added advantage.

This depletion factor explains why it is to the player's advantage to play against a lesser number of decks, and to the house's advantage to have more. So even though this isn't a rule variation in itself, it should be considered as if it were a rule variation. The difference between increasing from one deck to two decks results in a player's disadvantage of .35 percent, from one to four of .51 percent, and from one to six of .60 percent.

In determining what rules of blackjack to have and which ones to avoid, the first thing the casino manager has to do is to evaluate the competition and see what it is offering. This, of course, presupposes that the manager has the option to make rule changes and that these aren't dictated by the state, as they used to be in Atlantic City and still are in Puerto Rico. Even where rules are prescribed by the state, the casino managers could make a case for change if they understood exactly how the rules affected their operation. I previously gave the example of how this was done in Atlantic City, where blackjack rules dictated by the state gave the player an advantage over the house. The controversial rule in that case was early surrender, which was favorable to the player by .62 percent. Early surrender allows the player to forfeit half of his or her bet on the first two cards of play even if the dealer is showing an ace up.

Where casino managers can determine what betting rules they will have, subtle changes will be observed. For example, Las Vegas Strip rules are traditionally more favorable to the player than downtown and northern Nevada rules. The main rule that differentiates the Strip and downtown rules is the one that allows the dealer to hit soft 17. This rule is unfavorable to the player by .20 percent. At least two casinos on the Las Vegas Strip offer conventional surrender although they don't advertise it. The advantage to the player of this rule is minimal, a mere .02 percent on single deck and .07 percent on multiple deck. Another rule that differentiates Strip casinos from downtown casinos is the double down rule on split pairs, although not all the casinos offer this option. That rule is favorable to the player by .13 percent. In all, these three rules bring down the house advantage to .40 percent for those casinos that offer them. But there's yet another twist in the rule variation scheme. Some casinos will offer games with fewer decks within the same casino. In the example above, were a casino to retain the same rules throughout regardless of the number of decks, the player could have an advantage or reduce the advantage substantially. If the casino were to offer single deck, the player would have an advantage; if it were to offer double deck, the player would have a slight disadvantage. Either way, blackjack is a game that presents the house with serious complications. To avoid this predicament the house makes internal rule changes that apply solely to the single or double deck games.

Let's not forget that these percentages apply only to those players who play perfect strategy. All other players will have a disadvantage according to their level of play that is determined by the number and type of mistakes they make. I note this distinction because ordinary players aren't consistent, and their play can vary depending upon what other players do, how much they're winning or losing, and how they feel at the time they're facing the play decision. Also, the play disadvantages and advantages that I have presented are on the average and don't apply to specific plays on the game.

Other rules favorable to the player include drawing on split aces, which has an average advantage to the player of .14 percent; re-splitting aces, which has an average advantage of .03 percent; and doubling down on 3 or more cards, which has an average advantage of .20 percent. To the casino's advantage are rules such as no doubling down on hard 9 (.14 percent), no doubling down on soft counts (.14 percent), no hole card for the dealer (London Deal) where the dealers don't return splits and doubles if they have blackjack (.13 percent), and no re-splitting of pairs (.05 percent). For further information on the subject read *Million Dollar Blackjack* by Ken Uston, *Playing Blackjack as a Business* by Lawrence Revere, *Professional Blackjack* by Sanford Wong, or *Beat the Dealer* by Edward O. Thorpe.

In Craps

The next table game of importance to the casino operation is the game of craps. In reality, only two rule changes can affect the house advantage in the game of craps. One is to increase the amount of odds taken and laid on pass line, come, don't pass, and don't come bets. The other is to change the winning combinations on the field bet. All other house advantage variations are the product of either the introduction of an additional bet or a change in payout odds for a given bet. Let's begin by observing how the number of odds taken or laid affect the house advantage.

An odds bet, as I defined in Chapter 3, is a free bet. It is the only bet in the casino where the house doesn't collect a tariff or percentage. There's only one catch: The player must make a pass line, come, don't pass, or a don't come bet in order to be able to make it. Because the odds are attached to these low percentage bets, they're added together as one bet. So, by virtue of this union, a player who takes more odds than another will have a greater percentage of the bet non-taxed, which means that the disadvantage will be diluted more than the other player's bet. For example, if one player has a $10 bet and $10 odds, 50 percent of that bet has a disadvantage of 1.4 percent, and 50 percent of that bet has no disadvantage. The other player has a $10 bet with the same 1.4 percent, but this is only 33 percent of the total bet since he has $20 odds. It is easy to assume, because of this example, that the single-odds player would have a disadvantage of .70 percent and that the double-odds player would have a disadvantage of .47 percent. But statistics in gaming aren't that simple, nor are the odds rule variations that fluctuate from place to place.

If we take single odds to mean that the exact amount will be bet as odds, the player's disadvantage is reduced to .85 percent on the pass line and .83 percent on the don't pass. If we take double odds to mean that the exact double of the front line bet is to be wagered as odds in the back, then the house advantage is reduced to .61 percent for the pass line bettor and .59 percent for the don't bettor.

Yet there's another situation that we haven't considered. In most casinos, players are allowed to bet odds in increments that relate better to the odds payoff. This addition to the odds bet is called *breakage*, and the resulting odds bets are called *true odds*. True single odds reduce the house advantage to .73 percent on the pass line and true double odds reduce the house advantage to .50 percent. For those of you who are curious about the Horseshoe's 10 times odds, simple 10 times odds on the pass line would give the house an advantage of .18 percent.

The field bets can be manipulated to pay off different ways. Most casinos have field bets that pay on 2,3,4,9,10,11,12, paying double on the 2 and 12. This sets the house advantage at 5.26 percent. In Puerto Rico, field bets pay on 2,3,5,9,10,11,12, and this sets the house advantage at 5.56 percent. Some casinos pay triple on 2, double on 12, and even on 3,4,9,10,11, and this sets the house advantage at 2.56 percent. Many different combinations are possible and will affect the

house advantage on this bet. Since this is an impulse bet and it is self-explanatory, many newcomers to the game of craps try it. Also, because of its fast action, it is a bet that is used with some frequency in crap tournaments when players must catch up in a hurry. All these factors make the field bet one that can have a definitive impact on the total house hold of the game. I believe this bet can play a greater role in the crap game if it is manipulated to pay off at a low percentage and marketed accordingly. It would take a while to remove the sucker bet image and a new name may be necessary, but the results would be highly beneficial because of the fast action of the crap game.

There are many bets that have been introduced on crap layouts around the world. The addition or deletion of some of these bets may affect the overall percentage hold of the game, but not the house advantage on any given bet. For example, in Puerto Rico it is permissible to bet don't place bets. Don't place bets are equivalent to the wrong or losing side of the place bets on the right or win side. A casino that has this bet will lose action on the lay bets against the 6 and 8 and the 5 and 9. The reason for this is that place bets to lose on these numbers have less of an advantage for the house. If the casino gets a lot of don't play, this will affect the house hold on the crap table. However, most casinos don't get much don't play, so this is rarely a factor. A proper marketing campaign could make the availability of this bet a good attraction.

Other bets that can be adjusted to pay off differently are some of the proposition bets. For example, some casinos will pay off 15 to 1 on 11 as a 1 roll shot, while others will pay 15 for 1 (actually 14 to 1). At 15 to 1 this bet has a house advantage of 11.11 percent and at 15 for 1 this bet has an advantage of 16.67 percent. This is a big percentage difference, but people who make these bets possess little knowledge about the game, even though they may seem knowledgeable. These payoff variations exist for all proposition bets and can make a difference on the house hold depending upon the volume of proposition play the casino gets and the way the bets are marketed.

So, craps is another game that is greatly affected by rule variations, and a clear understanding of these mechanisms is a plus when determining how to set up and market the game.

In Roulette

The next game in popularity, on the average, is roulette.

There are few rule variations in this game. Two of them, however, have an impact on the house advantage and were implemented in Europe after the popularity of roulette began to dwindle due to the great losses suffered by gamblers. One variation is the elimination of the double zero, and the other one is the imprisonment rule. Elimination of the double zero sets the house advantage at 2.70 percent, and imprisonment sets the house advantage to those making outside bets at 1.35 percent. Attempts have been made to introduce these playing rules in American casinos, but for the most part they have come and gone. One reason for this could be that the rule changes failed to draw the extra business that was expected. Yet it is unrealistic to expect changes like these to have an effect overnight, especially since the damage to this game was done almost a century ago.

Most Americans developed an aversion to the game because it was a bloodsucking game when introduced into the United States. The first American roulette wheels had only thirty-one numbers and had three symbols that resulted in losses to anyone who wasn't playing them. They paid off single number bets at 27 for 1, giving the house an outrageous advantage of 12.9 percent. The other bets allowed on the layout paid 9.68 percent. Today, for the most part, American roulette wheels pay off at 5.27 percent, but they have lost out to the momentum of the blackjack and crap games, which are fairer to most players.

Since roulette has a steady stream of faithful followers and a high house advantage, most operators have opted to leave things the way they are. But an insightful manager might find a way to instill new life into this game and market it accordingly, keeping in mind that some things, *like good businesses*, take time to grow and mature.

In Baccarat

The next major game on the casino floor is baccarat. On the whole, baccarat enjoys the smallest house advantage of any casino game. Because of this small advantage, baccarat has become the favored game of players with huge bankrolls, especially foreigners. This fact makes the probability of any major changes in the rules of this game quite unlikely. But like any other game, rule changes can be made that will affect the house advantage. One rule that has seen change is the payout odds on the tie bets. American casinos, for the most part, pay tie bets at 8 to 1 odds, although some casinos used to pay them at 9 to 1. At 8 to 1, the house enjoys an outrageous 14.36 percent; 9 to 1 odds set the house advantage of this bet at 4.8 percent.

Another way by which the casino can alter the house advantage on the baccarat game is to charge a lower commission on the bank bets. One casino in Las Vegas has done this. A reduction in bank commissions from the customary 5 percent to 3 percent sets the house advantage on bank bets at a diminutive .18 percent. This gives the house very little to work with. Other commission changes that affect the house advantage would be to charge 3 percent on bank bets win or lose. This sets the house advantage on bank bets at 1.66 percent. To charge 2.5 percent would reduce the house advantage to 1.16 percent.

These are the major casino games. Many other games could be included, but that would extend this discussion unnecessarily. The main idea is that rule changes can affect the way casinos make money on their games. This knowledge is important in determining what strategies to employ to improve revenues and the operation in general. Only by knowing how these games work can a manager make effective change decisions for marketing purposes.

GAME MIX AND RATIOS

What games to have and in what quantity are questions to answer when setting up casino operations or when analyzing a casino's games efficiency. State regulations, geographical differences, and targeted markets will play an important role in determining the mix. I have already discussed how state regulations can determine limits, and in the same way they can determine allowable games. For example, the states of Colorado and South Dakota will only allow blackjack, poker, and slot machines in their casinos. In Puerto Rico, the government will only allow blackjack, craps, roulette, baccarat, and slot machines. Indian casinos are subject to the compacts they sign with the state governments, and these will vary from state to state. The most liberal states regarding allowable games are Nevada and Mississippi, with Illinois and New Jersey gaining ground in this respect.

Geography often determines the table game mix in a casino. This can be influenced by the local trade, or it can be influenced by the tourist who frequents the location where the operation is. Americans in general, for example, favor blackjack and craps, while South Americans and Europeans favor roulette and baccarat. This is the reason most casino operations in the continental United States will have more blackjack and crap games than roulette and baccarat. Based on this information alone, you could set up a casino operation with blackjack and crap tables in the United States and achieve some success, but the ratio you used would determine whether or not you would turn a profit. If, for example, you were to set up a casino on the slower side of the Las Vegas Strip with a 1 to 1 ratio of blackjack and craps tables, you would fail for two reasons. One, blackjack enjoys more popularity than craps in general. Two, a craps table accommodates twice as many patrons as a blackjack table does. A craps table requires 2.66 more dealers and 1.5 more supervisors. It produces more income on the average, provided that the business is there, which I sincerely doubt in this case. A 4 or 5 to 1 ratio would seem more realistic on the average for this location.

The farther you get from the Las Vegas Strip the greater the blackjack/craps ratio is going to be. That is because craps, with its diversity of bets, is a game that generally attracts customers who have more money to put into action. This also happens in locations that cater mostly to a local market. Locals, contrary to tourists who save up for annual gambling trips or serious gamblers with heavy gambling budgets, must limit their gambling budgets for as many gambling outings as they intend to take during the year. This forces them to be more conservative and to choose games that will give them more fun for their money. Also, because locals for the most part aren't serious gamblers, they tend to choose games that are simpler and less intimidating than craps.

The market you target has a great bearing on the game mix. If you're going to cater to the Asian population, you'll have to provide a greater number of baccarat tables than you normally would. This is going to depend upon the number of Asian customers you wish to attract. If you're going to cater to European and South American groups, you're also going to have to increase the number of baccarat and roulette tables. If

you're going to rely heavily on casino junkets, for the most part you're going to have to increase the number of crap tables.

There's no hard and fast rule here. You have to take the time to research your markets. When dealing with junketeers, you must gather information about the composition of their player lists so you have a better understanding of their table game needs. When analyzing the location you intend to compete in, you have to study the competition to see the game ratios that they're employing in regard to where they're marketing. You also have to analyze the surrounding markets, depending on your competition, up to an approximate 300-mile radius. Five or six hours is the most people are going to drive to reach your location, provided there isn't a better and closer location than yours. Flying distances have to be compared to other locations in order to determine viable markets.

So the gaming mix is a product of the regulations that limit them, the location where they're going to be set, and the markets that are going to be targeted. There are no real rules of thumb that apply here, just an awareness of these factors and a definite need to do extensive research before determining the mix.

Another thing to consider when determining which and how many games to have is if there are special needs that can be supplied by your operation. Most people are familiar with the four basic table games: blackjack, craps, roulette, and baccarat. Yet there are other games such as Caribbean stud poker, poker, paigow, paigow poker, casino war, let it ride, red dog, big six, keno, bingo, etc., that attract certain patrons or ethnic groups. Except for poker, where the house takes a percentage of the rake or pot or a set fee, the other games are high-percentage games, extremely favorable to the casino. So, it would be advantageous to the casino to have as many of these as possible. But unfortunately most customers learn very quickly that these games are bad for their financial health. The speed with which people lose money on these games makes them unpopular. Nevertheless, strategically placed, they can be a good source of income for the casino.

The best thing to do, again, is to know your market. Find out if there are requests for any of these games or check to see what the competition is doing with them. Find out if there are any other games that might be attractive to the market you are drawing. Then, when you decide which, if any, of these games you are going to go with, place them in areas of heavy traffic, preferably where they will be one of the first games people see as they come into the casino. Have the dealers aggressively call attention to these games by keeping equipment in motion and by vocalizing calls or references to the game. Like any other hard sell, these games require aggressive exposure. If you can manage to do that, you will have added an important element of variety to your operation.

If you do decide that certain games add something to your operation that it needs, monitor them closely to make sure they are cost effective. Their cost effectiveness isn't only measured by the revenue they produce minus the labor required to operate them, but also by the added business they may bring in. In other words, let's say that groups of people go out regularly to gamble but have varied preferences regarding table games. It may be that your establishment will become a regular place of action to them because you can accommodate all their gaming tastes. In this instance, that specialty game has done more than produce its own income; it has helped produce other income.

Quite often new games are developed and are introduced into the market place. Gambling expos are usually a good place to go to examine these new developments and to get first-hand knowledge of them. You must keep an open mind when examining and analyzing these games because out there might be the game to replace blackjack as the most popular game for the twenty-first century, just like blackjack replaced faro (the most popular game of the nineteenth century) and became the most popular game in the twentieth century.

CHAPTER 8

ANALYSIS OF NEW AND EXISTING GAMES

Table games are rapidly losing ground to slot machines, and there seems to be no indication of a reversal. In 1994, slot win accounted for 61.47 percent of the casino win in Nevada and 67.18 percent in Atlantic City. This compares with 60.57 percent in 1991 in Nevada and 61.88 percent in Atlantic City. On the other hand, table game revenues weren't only down in relation to the slot win advance but also in relation to the amount of actual income produced from the year before, for the first time in many years. Many experts attribute this trend to the simplicity of the slot machine operation and to the creativity of manufacturers who have turned out a steady stream of innovations in slot technology. Responding to this trend, industry innovators have developed new games to try to spark a renewed interest in table games. So far it hasn't worked, but some of the new developments in table games do produce interesting results that are worth considering. Among the new games getting a lot of press today are multiple action blackjack, super sevens, over and under thirteen, double down stud, royal match 21, 9's up, mini craps, Carribean stud, let it ride and war. In fact, one of the leaders of the gaming industry, Caesars Palace, has adopted three of these new games: multiple action blackjack, super sevens, and over and under thirteen. Because a major casino operation such as Caesars has implemented these games, I believe they deserve further analysis.

NEW GAMES

Although there are quite a few relatively new games on the market today, I will restrict my discussion to multi-action blackjack, over and under thirteen, and the innovative game called Caribbean stud, let it ride, and casino war.

Multiple Action Blackjack

Multi-action blackjack was created by Dick LeVasseur, who is the marketing vice president of the Four Queens in Las Vegas. Mr. LeVasseur claims that the game adds 2.1 decisions an hour to the game yet doesn't alter the house advantage of the game. These additional bets, he claims, account for increasing the hold on the blackjack game to 22.5 percent at the Four Queens since December 6, 1991, when the game was first introduced. In an article in the October 1992 issue of Casino Journal, he compares this hold to an average of 12 to 16 percent on other blackjack games.

I believe this game to be an interesting development which is favorable to the casino because it increases the action and adds a little variety to the casino operation. However, I don't believe it will have the impact that Mr. LeVasseur is hoping for, or that it will stimulate a rise in table game activity. First of all, since I don't have statistical information available other than what LeVasseur has provided, I have to use it at face value for the purpose of this analysis. This may actually be to his disadvantage since my first impression is that by placing three wagers simultaneously, a number of decision far greater than 2.1 should be expected.

So what does it actually mean that you are able to get 2.1 more decisions per hour at a blackjack table? Depending on the source of information you use, you find that the average number of decisions per hour in blackjack range from sixty, which is used by most casinos, to one hundred, which is used by Ken Uston in his book *Million Dollar Blackjack*. Actually, the number of decisions per hour is going to vary according to the players on the game and the speed with which the dealer operates the game. It has a direct relationship to the number of players, how fast they play, how many additional wagers they make and, of course, the speed of the dealer. Yet for the purpose of this analysis, I am going to use what in my experience is the industry average of sixty decisions per hour.

At sixty decisions per hour, 2.1 additional decisions would represent an increase of 3.5 percent decisions per hour. If you use the industry average of 2 percent house advantage for blackjack, the 3.5 percent increase in decisions per hour would be the equivalent of raising the house advantage to 2.07 percent, or eliminating conventional surrender (.07 percent) in a casino that has that rule. You realize that house advantage is directly related to strategy; however, in order to make a meaningful explanation, it is necessary to equate increased decisions to P.C. To understand how I arrived at this conclusion, reflect on this: At 2 percent and 60 decisions an hour, a player betting $100 a hand in blackjack is going to lose $120 (2 percent x 60 = 120 percent). If instead you multiply the 2 percent x 62.1 decisions per hour, you arrive at $124.20. If you divide $124.20 by the industry average sixty decisions, you find that the house advantage is now 2.07 percent. So, this game has managed to increase the house advantage on the 2 percent player seven one-hundredths of a percent (.07 percent) and in the basic strategy player at an average of .5 percent, only .0175 percent. This doesn't take away the merits of the game, but you do see it in a different light.

It's obvious that what Mr. LeVasseur was alluding to in an effort to market his product is unrealistic. The comparative mathematics of a game that has an advantage of 2 percent as opposed to one that has a 2.07 percent advantage isn't going to account for a difference in hold percentage from 12 percent to 22.5 percent. How do you explain this?

Mr. LeVasseur is a vice president of marketing, and as a marketer his job is to sell. He doesn't say at any time that the game is expected to hold 22.5 percent; he just mentions that this is the result they achieved at the Four Queens from December of 1991 to September of 1992. He doesn't mention what the hold percentage at similar blackjack games in his establishment is; instead, he uses a reduced assessment of what he believes to be the industry ranges. But in actuality, these aren't the industry ranges. And those casinos that do show hold percentages in the range of 12 percent to 16 percent do so because their rules are much more liberal than the Four Queens' and their volume of play is much greater. They also have a better caliber of players and a lot of inflated drop that brings the hold percentages down. So this explains the mathematical discrepancies.

LeVasseur further explains that another reason for the increase in hold percentage is the conservative strategy that the players employ because they're betting more. Whether this conclusion is sound or not I am unable to say. However, since he has drawn a conclusion to that effect, I believe it is my responsibility to comment on it. First of all, it would seem a natural reaction for some people to divide their bets into three, especially those who are budget-minded. Granted, for the person who is accustomed to betting the table minimum, this may not be possible; then again, that person might not even consider betting on the game in the first place since at first impression it would seem as though he or she would have to bet three times the minimum of the table per hand. Second, strategy decisions are usually pretty consistent and are based on the dealer's up-card. Since the up-card isn't going to change for three decisions, I don't see why this would make a difference to the player. This would be the same as customers on regular blackjack games basing their strategy decisions on whether or not they think they're going to lose the next couple of decisions.

The fact that LeVasseur uses the example of conservative play as a player neglecting to hit a sixteen against a ten when he could have used much better examples (this play is basically an even proposition either way) makes me believe he lacks expertise in this field. That's part of the reason his explanations, in my opinion, don't hold water. Nevertheless, his accomplishment can't be denied, and he is worthy of praise for developing a variation to a game that was basically stagnant—a variation that in fact has a positive effect on casino revenues without being a major detriment to the players.

A final comment on the game would be to try to predict its acceptability in the marketplace and its future. I would like to say that this game has a brilliant future in the gaming business and that it is the stimulus needed to create an upsurge in the lagging table games revenue. It certainly is a step in the right direction, yet I see in it two faults that I believe will eventually lead to its demise. One, most people tend to focus and linger on the negative, and this attitude is going to make them feel as if they will get stuck with bad decisions. Obviously, since the house has the advantage over the player, the player is going to have more bad decisions (at least from the player's point of view) than the dealer. The player is going to remember more the times when he was stuck with a 13, 14, 15, and 16 for three long decisions in a row. This is an inherent fault of this game. The other fault is that some players are going to look at their wagers as three times the minimum of the game and that may cause them to stay away. These faults, added to the fact that this game is so closely related to the most popular game in casino gaming, make it a tough-win situation for its future.

Financially, this game is currently being offered at a rate of $500 per table per month, which comes to $16.67 a day. If you round off the industry average drop for traditional blackjack at $5,000 and the average hold at 16 percent (which is close to what it is claimed to be), you find that the daily win is going to be $800 per game. That's pretty close to the Nevada average for 1994, which was $773. Now, in order to determine what difference multiple action blackjack is going to make on these games, we have to determine what effect the added decisions are going to have on the win figure. Earlier I drew a parallel between additional decisions and the house advantage for the purpose of comparison. I'm now going to use those percentages to determine the win difference. To simplify the process, let's assume the $800 win was obtained by a single player betting $100 a hand, and there was another player playing $100 a hand on the multiple action blackjack game next to it. After the first five hours of play, the traditional blackjack game had won $600 (60 decisions x 2 percent = 120 percent x 5 hours = 600 percent of $100 = $600), while the multiple action blackjack game had won $621 (60 decisions x 2.07 percent = 124.2 percent x 5 hours = $621). (I wanted to keep it in even numbers to make the concept easier to grasp.) However, you still have $200 left to account for. If you multiply the $200 by 3.5 percent, which is the additional percentage of decisions dealt out on the multiple action blackjack game, you find that seven additional dollars will be made. Therefore, multiple action blackjack, on an average $5 to $1,000 game, will have produced an additional $28. You could have multiplied the $800 times 3.5 percent and arrived at the same $28. Subtract that from the $16.67 license fee and you have an additional $11.33 profit, provided that all other variables remain equal.

Multiple action blackjack marketers claim the game increases the average daily win 49.4 percent to $1,203 with a hold percentage of 21.9 percent. As I have illustrated, theoretically at least, this isn't so. So there has to be a reason for this discrepancy. Without having been present at these trials I can only speculate on the variables that contributed to this difference. Science calls it the *experimenter's effect*. This means that, consciously or unconsciously, you tend to prove your premise. There are differences inherent in gambling experiences, not only from the games themselves but also from the environment in which the trials are conducted. Therefore, even though theoretically you can expect a performance difference between the games, realistically, time coupled with experience will tell how this new game performs in comparison to traditional blackjack.

At the Isle of Capri in Biloxi, the game was tried without much of a response, and I have no indication that the game is starting a blackjack revolution anywhere in the country. As with other games that have been introduced in recent years, this game has the disadvantage that it is up against proven winners that have withstood the test of time, that is, blackjack, craps, roulette, and baccarat. I believe the game has merit, but it isn't the answer to declining table game revenues.

Over/Under 13

Born out of the inspiration of the over and under on a football game and designed by Ken Perrie, who was then dealing at Caesars Tahoe, this game seemed to mark the beginning of the new wave of casino games. Perrie is also the co-developer of the Super Sevens addition to blackjack.

Over/Under 13 is a valuable addition to the game of blackjack, was well received by the gaming industry, and accounted for more than 500 tables worldwide as of the February 15, 1992, edition of *International Gaming & Wagering Business*. Its warm reception lay in the simplicity of the payoff odds (even money) and the high house advantage. On the *over* side it is roughly

equivalent to a place bet on the 4 and 10 in craps or to a roulette bet, and on the *under* side it is roughly equivalent to the big 6 and 8 and the hardways. In other words, this is a very good bet for the house.

Like the field bet in craps, this bet gives the inexperienced player the illusion of a good deal since, except for one number, the bet has the look of an even proposition. Also like the field bet, the *under* gives the impression of being a better bet than it is because it has 11 numbers that win as opposed to eight numbers that lose. Contrary to the field bet, however, it doesn't have as many decisions per hour. Therefore, the player doesn't notice as quickly how bad a bet it is. This camouflage effect is what makes it an ingenious development. What this means mathematically is that, while a field bet at 5.26 percent house advantage seems a better bet than the over bet at 6.5 percent house advantage, the field bet is going to have approximately 175 decisions per hour (industry averages vary from 150-200) as opposed to sixty for the Over/Under. This means that a customer will lose 921 percent of an average bet in one hour on the field as opposed to 390 percent on the over bet. The field bettor will lose 2.36 times more.

This addition to blackjack is an achievement in gaming, but it is not without flaws. It could present an opportunity for card counters, given the right circumstances. But because of the high percentage against this bet, the advantage to the card counter in all likelihood will never be exploited.

A very high plus count and a complex variation to counting systems would be required to take advantage of this deficiency. It is only after true counts of over plus three that the card counter enjoys an incredible advantage. At true plus three and true minus three, the bet is even on both the over and under bet. But since high true counts rarely occur, the chances of any one counting down multiple shoes and keeping separate counts of aces to exploit this advantage are very slim. At true plus four, the player obtains a whopping advantage of 7.7 percent on the over, and at true minus four, the player has an advantage of 4.8 percent. Either one of these advantages is what players dream of. It is even more dramatic when you move on to true plus six, which has an incredible advantage of 14.36 percent. A true minus six has an advantage of 13.2 percent on the under bet.

If high true counts were more prevalent, then the beauty of a card counting system that incorporated these bets would be that the counter could throw off the supervisor by increasing bets when the count was either positive or negative. To give an example of how strong a system like that could be, let us compare it to an advanced card counting system. With a count of true plus four, the Uston Advance Point Count System with four decks remaining has an advantage for the player of .9 percent. In order to obtain this advantage, the player must maintain perfect strategy. The over bet, regardless of how many decks are left, will have an advantage of 7.7 percent (8 $\frac{1}{2}$ times greater!), and the player doesn't have to remember any play variations to do it. At true plus six, Uston is at a 2 percent advantage, and the over bet is at 14.36 percent!

To see an even better example of how a system like this can work, imagine this: The count is true minus six, and the counter has an approximate disadvantage of 2.3 percent. The under bet at this time has an advantage of 13.2 percent. So the card counter puts down a bet of $1,000 on the regular bet and $1,000 on the under bet. The supervisor who has been counting this player down scratches his head, confused, *"What the hell is this person doing?"* Since the regular bet has a disadvantage of approximately 2.3 percent, the player will lose $23 every time he or she makes the bet, but will win $132 every time he or she makes the bet on the under bet. This leaves this person with a profit of $109 out of the $2,000 action for a percentage win of 5.45 percent. And it happened exactly when this player was expected to lose.

On the plus side, the results are even more dramatic since at true plus six, the card counter would have an advantage of around 1.6 percent (with four decks remaining) while his or her over bet would have an advantage of 14.36 percent. Assuming the same $1,000 bets, the player would win a total of $159.60 for a total advantage 8 percent. How's that for a power play?

Another plus to this system is that, contrary to a card counting system where bets have to be made every hand, the player doesn't have to make a bet on the over/under until it is advantageous. Unfortunately, the added work load for the card counter isn't worth the reward since true counts over four rarely happen. And even if someone were this tenacious, that player wouldn't represent much of a risk to the casino. More-over, the added volume of play generated by the bet is more than enough to offset whatever damage a few stray, testy card counters can do to it. Casinos take precautions against this bet by limiting the maximum wagers.

Caribbean Stud Poker

The idea of a large jackpot such as those that occur on a slot machine is innovative and in tune with what is happening today in gaming. The incorporation of these jackpots is a giant step in the right direction.

The developers of this game claim the progressive jackpot handle increases the game's hold by 2 percent for every 10 percent of game hold. As a marketing tool they use statistics from the Grand Holiday Casino in Aruba that show a hold percentage from 24.9 percent in 1989 to 29.1 percent in 1990. I know for a fact that in some casinos in Mississippi this game is holding over 45 percent and enjoying extraordinary success with an average win per day per unit of over $2,000. This is a very strong hold percentage and is bound to attract many casino operators. Initially the developers of this game claimed a house advantage of 2.56 percent using basic strategy. Now they're saying it is 5.3 percent based on 65 billion decisions. The previous house advantage projection was based on 65 million decisions. I question how such a sharp increase in house percentage could have occurred based on a sampling larger than 65 million decisions. Something had to be wrong with programming.

At 2.56 percent Caribbean stud poker had the qualities a casino wants to increase win figures. At 5.3 percent it faces difficulties because the average will be much higher and, therefore, it will destroy the opposition and fall into disuse. However, this hasn't been the case so far. It is probably the most popular and successful of all new games, possibly because it offers the possibility of high payoffs, in addition to what can amount to an extraordinary progressive jackpot. The element of greed is highly represented in this game.

Though an interesting game, I doubt that it will draw customers from real poker games since the challenges of that game are missing here. There are no major decisions to be made and no bluffing. Nevertheless, for those who feel intimidated by the actual poker game, this game presents a fun alternative. If it is marketed so that customers understand the rules, it can continue to enjoy the success that it has enjoyed until now.

One saving point that this game has is the quickness with which the progressive jackpot escalates. Obviously, the higher the jackpot, the more excitement the game will generate. This is the seductive factor that could offset the negative high house hold. At worst it offers an extra game to spice up the mix, at best it offers a fantastic revenue machine for the casino. The future will tell if it can continue its momentum, but for a while, at least, Caribbean stud poker is the king of new games.

Let It Ride

The success of video poker games and Caribbean stud poker has brought about the design of other poker-related games. One such game is Let It Ride, a poker game based on five-card stud that allows the player to bet equal amounts in three different betting circles, yet on the same hand. The advantage of doing so is that players are favored on the first two bets, since they can withdraw their bets if they choose to do so. If they have winning combinations, they would obviously stay with it. What could be better?

LET IT RIDE
Pay Table

HAND	PAYOFF
Pair Tens +	1-1
Two Pair	2-1
3 of a Kind	3-1
Straight	5-1
Flush	8-1
Full House	11-1
4 of a Kind	50-1
Straight Flush	200-1
Royal Flush	1000-1

There's obviously a catch. The final bet cannot be withdrawn. That bet nets the house a whopping 37.28 percent. However, the advantage on the preceding wagers is so strong that when the final tally of wagers versus payouts is in, the house nets 2.4 percent, if the player has played smartly. It doesn't take a lot of savvy to decide when to stay in.

This game has three of the prerequisites the house looks for in a casino game. One, the house percentage (PC) is a favorable 2.4 percent or more; two, players have the illusion that the game is favorable to them because they can withdraw their first two bets if they aren't good for them and, three, the high payoffs of some winning combinations are extremely attractive. These payoffs are subject to a cap that is established by each individual operator. They could vary from $10,000 to possibly $100,000.

One drawback to the game is that, because of these high payoffs and the strong payoff advantage on the first two bets, the game's house hold is reported to fluctuate greatly. In other words, one month could show a house hold of 30 percent while the next month could show a house hold of 5 percent, with many losing days in between. Let It Ride May, 1995 figures in Nevada casinos show a house hold of 21.57 percent and the win per day of $924.

These initial reports are not strong; however, the game is still young and rising in popularity. As the game continues to draw loyal fans, it should begin to stabilize at higher rates. Already that loyal following has begun to show as different companies (Bally's, the Four Queens, the Las Vegas Hilton, the MGM Grand and the Riviera in Las Vegas; Buffalo Bill's and the Eldorado in Reno; and Harvey's in Lake Tahoe) have banded together to produce a million-dollar tournament. This is an indication that there is obviously a lot of interest in the game.

I don't expect Let It Ride to catch on like wildfire, but I do expect it to do well. The game isn't difficult to explain and understand, and it certainly has a lot of attractive components. Expect to see more of these games on casino floors.

Casino War

This powerhouse game has produced astounding preliminary results. The objective of the game is to have a higher card than the dealer. Since you win as many hands as you lose this way, the only way the house can make money is by collecting on the ties. When a tie occurs, the house gives the player the option to go to war or to relinquish half the bet. If the player decides to go to war he or she must put up an equal amount or less, while the dealer does not have to do that. From there derives the house advantage, even though if the player wins the war the house will pay the winner at a rate of two to one.

This is another game that has some of the qualities the casino looks for. The house PC is 2.88 percent and the house hold is outrageous, in some places surpassing 50 percent. The reason for this enormous house hold is because of the inordinate amount of decisions on the game, which becomes obvious when you realize that only one card is being dealt to each player. BET Technology, Inc., who is the developer of Casino War, claims that an average of 900 hands will be dealt on the game in an hour. If we assume an average of four players on the game, that would mean we could expect 225 decisions in that hour.

Assuming that we are playing an average of $5 every hand, we can expect to lose $32.40 in that hour. Compare that to $1.50 in blackjack playing perfect strategy on a shoe game. Quite a difference, isn't it? That's why the Mississippi Gaming Commission made the Isle of Capri (which was the casino that tested the game in Mississippi) increase the payoff to 3 to 1 when the house goes to *war* and ties with the player. This gave the player slightly better odds, but not much more. The real killer is the number of decisions per hour.

What I can't understand is how the Commission can feel that 2.88 percent and 225 decisions an hour are outrageous, yet they say nothing of the 10 percent and 360 to 720 decisions an hour that a player gets on some slot machines. Here is another instance where a governing body is poking its nose into something that should not be its concern and of which it has no knowledge.

Returning to the game of *war*, it seems obvious to me that this is a great game for the house and that its simplicity will make it very popular in the beginning. Casinos should avail themselves of this game while it is still popular. However, like most killer games before it, it will eventually fall into disuse because of its high hold percentage. I don't think that it will become extinct because of its simplicity and because of the illusion that both player and dealer have equal opportu-

nity. Also because it is a game that is so familiar to everyone.

I believe this game will flourish through the next year or so and then it will become a game that is mainly for novices and tourists.

New Game Commentary

We have seen how new games are affecting the casino environment. Never before in the history of gaming have so many games been introduced in such a short time. Declining table game revenues help to foster this creative sprint. But what of the casino games that have been the trademark of the gaming industry? Are they doomed?

The first thing I want to make clear is that the decline in table game revenues doesn't necessarily mean that the gaming public has lost interest in those games. Casino owners don't complain about declining table game revenues. The obvious reason is that slot machines are far more profitable and efficient than table games. Slot machines cost less than people, don't get sick as often, and produce a lot more revenue. For example, a single blackjack table per three shifts requires four dealers and one floorperson to operate. Over the course of five years the average labor cost, not including company benefits, would be $351,800 to produce gross revenues of $1,040,000 at $800 per unit per day. The labor cost equivalent in slot machines would be 70.36 slots at $5,000 per machine. Assuming an average win per day of $75, the slot machines would produce $6,860,100 in the same span of time and would still have many useful years ahead of them. The life expectancy of a slot machine is 10+ years. The cost of maintenance and change personnel is easily offset by the cost of employee benefits in the table game operation.

A reduction in table game revenue will have a negative effect on labor needs and requirements. As long as the gaming boom continues, this isn't going to be felt, but once it's over, the house of cards is going to come crashing down and it's the table game employees who are going to get crushed. It will be up to innovators in the gaming field to develop ways to prove to casino operators that a smile, a friendly handshake, and human warmth, in the right circumstances, can be more productive than the cold steel and taut body of a slot machine. It isn't going to be easy.

EXISTING GAMES

Blackjack

Blackjack remains the most popular casino table game. Boasting a reported win of almost two billion dollars in 1993, it is the obvious medium for table game expansion. The move to introduce variations in the game of blackjack is under way, but it is too early to determine if the innovations will mean more profits.

Blackjack itself in its classic form or with variations will remain popular because it allows the player to exercise certain control over the events of the game. Rules are simple, the payoff is uncomplicated, the proximity of the dealer and players allows for human interaction, and the normal give and take of the winnings and losses, almost at 50-50, gives the players the impression they can win. These conditions have made blackjack enormously successful. Any game that wants a chance at success in the future should factor in these guidelines.

Blackjack, depending on rule variations, has an average house advantage of 2 to 3 percent. This is sufficient to produce good revenues. However, government regulations and competition continue to negatively affect the house advantage and this, added to the growing knowledge of game strategies by the players, has managed to significantly reduce the house advantage.

If we think in terms of inflation, obviously we have a no-win situation. Our hold percentages should increase to keep up with inflation and maintain profitability, but they are decreasing, and our profits will eventually succumb to inflation. A technique that operators use to increase hold percentages is to have dealers deal more hands per hour. I've discussed the drawbacks to this approach: Customer relations often suffer when there is too much speed in operation. Added pressure on the dealers works negatively against employee relations, resulting in conflict, turnover, and low morale.

If dealers can be motivated to increase their production while maintaining the same degree of customer service and friendliness, the hold will improve. But this isn't something easy to achieve. Motivating dealers is one of the great challenges to casino managers. Michele Comeau, co-author of *Casino Customer Service—The Win Win Game*, says a survey conducted by Richard Darder and reported in his 1991 master's the-

sis at the University of Nevada-Las Vegas found that dealers are motivated more by good wages than by job security. Working conditions placed third. This is only one study but, assuming its validity, we could conclude that, if we were to offer dealers better wages to have them increase productivity, they would be likely to oblige. But how do you define productivity?

Doug DuCharme, Director of Gaming at Fitzgerald's in Las Vegas, believes he has the answer to that problem. He devised a concept called *productivity gain sharing* whereby dealers were rewarded for surpassing 375 hands per hour (approximately 75 decisions) after determining, through surveillance and pit personnel, the average decisions per hour that were being dealt. The trial period for this program was four months. An increase in productivity was achieved. Dealers who maintained consistent production, *error free,* over the decisions per hour requirement, were awarded $300 cash or a trip to Disneyland for two plus $100. According to DuCharme, eighteen dealers made or broke the prescribed number of decisions. *Incidentally, it is a human impossibility to deal four months full time without committing an error.* So, aside from this *error* in design, the program did seem to have merit. Again, without having been there or duplicating the experiment, it is impossible to assess if there was any fallout due to the increase in speed. It wouldn't be cost effective to involve pit personnel and surveillance personnel to monitor this. Still, there is a pace that will increase decisions per hour while not souring customer service or breaking the spirit of the dealer.

One way casinos can increase revenue production and hold percentages is to regulate competition to the point where destructive practices are controlled. This requires government intervention or the forming of an organism to set realistic minimum percentages for different games—sort of like what OPEC is to oil-producing countries. This could work effectively, especially with comps; it would prevent some operations from self-destructively giving the store away. But this will never happen because the more solvent companies like to maintain their edge over the smaller, less profitable casinos and the larger more leveraged companies. Still a solution must be found because every year comp expenses continue to rise.

The way to increased revenue production and hold percentages is to keep customers playing the games longer. If a person buys in for $100, makes $5 bets and spends two hours at a blackjack game that has a house advantage of 2 percent, he will lose $12, which translates to a 12 percent hold of the $100 buy-in. If that person stays on the game for another 30 minutes, the casino wins another $3, and the hold percentage increases to 15 percent. This is the theory behind the *one minute more* concept promoted by Lyn Baxter, vice president of casino operations at the Rio Hotel in Las Vegas. Baxter estimates that, if customers stay on the games one more minute on an average stay of two hours, the bottom line is increased by 1 percent without any additional cost. The mathematics don't hold up on that one, but the idea behind it is solid. The longer the customer stays on the game, the better it will be for the house hold. The question that needs to be answered is: *How do we keep the customer longer on the games?*

Lyn Baxter's suggestions all deal with customer service. Employee evaluations reflect what is expected of dealers: (1) Do dealers encourage hesitant guests to join the game? (2) Do they greet guests promptly and courteously? (3) Do they provide information about the game if needed and make new players feel comfortable? (4) Do they create an environment where guests have fun at their table? (5) Do they thank guests for playing at their table and encourage them to return?

I agree and can't stress too strongly the importance of the relationship that dealers establish with their customers. Blackjack provides the opportunity for intimacy between the players and the dealer. These goals should be a focus for every casino operation.

I would take this customer relationship a step further to include the floor supervisor, whose main function should be customer relations. There's much a floor supervisor can do to make customers feel welcome and appreciated. Customers like the attention they get from supervisors; it makes them feel important. A casino that fails to project this feeling to its customers is doomed to fail.

Another interesting thing that Baxter tried in an effort to make customers feel more comfortable was to lower a blackjack table to give it a kitchen table feel. Baxter says it worked, claiming customers are less intimidated by the dealer, and their feet are set comfortably on the carpet instead of hanging on the chair. It's an interesting concept that should be explored fur-ther. Anything that makes customers feel more *at home* is going to make them stay longer. You should take a closer look at this and evaluate your findings.

The casino environment affects how comfortable a customer feels. In this respect, the Rio has also been innovative. Their jungle is surrounded by foliage and has TV monitors on each machine. This gives players a feeling of seclusion and family room comfort. It also sends the message that the casino cares about customers' comfort. Concepts such as these do keep the customer in the casino for longer periods of time.

Larry Smith, vice president of casino operations at the Sands in Las Vegas, attempted to remove the intimidation factor from the table games by distributing WIN cards to players at the Dunes before it closed. WIN cards are plastic cards with a dial that tells players how to play blackjack, craps, and roulette. They were developed by Ted Gottlieb, a former Sahara Tahoe blackjack dealer and founder of Gaming International Stateline, which distributes the WIN card. Larry Smith reports that 1,500 WIN cards were given out the first week they were introduced and that they showed a positive effective on revenues for the six months before the casino closed. The Dunes went further by giving players match play chips and dealer bet coupons in exchange for the money. This gave everyone, including dealers, an incentive to promote the program. Some operators feel uncomfortable educating their customers and converting them to a .5 percent player from a 2 or 3 percent player in blackjack. This approach requires foresight, but it gains loyalty and profits over time. Obviously, it doesn't pay to take away a once-a-year tourist from a 5 percent to 10 percent slot machine to convert him or her into a .5 percent blackjack player. But it can pay off if you make a regular player out of someone who can visit you more often.

Craps

The major problem with craps is that it is the most intimidating of all casino games. One reason is the variety of possible wagers on the layout. Another is the excitable crowd that usually surrounds it. In order to really appreciate the game of craps, a crowded layout is required. This situation in itself places a barrier between the observer and the game, since players in craps have to stand up, and by doing so, they block the view of the game from the outside. This is probably the reason that from 1982 to 1990 craps was the least improved of the four major casino games in terms of reported win, showing an increase of only 30.4 percent. It only increased 2.3 percent from 1989 to 1990, and in 1991 it reported a decrease of 9.4 percent. This 1991 decrease was only surpassed by baccarat at 11.65 percent, but baccarat's decrease was mostly due to less participation by foreign nationals. This means that craps had the highest decrease in terms of our national market, which is basically the market that supports it. However, from 1993 to 1994, craps experienced an increase of 6.67 percent in Nevada.

Removing the natural barrier that the game of craps presents isn't an easy task. The game can't be simplified without working against what you're trying to achieve. This isn't to say that the layout can't be improved upon. Instructions such as we see in blackjack (dealer must hit all 17's and stand on 16, and insurance pays 3 to 2) can be added to crap games. Obviously, crap instructions are more complicated but they can be placed on signs above the game. Example: Pass line: Wins on 7 and 11, losses with 2, 3, and 12 on the first throw. A picture of a small layout with the puck in the off position should accompany that. A second graphic with the puck on the different numbers should read: *The following throws will result in a win if the point total is repeated* [graphic showing the different dice combinations] *and will lose if a 7 is thrown before.* This should be the minimum explanation on the crap game. More explanations are even better. Since the crap table is pretty lengthy, there's a lot of room for explanations across it with a sign that hangs from the ceiling. Of course, this produces another problem, which is the surveillance coverage, but that can be dealt with.

Another thing the casino should do is exhort their supervisors and dealers to teach players at least the basics of the game and to be ready to answer any questions. Many times I've observed dealers and supervisors turn players away and direct them to the security booth, the cage, or the inspector's desk for information booklets rather than taking the time to offer a simple explanation. Employees who do this deserve to be disciplined. It isn't always possible to make explanations to customers during a fast-moving crap game, but usually there's someone available who can give an explanation and should do so. A dealer who doesn't have a heavy work load can make explanations without losing control of the game.

Explanation booklets on craps are often difficult to understand. They are usually readily available, incomprehensible color brochures that cost a lot of money. A simple white cardboard sheet or card, with explanatory drawings and easy-to-understand wording, would fill the bill. These should be in ample supply in the pit.

Craps can also be revitalized by offering bonus chips specifically for different betting areas, accompanied by the explanatory gaming booklet. This way the player will learn how to wager on the betting area for which the chip is designed. The chip can be offered as part of a package that is given out once a day, as part of a tour package, or as part of a promotion. One chip can only be used as a place bet—maybe even a specific place bet, another can be used on the field, another on the hardways, and still another on the proposition bets. Proposition bet payoffs can be reduced in half for this promotion, but even if you keep them at true value, you should keep in mind that if someone hits a 15 to 1 payoff on the first shot, it not only is good promotion, the person is probably going to continue to try to hit it again since it was so easy. The majority of these bets you don't have to worry about—they lose. Casinos spend millions of dollars in advertising. This simple type of promotion will keep players coming back, inviting others, and promoting your giveaway, and chances are folks will leave a lot more money in your casino than they will take with them.

And how about a we-teach-you craps tournament with low limits for beginners? You double the excitement of the game while cultivating a new crop of players. A simple explanatory booklet or sheet should be mailed with the entry invitation. This gives any player a chance to get better acquainted with the game before putting money up. Because it's inexpensive (comparatively), it should lure new players.

Crap dealers should be trained to promote proposition bets. Variations should be explored, such as $1 multi-bets for players with smaller budgets. The idea of letting a player make a $1 horn bet seems ludicrous to most casino personnel but, if you think about it, a $5 bet on the pass line will lose $3.50 while $1 bet on the horn every roll will lose $20.25, based on fifty pass line decisions (168.75 rolls). This, of course, presumes that we apply the same paying procedure and house advantage of 12 percent. Since it can't be done, you would short the player when the high side hits and pay him only 6 to 1 instead of 6.75 to 1. This raises the house advantage on this wager to 14.8 percent. Thus, instead of winning $20.25, the house would win $24.98. Keep in mind that this is five times what the house makes on the pass line bet.

The actual horn bet can be modified to be paid in unison at 9 to 2 odds for a house advantage of 8.33 percent or at 19 to 4 odds where it has an advantage of 4.17 percent. This could increase the action on these bets. A world bet can be modified into a natural bet with all combinations paying equally at 9 to 5 odds for a house advantage of 6.67 percent. It's not always recommended that you bargain with house percentages, but these are bets that are outrageously assessed to begin with, so it doesn't really hurt the house to bargain with them if it increases the action on the game and stirs more interest. This probably won't even make sense to most operators. That's fine, but my intention is to stimulate your thinking in this respect. There are better ways out there, and you can find them.

Roulette

The game of roulette definitely needs revitalization. Of all the casino games, roulette holds the greatest potential for improvement. It is a simple game and doesn't require much explanation. This is a game that has been traditionally popular in Europe and Latin America and has yet to live up to its potential in the United States.

The main reason for its fourth rating among casino games in the United States is because of its high house advantage (5.26 percent compared to .5 percent to 3 percent in blackjack, .5 percent to 16.7 percent in craps, 1.25 percent in baccarat). When the popularity of roulette began to lag in Europe because of the amazing speed with which customers were losing their money, casinos responded by making the odds more attractive for the player. They eliminated one zero bet, and they gave the outside bettors a second chance with the imprisonment rule. For some reason, when roulette was introduced in the United States, it was the game that had already fallen into disuse in Europe. This put it at a great disadvantage against games that had already outdone other unhealthy games such as faro.

Faro no longer exists today and that is the fate of any game that doesn't give the player a fighting chance.

A testimony to roulette's great potential is the fact that in spite of its limitations it has risen in popularity. It experienced a 96 percent increase in reported win from 1982 to 1990. It went from $133,096,939 to $261,524,000. Some operators may reason that, because of this trend in roulette, it should be left alone since it is doing just fine. In other words, "If it ain't broke, don't fix it!" But that approach is near-sighted.

Today's casinos must factor in increased player sophistication. Games must be reevaluated with that in mind. Look at slot technology. The new video machines are becoming more favorable to the player. In fact, Bob Stupak installed video poker machines at his Vegas World Casino that actually gave the player the advantage if he or she played perfect strategy. This is just one indication of change in the gaming world thinking. Punters will abandon games that are too heavily weighted against them.

Roulette is the natural game for introducing new gamblers to the table games. It is possible that the increase in foreign junkets plus the game's simplicity have been factors in the increase observed in roulette win during the last decade.

Casinos have introduced lighted number boards that indicate what numbers have previously come out. This board is a standard in European casinos, where roulette is the main game. What it does is give the player a sense that he or she can predict the numbers that are going to come out based on the numbers that have previously come out. The Rio and the Mirage have used this board successfully, and I believe it is something to be seriously considered to promote the game of roulette. With a single zero, the roulette game has a disadvantage of 2.70 percent on the inside, and with imprisonment the outside bet has a disadvantage of 1.35 percent. This makes the game almost as good as baccarat for the player on the outside with the potential for more excitement. The level of excitement increases with the size of the payoff odds. And although this wouldn't be applicable to the outside bet, it would be applicable to the inside bet where a 35 to 1 payoff is possible. The equivalent in baccarat would be to hit the 8 to 1 tie bet, which carries an outrageous 14.36 percent disadvantage. Obviously, roulette has the advantage there.

I repeat my belief that roulette has excellent potential for improvement and holds great promise. To overlook it would be poor management.

Baccarat

Baccarat's strength is baccarat's major weakness. This may seem contradictory, but it is true in the sense that the elaborate and secluded atmosphere of the baccarat pit is intimidating to some casino customers. Prestige and the high wagering associated with the game scare the everyday player. A player when first introduced into casino games is usually very cautious and conservative. That's why the slot machines have so much appeal to newcomers. At the slot machines, a player can wager a nickel, a dime, or a quarter. Not so in the baccarat pit games where $5 is the least that can be bet, and where a $25 minimum is more common. Obviously, if you can't capture the player's attention in the beginning, chances are you're not going to catch attention later. And so, baccarat, for the most part, has remained a game for the serious gambler. With its high limits and low advantage percentage it has maintained a loyal following, especially among foreign visitors. It is precisely foreign loyalty that has made this game the most progressive of all casino games.

In 1982, the reported win for baccarat in Nevada and New Jersey was $225,611,107. In 1990, the reported win for baccarat escalated to $541,723,000. This is an incredible 140 percent increase. And it was a trend that until that year was still on a rapid ascent, showing a 54.83 percent increase from the win figures of 1989. In 1991, the world-wide recession took its toll, and the dependency of this game on foreign players became evident when their numbers diminished and baccarat showed the greatest decrease of all games at 11.65 percent. The 1991 reported win figures were $478,623,000. Yet in 1994 Nevada baccarat win exceeded $491,000,000, an increase of 42.44 percent over 1993!

Obviously, in some circles, baccarat is alive and well. But in order for baccarat to expand its appeal, it must remove the fortress impression and make itself more player-friendly to newcomers. An indirect attempt at this has been made with the introduction of mini baccarat. Mini baccarat has succeeded in gaining ground in the gaming world. In 1990 it accounted for a reported win of $16 million, an increase of 58.87 percent from 1989, and in 1991 it reported a win of $20,586,000 for an increase of 28.5. In 1994, Nevada reported a win of $44,512,000 in mini baccarat.

Conclusion

Why spend large sums of money on promoting low percentage games when you can spend the same amount of money promoting your high percentage games, such as the slots? After all, it wasn't total gaming win that decreased in 1991, it was table game win. Total gaming win increased by 1.7 percent, as opposed to table game win that decreased by 6.2 percent. So generally speaking, casinos didn't make less money; they made more, and they made it where their costs of operation are less. The question is, did these people just gravitate to that slot operation or did casino operators direct them there? In Spain, slot machine revenues in 1991 accounted for 15.9 percent of total gaming revenue. In Holland, it was 37.7 percent, and in Puerto Rico, in 1993 it was 51.53 percent. I believe the body of evidence before us clearly indicates that casino operators are purposely directing their gaming revenues to where they can better serve the operation. From a business and management standpoint this makes all the sense in the world, and it also forces the table game operation to reach deep within itself for survival. It becomes sort of a friendly competition where, hopefully, the table game operation will respond to the challenge and make casinos more profitable.

Many people may feel that the casinos don't have to go to these lengths to procure profitability (favoring the slot operations). But as Donald E. McGhie, the president of a Reno-based consulting firm, has pointed out: One-third of all casinos in Nevada and New Jersey declared operating losses in 1990. That's an astounding fact in an industry that people describe as having "a license to steal"—a belief so prevalent that casino stocks soared during 1992 to the beginning of 1993, outperforming all the leading stock market indexes.

Table games employees must realize that their conduct affects their jobs. They have to understand that the patrons who contribute to their coffers pay their salaries. A dealer should see every customer, regardless of the amount of money gambled, as a friend and benefactor and treat that person accordingly. Only by doing this can we establish a difference between ourselves and the slot machine, only this way can we hope to keep this customer by us a little longer. It is painful to say that I have observed slot machines that are more animated than some dealers and supervisors.

As for the casinos, there's a large, untapped market out there in need of discovery. All the potential customers are waiting for is the right invitation. In the April 15, 1992 issue of *Gaming & Wagering Business,* Phil Hevener states that studies he has seen indicate that only 15 percent of Americans have ever been in a casino. Let us assume that a Gallup poll reported in the November 15, 1992 issue of *Gaming & Wagering Business* accurately represents all of America. In that poll, 80 percent of the people stated that they enjoyed gambling activities. If that is correct, it means that at least 65 percent of Americans haven't received the right invitation or are still waiting. It means that 100 million people are ready! What are we waiting for? Let's roll out the red carpet, dress up for the occasion, polish up our layouts, and ask them over with a smile. If we show them that our home is theirs *(mi casa es su casa),* maybe they'll want to spend another night.

CHAPTER 9

PIT PROCEDURES

GENERAL PIT PROCEDURES

Opening Pit Procedures

It is only proper to begin pit procedures at the time when the pit is about to commence operation. However, the commencement time could be before the casino opens to the public (in the case of operations that close) or it could be when the incoming pit manager arrives to take over the shift. The pit manager will usually arrive twenty to thirty minutes before the shift or casino opening and prepare the pit for operation. This preparation will entail getting all necessary information about the operation as it stands at the time the pit manager is taking over, or an inspection of all paperwork and pit tables if the operation is closed.

The inspection of the tables should include verification of bankroll totals, verification of bankroll security (lid inspection), inspection of drop boxes (making sure that numbers correspond to tables and that there's a box present and locked), and verification of credit transactions. Paperwork will be checked for recording and mathematical errors, fills and credits will be verified, and the incoming pit manager's paperwork will be readied for the operation. This paperwork would include table game inventory sheets, the table game routing sheet, and the shift transfer sheet. Scheduling changes and adjustments, as well as substitutions for call-ins, would be done at this time.

The floor supervisor will be the next to show up at his or her assigned section of the pit. Usually, the floor supervisor will be required to be in the pit twenty minutes before the shift begins to make preparations for opening, or to relieve the previous supervisor who had to start twenty minutes before shift. The pit manager will check off the floor supervisor and will relay any special instructions that are to be given for that day. These instructions could include a new rule or procedure that is in effect or information on the expected arrival of a special group or player.

Instructions for the handling of these customers could be provided at this time. An example of this could be the arrival of two junkets, one that must be rated and has red identifying buttons, and one that doesn't necessarily have to be rated and has blue buttons. This simplifies the floor supervisor's job.

Once the floor supervisor has gotten situated in the right section, he or she will proceed to set up the paperwork. This usually consists of a table games card or cards, where the floor supervisor will write down the inventories of each individual game under his or her supervision. The paperwork will also include the total count of major chip categories like $10,000, $5,000, $1,000, $500, $100, and $25. Smaller denomination chip totals such as $5 and $1 are rarely annotated, although in casinos that mainly cater to this clientele the supervisor will keep a mental note of what is there and where it is going. Other useful information that may be kept on the table game cards could be markers, fills, credits, and the names of ratable players. This can come in handy when these players return to the supervisor's table later on or when they make a request for a marker. It is always embarrassing to ask a player's name a second time during the same shift. Some casinos record markers on a marker card at the tables where they were issued. The net amount credited to the table will be displayed by a numbered button in the table's bankroll rack.

The floor supervisor will also have to handle the rating cards. Filling out rating cards is possibly the most important paperwork function the floor supervisor has to deal with. It is necessary to be very careful to fill these cards out accurately because many times ratings will be the subject of disputes. Valuable information included in the rating card is the name and account number of the player, date of birth, the player's credit line or cash cage deposit, and the amount of credit still available. Also recorded on the rating card is the player's average bet, when the player's play began and when it concluded, the total amount of time played, the amount of cash, credit, or chip buy-in, and how much this individual won or lost. The floor supervisor's signature and employee number are also important in case the supervisor must be tracked down to resolve conflicting information. (Examples of forms can be found in Appendix C.)

Fill and credit request slips are also part of the floor supervisor's paperwork in the normal course of a working day, and these should be close and ready if needed. Where markers are issued manually, the floor supervisor will usually have these set up by denomination nearby. Some operations don't allow a floor supervisor to issue markers, so the pit manager does it. But the floor supervisor still has other paperwork to do. In dealing with junkets, the floor supervisor will have to fill out time and action cards or use special rating cards that identify the group in question. Sometimes an identifying number and color on a regular rating card will suffice. Filling out evaluation and rating sheets of dealers and disciplinary action forms for employee misconduct are also part of the additional paperwork the floor supervisor has to do.

The next table game employee to the pit is the dealer. Usually, the dealer will be required to show up at the pit five to ten minutes before starting time because the opening procedure of the game requires certain preparations. In blackjack the dealer may be required to remove the shoe from the shoe box, inspect the cut cards, remove the lid from the chip bank and store it, and inspect the cards as they're handed over by the floor supervisor. After the cards have been inspected, the dealer will neatly spread them across the layout so they can be inspected. This may be done in either of two ways depending upon in-house or state regulations. The cards may be spread in a fan-like formation in two columns of three or four decks each, or else they can be spread straight across the layout, in two rows. If the table bankroll needs to be adjusted and filled, the dealer will make the floor supervisor aware of this.

The crap dealer stands at an assigned position, which is usually named first, second, or third base. The dealer may assist the boxperson in fixing the bankroll if asked, but other than that, major preparation is to place the number marker (puck) inside the don't come box, set it to the off position, and stand straight and ready for business. The stickperson will store the chip bank lid under the table and place the dice bowl against the mirror. The game is then ready for action.

The roulette dealer must remove the lids from the wheel and from the chip bank and then position the chips in whatever way they best serve that individual's dealing style. The roulette dealer always places the value chips toward the center of the table to allow better supervision. He or she spreads the nonvalue chips in color groups and rows of four along the wood railing, which prevents them from falling under the wheel and off the table. This railing curves toward the back of the table, allowing enough room to spread out the different colors and leave enough room between them to accommodate anyone's hand. After verifying and signing the inventory sheet, the dealer spins the roulette wheel counterclockwise and waits for business.

The baccarat dealer has opening procedures similar to those of the blackjack dealer: verifying and signing the opening inventory sheet; inspecting the cards as they're handed over by the floor supervisors; and spreading them neatly on the table for proper inspection, much as the blackjack dealer does except that baccarat usually requires eight decks.

The Twenty-Four-Hour Operation

In twenty-four-hour operations such as Atlantic City and Nevada, some of these procedures only apply when opening additional pits and table games. Once the operation is in progress, the pit manager supervises the pit, ensuring that all employees are adequately performing their duties. The pit manager will carefully inspect all paperwork for accuracy and ask questions in the event of any inaccuracy. Both the pit manager and floor supervisor have been known to falsify information on rating cards in order to accommodate customer requests from which they may profit in some instances. The pit man-

ager should be aware of this and be ready to question ratings that don't seem accurate. Mistakes can be intentional or unintentional, although most of the time they're unintentional. The pit manager must be ready to spot inconsistencies.

When pit managers aren't handling paperwork, they will walk and inspect the pit. They will look for unusual play, suspicious-looking customers, and employees who aren't paying attention to their jobs or are displaying improper supervision or dealing techniques. They will ask questions about what is happening at the tables; they will greet known customers and initiate friendly conversation with them.

Pit managers must make sure that all customer needs are satisfied and, if not, offer to help them (within reason, of course). They should ask questions about new players (especially good ones) and then make sure to meet them. Finally, they can express interest in their employees to let them know that the pit manager cares. All this, in a good day's work. At the end of the shift, the pit manager will pass along inventory to the incoming pit manager and summarize the day's operation on the shift transfer sheet and by oral transfer to the incoming pit manager.

The floor supervisor will cautiously watch all of the games assigned to him or her, looking for unusual occurrences and suspicious moves by dealers. Although most dealers and customers are basically honest, there are exceptions to this rule and it's because of those that the floorperson must be on the alert.

Stealing or cheating probably occurs a lot less than casino executives believe. This not only speaks well of human nature in general for its honesty, it also reflects the many controls that are in place in a modern casino. But cheating and stealing do exist despite these controls.

Aside from looking for suspicious activity, the floor supervisor should anticipate customer needs. A customer with a cigarette in hand who looks around for something, may be looking for an ashtray. A customer who is hesitating before making a decision on a play may not understand the options. A customer who stands up from the game and is hesitant about getting the floor supervisor's attention might be shy about asking for a complimentary or something that the casino would be glad to provide. A customer who is running out of money and has credit available may need assistance. Even without credit available, the customer may need the floor supervisor's assistance to make a call bet, to request an extension of credit, or to be guided through the credit process. There are many ways in which the floor supervisor can anticipate customer needs, and doing so should be a very great concern.

Filling the table game racks with sufficient chips is another concern. The floor supervisor should be able to anticipate needs according to the action that is taking place on the game. Certain groups or players may have specific needs. The amount of credit or cash deposit a customer has can be an indication of a possible need as well as the range of his or her bets. Accommodating these special needs will require the floor supervisor to remove some denomination chips from the game. This action is called a credit.

During the course of the day, the floor supervisor will also be required to issue markers. In Atlantic City, the supervisor turns the marker request over to the pit clerk, who verifies the customer's line of credit. When the pit clerk returns with the counter check, the customer needs to sign it. The floorperson then verifies that the marker has been signed before instructing the dealer to hand off the money. After the chips have been handed to the player, the floor supervisor then verifies the drop of the marker into the drop box.

In Nevada, the floor supervisor places the marker button on the table and instructs the dealer to cut out the chips. After verifying that it is correct, the supervisor will authorize that the money be handed to the player. After the player has received the money, the floor supervisor then proceeds to have the player sign the marker. Once the marker has been signed, the floor supervisor takes it to the dealer, who then signs the drop box stub or portion of it, drops it into the drop box, and then removes the button from the table and puts it in the rack. Unlike the floor supervisor in Atlantic City, the floor supervisor in Nevada has the authority to approve the marker and issue chips before the customer signs it. The floor supervisor who doesn't know the player will ask the pit clerk to verify the player's credit line.

Marker redemption is another function of the Nevada floor supervisor that the Atlantic City supervisor doesn't have. In Atlantic City, the customer must go to the cage cashier in order to redeem markers. In Nevada, they are paid right at the table, unless they have been transferred to the cage. The floor supervisor will ask the pit clerk to produce the marker that the customer is requesting, then will instruct the dealer to bring in the cash or chips from the customer and count them in the center of the table. Once it is verified, the floor supervisor will instruct the dealer to place the money with the marker button in a strategic spot that will depend upon the game. The marker is then returned to the player. The floor supervisor makes the necessary adjustment to the table marker card, signs it, and has the dealer sign it. The dealer then drops the money or returns the chips to the bank. The supervisor then removes the marker button from the table.

I've elaborated on the marker procedure because Nevada's system differs from Atlantic City. All other functions are similar. In both places the pit manager issues comps, and this will probably be based on the player's rating card, unless the player has play history that merits the comp. They both hand their fill and credit requests to the pit clerk, unless a pit clerk isn't available or isn't used. In either case, the transaction will be completed through a security guard who has the appropriate form. They both look basically for the same things in the operation of their games. And at the end of the shift, they both record the new inventory figures and cards that will be used by the following shift.

Dealing procedures are written in company manuals which the dealer must abide by. They're going to vary from game to game. Procedures that apply to all are procedures such as the time period required for calling in when sick. This varies from casino to casino, and it ranges from two to four hours before the shift. Dress and appearance codes are another thing that most operations have in common. Most casinos will not allow employees to wear beards, and will restrict the length of sideburns and earrings. At Caesars you can't have a mustache.

A generally clean and well-groomed appearance is required. Irrational, aggressive, or attitudinal behavior toward customers or supervisors must not be tolerated. Absenteeism and tardiness should be kept to a minimum. In fact, supervisors are expected to have perfect attendance, and calling in sick, justified or unjustified, is frowned upon. A few absences could cause a supervisor to be rated substandard.

Other general procedures include when and where to enter the pit—usually at the beginning or at the end of the pit. Side entries are not permitted. Calling out change and cash transactions and waiting for authorization on hundred-dollar buy-ins and up are also common in all casino operations. Calling out decisions in blackjack is enforced in Atlantic City yet not given much attention in Nevada.

Paying strict attention to the game and layout is strongly enforced in New Jersey and, although Nevada casinos do enforce this, they are more lenient, but not as lenient as Puerto Rican casino operators have been through the years. It was so lenient in Puerto Rico that when Caribe Hilton employees were asked to tighten up their gaming procedures, especially the rule that obliged them to clear their hands before leaving the game, they went on strike for almost a year!

PIT ACCOUNTING

The pit manager, along with the pit manager being relieved, counts down all the table racks. This can also be done by subordinates appointed to perform this function such as a *backup* or assistant pit manager. Table inventory slips are handled by one supervisor while the other handles the routing sheet that has every game on it. One of the supervisors will stop the game, and either the dealer or one of the supervisors will call out the cash value of the total amount of chips in each denomination category. This figure will be recorded both on the routing sheet under the corresponding game and denomination column and on the table inventory sheet that the other supervisor is handling. Some establishments don't stop the game.

When each denomination has been called out and verified, both supervisors add up the figures and total them. If both agree on the total, the sheets are separated, the original is dropped, and a copy is left on the game to be dropped in the box. The third copy goes either with the supervisor to the next game or is handed to the floor supervisor to record the totals on his or her table games card, who will later hand it to the pit clerk. After the table inventory sheet has been dropped in the drop box, the dealer removes the paddle so that security can exchange the drop box.

The pit manager then moves on to the next table, and does the same thing until all the tables have been counted down. Once all the tables have been counted, the pit manager proceeds to add all the table inventories. That figure, with the total estimated cash drop and the total amount of all markers issued during the shift will be compared against the pit need figure, which is the opening bankroll plus the fills that were required to keep the games operating, minus any credits for chips that were sent back to the cage.

If the need figure is less than the inventory plus cash and marker transactions, the pit will show a win figure balance. If it is more than the inventory plus cash and markers, the pit will show a loss figure. Most pit inventory balance sheets will first record the opening inventory, add fills, subtract credits and the closing inventory to determine the *need* figure. The cash drop and markers are compared to that to determine the *win/loss*.

Estimating cash drop is done in various ways and can depend on management directives on whether or not floor supervisors are required to track cash drops. This is the most common way cash drop is estimated: The floor supervisor or the boxperson will keep track of all $100 buy-ins. In craps, all buy-ins are counted. The pit manager will then add to this figure a certain percentage or a certain amount per table according to the amount of business that the shift experienced.

A pit manager in doubt will ask the floor supervisors if they had a lot of small drop or if they had a small number of small bills. There's really no steadfast rule to determine cash drop this way since it is dependent on the business at the time. High-limit pits, for example, get mostly large buy-ins and, therefore, the amount of small cash will be 5 to 10 percent, depending upon the amount of action and the floor supervisors' previous accuracy.

Average pits will add 20 percent or more, depending on the amount of the action. Some pit managers add a certain amount of cash per table, depending upon the minimum bets allowed on the average. There's another way pit managers estimate cash drop when floor supervisors aren't allowed to keep track. They will estimate the cash according to the table minimum. This will range, on average, between $500 to $1,000 for $1 and $2 tables; $1,500 to $2,500 for $5 tables; and $5,000 to $10,000 for $25 tables.

The total of markers or customer credit per table is entered into the computer and is kept separately on each table or on table cards that the floor supervisors have, in addition to the pit manager's own record. Pit managers will then verify that the computer total matches the totals of their records and the totals given to them by the floor supervisors. If they match, the pit managers then add it to the cash drop and the table inventory. If it doesn't match, the pit managers must investigate to see why there's a discrepancy. Once they determine who is in error, the correct amount is used to complete the shift report.

Uncovering the discrepancy involves checking the cards against the computer entries to see what is missing or has been entered more than once. If there's still a discrepancy, the actual counter checks will be compared to the markers that have been entered into the system. In Nevada, where chips are given out before markers are signed, the discrepancy could result from a marker recorded but not yet signed and entered. This doesn't happen very often, but it can happen when floor supervisors get very busy or when they're inexperienced. That's another reason the pit manager should be paying attention to employees' needs, and help them when necessary.

There's yet another form of accounting that the pit manager must handle, and that is the Cash Transaction Report. The Treasury Department requires all casinos to report cash transactions in excess of $10,000 by a single patron in a twenty-four-hour period. This report must be accompanied by the social security number of the customer and must be verified by another valid form of identification with a picture I.D. This identification must be government-issued. A separate record is kept where cash transactions of $2,500 at one time or an accumulation of such is registered. The starting point on this form can also vary from casino to casino. Since only when the patron passes the $10,000 mark is the pit manager required to get the information previously stated, the pit manager must then keep a running count of the cash and transfer this information to the incoming pit manager.

Aside from periodic rundowns to assess the financial status of the pit, the above is the extent of the internal pit accounting. There's a general pit accounting that is kept in the data banks of the computer, but this information is used by other departments. Financial records for individual games are kept, which can be compared against scheduling records in case of discrepancies and/or suspicious trends. Even productivity records can be accessed this way.

SCHEDULING AND TABLE ASSIGNMENTS

Some games departments have a scheduling office that assigns positions to employees according to their qualifications and pit manager recommendations. Others do scheduling within their own pits, either by the pit manager or a person whom the pit manager assigns. Scheduling from an office has the advantage that the computer system can be used to ensure fairness and accuracy. Pit manager recommendations are still given priority but, by doing it this way, the pit manager is obliged to take responsibility for biases and unusual requests. This makes it more difficult for pit managers to use favoritism in assigning days off, starting times, table games, and sections.

Where pit managers take on this responsibility (which is usually the way smaller places operate), a subordinate may be required to schedule dealers while the pit manager schedules the supervisors. Both at the pit level and office level, off days may be assigned by seniority, by need, by request, by the pit manager's whim, or by rotation. Seniority is usually the predominant choice and is preferred by most employees because it allows them to make plans in advance. Some casinos use a variation of both methods where a certain number of employees on the top of the seniority list enjoy regular days off while those at the bottom of the list rotate and take what best suits the needs of the pit manager or the casino.

Time starts also vary according to company policy. Policy may establish a seniority system, a random system, a rotating system, a system based on employee evaluations and ratings, or a pit manager's choice system. Random systems, evaluations and ratings systems, and pit manager's choice systems can all be influenced by bias and shouldn't be used where employee morale is a concern, as it should be.

That leaves two systems that are fair: *the seniority system* and *the rotating system*. But they're fair to different groups of people. The system that shows the most respect for equality is the rotating system, yet employees who have more seniority will sometimes complain that they can't set common times with their spouses or friends who many times also work in the gaming business. They will also complain that they have earned the privilege to have first choice because they have been with the company longer. They may have a point but, unlike days off where they have to wait a long time to have the same days as their spouses, time starts are usually three choices that are two hours apart, which means that 33 percent of the time they will have the desired time start, and 66 percent of the time they will be either one or two hours off. Weighing the pros and cons, I believe that time-start rotation is probably more helpful to the operation because it promotes better employee relations.

The next step in scheduling is the assignment of sections and tables. Supervisors should be able to handle any section of work within the casino; otherwise they shouldn't have been hired or promoted. Unfortunately, incompetent supervisors do get hired and do get promoted. Because of this, pit managers are reluctant to assign sections of heavy action to supervisors they judge to be incompetent and green. We can't blame pit managers for this attitude; after all, they're held responsible for what occurs in that pit. The problem is that pit managers soon find faults in everyone but a few hand-picked favorites. If the casino were a nuclear reactor or a highly sophisticated weapons station, or the brain of a human being in need of surgery, we would say the manager has all the right to have nothing but the best. But front-line casino jobs are so simple that anyone who knows basic arithmetic and how to read and write can perform them. If we assume that almost anyone can do the job, then from where comes this necessity to have just a certain few assigned to some sections? Pit managers should be willing to train employees and help them develop their skills.

Attitudes, responsibility, and character should be used to determine the best employees at the supervisory level. If they care for the customer, for the employee, and for the company, their job will get done efficiently, and the good they bring to the job will outweigh any mistakes they make.

There are two things we should keep in mind when evaluating employees: One, everyone makes mistakes every day and, two, the biggest and most costly mistakes in the casino aren't committed by people who don't know, they're committed by people who don't care. This is just something to keep in mind when deciding if an employee can handle a section or not. Instead of rotating that person to another section, maybe it would be better to give a hand so he or she can learn the job better. After all, we have to earn our salaries.

Another problem when relying on a limited number of people all the time is—what happens when those people aren't available because they're on vacation, they quit, or it's their day off? Sooner or later you have to use someone else, and it is better to introduce that person slowly into demanding jobs than in sudden desperation when there's not enough time for the person to learn the task. By rotating employees, you raise the level of skill of your employees, and you also raise morale because you avoid insulting employees by associating them only with simple, ordinary tasks. If you truly have a star employee under your supervision, you can acknowledge it by recommending her or him for a promotion or a raise.

Assigning dealers to a certain section makes more sense because dealers are the operators of the game and because dealers are the entry level position of the table games. Contrary to the supervisor who is required to have experience and good knowledge of the game, the dealer is many times an apprentice who is practicing a skill learned at a school or by observation.

There's no task on the casino floor that can't be mastered eventually by any individual unless that individual has a learning disability. And I must say that I have seen individuals who have had certified learning disabilities who have been able to master the games that are considered most difficult (craps and roulette) on the casino floor. I have also noticed there's a direct correlation between the exposure to more difficult tasks and the time it takes to master them. Although this assumption is based solely on empirical observation, I don't think that anyone who is familiar with the early Atlantic City experience will argue that in a few months, due to the exposure they had, Resorts International dealers became as competent as any other dealers in the world. This seems to dispel the notion in the gaming industry that it takes three years to make a good crap dealer. It makes the old Puerto Rican school of gaming look like fools, with their belief that crap dealers should spend months on the stick before they're allowed to deal to small action. So we should exercise caution when assigning games to dealers, but we should also try to get them into the mainstream as soon as possible. Sometimes it is our expectations of the way a game should be handled that are limited and not the abilities of the dealers.

Some casino managers believe that by keeping crews together for weeks and months it is easier to monitor their performance, similar to limiting the independent variables in an experiment. Although this does limit what has to be done in terms of paper searching, there are still too many independent variables that can't be controlled. One is the fact that the dealer is going to be relieved and that more than one person is going to be working on that game. Another is that most of the fluctuations in a casino are going to be ruled by chance, and they're going to send the researcher on constant wild goose chases. A task force would have to be hired for this function alone.

The bottom line is that the system isn't going to be any more efficient than random selection and supervision, and costs more in terms of time and resources. In the end, you're still going to have to rely on and entrust to others the task that your busy schedule won't allow you to do. So it won't be very effective, from a manager's point of view, and it definitely won't be appreciated by most employees, who will get tired of the same scenery every day.

I have concluded that the best system is to rotate dealers. You can monitor their progress so that new dealers and those who have to improve can gradually be brought into the mainstream system. Any necessary productivity study or security research can be done with the aid of scheduling sheets and the casino dailies. Other than that, scheduling is a matter of printing forms with all the employees' names on them, determining what the personnel requirement for each day of the week is going be, making allowances for special events, making allowances for vacations and medical leaves, determining how many employees are going to be needed at what time, and assigning days and time starts to the employees by whatever system has been chosen.

The computer system facilitates this process a lot. It can remind the scheduler of special requests, vacations, leaves, and special events. It can also compare data from the previous year to determine how special events affect the operation and enable the scheduler to predict the casino scheduling needs. It can help predict how employee cutbacks will affect the overall operation. And best of all, changes can be made to the very last minute and a neat schedule is always available. Storage of scheduling information is much more efficient this way, and the pit sheets that are printed out can then serve as a backup to the computer information.

The weekly scheduling sheet usually shows the week dates, the shift number, and the pit number. It also has all the dealer or supervisor names. There will be a column for each day of the week and rows that start at the name of each employee. The bottom row will show the total number of employees that are needed for each day of the week, and each row beyond the employees' names will show what time starts they have on each day they work. When all the time starts are added in a column, they must total the need figure at the bottom of the page. The need figure always includes extra dealers to cover for employees who may call in sick. This includes supervisors also, since these employees are always expected to show up for work and no allowances are made for them. A dealer who has a dual status of both dealer and supervisor will cover for a supervisor who fails to show up at work.

The daily schedule can reflect the table assignments of each employee or they can just name the employees assigned to the pit at their prescribed starting time. In the latter case, the pit manager will either fill in the table assignments or use what is commonly known as the *rubber band*. The rubber band is nothing more than arranging employee names on a sheet of paper, and assigning most of them initially to a game while the rest go on break. The breakers will return twenty minutes from whatever time is designated as the break time in the case of the dealers and boxpeople, and twenty or thirty minutes from the break time in the case of the floor supervisors.

Break times are usually staggered so that everyone isn't changing positions at the same time. For example, dealers and floor supervisors could start breaking on the hour, while boxpersons could begin breaking at ten minutes after the hour. When these employees return from their breaks, a designated floor supervisor or the pit manager directs them to the person whose name appears below the rubber band that has been placed above the names of the employees on the list.

Another way to do this is to place the supervisor's name on a column list and mark the row corresponding to the break that is being given. This can work both as a rotating system or a system with assigned games and relief persons. Most pit managers prefer to assign floor supervisors to designated games, thereby making them responsible for what happens on those games.

The rubber band system is fairer to the employees in that it helps distribute breaks evenly. Dealers also like the idea of moving to different games. It helps in the sense that some sections and games, because of their location and minimum wagers, can be busier than others and the dealers who are assigned to those games will work harder. In craps, where four dealers are assigned to one game, this system doesn't work effectively and it is rarely used. Also, where assigning tables is the preferred method, pit managers can direct extra dealers in a rotation that would spread breaks equitably.

Assigning sections on a daily basis makes sense for the floor supervisors because it facilitates record keeping. It also makes supervisors responsible for their section or game, forcing them to pay attention. It helps the pit manager because he or she doesn't have to track down the person responsible for the games when a given situation occurs. So in this case, and on a daily basis only, the assigned sections are more effective. They also help improve communication between pit manager and subordinate supervisor, and employees in general.

Scheduling is a controversial issue. Because of that it should be approached with care. It is the issue employees complain about the most. Richie Zappula, the ex-director of casino operations at Trump Castle, said, *"We try to please everyone, but nothing is 100 percent. We can only hope that our efforts please most of the people most of the time."* That should be the objective of the scheduling policies of every casino. How efficiently it is dealt with can make a big difference in the operation of a casino both from a financial point of view and from an employee relations point of view. Only by applying blind justice and by keeping your ears open will your efforts be directed to *please most of the people most of the time.*

SUPERVISION OF EMPLOYEES

Employee supervision in the casino goes through many levels. Since casinos are insistent on the chain of command, supervisors will rarely interact beyond the immediate level of subordinates directly beneath them unless a matter is brought to them by a subordinate. This is true until you enter the pit manager's domain. Although the chain of command applies here also, the interactions of the pit require that everyone come in close contact with each other on a daily basis. Because of this proximity, pit managers will many times find themselves issuing orders directly to dealers while the floor supervisor is busy supervising his or her section. Most of the time, however, the chain of command does apply, and each superior issues orders to an immediate subordinate, who then passes on the information to an immediate subordinate.

Supervision at the top level of management mostly entails analyzing reports and noting any changes that reflect work performance, marketing programs or advertising campaigns. For example, the vice president of casino operations might notice a drastic decline in the table games hold percentage, or in the hold percentage of a specific game category. This might induce the vice president to observe the table games to see if there's any behavior pattern that might contribute to this downward trend. Noticing in passing the crap pit that dealers aren't paying much attention to what they're doing and that they're deeply involved in conversation, to the point that players are having difficulty getting dealers' attention to place bets, can provide a clue. This super-relaxed working environment could be one of the causes for the decline in the hold.

Next, the vice president seeks from the casino manager or assistant an explanation of the behavior. When the vice president visits the casino manager's office, the casino manager isn't there. A call on the cellular unit gets no response. The vice president then revisits the casino manager's office and notes that there's no sign of habitation. Either the casino manager is very neat, or not spending much time there. The vice president then leaves a message to call with the casino manager's secretary. The vice president doesn't get a call until the next day. What's wrong with this picture?

Two things. One, the casino manager isn't doing the job and, two, the vice president hasn't been effectively supervising. The Webster definition of supervision is to oversee or direct. And although that is what is required, good supervision should have a definition more in tune with the qualitative aspect of the word. *Super* as in over and above, on top, higher, greater in quality, extra and additional, surpassing, and beyond what is expected; and, *vision* in its true sense of seeing. In other words, *to see further and beyond that which is obvious and routine.* This is the true mark of a good supervisor.

A shift manager at the Claridge said to a supervisor, *"I rate everyone average because I don't know what's in their head. I have no idea what they know."* As ratings and evaluations go in the gaming business in general, this may be a fairer assessment than most, but it says something about that shift manager's supervisory skills that he or she may not want to admit. No true effort was made to know subordinates, and the shift manager didn't watch them as closely as should have been done—*above and beyond that which is obvious*. Many others fall into this category. Actually, this manager is far better and more honest than most.

Keeping the above definition in mind, let us see how this skill is employed throughout the casino. From the top to the bottom, each supervisor keeps an eye on subordinates, with the other eye on what is happening below them, which is indicative of how well his or her supervisory skills are being employed. For example, the shift manager might notice that the pit manager is always busy, and that's good, but also observe that the pit employees aren't doing their jobs, and that's bad. So the pit manager is a good worker but a bad supervisor. Since supervision is the main function of the job description, the pit manager could be categorized as a poor manager.

Casino managers should ensure that the shift managers are doing their jobs and that the casino is operating smoothly. Observing whether or not the shift manager is doing the job isn't as simple as determining whether or not the operation is running smoothly. The reason for this is that one isn't necessarily a consequence of the other. This has to do with the reality that there's more than one shift manager, and there are also other supervisors below the shift manager who take pride in what they do.

A casino manager may have a disruptive shift manager or two within the operation and not know it until lots of damage has been done. The blame for this can only be attributed to the casino manager's lack of supervision. One eye was closed while the other was looking in the wrong direction.

Well-intentioned casino managers sometimes have their programs and objectives sabotaged by shift managers with authoritarian complexes. These disruptive figures believe that they're the maximum authority and establish rulings and directives as if the casino operation belongs to them. The authoritarian figures tend to impart discipline in a very strict way with punishments grossly outweighing the infractions that are committed by employees. Many times these infractions are due to faulty communication of senseless directives. Once violations occur, those with authoritarian complexes will take them personally, as an affront to the shift manager's authority and person. They're never forgiven but kept in the back burner until another infraction or interpreted infraction spreads the fire. Casinos with authoritarian figures such as these usually end up with higher turnover and employee termination rate. Actually, these people believe this is a necessary pattern to maintain a smoothly operating casino.

It makes no sense that a casino manager would allow this to happen, but many of them do it unknowingly. This is because they get so involved in the paperwork and administrative side of their job that they depend on the shift managers to oversee the operation. They feel comfortable doing this because many times the shift managers are people they trust. Yet, as they will eventually learn, there are two sides to every person. One is the side the person wants you to see; the other is the side that the person truly is. In some people they're one and the same; in others they're not. Unfortunately, people in power only get to see one-sided people face to face. That's why our definition of supervision is much more comprehensive. The only way a supervisor is going to be able to see the other side of the two-sided person is *to see above and beyond what is obvious and routine.* Easier said than done, right? Right. But it can be done. It's up to the individual supervisor, regardless of capacity, to uncover the mask. This takes maintaining an open mind throughout the process. Don't focus on what people say but on what they do. We can't focus on isolated instances but on the whole picture. As mentioned before, people make mistakes everyday and the majority of them aren't caught by anyone. So if we focus on the one or two mistakes and divide our subordinates in two categories (the ones that do and the ones that don't), we have simplified this process to the point where it doesn't make any sense. This happens quite often, not only in the gaming business, but in other businesses where mistakes can't be quantified by the end product. This is called jumping to conclusions, and what it does is give the supervisor a false sense of trust in employees who haven't been caught in an error, while focusing on the ones that get caught.

In the meantime, letting the guard down opens the door for a big surprise. Only by looking at the total picture can you understand how well the operation is functioning. Supervision involves taking a step back and looking at things from a distance so you can see more of what is happening. Only then will you be able to see things that are out of place and deserve closer inspection. Only that way can you see everyone, and not only those whom your prejudices single out.

A way to gauge subordinates is to query those with whom they relate in the performance of their duties. That would mean questioning their subordinates and the customers they service. These queries should be done intelligently and in an unbiased way. Questions like, *"Harry is doing a good job, isn't he?"* give the impression that the questioner is convinced of it. If this person is a person of power, the answer won't be contrary. If instead you ask, *"Which supervisors can you really count on when you have a problem on the game?"* *"Who is really outgoing with customers in this pit?"* *"If you had a personal problem, which supervisor would you confide in?"* *"Who is strong on enforcement of rules and regulations?"* Specific questions like these, without lead-ins, should produce truthful answers, unless, of course, the supervisor through actions has made it clear which employees he or she favors.

Once the weaknesses and strengths of all employees have been determined, the next step in the supervision process is to remedy weaknesses and reward strengths. Your goal as a supervisor should be to help make all of your subordinates excellent employees and not to determine who is good and who is bad so that you have some variety to report when you do your evaluations. If you turn in evaluations that say everyone is doing an excellent job, you are going to have your supervisor breathing down your neck and asking you how the hell is that possible. But that should be the least of your concerns. If you managed to accomplish such a feat (anything is possible), then let your supervisor prove the contrary. That is likely to happen, but at least you'll have the personal satisfaction that you managed to do what you set out to do.

PRINCIPLES OF SUPERVISION

Instead of going through each level of supervision and determining what constitutes good or bad supervision, it is probably best to see supervision from the level that is closest to where the action is. Most of the principles that will apply at this level will probably apply at all levels of supervision.

The floor supervisor is the supervisor who mostly relates to the employees who carry out the main casino function and to the customers who support the operation. As a supervisor, it is the job of the floorperson to ensure that the dealers carry out the mechanics of their jobs with efficiency and that they maintain an attitude of respect and caring toward the patrons who support the casino operation. Floorpersons must serve a customer relations function and look out for customer needs both as individuals and as supervisors. Protecting the game, a primary function of the floorperson, also falls under supervision since it relates to watching what is happening above and beyond the games. It entails looking for suspicious maneuvers both by the dealers and customers.

Games are supervised most efficiently when the supervisor can see almost everything that is happening. I use the word *almost* because there really isn't any place on the casino floor that allows a supervisor to see everything. Actually, the floor supervisor focusing on one particular game *still* would not be able to see everything on that game. This may be hard to understand, but it has to do with concentration, as previously discussed.

The vantage point that best accomplishes the *see almost everything* capability is going to be found at one of the extremes of the section of tables or table that is being supervised. Usually there will be obstacles to viewing such as columns, desks, podiums, computer terminals, and so on. It is up to the supervisor to find the place that has the fewest obstructions. Even then some circumstances are going to require adjustments in perspective. (Incidentally, a Mississippi casino put artificial palm trees in the middle of its pits. The above concept was definitely not taken into consideration when that casino was designed.)

Sometimes the action on a game gets so heavy and complex that you need to supervise it more closely. This is going to require getting closer to the game that has the extra need while keeping the other games in view. When two games on the same side have heavy action or require special attention, the floor supervisor is going to have to trade off on the security of the other games. The best thing in that case is to rotate your posture so you can glance over at the other games with a certain amount of consistency. Of course, a supervisor having high action on two games shouldn't watch any other games. The pit manager should find someone else to cover those other games.

One last comment: Just because there's a best position for watching the games doesn't mean the supervisor's position is supposed to be stationary. That position is where the most time will be spent; however, moving around is essential.

In the case of craps, where a supervisor usually watches one table, a position at one of the extremities of the table is usually not going to be appropriate since the complexity of the game requires close inspection and the view from the far end is often obstructed by customers, dealers, and boxpersons.

Fortunately, the craps floorperson has four extra pair of eyes to help with the supervision of the game, and in some instances five. That individual is assisted by the boxperson, who for the most part watches the shooter's side of the game, and by the stickperson, who watches the side where the dice land. Since both sides of the craps layout are covered, the floorperson can then look at the total game and concentrate on those areas that appear to need extra attention.

As in the case of multi games, a couple of steps back often prove effective in producing a better perspective. This allows the supervisor to view the crowd, serve customers better, and become more alert. By being a few steps back, the floorperson can see a total view of the layout in the mirrors. With a slight movement of the eyes (which can move up to seventy times per second), the floor supervisor can focus on either side of the crap game in a fraction of a second.

Some people have difficulty watching games in the mirror since the perspective is altered. This difficulty gives rise to the argument that the game is better supervised at close range, with the supervisor's body almost in contact with the table. However, our contention is that it doesn't take long to distinguish the relative positions of the layout in the mirrors and, by doing so, the supervisor increases the capacity to observe. It's like being able to see twice as much with the same pair of eyes. I say: *The mirrors were put on the tables to serve a valuable purpose. Use them.* This also goes for the boxperson whom the floor supervisor often trusts with the total supervision of the game.

In cases where the floor supervisor must monitor more than one game, the boxperson's role increases in importance because the floor supervisor can watch only one crap game at a time effectively. This situation also occurs when the floorperson, for whatever reason, must leave the game. The boxperson is then left with the sole responsibility of supervision. If the boxperson then buries his or her sight on one side of the table, the other is left to the supervision of a dealer who also has other functions to perform and sometimes doesn't have the experience to do an effective job.

If there's heavy proposition bet action, unless the boxperson glances over every once in a while, no one will be watching that side of the table. And craps isn't a game like blackjack where players wait in turn to make decisions. The action in craps is sometimes fast and furious with many demands being placed on the dealer. So unless another pair of eyes is there to help, oversights and errors will occur. Good boxpersons not only watch their side, but also keep an eye and an ear out for the other side. We were born with two of each, we might as well use them.

The floor supervisor who must watch more than one crap table must determine which table requires the most attention and move closer to that game while still keeping a sporadic eye out on the other one. A forty-five-degree body angle, while being close to the heavier game, is usually quite effective in this situation. In Atlantic City, the Casino Control Commission requires that four supervisors watch two crap games. This could either be two floorpeople and two boxpersons or one floorperson and three boxpersons. That means that the single floorperson has the option to place the extra boxperson on the game believed to require the most attention. Also, there will usually be an extra boxperson or two that can cover the other game, if needed.

Although these extra measures facilitate the floorperson's job, the ideal situation in terms of supervision is to have one floorperson assigned to each game. When crap tables get busy, the amount of work required of the craps floorperson can be overwhelming. Not only is that person responsible for the supervision of a complex game, but also the paperwork on games that can hold sixteen or more ratable players.

Roulette games supervision depends on the number of games being supervised and the possible obstacles in the way of supervision. If two games in line are being watched, an unobstructed position somewhere in the middle of both games gives the best perspective. Roulette tables that are on opposite flanks of a pit are better supervised from one of the extremities, standing closer to the one that has the heaviest action.

As with the other games, baccarat is best supervised from a position that allows an unimpeded view of the table layout. This position can vary depending upon where the table is located and how many are playing. If the play is only on one side of the table, then the opposite side gives the best perspective of the game. Usually, spots that aren't occupied by customers give the best perspective of the total layout. On crowded games there's usually more than one supervisor and each can find a vantage point that allows a view of each of the betting areas in addition to the rack and the dealers. High chairs provide a great perspective until people get up and obstruct the view. On the floor, the supervisor can shift position to remove the view obstruction but on the high chair a lot of uncomfortable maneuvering is required.

There's one more subject that needs to be covered and it is how supervisors deal with violations of laws, rules and regulations. The authoritarian shift manager deals with violations in a ruthless way and imposes sanctions that far exceed the violation, assuming that the severity of the penalty will serve as a deterrent. Yet as I mentioned before, deterrence often isn't the sole motivation behind the penalty; there's a personalizing of the operation and a sense that the violation was a violation to the shift manager's own persona. In other words, *you don't do that to me!* This is irrational, unproductive, and can have a serious negative effect on the casino operation. This type of thinking may conflict with civil rights and labor laws and can open a casino to lawsuits.

I make this point for two reasons: First, accusations of cheating without proof to substantiate the accusations are defamation of character and are going to cost the casino money if a court battle ensues. A shift or casino manager may be upset about a player who switches dice on a crap game and beats the operation out of a lot of money, but without the extra dice, a videotape of the switch, or a reliable witness, an arrest isn't possible, and an accusation is dangerous. Second, unlawful termination in today's pro-labor climate won't be tolerated.

As supervisors, when we approach situations that we interpret to be violations, we must keep an open mind and be as objective as possible. Our attitude or demeanor should be unemotional and rational. Once we have determined exactly what the facts are, then we can proceed to administer punishment befitting the violation, or make a report that sticks to the facts and not our interpretation of the facts.

If a violator is a low-level employee, such as a dealer, the right moment to deal with the violation must be found. Customers may feel uncomfortable if a supervisor reprimands a dealer in their presence. Nor will the dealer feel happy about it, especially if he or she has committed only an insignificant procedural violation. If the procedural violation is of such nature that it requires immediate attention, the supervisor should approach it so as to give the impression that the dealer is being taught something.

If the supervisor feels the procedure was explained enough times to the dealer for the violation to constitute an act of insubordination, then he or she should wait until the dealer leaves the table or tell the pit manager so that disciplinary measures can be taken.

In dealing with subordinates or customers, avoid profanity, insults, and hostility. Your objective isn't to provoke the offender but to identify the offense, report it to the proper authority, or correct it if it is your place to do so. Remedy the situation in a manner that seems fair to all those involved.

CHAPTER 10

PLAYER TRACKING AND COMPLIMENTARIES

PLAYER TRACKING

I have already discussed player tracking. Remember that it starts from the moment the player starts to play. The importance of tracking players became evident in the early 1980s when competition forced casinos to find a better way to attract and serve customers. In fact, although rudimentary tracking existed from the beginning of organized gambling, it wasn't until the complimentary explosion that a need to justify these giveaways became apparent. The rating card was born, and computers were programmed to receive and analyze their data.

The actual rating begins when the player makes the first bet. However, a floor supervisor who made a rating card for every customer who sat at the table would end up doing an inordinate amount of work, much of it wasted. That is why the usual rule of thumb is that supervisors will rate patrons when any of these conditions is met: the customer buys $500 or more worth of chips; the customer plays at an average bet of $25 or more; the customer wins or loses over $500; the customer takes out a marker; and the customer asks to be rated. These are basic player tracking rules though they can vary from casino to casino and even within the same casino. For example, a person who met all of the above requirements would not necessarily be rated in the baccarat pit of the MGM, Caesars, the Mirage, or the Hilton.

Some customers who don't meet the above rule of thumb for rating at first may eventually meet those requirements. Because of this possibility, customers who buy-in for $200 or more or are betting close to the $25 average should be monitored even though a rating card isn't started. Some supervisors will start nameless cards on players like these just in case they later meet the requirements.

Once customers merit being rated, floor supervisors will introduce themselves and welcome them to the casino, and preferably make physical contact by way of a handshake. Then the customers' names are asked for along with other identifying information such as city of residence or date of birth. Date of birth is preferable, although some might be reluctant to give this information. A driver's license makes this easy, as does a player card.

The reason it is important to get the city or date of birth is to distinguish that customer from any other who may have the same name.

Friendly conversation is in order at this point and helps establish a rapport between the supervisor and the customer. It could turn out to be the only thing that swayed the customer into returning to the casino. It also can turn out to be the deciding factor if a dispute should arise on the game. *It always pays to make friends of the customers.*

When to approach a customer is also important. Some customers will become upset if the floor supervisor approaches them while they're in action in a game. The supervisor must use good judgment to determine the appropriate moment for the interruption. This will vary from game to game. In blackjack, shuffles occur quite often, and this allows enough time for the supervisor to obtain the information. In craps, the moment after a customer has made the customary bet is an apt time to get the information. Some players are superstitious. They're reluctant to give this information until a decision has been made on the game. The floor supervisor should exercise caution with such a customer and politely say that he or she will be in touch later.

This is a standard practice when having markers signed in Nevada, where floor supervisors will usually wait until the shooter has either made a pass or thrown a losing seven combination. In baccarat and roulette, where placing a bet is the extent of the customer's decision, the moment after the wager is made is usually a good time to get the necessary information. Again, the floor supervisor's judgment is needed to determine if there's anything going on that would make an approach inappropriate.

Once a relationship has been established between the floor supervisor and the customer, the supervisor can begin the rating process. Observing the first few bets the customer makes is helpful in establishing a playing pattern. This average should be recorded but not made part of the permanent record because it can change. The average bet should be a true appreciation of the fluctuations that occurred in the betting pattern of the customer during the time played. If, for example, the player's bets fluctuated but averaged $25 for the first hour, $50 for the next hour and $75 for the third hour of play, the average bet should be recorded as $50. Does the player get credit for pressing his winnings? This shouldn't be at issue when rating. The fact is that a player who presses his or her bets will lose more than the player who maintains a flat bet average. This happens because the player who presses puts more money into action. If the player who presses his or her bets is rated at the same level as the player who makes only flat bets because of starting at the same level, the pressing player will be denied rightful credit in the rating.

One position is that the pressing player who enjoys a good run on the game will be playing at a level at which he or she doesn't belong. The player rated at that level would be entitled to complimentaries of a player of a higher level. Say, for example, that the player in question caught a good run and ended up with an average wager of $200. A complimentary room and dinner would normally be given the player who plays at that level. However, the position of some managers is that the pressing player doesn't deserve these perks because his or her play doesn't reflect the same assets as the normal $200 bettor. Yet, if we check the computer, we find the normal $200 player visits the casino once or twice a year while the pressing bettor has visited the casino fifty times and has lost ten times the amount that the normal $200 bettor has. Who is more deserving of that meal and room?

Another way to resolve this controversy is through simple mathematics. I established that player worth can be determined by multiplying the house advantage on the betting system the player uses times the amount of time used. This is a blind system that doesn't take into account the status of the player but only the way he or she plays. It will tell you, mathematically, how much money the casino can expect to make off the player's betting strategy and the time used. Unlike the pit manager or floor supervisor, the computer doesn't base judgment on whether or not the player has $50,000 in his bank account or in his pocket, information that, in the first place, the pit manager or floor supervisor has no way of knowing unless the player reveals it.

A player whose bets fluctuate between $25 and $200 may end up with a $100 average over a period of four hours, yet might be rated at $25 or $50. Based on this action, this person will get a dinner comp for the coffee shop, and that's it. Another player might play two hours and be given a $200 average for consistent play and be issued a comp to the gourmet room and have his or her room comped. (This policy is not in effect everywhere.)

Let's say that the first player had a 3 percent disadvantage and was playing on a game that had seventy decisions per hour, and ended up losing, on the average, $840. But since this player has played on different tables, the floor supervisors inaccurately assess the losses, and they appear to have been only $300 (it happens many times). The other player is on a slow game that is putting out forty-five decisions per hour and is playing perfect strategy. This is happening at the Mirage (hypothetically), where the house advantage over this player on a double deck game is approximately a quarter of a percent. The total win for the casino in these circumstances would be $45! So even though the pressing player lost $18\frac{2}{3}$ times the amount of money the *high roller* lost and will probably forever lose, the pressing player wouldn't be able to eat anywhere near the other player and would also have to find a warm corner out in the street somewhere if out of cash and had forgotten credit cards.

Although it may sound like it, this isn't fiction. People get lost in the casino shuffle all the time and are discriminated against because of irrational, antiquated, and preconceived ideas. At the same time many players are overrated and cost the casinos a lot more than their play justifies. This is bad business. Managers aren't totally at fault because they are unaware of the rating practices of their subordinates. They assume that this is a clear proposition and that any inconsistencies can be solved by a lower-level manager. But it doesn't happen that way. In the same pit, three or four supervisors will be rating in different ways and the pit manager, who hasn't bothered to be specific, doesn't realize this until a rating card comes in. That's when the manager will realize that the floor supervisor has a different view of the player's action.

And it may be that it is the pit manager who has the wrong concept and is propagating it. The shift manager is unaware because he or she supervises the pit manager far less than the pit manager supervises the pit supervisors. Then again, it could be that these directives come from any of the levels of management straight to the top.

Wherever these mandates or ideas stem from, the important thing is to realize they break many fundamental rules: One, *justice for all*. Justice means to give to each what each deserves. Two, *all men are created equal*. In the casino, as in George Orwell's *Animal Farm* it seems that some people are created more equal than others. Three, *good business is to attempt to profit from your production*. You can't profit if you sell your goods at a price below what they cost to produce, nor will you profit if you continuously deny those who support you the respect and consideration they deserve.

Having established a philosophy of player tracking, let's proceed to see how the process evolves. After the player finishes play, the floor supervisor ascertains the average bet and the win/loss. The win/loss is determined by the amount of cash, markers, or chips the player put into action minus the amount of chips held at the end of the play. The player who buys in for $2,000 and leaves with $500 in chips has lost $1,500. If he or she comes to the table with $300 in chips, buys in for another $500 in cash, and leaves with $200 in chips, the loss is $600.

A word of caution here: A player can't be in chips that he or she doesn't lose. So in the case above, the floorperson will report that the player was in $500 in cash and $100 in chips and lost it all. Where markers are redeemed at the table, as in Nevada, each marker will be recorded separately on the rating card and circled if the player buys them back. At the end of the play, whatever markers aren't circled are the total amount owed by the customer. This, added to the cash and chips, if any, will constitute the player's buy-in.

If the chips the player has left aren't sufficient to cover the markers, that amount is subtracted from the total buy-in to determine win/loss. If the amount of chips is more than the markers, the floor supervisor is supposed to make an attempt to have the player redeem the markers. In some places, even partial amounts are supposed to be redeemed.

After the win/loss has been determined, the rating card is signed and passed on to the pit manager. The pit manager usually has a box where these ratings are stored. From that box, the pit manager will pull out cards and check to make sure no information has been left out. Sometimes supervisors will forget to circle the shift, to enter play times, average bet, etc. Once satisfied that the card is accurate, the pit manager will copy any information that is relevant and pass it on to the pit clerk, retaining one copy. Pertinent information usually is a substantial win or loss of a known player whose play needs to be tracked. This information will be recorded on a player action sheet.

The guidelines for the player action sheet vary from casino to casino. Some casinos will record any win or loss of $500 or more in addition to marker play, while some pits that have extremely heavy action will record wins or losses of $5,000 or more. The average for premium casinos is $1,000. Once a player's name is on the list, every subsequent rating card total will just be added to or subtracted from it until the shift ends.

The pit clerk, upon receiving the rating card, brings up the entry screen in the computer for that particular player and types in the data. That information will become part of the player's permanent record. From then on the capabilities of the computer program determine what kind of information will be available for analysis. Most programs provide a history of all the player's trips for the year up to a certain amount with up-to-date figures. Totals from previous years are also available in some.

General information that can be found includes average bet per trip, total amount of time played, cash buy-ins by trip, total credit, total win/loss, and a comp history. All of these will also be averaged for the year. Some

computer programs will show a theoretical loss, others will show comp points accumulated according to the theoretical loss, or both. The programs that have these capabilities can signal warnings when players' comps exceed their worth. In many instances the computer records will show that comps issued to a player exceed that person's theoretical loss. In spite of this, some managers will blame computer error and continue to issue comps to these players. This is something that should be given a closer look by auditors, owning entities, and top-ranking company officers. It may be that the manager, shift manager, or pit manager is justified in extending comp privileges based on the customer's potential. If that's the case, fine. But it can also mean that these managers are either incompetent or have a personal motive contrary to the company's best interest. The moral: *If the computer raises the red flag, look into it.*

As I have said, player tracking serves more than a customer relations role; it serves a security role. It places customers and employees at certain times and places and it helps make employees responsible for their interaction with players. Any unusual occurrence can be tracked down, further analyzed, and investigated. Excessive comping, which is another form of stealing in casinos, can be audited and investigated, thanks to the player-tracking systems.

Player-tracking systems can also be used as mailing lists for special events and for other marketing purposes. This *is* the information age, and the player-tracking system can be an efficient information system.

For some time now, automated table player tracking systems have been in place dating back to the early 1980s. The first models produced rating cards, today's models interface directly with your computer system. One such system is Pit Trak. With Pit Trak, the player simply inserts his or her player card into a slot at the table and his information is readily available on a flat monitor that is mounted on the table. This makes the supervisor's job a lot easier, and reduces the need to have input clerks. It also reduces the chances of having input errors due to the difficulties associated with reading poor handwriting.

COMPLIMENTARY MANAGEMENT

Comping policies vary from casino to casino as does the way rating information is compiled. It used to be that if you were betting $25 for one hour on a game, you were eligible for a comp for two to the coffee shop. Some places still do that, but most casino operators have learned that a $25 average bet for one hour doesn't pay for a $50 comp to the coffee shop. So how do we know how much is enough? A well-programmed computer can answer that question. Usually the comp value of a customer's play is said to be 30 percent of the theoretical loss. Seventy percent is supposed to pay for the high cost of operation associated with a casino, with a small allowance for profit. How small? Actually, very small. The cost of operating a casino compared to other businesses is high. Casinos are labor intensive. They require a lot of employees, many of whom are paid comparatively high salaries. The Mirage, for example, employs almost 7,000. Add to that electric and water bills, the mortgages, the marketing and advertising expenses, and the other operational costs, and you can see why 70 percent of what you are expected to win doesn't leave much room for profit. Not everyone requests comps. Yet this gives you an idea of why some casinos have gone bankrupt.

So, one way the pit manager can determine if a player's action merits a comp is to ask the computer. This is usually the second step the pit manager will take before issuing a comp. The first one is to evaluate the present rating. It very well may be that the action recorded on the rating card is so obviously favorable that the pit manager doesn't have to go any further. Let's say that, if the player has been playing for four hours at a $200 average and has lost $1,000, the trip to the computer is really an unnecessary one. But a pit boss may go anyway because there might be information in the system that warns against comping this player. It may seem illogical in the circumstances, yet many things can prompt such an action. One could be that the player is a card counter who, unfortunately, had a bad run. Another could be that he or she caused serious problems. Either way, to issue the comp in these circumstances could cause trouble.

Now, the reverse situation could also be the case when a comp request is made. The player's action may not merit the comp, but a look at the history may reveal that the player is more than worth it.

Let's assume the player has no previous history and that the comp must be determined by the present action. The pit manager could have the pit clerk enter the card into the system and wait for a response, which could take some time. Or what will most probably happen, the pit manager will make a determination on his or her own (which is one of the reasons for becoming a pit manager to begin with). A commonly accepted rule of thumb today is that a player will lose one bet more than will be won per hour of play. Based on what we said before, the pit manager could use this hypothetical loss as a guideline. Another basis for a decision could be a substantial loss. If a player has lost $500, it is pretty hard to deny a $50 comp, even though his or her average or time alone wouldn't qualify for it.

Some places have written or verbal guidelines for the issuance of comps. They will say, for example, that in order for players to get comps to the coffee shop, they must have an average bet of $25 for four hours of play. A buffet comp would require $25 for two hours or $10 for four hours, and a comp to the gourmet room would require $100 average for four hours of play. By the way, those were average guidelines in the gaming industry where computers weren't used; however, competition has loosened those requirements.

When issuing complimentaries, management personnel have some leeway to deviate from the standards that are established by the company. This is done because there are many variables that aren't taken into account when setting these standards. Factors like the frequency of the customer's trips to the casino, the potential in terms of worth, associations that the player may have with other valued customers, the projected losses due to the player's betting strategy, and the actual losses themselves.

Management will usually carry a player whose financial circumstances have changed until it feels certain that a return to the previous level of play isn't possible. How many trips this entails is entirely up to management and depends on the status the player enjoyed before the change in financial situation. For some players this could mean quite a few. For others it could be just one visit. Some computers are programmed to factor this in and begin to subtract comp points as the level of play declines.

Customers will be able to initially obtain perks and complimentaries based on the amount of cash they deposit into the casino's cage or based on the amount of credit they establish. Players who establish a $100,000 credit line will be given fight or major event tickets and comped room, food, and beverage based on their potential losses. However, if customers don't play up to their lines, complimentaries will gradually be reduced to what they are actually worth to the casino. This could happen after one trip, or it could happen after a few trips depending on what the manager sees in the customer's play. The theory is that players eventually find out that the only way to make serious money at the tables is to bet heavier. This is a very sound principle since most people are ambitious and, as gamblers, dream of making a big score. From there the repeated slogan: *The more you bet, the more you get!*

Often valued customers bring friends and acquaintances on gambling trips who don't play at the same level they do, but they'll want their friends to enjoy the same benefits that they do. In many instances, these associated players are pretty close to the requirements needed for the complimentaries they seek and their association will be the deciding factor in the issuance of these complimentaries. However, if they're far from the requirements for the comp they seek, a closer look is required. It may turn out that the main customer's play is good enough to merit adding a person or two to his or her complimentary budget. But there could be two other situations: One, the main customer is barely strong enough to justify his or her comp load and, two, the relationship between the players isn't as close as the associated player would have us believe. In either of those instances, the chances are that the complimentary status is going to be denied, and rightfully so.

As I mentioned before, players' betting strategies will determine how much money the casino is going to retain from their play. A player who bets the outside numbers and proposition bets on the crap game is more valuable to the casino than a player who bets line and come bets. Actually, the former player, on the average, is ten times more valuable, assuming that they're betting the same amount of money. The same holds true for the blackjack player who makes a lot of decision mistakes in comparison to one who plays perfect strategy. A roulette player would enjoy this same *bad player* status since the 5.27 percent disadvantage played against is also ten times as much as the .5 percent disadvantage the double odds line bettor in craps has. It would be twenty times the disadvantage a double deck perfect player playing to liberal rules would have. Because of this reality, some managers will make special concessions to these unfortunate players and

upgrade their status to represent their true worth to the casino. Most managers, however, will not.

There are two main reasons most managers will not make exceptions in the above-stated case. One is that casino managers assume these players will either quickly lose their gambling resources and won't come back, or they will realize their stupidity and reduce the amount of money they wager. Either way, the managers reason, these players will not be the resource they are today for long and, therefore, aren't worth special consideration. But that isn't always the case, and it brings me to the other reason casino managers won't make exceptions in this case: *ignorance.* Technical and information system ignorance is rampant throughout the gaming business.

Regardless of whether or not customers' future potential is judged to be poor, the casino can't go wrong by treating them according to their present worth. If it is wrong and you treat them with disregard for their present worth, they may end up as a strong customer at somebody else's place.

The next area of consideration is where some managers will argue that they do value these high-worth customers. They'll say, *"OK, if the customer loses a few thousand dollars, we'll be happy to comp him for the gourmet room or comp his room."* But they won't make this decision based solely on this. They'll also ask: "How long did the customer play? What was the average bet? Did that person have any money left that you know of?" Then they'll hesitate and think about it, but hardly ever will they ask what the player's betting strategy was like. I can't attest to how prevalent these practices are, but I can say that they're known to happen quite often.

As a general rule, casinos establish comp guidelines in writing. These usually require that customers have a specific minimum amount of cash or credit buy-in or line. Smaller comps such as for drinks, buffets, coffee shops, and show tickets have small cash buy-in requirements and are issued by the pit manager or floorperson. Even though a company may establish a $500 buy-in requirement in order to issue some of these comps, at this level it is a lenient requirement hardly ever adhered to.

The next comp level is mostly beyond the comping authority of the pit manager. This level includes room comps, gourmet restaurants, spa comps, limousines, headliner shows, and special events. This level of comping falls under the authority of hosts and shift managers. Room comp guidelines vary and depend on availability and the clientele to whom the casino caters.

General guidelines start with a $3,000 credit line or cash deposit together with average bets of $50 for four hours a day. With a cash or credit line of $5,000 and an average bet of $75, some casinos will comp a player for room, food, and beverage. Most will not. Room, food, and beverage comps (RFB) usually begin at an average bet of $100 for four hours of play up to $150. Some places that choose to use a lower average bet will limit the amount of food and beverage, from there the *limited RFB* and *full RFB*. Even full RFB customers require special approval for certain beverage requests such as *Don Perignon* and *Cristal Champagne*. The El San Juan in Puerto Rico places a dollar amount on daily consumption of food and beverage depending upon credit line or cash deposit and the average bet and time played. For example, a player with a line of credit of $10,000 and an average bet of $100 in blackjack is entitled to $150 in food and beverage, while a customer with a line of $20,000 and an average bet of $200 is entitled to $200 in food and beverage. This certainly doesn't follow a mathematical progression, which would have doubled the customer's limit. This is because other complimentaries may be issued to this player that aren't available to the $10,000 player. Among other things, the $20,000 player qualifies for limousine airport pickup, a better room, and $200 more toward air fare reimbursement. However, in order to qualify for these, the player must play for at least twelve hours.

Most casinos have similar guidelines, but they may vary in the interpretation of average bet. In the example above, the $10,000 blackjack, roulette, and baccarat player all are required to bet at an average of $100 to receive the same benefits the $10,000 crap player gets betting at $150. This discrimination against the crap player is inconsistent, specially since the odds of the crap player's bets aren't counted. Caesars, for example, used to require the crap player to have a higher average bet per comp than players of the other games, but will count the odds. Casinos design systems to suit their own needs.

Spa rooms, mini suites, one and two bedroom suites, and luxury suites also fall under this level of comping. These specialized rooms are given to play-

ers with lines of $15,000 and more. In some instances, players with smaller lines qualify based on their table action and availability of the rooms. Two-bedroom suites need a $20,000 line but exceptions are made depending on play quality or the quality of the resort. It is also possible (and it does happen), that a player will be bumped out of a suite because a player of higher money action shows up. Someone will apologize for the "booking error" and the player will never know that his suite isn't available because a "bigger fish showed up in the pond." Luxury suites are given to players with lines of $25,000 to $50,000, depending upon the particular hotel and depending upon the quality of play associated with the line.

Expectancies are that the player will bet from within 1 to 2 percent of his line, on the average. If on the low end of the equation, the player will be considered mostly as standard. At the high end of the equation, however, the player is now elevated to the level above which he or she would normally qualify for.

The next comping level requires the shift manager or someone higher, although in some places if you are an executive host, you can handle these, also. This level involves air fare and cash reimbursements. These are considered *hard comps* as opposed to *soft comps* because they require the disbursement of *hard* cash. These disbursements as well as commissions paid to junketeers are watched very closely by auditors and state regulators. They have been the object of many investigations and legal proceedings by state regulators and other enforcement agencies.

From the need to import business grew the need to provide transportation to facilitate that importation. That is the basis of casino junkets. Chartered planes have supplied this need. Chartering planes is slowly falling into disuse because of the escalating costs. It's more cost effective to pay the air fare of players who warrant it.

Casinos won't provide air fare unless the customer shows a minimum line of $5,000 and at least a $100 average bet for twelve hours of play. Some casinos require higher credit lines or cash deposits and some require higher average bets. They also vary in the cash limits they impose according to the quality of play. Las Vegas and Atlantic City casinos, for example, will pay less than Puerto Rico casinos for air fare reimbursement. This is probably due to the higher cost of air transportation to Puerto Rico from most mainland cities and also because Puerto Rico casinos have a greater need to import business. The average Las Vegas and Atlantic City casino will reimburse up to $500 in air fare to a player with an average bet of $150 while Puerto Rico casinos will reimburse up to $700. All casinos will make exceptions to these rules according to the circumstances, but not without substantiating their decisions. These circumstances could be heavy losses, slow business, or a good customer history. People who bet over $500 a hand usually get first-class fare.

There are other comps issued by the casino that also fall under this restricted category. These are helicopter fees, private jet and airplane expenses, and special event tickets that require cash disbursement such as sporting events and shows. The bottom line is that when cash is to be disbursed, it is going to be highly scrutinized, and it will be based on high credit or cash line requirements and high average bets and time played.

Just to give you an idea of how sensitive this can be, let's assume that the $150 player loses the rule of thumb one bet per hour. That comes out to be $1,800 in the twelve-hour period. Assuming that we reimburse $500 in air fare, pick up the room for $450, cover the food and beverage bill for $450, provide limousine transportation worth up to $150, and give show tickets that amount to $100, the total cost of this player is $1,650, leaving us with a profit of $150 over a three-day period. That, assuming you don't buy a jacket at the gift shop for this player and that you didn't send him or her to a special event. Using the 30 percent formula, we should have reimbursed this customer $540, which would enable you to pay for his or her share of the cost of operation plus make a small profit. Granted, $1,150 were soft costs, if the limousine is casino-owned. Yet how much of those soft costs are actually hard costs? What is obvious is that a substantial amount of those *soft costs* are in fact *hard costs*, and if you don't control them, you'll lose money. And remember, we used the one-bet-per-hour rule of thumb, which we have seen doesn't apply to all players. The thing to remember is that general rules don't always apply and that informed decisions must be made to compensate for the gaps. It is better to lose an unworthy customer's business than to give away your operation and end up losing money.

CHAPTER 11

TABLE GAMES PROTECTION

The integrity of the games in a casino concerns both the casino and the players. Game protection is an all-inclusive term that is used to identify the measures that must be taken to protect the games from cheating and stealing. Every year, casinos spend millions of dollars in protective equipment, seminars, conferences, and other measures to try to stop an inevitable consequence of the games themselves—cheating and stealing. And every time the casino finds a way to prevent these acts, the cheaters get more innovative. This vicious cycle will probably exist until the end of time. But the inevitability of this situation isn't as much a concern as what can be done to minimize the damage.

Game procedures are written with the protection of the games in mind. That is why enforcement of the game procedures is so important. Yet supervisors who work in different areas will notice that some areas are more relaxed in their procedures than others. For example, until recently casinos in Puerto Rico were extremely lax in their dealing procedures. They were so lax (and still are in some operations) that, as I mentioned before, labor disputes and strikes occurred when tighter measures were proposed. They were lax to the point that operations had to be closed down because of the amount of stealing that was going on. There was no surveillance; there was no tracking of fills and credits (chips were handed from one table to the other); there was no separate department to handle markers; there was no discipline for inattentive dealers even if they were caught away from their games; and often there was little or no supervision of games.

Regardless of the procedural philosophy under which casinos operate, it is inescapable that procedures to increase the security and efficiency of the operation must be available. If management or government regulators have taken the time to write them down, employees should be advised to follow them.

Let's take a look at some of these procedures that improve game protection and see how they accomplish this function.

CHEATING IN BLACKJACK

In the game of blackjack, the cards can be dealt to the players out of the hand or out of a dealing shoe. When the cards are dealt by hand, there are several ways the dealer can cheat the casino, in addition to the many ways which would apply to all games in general. These are: (1) to deal seconds, (2) to set the deck and false shuffle, (3) to mark the cards, (4) to aid an agent, and (5) to introduce a "cooler."

Some of these techniques require a lot of ability and practice on the part of the dealer. One involves dealing out the second card of the deck while the top one remains. Another involves setting up the deck when picking up the cards, mostly through a method called the *high-low pickup*. Another involves crimping, bending, scratching, daubing, sanding, or blistering. Aiding an agent could be anything from flashing the hole card, peeking, and signaling, overpaying and leaving losers, or just plain looking the other way while the agent presses, pinches, hand mucks, plugs the deck, or switches cards with another player, or outright switches the deck. The last one, the introduction of a cooler, requires a gutsy move by the dealer to either switch the deck or substitute or add certain cards.

All of these methods of cheating require an agent on the outside to split the profits with the dealer. That agent is the one who's either going to receive a favor-able card when it is needed, or is going to collect when the dealer breaks his or her hand with the second card. The *high-low pickup* involves separating the high and low cards as they're being picked up. Sometimes moving a couple of cards is all that is required. Marking cards, flashing hole cards, and other aids to the agent are self-evident.

These cheating techniques were among the main reasons the New Jersey Casino Control Commission would not allow hand deck dealing in Atlantic City. But dealing shoes aren't foolproof either. There are a few things a dealer can do to cheat when using a shoe. One option is to allow an agent to switch shoes on him or her, introducing what is called a *holdout shoe.* This would be very difficult to accomplish today because shoes are chained to the games and because the relief dealer would probably notice something funny about the shoe, which is built to deal seconds and has a prism for identifying cards. But the dealer can aid an agent in switching the decks of cards or by helping the agent introduce a plug.

The first technique is called putting in a *cooler,* the second involves placing a prearranged set of cards or a concentration of high cards. The dealer can plug the deck by setting high cards together when picking them up. Another way a dealer can cheat both with the hand deck and the shoe is to flash his or her hole card to an agent. The dealer could also mark the cards so that the agent knows what the hole card is and what is coming out of the shoe.

There are other ways a dealer can cheat in blackjack that also apply to almost any other game. The dealer can pass off chips to an agent, pay ties, refuse to take money when an agent loses, overpay or give the agent excess change, and add on to his or her color changes. All these ways of cheating constitute methods that are aided by inside help or considered to be an inside job. But as you'll soon see, people on the outside aren't afraid to take a chance.

Where players are allowed to handle cards, they can use this to their advantage. One way is to *hand muck.* Hand mucking involves palming the two top cards of the deck when the dealer offers them for the cut. It doesn't matter which cards these are because they can later be switched for better ones.

Another way is the *money switch.* The money switch is performed by first preparing the switch envelope, which is nothing more than two bills fastened together with one opening through which a blackjack combination will be stored and later switched for the cards dealt to the player. When the cards are dealt, the player picks them up with the same hand that holds the stack of bills, then quickly makes the switch and drops down the winning combination. It is not as simple as all that; a little playacting, usually by impersonating a drunk, is required. A one-armed person would have even a greater effect. The idea is to have one hand occupied so as to justify picking up the cards with the same stack of bills from which you peeled off the bet.

Another way to cheat with hand-held decks is to *front load.* According to Darwin Ortiz, one dealer in a hundred has a problem with front loading. This refers to a slight lifting of the hole card, which is done unintentionally and can only be seen from a certain angle on the game, which varies with the dealer.

Cheaters search for front-loading dealers and calculate the angle from which the cards are exposed. They then sit on that spot as low as possible without calling unnecessary attention to themselves. Even dealers who keep their cards low have to expose cards somewhat when dealing out of the hand. This has prompted cheats to use a reflective device like a shiny lighter to peek at the dealer's hole card. The artifact used to do this is called a *glim.*

Front loading doesn't occur when using a shoe because the card slides out of the shoe onto the surface of the table and from there underneath the dealer's hole card. This prevents the use of the glim, also. In Puerto Rico, however, a shoe which has an elevated lip is used and turns almost every dealer into a front loader. Yet even when dealers aren't front loading there's still a way that their hole cards can be exposed. It is called *spooking,* and it refers to the act of checking the hole card from an angle behind the dealer. It requires more than one person and can only be done when dealers peek at their hole cards to see if they have blackjack.

Marking cards is another way by which casinos can be beat out of a lot of money. This usually occurs by marking the ten cards in the whole deck. Knowing when the dealer has a ten under an ace by itself gives the player a 2.5 percent advantage over the house. That's pretty strong considering that there will be many other instances when that ten knowledge will come in handy. There are different methods that can be employed to mark cards. One method is to use a *daub.* This sticky substance can be read from the shoe hole and when the dealer places it under his or her up card. There are many other ways to mark cards with foreign materials such as ink, vaseline, whiteout, and even the oil a person's own body secretes. A very recent substance has been developed that is a combination of various chemicals that are totally invisible to the naked eye and cannot be detected with black lights or other devices used to uncover card markings. A special camera with five different lenses is used to transmit the image to a remote location. The substance can be placed on a dollar bill (invisibly) then touched by the player when he or she wants to mark the card. The camera used measures 2" x 3" and can be housed in a tall cowboy hat. Through a listening device information is communicated to the player from a remote location such as a van in the parking lot. This unit costs $20,000.

The second method is *nail nicking.* This refers to the nail markings that are placed on the front edges of the cards if dealt from the hand and on the side edges of the cards if dealt from a shoe.

The third method is *crimping.* The crimp is a crease in the back of the card that can be seen when dealers place the card under their hole card or on the top of the deck if they aren't careful.

Aside from using the cards to cheat, the player can use the money. There are two methods employed to do this: One is called *capping,* the other is called *dragging.* Capping refers to the act of increasing the bet by placing additional chips to the bet once the cards have been dealt. A similar procedure involves slipping a higher denomination chip under the player's bet in order not to cause suspicion. Dragging refers to the act of reducing one's bet when the hand isn't favorable. These procedures are used by amateurs and professionals alike. The methods used by amateurs are of course crude and easier to detect since they basically rely on the lack of awareness of the dealer. The effectiveness of this method is increased, as in all cheating, by sitting at the periphery of the table where the dealer's vision isn't as good. Where players are allowed to handle the cards, these procedures are facilitated by picking up the cards and redepositing them. Capping is usually achieved by palming the chips to be pressed and depositing them when cards are returned to the table, and dragging is usually achieved by flicking the top chip with the edge of the cards into the other hand, where it is palmed.

In the computer age we live in, it wouldn't seem right if a device hadn't been invented to cheat on the games. And true to this thought, the computer world has developed a device that aids the player in tracking the cards and making play decisions. These tiny computers start around $6,000 and were initially sized to fit in the heel of a boot. But boot computers made their users look so guilty of mischief that a different version was needed to conceal the operator's intention.

Body units have been developed that either can be operated by a single user or in conjunction with an accomplice who processes the information and then relays it by remote control to the player. One method involves a sort of tap dance. With the toes of the feet, the operator feeds the computer information about the cards that are coming out of the shoe. The computer then feeds back a signal that tells the player how to bet and how to play the hand. Another method has the terminal either strapped to the player's waistline or another accessible body part, or is attached in a similar manner to the accomplice. Just as before, the card values are put into the computer and the computer signals back, through coded vibrations, the manner in which the hand should be played. This may sound like science fiction, but you'll see signs posted throughout the casino prohibiting the use of electronic devices in the casino. It is against the law. Anyone caught with the device is usually arrested, and the device is confiscated.

There are probably other cheating techniques out there that have been developed or are in the process of being developed. I don't pretend to know all of the possible ways of cheating or all of the ways to defend against cheaters. I do, however, believe that there are measures that can be taken to minimize the risk of being cheated. That's what game protection is all about.

PROTECTIVE MEASURES

The general measures the casino takes to protect itself against theft include electronic surveillance, plain clothes security and spotters, floor supervisors and pit supervisors, and the use of gaming equipment that's as foolproof as possible. These measures apply to all the games. In blackjack, the dealer is handed a procedure manual that details each aspect of the game and how

it is to be performed. The floor supervisor receives the same manual with an addition that details his or her job function. Most of what is written in those manuals pertains to the security of the games. Incidentally, not all casinos issue procedure manuals. Some of them have a general employee manual and assume that, since they hired experienced help, employees should be aware of general security measures.

Walking the Game

The game of blackjack is most vulnerable from the dealer's standpoint, so it is only proper to present some of the procedures that aid in the protection of the game at that level first. One of the most underrated procedures in Nevada and Puerto Rico is the walking of the game. I have mentioned how cheats prefer the periphery of the games because of the limited visibility. This should be enough reason for dealers and supervisors to be extra cautious about these spots. Walking the game allows dealers to broaden the scope of their perception by positioning their bodies in angles that take in more of the game. This is achieved by a left-to-right movement as the dealer is distributing the cards and scanning the layout, then by standing at the left side of the table, slightly angled toward third base (the last spot to the right from the dealer's perspective) while calling for decisions on the hands. The dealer's body moves toward the right and begins to straighten when the middle of the table is reached. Instead of turning the body toward the right when calling for a decision on third base, the dealer's body is slightly turned toward first base, keeping the player on first base in sight. This maneuver makes it more difficult for a player to press and drag bets, to introduce a cooler into the game, to switch cards, and to mark the cards. It is one of the most effective game protection techniques in use today. It is really puzzling that Nevada and Puerto Rico casinos haven't made better use of it.

Change Transactions

Requiring the dealers to *call out change transactions* is another strong anti-theft procedure. A dealer who doesn't do it or does so only intermittently immediately becomes a suspect. This doesn't mean that the dealer who occasionally forgets to call out change transactions is stealing. Unfortunately, enforcement of all procedures is sometimes lax. However, if strict enforcement has been in place long enough to make the procedure routine, a violation of it does give cause to suspect the violator. Even places that have established change procedures will many times get lax with the enforcement and won't caution dealers when slight deviations occur. For example, the procedure of calling for color change requires that the dealer request permission to bring the chips in by saying, "Color coming in." But many times dealers will call for color when they already have the chips cut out in front of the rack. The same is true of chip changes. This action defeats the purpose of the procedure. The dealer could virtually come out of the rack with the chips or palm chips and add them onto the player's color.

Body Language

Dealers have been known to store chips and cash on their bodies. This is one of the reasons dealers are required to use aprons and why they're not allowed to have shirt pockets. Yet even with these provisions, dealers have managed to steal by using secret compartments inside their clothing and by using their mouths as storage, also. That's why the supervisor should randomly check to make sure money is being deposited in the drop box and that dealers don't make any hand movements toward their bodies. If for any reason dealers must go to their bodies, they should first ask permission, then clear their hands. The action of hand clearing should be executed appropriately, with the hands and fingers spread wide open and rotated 180 degrees, palms up, at least twice after clapping them together. Some dealers have their own variation of this movement, which is done so quickly that it could still allow them to palm checks.

Talking the Game

Talking the game is another procedure that not only prevents players from making unwarranted claims; it also speeds up the game because it helps slow counters to make decisions, plus it gives the customer the impression that an immediate response is required. It also helps the dealer remember the count totals on the layout and associate them with the bets. This has two advantages: One, the dealer will remember which bets to pay and which ones to take (speeding up the game in the process) and, two, if someone has managed to make a switch on the game or a press, it'll be easier

for the dealer to remember. There's one more important thing: The supervisor doesn't have to look to know what is happening on the game.

Card Handling

It is difficult for card cheaters to mark the cards if they're not allowed to touch them. This, of course, is a very good rule to have, but one that the nature of some games makes difficult to impose. Traditionally, single and double deck blackjack has been a game where players are allowed to manipulate the cards because they're dealt face down. A lot of players like this sense of privacy, and the casino likes the idea that a card counter has an obstacle in the way, although this won't stop a potential cheater. Casino operators reason that, since this game is a good draw, it is a good marketing tool to have as long as the right controls are in place. Casino operators feel that, as long as dealers tilt the decks up toward their bodies and place their hand in such a way as to cover the front edge of the cards, half the battle against cheaters has been won. The other half is dependent on an alert dealer who knows what to look for in a cheater and who won't allow customers to break the card handling rules of the game. One thing that must be insisted upon is that the customer use only one hand when manipulating the cards. This makes cheating techniques more difficult to accomplish, but it doesn't prevent them.

I'm not sure that the hassles associated with blackjack using single and double decks are really worth the aggravation. The dangers and skills associated with the game require that the dealer who operates it be very competent and honest. This can present scheduling problems and, as more and more casinos restrict the availability of these games, it is going to become more of a problem to find competent dealers. Casino operators will eventually have to decide if this casino art form is worth preserving or not. The popularity of the game, because of its fairness to the player, may manage to keep it alive. But as a manager who'll make this choice, make sure that you have considered all the pros and cons as they would apply to your operation. Don't do as they did at the Dunes about a year before they closed. The game was brought in hoping to salvage the operation, yet instead became a source of constant tension. If you're going to sweat the games, then maybe you should use a shoe.

A shoe with a covered hole also ensures that a dealer or player who still manages to mark the cards won't be able to use this information coming out of the shoe. The player would enjoy a sizable advantage by identifying the hole card, but at least the advantage has been greatly reduced, especially if this person is sitting at the end of the table. I know it is unbelievable that someone would be able to mark a deck when not allowed to touch the cards, but it can be done. That's why it is so important for the dealer to be attentive and to walk the game, which is easily accomplished. Otherwise, anything can be done.

Another important dealing practice on the blackjack game is to retrieve the cards in order. This procedure allows the dealer to reset the game as it was played to settle disputes and makes a dealer trying to rearrange cards a suspect. As I mentioned earlier, setting cards for a plug is one way a dealer can cheat with an agent. If when a dealer is asked to reset the hand that was just in play, the cards aren't only out of order but also separated into high cards and low cards, the supervisor should suspect that something is wrong.

The Shuffle

A good shuffle procedure prevents the dealer or a player from using plugs. It used to be a common procedure in Puerto Rico to divide the four decks of cards in half and then shuffle each stack two or three times. Some dealers even prided themselves on their ability to shuffle all four decks at the same time. It requires a lot of skill. But it is a move that makes card location a cinch, as is the other shuffling procedure they employed where the basic rule was to get it over with quickly. Card location refers to finding the position of a cluster in the deck and then increasing bets accordingly when the plug is ready to come out. That's why a good shuffle should be thorough. The decks should be broken apart at least four times, preferably six. Half decks should be intermixed between the different stacks in a prescribed fashion so the dealer can't deviate from the procedure, and plenty of stripping should follow. The cards should then be intermixed again from two stacks and left with the interlacing visible on the final procedure so that the supervisor can verify that the shuffle occurred. This method will break down most plugs and make it extremely difficult for the card locator to follow it. Even a false shuf-

fling mechanic would find it almost impossible to fake the lacing.

Card Placement

The placing of the cards on the layout also helps protect blackjack against theft. Cards that are bunched together and hard to read make it easy for dealers to pay agents who have lost their hands. It also makes it easier for dealers to make mistakes since they may believe that the point total isn't what it shows. The same occurs from the supervisor's perspective. When the supervisor is far away from the game, it is especially difficult for him or her to read the cards. In this instance, the only way the supervisor is going to be able to identify the point total of cards is to read the suits. The way the hearts, diamonds, spades, and clubs are arranged on a card identifies the card to the supervisor from a distance because the total figure of the suits makes for a much larger object than the number or letter of the card. If the cards are then covered or bunched to the point where the supervisor can't distinguish one card from another, it is impossible to know what the point total is. In order to avoid this mistake, the dealer is instructed to place each subsequent card to the bottom left side of each card. This leaves from 60 to 75 percent of the card visible and identifiable to the floor supervisor. This arrangement also makes it a lot easier for the dealer to pick up the cards because each card slides underneath the other.

Peeking

One more measure of game protection on the blackjack game that is very important is *peeking*. When I mentioned front loading, glims, and spooking, you saw how cheaters go to great lengths to identify the dealer's hole card in order to achieve an extremely valuable advantage in strategy play. There are various ways in which the casino can protect itself against this. One way, which is used in Puerto Rico and England, is to have dealers give themselves a hole card after all the players have completed their play. This is the safest measure that can be employed in this case, but it is one that doesn't fare well with players who are leery of the house. It also has another disadvantage: In England, it increases the house advantage .13 percent, and this doesn't satisfy players either.

In Atlantic City, cards are dealt out of a shoe, and dealers aren't allowed to peek at their hole cards. This procedure is effective, but the house loses valuable time because it has to play out the hand. The fact that the house can't take double downs or splits until the hand is over also delays the process. The next best thing is to have the dealers be extremely cautious when inspecting their hole cards, making sure that they slightly and quickly lift the bottom left corner of the card while protecting it from exposure by covering it with both hands. If the cards are covered properly, it would be extremely difficult to catch a glimpse of the card. Unfortunately, some dealers aren't that cautious. They believe that this knowledge doesn't produce that great an advantage. They also believe it is almost impossible for a person to see the card from behind when the dealer is only lifting a corner of it. This is another one of those instances where effective communication can be of great value.

An alternative position that some Nevada casinos have taken is to have the dealers only peek when they have an ace up. They figure that since the chances of the dealer having a blackjack with an ace up are four times greater than with a ten, and since the ace comes up four times less, the risk is reduced while the amount of hands per hour is increased. There's one more added advantage to this method—the dealers know their hole card four times less. Of course, if dealers are cheating with agents, it doesn't matter if they know the hole card or not, except that flashing the hole card is easier to detect than a hand signal or body language.

The Peek Machine

Technology has had a role to play in this controversy, also. A prism has been developed that aids the dealer in identifying an ace or a ten when the dealer passes the card through it. The Mirage used it for a short period of time yet was unsatisfied with its performance and later withdrew it from the games. The exact reason the company was dissatisfied with the peek machine is unknown. However, I do know that the majority of the casinos aren't employing the device.

In evaluating what system is more effective, we are put in a position of having to measure the additional productivity loss and compare it to the potential security risk in quantitative terms. This is so hypothetical that it is impossible to measure. We can measure, to a certain extent, what the loss is going to be in terms of decreased production of hands per hour. For example,

we know that blackjack occurs 4.77 percent of the time. If we find that the average hands per hour in our casino is sixty, we know we're losing 2.88 hands per hour (additional hands that could be dealth), per table. Assuming all other variables to be equal (which they wouldn't be), we can assume that in a twenty-four-hour period the casino will have lost 69.12 hands per table, or the time equivalent of one hour and nine minutes of gaming time. Now let's assume that our daily win per table is $1,200 which, divided by twenty-four hours, is $50. The resulting monetary loss would be $50 for one hour plus $7.50 for the additional nine minutes. If this casino had ten active tables, at this rate the casino would lose $575 a day. I sort of cross-referenced here when I applied theoretical assumptions to actual win figures, but I did it to give a clearer picture of how this concept applies.

Down strict theoretical lines, I would have made assumptions such as an average bet of $10 per person times six people on the table totals $60 average bet per hand, which at an assumed 2 percent house advantage produces $1.20 per hand. Since I already determined that the casino loses 69 hands per twenty-four-hour period, we end up with a total loss of $82.80 per table, times ten tables adds up to an $828 loss for the casino, per day. On a yearly basis, the casino would lose $302,220. Each individual casino's situation is different, and it is up to management to determine what its potential losses are going to be due to the reduced productivity and compare this loss to what they feel the machines will cost them. There's no way to determine the latter.

Hand Signals

Hand signals are another way of protecting blackjack against cheats and opportunists. Many times arguments will ensue because players will claim that they intended to stay, or they intended to hit, or they intended to split or double down. Nothing can really prevent this from happening since human nature will make both the dealer and the player believe they're right. But the only way the casino can effectively reduce most of these disputes is to force the players to give a clear hand signal. It is the dealer's responsibility to make sure that the player complies with this rule. A scratching motion with one or more fingers is required for a hit, and a horizontal movement of the hand, palms down, is required for a stand. Double downs and splits are requested by placing the additional number of chips to the left side of the bet before the dealer comes to the player's hand. This is just another example of how body language speaks clearer than the spoken word.

Checks Play or Table Limit

One final procedure in blackjack deserves to be mentioned, and that's making the supervisor aware that a substantial bet has been placed on the layout. Most casinos have the dealer call out, "Checks play!" to acknowledge these large bets. This is an important procedure because it informs the supervisor of a potentially dangerous situation on the game. The amount that constitutes a large wager varies, but in most casinos it is $100. Some casinos even establish rules that require an automatic shuffle if a wager of $500 and above is placed. This extra measure of protection, if all other game protection procedures are in place, would only protect against a *shadow counter or partnership counting.*

A shadow counter is a card counter who counts from a distance and then sits down to play. Partnership or team counters are counters who have one team member sit at the table and count. This member gets up when the deck is highly favorable to the player so that the other team member can sit down and exploit the richness of the shoe without causing suspicion. Management's feeling is that, although breaking the deck has some justification, counters who place a substantial bet in these circumstances have broken two fundamental rules of card counting: The player has brought attention to himself or herself, and has become a gambler even though betting on a slight advantage. This type of card counting doesn't allow players to get in enough trials to let the law of averages work in their favor. There aren't advantages or disadvantages here, but it would be unfortunate if other good players who were sitting at the table at the same time decided to leave because they felt the house had been unfair to them. It would also be unfortunate if the player who places the bet happens to be a good resource who otherwise would have played at your casino, but decides to go elsewhere because of your attitude.

The main concern of the supervisor in the above circumstances should be to find out what the nature of the increased wager is. Upon being alerted, the first thing the supervisor should do is to locate the wager, see how much it is, and see if the player is recognizable. It could be a player who is known to the supervisor as a regular player or it could be a player who's a known cheater or card counter. If the player is neither of those, then the floorperson has to watch that game closely, perhaps consulting with an adjoining supervisor or making the pit boss aware of the player. The dealer shouldn't be allowed to continue dealing until the floor supervisor gives authorization. This is another procedure that is routinely violated because some busy supervisors respond to it as if it annoys them or respond even when they aren't looking. Dealers notice this and get the impression that it is not that important to that supervisor. But it *is* important, and supervisors shouldn't allow dealers to continue to deal until they've had a chance to assess the situation. Dealers who have agents on the game are going to be reluctant to call attention to them and they aren't going to call out if the casino is lax on the enforcement of this rule. Since there are so many potentially dangerous reasons why players may be increasing their bets to this level, it is essential that the floor supervisor enforce this rule strictly and pay close attention to the game.

Communication

The procedures described above are the main methods used to protect blackjack games from the dealer's point of view. There are other things dealers can do to protect the games. Whether dealers do these things depends upon their rapport with the supervisor. An example of this is that the dealer who notices odd fluctuations in players' bets, odd plays or odd behavior, both on the table and outside the table, should notify the supervisor. You must remember that a supervisor in blackjack may be watching four games while the dealer is only watching one game and, therefore, can observe much more. A good dealer will inform the supervisor of these abnormal situations, provided that supervisor maintains an open line of communication.

In the chapter on communication I made the point that if a supervisor makes subordinates feel like idiots or unappreciated when they communicate something they feel to be important to the supervisor, the chance of receiving another communication of this type is greatly reduced. Although there are some things you can make dealers responsible for, there are others that you can't. For example, let's assume that the dealer notices that the player in third base has consistently hit 14, 15, and 16 against the dealer's higher cards. The dealer also notices that the player is doing well and hit at one time with a point total of 18. Now, all of a sudden, the player stays on a 12 against a 10. Something is obviously strange, and although the dealer feels a need to communicate this to the supervisor, he or she remembers that upon making this particular supervisor (or maybe even another supervisor) aware of a similar situation, the supervisor responded with ridicule. What do you think the chances are that the dealer will communicate this situation this time? If I have made this point clearly enough, you may conclude: *Very slim.*

The Equipment

Games are also protected by the equipment. In blackjack, shoes are a protective device. They're usually numbered and attached to the game by a chain. Some of them have covered the hole of the face plate either with a plastic cover, a cloth curtain, or a set of bristles that the dealer forces out of the way to pull the card out. Baccarat shoes have top covers, also. Some supervisors even believe that the dealer should deal with one hand and keep the other one on the shoe to protect it. Most casinos today allow blackjack dealers to pay up to the first three bets with the left hand, while some of them insist upon it. This procedure protects the right flank of the dealer, which is where the discard rack is, a great number of the cards are, and the right side of the chip bank is. However, you'll notice that banks are laid out in such a way as to place lower denomination chips to the outside of the rack and higher denomination chips toward the middle. This is a protective measure in case a player reaches into the rack for chips. The higher denomination chips are protected.

The discard rack is covered on the side that faces third base and on the side that faces the back of the table. This makes it a little more difficult for the player on third base to access the cards and also prevents the cards from falling off the table. Another safety feature of the discard rack is its red plastic construction. This allows some marks to be seen easier than with the naked eye. This brings us to the most important piece of equipment on the blackjack layout—the cards.

Cards are handled by many people before they reach their final productive destination, which is the game table. It is possible, although highly improbable, that someone in this long line of handlers could slip in cards that are either marked or stacked heavily in favor of either interested party. In the case of marked cards, the alerted player would be the one to benefit, and in the case of the stacked deck, it could be either, depending upon how it is stacked. A deck heavy of low cards benefits the casino, and a deck heavy of high cards would benefit the player. In organized and regulated casinos the chance of the latter happening is extremely slim because too many people would have to be involved. This scam could be limited to two or three people, but in that case we would be talking about a separate set of cards introduced by inside help and not the ones that came from the warehouse. Marked cards, on the other hand, wouldn't require as many participants, though they would still require a few. Because this is conceivable, some managers and supervisors are leery when heavy losses occur on games, so they have the cards inspected and run back tapes on the game to see if anything went wrong.

Distribution and Inspection of Cards

To make it more difficult for foul play to occur where the cards are concerned, the casino stores them in a locked compartment or room with limited access. In some places, a security guard and usually a shift manager then remove the cards from the storage room and transfer them to the pit areas where they'll be used. There, the pit manager stores them in a locked compartment until they're needed. When it is time to distribute the cards to the tables, the pit manager delivers them personally to the supervisors, or assigns a supervisor to do it. After receiving the cards, the supervisor first checks to make sure the plastic wrappers are intact. If they are, the supervisor will tear the wrappers off, then break the seal that covers the opening of the deck of cards. The wrapper and the seal are two protective measures that the manufacturer throws in to protect the casino; however, this method isn't infallible since cards can be taken out of the side of the page, marked, then replaced. The package is re-glued and re-wrapped while the seam remains intact. Once the cards have been unsealed, the supervisor will place them on the table game, where the dealer proceeds to inspect the cards.

In some places the inspection of the cards is initiated by the floorperson, who spreads the cards to make sure they're all there before handing them to the dealer. The dealer then proceeds to recheck them and to inspect the back of the cards also. Back inspection is more comprehensive than face inspection because markings will identify the cards to the player. Yet most dealers take as much time inspecting the back of the cards as they do the front. This is a mistake because on the face of the card, all they need to see is the number, which is in an order that is easily visible. The back, however, should be totally exposed and scrutinized with the reflection of the light that shines on them. Most dealers will expose them halfway with their fingers and continue to do the same with the next. The main reason for this is that the supervisors and managers instill in them the need to have the games opened as quickly as possible. Supervisors aren't too concerned because most of them don't believe cards can be set up if they're in sealed wrappers. But since this inspection only happens once a day, the supervisor is better off having the dealer spend that extra minute to inspect the cards correctly.

In Puerto Rico, the government doesn't trust the casino to do its own inspecting. The government sees itself mainly as a protector of the citizens who come to the casinos to play and less as an agency to protect the interests of the casino. Because of this reasoning, all casino equipment, including cards, is inspected by a government inspector, who's on property at all times. It is the government inspector who tears the wrappers, and breaks the seals on the cards, checks to see that all cards are present in a deck, and that there are no apparent markings. Part of the equipment that's handed to the government inspector is a red plastic sheet that's used to uncover hard-to-see markings. Inspectors rarely use these, and the task of inspecting all the equipment of a casino may be too burdensome for one person.

The above limitation was evidenced at El San Juan in 1978. A player was losing a lot of money on a blackjack table when a blank card showed up out of the shoe. The player started yelling that no wonder he had been losing since the cards in the casino weren't on the level. The player caused such a commotion that other customers refrained from playing and were coming to listen to him more closely and to take a look at the white card. Much to his displeasure, the casino manager had to call the inspector to resolve the conflict. But instead of using a diplomatic approach, the casino manager

told the inspector that he had to inspect the cards before the player to prove to him that they were on the level. He even implied that in a way it was the fault of the inspector who didn't check the cards properly.

The Puerto Rico regulations require that any claims regarding the integrity of cards on a table are to be settled after the gaming operation is over and in the presence of a casino official and the complaining party by the government inspector. The inspector is supposed to bag the cards, seal the bag, and secure the bag until he is ready to inspect them. So in effect, what the casino manager was asking the inspector to do was to break the law, and it was done in a way that sounded like a threat. The inspector picked up the cards from the table, recited the regulation to both the casino manager and the player, and left. The manager followed the inspector and continued to threaten him, telling him that he was wrong about the regulation and making reference to his connections in the gaming commission, where he had previously been a director of investigations. This tactic didn't work either. (By the way, it hadn't been this inspector who had checked the cards at the beginning of the operation.)

After the inspector left, the manager returned to the main part of the casino, where the situation was getting worse. A few minutes later, the manager came over to the inspector, who was doing paperwork and wouldn't look up to acknowledge him. The manager sat by the inspector and in a soft tone asked him to please do him this favor because the customer wasn't calming down, and no one was playing at the tables. The inspector looked up from his paperwork and said, *"You know, if you would have asked me this way the first time, I wouldn't have had a problem with your request. Go tell the customer to come over and we'll check the cards now."*

The casino manager was lucky to be dealing with an open-minded person; otherwise the casino would have lost a lot of revenue, and its image would have been tarnished in the eyes of the people who were there that evening and who probably would have spread the word to others. As it turns out, the white card was nothing but an unprinted extra card the daytime inspector failed to see when inspecting the cards.

This story had a happy ending because the manager changed his faulty communication approach and the inspector was a fair-minded person. On one side was a person who wasn't communicating at all, and on the other was a person who was communicating clearly because of seeing the whole picture and not just a fraction of it. He also had the capability to put himself in the position of the other person, which is essential to good communication. Although communication isn't the subject matter of this section, I feel the need to bring the subject up every time there's cause for it because it is of enormous importance in every facet of the casino operation. *Communication is essential in game protection.*

As for the inspection of the cards, it is important that this repetitive task not be carried out by one person, because it requires a lot of care. You have seen how not only can the casino lose by being cheated, its reputation can plummet if the job of inspection isn't carried out appropriately.

Exercising Caution and Taking Control

For the supervisor, game protection entails making sure that the dealer is protecting the game and, if not, the supervisor must call attention to the fault and make sure it is corrected. If the dealer fails to correct the fault, then stricter measures have to be taken to ensure compliance. Game protection isn't something to be taken lightly. The supervisor has to be on the lookout for situations that might escape the dealer regardless of how well he or she protects the game. This refers to actions on the game and outside the game that may lead to or be an indication of trouble on the game, such as suspicious-looking people or suspicious bets or plays being placed. A person who is standing on the outside of a game looking nervously around at the rack may be planning to steal from the rack or from a person on the game. As I have expressed many times before, body language is important when trying to anticipate what another person is trying to communicate. Glances and signals between players and between players and dealers can be all a supervisor needs to see to uncover a scam. That's why the supervisor has to be scanning the games constantly. People who ignore each other one time and seem well acquainted at another time are worth closer inspection.

Card Counters and Computer Cheats

Card counters and computer cheats are two other foes the supervisor has to contend with. I've already expressed my position on card counting and, although I believe that for the most part this dying breed is harmless, it is important to recognize that some aren't. How much damage they can do depends on their resources and the resources of the casino. Many operators feel that they must eradicate these *vermin*, and they go to great lengths to do it. In the mid-eighties, some casinos were breaking down decks on $5 players who raised their bets to $15. This still might be happening. Yet this doesn't make any financial sense, except in the minds of those who take these things personally.

When the need does exist to remove these *vermin*, the supervisor has to be ready for the challenge— either by personally learning to be a good card counter or by employing the assistance of someone who is. The first thing a supervisor has to know in order to uncover a card counter is basic blackjack strategy. Surprisingly enough, most supervisors, including pit managers and shift managers, don't know perfect basic strategy even though most casinos make this an unspoken requisite. If it turns out that you failed to recognize a play, this may turn up in your next evaluation. The rules are varied, and if they're not practiced they're going to be forgotten. So this is one of the things the supervisor has to do on a daily basis while watching the games. He or she should also be required to carry a basic strategy sheet as a memory aid, one that shows the deviations of the plays that a good card counter would make in order to maintain the maximum advantage. These are also the plays that a good card counter makes with confidence even when being watched because there is no expectation the supervisor will understand why it was done. Card counters' knowledge of the game is such that they can sometimes make purposeful mistakes so close to an even bet that they'll usually throw the supervisor off, and yet they have barely hurt themselves.

Examples of plays that will probably throw most supervisors off are splitting tens, even more so against a 4, splitting sevens against an 8, splitting threes against an 8, not splitting fours against a 6, not doubling down on 10 against an 8, not doubling down on 11 against a 9, and not doubling down on the soft counts against a 4, a 5, or 6. All these plays can be good plays depending on the count.

Plays like hitting 12 against a 4 or a 6, staying on 16 against a 10, doubling on 8 against a 6, doubling on 9 against a 2, not doubling on 9 against a 3, doubling on 11 against an ace, not splitting threes against a 2, splitting fours against a 4, not doubling soft 13 against a 6, doubling soft 14 against a 4, not doubling soft 15 against a 4, not doubling soft 17 and 18 against a 2, and doubling on soft 19 against a 6 or a 7 are all plays that require very little variation or none at all to be an even proposition to the counter. So as you can see, there are many legitimate plays the counter can make to confuse the supervisor.

Yet the supervisor having a basic strategy card with a variation index table will be able to uncover even the best counters, even if the counter is using a system different from the hi-lo system used for the examples above. Most of the plays are going to be similar, and the critical hands are going to be the same. For more information on counting systems, refer to Ken Uston, Sanford Wong, or Lawrence Revere.

Computer play keeps a more precise account of the status of the deck and the plays that would be appropriate according to that status. Some plays and presses are going to vary, but for the most part, computer play will follow close to the general pattern of advanced counting systems. The giveaway, both of the counter and the computer player, is that they're going to be paying attention to the cards, and their bets are going to be fluctuating, not necessarily when they win or lose, but when high concentrations of high cards and low cards are discarded at any given time. Don't be fooled by apparent lack of interest, because a good card counter needs but a glimpse to follow the game, and just a second or two to take a glance at the whole layout. But if you watch good card counters, you'll notice that they'll look at the cards even if it seems out of boredom or out of the corner of their eyes.

Computer players stand out because their play is more precise, and usually they are making suspicious body movements to key-in information to the computer. Sometimes a partner does the clocking of the game from a distance and relays play information by remote control to the one who's playing on the game. Wearing boots with a large heel to hide the apparatus used to be the trend, but that's not the case any more because foot movements are more awkward than hand movements. Yet the easiest way to detect computer tracking is to have a portable radio available in the pit. If the unit is set between stations, the radio will pick up the radio signals the computer emits as the information is being input. Radio waves released by electronic equipment are the reason operators are prohibited from using these devices during takeoff and landing of aircraft.

Once it has been established that a card counter is on the game, the supervisor must decide how to handle it. In Nevada, casinos can refuse to deal to anyone, and that includes card counters. The other option is to reduce counters' edge by cutting the deck in half. Since counters are struggling for every tenth of a percent they can add on, this move is really annoying and they usually leave the game. For the stubborn ones, another move employed is to shuffle every time counters increase their bets substantially. This usually works but we also have to realize that there are other people on the game and that they, too, will get annoyed. So we have to measure the threat that's involved against the possibility of losing other patrons because of our cat and mouse games. Also, ethically speaking, we would be cheating those other people out of an advantage that is rightfully theirs at that time. In my estimation, card counting is highly overrated and shouldn't be handled in any way further than to cut the deck in half, and even that measure should be used only against those who really constitute a threat.

The computer player is treated differently because of using an extraordinary device to achieve an unlawful advantage. Since the law has a remedy for this violation, there's no need to cut the decks in half or to shuffle each time a bet is increased. This is one of the times when the surveillance team is alerted and a visual record of the play is taken. This tape will prove that the plays made by the player were a threat to the operation, and it'll also prove that the player made the suspicious moves associated with computer play. With this tape in hand, the casino security can detain the suspects until the commission agent arrives to do the search, or in the case of Atlantic City, the Division of Gaming Enforcement agents will bring the suspects in for questioning themselves.

This is the way all serious violations are handled. The supervisor alerts the pit manager who then alerts surveillance and security, who, in turn, alerts the state agents who are in charge of enforcement. Sometimes, as in the case of a rack or rail thief, the supervisor doesn't have time to call for help and must act immediately in order to stop the crime. If wrestling with a criminal isn't the supervisor's style, he or she can at least alert the victim, get a good look at the thief, and call out for security.

Other Protective Measures

Other ways for supervisors to ensure the security of blackjack is by keeping accurate counts of the bankroll and by knowing where the money is going on the game. If the dealer has been trained to properly call out change transactions, this shouldn't be a problem. All other major bankroll transactions will be evidenced in the record the supervisor keeps with the rating cards and by the cash and credit transactions that he or she also record. Any unexplained discrepancies that show up are then investigated more closely.

If an explanation can't be found, then the dealer or dealers who were on the game when the discrepancy occurred have to be watched more closely. A casual conversation (one that doesn't accuse any dealer directly) with another supervisor on the subject might shed some light on the problem. If it turns out that another supervisor had a similar situation with one of the dealers on the game, then it is time to alert the pit manager and put the surveillance team to work. A visual record of stealing or cheating is acceptable and indisputable in any court.

Watching the Shuffle

The shuffle is another aspect of blackjack that requires close attention since the dealer can manipulate the cards to the advantage of an agent or aid the agent in making an exchange. For this reason, dealers are required to call out for the shuffle and the cut. This isn't the only time a *cooler* or a *plug* can be introduced into the game, but it is when it can be done most effectively. Some cheaters will dispute this since they probably believe that the best time is when the cards are in the discard rack and a cheater positioned at third base can monitor the attention of the players, the dealer, and the supervisor. However, there are many things that can happen when all the cards are out of the shoe or during the shuffle that do require the supervisor's attention. The supervisor should insist on an audible call for the shuffle, and for the dealer to wait until it is acknowledged before the remaining cards are brought out of the shoe. At the end of the shuffle, the cards should be

visibly interlaced in evidence that a good riffle was performed. If clusters of cards remain unriffled, the dealer should be counseled in this respect. A dealer whose ability to riffle is deficient should be advised to practice at home until even riffles and interlacing of the cards are achieved.

Watching the Cut

The cut should also be monitored so that it isn't aided by the dealer and so the supervisor should visually follow the cards into the shoe. If no one wants to cut the deck, then the supervisor should be the one to cut it. After the cards are in the shoe and play begins, there are several things that the supervisor should be aware of. From time to time, players will ask the dealer for advice on how to play their hand. This is usually an innocent request, but in some isolated cases it could be a clarification of a signal that has been confused by an amateur agent. Because of this possibility and of the possibility that the dealer might want to be a little too helpful to someone he or she fancies on the game, the dealer shouldn't be allowed to give advice to players on strategy. However, it is good public relations for the supervisor to aid the player in this respect once in a while, even though the house would probably be better off with the advice that the dealer would give since dealers usually aren't as knowledgeable on playing strategy.

Watching the Dealers

Dealers with roving eyes are dealers to watch out for. Dealers who looks around too much are security risks to the casino for two reasons: One, they are not paying enough attention to their game and, two, they might be trying to figure out the location of the supervisor to make their move on the game.

Supervisors must be aware of their games at all times, regardless of what they may be doing at the moment. Corrupt dealers and cheats will target unaware supervisors. They'll distract supervisors by creating arguments and disputes on games, or by engaging supervisors in conversation. When these things happen, the first thing supervisors have to do is scan the tables—something else might be happening. Other vulnerable moments are when the supervisor issues markers, does fills or credits, gets relieved by another supervisor, does the count or table game accounting at shift change, or assists the dealer where a drink was spilled over.

Added Measures

Aside from the measures that must be taken by the dealers and supervisors to protect the games, there are other measures taken by the pit manager. The pit manager serves as an extra pair of eyes to look for the same things the floor supervisor does, and makes sure to do an adequate and honest job. The pit manager is also responsible for the keys to the cabinet that stores the cards, the box that stores the dealing shoes at the tables, the lock on the lid covers that secure the bankrolls. When not in use, these keys are to be locked up in a drawer to which only the pit managers have access.

IN CRAPS

The game of craps presents its own security risks both by the way the equipment is handled and the amount of action that's possible on the game. In 1991, a craps table full of players betting $5 dollar chips lost over $200,000 in two hours at the Dunes in Las Vegas. Such is the financial power of the game of craps. There was nothing illegitimate about this game; it was just one of those vagaries of chance where the dice were held for over two hours. Yet this unlikely occurrence shows what can happen when the integrity of the game is violated. Because of the fast action and the multitude of bets, if instead of $5 players the game had been full of $100 players, this casino would have been ruined in that amount of time. Instead of closing in 1993, the Dunes would probably have closed that night.

The Dice

The most obvious and harmful way to cheat the casino in the game of craps is to tamper with the dice. This can be done either by an employee or by a player. The easiest way for the employee to do it is from the pit stand. This would require the pit manager to have the authority to place the dice on the game without scrutiny, then place a weak boxperson on a busy game who would receive the tampered dice as the shooter sevens out. As a result, the boxperson would feel there wasn't time to inspect the dice and just take the old ones out and put the new ones into play.

There are various ways pit managers can affect the outcome of the game from the pit stand: One, they can bring in a set of dice already set to affect probability in a certain way; two, they can steal a pair of dice and have them set, and three, they can do their own setting up at the pit stand. The first two ways are more complicated because one involves finding an artisan who can copy the company's logo and fix the dice, and the other involves removing a good set of dice in hope that no one discovers the switch before the dice are prepared and brought in to be placed on the game. The third method involves shaving or sanding the edges or corners off the dice or rounding them off. This maneuver can be easily performed by the pit manager at the podium, provided that the nearest supervisor is kept busy.

In the early 1980s a pit manager was caught shaving dice at Resorts International in Atlantic City. He was turned in by a floor supervisor, who informed management of what he saw. At first it was a joke, because evidently the pit manager's intention was to stop heavy losses at a crap table under his supervision. But quickly the casino realized the implications of the act and proceeded to report the pit manager to the Casino Control Commission, who suspended his license indefinitely.

Dice Switch

Where supervisors and boxpersons are required to inspect the dice before putting them on the game, the chances of getting away with this last method of cheating are very slim, unless these two supervisors are involved in the scam, also. In fact, either of these two supervisors could introduce bad dice into the game. The other employee who has the opportunity to switch dice is the stickperson, since the two base dealers hardly ever handle the dice, and when they do all eyes are centered upon them. In order for stickpersons to make the switch, they have to be professionals. They have to be even better than the hustlers who switch the dice off the game, and they have to be working either for the casino or in conjunction with agents on the game. In regulated casinos, I sincerely doubt that the house would employ a hustler to cheat the players. So for the most part this represents the stickperson as a collaborator to agents on the game.

There are two techniques used to switch the dice: the thumb switch and the palm switch. In the thumb switch, the cheater traps the good dice in the crotch of the thumb while releasing the bad dice, which are cupped in the fingertips. In the palm switch, the cheater picks up the casino's dice with the fingertips, then releases the crooked dice, which are based at the palm of the hand. It sounds simple, and to a certain extent it is. I happen to disagree with Darwin Ortiz, who feels it takes at least six months to master this technique.

Of course, mastery can be defined different ways. But in essence, an amateur can learn to switch dice well enough for most casino situations within a day or two, but it will take time to perfect an act and to gather the courage to pull off the stunt in a live game situation. This is why it is so important to be alert on a crap game and to have strict game protection procedures in place. I would venture to estimate that at least 50 percent, if not more, of the crap tables in this country are susceptible to amateur dice cheaters.

Crooked Dice

There are many kinds of crooked dice. Some alter the percentages of events happening on a crap game, and some stop the event from happening at all because the numbers required for the event to occur aren't on the dice. *Percentage dice* are dice whose shape has been changed somewhat so that the dice are no longer perfect cubes, or dice that have been drilled and loaded, making them heavier on one side than another. *Shapes* can be *flats,* which are dice that have been shaved down on one or more sides, making the dice rest more often on those sides, or *bevels* and *cut edges,* which are dice with edges that have been sanded or cut to have the dice roll off that edge more often than probability.

Loaded dice are dice whose surface has been drilled to accommodate a heavy substance such as gold, platinum, or tungsten amalgam. Obviously, the dice are going to rest more often on the side that has been weighed down. How often will depend on the amount of weight used. In today's regulated casinos, the dice that are used are transparent and therefore weights can only be placed under the cover of the white spots. Since these white spots are only seventeen one-thousandths of an inch, there's not much room for the weights. This makes it difficult for the cheater to have a large advantage, but it is big enough to net a good profit. These dice have the added advantage that they don't have to be removed from the game since only close scrutiny will detect them.

Misspotted dice are dice that are missing one or more numbers. They're also called *tops, bottoms, busters,* and *Ts.* Misspotted dice come in different combinations depending upon the numbers the cheater wants to make. For example, a set with two, three, and six on them will make fours, fives, sixes, eights and nines. A set with one, three, and five will make fours, sixes, eights and tens. Numbers four, five, and six are good dice for field numbers. Many mechanics will alternate the dice in order to cause less suspicion, then when they notice the supervisors getting edgy, they'll switch back to the original dice and let them *seven out.* Another variation of the misspotted dice is the double number. These dice are less likely to be discovered because only one number is missing. The number that is doubled is going to affect the probability of certain numbers on which the mechanic's partner will be betting heavily. And this is another thing to remember: *Rarely will cheaters bet heavily on the game.* As a matter of fact, sometimes they employ what's called a *beard.* This is a well-known high roller who doesn't cause suspicion when making heavy bets. With this maneuver, the casino can lose a lot of money, and it may seem to them business as usual—just a lucky day for Mr. Big.

Sliding the Dice

Aside from cheating with their own dice, dice hustlers have practiced ways to cheat with honest dice. In today's gaming environment, most of those practices have become obsolete because casinos are alert to controlled shots. The most popular and effective of all the control shots is the *slider.* In Puerto Rico, for example, the government has gone to great lengths to protect against sliders by placing a string across the middle of the game that acts as a trip wire. The shooter must pass both dice over the string in order for it to be a valid roll. Although this will prevent sliding the dice flush on the table, it won't prevent the sliding, especially if the pass is made from the spot next to the stickperson. Yet even where one is required to hit the back wall with both dice, the shooter can still manage to slide the dice if the employees on the game aren't paying attention. Some hustlers will confuse the issue by hitting one die against the back wall and sliding the other. The very best of them will make both of the dice hit the back wall while still making one die maintain the slide. This one is obviously more difficult to detect.

Check Moves

Just as in blackjack, players in craps can cheat by pressing their bets when they have the advantage or by reducing their bets when the bets are at a disadvantage. However, craps players have still another advantage in these circumstances. They can remove the totality of their bets or place a bet after an advantageous situation occurs and possibly escape detection because there's nothing but the bet to identify them as players. Blackjack players would look odd with cards sitting in front of them without a bet and they stand a very small chance of getting paid on a bet without cards. The act of placing a bet after a decision on the crap game, or after a point has been established, is called past posting. This usually occurs when a point four, five, nine, or ten is established on the don't pass, or when a winning combination is thrown on either the pass line or the don't pass.

Withdrawing bets happens on both lines but is illegal only when a losing bet is withdrawn or when a pass line bet is withdrawn after the point has been established. The don't pass bet can be withdrawn after the point has been established and that move is to the casino's advantage. The same happens when players place a pass line bet or press their pass line bet after the point has been established. Because this is a move that is advantageous to the casino, Nevada regulators have allowed it. New Jersey regulators, however, will not allow players to place or press bets on the pass line once the point has been established.

Claims

More so than blackjack, craps is a game that is constantly inundated with claims of all kinds. This is partly due to the fast action and also the complexity of the game and the number of different ways that can be wagered. This inordinate number of claims requires that craps personnel be constantly on their toes and ready to respond effectively. This is one of the reasons New Jersey casino operators are so insistent on employee communication on the game. All bets must be repeated so that a spoken record exists and a contractual agreement is entered into by the person booking the bet and the one making it. Otherwise there can be chaos with the extraordinary number of bets that are sometimes tossed around in a game of craps.

These measures have been hard to impose in Nevada, where dealers are accustomed to their tradi-tional ways, which they seem to feel work better for them. This isn't to say that all Nevada dealers don't book their bets, or that they don't book all their bets all the time. Yet if we had to compare the booking pattern of New Jersey dealers against Nevada dealers, we would have to conclude that New Jersey dealers are more effective in their booking of bets and more conscientious toward the process.

I mention the above because claims on the game are a way of cheating, and they cost the casino a substantial amount of money. As in blackjack, a lot of claims can't be avoided, but many of them can by being more attentive and giving verbal confirmations of the bets or asking about money when it is thrown down on the layout. The latter is a very common way of cheating. A player will throw in a chip or chips and not say anything at all. Then when the combination hits, the player will claim to be a winner and argue incessantly about it. At the very least the contentious player will get his or her money back.

There are different philosophies applicable to claims on the game of craps. One philosophy is to allow every player the benefit of the doubt at least once, depending on the size of the wager. If a player is betting $5 on the line and claims to have thrown in $10 on 12, which involves a $300 payoff, I sincerely question whether that player will get the benefit of the doubt. Nor should such a patron get paid, because the claim isn't remotely consistent with his or her betting style. Now if the same customer claims to have thrown in a dollar for that bet and there's an extra dollar on the layout, there's a good possibility that he or she is telling the truth. But that isn't going to get the patron the benefit of the doubt unless someone recalls having heard something to that effect even if he or she can't actually say it was the customer in question. In such case, the customer will get the dollar back.

Another claim philosophy will take status into consideration when making claim decisions. In other words, if the customer is a minimum wage bettor and nobody can verify the bet, then the customer isn't going to be paid. However, customers who are big bettors at the casino, whether someone heard their bet or not, will get paid because the casino will be afraid to lose their patronage. This is a practice that is quite common, and understandable, but it is quite unfair to the other person who may be on the game at same time and didn't get paid in the same circumstances. It'll make this person feel unwanted and discriminated against. That's why giving everyone the benefit of the doubt at least once, regardless of play, is a much better and fairer system.

The last philosophy isn't worth mentioning, but I will, since it does happen in some places. This practice is to make no exceptions. "If the bet wasn't booked, if the chip isn't here, if you didn't pick it up, or whatever, we're sorry but we can't help you out." This is a philosophy that's in direct opposition to *the customer is always right*. Here, the customer is always wrong, and had better watch out or he or she'll get thrown out. This is a bad business philosophy.

Unfortunately, leniency with claims is what the cheater is counting on, and because most casinos do want to be fair to customers, they're going to succeed in getting many claims on. But after a while they're immediately recognized and can no longer make these claims.

Palming

The easiest thing the craps dealer can do to steal on the game is to palm chips. The craps game is set up so that dealers constantly have their hands on the vertical stacks of chips, and this facilitates palming. All they have to do then is straighten up their pants and drop the chips into a *sub*, or cough or sneeze and deposit chips into their mouths. The latter move they'll usually make when they're ready to go on break because in that way they don't have to talk that much with the impediment in their mouths. We must realize though that, although a chip in the mouth does impair speech, it doesn't make it impossible. People speak with food in their mouths all the time and the great Greek orator Demosthenes used to put pebbles under his tongue to better his speech.

Dealer Collaboration

Dealers can also cheat by setting up bets for an agent on the craps game. A base dealer can place two $25 chips and two $1 chips from his or her stacks next to the boxperson and call out, "Fifty-two dollars across next to me." The floorperson could be busy with a marker at the time, or could be answering a question or settling a dispute on the other side of the table. When the game is busy and many proposition bets are being thrown in, the base dealer or the stickperson can vouch

for a proposition bet that's claimed, or throw one in on their own. With this kind of assistance, the agent could walk away with thousands of dollars, if greedy, or with hundreds, if conservative. This doesn't even take into consideration overpayments, excessive change, or skipping the agent's bet when it loses.

From the stick position a dealer can cheat by setting up bets for an agent, backing up the agent when there's a claim, by working in collaboration with the base dealer, by allowing an agent to make a switch, or by personally making the switch, which is the most unlikely of all these possibilities.

The boxperson can work in collaboration with the dealers, with an agent on the game, or steal directly from the rack or from the cash that's to be deposited in the drop box. Some boxpersons have been caught with over a thousand dollars in chips in their coat pockets. They have plenty of storage room in their pockets, they have a huge bankroll in front of them, and they usually know where the supervisor is. On busy games, the dealers don't have much time to look around and notice what the boxperson is doing.

The floor supervisor doesn't have access to the money but has the power to adjust the bankroll and to justify where the money is going. Because of this power, the supervisor can work in collaboration with the boxperson to cheat the casino out of a large amount of money. Marker chips can be handed to customers and never signed for, big numbers of chips can disappear while rating cards can be written to explain where they went, and a bogus set of dice can be placed on the game with little scrutiny. On their own, supervisors can falsify rating cards and can return markers to customers without them being paid back. They can also settle disputes in favor of agents on the game and have the dealers set up bets for agents, claiming that they're transferring a bet or change from another game.

The craps table is a very vulnerable spot in the casino in need of strict controls and good supervision. The question is: *How do you protect yourself against all these possibilities?* The answer is you can't, but you can have controls in place to minimize the risk. These controls are the basis of game protection.

Dice Inspection and Handling

First of all, dice inspection is taken too lightly in most casinos because the pit manager or the gaming inspector (in the case of Puerto Rico) assume that the dice manufacturers and the casino managers are basically honest and make good enough money that they don't have to steal. Although that may be true for most people, exceptions to the rule do exist. That's the way of human nature.

So the pit manager or whoever has this assigned duty shouldn't be complacent and should do a thorough inspection of the dice, using all the equipment that's available. This equipment should include at the very minimum *a micrometer, a balance caliper (spinner),* and a *scribing tool.* The *dice square* can also be helpful, but the micrometer can pick up angle deviations also, if used properly. Since the dice are cubic, they have to be measured for height, width, and depth. At least two positions, if not more, should be measured on each side because variations of size on the same surface do occur and will affect probability. A deviation within two ten-thousandths of an inch is ideal for the three-quarter-inch cubes, although a slight deviation from this may be acceptable. Anything higher than that is bad quality control on the part of the manufacturer and should be rejected. Exactly how much of a deviation will affect probability enough to be advantageous to the cheater is hard to tell and depends upon the speed with which the cheater intends to score. The normal gauge that most conservative dice cheaters usually use is around twenty ten-thousandths of an inch.

The next tool that should be used carefully is the *balance caliper.* The balance caliper is thrown off by deviations in weight and will rattle if a big difference exists such as in a loaded die. Obviously, the heavier side is going to end up in the bottom all the time, but the main indicator is going to be the shimmy. Some supervisors get discouraged with this apparatus, because it has a tendency to come up with the same combination quite frequently. That makes them feel that the balance caliper is inaccurate, yet it is the dice that cause this problem because there's rarely a perfect die. But they're close enough to perfection that they serve the purpose they were designed for. So it is my recommendation that the balance caliper be used at all times, especially since it has been established that in a business where money is so accessible, anyone is a potential candidate for theft and cheating. Yet I want to make it clear that the majority of the people who work in the gaming business are honest, in spite of this accessibility.

Many supervisors and managers frown upon the use of the scribe to place imperceptible markings on the dice that can positively identify them. Their position is that the chance of a switch is remote in itself, and that the chance of a switch where the mechanic has an identical pair of dice is almost impossible. The mechanic would have to personally shoot the dice first, record the serial number on the dice, then leave the game to find a die maker who can duplicate the logo and number. If die-making an art copy were something only a great artist could do, I'd say the chances of this happening would be extremely remote. Even so, it wouldn't be remote enough to be impossible. However, the skill required to do this is within the abilities of any good die maker and within the ability of any commercial artist or professional engraver. It is, therefore, within the realm of possibilities and so undetectable to casual inspection that, for all we know, it may have happened many times without being noticed. Even when heavy losses occur on the game and the dice are inspected, we have noticed that most of the time the floor supervisor will do a close visual inspection and then, maybe, use the micrometer. Neither of these inspections will detect a good pair of loaded dice. Only if the job were done in a hurry and the drillings on the loaded side are too deep, or if the person doing the visual inspection knows what to look for, will the visual exam work. If you compare the depth of the loads to normal dice, you will be able to notice the difference. And an experienced hand will even notice it just by the weight.

Because *perfect dice switching* is a possibility, the casino supervisor should spend an extra minute a day to reduce the risk of this occurrence, which could be quite costly if it happened. This is a precaution that doesn't cost the casino any more money.

Once the dice have been properly inspected and scribed, the pit manager will hand them to the floor supervisors, who should be obligated to visually inspect them. The supervisors should make a mental note of the serial number and the scribe mark. If they don't have an adequate memory, they can record the serial number on their table game cards. Pit managers should later come by the game and request to see the dice that are in the bowl to make sure the dice they inspected were transferred effectively to the game. From the supervisors, the dice will be passed on to the boxpersons, who will also do a visual inspection, unless they're the ones who must do the actual dice inspection, as some places require. If that is the case, then the supervisors should make sure the boxpersons do a thorough inspection job. The dice are now ready to be put into action.

When the old dice are replaced by the new ones, the boxpersons should inspect the old ones to make sure that these were legitimate dice. The fact that nothing unusual happened shouldn't stop the supervisor from inspecting the dice. It could be that a switch was done too late in the day, or that the mechanic was unaware of the dice-changing routine, or the dice-changing routine was changed since the last time the mechanic had cased the casino, or the percentage dice weren't weighed heavy enough to make a significant difference, or the cheaters were conservative, or there was heavy betting outside of the combinations that were targeted. All these possibilities could account for a normal day at the crap game when it really wasn't. Regardless of whether it is too late to do anything about it, the casino should be aware of any breach in security such as this one. So checking the dice after they've been withdrawn is essential to the security of the casino.

Employee Behavior and Reasons for Caution

The next security item on the agenda is the behavior of the employees who run the game and their role in game protection. First, *all employees should pay strict attention to the operation of the game*. This isn't to say that I support a regimented environment where the employees aren't allowed breathing room or the opportunity to communicate with the customers in order to make them feel welcome and appreciated at the casino. Employees can pay strict attention to the game and still manage to make their job enjoyable and pleasing to the customers. Just because employees occasionally talk to customers or have short casual exchanges with other employees on the game doesn't mean that they are not aware of what is happening on the game. Human beings are capable of doing two or three things at the same time. It is up to the supervisor to use prudence in evaluating the capabilities of

employees and to know when conversation and lack of concentration are getting in the way of adequate job performance.

The posture of the employees is also important. They should stand up straight and face their work area at all times. They shouldn't be allowed to turn around or lean on one side or on one hand when performing their job tasks. This lazy appearance relays a bad image to the public and is an indication to cheaters that these employees are easy targets for scams. The stick position on the craps table is an especially vulnerable spot. This position controls the tempo of the game and safeguards its vulnerable equipment. It is also responsible for part of the supervision of the game. It is such an important position that it is surprising that in the past, and even today, some casinos have insisted on having inexperienced dealers perform this function.

When the casino opens for business, it is the stickperson who puts the dice into play. At this moment the casino is very vulnerable. A mechanic on stick could switch a pair of dice at any time from the moment they're rendered into his or her custody. For that reason, boxpersons should keep the dice in the bowl and in front of them at the center of the table until they're put into action. When they're ready to be put into action, the boxperson should watch the stickperson dump the bowl of dice onto the layout, without allowing touching of the dice. The stickperson is then going to move the dice over to the shooter, with the stick. But when the shooter has made a selection, the stickperson is going to retrieve the dice and put them into the bowl with his or her hand. This would be the stickperson's next opportunity to make the switch.

Unless the boxperson has reason to suspect the stickperson, the first responsibility is to watch for the security of the dice that are going to be put into play. This is the responsibility of the stickperson, yet it is such an important function that it can't be left to the sole responsibility of one employee, especially since many times the dealer will neglect this responsibility, and a reprimand isn't going to reverse the consequences. When the player makes the selection, the boxperson's concentration remains on the shooter although his or her peripheral vision is trained on the stickperson. Then when the shooter releases the dice, the boxperson's eyes should remain fixed on the shooter's hand. If the shot was a clear forward movement that ended with the shooter's palm exposed, the boxperson is assured that the toss was legitimate. The boxperson can then quickly change viewpoints and focus on the stickperson's hand. If no awkward or unusual movements were detected out of the corner of the boxperson's eye, the boxperson can then assume that if the grab hand of the dealer is relaxed and apparently empty, chances are that a switch didn't occur. The grab hand should always be the one closest to the shooter so that the stickperson's body doesn't have to turn as much to retrieve the dice. At the same time, the grab hand remains closer to the boxperson's field of vision when the shooter has the dice.

If instead of a clear toss, the shooter uses a suspicious back and forward motion or a palms down ending to the throw, the shoot is questionable. Unfortunately, some legitimate players use a back and forward movement, and there are also those who end up with their palms down. The first thing that has to be done in this case is to stay with the shooter. The boxperson doesn't bother to verify the call of the dice but instead watches the shooter to see what is going to be done with that closed hand. Until that hand is open, the question will still remain. If the closed hand leaves the table and is placed out of sight of the boxperson, the question is going to remain, and the answers are going to have to be sought elsewhere.

We can't request that the player open the hand, so the first thing the boxperson has to do is request that the stickperson square the dice in front of him or her and parallel to the bankroll. With the dice squared and slightly separate so that the boxperson can see the inside numbers, the stickperson can turn them over slowly with the stick, at least twice. At the end of the procedure it is also helpful to slightly push the stick through the middle of the two dice so that they end up in a two-diamond formation in front of the boxperson. This allows the boxperson to see all sides of the dice except for the bottom, which should have been seen clearly when the stickperson began the turning procedure. Remember that the mirrors will show the backside of the dice. This procedure should be a standard safety measure after every come out roll.

In normal circumstances, the turn procedure lets the boxperson see all the numbers on the dice, that the edges are in good shape, and the logo and serial number are present on the dice. In the above case, where there's a possibility of a switch, a closer inspection is needed. The boxperson then takes the dice off the layout and takes a closer look at them. The object is to see if some spots are deeper than others, if they're all too deep, or if one side of the die is smaller than the rest. The latter can be checked by placing the dice next to each other and rotating one of the dice on all its sides. If the dice pass this inspection, they should be all right, yet there's still a small possibility that it is a very good load job and these dice have been designed for a slow gain. After putting the dice back into action, the boxperson should look to see if there's a player on the game who is betting heavily. If so, the betting pattern of the player should be followed so it can serve as a frame of reference later on.

The description of both the shooter and this player should be fixed in the boxperson's mind in case he or she later has to identify them. If the rest of the day's action continues in a normal pattern and there doesn't seem to be a connection between the shooter and the heavy betting player, the boxperson has nothing to worry about. However, if the heavy betting player only increases bets when this shooter has the dice and betting pattern changes accordingly, there still might be something to worry about, especially if the heavy bettor is winning a substantial amount. If a connection can be made, the supervisor should be informed, who should then inform the pit manager, who'll alert surveillance.

Of course, there are quite a few different types of gaffed dice that the casino and the boxperson should be on the alert for and possibly many others that are in the process of being invented or in the creative process of somebody's mind. There's another type of dice that deserve to be mentioned and they're the *magnetic dice*. These are switched into the game by one mechanic while another operates a gadget that affects the roll. This gadget is usually worn around the waistline, and the telltale symptom here is basically the same as in computer tracking with cards; the operator acts suspiciously while operating the device on the table.

Much in the same way, the stickperson watches the release of the dice. If they have reason to suspect the throw, they'll watch to make sure the shooter's hand is empty. If the shooter's hand movement is suspicious, the dealer can ask the base dealer to make the call of the dice and continue to observe the shooter. If still in doubt, the dealer will ask the boxperson to take a closer look at the dice. This is something that seems obvious from our point of view, yet I find that a great number of dealers fail to do this. In fact, if I had to guess, I would say that the majority of dealers don't watch the shooter's hand on every release of the dice. Many supervisors and managers don't enforce this procedure. The reason they don't is that most of them don't believe anything is going to happen. I say, *"It is going to happen,"* and it is going to happen when you least expect it. To ignore the possibility is an invitation to the cheater.

Dealing Procedures

The next procedures that need to be mentioned are the proper use of hands on the crap game. As dealers stand on the base position, they have one hand that faces the boxperson and one hand that faces one of the extremities of the game. The hand that faces the boxperson and the center of the game is the inside hand, the other hand is the outside hand. The use of the inside hand limits the visibility of the boxperson because the dealer's body shields part of the view field while the arm and the hand itself will also obstruct the view. For this reason, the dealer should not be allowed to hand off any change or payoffs with the inside hand. The dealer can make mistakes or purposeful overpayments that may escape the boxperson's scrutiny or that may end up in the customer's rack by the time the boxperson is aware of what actually happened. This always makes for an awkward situation and can be the subject of a heated argument.

Change transactions, markers, and payoffs other than the pass, don't pass line, and the field should all be laid out in the come line before being handed off to the player. This allows the boxperson sufficient time to make a correction if needed. Change transactions, markers, proposition bet payoffs and most payoffs are to be cut out in the come line with the inside hand. The inside hand is then lifted to allow the boxperson to make a visual inspection of the amount of money there. For the most part this is just a split second except when large change sums or markers are involved. Some payoffs will require the use of both hands, but again, the boxperson has to have a clear visual field of the payoff at some time before the bet is handed off, and the bet is to be handed off by the outside hand. Only in one instance is the inside hand acceptable, and that is when

handing off to the player who is standing next to the stickperson, yet it still might be preferable to use the outside hand.

This is a problem that Puerto Rico supervisors have had to contend with for some time. Puerto Rico crap dealers take great pride in their ability to drop-cut chips and will use drop-cutting whenever they can. This may seem to speed up the game, but when a supervisor has to stop the action of the game to ask for the return of an incorrect payoff, or one that seemed incorrect, the possible gain is lost. Worse yet, the boxperson may be reluctant to ask the customer for the money, or may be unsure of a payoff and lets it go because of not wanting to hold the game up or feeling embarrassed to have figured it out a bit late. Cutting out the payoff in the come area gives the boxperson enough time to figure out any difficult payoff and to correct a mistake before it gets to the customer's hand. In terms of the speed of the game, there doesn't seem to be any difference in spite of the cutting procedures. Whenever possible, dealers should size into bets. This makes the payoff very clear.

The dealer and the boxperson should both be aware of two blind spots on the layout. One is next to the stickperson, and the other is next to the base dealer. These are prime spots for past posting. This can occur on the pass line, the don't pass, the don't come, and the field. It can even happen in the come line with a dealer who isn't alert. Not only are these locations vulnerable for past posting, but they're also prime locations for a free ride. The don't come and the don't pass should be scanned regularly because these are the most popular locations. The boxperson should be especially careful about the spots next to the dealer because of limited visibility of this area in which a good view is possible only through the mirrors. The dealer could easily place a bet there at any time.

When paying the pass line or the don't pass, the boxperson should make sure that the dealer pays the first bet with the outside hand and that all bets are sized into unless a total payoff of the flat bet and the odds is clear enough for everyone to understand. A verbal explanation of the total should be made to the customer since the customer may not understand what is being paid, and this could delay the game if an argument occurs. These explanations should be standard procedure whenever a complicated payoff is being made to a customer. It leaves no doubt in the customer's mind of fair treatment. When odds bets are stacked over five chips, these should be broken down for clarity. If the same color is going to be used for the payoff, the most efficient way to make this payoff is to size into the bet, cut that portion of the payoff in half, and size into that half one more time for the point five and nine, or place the extra portion of the payoff on the side for the point six and eight. Doing it this way saves one move. Never allow the dealer to break down the bet with the hand that has the same color chips in it. This would allow adding chips to that bet.

As I mentioned before, having the dealers repeat their bets is a good measure of game protection. It adds clarity to the game and avoids unnecessary claims. It also discourages potential cheaters from taking shots on the game and allows the boxperson to know what's happening at all times. *Booking bets makes dealers responsible for them.* Bets should be repeated exactly the way the customer requests them, except when clarification is needed. The bet should be repeated in a tone of voice that allows the supervisor and anyone passing by the game to hear it. It should be spoken clearly, identifying the bet, the amount being bet, and the location of the customer who's making the bet. If the money used to make the bet requires change, the chips or cash handed to the dealer are deposited in front of the boxperson for verification. The bet is called out and is said to be taken out of the money that's given to the dealer. If the number of chips given to the dealer is exactly what the dealer requires to set the bet up, the dealers will use the expression, *"using player's money."* Most New Jersey dealers have been trained this way and will book bets this way. In Nevada and Puerto Rico dealers haven't been required to be this precise with their booking of bets and, when asked to do so, offer resistance. The safety of the game, however, is better served by this precision, which will avoid unnecessary and costly surprises to the supervisors and the casino. Booking bets properly is a courtesy and responsibility the dealers owe both to the customers and to the casino, so supervisors shouldn't be reluctant to require them to do it appropriately.

When making change or placing bets for customers, dealers should never be allowed to take the money out of the customer's hand or out of the cus-tomer's rack. The only exception to this rule would be in the case of someone whose incapacity prevents the performing of this function such as a blind person or a person whose arms are handicapped. Change transactions must go directly to the boxperson and should be verbalized clearly.

The Safety of the Bankroll

The safety of the bankroll is a responsibility that the boxperson shares with the supervisor. The action of the crap game is going to determine which part of the bankroll is going to be used at any given time. If customers are betting $1 and $5 chips, there's no need for dealers to have a stack of $25 chips in front of them. Once the action starts to increase on the game and there's a need for the $25 chips, the dealer may be allowed to access these chips. However, if the action subsides, the boxperson should remove the stack of $25 chips. When using $100 chips and above, they should be accounted for entirely and should be put out by the boxperson only. Boxpersons should know what the total count of their $100 chips is, and should keep a running count of whatever number of chips they put out for the dealer. They should know at all times which customer has these chips and how many. In games where the overwhelming action makes it impossible for boxpersons to know exactly where each chip went, they should be able to keep track of almost all of them and have a pretty good idea where the rest of them went.

Supervisors have a written inventory of the bankroll, with total counts for chip denominations $25 and above. They must adjust those counts as the action of the game depletes the bankroll. Rating cards should reflect the fluctuation in the bankroll, even though a normal depletion is expected. Pit managers are going to want to know who took the money off a game, especially on a game that is losing. This is one way the pit manager knows if the supervisor is doing the job. Of course, floor supervisors will falsify rating cards from time to time or inflate the winnings or losses of other rating cards to justify themselves when they really don't know where the money went. *This is the main reason casino statistical studies show that rated play has a very low hold percentage.* Pit managers should stay on top of supervisors to make sure the information they're getting is accurate.

ROULETTE

Past Posting

A roulette table is larger than a blackjack table, and in addition to this the wheel head is at the extreme opposite of the end of the betting layout. This makes it difficult for a dealer looking at the roulette wheel straight on to see the whole layout. It makes the dealer especially vulnerable at the bottom three columns. This area of the layout is a favorite location for past posting. This can occur, most likely with a dealer who doesn't pay much attention to the layout. Cheaters can actually use diversionary moves to place their past posted bets, especially when they're sitting or standing opposite each other. When the dealer gets dubious about one player, that player will stand up and move suspiciously toward the layout while the other makes a move. Players can also past post knowing their late bets will be removed; however, they will have placed team players' checks under theirs, which in all probability will remain on the number after the bet is removed.

Diversions can be made in many different ways, and the objective is always the same, to draw the dealer's attention away from where the move is being made.

The Computer

The computer age has also played a part in roulette cheating. Although not as accurate as blackjack computers, roulette computers do exist that attempt to predict in what sections of the layout the roulette ball will fall. The cheater must clock the speed of the ball and the speed of the wheel. The computer can then determine the most probable landing section for the ball. The design of the roulette wheel doesn't make this easy since there are obstacles called breakers in the way of the ball's path. Approximately 25 percent of the time the ball sneaks through these obstacles and falls in the general vicinity the computer has mapped out. This knowledge alone would give the player considerable advantage at the wheels were it not for the technical difficulties computer users have encountered. The main problem is that the operator must get as close to the wheel head as possible. A person constantly standing by the wheel head making suspicious moves is definitely going to draw attention and will probably get caught. A cowboy hat with a camera in it has been used for this purpose. A gem in the center of the hat is the lens. It is against the law in Nevada and other states to use electronic devices in a casino. Yet even though there are difficulties for the computer cheat, we shouldn't get complacent because a better system is bound to be developed, if it already hasn't been.

Gaffed Wheels

Illegal operations have been known to use electromagnetic fields to alter the natural trajectory of the roulette ball, as well as pins to trip it and direct it to a desired location. I doubt that any legitimate operation would use such equipment, since the casino's existence depends on its honesty. Besides, the edge in roulette is so great, they really don't have to. There does exist a device that is powered by electromagnetic energy capable of altering the natural spin of the ball and which depends on the possibility of introducing a gaffed ball into the game. This particular device is very sophisticated and costs around $20,000. Because of its cost, we don't expect this to be a widespread cheating method; however, it is a natural conclusion that the stakes are going to be high when it is in use, and this presents a great risk to the operation.

When the number receptacles are loose or separated from their base so as to provide cushion for the ball when it lands, this action is going to allow that number to come more often than probability. This action, intentionally or unintentionally will affect probability and the integrity of the game. Also, roulette cheats have designed a hollow section of the wheel which they insert over the number receptacles so as to blend in with the wheel. This unit is made out of lead and has the same cushion effect that a loose receptacle would have.

One thing to keep in mind is that, in roulette, as in any other game, when something out of the ordinary happens, we have to keep an open mind and an open eye. Unusual winning streaks, unusual betting patterns, and unusual movements by the wheel or the ball all deserve a closer look and analysis. If a ball all of a sudden loses momentum and drops, we have to ask ourselves, why? If a player watches the wheel or the dealer with intensity, we have to take a closer look. Cheaters and thieves are always going to be a step ahead of the game. The only way we can catch up is to be suspicious, to doubt everyone and everything. But I want to emphasize that to be suspicious doesn't mean that we sweat the games or that we draw unfounded conclusions.

The Spin Skill

The dealer can affect the outcome of roulette in various ways. Some of them I have already mentioned when relating to other games, yet there are others that are peculiar to roulette. One way commonly used by roulette dealers with agents is the marker or dolly drop. The dealer places either nonvalue chips or regular chips under the marker and places the chips and the marker on the winning number. This is a very simple move that can only be detected if the supervisor has assessed the winning number before it is marked or he or she catches the dealer setting up the dolly.

Another move involves the ball drop. An agent on the game sits or stands close to the wheel head and gets up to place a bet just as the ball is about to drop. The agent's body blocks the view of the wheel while the dealer places the ball on the desired number. The agent is also on the lookout for the supervisor and won't make the move unless the supervisor's attention is elsewhere.

The final maneuver is the subject of a lot of speculation and is believed by most experts to be ineffective, the most prominent of whom was the late John Scarne. It involves the dealer's accuracy in purposely placing the ball in a given section.

Many old-time dealers will swear to it, and still many others will swear they know someone who can do it. We have known many of these dealers, yet are still to see anyone throw sections with accuracy. However, we can't infer from this that it is impossible to cheat this way since, to be able to do it, all the dealer would have to do is to alter probability by just a couple of trials. If, for example, the probability of hitting a six number section on a thirty-eight number layout is 15.8 percent, or one in six and a third times, and the dealer is able to hit it one in five, an agent for the dealer would have a whopping 20 percent advantage. At a table where a conservative forty spins an hour are being dealt, with an average bet of $30, the player would make $960 in four hours. If the player bets $25 per number he or she now has winnings in the amount of $4,800. After twelve hours of play, he or she can call it a night at $14,400. Even if you suspect that something is wrong, it would be hard to prove.

Charts can be designed to record the position of the numbers that are thrown, to see if they are landing more prevalently in any given section. One such chart has been designed by Jerry Tobish, who is at this writing Director of Surveillance for the Isle of Capri in Lake Charles, Louisiana. If we notice a pattern, we can then review the tape to see if the dealer is purposely setting the wheel speed at a constant and delivers the ball at constant speed from the same guide point number every time. If those conditions exist, we can present a case for cheating. Whether we can prove it or not in court is a different matter altogether.

This is the kind of proposition that requires an open mind. Previously when I said that the computer's job was made difficult by the breakers on the wheel, I accepted that one out of four times the ball sneaks through. This would give the dealer only a 25 percent chance of hitting the target, assuming it could be done every time. Those aren't very good odds, but still would allow for the possibility of obtaining an advantage. However, let's assume that the dealer is talented enough to also figure out where the displaced shots will end up. The agent has to cover more numbers, but still manages to beat probability and make a profit. What if the dealer has the wheel's rhythm down so well as to be able to slip through the breakers two out of four or three out of four times?

We have to admit that the level of difficulty for such a feat has to be incredibly high, yet haven't we seen exceptional human beings defy incredible odds before? The average person can't shoot a basket from three-point range at a basketball court, yet there are some people who can do it at better than 50 percent. The average person can't bank a shot on a pool table, yet there are people who can do it almost all the time, some of the shots involving multiple banks. Dealers who claim to be able to throw sections say they can maintain a constant speed of the wheel and that by using a point of reference on the wheel they can spin the ball to die down at approximately the same place on the wheel, *all the time*. Whether this is true or not, we doubt we will ever be able to verify it, at least not on a voluntary basis. Since it's impossible for us to certify this one way or another, we do want to remind the reader that almost anything is possible. *Our best advice is to always keep an open mind and to expect the unexpected.* If you believe what is happening on the game is unusual and doesn't feel right, follow it through. If you think the dealer is doing something out of the ordinary, document it and keep an eye on him or her. Who knows? Maybe some day we'll be able to know with certainty if this is a myth or if in fact this is another human talent. Yet either way, we know that roulette computer developers believe it.

Protecting Roulette

So how do we protect roulette against all this? First of all, we watch our games and closely observe the players and the dealers. We make sure that the dealers are doing their jobs properly, following procedures to the letter and intent. Dealers should be positioned as far back as possible so as to have a broader perspective of the game. They should be facing the layout at all times, should call "no more bets" a couple of rotations before the ball falls, and should be on the alert for any movements thereafter. The call for "no more bets" should be accompanied by hand signals, palms down and parallel to the surface of the table so there's no misunderstanding as to the finality of the call. Dealers should maintain their face-forward pose as the ball lands, and catch the number with a quick eye movement. Of further aid to the dealer is to visually survey the layout, paying close attention to the outside bets, especially the three columns at the bottom of the layout. Dealers should be adamant in preventing customers from making wagers while they are still paying off bets. All payoffs and transactions on the layout should be clearly verbalized and any transaction or payoff of over $100 should require the authorization of the supervisor.

The supervisor should make a habit of verifying the call with the payoff and watching the periphery of the layout closely.

The supervisor should regularly look at the crowd and not permit anyone to lean on the glass around the wheel head. Anyone lingering by the glass should be observed closely. Watch for suspicious movements, suspicious attire (anything that could be a lens), and for body language directed at someone on the table. If for any reason you should become suspicious, don't appear obvious. Move around, pretend to be busy with paperwork or talking to someone else. Remain calm and notify your pit manager, who will notify surveillance and the suspect will be put on camera.

BACCARAT

Throughout history, the game of baccarat has been the scene of some very interesting scams. Because of the high volume of play in baccarat and because baccarat shoes have eight decks, a scam in baccarat can be particularly dangerous. It is no wonder that most baccarat games have three dealers and two supervisors. Yet even with this many employees, casinos have been hit with scams. The reason is that there are some very talented cheaters out there and, after a while, the game becomes a boring routine to employees who don't give the game as much attention as they should.

The Equipment

In any game where the players are allowed to manipulate the cards, the casino's level of vulnerability is going to increase. In baccarat, not only do the players manipulate the cards, they also manipulate the shoe. Because of this, the casino is twice as vulnerable. The obvious thing to watch out for is the marking of cards (this would apply to casinos that don't replace them after every shoe). Where the cards aren't replaced after every shoe, the player is going to have multiple opportunities to crimp them, scratch them, and daub them. As in blackjack, another thing to watch out for is card switching or hand mucking. This could happen as the cards are being plucked out of the shoe or when the player gets to view his cards. With the amount of time some players take to view their cards, even a gutsy amateur would be able to palm cards and perform a switch. It is reported that sometimes only two shoes have been dealt in an eight-hour shift in busy luxury mega-resorts. This allows ample time to get on any scam.

Even when casinos change cards after every shoe, because of the high volume of play on baccarat games, some pit and shift managers fear that there's always the possibility that somewhere along the way, someone may have introduced marked cards. There are, of course, many controls in place in most operations to prevent this from happening, yet as we all know, when it comes to scamming large sums of money, the mind of the thief can be very creative. In places where the action leaps into million-dollar figures, the incentive for a scam is unquestionable.

In the movie *Indecent Proposal*, the vulnerability of the human spirit to extreme monetary temptations is graphically exposed when a couple prostitutes themselves for the sake of a great reward. People all over were asking themselves: *Would I do that . . . for a million dollars?* The truth is that many people will answer yes to this question.

It is, therefore, conceivable that the previously mentioned scenario that troubles some casino operators has validity. We then have no choice but to consider it a possibility; thinking that somehow from the manufacturer to the game, someone has altered the playing cards.

A holdout shoe could also be used in baccarat just as in blackjack, yet more than one person would have to be involved in the scam. This would be a very daring move, but not inconceivable.

Slugs and Coolers

What we do know for sure is that slugs and coolers have been introduced into baccarat games. In 1989, a slug was introduced into a baccarat game at Trump's Castle in Atlantic City. A dealer placed the slug at the top of the decks and then acted in unison with an agent to facilitate a false cut. The slug was part of the cards the dealer was supposed to use to lace the deck. It is because of this that Mirage Resorts no longer allows dealers to lace the baccarat decks. It is a shame that this measure was necessary since the act of lacing the decks in baccarat contributed to the sophisticated flare of the game and required a certain amount of dexterity on the part of the dealer.

With four or five people on the game, the chances of introducing a cooler or replacing the shoe are very slim. A major disturbance or some extraordinary circumstance would have to occur. However, unusual things do happen on games that will draw a lot of attention. Fist fights are one of them, a fainting person another. The one that ranked among the highest occurred at the Claridge in 1982. A well-endowed southern belle kept lifting her blouse at one of the crap tables, exposing her voluminous breasts. All eyes on that table, including pit personnel, were centered upon her, every time she did it. The woman in question, obviously, had had a little too much to drink, and nothing illegal (at least not to our knowledge) occurred on that game. But it sure was one hell of an opportunity, the kind of opportunity that allows for anything to happen. Again, if more than one person is involved, then it is a lot easier.

Card Counting

In blackjack, you saw how card counters have made a living on the blackjack tables with their trade. In baccarat, although card counting is possible, no one really takes it seriously because the few systems in existence are either too complex or the possible advantages are minimal. In fact, Peter Griffin states that, with the aid of a computer and a very large bankroll which would allow the player to make $1,000 wagers, the player could achieve an advantage of 2 percent for one bet in a shoe. So the gain would be $20 for about one hour of work. In the meantime, that advantage would be lost to the bets that would have to be made in order to remain on the game.

For example, a plus minus system in existence plays a whole shoe to make a tie bet. Assume that the player has been counting down a shoe and that the last hand is about to come out. There are fourteen cards behind the cut card and a maximum possible six cards for the last hand. Let's say that the running count at that time is plus ten. This means that 50 percent of the cards remaining are ten value cards. At first sight it would seem there's a pretty good chance that a zero-to-zero tie can happen, since the six ten value cards required for this are available, with four to spare. That is the whole basis for this system. But a closer inspection shows us that the chance of one ten value card coming out would be one in two; two consecutive ten value cards would be a little less than one in four (23.7 percent); three consecutive ten value cards would be less than one in nine (10.5 percent), and we still have three more cards to go before we can tie. Since tie bets in most places pay 8 to 1, whoever invented this system either didn't bother to figure this out or wasn't very good at math. Even if we believe the remaining cards can contribute to a tie, if we assume all other permutations to be random, the probability of a tie should not increase.

The fact that this system and most baccarat systems aren't effective doesn't preclude someone from developing a system that *is* functional and effective. Like blackjack, baccarat uses a depleting resource and is therefore subject to probability changes through the shoe. This in itself is a sufficient reason to exercise caution and to keep an open mind toward future developments. However, even in this instance the general drawbacks to card counting would apply. The only way to shield ourselves is to stay alert and to maintain open lines of communication with the gaming world. *Never assume the impossibility of any cheating or counting method until extensive analysis and research have been conducted.*

Protecting the Game

The best way to protect the game of baccarat is to carefully inspect the cards on both sides. Watch the shuffles carefully and make sure the dealer shows an even riffle and plenty of stripping before offering the cards for the cut. Preferably, the dealers should leave the cards laced (intertwined) until a supervisor has had the opportunity to examine the riffle and authorize the cut. The dealer can then push in the intertwined cards to even them out and offer the cut. Make sure that the cut is deep and not superficial; preferably at least one deck should be cut. Once the cards have been secured in the shoe, we must never lose sight of the shoe. When not in use, it should be brought to the center of the table and carefully guarded. At no time should the shoe's face plate point anywhere other than forward toward the operators of the game. Don't allow players to over-handle the shoe and to use any device that may leave markings on the cards. Where wagers are allowed (although they shouldn't be) before cards have been exposed, yet after they have been drawn from the shoe, make sure that the shoe operator isn't flashing the cards as they come out of the shoe. Remember, the player doesn't have to lift the card that much to expose it. This is one of the reasons most casinos won't allow players to make wagers after the first card has come out.

When the player handles the cards, make sure that he or she only uses one hand and watch that hand carefully. Before placing the cards in the discard bucket, make sure the dealer does a quick inspection of the back of the cards. Another thing you want to watch out for is that the cards are delivered in the proper order. This not only prevents disputes, it insures that cards aren't being rearranged after being identified by cheaters. Always be on the lookout for suspicious behavior on the game and suspicious-looking people. People with tinted glasses can be suspicious if actions on the game seem unusual. Take a closer look and try to notice how carefully that person watches the cards. Remember also that shiny objects can be used to read barely exposed cards on the layout. Finally, if you have any doubts, have surveillance review game tapes and have the cards carefully inspected after the game is concluded. Never be afraid or ashamed to exercise caution. You may be ridiculed, but you're providing an invaluable service to your company.

PART IV

OTHER DEPARTMENTS

CHAPTER 12

THE SLOT DEPARTMENT

This is a satellite department that used to be held in very low esteem, yet the power of its income production has made this department soar into prominence. Although it is under the control of the casino manager, who has only limited knowledge of it, it has caught the attention of casino operators who now realize that without this department they can't survive. In some casinos such as those in Colorado where gaming space is so limited, the slot operation *is* the casino. Table games are mere adornments and, frankly, in some instances, in the way. However, it is fair to say that, due to the low limits required in the state of Colorado, the table games are in an unfair competition with the slot operation. Nevertheless, it is undeniable that with almost a 2 to 1 comparative ratio where income is concerned, the slot department has risen prominently above the table games.

The above fact is going to be of increasing importance in the years to come. Competent slot personnel will become scarce and, inevitably, a power play between slot managers and table game managers will come to a head despite the peace that seems to exist between them at this time. Ironically, slot managers and slot shift managers are always subject to the table games management approval, and these managers can't authorize their own high jackpot payoffs even though they're more qualified to do so than the management of table games.

When we look at the slot operation, what we immediately see is a relatively low cost enterprise if we compare it to the table games. We have one director who oversees the operation and responds directly to the casino manager or the general manager, the shift managers who respond to the director, the slot supervisors who all answer to the shift managers and director, and the slot attendants who are under the supervision of the slot supervisors. Change personnel can either be under the supervision of the slot department or the cage. In most places they're part of the slot department and are under the supervision of the slot supervisors and shift managers. It is also important to note that there can be various categories of slot supervisors depending on the size and gaming philosophy of the casino. Also, there are going to be slot technicians that can be divided into mechanics or video technicians. One repairs mechanical machines, the other works with video boards.

SLOT DIRECTOR

The slot manager or director oversees the slot operation. This executive directly supervises the slot shift managers and makes the ultimate disciplinary decisions regarding the personnel of the slot department. Jackpots over a certain amount of money, usually between $5,000 and $10,000, are authorized by this executive up to a pre-established cap that requires the signature of the casino manager or the general manager. This cap is usually around $25,000 to $50,000. Aside from these functions, the slot manager sets hold percentages, trains personnel, submits budgeting, marketing, and operational plans for the department, and reviews those that are presented by the marketing department or the corporate office.

It is also the function of the slot manager to review a myriad of reports and compile them in a meaningful order. These reports will be full of statistical data that are used as indicators of the proper functioning of the department. For example, one of the reports to be analyzed by the slot managers is the report that singles out the losing machines. If this losing pattern has been consistent for a reasonable period of time, the manager will request that tests be conducted on these machines to determine their proper functioning. It is understood that in normal circumstances fluctuations will occur and that they're part of the probability distribution. However, there are instances where these fluctuations aren't the product of randomness and that a faulty chip, program, meter, or diverter gets the blame for the inconsistency. In that case the malfunctioning part will be replaced so that the machine can return to its proper functioning and profitability. This is the task that is given to the slot technicians when a pattern of losing occurs.

Other considerations that have to be addressed by the slot manager are whether or not to replace, update, or exchange the existing equipment. We must understand that, in an increasingly competitive environment, the advances in slot machine technology appear in leaps and bounds. Every year growing numbers of different games and slot-related equipment hit the market and must be looked at because these developments can be used by the competition to achieve an advantage in the marketplace.

In recent years, machine technology has seen the advent of touch screen video machines, a variety of bill validators, a variety of video games, a variety of tracking devices, change machines, and much more. The analysis of these advances and their applicability to the gaming operation are the concern of the slot manager. Only by keeping abreast of all these new developments can the slot manager maintain the required level of competence in this increasingly competitive environment.

SLOT SHIFT MANAGERS

The slot shift managers are the extension of the slot manager on the casino floor. They're usually authorized to sign jackpots between $5,000 and $10,000. They're required to inspect all jackpots for legitimacy and to handle hopper fills. Slot attendants and technicians are also under the supervision of the slot shift manager and, in many instances, so are the change cashiers. When irregularities or inconsistencies are found by slot managers, they will advise the slot shift managers and will entrust them with the testing and inspection of suspect machines as well as suspect personnel. The slot shift managers rely on technicians to assist them in testing suspect machines, and then they make a report of their findings.

Slot shift managers also help monitor the performance of the machines and are usually allocated computer systems to aid them in this function. Two common systems that are used to monitor machine progress are the EDT (now IGT) and the SDS. These systems monitor all performance of the machines and track the slot drop process.

SLOT TECH MANAGER

This executive usually plays a double role, acting as a slot shift manager and as the direct supervisor over the slot technicians. Like the slot shift managers, the slot tech manager monitors the performance of the machines and brings to the attention of the slot manager those that aren't performing at expected hold percentages. Again, I must clarify that slot machine hold percentages can and will vary constantly, yet their fluctuations are expected to follow a tighter pattern than the table games. If a machine program is set to pay off 90 percent, which means that it retains 10 percent, a payoff of 87 percent or 93 percent is acceptable. After an extended period of time, say one year, the payoff schedule will be close to that 90 percent expected. However, if the machine is paying off at a rate of 98 percent or over 100 percent, the machine is then suspect. It is the slot tech manager's function to bring this to the attention of the slot manager and assign a technician to run tests, find the fault, and make a report on the findings.

Scheduling maintenance schedules on the machines is another function of the slot tech manager. Like any other piece of machinery, slot machines are going to require maintenance in order to function properly. They will also break down and will have to be scheduled for repair or substitution. All these fall under the duties of the slot tech manager. Ordering and maintaining a supply of replacement parts for the machinery are also functions of the slot tech manager. It is costly to the slot operation if a part for a machine is unavailable, and the machine has to be put out of commission. In Mississippi, where slot machines were averaging $300 a day in revenue, a two-week wait for a part would be the equivalent in revenue lost to the cost of the machine.

SLOT ATTENDANTS

The slot attendant, also called slot floorperson, is the casino's main link to the slot players. It is because of this that a personable individual must be chosen for this function. In some places this individual is also considered a slot host, even though in busy operations this employee works hard and has little time to be a host. If you've been to a casino and noticed many lights blinking, bells ringing, and the top light of the slot machines lit, you've been to a casino that is very busy and probably is short on slot attendants. The slot attendant travels from one blinking light to another to assess the different problems that have occurred at the machines and for which people are awaiting service. Problems at the slot machines can be jammed coins, jammed hoppers, failure to pay out, insufficient payouts, a tilted machine, and so on. This employee also assists in jackpots, fills, and even change. In some places, due to the shortage of personnel, he or she may be required to give out change.

SLOT TECHNICIANS

As I mentioned before, there are two kinds of slot technicians: one who is a mechanic and deals with mechanical machines and mechanical moving parts, and one who is a video technician and deals with video games and program boards. The technicians are invaluable to the casino operation; they not only keep the machines in working order, they also make recommendations and implement changes concerning the machine when necessary.

CHANGE PERSONS

Where change machines and bill validators don't exist, change persons represent the front line of the slot operation and are possibly its greatest asset. In fact, when making the decision on whether or not to purchase bill validators or change machines, slot managers are faced with the dilemma of sacrificing customer service and relations for efficiency. These aren't easy choices. In an ideal world both objectives can be achieved but, as some busy operations have found out, it sometimes is difficult to get change out to customers even with adequate personnel. Crowded conditions make giving out change difficult. If you add to that the insistence of some operators on using archaic formulas to determine how many change personnel to employ for a specified number of machines, you find yourself with inadequate human resources at your disposition. This is the mistake a Mississippi casino made upon opening. It didn't hire enough personnel, and on top of that they paid meager wages that didn't inspire anyone to perform the demanding job. They had to hire constantly to compensate for a heavy turnover.

So that's why bill validators and change machines came to be. They don't get sick, they're never late, and they don't complain. Very efficient. But they don't say, *"Hello, how are you?"* in a friendly tone. They don't say, *"Good luck!"* and they don't give you a friendly smile or shake your hand and congratulate you when you win. These are all the things that people look for. People want to experience things, but they want to share them with someone. People *need* to share them with someone. So maybe a combination of both efficiency and customer relations is the answer.

The change person is the one who walks the casino floor with a coin pouch strapped around the body, strolls a change cart around the floor, or stands in a change booth somewhere on the floor. The change person works out of an imprest bank and is accountable to it at the end of the day.

THE SLOT OPERATION

Casino Cage Transactions

Currency and chips must be sent to the casino cage by locked box. The slot department buy sheet is usually a three-part form. The yellow and pink will accompany the money in transit while the white copy is retained by the carousel attendant. A buy sheet is originated by the attendant for each transaction from the cage with the following information being recorded on the buy sheet:

A. Carousel number.
B. Listing of all items being turned in.
C. A total.
D. A list of all items being exchanged.
E. A total.
F. Date and shift.
G. The carousel attendant's signature.
H. The floorperson's signature.

An adding machine tape is prepared listing each separate item of the turn-in with a total figure, followed by a list of each separate item being exchanged for a total figure. This adding machine tape is stapled

to the top left corner of the original buy sheet. The yellow and pink copy of the buy sheet and the locked box are given to the supervisor who will perform the transaction. The cage will open the locked box, count the contents, and announce their totals against the buy sheet figures. If there's an error, the entire contents are placed back into the box, locked by the casino cage, and returned to the attendant for correction or verification. If there's agreement, the transaction is completed by the casino cage and the supervisor, and a security officer then returns the locked box to the carousel. Using the attendant's copy of the buy sheet, the attendant will verify all items (credit slips, money, etc.) as being returned as requested. He or she will then sign the yellow copy of the buy sheet as a completed transaction. The yellow copy will be given to the supervisor, and the white copy will be retained by the carousel attendant. The supervisor will deposit the yellow copy in a locked box.

Coin Room Buys

A buy sheet is originated by the carousel attendant for each buy from the coin room, with the following information:

A. Carousel number.
B. Accumulated credit slips.
C. A total.
D. A list of all items being bought.
E. A total.
F. Date and shift.
G. Carousel attendant's signature.

An adding machine tape is prepared listing all accumulated credit slips, with a total figure, followed by a listing of each separate item being bought with a total figure. This adding machine tape is stapled to the left corner of the original buy sheet. Coin room personnel will pick up the buy sheet on the graveyard shift. The yellow copy is given to the coin room personnel, while the white copy is retained by the attendant. Coin room buy will be made with credit slips only. When the coin room personnel returns with the coins, the attendant will use his or her copy of the buy sheet to verify that the transaction was correct as originally ordered, and then will sign all copies of the buy sheet. The pink copy will be given to the cage, the yellow will be given to the coin room, and the white copy will be retained by the carousel attendant.

Carousel Operation

Each carousel attendant is assigned to work an individual carousel. No one other than the assigned attendant is allowed access to the carousel, except during supervisory countdowns or during the restocking of money, both of which are done in the attendant's presence. The attendant is required to verify the correct total of money upon checking in and upon checking out. He or she is also required to have the signature of a relieving person in the slot department countdown sheet.

The carousel to which the attendant is assigned will have a fixed dollar value. The attendant will be held accountable for these funds during the shift. If, at the end of the attendant's shift, he or she is over or short of this fixed dollar value, the casino's procedures for overages and shortages will be followed.

The attendant is always expected to keep the carousel neat and orderly, as this will avoid confusion when preparing a buy, performing a supervisory countdown, or checking out. Paper money should be kept so that all bills of the same denomination are together and facing the same way. The attendant must record his or her name, department, carousel number, and date on the strap. All paper bills will be strapped or clipped together in accordance with basic cashier procedures. The table below shows these groupings.

Denomination	Clip	Strap
$1.00	$25.00	$100.00
$5.00	$100.00	$500.00
$10.00	$250.00	$1,000.00
$20.00	$500.00	$2,000.00
$50.00	$1,000.00	$5,000.00
$100.00	$2,500.00	$10,000.00

Carousel attendants are expected to sell all denominations of rolled coin and mustn't break rolled coins for a customer. Rather, the roll should be handed unbroken to the customer. Loose coins will be provided by customer cash outs and will aid the attendant in performing his or her job satisfactorily. Most operators instruct their carousel attendants to remain in their positions even when observing a large machine payout. They believe that rushing over with a rack or cup is interpreted by many guests as a form of hustling for tips, which guests resent. It is always preferable to wait until the guest requests a rack and then provide one for him.

Another thing a carousel attendant should avoid is accepting hand-rolled coins from guests. If the guest makes such a request, the attendant should give directions to the nearest change booth or cashier's cage for service. Carousel attendants should not be permitted to hang over the top of the machines since this displays a lazy and intrusive attitude. They should be instructed to be cheerful, give quick service, be courteous, but not carry on lengthy conversations with the customer or other employees which may deter them from performing their duties. For the most part, the carousel attendants will be expected to walk around their work area facing customers. Yet in no circumstances should they be allowed to steer customers to specific machines.

It has become fashionable and quite public for minors to frequent casinos, especially in the slot area where they can sometimes conceal their age in the anonymity of the hundreds of machines. It is imperative that carousel attendants be on the lookout for minors who may be around their work area. By doing so they can prevent unnecessary legal proceedings that will be painful for both sides of the issue.

As an added measure of security, carousel attendants should not be allowed to exchange any money with other employees without the express consent of their immediate supervisor, unless it is a slot business transaction. Along the same lines of security, carousel attendants should not be allowed to count their banks down prior to check-out time unless instructed to do so by their shift supervisors.

Check-In/Check-Out

Carousel attendants must keep their conversation to an absolute minimum during the check-in and check-out process to aid in reducing count errors and to expedite the shift changeover. Attendants are expected to conduct themselves in a businesslike manner, proceeding with the countdown in a timely and orderly manner.

Similarly, carousel attendants should not attempt to provide guests with service while the check-in or check-out is in progress because of the same possibility of committing count errors and also because it will hold up the shift changeover. Outgoing attendants should be attentive and are required to observe closely the count-in by the relieving person. Likewise, the relieving person should have full attention on counting the bank. Since the relieving persons have not accepted the bank, they are precluded from conducting business with guests. If guests should need service while the attendants are in the process of turning over the bank, they should be politely informed that they will be serviced in a few minutes.

The check-out sheet must be filled out at the end of the attendant's shift. This must be done accurately and in ink. If an error is made, some places will allow the attendant to cross out the incorrect number and write the correct amount next to it and initial the correction. Other casinos, especially highly regulated ones (as in New Jersey) will not allow this practice. In this case the form must be voided and a new one made. In no circumstance should white-out be used.

Most operations will not allow outgoing attendants to close their carousels sooner than five minutes prior to the end of the shift. At that time the checkout sheet must be filled out to count down the bank and record the figures on the slot department countdown sheet. Similarly, the incoming attendant isn't usually allowed to enter the carousel sooner than five minutes prior to the start of the shift to count down the bank. The outgoing cashier will remain inside the carousel to observe the incoming attendant's countdown of the bank.

If the incoming attendant disagrees with the total figures of the outgoing attendant, then both will recount the area of disagreement and resolve the disputed count. If the dispute can't be resolved, a supervisor will be called.

The incoming attendant will prepare an adding machine tape of all recorded figures and enter the check-out total figure on the countdown sheet. If the bank is over or short the beginning check-in total figure, a supervisor must be called. If no discrepancies are encountered, the incoming attendant will sign on the *Open Signature* line of the outgoing cashier's countdown sheet, accepting accountability of the carousel's money. After that, the incoming cashier will immediately open the carousel for business.

If the carousel bank isn't to be used for one or more shifts, the slot department countdown sheet is placed in the bank's cash drawer by the relieving slot supervisor or the relieving cashier, and it remains there until the carousel is open again.

Handling Complaints

When a customer makes a complaint regarding incorrect change, the attendant will stop selling change immediately and will call the shift supervisor. It will be the supervisor's decision, based on the circumstances, whether a countdown in the presence of the customer is required or if it should wait until the normal countdown at the end of the shift.

When there's a customer complaint about a machine, the carousel attendant will inform the customer that a slot attendant will provide assistance shortly. When the attendant arrives, the carousel attendant will be expected to allow the customer to explain the complaint to the slot attendant and not attempt to do it for her or him.

On occasion, customers will attempt to cash gaming chips for cash, assuming that the carousel attendant is similar to the cage cashier. This could result in customer complaints since the carousel attendant should not cash chips for cash, yet may be allowed to accept them in exchange for tokens or slot change. Also, where applicable, customers will attempt to cash foreign gaming chips (from other casinos) or foreign currency, and, as in the situation above, will have to be referred to the casino cage for service.

Slot Jackpots and Fill Procedures

When a slot fill is required or a slot machine hits a jackpot requiring a manual payout, the slot floor supervisor will request a slot payout form from the booth cashier or the cage cashier and will record certain information: In the case of a jackpot, the floor supervisor will record the machine number, the floor location, the machine type, the coins registered, the line hit, the reel symbols, and the amount of the jackpot. In the case of a fill, the floor supervisor will record the machine number, the location, the machine type, and the amount of the fill.

The slot supervisor then signs the payout form and returns it to the booth cashier or the cage cashier, who then dates and time stamps it. The booth cashier or cage cashier will review the payout form for accuracy and completeness. After reviewing the payout form, the booth cashier or the cage cashier will give the form and the money to the slot floor supervisor authorized for the particular transaction. The requirements for signatures on jackpot and fill forms can vary from casino to casino but for the most part range around the following parameters:

If the jackpot or fill is $249 or less:

A. Two slot floor supervisors (one if a security person signs).

B. Booth or cage cashier.

C. Security officer (optional in a few casinos).

If the jackpot or fill is over $250:

A. Slot floor supervisor.

B. Booth or cage cashier.

C. Security officer.

If the jackpot ranges from $1,000 to $5,000:

A. Slot shift supervisor.

B. Slot floor supervisor.

C. Booth or cage cashier.

D. Security officer.

If the jackpot is over $5,001:

A. Casino shift manager or slot manager.

B. Slot shift supervisor.

C. Slot floor supervisor.

D. Booth or cage cashier.

E. Security officer.

All jackpots have to be visually verified by all the above except the booth cashier or the cage cashier. The original will be retained by the slot cashier or the cage cashier and will accompany the end of shift paperwork that is subsequently forwarded to soft count. However, before it is given to the cashier, the slot supervisor takes it and gets all signatures on it. The pink or third copy is retained by the jackpot fill dispenser which is later retrieved by someone from the accounting department, usually from internal control. The remaining copy, the yellow one, is deposited in the accounting box located somewhere on the casino floor.

Where booth cashiers are in use, the duplicate copies will be returned to the originating slot booth cashier. The booth cashier will enter the information contained in the slip on the *Slot Machine Fill and Payout Form*. This three-part form is pre-numbered and located in the change booth. Part two of this form will stay with other slot documents for reimbursement by the casino cage. Part three is placed in a basket in the slot booth to be picked up by the director of slot operations or the slot manager the next morning.

The *Slot Machine Fills and Payout Form* contains the machine number and type, booth number or cage, denomination, date, amount (alphabetical and numeric), shift, voucher number, and booth cashier signature.

Initial Slot Fills

Initial slot fills are fills that are made when a slot machine is placed into operation. The fill is requested by the head slot mechanic or slot tech manager for bagged coin from the coin room. A fill is recorded on the slot department's accountability, consequently increasing the accountability of the slot department and decreasing the coin room's inventory. This procedure is verified by an accounting representative, a casino cage cashier, and a representative from the slot department. The head slot mechanic or slot tech manager will prepare the necessary documents noting the date, the machine number, the denomination, and the amount of the fill. The documents are retained to update the slot accountability and to record the addition (source document for computer input). The coin is taken from the slot change booth or from the cage cashier, whichever may be the case. Subsequently, the updated slot accountability is taken to the casino cashier's cage to replenish the slot change booth, where booth systems exist.

Slot fills are generally $5,000 for $100 machines, $2,500 for $25 machines, $1,000 for $5 machines, $300 for $1 machines, $300 for $.50 machines, $200 for $.25 machines, $100 for $.10 machines, and $50 for $.05 machines.

Slot Machine Fills

Fills to the slot machines are recorded on the same *Slot Payout Form* and *Slot Machine Fill and Payout Form* as previously mentioned. Both fills and payouts are recorded on the same summary sheet and made by booth or cage cashiers. Where booth cashiers are used, fills are sold to the cage at the end of the shift, or before the end of the shift if conditions warrant a coin buy. All other form procedures are the same as jackpot payouts.

Loose Slot Change Booth Coin

In casinos that have three shifts, at the end of the graveyard shift each day the booth cashier prepares a coin buy sheet showing what wrapped coin is needed from the coin vault. The sheet also denotes what loose coin they will be sending to the coin vault. The change booth accumulates loose coin in canvas bags by denomination.

Each canvas bag is scaled and tagged by the booth cashier noting the denomination, the dollar amount, the date, and the initials of the booth cashier and is verified by the slot floor supervisor or slot shift supervisor. The buy is accomplished by use of the marker slip. Where booth cashiers aren't used, the same procedure is followed by the cage cashiers and is verified by their supervisor.

The bagged coin is weighed, and if no unusual variance exists between the weighed amount and amount per tag, the coin is immediately wrapped. The wrapping is completely separate from the wrapping done for the drop. If an unusual variance does occur, the slot floor supervisor or the cage supervisor is notified and that person decides whether to weigh and wrap the coin or to investigate the variance. The investigation will ascertain the reason for the variance and who is responsible for the overage or shortage.

Overages and Shortages

Overages and shortages discovered during the checkout and reconciliation procedures are noted on the Slot Booth Check-Out Sheet and Change Person Check-Out Sheet. The slot floor supervisor is notified of all employees involved and the amount of the shortages. In a few casinos, genuine shortages (i.e., no offsetting overage) must be paid immediately by the responsible individual. The *Marker Stamp* notes the amount, date and time stamped, and is signed by the booth cashier or the slot change person and slot shift supervisor or cage supervisor, whichever may be the case. This procedure will facilitate determining the necessary coin to buy to bring the slot change person's bank or booth cashier's bank to the correct imprest amount.

The information placed on the marker is also recorded on the *Marker Control Sheet*, which is under the control and custody of a specified slot change booth. The *Marker Control Sheet* is also used for checkout and reconciliation purposes (slot change booth) and it, too, can facilitate the necessary coin buy to bring the booth cashier's bank to the correct imprest amount. The *Marker Control Sheet* will indicate the date, the signature of the slot floor supervisor, and the booth cashier or slot change person, the amount, the date and the amount paid, and the booth balancing (running balance).

In the case where shortages must be paid, the payment is recorded on the *Marker Control Sheet,* and a copy of the *Marker Stamp* is given to the booth cashier or slot change person if requested. All overages are accumulated by the slot floor supervisors or the cage supervisor, depending on the circumstance. The overages are recorded on a daily tally sheet with the amount of the overage, the date of the occurrence, and the signature of the slot floor supervisor or cage supervisor.

The overage money is then placed in an envelope, which is sealed. The sealed envelope is locked in a drawer located at a specific slot change booth (the drawer is accessible only to the slot floor supervisor and the slot shift supervisor). When the overage reaches $500 or over, the amount is transferred to the casino cage by the slot shift supervisor or slot floor supervisor. There the overage is counted and verified by a cage cashier. Then it is recorded into the cage accountability.

Short Pays

For short pays of ten dollars or more a slot payout form is completed and handled in the same manner as for a jackpot. Short pays involving a single token in a denomination higher than ten dollars are handled without the above documentation. However, the machine access record must be completed with the date, signatures of two witnesses, and the reason.

Shift Close-Out or as Needed

At the end of the shift or as conditions necessitate a coin buy (resulting from manual jackpot payouts and/or fills), the slot booth cashier will close the slot machine fill and payout form by drawing a line through the center of the line below the last line of entry, crossing out the remainder of the sheet, and totaling the sheet. The booth cashier will then attach the first duplicate copy of the slot payout form to the original copy of the slot machine fill and payout form. The slot shift supervisor will review and initial the form. The booth cashier retains the first and second duplicate copies of the slot machine fill and payout form and second duplicate copy of the slot payout forms.

The slot shift supervisor or a security officer will take this form to the cage for reimbursement. The casino cage cashier will verify that the total of the slot payout forms attached to the slot machine fill and payout form are in agreement with the total reimbursement requested. The casino cage cashier then signs the original slot machine fill and payout form, and gives the money to the slot shift supervisor or security officer to take to the booth cashier. The original of the slot machine fill and payout form and the first duplicate copies of the slot payout forms attached are retained in the cage.

The slot shift supervisor or security officer will then deliver the money to the booth cashier originating the request, who will sign the duplicate slot machine fill and payout forms indicating receipt of the money. The second duplicate copy of the slot machine fill and payout form is retained by the security officer for filing.

The original slot payout forms that have been placed in the slot box in the slot cashier's booth are delivered first to the redemption booth to update player information for promotional purposes and then to the accounting department. The forms are placed in numerical order, totaled, and checked to make sure they agree with the amount paid out by the casino cashier's cage for each day.

The booth cashier will attach the second duplicate copies of the slot payout forms to the first duplicate copy of the slot machine fill and payout form and forward them to the director of slot operations or the slot manager for review and retention. He or she will count down the bank at shift end and record the totals on a slot booth check-out sheet. The change person will count his or her bank down at shift end and record the totals on a change person check-out sheet.

Drop Procedures

Prior to the commencement of the drop, an accounting representative counts the coin vault and verifies that the amount is that which has been entered on the coin vault inventory sheet. He or she then prepares a new coin vault inventory sheet. The following functions are performed in the removal of the slot drop:

1. Audit clerk function (rotated on a regular basis)—performed by an accounting representative.

2. Observation function—performed by a security officer.

3. Laborer function—performed by hard count team personnel.

As each machine is opened, the person performing the labor function replaces the drop buckets under the slot machine with an empty bucket. The buckets are placed in a cart and transported to the coin count room. During the drop, the coin buckets on the cart are watched by the security officer prior to being put in the coin count room. The drop will require more than one trip to the coin count room, so between trips the filled buckets are left secure in the locked coin count room until the drop is finished. This entire procedure is filmed and monitored by surveillance cameras.

Count Procedures

The coin count is performed in the coin room where the slot drop coins are weighed and the weighed coins are subsequently wrapped. This is done under the control and authority of the comptroller, who is responsible for the coin room personnel and procedures. The coin room is subject to continuous observation by electronically controlled video cameras from the surveillance room, and it is also usually monitored by magnetic taped recordings to verify the verbal counts. In the coin room, the weigh and wrap of coin is performed by an audit clerk who represents the accounting department and the coin wrappers.

Weigh and Wrap Procedures

Prior to the weighing of the coin, the scale is tested with a weight to verify that the calibration is working correctly. As each bucket is emptied into the scale, the accounting representative puts the machine number into the scale keyboard. After the coin is settled in the scale and the amount appears on the scale screen, the accounting representative depresses the enter key, and the machine number and the amount are recorded on the tape. At that time the amounts are automatically transmitted from the weigh scale to the computer by interface through a wall data box. In the same manner, each bucket is emptied into the scale by a coin room employee.

It is imperative that three members of the weigh count team be present during the count. One should be from the accounting department, and two should be coin room employees. The accounting representative records the count on a *slot wrap sheet* and any discrepancies between the count of the wrapped coin and the weighed amount are reconciled. Any errors on the slot count data sheet are crossed out and initialed, in ink, by two count team members.

The accounting representative is present throughout the weigh. After observing the whole process and ensuring that the coins are wrapped immediately after being weighed, he or she, along with one other member of the weigh count team, signs the tape of the weigh scale. When the weigh is finished, the accounting representative prepares, in ink, a *slot wrap sheet* showing the results of the weigh count by denomination.

Each drop is completely weighed and wrapped so that there's no commingling with the next drop funds. At least two coin room employees should always be present during the wrapping of the coin. Also, at this time, the coin vault is counted down by the coin wrapper and accounting representative and later the cage cashier. A new coin vault inventory sheet is prepared and signed by all counters and placed in the coin vault. The casino cage cashier should also verify the weigh and wrap amounts and the variance between them. The old coin vault sheet is retained in a coin room cabinet for reconciliation and verification. The slot wrap sheet is signed by the accounting representative, all coin room employees who participated in the weigh and wrap process, and the casino cage cashier who verified the funds. Large discrepancies between the weigh and wrap will be investigated by management instead of the slot department. This investigation will be documented and filed.

The accounting representative transports all currency (from machines that take currency) and all coins or tokens in amounts less than one full can or rack, as applicable, to the cage. The transfer of coin and currency from the coin room to the casino cashier's cage is observed by a security officer who will be escorting the accounting representative to the cage. The casino cage cashier receiving the coin and currency will sign the slot wrap sheet and add the value of coin remaining in the coin room to the cage's coin room balance in the cage accountability. A copy of the slot wrap sheet will be retained by the cage, with the original being forwarded to accounting.

Transfers of coin out of the coin room during the wrap will not be permitted except in emergency situations in some casinos. If a transfer is necessary, it is well documented, and the amount is accounted for in the total wrap amount. These transfers are observed by an accounting representative and a security officer, where permitted. The form the transfer is recorded on is signed by the accounting representative, the security officer, the cashier receiving the coin and another member of the count team.

The cage will remove the fill and jackpots equal to the fill and jackpot amount on the slot wrap sheet from their cage accountability. The difference between the coin added and the jackpots and fills is recorded on the cage accountability sheet as slot win. The cage forwards a copy of the accountability sheet and supporting documentation to accounting on a daily basis. The accounting detail for the weigh and wrap process is brought to the accounting department by the accounting representative.

Meter Readings

All slot machines record total coins in through the *in-meter*. The in-meters for all the machines are generally read on a daily basis although some places may do it on a weekly basis. Accounting representatives assigned on a rotation basis record the in-meter reading of each machine on preprinted computer sheets, which have listings of all active machines. These preprinted sheets will show the floor location of the machine, the machine location within that floor, the handling meter reading from the previous drop, and will also have blank spaces for the current meter readings.

Where the machines are managed by route operators, the in-meters are read by the vendors who service those machines as well as an in-house representative. The machines are listed on the report in floor number sequence to facilitate the entering of current meter readings and the current coin count as the drop is taken. An accounting representative reviews each machine's meter readings for reasonableness. For meters that aren't reasonable, a second check will be made to see if it was read correctly. Auditors check and compare previous readings with current readings to try to explain any significant variations. Any adjustment will be noted on the preprinted computer sheets. Any major problems will be brought to the slot manager or director's attention.

Slot revenue, handle, and percentage are calculated on the daily operations report for the day, month to date, year to date, month to date last year, and year to date last year. Any corrections to the original slot payout forms are completed in ink and brought to the attention of management by the accounting representative.

Equipment Control

Access to the weigh scale calibration module of the coin-weighing scale is limited to authorized representatives of the scale company and the accounting department representatives. All keys allowing access to the weigh scale calibration module are secured in the accounting department vault, whose access is controlled in a log where the date and time, the signature of the person receiving and returning the key, and the signature of the accounting department personnel (verification) is noted. The company technicians will perform most of the repair service and routine maintenance on the coin-weighing scale. An accounting representative should be present at all times when the calibration module is unlocked, yet this accounting representative will not be involved in the weigh count function. Copies of all service invoices will be retained by the accounting department and will contain the date the service was performed, the type of service performed (if the calibration module was unlocked, it will be so noted), the signature of technician or representative of the scale company who performed the service, and the signature of the accounting representative who was present during the performed service.

On a quarterly basis, the calibration of the weigh scale should be tested. At that time an accounting representative, who isn't a member of the count team, will be present for the test along with the scale company technician. On at least a semiannual basis, the internal auditor should do a surprise test of the weigh scale calibration, and these tests should be documented. The documentation is kept on file for future reference.

KEY CONTROL

Coin Vault Keys

There are two keys required to gain access to the coin vault. The cashier's cage has custody and keeps control of one key, which is released to authorized personnel only. The table below shows who is considered "authorized personnel." The security department will keep copies of all controlled keys and will also have a list of all personnel authorized to enter the coin room. To access the coin room, the use of a buzzer should be required in addition to the use of the proper key.

Drop Cabinet Keys

Drop cabinet keys are maintained at the security office and should be issued to authorized personnel only after the authorized person is entered into the key log with the following information:

1. The date and time the key was issued and returned.

TITLE	ACCESSIBILITY
Slot Manager	Slot drop cabinet keys, slot burglar alarm, coin vault.
Slot Shift Supervisor	Slot drop cabinet keys, slot burglar alarm, slot coin storage cabinets (casino floor area), slot machine keys, coin vault.
Slot Floor Supervisor	Slot coin storage cabinets (casino floor area), slot machine keys.
Slot Tech Supervisor	Slot machine keys.
Slot Technician	Slot machine keys.
Booth Cashier	None
Change Person	None

2. The reason it was withdrawn.

3. Whom it was issued to and who returned it.

4. The security officer's initials.

A minimum of two persons should be required to accompany the keys and observe as the drop cabinets are accessed. In some places one person can do it as long as surveillance is notified and observes the person throughout the period that the keys are checked out. However, drop cabinets should never be accessed without surveillance coverage.

Change Bank Keys

The slot floor supervisor or the cage supervisor will have custody and control of the change bank keys. These keys are issued to oncoming slot change persons at the conclusion of the shift and completion of the check-out procedures. The outgoing slot change person will relinquish the key to the slot floor supervisor or the cage supervisor, who will issue the key to the oncoming slot change person. No log will be used since the keys are issued on a shift basis and the use of the key is for an assigned area (change bank).

Bank Keys

Each bank has two separate locks: One is the bank lock, and the other is a security lock. Carousel attendants will have the keys to the bank locks, while supervisors will have the keys to the security locks. Change persons have the keys to their individual imprest banks. It will not be necessary to lock the security lock in the carousel bank unless it is in an isolated area or the bank is being closed down because there's no relief person. Bank keys must be kept in the possession of the attendant until the end of the shift, at which time the bank keys are given to the incoming person assigned to work the carousel after he or she has signed the slot department countdown sheet accepting accountability for the bank, or the relieving slot supervisor after he or she has signed the slot department countdown sheet accepting accountability for the bank.

Documents

Carousel attendants will be required to complete or be familiar with the sign-up sheet, break card, countdown sheet, buy sheet, shortage slip, credit slip, job rules, descriptions, procedures, and customer buy sheet.

OTHER SLOT DEPARTMENT FORMS

Slot Payout Form

This is a three-part form used to record slot fills and manual jackpot payouts. It includes the date, the booth number or cage location, the denomination of the machine, the machine number, the amount of the payout, and the authorizing signatures.

Slot Machine Fill and Payout Form

This form is used to summarize the slot payout forms. More specifically, it is used as a basis to reimburse the slot booths for payouts made for fills and jackpots.

Slot Meter Sheet

This a preprinted computer input sheet used to record slot meter readings. The machines are listed individually with the meter readings from the previous slot drop already recorded on it.

Slot Wrap Sheet

This form is a summary of the slot coin count. It includes coins weighed and counted, the dollar amounts of the counts, the jackpots, and the net results for each denomination of machines. The sheet is signed, in order, by the accounting representative weighing the count, the coin wrapper wrapping the coin, and the cage cashier accepting the increase in total cage accountability.

Slot Department Credit/Fill Credit

This three-part preprinted form is used to record the transfer of currency from the slot department to the cage (credit) or the transfer of coin from the vault to the slot floor. It includes the reason the credit was made, the date, the time, the shift, the dollar amount, the written amount, who issued it, and who received it.

Progressive Meter Reading Sheet

This form is used to record the changing meter readings by day. It includes the machine number and the daily meter readings that are used to ensure correct rotation of meters. Records are maintained for each progressive slot machine.

Booth Buy Sheet

This form is used to record the currency and coin sold to the cage or sold to the booth cashier and it includes the *Summary Fills and Jackpots* forms turned in by the booth cashier. This form should have the date, the shift, the denominations, the total amounts, and the signatures of both the booth cashier and the slot shift supervisor.

Form control

The *Slot Payout Forms* are three-part forms that are pre-numbered. Unassigned slot payout forms should be stored in a secure area within the accounting department under the custody and control of accounting or internal control.

The slot payout forms are assigned to the slot department or the cage in numerical sequence. The assigned slot payout forms are subsequently issued to the slot cashier's booth or to the assigned cashier's cage in numerical sequence. The numerical sequence of all assigned and issued slot payout forms is accounted for by the accounting department through use of a log. Missing slot payout forms should be investigated by an accounting representative and reported to the director of finance or the controller, who should then report it to the director of casino operations.

SLOT MACHINE REMOVAL

Before a slot machine is removed from the floor, the entire contents of the slot hopper are placed in a bucket in the drop cabinet. The drop bucket remains in the cabinet until the next drop. However, the drop bucket is set aside within the cabinet so it doesn't get mixed up with the drop amount of the new machine.

The head slot mechanic or the slot tech manager will give the booth or cage cashier a list of machines to be deleted. The booth or cage cashier will prepare the necessary slot payout form (fill purposes) for each machine. Then when the drop is done, the drop amount of each machine is reduced by the fill amount. The original fill amount isn't segregated, but commingled with the drop, which necessitates the fill reduction.

The accounting representative, the cage cashier, and the slot department representative all prepare an updated accountability report, recording the decrease in total initial slot fills.

Slot machines that are removed from the floor are noted on the *Slot Machine Addition and Deletion* form submitted to accounting. This form will be used to

add machines, to change any reel setting, to change payoff schedules, and to recalculate the theoretical hold percentage resulting from any changes made. Changes to a slot machine number are documented, and the documentation is kept by the accounting department.

STEPS IN PLACING A MACHINE OUT OF ORDER

1. The slot mechanic completes the out-of-order card with the required information. The hard copy of the form is placed in the inside of the reel glass.

2. An out-of-order sticker is placed over the coin head.

3. The soft copy of the form is taken to the nearest change or cashier booth. The information is then transferred to the machine log and the copy is clipped to the board.

JACKPOT PROCEDURE

1. The slot supervisor records the winning machine number, the machine location number, the amount of the jackpot, the winning combination, and the denomination of the machine on a scratch pad. At this time he or she should notify surveillance for verification.

2. The slot supervisor will then go to the nearest change booth, carousel or cage that has a jackpot dispenser and either fill out the payout slip with the recorded information or, ideally, give this information to the cashier to have it recorded on the form.

3. If the jackpot is $1,200 or more, the slot supervisor will be required to get two forms of identification from the winner (one of them a valid picture I.D.) and complete a W-2G form. In most states, the winner will be required to pay state taxes immediately, and this will be deducted from the jackpot payoff and reflected in the W-2G. If the winner refuses to provide identification, he or she will either have to return with an identification or accept a federal tax deduction at the maximum rate.

4. Depending on the casino, if the jackpot is in excess of $5,000, the shift manager will be immediately notified of the amount of the jackpot and the location. The shift manager will then determine whether the jackpot should be written up in the cage. In casinos where the cage pays all jackpots, this is a moot point. All the shift manager will have to do then is show up

at the cage to verify and sign the jackpot slip and then verify the jackpot. Depending on house procedures, this can be reversed. Although $5,000 is a very common figure, some casinos place the threshold at $10,001. This adds to the responsibilities of the slot shift manager, who is usually more qualified to verify and approve these payouts.

5. In some places, the shift manager is notified of the jackpot and its location, then the slot supervisor removes the payout slip from the dispenser and reports to the jackpot machine so as to meet there with the shift manager.

6. Once the jackpot has been verified and paid, the attendant will instruct the winner to deposit a coin to erase the jackpot or reset it manually if the patron refuses to do so or doesn't have a coin or token to do it with. The jackpot slip with all the appropriate signatures will then be returned to the booth or cage.

HOPPER FILL PROCEDURE

1. The slot supervisor records the fill machine number, the machine location number, the amount of the fill, and the denomination of the machine on a scratch pad. At this time he or she should notify surveillance.

2. The slot supervisor will then go to the nearest change booth, carousel, or cage that has a jackpot and fill dispenser and either fill out the fill slip with the recorded information or, ideally, give this information to the cashier to have it recorded on the form.

3. If the fill is $1,000 or more, the slot supervisor will be required to call the slot shift manager to verify and authorize the fill.

4. In some places, the shift manager is notified of the fill and its location and then the slot supervisor removes the jackpot slip from the dispenser and reports to the fill machine to meet there with the shift manager.

5. Once the fill has been verified and performed, the attendant will return the fill slip with all the appropriate signatures to the booth or cage. If a machine has had more than two fills, the shift manager will be informed so that a technician can inspect the machine.

COIN BUY PROCEDURES FOR CHANGE PEOPLE

1. A two-part change bank buy sheet will be filled out at the respective bank where currency turned in should show on one-half of the form and the coin purchase amount on the other. This method is to be used when change persons don't have access to their own imprest bank.

2. Where money runners are in use and they're on duty, he or she will complete the buy transaction for the change person. If money runners are busy, unavailable, or not working during the change person's scheduled hours, the change person will go to the nearest change booth, carousel, or cage.

3. The money runner, booth or cage cashier will verify the currency, issue the coins and sign the buy sheet. The yellow copy sheet will be returned to the change person and the runners or cashiers will retain the original or white copy.

4. If there should be a mistake in the paperwork or the buy money, the runner or cashier will stop the transaction and return all moneys and paperwork to the change person for correction. To avoid confusion, all tokes or tips are to be kept separate from the bank money and may be cashed in at the designated cage at the end of the shift.

THEORETICAL AND ACTUAL HOLD

The theoretical hold is the percentage of coins-in that the slot machine is set to retain on the average. Since the machines are equipped with program chips that have been randomized, there are going to be fluctuations in the retaining percentages which would mimic what would happen if the reels were to move freely. This randomness accounts for the deviations that are noted in actual hold from the expected or theoretical hold. Minor fluctuations are expected, just as they would happen with a mechanical machine with free-moving reels. However, abnormal fluctuations require a closer look. To assess the cause of these abnormal deviations, a number of controls must be set up. In this respect, the casino establishes the following:

The slot machine area is patrolled and under the observation of security officers at all times. These officers are expected to observe the area during the time of slot hopper fills, the handling of slot machine coin jams, and all other times when the slot machine door is opened, and the slot hopper or any other integral part of the machine can be accessed. Also, slot attendants and technicians are required, or should be required, to notify surveillance when accessing the inside of a machine. Surveillance should also be notified of the purpose of the intrusion.

Aside from these physical controls, the accounting department maintains the following records for each individual machine:

1. The reel settings that have been established in the slot shop.

2. The payout schedules that have been established in the slot shop.

3. The theoretical hold percentage as computed in reference to the reel settings and the payout schedules that have been established in the slot shop.

4. The date the machine was originally placed into operation.

5. The date the machine is removed from operation.

6. The date the machine is placed back into operation.

7. The summary of hand-paid jackpot payouts.

8. The date changes were made on the reel settings.

9. The date changes were made to the payoff schedules.

10. The actual changes made to the reel settings and payoff schedules.

11. The recalculation of the theoretical hold as a result of the changes made to the reel settings and payoff schedules.

STATISTICS

The accounting department receives a report every day corresponding to the slot drops. This in turn is consolidated in a week-ending report and a month-ending report. A reference to year-to-date is always made. Sometimes comparisons are made to the same period the year before. Any additions or deletions have to be noted on a computer form showing machine number, in-meter, par, and date. This includes any changes made on reel settings that would affect the par of the machine. The following are the reports that are forwarded to the accounting department and the information that these reports are required to have:

1. Slot Drop Analysis. It is a computer-generated report that contains the machine number, location of the machine, model number, average win per day, date, total handle, actual drop, dollar amount of jackpots, super jackpots, hopper fills, win calculation, the par, hold percentage, and the off par percentage. The report

provides current, month-to-date and year-to-date figures, totals by denomination, and grand totals for all slot machines.

2. Drop Transaction Error Warning Register. It is a list of those machines for which drop or fill data was found to be erroneous while processing. This register also lists validity warnings for those machines that the coin count or the computer handle play is found to be either lower or higher than the expected amount.

3. Slot Revenue Report. It is a revenue breakdown by machine type and by denomination. It contains the dollar amount of the total handle, dollar amount of the total drop (computer-estimated instead of actual coin count), dollar amount of the total fills, dollar amount of the total win, average par, average hold, average variance (the difference between the theoretical hold and the actual hold), current number of machines, and current unprocessed fills. The report provides current month-to-date and year-to-date figures as well as the previous month-to-date and year-to-date figures.

4. Cross Reference Listing, Machine Number Sequence. This is a listing of all machines in numbered sequence order. It contains the following:

   a.   The machine number.
   b.   The floor number (AREA).
   c.   The serial number.
   d.   The machine type.
   e.   The model.
   f.   The par.
   g.   Data installed.
   h.   The status of the machine.
   i.   The access codes.
   j.   The drop schedule.

5. Slot Maintenance Register. This listing is produced during the file maintenance run. All changes, deletions, and additions submitted to data processing are listed on this register. If any file maintenance data isn't processed, a printed explanation is required. This report provides information concerning the dates these machines were put into operation and the changes that are made to reel settings. The head slot mechanic or the slot tech manager also keeps a history on each machine.

Copies of the preceding reports are distributed to the director of slot operations and to the accounting department. Slot department management and casino management personnel review these reports on a monthly basis (at least). If any large variances should occur between the actual hold and the theoretical hold, the director or manager of the slot department will demand an investigation. A report of such investigations and their findings is kept by the slot director or manager for future reference. If any adjustments or replacements are made, these will also be documented and kept on file.

This is a comprehensive view of the slot department. It is my belief that it requires a better understanding than most casino managers achieve. However, to neglect this department is equivalent to airplane pilots assuming they can operate helicopters just because flying is their profession. In both cases, the casino manager and the airplane pilot had better brace for a crash landing if they neglect to inform themselves of the operation of their respective vehicles.

CHAPTER 13

THE MARKETING DEPARTMENT

STRUCTURE

Marketing departments are run by vice presidents or directors. Some departments even have vice presidents of different sections within the department. This importance of marketing within the casino is exemplified by the six-figure salaries the key personnel in marketing command in today's major resorts. In most casinos, marketing means the development of high-caliber players. Yet since there's a limited number of high-caliber players, marketing hosts and marketing personnel are primarily concerned with bringing in more players to the casino. As an added incentive for bringing in a higher quantity and quality of players, most hosts and representatives get bonuses for the amount of play they contribute to the operation.

After the vice president there might be directors of different departments in marketing who are assistants to the vice president. Different cultural sectors usually come at this level, although this mainly applies to the major casinos. Casino hosts are the heart of the marketing department. Hosts can be classified in different ways. There are executive casino hosts, junior casino hosts, credit hosts, Latin American hosts, and Asian hosts.

The final category in this department can be attached to V.I.P. Services and is filled by the clerks and assistants who aid the marketing department. The marketing department is comprehensive, and it is of extreme importance to the casino's survival. Without a good marketing program, casinos in today's gaming environment are destined to fail.

With the expansion and evolution of the gaming business, a separation of this department has been seen. Basically, what we are seeing is a division along the lines of high caliber patrons (VIPs) and those who are considered the general public. To that effect, some casinos have divided their Marketing Department into two separate departments, one called Player Development, VIP Services, or Guest Services, and another called Marketing or Sales. The objective of the Player Development Department is to increase the quantity and quality of high caliber patrons in the casino whether they are table game players or slot players, and the objective of the Marketing or Sales Department is to increase the number of patrons period.

The Player Development will create, organize, and oversee gaming tournaments, entertainment events, dinner parties, cocktail parties, sporting events, etc., while the Marketing Department will do the same with busing programs, general promotions and giveaways, senior programs, and all advertising campaigns.

Because the Marketing Department seen in the above sense follows along the lines of basic marketing concepts and theory, I am going to concentrate more on the Marketing Department as it is seen in most major casinos. Obviously, there are better texts that can explain general marketing principles. Yet, my discussion on the subject of marketing will cover many of the functions of the Marketing Department as seen in the above manner.

THE DELEGATION OF AUTHORITY

The matter of authority within the marketing department is directly related to the income power represented within it. In many instances the marketing department is stronger than the casino department itself. So even though the delegation of authority within the marketing department is supposed to follow a direct line down from the vice president or director, when a powerful premium player is involved, the host who represents him or her can overrule high-ranking officers

in the casino, even if procedural matters are concerned. In some casinos, the vice president of marketing is second in power only to the president of the company, excluding, of course, the chairman of the board.

Usually the chain of command in the marketing department goes from the top executive to the directors of the different cultural departments, then to the executive hosts. Any of these executives carries a lot of decision-making power, to the point where they can approve credit or extraordinary complimentaries and bend rules. In a highly regulated environment such as New Jersey, the power of the marketing department is felt, yet the watchful eye of the state prevents it from exerting the power that it has in Nevada. Executive hosts can issue credit and some extravagant complimentaries, but there are boundaries they can't surpass, especially when it comes to state regulations.

OBJECTIVES

Even though player development does play an important role in today's casinos, it can be seen in many ways where marketing principles are going to be relevant. Although the title suggests that there's more than one objective to be established by the marketing department, most concern themselves with increasing the drop. To base this important department on one objective is to limit its potential and value to the organization. Market share and profitability are other important objectives that should also be considered. If we fill the casino with customers that buy-in heavy amounts of cash and credit but then don't play, we've achieved our objective of increasing the drop, but we've done nothing to improve the revenue of the casino.

This is where casinos have to be very careful. Today, more than ever, casinos are buying business at an alarming rate. This expenditure has continued to rise every year since the early 1940s, and if it continues this way it will no longer be profitable to operate a casino. That's why profitability should be a major objective of the marketing department. Anyone can sell a five-dollar bill for four dollars, but who really wants to? Yet that is exactly what many marketers do when they overcomp the players they bring in. There has to be an understanding of profitability.

Unfortunately, too many people in the casino business don't understand the mathematics that determine profitability. Managers keep getting promoted over and over again without having a clue as to why a game has a disadvantage of 3 percent, except that it says it in the book or somebody told them so. The source's mistake can be our downfall if we don't understand the basis of the games we manage.

At the very least, the objectives of the marketing department should be to increase the drop, to try to capture a strong percentage of the markets we decide to compete in, and to make sure that the business we produce is sound business that allows the company to derive a decent profit. To restrict ourselves to a single objective in marketing is to blind ourselves to the opportunities that exist.

OPERATIONS MANAGEMENT

The Director of Marketing

Like the casino manager, the director of marketing must ensure that his or her directions are being followed and the declared objectives are achieved. To do this, the directors must hire qualified personnel to whom authority can be delegated and who can be depended on to communicate the declared objectives to their subordinates, and to make sure the goals are reached.

First the plan is laid out. Afterward the organization of the work tasks is determined, hopefully, with the input of the lower department heads. The work has to be organized at the company level to see how this new business is going to be handled. All organizational decisions are made between the vice president or director and the subordinate directors. It will be up to the subordinate department heads to organize their assistants and hosts to carry out these tasks.

Casino Hosts

One major problem that most marketing departments have is that, in order for the hosts to be effective, they must be given freedom of movement. This liberty lends itself to laziness if the host isn't motivated to work. There are various ways by which department heads can monitor the hosts to see if they're performing their jobs effectively.

MONEY AS A MOTIVATOR The greatest motivator in the marketing department, of course, is money. Casino hosts in most major casinos make comparatively high salaries and bonuses, and many get car allowances. But are these really good motivating tactics, and are these

individuals really deserving of them? Casino operators believe that, in order to acquire the right individuals, it is necessary to pay high salaries. Some of these individuals do bring in enough play that the revenues produced more than pay for their outlandish salaries. And it's obvious that if the casino doesn't pay these big figures, they aren't going to obtain the services of these individuals. But once the contract is signed, the salary is no longer a motivator. So the casino must find another way to motivate these highly paid individuals.

BONUS INCENTIVES The next motivator the casino chooses in most cases is the bonus incentive. This can be based on the amount of drop produced during the year or it can be in line with the host's status within the company. Bonus incentives based on the drop are a disadvantage to the casino, yet they are advantageous to the host. Because of this, many casinos choose other ways of compensating hosts for their efforts.

THE JOB AS A MOTIVATOR In many instances, the job itself turns out to be a motivator. The job offers freedom of movement, the opportunity to attend special events that would otherwise be difficult or costly to attend, the opportunity to partake of most casino services including gourmet meals, and the power to issue casino complimentaries, which in itself is a powerful resource. Many scams have been uncovered related to the exchange of favors for complimentaries. This is a problem that the casinos have to contend with since casino complimentaries have escalated to extraordinary proportions. Business cost continues to escalate every year and must be controlled if casinos are to survive.

The power to issue complimentaries as a motivating factor is a dangerous though necessary evil. Without it, the host can't do the job effectively and wouldn't feel comfortable doing so. Restricting this power is an extraordinary challenge and one that most casinos don't want to tackle because of the negative consequences that can arise in the attempt. The most important is the business loss due to shy comping policies.

JOB INSECURITY AS A MOTIVATOR The reverse motivating factor in the marketing department is the speed with which hosts disappear or are terminated. It is a job that in many places doesn't offer longevity to the host. The casino hires many of these people because they present themselves as producers of revenue. When they fail to do so, they're terminated, unless they can demonstrate other redeeming qualities. Where the hiring of the hosts isn't based on their contacts, their longevity is dependent upon the kind of service they give, how they get along with their superiors, and the changes in administration. The possibility of losing their jobs becomes an important motivating factor.

Smart casino management treat their hosts very well because they realize they serve an important function within the casino. Who else but the casino host can exemplify what service means in a business that lives and dies by customer service?

COMPUTER REPORTS

Computer reports show the comps that each individual host issued and, if programmed correctly, will also show how the players assigned to or developed by each individual host performed. These two reports, along with feedback from the casino floor, will give us an indication of the work performance of the hosts.

WHAT THE REPORTS DON'T SAY

If all figures are good, the event will be considered a success. The problem with this thinking is that many times things go wrong, and those problems eventually cost the casino a lot of business. The effect of this inefficiency isn't immediately reflected in the casino's win figures, and the casino may never know this because the customer might believe it's a waste of time to complain. Besides, it's always possible to go somewhere else and get treated better. Also, employees might feel intimidated by the person who commits these customer service violations or don't think anyone cares, so they don't report them.

Supervision in the marketing department is just as important as that in the games department, if not more. Employees should be closely monitored to ensure that they provide good and prompt service to their customers, and to all customers in general. Because of the delicate nature of the hosting job, the casino should have spotters to monitor their work-worthiness, their attitudes, and the relationships they establish with customers. Some of these relationships can be detrimental to the operation.

Another way to monitor the marketing department's effectiveness is to survey the people whom it services and the people with whom it comes in contact on the job. Traditionally, casinos have been reluctant to ask subordinates about their executives and supervisors, but this is a mistake. All superiors should be evaluated by their subordinates because these employees know better than anyone else the good and the bad about their boss. Employee relations may suffer a bit, but a supervisor who can't handle criticism should not be a supervisor. In the end, the marketing department *has* to be evaluated in qualitative terms.

GENERAL PROCEDURES

Vice President or Director

The vice president or director is the manager of this department and will play an active role in planning, establishing, and implementing procedures. This includes receiving daily and monthly reports which will enable monitoring the activity on the casino floor and within the department. On major occasions, the director also serves in a customer relations role and usually introduces himself or herself to important patrons and participates with them in special activities, parties, and dining engagements.

The director will also monitor the progress and effectiveness of the department by having frequent meetings to plan and make projections for future events with subordinate directors and supervisors. All special preparations will be ordered and coordinated at this level.

Directors of Subordinate Departments

Directors of subordinate departments must fill hands-on positions. These middle managers coordinate the activities of special groups—usually ethnic groups with special needs. The directors are considered to be hosts even though the title may be vice president. Pursuant to their status, these individuals are empowered with higher comping privileges and are allowed to approve higher credit lines than the credit hosts under their supervision. These employees also serve as junket coordinators with the junket representatives who bring in groups that fall within their departments. They also supervise the commission reports that their subordinates prepare pursuant to the players the junket representative brings in. Before a check can be made out to the junket representative, this director will approve the commission report.

When difficulties arise with esteemed customers of these departments this employee must find a way to satisfy both the customer's gripe and the casino's best interest. This is where gaming knowledge and insight into human nature play an important part of this supervisor's background.

This executive must ensure that all hosts under his or her supervision are carrying out their hosting function properly and are in fact servicing casino customers as they deserve. Here is where the major weak link in the marketing department exists, since the supervisors or subsidiary departments usually neglect this important supervisory function in favor of performing their own hosting functions as they see fit.

Casino Host

The casino host carries out one of the most important functions in the casino. It is this employee's duty to maintain customer service at a level that ensures customer satisfaction and repetitive business. In busy casinos, pit personnel depend on casino hosts to take care of customer needs such as complimentary meals, rooms, and transportation. This function is shared by the pit bosses and shift managers, but they're so busy at times with the management of the games that it becomes difficult for them to fulfill this function. This is when the casino host becomes invaluable. However, some casinos have difficulty locating the hosts, and this becomes a problem. Pit bosses can issue the complimentary to the customer, but they can't always abandon their supervisory positions to accompany patrons to restaurants and limousines, as the casino host should do.

Because of their freedom of movement, casino hosts don't only issue the complimentaries, they also sustain friendly conversations with casino customers and escort them to their destinations, wherever these might be. They can alert the maitre d's of restaurants as to the importance of certain patrons, what they can order, and what they can't. They can also assist them in directing them to wherever it is they wish to go, where to meet their limousine, and so on. They can even join these customers in attending special events, dinners, and shows. They can make the customer feel like a wanted friend, as we should make all of our customers feel.

Deciding who should be awarded what complimentaries is a function that today has been made a lot simpler than it was a couple of decades ago. Even in newer casinos such as the ones that are popping up all over the country with the establishment of riverboat gambling, new and inexperienced hosts can be aided by computer programs designed by different companies. These programs determine, by defaults input into the system by company executives, what the player's comp worth is in accordance with the way he or she plays. These programs establish a comp worth in dollar amounts. This dollar value tells the host if the complimentary the customer is requesting has been earned. If he or she hasn't earned enough comp dollars, the host may override the system based on a judgment of the customer's potential value. It is here where common sense and experience assert themselves, and where the host's function becomes more important.

Aside from the above function, hosts must seek out customers to cater to. They must roam the pits and slot areas in search of anyone betting above normal averages. These are ideal targets for the casino host. Such persons should be approached and welcomed, with introductions exchanged. Guests should be made aware of their importance to the casino and told how much their presence is appreciated. Upon guests' departure, at very least, the host should offer a business card and invite customers to call if they should need anything the establishment has to offer. No exchange of this nature should end without a warm handshake and a friendly smile.

VIP Clerks

VIP clerks are important because they do the leg work for the casino hosts and in some instances input the information that facilitates the host's job. These employees are in the background, yet in busy casinos their function is so important that the whole hosting department would come to a standstill without their involvement.

Efficiency in this department is of the utmost importance and, to ensure it, these employees must be recognized and treated well. Many times these very important people are unnoticed and unappreciated.

SPECIAL EVENTS AND PROGRAMS

The Bus Program

Possibly the most controversial of all casino programs is the bus program. It requires high expenditures in an effort to generate low-end business. Early unpublished and unofficial studies tended to indicate that bus programs were unprofitable in Las Vegas, Atlantic City, and Mississippi.

So why do casinos bother? This is a good question, and it has puzzled me so far. It is true that slow periods are costly to casinos since they must remain open with almost the same expenditures as if they were working at full capacity. In light of this reality, the idea that any business is good business surfaces immediately as an answer. Yet in terms of efficiency in management the question has to be answered from the balance sheet.

To begin with, the bus program encounters the same difficulty that other marketing programs do—the cost factor has to allow for a net return; otherwise the program is a failure or a loss to the company. The problem with bus programs is that the intended market is a low-end market that usually doesn't have a lot of disposable income available. So the first problem we encounter with the bus program is that the income potential is low. If the right volume exists, this isn't a problem since the quantity will make up for the quality deficiency. However, some marketers have found that not only is the quality limited with bus programs, but the quantity is also. When that happens, the program is definitely a loss.

So why do marketers bother? Because bus programs usually fill in those high percentage slot machines that make the casino so much money and also because bus patrons don't have to be catered to with expensive meals, rooms, shows, and luxury transportation expense. So the price of buying this business isn't remotely as high as buying high-roller business. Another advantage is that bus programs fill in those slow times when the casino needs business. The catch is that it does carry a price tag, and that is where the accountant has to sharpen the pencil to see if it's worth it. There's also another problem: Bus programs insist on a trade-off where they're allowed to bring in patrons on weekends—when the casino doesn't want their business.

Because your casino isn't the only casino that is competing for these patrons, incentives have to be included in the package to make customers choose your property over others. These incentives can include meals, shows, cocktails, drawings, slot tokens, and match play coupons. The incentive can be a cash reimbursement upon arrival at your property for the amount charged to them by the bus representative. These incentives can take many shapes and forms but, however we design them, there's no escaping the cost to the operation. This cost has to be measured and compared to the revenue that it produces.

In some instances, provided the proper measuring devices are in place, this can be accomplished with a certain amount of accuracy. In others it is mainly a conjecture. Where the casino has player-tracking devices such as computer cards that are inserted into slot machines, cash and play tracking is made easy. It is also facilitated if the customers are identified with junket buttons that they wear on their clothing so the floor supervisors can track their play on the tables. In any event, the following pages provide examples of forms used to analyze the bus programs' success.

On these forms, the bus department or the entity within the marketing department in charge of coordinating the bus program will record and evaluate the information and draw financial conclusions as to the effectiveness of the bus program. The accounting department and internal audit will surely have questions about the effectiveness of the bus program if the cost figures continue to overrun the revenue figures. However, most of the time these reports are held internally, and the only report the accounting department receives is the cost reports. Since the revenue reports are subjective, a creative analyst can make the program read whichever way he or she wants it to read. The difficulties arise when the customer-per-bus rate is too low, and the high-income contributions ascribed to these patrons can no longer be substantiated.

Junket Programs

Junket programs were very popular in the last three decades and to a certain extent they continue to have some popularity. However, they have lost a lot of appeal due to their high costs, partly because airline charter costs have escalated tremendously. For those who don't understand the concept of a casino junket or the word itself, it basically refers to groups of individuals who are brought together by a representative to do gaming in a property with which the representative is associated. There are various types of junkets and there are different ways by which the representative negotiates fees and commissions. There are also different ways

BUS PROGRAM DAILY COST REPORT

Tour Type	Tours	Cost Per Person	Total	Buses	Bus Comm.	Total	Agent's Comm.	Number Hours	Additional Costs Per Bus Per Hour Per Customer
One Hour First									
Two Hour First									
Three Hour First									
Four Hour First									
Eight Hour First									
One Hour Second									
Two Hour Second									
Three Hour Second									
Four Hour Second									

BUS PROGRAM MONTHLY REPORT

CATEGORY	JAN	FEB.	MAR	APR	MAY	JUN.	JUL.	AUG.	SEPT.	OCT.	NOV.	DEC
Buses												
Customers												
Customers Per Bus												
Expenses												
Cost Per Bus												
Cost Per Customer												
Slot Win												
Table Win												
Total Win												
Net Win												
Dollar Win												
Vs												
Bus Costs												

in which a junket representative is qualified, depending upon the state he or she is dealing with.

There are four basic types of possible junkets: regular junkets where most individuals qualify for complimentaries because of their play, splinter groups that consist of high rollers and could actually consist of one individual, up-and-back groups that come for the day and are usually composed of low-limit players, and low-limit junkets or $5 bettor programs that are nothing but package deals, usually including match play chips or coupons, plus a cash incentive to help pay for transportation costs in exchange for a prescribed amount of time played.

REGULAR JUNKETS Regular junkets are usually quite profitable since the main participants are valued players who put into action a lot of money. They usually have credit or cash lines in excess of $5,000 and minimum bets in excess of $25, with the average being around $100. Complimentaries for these preferred players generally are based on the amount of money put into action and, therefore, the casino usually recovers its costs. In recent history, however, it has become increasingly difficult to gather a substantial number of these individuals into a group, and representatives have had to fill in the gap with less qualified individuals who cost the casino money. If the casino doesn't have to pay for the transportation, however, it has a better chance of recovering cost. It then has only to concern itself with paying the representative a commission and the complimentaries for which it will be liable.

Casinos determine commissions in different ways. Some casinos pay what is called a *head count*. A head count refers to a fixed dollar amount for each individual brought in. The head count value will depend on the caliber of player being brought in. It usually averages around $100. As an added incentive, most casinos will throw in a bonus commission based on the credit or cash line the customer establishes, the amount of money the customer puts into action, and the amount of time the customer plays. It is usually based on a formula that determines the casino's theoretical win, a percentage of which will be given to the representative as a bonus. This bonus can be as high as 16 percent. Some casinos will base the bonus on the amount of money the customer loses. Again, a percentage of that will be given to the representative.

When credit play is involved, casinos work the commission in two different ways. Some will advance the commission and deduct it from future revenue if the customer doesn't pay, and some will wait until the markers are paid off before disbursing the bonus commissions. In any event, these are usually paid through monthly statements that take a while to be paid.

SPLINTER GROUPS Splinter groups are individuals who travel mostly by themselves and who expect to have their expenses reimbursed in exchange for their play. They're usually very good players whose average bet exceeds $100. These individuals may come in for anywhere from one day to a week and will be expected to play a certain amount of time in order to be compensated for certain expenses such as air fare.

A typical situation is the splinter individual who travels from the East Coast to Las Vegas, Lake Tahoe, the Bahamas, or Puerto Rico, and will usually stay three nights. This individual will be required, on the average, to play for twelve hours during his or her stay in order to get compensated for air fare. Depending upon the average bet and credit line, he or she will qualify for a range of complimentaries that are stratified according to the individual's worth to the casino. These will vary from standard air fare for one individual to first-class air fare and private jets for several individuals. Regular rooms to penthouse suites and villas are also complimentaries. Coffee shops, unlimited gourmet restaurants, and airport transportation by limousine may be included too.

Junket representatives are compensated for splinter groups much in the same way they're compensated for regular junkets.

UP-AND-BACKS *Up-and-backs* are usually mixed groups that include both high rollers and low-limit players, although some of them are mostly low-limit play. These groups usually work on package deals or certain incentives such as partial reimbursement of transportation costs and possibly a free complimentary meal and/or show. The junket representative usually negotiates a flat head count commission, to be received regardless of whether or not the individuals play. Some casinos have become aware of this and have placed certain restrictions to ensure that bona fide players are brought to their property. Bus programs are a type of up-and-back program.

Up-and-back programs can fill in a certain need at certain times of the day and certain slow periods of time, but for the most part they're difficult to put together because people tend to want to visit the casino at busy times. The incentives required to put these groups together usually cost the casino more money than they produce, and that is negative. The only time these groups are productive is when the incentives are limited and monitored and when the customer mix is such that good players compensate for the ones who don't give enough action and just come for the ride.

LOW-LIMIT JUNKETS Low-limit junkets have been popular in some places, but they're not the answer to gaming survival. In Puerto Rico, for example, low-limit junkets are welcome in the off-season when the casinos are hungry for business. Since the season is very short, from Thanksgiving to March 15, low-limit junkets are welcome most of the year. In Las Vegas, the Riviera has had the longest-running low-limit junket program and still continues to offer it. Bob Stupak's Vegas World offers incentive packages much in the same fashion. The Four Queens and the Tropicana in Las Vegas experimented with low-limit junkets with little success and so did the Landmark and the Dunes. So, two of the hotels that offered such a program no longer exist, and two of them are experiencing financial difficulties.

If the above is true, then why do casinos put such a program into effect? Some believe that, although low-limit junket programs are costly, they increase traffic on the casino floor and that condition in itself attracts other players, who like busy establishments. Others believe that the average bet on a low-limit $5 program, isn't $5 but $25 and, therefore, there's much more revenue potential than meets the eye. If any of the above statements were true, the low-limit junket programs would be an outstanding success. Evidently they're not, and history can make a very good argument in that respect.

The main problem with low-limit junkets is that cost considerations are usually underestimated, as happens with so many other programs casino marketers dream up. It doesn't always work out badly, but it certainly is food for thought and another wonder attributed to casino marketers.

Regardless of what type of junket program, if any, a casino chooses to establish, the casino is going to have to monitor its effectiveness. It can do so in different ways. The most effective way to monitor junket profitability is to keep track of cost and performance. The following pages will show different forms used to monitor junket efficiency.

On the following pages you will also see cost ratios. These ratios used to be kept low in order to ensure profitability, yet with the fierce competition that has existed for the past decade, they have escalated enormously. For example, it used to be customary to keep commissions within 1 percent. However, today some casinos pay up to 16 percent of the theoretical loss of some patrons in addition to a head count that is usually around $100 for premium players. With those kinds of incentives, the cost ratio of commissions has no chance of staying remotely close to 1 percent, since the theoretical loss is supposed to match the actual loss even though it never does. Air fare costs have also escalated, as well as all other costs associated with gaming. Most computers today are set to return between 30 percent to 40 percent of the theoretical loss, while at the beginning of the 1980s, 10 to 11 percent was considered average. Anything over that was excessive.

You can see by the facts above why it has become so difficult for casinos to make a profit and why most casinos are shying away from junket programs and competing for premium players. In the emerging new markets, junkets have not yet been a factor.

Before I end this section of the casino business, I would like to show by way of example how marketing programs are implemented and how they're planned in accordance with sound business principles.

CASINO MARKETING PRO FORMAS

Pro formas can be prepared for single events as well as an ongoing program or campaign. It is a plan that takes into consideration what the event, program, or campaign entails, what the associated costs are, and what the expected return will be, given known factors that can be measured. In the end run, it will be nothing more than an estimate or projection; however, managers sometimes live and die by these projections.

A long-term program or campaign would employ more or less the same criteria except that the period comprehended or projected would be specified and

JUNKET GROUP ANALYSIS

RUBEN MARTINEZ
Rockford, Illinois

August 30 to September 3rd, 1995

NAME	LINE	FACTORS	DAY 1	DAY 2	DAY 3	DAY 4	DAY 5	TOTALS	COMM.
Alphonse, Al	10,000	Markers	2,500	1,500	4,000	2,000		10,000	
		Average	125	200	175	150		163.31	
		Time	4.25	5.5	3.5	6		19.25	
		Comps	125	195	155	185		660	
		Transport	75			450		525	477.25
Brown, Steve	15,000	Markers	3,500	2,500	3,000	3,500		12,500	
		Average	175	200	150	250		197.79	
		Time	4.5	4	3.5	5		17	
		Comps	225	205	255	175		860	
		Transport	75			650		725	503.5
Geiger, Michael	20,000	Markers	3,000	3,500	4,000	5,000		15,500	
		Average	175	300	250	250		247.86	
		Time	4.5	6	2	5		17.5	
		Comps	350	250	365	275		1,240	
		Transport	75	75		550		700	620.5
Phan, Adam	7,500	Markers	1,500	1,500	2,000	3,000		8,000	
		Average	125	100	100	150		118.28	
		Time	4.25	4	4.5	4		16.75	
		Comps	175	205	155	175		710	
		Transport				350		350	337.75
TOTALS	52,500	Markers	10,500	9,000	13,000	13,500		46,000	
		Average	150.71	210.26	154.63	200		181.91	
		Time	17.5	19.5	13.5	20		70.5	
		Comps	875	855	930	810		3,470	
		Transport	225	75		2,000		2,300	1,939

GROUP STATISTICS

RUBEN MARTINEZ
ROCKFORD, ILLINOIS

JUNKET STATISTICS REPORT
SEPTEMBER 30TH TO OCTOBER 3RD, 1993

PLAYERS	ROOM NIGHTS	AIRFARE	LUGGAGE	LIMO	COMM.	R.F.B
4	16	$2,000	0	$300	$1,989	$3,470

| TOTAL EXPENSE | | COST PER GUEST | | | | |
		AIRFARE	R.F.B	LIMO	COMM.	TOTAL
$7,759		$500	$867.50	$75	$497.25	$1,939.75

| CREDIT | CASH | TOTAL HANDLE | HOLD 18% | REVENUE | | |
				CASINO	HOTEL	TOTAL
$46,000	0	$46,000	$8,280	$521	$3,470	$3,991

AVERAGE REVENUE PER PLAYER	AVERAGE ROOM REVENUE	AVERAGE BUY-IN PER PLAYER
$997.75	$249.44	$11,500

COST RATIOS

TRANSPORT	HANDLE	R.F.B.	HANDLE	COMM.	HANDLE	TOTAL
5%	$46,000	7.54%	$46,000	4.32%	$46,000	16.87%

MONTHLY JUNKET REPORT

AUGUST, 1995

GROUP	PLAYERS	ROOM NIGHTS	AIRFARE	R.F.B	EXPENSE	COST PER PLAYER		BUY-INS	WIN/LOSS
						AIRFARE COMM.	R.F.B.		

GROUP	PLAYERS	ROOM NIGHTS	REVENUE		TOTAL REVENUE	REVENUE PER PLAYER	ROOM REVENUE	BUY-INS PER PLAYER
			CASINO	HOTEL				

SPECIAL EVENT PROFORMA
NAME OF EVENT OR PROGRAM
DATES OF EVENT OR PROGRAM

OFFICE OR DEPARTMENT:	SLOTS, MARKETING, TABLE GAMES, ETC.	
TARGET GROUP:	BLACKJACK PLAYERS/CRAP PLAYERS $10,000 PLAYERS/GOLFERS	

	ESTIMATED	ACTUAL
Number of Invitees		
Number of Players		
Credit or Cash Line		
Slot or Table Games Handle		
Projected Revenue:		
Casino		
Hotel		
Entrance Fees		
Other		
Promotional Expenses:		
Limousine		
RFB		
Invitations		
Mailing		
Tickets		
Prizes		
Airfare		
Brunch/Dinner/BBQ		
Cocktail Parties		
Decorations		
Specialized Personnel		
Equipment Rental/Purchase		
Uniforms		
Photography or Video		
Trophies/Gifts		
Miscellaneous		
Publicity		
Advertising		
Signs		
Entertainment		
Musicians		
Magicians		
Headliners		
TOTAL REVENUE:		
TOTAL EXPENSES:		
PROFIT:		

evaluated for the long run. If, however, the program were to show very slow growth, a preliminary evaluation would be certain to occur. This brings me to the analysis of the marketing program I believe to be ill-conceived and my explanation of what occurred and what should have occurred.

DOUBLE JACKPOT PROMOTION

When a Mississippi casino decided to initiate a slot promotion offering double jackpots on hand-paid jackpots in order to compete with a casino that had much more to offer, the slot manager and the casino manager vehemently opposed it. Their reasoning was that this type of promotion was not only extremely expensive, it would in fact tie the hands of the slot manager and impede him or her from reacting effectively if a competitor were to lower the casino's slot percentages. They further argued that the enormous cost of the program, which could total up to $12 million a year, would be better served if customer service were to be improved by facilitating change operations and increasing salaries and incentives to slot and change personnel that would take better care of customers. This extra cost could also be used to pamper customers with dinner and cocktail parties in their honor.

The company president's argument was that in evaluating the situation, the managers had used historical data that in reality didn't prove anything, since the future couldn't be predicted. The reality, the president said, was that their competitor was surely going to bury them because of their improved facilities. He proceeded to use one of the manager's arguments against himself. The manager had said that it was senseless to worry about a player who wins $20,000 on a crap game because he was surely going to lose it back. It was then, by the same token, conceivable that those $12 million dollars in extra jackpot money would eventually return to where they came from. Needless to say, the program was implemented.

There are some inherent problems with a double jackpot program. One problem is that the extra payoffs decrease the house hold percentage, yet since the programs of the games aren't set to that lower percentage, in some states, the operation may not be able to advertise lower hold percentages. If the competitor decides to lower its hold percentages, it would look as if it had the better deal, even if it didn't. In order for this casino to compete, it would have to lower the game's percentages to a very low hold, in an environment that probably doesn't warrant such a measure.

Another problem with double jackpots is that it caters to a small percentage of patrons—those who hit the bigger jackpots— and that doesn't happen often. The majority of the patrons are going to leave the casino empty-handed with the impression that the double jackpot campaign is just a hoax, that in order to give out the extra money, the casino is taking it from them, the losers.

Finally, with such a big giveaway, the casino has very few promotional resources left for the slot department. Parties, prizes, and programs that have a more personalized character can't be enacted often because of the added expense.

On the positive side, double jackpots do give the impression of a great giveaway. In fact, the effect of double jackpots on the Mississippi casino referred to has been equal to lowering the house hold 1 percent. Since this casino has met with great success, at least for now, we must give the promoter his due and mention *double jackpots* as a marketing tool to keep an eye on.

CHAPTER 14

CASINO CREDIT

Casinos have become increasingly dependent on credit, to the point that according to Robert H. Davis of Hamilton & Hawkins International, 40 percent of all play in Las Vegas is based on credit. The Asian market is even more dependent on credit, accounting for 90 percent of all play. Every year casinos write off amazing amounts of bad debt, which in actuality isn't the total amount of past-due markers. For example, in 1990 when Roger Wagner became president of Trump Castle, he wanted to start with a clean slate, so he ordered the credit department to buy back approximately $13,000,000 in past-due markers at a discounted rate. The casino reported a loss of $6,327,000 in noncollectibles. In 1991, Atlantic City casinos wrote off $38,394,000 in noncollectibles, and casinos with revenues in excess of $1,000,000 in Nevada wrote off $166,556,365. Clark County casinos accounted for $150,475,154 of that total. In 1992, Atlantic City reported $24,394,000 in non-collectibles, while the same Nevada casinos reported $105,276,379. Clark County accounted for $86,928,012 of that amount.

As the above indicates, it's not spare change that is being lost to bad debt. These are significant sums of money. Part of the problem is that increased competition and new properties struggling to position themselves in the marketplace increase credit lines indiscriminately to draw business to their properties, sometimes doubling and tripling what others have approved. If we look at the figures from the Taj Mahal, we see that in 1990 they wrote off $6,577,000 even though they opened on April 4th of that year. In 1991, they wrote off $8,437,000 and in 1992, they wrote off $6,041,000. The practice of increasing credit lines indiscriminately can carry serious consequences, as evidenced by the Casino Control Commission investigation of Trump Castle in 1988 when an excessive amount of credit was improperly approved for Richard Hartman. The casino was fined $175,000 for this violation, and stricter measures would have been taken if the Commission had determined that the violation was done willfully and maliciously. Therefore, this type of situation is best avoided.

We can see that, in 1992, both Nevada and New Jersey decreased the amount of bad debt they wrote off. This could have been due to a concerted effort to reduce this expenditure, but it most probably was due to the decline in Asian business, which is heavily based on credit. If that were the case, it doesn't represent a change in attitudes; it represents a fluctuation in the market.

Competition is going to increase as new markets and new casinos open. If the past trend holds true, more bad debt is going to be reported in the next few years. Casino operators must take a good look at their credit policies to determine if this bad debt expense, along with the cost of buying this business, is really worth the rewards they will reap from it. At face value, even though the figures I mentioned may seem alarming, the 1991 Atlantic City's uncollected debt figure is only 1.3 percent of the casino win, and assuming that 40 percent is credit, that means that 3.2 percent was uncollected. The 1992 figure is only .76 percent of the casino win, and with the same 40 percent assumption, it would be 1.9 percent uncollected debt. Even the Taj Mahal figures that seemed so outrageous were only 2.2 percent in 1991 and 1.5 percent in 1992. Using the 40 percent credit assumption, that would mean that 5.5 percent was uncollected debt in 1991 and 3.8 percent in 1992. If we compare these figures to delinquent

credit in the banking world, they're not so outrageous after all. If we compare them to Nevada figures, they're also below average. The 1991 figures for the casinos with over $1 million in revenues was 3 percent of the total win, and the 1992 figures were 1.9 percent.

There are two reasons for the differences between Atlantic City and Nevada. One, New Jersey credit regulations are far more stringent. Two, there are many collection problems associated with foreign credit, and Nevada casinos cater heavily to foreign markets. Nevada might still be on the high side when it comes to uncollected debt, but it's not far from the averages of the FHA, personal bank loans, and credit card loans. So without weighing other factors such as the cost of generating this extra business or the deficiencies of some executives in issuing credit, it would seem that most casino credit policies are reasonable, although not necessarily efficient.

DEPARTMENT STRUCTURE

The credit department is run by a director, or in a more informal setting, a credit executive who usually has an office within or by the casino cage. The director has obligations just like any other department manager, with an added function—the power to issue credit and the responsibility for it. This executive is also responsible for the implementation of company credit policy and the adherence to it. It is a great responsibility since credit policies have changed dramatically in the last decade. When Bill Friedman revised his *Casino Management* book in 1982, he stated that credit executives were limited to approvals of $10,000. Anything higher than that required the approval of a credit committee composed of a few of the casino's higher executives or someone high in the company hierarchy. Today, some directors of credit and credit hosts can approve credit well into six figures. That kind of power makes this executive highly vulnerable and the constant object of scrutiny.

Because the function of the director of credit and credit executives places them in direct contact with the casino patrons, they also perform a customer relations function. This function requires that they be able to issue complimentary services at the same level that a shift manager and above would. In most Nevada casinos the credit executive is a casino host with the added function of credit approval.

Below the director of the credit department are usually two assistants or credit executives, most probably one for every shift. These executives usually have a lower credit approval rating than the director, but strong enough that they will be able to handle most credit requests by themselves and will be able to cover the director when he or she is absent. If a credit request exceeds the authority of these executives, they will contact the director for a decision, based on the information they have available on the credit request.

Busy casinos will have other employees who can approve credit up to a certain limit. These could be considered junior credit executives or credit assistants. These employees usually don't have the authority to issue complimentaries, or if they do, they're limited to what complimentaries they can issue. Some Nevada casinos will allow cage personnel to issue low levels of credit and to approve check cashing up to certain limits (which are usually low), provided that proper identification is offered.

GENERAL PROCEDURES

There are various procedures by which casinos issue credit to customers. They may allow the customer to cash personal checks, to make a call bet (a verbal wager without showing the cash or chips), to play on rim credit (a table marker), to sign an IOU based on a personal check or a second-party check or a payroll check, to use cash advances on credit cards, and to establish a line of credit and draw markers. Up until recently, the final two ways were the only ways in Atlantic City. However, casino cages in Atlantic City can now accept checks.

Check Cashing

The check-cashing policy in the casino is similar to that of issuing a credit line. The customer must fill out an application, and the line of credit must be approved by an executive. Once the application is on file, the cage cashier can cash checks for that customer up to the limit established by the executive. Anything over that would require an executive's authorization. In Nevada, almost every casino will cash checks up to one hundred dollars with the proper identification and up to two hundred dollars for hotel guests. Some casinos will cash almost any paycheck for local customers.

Rim Credit

Rim credit is convenient for customers but inconvenient for casino personnel. However, since some premium players are used to this privilege, casinos are forced to oblige. Basically, the customer sits at the gaming table and makes the request for credit. If the supervisor knows the customer, the supervisor will immediately place a lammer button on the table representing the amount of credit requested. The dealer will then cut out the amount represented by the lammer and wait for the floor supervisor's authorization to hand off the money. If the supervisor doesn't know the player, he will call the pit supervisor for authorization. Sometimes the player will not be known to the pit supervisor either, and he or she will have to call the cage for verification.

In addition to the lammer on the table, a player activity card will reflect the name of the player and the amount of the transaction. Both the dealer and the floor supervisor will sign the player activity card. The rim player may decide at any time to sign a marker for the amount of money he or she has taken out in credit.

How long the player will be allowed to play on rim credit depends on casino rules. Sometimes a player is allowed to continue to draw rim credit until his or her trip is over. When the player leaves the table, the lammer buttons remain, and the player activity card still reflects the amount of credit owed. As the player continues to request credit, the supervisor crosses out the previous amount owed and writes the new total owed on the next line. Each transaction will require the initials or signature of the dealer and the floor supervisor. If the player wishes to reduce the amount owed, he or she will hand the dealer the chips or cash to reduce it, and the floor supervisor will convert the lammer button to the new amount and will cross out the existing amount owed on the PAC, and write the new amount on the next line. A notation of how the amount was reduced is usually part of the record, in other words, whether it was with cash or chips. If the player pays off the amount in full, the floor supervisor circles the amount owed and writes beside it in which way it was paid, signs it, and has the dealer sign it. The lammer button is then removed from the table. Some places that are extremely flexible in their handling of rim credit will allow the player to go rest while the rim remains unpaid. Even if the table closes after the player has left, the lammer will remain in his or her spot on the game, and the player activity card will be placed somewhere in the pit. I believe this practice to constitute a security risk, especially since I have observed player activity sheets lying unguarded for up to a week.

Call Bets

Call bets are one-time verbal wagers that are allowed as a courtesy while players are waiting for confirmation of their credit lines. They're also wagers that are allowed for players who first come up to the table and want to get in on a hand before they have had a chance to buy in. Sometimes players will run out of chips and make a call bet. Since the supervisor isn't sure if the player has any money left, he or she will usually give the player the benefit of the doubt and accept the wager. Casinos will vary in their flexibility regarding call bets. Some have a policy that, because they cater to premium players, call bets up to a certain amount will be accepted. It isn't uncommon for some baccarat pits to accept a call bet in the range of $5,000 to $10,000. But for the most part it is a judgment call that will depend on whether or not the person seems qualified for it and also on the size of the bet. Except for Nevada, most casinos won't accept call bets.

IOUs

IOUs are documents or counter checks that customers sign at the casino cage that allow them to draw markers at the tables. These IOUs are usually based on personal checks, payroll checks, or second-party checks on which the casino puts a lien. The player then draws markers at the table based on the amount that has been approved. It is a crossbreed between a credit line and front money credit. The customer at the end of play will either redeem the markers and have the check returned, will allow the casino to cash the check, or will return at a later date with the money owed in exchange for the check.

Credit Cards

Cash withdrawals on credit cards work like they do with banks. The player will be sent to the casino cage, where the cashier will check the list of stolen and lost cards, then call the card company and obtain a pay authorization. Once the authorization is obtained, the cashier will have the customer sign the voucher and give him or her the money. There are also self-service

teller machines on the casino floor of almost every casino that allow customers to handle this transaction by themselves.

Markers

The marker systems in New Jersey and Nevada are very different, although some similarities do exist. In common they have the serial numbers on the counter checks. This is to avoid marker scams where supervisors tear up markers after the money has been issued to the player. This was a very common way of stealing in the past, and is believed to be the reason a casino was forced to close several years ago in Puerto Rico. Sometimes errors will be made that require the marker to be voided, but it can't be disposed of. It will remain on record as evidence of a failed transaction.

Another similarity is that in most Nevada locations, a pit clerk will verify the customer's line and eventually handle the paperwork. The clerk will be responsible for updating the customer's account, but will not secure the customer's signature. This is one of the ways Atlantic City differs. There, the pit clerk is obliged to take the marker to the customer for signing. The pit clerk then hands the marker to the floor supervisor, who also signs it and gives it to the boxperson or dealer. By doing this, the casino has one more person involved in the transaction, and that makes it more difficult for collusion to occur. The fact that the pit clerk is part of the finance department also makes a difference since he or she isn't accountable to the pit supervisors. Another difference in the New Jersey marker procedure is that markers begin as a signed request that is verified against a signature card before the marker is generated. After the marker request has been cleared, the pit clerk then generates the marker in the computer and prints it out. The customer doesn't receive the money until it is signed by him or her, the pit clerk, the floor supervisor and the dealer or boxperson. In some instances, the pit boss is required to initial it.

In Nevada, the customer is given the money immediately upon requesting it if he or she is known to the floor supervisor. The floor supervisor will place a lammer button on the layout and will instruct the dealer to cut out the amount for the player. After verifying the amount, the floor supervisor will authorize the money to be handed to the player. Depending on the casino, the floor supervisor will either prepare a manual marker or instruct the pit clerk to issue a computerized one. The computerized marker, as well as the printed manual one, will probably have another security measure in common with New Jersey. The amounts of the counter checks will already be printed on the marker. Where manual markers are issued, sometimes they're color-separated by denomination so that supervisors, spotters, and surveillance personnel can identify the amount from a distance.

Once the marker has been printed or filled out, the floor supervisor hands the marker to the player, who then signs it. The floor supervisor then signs the verification stub and fills out the table marker card with the player's name, account number, and the amount of the marker. As with rim credit, the markers are accumulated, added, and subtracted as the player takes out more or reduces them by redeeming them in exchange for cash or chips. The floor supervisor, after having both the marker stub and the table marker card filled and signed, has the dealer sign both. The stub is then deposited in the drop box by the dealer and the lammer is removed from the table. In most places, the lammer is placed somewhere in the rack, usually to the furthest right row where it can verify the amount of markers on the table. The floor supervisor will then hand the marker to the pit clerk, who updates the client's account and files the marker in an alphabetical file folder which he or she can later retrieve if the customer wishes to pay it back. Usually, once a day, the markers will be transferred to the cage and the player will have to go to the cage in order to pay them off. In high-limit pits where the casino caters to major players, the casino will have one of the supervisors redeem the markers for the player at the cage.

CREDIT APPROVAL

Central Credit

Credit approval depends on many things, but mainly is a function of the credit executive's judgment. To make a credit decision, the main source the credit executive uses is Central Credit, Inc. This is an agency that provides twenty-four-hour credit information on applicants. They provide information on check-cashing history, traveler's checks, credit cards, casino credit, and addresses. They also provide credit ratings and give recommendations. They can connect direct phone lines between casinos in different gaming states through

their own switchboard so that current information on a casino patron can be evaluated immediately instead of having to access each independent source separately. The scope of Central Credit is international, so that foreign nationals can also be scrutinized. When accessing Central Credit, executives should be aware that most casinos will not immediately report delinquencies on their best customers. It usually takes a second return or a refusal to pay by the customer to force the casino to report them.

Central Credit also provides a warning service that alerts casinos about frauds and large bad debts. They usually do this over the phone to expedite the warning and to prevent the situation from worsening. The agency also has a Don't List, which is a monthly computer record of patrons who aren't yet considered delinquent but have had outstanding casino credit for over ninety days. In-transit reports are also supplied by Central Credit. These reports are used when the casino suspects a customer might be gambling in desperation and taking advantage of all possible credit. Central Credit telephones every casino where the customer has established credit and requests information on any checks from this customer that haven't cleared the bank and also on the amount of outstanding credit that the person has. Speed is of the utmost importance in these cases since the casino wants to service the customer as quickly as possible with the least amount of risk possible. Since so many customers do establish credit lines with more than one casino, in-transit reporting is an invaluable source and one that should be taken seriously. Studies have shown that customers with credit in many casinos tend to have outstanding receivables for over 90 days.

Bank References

Once the person's credit has been checked, bank references are the next area of concern. Since the casino can't draw money out of a customer's savings account, the checking account is the most important bank reference. Not that the savings account isn't taken into consideration, but at this point it becomes secondary. This is one of the problems that issuing credit poses. Most people don't keep high balances in their checking accounts since the interest they receive for their money in that account, if any, is poor. In fact, some customers who are familiar with how the process works will temporarily transfer funds into their checking account, before requesting credit. Then when the credit is approved, they withdraw it. The casinos are aware of this, but they're not concerned since the credit report has a history of the account.

When the casino contacts the bank, the bank will not tell the casino exactly how much money the customer has in the account. Instead, the bank uses a code, which includes one word and one number. For example, low five means that the customer has a balance from $10,000 to $25,000. High six means that the account has a balance from $750,000 to $999,000. Based on this information and other determinants, the credit executive will establish a credit limit for the customer.

There are three ways a casino can obtain a bank account verification: by letter, by phone, and by teletype machine. The teletype is the most efficient because it is fast and leaves a paper trail. The letter is the least expensive, allows for a paper trail, but is very slow. It is a good method, however, when time isn't of essence. This would be the case when a premium player alerts the casino beforehand of an intent to visit the casino on a future date. The telephone is too expensive, takes more time than the teletype, and doesn't leave a paper trail. In the past, although it wasn't common, the telephone was used in credit scams.

Financial Information

Aside from the credit and banking information necessary for credit evaluation, the credit application will request information on the customer's employment or business. This information will be used in addition to the credit and banking information to determine the creditworthiness of the customer and the maximum credit line that can be approved. The credit executive will then determine whether the limit the customer is requesting is realistic. If it is, it will be approved. If it's not, then the credit application will be reevaluated to see if there's any other area of financial information that can carry enough weight to allow a little more flexibility on the credit executive's part. Sometimes that executive will contact the customer and advise that the amount requested is in excess of what the individual qualifies for. If the customer insists that he or she is qualified, then the credit executive may require other financial information or verification of certain assets.

In the end, if the customer is insistent enough and the executive's instincts indicate it is a good risk, the credit executive may decide to take a chance. After all, risk-taking is an important part of handling credit. The alternative is to talk the customer into a lower limit.

Risk-Taking

Credit risk can be seen in different ways. In one sense you are approving a noninterest loan that the customer may use for other purposes. Casinos try to monitor credit customers closely in order to avoid this. In Nevada, floor supervisors are required to insist on marker redemption before the player leaves the table. But most of the time, the player no longer has the full amount of the marker left when ready to leave. In that instance, the floor supervisor is instructed to have the player sign a marker for the difference owed and take in the rest. In practice, however, that doesn't occur since players will usually say they are going to move to another table and will use the money there. Or they will say they are going to go up to the room to rest or go to dinner, and will be back later on to play. In those circumstances, supervisors are reluctant to insist on the marker settlement because they fear insulting the customer.

Management's point of view is ambivalent. Although reluctant to insult customers, obviously they would like to remove the chips from their hands. So what usually occurs is that, for a while at least, they follow the movements of the customers to see if in fact they go where specified. If they do, the floor supervisor will contact the other floor supervisor with information about the situation, possibly handing over the rating card for the player. If the player does go in the direction of his or her room, then the floor supervisor has to assume that the truth was told, even if the player should decide to backtrack and head for the cage. If it's a considerable amount of money, the floor supervisor will alert either the pit boss or surveillance. Most cages are alerted to call the pits for verification of a cash out in excess $1,000 although a few limit it at $5,000. Yet this doesn't prevent customers from loan sharking in the casino.

In Puerto Rico, casinos have different chips for credit players. It is a hassle, but it prevents customers from cashing out small amounts of money in order to cash out their credit line, and it also makes loan-sharking more difficult. The loan shark would have to lend money to credit players only since a noncredit player with credit chips wouldn't be able to redeem them. Also, since credit players are monitored so closely, more chips in the player's possession would cause suspicion. In any event, the casino doesn't lose, since markers have to be paid before any cash will be disbursed. And cash isn't disbursed until the end of the customer's trip.

This system has several drawbacks: It requires a larger inventory of chips, it makes the dealer's job a little more difficult, and (biggest of all) it annoys the credit players. Credit players can't use these chips to gamble in any other casino, nor can they cash them. They also see it as an insulting measure against them. However, as Juan Causa, a legendary figure in Puerto Rican gambling used to say, "You give me paper, I give you paper. You give me money, I give you money." He said it with a flare of Spanish accents that made us all laugh, except those to whom it was being said.

In Puerto Rican casinos, this is the norm. But in mainland casinos no one does it, and I doubt that anyone would attempt it since competition is feared more than credit losses.

I believe that the casino should be concerned with the prospect of loan-sharking, at least, because the loan shark is producing false drop while taking outrageous amounts of interest from the casino's customers. The loan shark is making money that the casino isn't going to make. The Mirage has established its own cage for its own baccarat chips, which in a way is a toned-down version of the Puerto Rican practice. However, at the Mirage it has to do with all baccarat chips, not just those on credit. As it turns out, most of the play in the baccarat pit is on credit. Yet this doesn't prevent the customer from using these chips elsewhere in the casino and, therefore, there's a way around it.

Another way to see credit risk is the obvious one: that the customer will not repay it. This risk is greater in conventional lending than in casino lending since in casino lending, if the customer uses the entire loan in the manner in which it was prescribed, the casino isn't really out any money, except what was expended as a complimentary service to the customer. Although the complimentaries can amount to a substantial amount of money, the cost is usually far below the amount of the loan. If we compare this diminished risk to the added profits that extending credit brings in, this risk

becomes insignificant. So when weighing the risk of extending credit against not extending it, we need to look at the whole picture.

We have to consider what the monetary value of a conservative credit position is going to be in contrast to a lenient one. We have to try to determine at what point credit increases become financially negligible. There are two things that have been proven in credit approval policies: One is that the more credit is approved, the higher casino revenues and win figures are going to be and, two, that the more credit is approved, the higher the collection rate is going to be. The key to successful credit management is to determine at what point liberal credit policies begin to eat into casino net income. That is where casino credit policies have to draw the line.

Front Money

Before ending this section on credit approval, I would like to mention one method of credit approval that reduces risk tremendously. As a matter of fact, most casinos in Puerto Rico have standardized this procedure. It is commonly called front money and is basically credit issuance based on cash deposits into the casino cage. What Puerto Rican casinos do is issue an equal amount of credit to the amount deposited in cash into the cage. In this way, if players lose all of the credit issued to them, their own money has paid for the credit issued to them by the casino. This offsets whatever complimentaries were issued and still allows the casino to make a profit. This concept is by no means novel, and isn't only practiced in Puerto Rico. Yet as I mentioned before, in Puerto Rico credit risks are reduced by the inability of a player to cash out credit chips until the end of the trip.

Customers aren't usually made aware of *credit equal to front money* option, unless they're requesting credit beyond that for which they qualify. Most customers who use front money as a means to writing markers usually prefer using their own money rather than having credit extended to them. These are people who understand the dangers of credit play.

DANGERS OF CREDIT PLAY

There are dangers inherent to credit that both the casino and customers should be aware of. Some customers, like those in the last example of the previous section, are well aware of them. Others may be aware of them yet believe they can't be affected by them. Still others are totally oblivious to them and are taken in before they realize what has happened. This situation poses problems both for the customer and the casino.

The dangers to the customer are obvious; the casino, on the other hand, exposes itself to bad publicity, court battles, diminished revenues due to destruction of its customer base, and an unwanted contribution to the destruction of people.

There's no question that gaming has a psychological effect on people. No one likes to lose, and everyone likes to win. In gaming, both things are going to occur. When people lose, their character or their life's philosophy is going to determine how they react to the loss. Some people react aggressively and try to fight back by attempting to recover their losses. In order to do that, they must invest more money. For these people, credit is dangerous since they don't see beyond the moment. Like credit buying in stores, it is facilitated by the fact that it doesn't have to be repaid immediately. The borrowed money doesn't come out of their pockets right then, and people believe there's always the possibility that they will be able to repay it soon and even win. The person whose goal is to get even will eventually get ruined. This is because probability's certainty is manifest over long periods of time. So anyone who plays long enough is going to lose.

When people win, they tend to believe the casino odds are surmountable and that they're going to win again, possibly a lot of money, as so many people in campaign advertisements have been glamorized as doing. In this sense, winning serves as a great motivator. The win-seeking behavior is further strengthened by what behavioral scientists call intermittent reinforcement. Intermittent reinforcement is said to be the strongest behavior modifier. It refers to the act of giving a reward once in a while instead of every time the behavior is manifest. Behavior is increased to try to expedite the reward. The combination of both the win condition and the lose condition is what produces the aberrant behavior that is observed in gaming habituation and gaming obsessive behavior, which has led to institutions such as Gamblers Anonymous.

The danger to the casino is that it will quickly lose valued customers and contribute to their financial and moral ruin. As the French found out many decades ago

when they eliminated the double zero in roulette, it is better to get a steady stream of income than to ruin everyone at once. So in establishing credit policies, you must be well aware of the person's ability to repay credit and the impact that the total loss of the line will have on this person. This is also a consideration when you try to evaluate whether you should extend a customer's credit limit or not. Usually, when a customer requests a credit extension it is out of desperation and many times the customer is under the influence of alcohol.

Although a person is basically responsible for his or her own actions, a court decision rendered on February 25, 1993, by U.S. District Judge Joseph Irenas in the case of Leonard Tose against the Sands in Atlantic City gives us an indication of how our judicial system may see this issue. In that case the judge decided that the casino was responsible for Mr. Tose's impaired judgment by allowing him to get drunk. This decision permitted Mr. Tose to avoid paying $2.3 million he lost at the Sands during seven gambling days between 1986 and 1987.

The implications for the casino are obvious. Casino patrons who drink may escape responsibility for their debts. This decision of impaired judgment also opens the possibility that a future court may judge the casino responsible for the psychological impact of gaming. If this happens, no one will be responsible for gaming debts and casinos may be held responsible for the financial, emotional, and physical ruin of their patrons. If that ever happens, it will be the financial, emotional, and physical ruin of the gaming industry itself.

The lesson to be learned here is that we shouldn't be too eager to extend credit so that we can improve our drop figures at the expense of the people who support our business. And although it is true that people shouldn't have to be treated as children and should be responsible for their own actions, the casinos have to contend with the negative image that precedes them and make decisions accordingly. By doing so, we not only protect our operations, we also extend a bit of kindness and consideration to the human race. This may not be immediately appreciated by everyone, but it is appreciated by most people, especially those whose lives are affected by aberrant gambling behavior. Casino credit executives do have a social responsibility, as well as one to their managers.

Recently, in a major Las Vegas Strip hotel, a floor supervisor issued $100,000 to a well-known casino patron without verifying the customer's line. This was usual with this patron, and it is what casino supervisors are instructed to do with most premium customers in high-limit pits. Of course, this practice is acknowledged verbally, yet it doesn't appear in written procedures. As it turned out, the customer was overextended in his account by $800,000. The floor supervisor, upon learning this, panicked and notified the pit supervisor, who also panicked and notified the player's host. The host calmly opened another account with a slight variation of the player's name for $500,000. It is customary in this particular Strip hotel to have various accounts for premium players. The question is: How safe is this procedure? And what exactly are the casinos conspiring to hide?

Although it is obvious that, in some instances, allowing delinquent credit customers to play with cash allows us to recover part of our losses by getting a shot at the money they bring in, it is also true that by allowing them to play, we're furthering their difficulties. What's even worse, we're showing them our willingness to forget debt. This is dangerous for two reasons: One, the message is clear about the customer's lack of debt responsibility and, two, it offers an exquisite opportunity for casino executives to take kickbacks.

It is no wonder then that so much fuss is made about accurate accounting on high-limit games. And although this is essentially an important part of a floor supervisor's job, it is impossible for the floor supervisor to have an exact account when games get very busy. To insist that every dollar be accounted for, like some Strip hotels do because of the rebates that are offered to premium players, is ridiculous. This forces the floor supervisors to falsify rating cards and put their jobs and their casino license on the line. But it happens, and what is even worse is that sometimes casino executives themselves will alter rating cards because of allegations of errors by premium players and their hosts. This is an illegal practice, and it is disrespectful and detrimental to the floor supervisor. It is also a very dangerous practice since it also allows for a very sizable kickback. The relevance between this practice and credit is that 99 percent of the players for whom this is done are credit players.

People have been known to embezzle, to liquidate all of their assets, and to deprive and ruin their families because of an obsession with gambling. For most people, this process has been facilitated by lax credit policies. Let's not facilitate this corruption of the human spirit by taking credit requests too lightly. Let's approve credit conscientiously.

OTHER PROCEDURAL MATTERS

Many casino patrons who apply for credit don't visit the casino with regularity. For these patrons casino credit cards should be updated. A reasonable period of time, and one that is accepted by most casinos, is six months. But even in a few months the customer's financial situation may fluctuate, and credit executives should be cautious about that. A good way to update credit files would be to have the computer generate lists of patrons whose accounts will soon need updating and extend invitations to visit the casino, possibly tied to a certain upcoming special event. Invitations should include a reference to the obsolescence of a patron's credit application, with an invitation to have it activated. This procedure serves a dual purpose. It fulfills marketing objectives while it aids the credit department in keeping files active. It also serves to alert the casino to customer dissatisfaction, since some customers will inform the casino why they're not patronizing it any more.

Another rule-of-thumb procedure in credit goes beyond the credit department itself. It entails making the customer aware of nearness to his or her credit line limit. This is important since many times customers will lose track of how many markers they have taken out. It can mean the difference between a request for an extension of credit that may have to be denied, and having to deal with an irate customer who believes more money should be coming. The credit line limit assessment is the job of the floor supervisor, and it should not be overlooked. It may not change the circumstance of the credit extension, but sometimes it can.

Credit extensions are a difficult proposition and one that casinos don't want to deal with. In fact, some gaming corporations oppose extensions of credit. Yet this isn't an easy issue to resolve, since denying the extension of credit will usually lead to a threat by the customer to go somewhere else where additional credit will probably be forthcoming. Credit executives and casino managers know this, so whenever possible they try to accommodate the customer.

But as I indicated previously, the practice of increasing lines of credit can have serious consequences, and these should be taken into consideration when basing judgment on this issue. We should look at the total picture of the situation and not just the couple of pressing variables before us. If we believe that we can extend the credit limit of this customer without inflicting financial or emotional harm, then we should oblige. Otherwise, the decision shouldn't be made regardless of how insulted our customer feels, or if it means losing business. In this respect, credit executives should be held accountable for their decision. We must also keep in mind that credit approval does lend itself to irregularities and, because of that, credit procedures should be defined and restricted as much as possible.

Credit executives, because of the enormous financial power they have, should be scrutinized carefully. Computer printouts of the credit transactions they approved should be analyzed, preferably with the aid of the computer itself. The computer can be programmed to identify problem areas and unhealthy patterns that may lead to future problems. Casinos would be wise to take advantage of this technology and to do careful analysis of credit operations.

CREDIT RETURNS

The handling of credit returns is still surrounded by many complications. There are various reasons why a counter check will be returned: One, the signature doesn't match the one the bank has on file, and that means the casino has been the victim of forgery; two, there aren't sufficient funds to cover the check; and three, the bank is unable to locate the account, which means that there's a mistake or the casino has been the victim of a scam. Since the first and the last reason shouldn't occur if correct procedures are in place, let's consider insufficient funds.

Sometimes casinos will notify, especially premium players, that the counter check is due and is about to be deposited in his or her account. They're hoping that the check hasn't been redeemed because of an oversight by the customer. Usually customers will tell the casino to go ahead and deposit the check, but sometimes they will request an extension of the time period to pay the marker. If the casino can't locate the cus-

tomer, then it will proceed to deposit the check. Some casinos, however, don't believe in notifying players because they don't want to alert them, just in case they have no intention of paying. In some instances, they believe it is the customer's intent to have them deposit the check. In any event, when the check is deposited in the customer's account, many times it will be returned and marked as stopped payment, account closed, or insufficient funds. The first two reasons indicate greater problems than the last one. In those cases the casino will immediately call the customer to see what the problem is and how it can be worked out.

If the reason is insufficient funds, the credit executive will have to make a decision. If it's a first-time return, the credit executive might call the customer to see what happened and how the marker can be collected. The customer might tell a sad story and ask the credit executive to re-deposit it in one week. If it again returns with insufficient funds, the bank will probably stamp it and request that it not be deposited again. If the casino chooses, it can continue to present the check to the bank, but it has to do it in person. After a six-month period, the check will be considered *stale*. A *send for collection* order will be accepted by the bank for a period of fifteen to thirty days. By doing this, the bank clears the check if the customer's account balance reaches the required sum.

When a check can't be cashed, the casino will put it in a file and hold it for collection. It will then make attempts to collect it directly, and negotiate a settlement of the account if necessary. Collecting markers is troublesome since the casino must rely on junket representatives, hosts, and other casino executives to collect the money. The sums of money owed may be quite considerable, to the point that they're a huge temptation. A major Strip casino is still looking for one of their junket representatives who was supposed to have collected millions of dollars in debt.

Many years ago in Puerto Rico, a casino manager was sent to New York to collect $100,000 in markers. He claimed to have set the briefcase containing the money on top of a taxicab that drove away with it. The money was never recovered. Ironically, although the casino manager was fired, he promptly got another casino manager job, elsewhere.

If the casino believes the customer's financial situation has deteriorated to the point where repayment of the debt in its entirety is impossible, it may negotiate a settlement of the account. This is usually the best thing to do in that case since at least the casino recovers part of the money owed. A customer whose financial situation improves will likely remember the favor and demonstrate loyalty. However, decisions to negotiate account balances as well as to write them off should not be entered upon by people who deal directly with the customers, since this opens the possibility of irregularities.

Finally, if the casino is unable to recover the debt through all its bona fide and documented efforts, the decision has to be made to write off the debt as an uncollectible. The proper documentation is filled out and sent to the accounting department, where it will become a deductible expense for income tax purposes.

CONCLUSION

Although it is obvious that at some point the value of increased credit lines becomes negligible because of the increase in noncollectibles, history seems to indicate that aggressive credit solicitation has paid off for many establishments, especially as they have attempted to increase their market share or find a place for themselves in the market when commencing operations. In many cases this has been the claim to fame of major names in gaming management. All it takes is a lot of courage with somebody else's money.

The losses due to bad credit aren't as significant as the losses that will occur in the future if credit policies aren't reviewed carefully. As gaming expands throughout the country, our credit patrons are going to gamble with more frequency and are going to demand more credit to do it. Since there will be more new places opening, it stands to reason that more inflated credit policies are going to be enacted. This increased action is going to burn out gaming customers at a faster rate, and casinos may soon find themselves with a huge uncollectible debt and a diminishing customer base. If casinos don't take protective measures themselves, government intervention may be necessary. This is something to think about when implementing credit policies.

A few credit monsters have been created in the past, like David Zarin, Leonard Tose, Mitzi Briggs, Akio Kashiwagi, Richard Hartman, and most notorious of all, Jeff Byrd. Mr. Byrd had his credit line increased progressively from $50,000 to $1,000,000. In one week he managed to beat the casinos out of $5,000,000. The following week, when he lost $3,000,000, he said he didn't have the money to pay it. Byrd is currently serving a prison sentence for an unrelated crime. Many more names like these will be added to this list if casino credit procedures aren't carefully reviewed.

Finally, in comparing the credit procedures of Nevada, New Jersey, and Puerto Rico, I find that the expediency factor in Nevada, although it evidently caters more to the player and allows the casino to have players' money in action sooner, has too many weaknesses. These security risks don't only affect the casino itself; they're risks that can directly affect the people who handle the credit process. I would advocate a controlled credit environment such as New Jersey's with the added credit accountability of the Puerto Rican system. I realize that a system like that wouldn't be possible to implement unless all the casinos agreed upon it, or unless the government stepped in and insisted on it. Yet if it were possible, the casinos themselves would avoid many headaches.

At first sight, the Nevada system may seem convenient, and Nevada gaming will swear by it. But the Nevada system is antiquated, as are many other procedures that Nevada gaming has been reluctant to change. Nostalgia may make us believe that the way things were is still the best, but in reality most things need to change to adjust to the times. Nevada's marker procedures are based in an era where casinos were operated by organized crime and where credit violations were handled in an unequivocal manner that made people well aware of the consequences of defaulting on credit or cheating the casino. Today, although some places may feel they still have that kind of strength, as evidenced by the recent incident between the Sands and an Asian lady out of Los Angeles, that isn't the case any more. The Sands suffered because of that incident, and I doubt that it will happen again.

CHAPTER 15

THE FINANCE DEPARTMENT

The finance department is usually headed by a vice president. This executive oversees the accounting department, the cage, and the credit department, and all the departments related to the distribution of money within the organization. This department prepares budgets for all the departments of the casino operation. Because of this, the finance vice president communicates closely with the owners and operators and is knowledgeable about their objectives and goals. All procedures and regulations pertaining to the handling of money must be approved by this vice president. In Nevada, most casinos apply the Nevada State Gaming Control Board's Minimum Internal Control Standards (MICS) almost verbatim to their operations. If any changes were to be made to these procedures, the vice president of finance would be the person to approve them.

Another responsibility of the finance department is to aid the organization in reinvestment. It has become a custom in today's corporate gaming world to redirect casino funds to investments that will yield higher returns instead of depositing them in the bank or having them lie stagnant in the casino cage. This tendency has brought with it certain difficulties, mainly that at times there's not sufficient cash in the casino cage to cover obligations. This may have been what prompted the Nevada Gaming Control Board to amend Regulation 6.150, which establishes the minimum bankroll requirements, on November 29, 1990. The casino is required to report when cash or cash equivalents fall below the minimum bankroll requirements, and failure to do so will result in sanctions by the Board.

Casinos can't be blamed for trying to maximize the return on their investments, and it is doubtful that this practice will end. It is, therefore, the vice president's responsibility to ensure that both the objectives of the corporation and the state are met. To do so, he or she must know the actual status of the casino bankroll. To aid in this, the accounting department reviews the cage's cash count sheet and the bank control sheet.

THE ACCOUNTING DEPARTMENT

The accounting department is responsible for auditing the monetary transactions of all the casino departments. These transactions are reported in documents that are funneled through the casino cage, since it is the cage that's responsible for distributing money throughout the casino. In some instances, the accounting department, not the cage, is responsible for bankrolls to certain, if not all, departments within the casino. But the cage still has the responsibility of issuing and collecting the departmental employees' bankrolls. When it does this, the cage inventory sheet isn't affected. The count team generates a report that goes directly to the accounting department and prepares the deposit which it turns in to the cage to be included with the cage's bank deposit.

The accounting department verifies all receipts and reconciles fills, credits, and markers deposited in the casino's drop boxes. If any inconsistencies are found, a report is generated, and the department head where the inconsistency was found will have to investigate and give an explanation.

Many Nevada casino managers are uncomfortable with the number of internal controls that have been forced upon them. Although they used to feel that overzealous accountants forced these controls, they now know it is the government that demands most controls.

THE CASINO CAGE

The casino cage is undeniably the center of the casino operation since through it eventually flows all the money of the operation. This makes it the most vulnerable part of the casino. Because of this vulnerability, cage controls are very stringent. It is also because of this that the cage has recently been a target of scams and robbery. Yet surprisingly, the number of theft in casinos is low compared to the inordinate number of bank robberies in Las Vegas. This speaks well of the security department, of the stringent controls, and of the designers of casino layouts, who usually place the cages in the middle of the casino floor, so that patrons as well as would-be thieves have to cross a large area in order to reach an exit. The location of the cage is not only a security measure; it is also intended as a temptation for impulse betting.

The cage is usually run by the cage manager, but smaller casinos may use other officers who perform dual and triple functions to supervise the cage. Since banking operations occur in the daytime, cage managers and credit managers usually work the day shift, leaving the other shifts to shift managers. Like any other manager, the cage manager is in charge of the supervision of the cage and all the employees in that department, on all the shifts. Since the function of the cage is mostly one of safekeeping and controls, the objectives of the cage are well defined and almost universal. Its main concern is to keep shortages to a minimum and to provide good customer services and coordination between the departments and the cage.

Cage personnel usually include a cage supervisor, a head cashier and, at the very least, cage cashiers. They may also include cage clerks. Where the cage and the credit department are integrated, there will also be a credit secretary and a collection manager. The cage cashiers carry out most of the cage functions. They're the front-line employees who deal with the public and handle all of the customer transactions such as chip exchanges, cash change transactions, currency exchanges, marker transactions, and check cashing.

Cage clerks mainly handle paperwork, document preparation, and the teletype machine. In many instances these functions are shared by the cashiers. The head cashier is usually the assistant to the cage manager and helps with cage responsibilities. The supervisor watches over the cage cashiers and the clerks. The credit secretary handles credit verification, and collection correspondence, and other duties assigned by the credit manager. These duties might entail billing credit customers, requesting credit information, processing credit applications, doing bank verifications, and dealing with junket lists. These duties could be extended to determining comp worthiness for future trips, based on an evaluation of the customer's action.

The post of collection manager is mainly found in large casinos that are greatly dependent on credit. This dependency generates a great number of delinquencies, and it is the job of the collection manager to seek payment and try to recover noncollectibles insofar as possible. This is the position that first determines what accounts should be written off.

Functions of the Cage

The main function of the cage is to provide funds to the different departments so that they may have the financial resources to operate. Of all the departments, the casino produces the most complications in this process since it generates the greatest diversity of paperwork and because it deals in chip banks that the cage must account for. The slot operation is complicated in itself, yet because it has its own cashiers and change personnel, it provides the cage with less work. There are some casinos that have change cashiers and personnel consigned to the cage.

The Chip Bank

Chip bank handling is a problem in itself since the casino must decide whether or not to assign cash value to the entire bank or just to that which has been issued to the casino and customers. The two methods used to record the chip flow are the cash value system and the memo-entry system. The cash value system treats all chips as cash, including those that are in the cage. The problem with that system is that it inflates the actual size of the cage cash inventory, and it can lead to shortages when decisions are made to reduce the bankroll under the assumption that there's more cash on hand than is actually there. This shouldn't happen, but it has. The memo-entry system doesn't count the cage's chip inventory and treats circulating chips as cash equivalent items because they represent a cage liability and therefore have to be paid upon demand. The advantage

to this system is that it doesn't inflate the cage cash count by including the chip inventory in the cage cash inventory. Also, the chip's outstanding entry will equal the value of chips in circulation, which is the current liability of the casino cage.

The Memo-Entry System

In the memo-entry system, each time the cage issues chips, it receives in return either money, checks, or fill slips. Since these chips will eventually return to the cage, the value of the money, checks, or fill slips will have to be balanced in some way. This is done by entering the value of the outstanding chips as a negative value in the outstanding chip category of the cage cash count sheet. At the end of each shift, all inventories will be counted, and the cage will deduct the amount of chips on hand from the chip bank assigned to it by the accounting department. This transaction will show the amount of outstanding chips.

The Cash Count Sheet and Minimum Bank Requirements

The cage cash count sheet will include the original cage currency bankroll issued to it by the bank, which will be added to the revenues produced by other departments. When the currency balance becomes low, the cage will either cash customer checks at the bank or request a check for a bank withdrawal from the accounting department. As mentioned previously, the Nevada Gaming Commission revised its minimum bank requirements on November 29, 1990. The formula to determine the minimum bankroll is as follows: All available cash (minus moneys in safekeeping and front money deposits) is added to the expected gross revenues for one month to determine what the total amount of available cash for the month will be. That amount will be subtracted by the casino's cash requirements for the month, which are the gaming activity cash requirement, payroll expenses, operating expenses, debt service, and other expenses.

The gaming activity cash requirement is the total sum of exposure from table games, slot machines, keno, race and sports book, other progressive payouts, and periodic payments that are owed. The table games exposure is determined by the average daily fills per game class in a one-month period (as evidenced in the NGC-1SR monthly gross revenue statistical report), divided by the number of days in that period, then multiplied by two days. This is done for each individual game category. If there were twelve blackjack games and the total amount of fills for those games in a thirty-day month was $864,000, you would divide that by thirty and come up with an average of $28,800 in fills per day in blackjack. You would then multiply that by two and find that your exposure in blackjack is $57,600. You would do the same for every game category.

The reserve for the slot machines is determined in one of two ways. The first way is by the average daily fill and jackpots multiplied by the greater of the number of days until the next slot drop collection, or two days. The average fills and jackpots are determined by subtracting the gross revenues from the drop, then dividing that by the number of days in the month. It is required that this information be taken from the latest NGC-1SR. For example, let's assume our NGC-1SR shows our gross slot win was $3,312,694 and our slot drop was $4,246,352. That means we filled the slot machines and paid out jackpots in the amount of $933,658. Assuming this was a 30-day month, we arrive at a daily average of $31,121.93 in fills and jackpots. We then take this amount and multiply it by two to determine part of our exposure. That comes to $62,243.86.

The second way the reserve for slot machines is determined depends on the kind of license we hold. Group I and II licensees will have to add to the above amount the greater of 20 percent of the total progressive slot liability; or the single highest available progressive or nonprogressive jackpot. If one of our jackpots is $100,000 and the sum of all of our progressive jackpots is $250,000, then we end up reserving $100,000 for the main jackpot since 20 percent of $250,000 is only $50,000. So, our total slot reserve would be $162,243.86.

Group III licensees must reserve the entire progressive liability and add it to the average fills and jackpots to determine their total reserve for slot machines. Slot machine payouts that involve periodic payments such as keno machines, and slot prizes that are paid in installments, aren't included in the slot reserve. They're accounted for in a separate category.

The keno game's reserve is the game's limit plus whatever the current progressive keno liability is. The race and sports book reserve will be the greater of

$25,000 or the sum of: (a) amounts held by the book for the account of patrons; (b) amounts accepted by the book as wagers on contingencies whose outcomes haven't been determined and won't be determined within thirty days after the wagers have been accepted; (c) amounts owed but not paid by the book on winning wagers. The Chairman of the Gaming Board may require a different amount if it is deemed there is good cause to do so.

The present value of the total amount owed to patrons for annuities or periodic payments as permitted in Regulation 5.115 must be included as a gaming activity cash requirement until those funds are fully funded. Any other progressive payouts in the casino, except those that apply to slots and keno, will be reserved at 100 percent of their value.

A sample of the bankroll verification worksheet issued by the Nevada State Gaming Control Board is presented on the next page. The State of Colorado Gaming Control Board worksheet is presented in the following two pages. The Colorado worksheet isn't as comprehensive as the Nevada worksheet because it only allows limited gaming on slots, blackjack, and poker, but doesn't allow cash deposits. Also, Colorado sets a value for the table game fills of $3,393 for blackjack. Poker doesn't figure on either sheet because players don't play against the casino.

Currency is kept in the cashier's drawers and in the casino vaults. For security reasons, the casino usually has more than one vault in the casino, where surplus currency is stored in case the cashier runs out. Most small casinos have only one vault. Some casinos will have separate entries on their cash count sheet for each individual drawer and vault. Usually cash count sheets will have a category for each denomination bill. There will usually be two columns on the cash count sheet, one for wrapped bills and another for loose bills. Wrapped bills will have the initials of the person who counted them so that responsibility for shortages can be assigned. These bundles are usually wrapped in the count room or by cage personnel. They can also come from the bank.

Occasionally shortages occur, and the cage manager and cage supervisors will have to trace the source and see if there's a pattern. Locating the source of a shortage isn't always easy since the shortage can be produced by the person who's counting as well as the

STATE GAMING CONTROL BOARD
BANKROLL VERIFICATION WORKSHEET

	Immediate Exposure	Thirty Day Exposure
Cash Available:		
Cash on Premises	$ xxxxx	
Less: Safekeeping and Front Money	(xxxxx)	
Cash in Banks	xxxxx	
Progressive Keno Game Bank Deposit	xxxxx	
Restricted Race/Sports Book Reserve	xxxxx	
Cash - Other	xxxxx	
Total Cash on Hand	xxxxx	$ xxxxx
Gross Revenues (1 month)	xxxxx	
Total Cash Available		$ xxxxx
Cash Requirement:		
Operating Expenses (1 month)		(xxxxx)
Payroll (1 month)		(xxxxx)
Debt Service (1 month)		(xxxxx)
Licensed Gaming Activity Cash Requirement	(xxxxx) (1)	
Other	(xxxxx)	
Total Cash Requirement	$(xxxxx)	$(xxxxx)
Cash Excess/(Deficiency)	$ xxxxx	$ xxxxx

Note:

(1)   Licensed Gaming Activity Cash Requirement -

Games	Average Daily Fill	x	2 Days	
Craps	$	x	2	$ (xxxxx)
Blackjack		x	2	(xxxxx)
Roulette		x	2	(xxxxx)
Baccarat		x	2	(xxxxx)
Big 6		x	2	(xxxxx)
Other		x	2	(xxxxx)
Total Games Exposure				$ (xxxxx)
Slot Machine Reserve				(xxxxx)
Keno Game Reserve				(xxxxx)
Race/Sports Book Reserve				(xxxxx)
Periodic Payments Owed				(xxxxx)
Other Progressive Payouts				(xxxxx)
Total				$ (xxxxx)

BANKROLL ANALYSIS WORKSHEET

	Immediate Exposure	Thirty Day Exposure
Cash Available:		
Cash on Premises		
Cash in Banks	$	
Cash-Other		
Total Cash on Hand	$	$
Adjusted Gross Proceeds (1 Month)		$
Total Cash Available		$
Cash Requirement:		
Operating Expenses (1 Month)		( )
Payroll (1 Month)		( )
Debt Service (1 Month)		( )
Licensed Gaming Activity Cash		
Requirement	( ) (1)	
Other	( )	
Total Cash Requirement	$( )	$( )
Cash Excess/(Deficiency)	$	$
Note: *See detail on page 3*		
(1) Licensed Gaming Activity Cash Requirement -		
Live Games	( )	
Slot Machines	( )	
Payout Requirement	( )	
Total Gaming Activity Cash Requirement	( )	

LICENSED GAMING ACTIVITY CASH REQUIREMENT

LIVE GAMES

Game Type	Number of Units	X	Daily Fill Per Unit	X	2 Days =	Cash Requirement
Twenty-One		X	$3,393	X	2	( )

SLOT MACHINES

Game Type	Number of Units	X	Daily Fill Per Unit	=	Cash Requirement
Penny		x	$10.00	=	( )
Nickel		x	$40.00	=	( )
Dime		x	$100.00	=	( )
Quarter		x	$250.00	=	( )
Half Dollar		x	$400.00	=	( )
Dollar		x	$800.00	=	( )
Five Dollar		x	$1,200.00	=	( )
Total Slot Fill Requirement					( )

Payout Requirement	
Greater of:	
20% of Total Current Progressive Liability	
or	
Single Highest Payout of Progressives	( )

person who previously counted the bundle. In many instances, shortages happen through bank personnel, or could be traced from one of their depositors. The bank acknowledges this error and makes arrangements to reimburse the casino for the shortage amount. The shortage will be recorded, and a pattern search will be done.

Another way cashiers facilitate cash handling and improve customer service is by clipping small stacks of bills. This is done by placing a clip on the upper left corner of the small stack of bills. By doing this, the cashier doesn't have to verify the whole bundle.

Coin Handling and the Slot Operation

Now that you've seen how cash and chips are accounted for in the cage, we can take a look at other cage transactions. Coins are mainly the domain of the slot department although the cage uses a small amount of coins for change and has a section on the cash count sheet for them. Where change operations are a function of the cage, the cage handles them the same way the slot department would.

The slot department, on the other hand, gets its coins from the hard count room or from a nearby vault. In some places, the cage accounts for them by recording all the denominations on the cash count sheet, while in others the slot department does its own report. In any event, the slot department works out of an imprest fund, from which it will make change for customers, pay off jackpots, and fill the hoppers. Since this is a limited bank, it may have to be replenished, while at other times it can have an abundance of coins or currency that may have to be sent to the cage. When the slot cashier's booth needs coins or currency, it sends a fill slip to the cage for the money. When it needs to return bagged coins, currency, chips, hopper fill slips, or jackpot slips to the cage, it sends a credit slip, and its bankroll is credited by that amount. If a slot booth closes, it sends back its imprest fund and also receives a credit slip in return. However, these transactions will be recorded separately since they're considered temporary transfers and won't affect the slot win. Once the slot coin drop count is done, the total value of the jackpot slips and the hopper fills will be subtracted from it to determine the slot win. After this has been done, the documents are sent to the accounting department to be audited.

The slot operation is basically a cash operation although many slot players do play on credit. As popular as the slot machine operation has become, it is surprising that to this day slot players must either get credit at the table games or at the cage. These credit buy-ins without play, if credited to the table games, effectively reduce the hold percentage of that department. This is money that will be considered as part of the table games drop, yet the table games won't receive any play from the marker. This may change in the future if moneyless slot machines are introduced into the American market. It may change anyway, if the slot operation continues its rapid ascent and the table games hold continues to lag behind. In any event, it is one less transaction between the slot booth and the casino cage.

Other Gaming Departments

Where sports and race books exist, opening fills are issued to both the writer's bank and the cashier's bank. Since the cashier pays the winning tickets, this bank will have to be replenished with fills from the cage. The fills and the returned cash at the end of the day will increase or decrease the cage cash inventory but won't affect the sports and race book win since this is the product of the total number of tickets written minus the total amount of winning tickets, which don't get collected immediately. Some places pay winning tickets from the cage when the sports and race book closes. In these places, one fill slip for the total amount paid out will be written at the end of the shift.

The poker room usually has its own imprest fund at the supervisor's podium or at a separate location within the poker room from which it handles all cash transactions. This is always a balanced fund since the chips that are purchased in the poker room must be redeemed in the poker room. The only money that goes into the drop boxes is the house rake; that money will constitute the house win. It used to be that the casinos employed shills in poker, and their losses would be deducted from the drop to determine the win. This law went into effect in January of 1974, but was repealed in February of 1979.

Keno and bingo transactions are easy to calculate because all fills are added together and totaled at the end of the shift. The opening fill plus the subsequent fills will constitute the shift need for those departments. If the total cash in the banks at the end of the shift exceeds this need figure, the department will show a win.

Other Operations Departments

Other departments such as restaurants, lounges, showrooms, hotel, etc., will begin with an opening fill and end with a closing bankroll that will reflect the amount of business for the shift. Two methods of shift transfer are used. One has the incoming and outgoing cashiers count the bank; the other has each cashier carry the bank to and from the cage. The latter method produces the least inconvenience to the customer, while the former produces the least inconvenience to the cage.

The Table Games Department

Most of the work load of the cage is going to be produced by the table games department because of the chip bank and because of the issuance of credit. The chip banks will have to be replenished and, to do so, the pit manager must ask the pit clerk to request a fill order. These fill orders are identified by the table number and include the different amounts of each denomination of chips that are needed for that table. The cage cashier or clerk then generates the fill slip accordingly, signs it, and fills out the order from the cage chip bank. The chips are then placed in a plastic container, ready for transportation to the pit. The cashier calls the security dispatch booth, who sends over a security guard to make delivery of the chips and returns the signed fill slip to the cage. Believe it or not, twenty years ago, and in some places even less, fills were a matter of reaching into another rack and transferring the chips with no paperwork involved.

Sometimes the blackjack racks get overcrowded with chips that were issued for a certain high roller and are no longer needed, so the pit manager must send them back to the cage, making out a request form and calling security dispatch. Security takes the credit form to the cage and they generate the necessary paperwork. The security guard brings the slip and a secured container over to the table. This time the cashier doesn't sign the slip since a signature would indicate receipt of the amount of credit requested. So the security guard takes the chip container to the floor supervisor, who then inspects the credit slip for accuracy and instructs the security guard to lay the container on the table once the dealer is ready to accept it. The dealer then places

the excess chips in the rack or racks within the container, and proceeds to sign it. Then it is signed by the security guard and the floor supervisor. A copy of the credit slip remains on the game but won't be dropped until the cashier's signed confirmation is returned to the table either by the security guard or by the pit clerk.

Other responsibilities that the cage handles for the table games department are credit, withdrawals from deposit accounts, and as a financial source for reimbursements to casino patrons who deserve them. Credit verification is usually handled by credit executives, credit clerks, or a cage supervisor. This is also true of cash deposits from which casino customers draw markers. In some casinos, cage cashiers may serve this function, also. To verify credit lines and signatures, the cage employee must pull the customer's credit card from the credit file.

In Nevada, at the end of the working day, all markers are turned into the cage for safekeeping, and the cashiers handle all paybacks. A computer slip is generated and sent to the pit where the table card is adjusted for the amount, and the marker slip is dropped into the drop box.

In New Jersey, all markers are sent to the cage immediately, forcing customers to redeem them there. The customer gives the cashier money, chips, or a combination of both, and the cashier writes down the form of repayment on the marker stub and signs it.

Premium customers will request that their air fare or other cash expenditures be reimbursed to them. In order to do so, the casino executive authorized to approve such an expenditure will accompany the customer to the cage or authorize a cage employee to make the reimbursement. A copy of the ticket or receipt will be made, and the customer will sign a document to acknowledge receipt of the funds. That document will be forwarded to the accounting department together with a copy of the expense. Other cash disbursements to customers such as walking money or cash backs will be handled in the same way. Caution should be exercised when issuing this type of disbursement. Recently in Atlantic City a promotions booth representative swindled a casino out of a large sum of money by using his manager's code to change customer names and obtain cash reimbursements and complimentaries for agents he brought in. This is another example of why controls are so important. No one is above scrutiny.

Other Functions of the Cage

Another important function of the cage is that it is the custodian of the keys to the count room, the drop boxes, and the slot drop cabinets. At the end of each shift, these keys are handed to a designated security person who collects the drop boxes and opens the count room for the count team. The slot drop cabinets are also opened by security personnel, and the drop buckets are collected and replaced. The slot train is then escorted to the hard count room where the change buckets are deposited for the count.

At the end of each shift, the cage banks are counted, and all other entries are made into the cash count sheet. The recorded value of the cage cash inventory is then compared to the expected accounted value on the bank control sheet. The value of the shift's closing cash inventory is supposed to equal the closing balance on the bank control sheet. Yet since so many transactions are conducted during the shift, shortages are a natural consequence of conducting high-volume business in a casino. Some managers will search for the shortages, but some believe that's a waste of time since, if the money were lost or stolen, it is not going to reappear, and if it is in the cage, it is going to show up on someone else's shift as an overage. The time wasted in the search is time that can be used to service other departments and also the customers better. In any event, the accounting department writes off the shortages either monthly or annually.

The CTR and the MTL

Although I have oversimplified the cage operation, one regulation that involves the cage, and other departments, deserves to be considered separately. This is the regulation that requires documentation of cash buy-ins in excess of $10,000 in a twenty-four-hour period, which is mandated by the Treasury Department. It is important because it is handled differently in different gaming areas, and violators of this regulation are subject to criminal prosecution, including those employees who knowingly allow cash transactions of this nature to go unreported. To give an example of the complexity of this issue, suffice it to say that a player in Nevada can buy in up to $40,000 in some casinos (although others set it at $30,000), without having to provide a Social Security number and a valid ID. In Atlantic City, $10,000 is the total amount. Why this disparity? Mainly because it is a matter of interpretation and also because of a certain betting methodology that's allowed in Nevada and not in New Jersey. The state of Nevada was smart enough to reach an agreement with the Treasury Department whereby they would police these transactions, in exchange for that leniency.

In Nevada, gamers will allow a customer to accumulate buy-ins as *money play, call bets, front money, cage cash buy-in,* and cash. If all these are added together, they would add up to $50,000. However, not all casinos use the same interpretations. What is even more confusing is that despite the fact that employees can be prosecuted for having knowledge of these excessive buy-ins and not reporting them, some casinos will instruct relief supervisors to disregard them, unless they have firsthand knowledge of them. This mandate, of course, is verbally issued. The Horseshoe Casino in Las Vegas recently paid over a million dollars in fines for this type of violation, and it almost cost the company its licensing in Louisiana.

Even though it is understandable that the casinos want to preserve the anonymity of their patrons and that the government is being excessively intrusive by establishing these rules, the immorality here is that by circumventing the law, casinos are risking the livelihood of their employees, who may be subject to prosecution. It is unfair competition in that, when state governments such as New Jersey hold casinos faithfully to the $10,000 rule, the New Jersey casinos are at a disadvantage with the Nevada establishments. We can't blame the state of Nevada for attempting to protect their industry and allow the flexibility in the $10,000 rule. From a management point of view, if it is legal, it is a valid recourse. But where some Nevada operators fail is when they take it a step further and place employees in the middle and expose them to financial and legal harm. This disregard for the people who help make the organization what it is constitutes poor management and is unnecessary. After all, they should be happy that they're being allowed to play with the law at all since it is obvious that the intent is to identify anyone who buys in for more than $10,000, period. The purpose of this law is to allow the federal government to identify individuals who may be laundering money or who may be accumulating unreported income from questionable sources. They want to be able to track how money flows throughout the United States.

Pertaining to the above regulation, the cage has two forms it must fill out. One is the Currency Transaction Report, and the other is the Multiple Transaction Log. Basically there are four instances in which the cage cashier will have to determine whether or not an entry will be required: when a customer buys in chips at the cage; when a customer cashes chips at the cage; when a customer deposits cash or chips to an account in the cage; and when a customer makes a wager in excess of $10,000 that will be paid in cash (Regulation 6A.050-1, State of Nevada).

If a customer buys in excess of $10,000 ($10,001), the cashier is obliged to request identification. This identification will be preferably a driver's license, but can also be a passport or any other government-issued identification with a picture that will provide the patron's address and nationality. The cashier is also required to get the customer's social security number. If the customer refuses to provide these items, the transaction can't be completed. Sometimes this process can be avoided if the customer is a known patron whose information is on file although, technically, this isn't acceptable.

Any cash transaction on the casino floor in excess of $10,000 on the casino floor, whether it is a buy-in or a cash disbursement by the casino, must be accompanied by a Currency Transaction Report. This means that a customer who requests cash for a jackpot payout of over $10,000 will have to provide identification. If a customer doesn't provide identification, he or she won't receive the money, and a Currency Transaction Report Refusal Form will be generated. This form provides a description of the customer and is accompanied by two surveillance photographs.

When any of the mentioned transactions is under the $10,000 limit yet exceeds a house prescribed limit, *i.e.*, $2,500, the cashier has to record the transaction in the Multiple Transaction Log. The Multiple Transaction Log isn't required; however, the casino has to have some written vehicle to track the cash transactions. In the MTL, in addition to the type of transaction that occurred and the amount involved, the cashier writes a description of the patron. The purpose of this record is to prevent the circumvention of the $10,000 rule. This methodology succinctly establishes the government's intent to foil violations of this rule. With this in mind, casino personnel in most states maintain strong communication to avoid violations.

CHAPTER 16

THE SECURITY DEPARTMENT

The security department is usually divided into two separate entities: surveillance and security. These two entities are within the same department, and they work closely together. Security officers don't take any action without involving surveillance, unless they must react instantaneously.

The security department has become increasingly important because of its responsibility to control theft. Since the gaming business involves large amounts of cash, it attracts opportunists eager to beat the system and walk away with a piece of the treasure. Even those who don't intend to steal become susceptible to the temptation that ready cash produces. So in order to safeguard the casino's vulnerable resources, a system of checks and balances, which included an independent guardian who protects the casino's interest, was implemented. This was the security department.

Security and surveillance departments today are far more sophisticated than their predecessors were. Their predecessors relied mainly on limited personnel who watched when asked or intervened when force was required. Although some establishments still operate in these conditions, most of them today are better protected. Most average casinos will employ from 50 to a 100 or more security guards and will spend over $100,000 in surveillance equipment up to and possibly over $1,000,000. This shows the importance ascribed to this department in modern-day casinos. Many operators believe that the security department pays for itself many times over by the amount of money it saves the company in theft prevention.

Aside from the invaluable role security plays in theft prevention, there are many other functions this important department performs. There are traffic coordination, parking security and allocation, theft prevention within parking facilities, customer protection and escorts, crowd control, crowd discipline, transfers and verification of money transactions, and property safety. Security's responsibilities are comprehensive.

SECURITY PERSONNEL

Director of Security

The director of security usually directs surveillance also, reporting to the general manager, to corporate security, and to the board of directors of the company. This executive supervises security supervisors of varying ranks and, possibly, the director of surveillance. Along with responsibility for the overall security of the establishment and ensuring that company rules and regulations are complied with, the security/surveillance manager determines personnel requirements and establishes performance standards. This director also plans and organizes company procedures for property security and, in addition, plans and establishes the job-training program for all security employees.

Since part of the function of the security department is to maintain order and compliance with company rules and regulations as well as local rules, regulations, and ordinances, the director will have to establish and maintain a working relationship with local law enforcement agencies. Through the surveillance department, this executive will maintain control of operational procedures that apply on the casino floor, in all bars, restaurants, and other money-handling operations of the property. A very important consideration of this sensitive position is that all reports submitted must be factual, not based on conjecture. It is because of this that the individual selected for this position must be above reproach.

Security Supervisor

Security supervisors, who establish the chain of command and the distribution of tasks and duties, are of various ranks. Among the security supervisors are the assistant director, the security shift managers of every shift, security supervisors, and acting security supervisors. There are also ranks among the security officers themselves.

Security supervisors direct, supervise, train, and guide all security officers assigned to particular posts. They are also responsible for the daily inspections of all security officers and their assigned posts to determine if they're conducting themselves appropriately and to ensure that all officers are properly deployed. In addition to this peripheral supervision, the security supervisor must supervise removal of all drop boxes and their journey to the count room. Since most casino departments require the assistance of the security department, these supervisors serve as a link between departments.

Security supervisors also scrutinize anything that may affect the safety of the property or the people contained within it. They are responsible for reports of fire or other hazards that are found on the property and are required to be constantly on the alert for any unusual happenings within the property. These persons also work to ensure the preservation of the integrity of the casino.

Security supervisors also establish work assignments for security officers and the inspection and evaluation of security officers. This evaluation will look for alertness, proper appearance, and proper performance of the security officers. In addition to these responsibilities, security supervisors are entrusted with the custody of security-sensitive keys which safeguard the integrity of slot machines, slot machine drop buckets, table game racks, table game podiums, table game jackpots, card and dice rooms, cage vaults, cage drawers, and cage equipment.

Security supervisors, along with the casino department, are entrusted with security-sensitive equipment such as cards, dice, controlled forms and counter checks, and value and nonvalue chips. They are usually required to log all disbursements of these items and are held accountable for them. Finally, security supervisors must be able to train and retrain all security officers under their supervision.

Security Officer

Security officers are the first line of defense of the casino operation. These are the employees who are there to enforce rules and regulations, in much the same way police officers do for the government. Like police officers, security officers will be entrusted with escorting, detaining, and arresting infractors on casino property. Of course, when an arrest is necessary, the security officer will work in conjunction with local authorities, serving only as custodian until local authorities can take over where civil laws apply.

To ensure safety and compliance with rules and regulations, security officers patrol or inspect several different assigned areas for irregularities. While doing this, they are responsible for providing protection to all employees, guests, and company property. They will have to monitor all activity on property to ensure that no unauthorized removal of company property occurs. If any incident takes place regarding the above-mentioned functions, the security officer will be required to write detailed reports. A separate function of the security officer is to administer first aid and provide assistance as needed. This may occur when a patron or employee suffers an accident or suddenly becomes ill. If necessary, it will be the security officer's responsibility to contact the nearest hospital for assistance.

While doing routine patrols, security officers are required to periodically inspect assigned areas, being constantly on the lookout for undesirable persons or irregularities. They must possess knowledge of all city, county, state, and federal laws and/or ordinances, since they are responsible for any violation. In sum, the most obvious function of the security officer is, of course, to provide security and protection for the casino property, its guests, and its employees.

On a daily basis, security officers are required to inspect fire protection equipment to ensure that it is operational. They inspect all areas for safety and fire hazards, and file reports regarding the outcome of these inspections. They write detailed reports regarding incidents of theft, injury, property damage, or other matters affecting the property and its customers. They monitor all activities of the casino's employees and guests, paying careful attention to unauthorized removal of company property. And perhaps one of the most overlooked and underrated functions of security officers is their role as public relations officers. In this capacity, security officers provide protective and informative services to guests and fellow employees who may require their assistance.

Security officers also carry out or assist in inter-departmental functions that are security sensitive. These functions include the escort and verification of jackpot payoffs, the escort and verification of table game and hopper fills and credits, the verification and escort of table game and slot drop boxes and buckets, and any other security-sensitive interdepartmental transfer.

SECURITY FUNCTIONS DETAILED

Public Relations

A security officer's work often brings him or her in contact with more people in a single day than some other employees meet in months. Because of this, there will be times when security officers will have the responsibility of stopping and questioning strangers. It is, therefore, of the utmost importance that persons selected for this function be schooled and polished in courteousness. This is especially true when the officer's assignments are primarily duties that require public contact. The success of the security officer in this respect will depend largely upon his or her ability to remain calm and even-tempered in all circumstances.

The casino environment presents a unique situation for new casino guests since, in most environments, patrons rarely come into contact with so many uniformed officers. It is because of this singular situation, to which most patrons are unaccustomed, that the security officers should be especially pleasing and tolerant. The security officer's attitude should be one of modesty, concern, friendliness, and helpfulness.

As front-line representatives of the establishment, security officers are expected to be as informative as possible to the patrons and employees, as long as their information doesn't breach the casino's security. All responses and suggestions should be thoughtful, courteous, and accurate. When uncertain or uninformed, the security officer shouldn't reply in conjectures or make suggestions that can be misleading; it is essential to call for advice so as to instruct the aid-seeking party accurately.

When information is solicited regarding the casino's delicate security matters, policies, procedures, products, processes, and records, security officers should refrain from divulging such information and should question the inquirer in return. The nature and result of this exchange should be reported to the security officer's supervisor.

Arrest Procedures

Security officers don't have the authority of law enforcement. They represent a private concern and, as such, can function only to safeguard that which relates to their employer's security. It is a preventive function. However, just like any other citizen, security officers can apply arrest procedures when laws are violated in certain circumstances. Following are examples of such circumstances:

1. A person has committed or attempted to commit a public offense in the security officer's presence.

2. The person has committed a felony, even if not in the security officer's presence.

3. The security officer has reasonable cause to believe that the person arrested committed a felony. When requested, a security officer shall provide name, badge number, and the nature of the assignment to any violator or other person who requests it, unless such action jeopardizes the successful completion of the security officer's assignment.

Every member of the security department must refrain from using unnecessary force when making an arrest or at any other time. The *force* applied during such instances should not be more restraint than is necessary for the person's arrest and detention, and it should not jeopardize the safety and protection of the arresting officer or the person being detained. However, in performing this function the arresting officer must be firm, decisive, and unyielding, exercising only the necessary means to properly perform his or her duty. If force is unavoidable, the circumstances that led to such action should be clearly expressed and should be justified in a written report. In no circumstance should security officers antagonize or use irreverent or insulting language in reference to a prisoner or any other person with whom they come in contact in such a situation. A prisoner is an individual who is confined for any length of time where freedom of movement is restrained.

Security officers should keep in mind that prisoners and suspects, regardless of the offense committed, are human beings and should be treated as such. Offi-

cers only show their ignorance or similarity to the detained person if they reciprocate in an aggressive or insulting fashion. It is unethical and inappropriate for security officers to humiliate, ridicule, taunt, or embarrass any person. Furthermore, security officers should refrain from striking prisoners or suspects or from using any other form of physical force except when force is absolutely necessary to prevent escape, for self-defense, or to prevent violence to another person.

When security officers make arrests, the right to protect themselves may justify a search for weapons the persons arrested might use to escape or to harm the security officers. Persons to be searched may or may not consent to such a procedure. If they don't willingly consent, security officers may force them in an effort to recapture casino property, only if it is clearly evident that the persons to be searched possess casino property that has been unlawfully taken. This is a very sensitive area and should be approached as such. The casino is exposed to legal repercussions if an illegal or improper search is conducted by the security officer.

When making arrests and detaining prisoners or suspects, security officers should take all precautions to prevent an escape, an injury to themselves or others, or damage to property. They should be careful not to place weapons or objects that can be used as weapons within the reach of any person detained or arrested. To do so is to endanger themselves, and to put other people at risk. Security officers should also keep in mind that not only are they responsible for safely guarding a prisoner or suspect but also for any personal property that they remove from the prisoner or suspect.

Female prisoners or suspects should be handled only as is necessary to take them into custody and to determine that they're not concealing weapons. However, a female officer should be present when at all possible and should be the one to perform the search. Women who are in the custody of security officers shouldn't be searched by male officers unless an immediate search is necessary. Such a search would be necessary if there's good reason to believe the person has in her possession a weapon, a poisonous substance, a powerful drug, or other like means of causing death or injury to herself or to another person. A male officer should not talk to a female prisoner or suspect alone in an interrogation room unless his actions can be monitored by other witnesses. Even then, it is best to have a female officer present or at least another female employee to serve as a witness.

Security officers should adhere faithfully to the law when making arrests and should keep in mind the rights of the citizen concerned. At all times, officers should be aware that they are neither prosecutor nor avenger of the offense and, therefore, should refrain from inflicting punishment. They should be aware of their responsibilities and limitations regarding the detention of a violator. In performing their duty, security officers must conduct themselves in a manner that will minimize the possibility of having to use force. After making the citizen's arrest, the security officer will promptly notify the local police department.

We should always keep in mind that the security officers and any other casino employees who might temporarily act in the capacity of security officers aren't law enforcement officers and, therefore, their actions should be limited to the investigation and reporting of incidents. Whenever possible, these individuals should avoid attempts to physically restrain or to eject guests or other employees from the premises. A high degree of caution should be used prior to refusing anyone permission to leave the premises, and only in instances of a serious nature should they try to restrain or coerce anyone into remaining on the premises for reasons of questioning and/or interrogation. The security officers should also refrain from detaining persons against their will unless the establishment's management is willing to sign a complaint.

The main concern of security officers is to assist the general manager and/or the director of casino operations and staff in the orderly administration of the casino's rules and regulations. Because this responsibility involves security officers in areas that affect the rights of both guests and employees, they must be well aware of these rights and should also be conscious of performing these duties with the utmost courtesy, consideration, and restraint. In all conditions, security officers are expected to use good judgment and common sense.

Security officers may need to take certain actions when confronted with disturbances, crimes, and threats to life and property that can at times make the casino or themselves a target for legal action. Because of this sensitive situation, security officers' actions will sometimes be scrutinized to see if they did something wrong. This should be standard procedure for any casino operation. In this way the casino will avoid future lawsuits and will be prepared if a lawsuit is brought against it.

Security officers may make a citizen's arrest if a felony is committed in their presence, or if they have knowledge that a felony has been committed and the person to be arrested is the person who committed the felony. However, when a citizen's arrest is made for a felony not committed in the security officer's presence, he or she must be absolutely certain of the facts if liability for a false arrest is to be avoided. Just like any other private citizen making an arrest, security officers will not be permitted any mistakes in the matter and will not enjoy the same latitude sworn police officers would be entitled to.

Misdemeanor arrests may be made only when the misdemeanor is committed in the presence of the security officer and when it disturbs the peace. A misdemeanor arrest should be made only after the security officer has exhausted all other means of resolving the problem. After an arrest, the person arrested must be turned over to official authorities as soon as possible.

Except for a felony or misdemeanor arrest as described above, no other detention or confinement is permissible, unless the person being detained or confined freely and voluntarily agrees to such action by the security officer. Both the security officer and the person being held must clearly understand what is happening. If an arrest is being made, persons being arrested must be clearly told that they are being arrested. If the detention and/or confinement is voluntary, detained individuals must clearly understand that they are free to leave whenever they choose.

Normally, the job of arresting criminal offenders is left to police officers. That is why in all cases where a criminal offense is committed in the casino, the police department should be promptly notified. Only if the police officers can't respond in time should security officers perform a citizen's arrest.

Security officers should clearly understand that, like any other citizens, they may make a citizen's arrest and turn these infractors over to proper constituted authorities; however, they should also clearly understand that this arresting power is valid only when the purpose of the arrest is to turn the person over to the proper authorities. Failure to turn these people over to the proper authorities can result in criminal and/or civil liability for the security officers as well as for the casino.

If the above action is taken without proper legal authority, it is considered a false arrest and false imprisonment. And although every false arrest is a false imprisonment, not all false imprisonment is a false arrest. A false imprisonment may occur without an arrest if individuals are confined for any length of time where their freedom of movement is restrained. Security officers should take this into consideration when making the decision to confine any individual. There should be an extremely valid reason for such action and plenty of supporting evidence such as videotape and/or strong testimonial.

Ejection of a Guest or Employee (Trespass Law)

Security officers should keep in mind that every person, excluding employees, on the premise of the property is a guest by invitation or advertisement and should not be ejected without sufficient reason. In no circumstance should a security officer eject anyone without a supervisor's approval or the direct order of a casino management official, usually of the rank of casino shift manager or above. In doing so, the following guidelines should be used to determine *sufficient reason:*

1. If a person is creating a disturbance that annoys the guests or that interferes with or prevents casino employees from performing their assigned duties efficiently.

2. If a guest or employee is caught stealing.

3. If a person is caught on the premise with the intent to prostitute.

4. If a person is apprehended while cheating or attempting to cheat any gaming table or gaming device.

5. If a person is known to be a cheat and is identified by casino personnel.

6. If a person loiters about the casino for a long length of time and the security officer believes him or her desirous of committing an unlawful act.

7. If a person is defrauding or attempting to defraud the casino.

8. If a person endangers the life or well-being of a guest or employee.

9. If the security officer, having personal knowledge of someone who has a previous felony arrest record, sees that person loitering about the casino or lobby areas and that person refuses to justify his or her presence when interviewed.

10. In a hotel setting, if a person is loitering in the rooming area without visible or lawful business and can't justify his or her presence, or anyone who peeks in the door or window or any room without visible or lawful business with the occupant.

11. If a person engages in lewd or dissolute conduct in any place exposed to public view.

12. If a person accosts any casino guests or employees for the purpose of begging or soliciting.

13. If a person is caught in the act of tearing down, mutilating, or destroying any casino property.

14. If a person enters the premises and commits a crime, attempts to commit a crime, or shows the intent to commit a crime.

CLASSIFICATION OF CRIMES

1. A crime is an act or omission by law and punishable upon conviction by death, imprisonment, fine or other penal discipline.

2. Every crime which may be punished by death or by imprisonment in the state prison is a felony.

3. Every crime punishable by a fine of not more that $500, or by imprisonment in a county jail for not more than six months, is a misdemeanor in most states.

4. Every other crime is usually a gross misdemeanor.

In order for a public offense to be classified as a crime, there must exist a union, a joint operation of act and intention, or criminal negligence. Intention is manifested by the circumstances connected with the perpetration of the offense, and the judgment of sound mind is ascribed to the discretion of the person accused. This person will be considered of sound mind if he or she is neither mentally incapacitated nor affected with insanity, and is at least fourteen years old, or if younger, that the person knew the distinction between good and evil.

No act committed by a person while in a state of voluntary intoxication will be deemed less criminal by reason of this condition; however, the fact of this intoxication may be taken into consideration in determining the purpose, motive, or intent in a crime. These precepts are accepted across most of the United States.

ESTABLISHMENT OF LIABILITY FOR PUNISHMENT

All persons are liable to punishment except those belonging to the following classes:

1. Children under eight years of age.

2. Children between the ages of eight and fourteen, in the absence of clear proof that at the time of committing the act charged against them they knew it was wrong.

3. Mentally incapacitated persons.

4. Insane persons.

5. Persons who committed the act or made the omission charged under an ignorance or mistake of fact, which disproves any criminal intent, where a specific intent is required to constitute the offense.

6. Persons who committed the act charged without being conscious thereof.

7. Persons who committed the act or made the omission charged through misfortune or by accident, when it appears that there was no evil design, intention, or culpable negligence.

8. Married women, unless the crime is punishable by death, acting under the threats, commands or coercion of their husbands, provided, from all the facts and circumstances of the case, that violent threats, commands or coercion were used.

9. Persons, unless the crime is punishable by death, who committed the act or made the omission charged under threats or menaces sufficient to show that they had reasonable cause to believe, and did believe, their lives would be endangered if they refused or that they would suffer great bodily harm.

GENERAL SECURITY FUNCTIONS

A security officer is primarily responsible for the safety and protection of the casino guests and the casino employees, both within the building and outside the surrounding property. Security officers should patrol all public and nonpublic areas of the property, both indoors and out of doors on a twenty-four hour-a-day, seven-day-week basis. While working their respective assignments, security officers should be on the lookout for any guest or employee in need of assistance. This may require giving directions, filing a report, or listening to a complaint.

Security officers are also responsible for maintaining law and order within the casino and in conjunction with local law enforcement agencies. The security officer handles all monetary transactions between the casino cage and the gaming tables in compliance with gaming regulations. This officer is also required to maintain the security of the casino cage, where large amounts of currency are held. If anyone, employee or guest, should require medical assistance, it is the responsibility of the security department to administer first aid and make the necessary arrangements to provide medical assistance to those in need.

Where entertainment facilities exist, the security officer must control show lines and enforce crowd control at special events and functions. On the casino floor itself, the security officer must constantly check for suspicious persons, activities, and juveniles who may desire service in the casino or bars and lounges.

Slot areas must be kept under close observation at all times, specifically for slot cheats, purse snatchers, and hustlers in general. Slot jackpot payouts, hopper fills, and the transfer of money to and from the cage are also the security officer's concern. He or she stands by while porters and maintenance workers perform duties that bring them into areas where money and sensitive equipment are in use.

Security officers make sure that all fire stairwells, hydrants, and exits are kept clear of obstructions so that, in the event of a fire, the casino is prepared to handle it. They check for illegally parked vehicles in fire lanes, driveways, and handicapped parking spaces. They observe all foot traffic arriving through employee entrances, especially looking for intoxicated employees, nonemployees who may be using this entrance, and new employees who may need assistance. They also monitor any property which may be being removed from the casino by employees.

Security personnel assist paramedics and/or police and fire department personnel in emergency situations that may arise on casino property. In order to assist them better, they should know how to use fire-fighting equipment and be able to immediately locate and extinguish any fires. To further assist the authorities and firefighters, part of the security training should include CPR and the use of firearms. Many casinos frown upon the use of firearms, so this is going to depend on the philosophy of the establishment in question. However, some knowledge of firearms is necessary regardless of whether officers are allowed to holster weapons or not, since they may have to deal with situations that involve the use of them.

Part of the security inspection process includes garbage and refuse being removed from the premise to see if it contains any casino property such as silverware, dishes, linen, or like items. They monitor employee activities in public and nonpublic areas, looking for misuse of casino property, the use of controlled substances or alcoholic beverages, horseplay, vandalism, and unauthorized consumption of food items. At times, officers will have to perform special functions and conduct surveys when so requested by other departments. Counting visitors would be one such function.

Elevators are especially vulnerable to crime activities and should be monitored closely by security personnel, who should watch for the activities of casino guests in the elevator lobbies and for unauthorized removal of casino property and vandalism. Elevators should be monitored for any suspicious persons exiting or entering the area, and security supervisors should be advised of these activities. All service areas should be kept under surveillance for unauthorized guests or employees, suspicious activity, and the removal of casino property. Security officers should also check the furniture and decorations of public areas to ensure that all items are accounted for, checking them for vandalism and ascertaining whether they are in need of repair or cleaning. Need for repairs or cleaning should be brought to the immediate attention of the supervisor, who in turn will notify the facilities department.

Security officers are required to know the complete operation of the fire control command centers and to provide wheelchairs and escorts, when requested, for casino guests.

GENERAL FIRE PROCEDURES

In the event of a fire report, a smoke report, or a smoke or gas order report, all non-emergency radio traffic should cease until the dispatcher has cleared the channel. The dispatcher should clear the channel (at the supervisor's direction) by announcing *"Control clear with emergency traffic"* (at whatever hours).

In the event of a confirmed fire report, all security officers on break should immediately return to their duty stations. The dispatcher will broadcast a call for all units to return to their duty stations.

In order to prevent possible panic among guests who may overhear radio traffic, the following definitions must be used:

a. The term *confirmed 402* will be used to define either visible open flame and/or the obvious presence of smoke or unusual heat.

b. The term *substance* will define the obvious presence of smoke.

c. The term *odor* will define any heat or smoke smell where no substance exists.

d. The term *640-A* will define any activated fire alarm.

The following is the appropriate response to reports of smoke, odor, or fire calls:

a. Supervisors call the dispatcher, who in turn calls appropriate officers to the area of the call to investigate. The designated unit will travel toward the nearest located fire cart or hoses in case they are needed.

b. The supervisor nearest to the area of the call responds to the call, while a second supervisor travels towards the security office.

c. The dispatcher immediately notifies the engineers. (On confirmed fires, the dispatcher is also responsible for notifying the fire department via direct line.)

d. An outside officer directs emergency vehicles onto the property through the appropriate entrance.

e. The first officer on the scene immediately gives a radio report to his or her supervisors in lieu of their arrival.

THE ROAMING OFFICER

The following are the functions of roaming security officers:

a. To make constant patrols through areas of the casino building.

b. To respond to and provide assistance to any security officer who is on an assigned security post and who is in need of such assistance.

c. To report and identify all fire and safety hazards in areas of the casino where there's no assigned security post.

d. To respond to and provide fire protection in all areas of the building.

e. To maintain constant communication with the security department dispatcher.

f. To monitor all fire fighting and first aid equipment on a daily basis during patrols and ensure that all equipment is maintained in a fully operational status.

g. To ensure that all office doors, storage rooms, and cold storage lockers are locked and secure when these areas aren't in use.

h. To be first on the scene when dispatched to any area of the building that doesn't have an assigned security post or when the security of guests, employees, or the building is in jeopardy.

i. To interview guests and employees and write the necessary reports regarding incidents that may occur during the course of the shift.

j. To investigate reports written by other roaming officers and be ready to do a follow-up report or a continuation report in reference to the previous officers' findings.

k. To obtain witnesses and/or employee statements, when needed, in reference to the investigation of any report.

l. To seal off and preserve the integrity of any crime scene when an outside law enforcement agency has been called in reference to a major crime. This would include arson or the discovery of a dead body found anywhere on the casino's property, even if the cause of death appears to be natural.

m. To identify and isolate any witnesses or suspects pertaining to a serious incident, prior to the arrival of law enforcement agents, when a local law enforcement agency has been called to respond to the casino property in reference to a major crime or other such incident.

n. To know the complete layout of the casino, the building, and the surroundings in order to expedite the arrival of any emergency personnel. The security officer must also be able to escort such personnel to whatever part of the building they're needed. Emergency personnel may be defined as follows: paramedics, ambulance personnel, police officers, and fire department personnel.

o. To write a report regardless of the limited information available.

p. To write a report that is totally unbiased.

q. To write a report where the findings are expressed clearly, concisely, and in chronological order.

r. To assist the proper authorized personnel in unlocking and opening various secured doors throughout the building when requested to do so.

s. To know the appropriate statutes, trespass warnings, and the limitations of them.

t. To know how to fill out a *Field Interview* card in reference to identifying anyone who is considered undesirable or a potential threat to guests, employees, or property.

u. To question any persons found in secured areas or who are in unassigned areas.

v. To watch for any casino or guest property which has been placed in a suspicious manner or concealed for possible pickup at a later time.

w. To patrol the premises on the lookout for burglaries, persons prowling the area, acts of vandalism, unsecured doors and gates, keys left in doors, signs of forced entry on a door or window, broken windows, torn wallpaper, burned-out lights, or for any condition that would be a threat or hazard to any guests, employees, or to the casino itself.

x. To make several patrols through the various areas of the building and grounds, and to be extremely vigilant for any unusual changes in any area that has been previously examined while on patrol.

PROCEDURAL ORDERS

A procedural order is a directive that establishes a course or method of action for the accomplishment of a specific task. Following is a list of procedural orders that a security officer must adhere to:

1. A security officer, accompanied by another, must take inventory of property that is found involving currency or high-value items. Then it must be approved and initialed by the on-duty supervisor.

2. A security officer must be accompanied by another when escorting an intoxicated guest.

3. A security officer must be accompanied by another when entering an occupied room where the occupants aren't present.

4. A security officer must refrain from handling suspicious persons without a backup officer or officers.

5. A security officer must be accompanied by another when interviewing a detained female out of public view.

6. A security officer, along with backup officers, must report to the dispatcher the mileage of the vehicle upon departing the property and the mileage upon

returning to the property when transporting a female guest or employee in a company car.

7. A security officer must verify guest registration prior to assisting guests in entering their rooms.

8. A security officer can only seek the assistance of one other officer when responding to a call, unless it is of an emergency nature.

EVACUATION PROCEDURES

Evacuation procedures may vary depending on the circumstances and the location of the property. Obviously, there are various reasons for implementing evacuation procedures. Properties that are located on coastal waters or near or on riverbanks can be subject to hurricanes, tornadoes, or flooding in addition to the other common reasons for evacuation such as bomb threats and fires. The following are general procedures for evacuation of patrons and employees from a gaming establishment in the above emergency situations:

1 . If there's a fire, security supervisors will deploy security staff on duty to analyze the problem and combat the fire if necessary.

2. In any emergency situation, security supervisors will deploy security staff to aid and remove injured persons.

3. Depending on the circumstances, security supervisors will instruct security officers to provide a secured perimeter of the affected area, disallowing entry to all unauthorized persons, insuring by this means the protection of guests and casino property.

4. If the area is deemed a crime scene, security officers will be instructed to secure the perimeter of the affected area until the scene has been released by the proper authorities.

5. Depending on the circumstances (whether a hurricane or tornado warning has been issued), security supervisors will devise an evacuation plan and will take charge of the initial evacuation plan (partial or total), if it is deemed necessary.

6. If necessary, the security supervisors will provide an initial first aid station to treat any injured guests or employees.

7. Security supervisors will also coordinate operations with the fire and police officials responding to the incident.

8. If the incident is a fire or a crime, security supervisors will maintain the integrity of the scene until fire, police, and the establishment's investigations are conducted, insuring that all necessary reports, statements, and photographs have been obtained and are complete.

9. It is also important to remember that only the senior official on the scene, or the police or the fire department can order the evacuation of the establishment. The senior official effecting this order should be the highest-ranking director or manager on duty.

10. An evacuation due to a bomb threat should follow the procedures established in evacuation because of fire.

11. If and when an evacuation is ordered by a senior official, prior to the arrival of local enforcement officials, the chief engineer will ensure that all electric, gas, and fuel lines are cut off as required.

12. If an evacuation is ordered by police or fire officials, the instructions of the official in command must be explicitly followed.

FIRE ALARM ANNOUNCEMENTS

The following announcements should accompany the onset of an audible fire alarm. If it is deemed to be a false alarm:

"Ladies and gentlemen, this isn't an emergency, I repeat, this isn't an emergency. An alarm has been activated; however, there's no emergency. Please resume your activities and enjoy your stay at our establishment. I repeat, this isn't an emergency."

If the audible alarm is, in fact, due to an emergency, the following announcement should follow:

"Ladies and gentlemen, may I have your attention, please. An emergency (or possible emergency) situation does exist and management requests that all persons leave the ... (name the area affected) ... immediately as a precautionary measure. I repeat, an emergency situation does exist and management requests that all persons leave the ... (area) immediately as a precautionary measure."

CLASSIFICATIONS OF FIRES

CLASS A: These are fires in ordinary combustible materials where the cooling or quenching effect of water or solutions containing water are sufficient for their extinction. (Example: frame construction, furniture, waste baskets, wood, paper, cloth, etc.)

CLASS B: These are fires in flammable liquids, grease, gasoline, paints, oils, etc., where air exclusion or blanketing is essential. (Example: deep fat fryers, gasoline cans, vats of cleaning solvent, etc.)

CLASS C: These are fires in electrical equipment where a nonconductive extinguishing agent is of the utmost importance. (Example: electric heaters, switchboards, transformer banks, motors, switches, etc.)

BOMB THREAT PROCEDURES

The following outline or check list is designed to ensure that key casino employees respond in a prescribed manner after a bomb threat is received.

PROCEDURES FOR EMPLOYEES RECEIVING THE CALL:

1. They will handle the call on a priority basis.

2. They will obtain as much information as possible from the caller, asking the caller to repeat the message, particularly the location of the bomb, the time of detonation, etc.

3. They will also record the message, and if a recording device isn't available, they will transcribe the message verbatim.

4. While taking the call, they will listen for background noises that may provide a clue as to where the call is originating from.

5. The receiver will pay attention to the voice of the caller so it can be identified should he or she hear it again. Particular attention should be given to accents, dialects, speech impediments, etc.

6. Immediately after the call the receiver will notify, in order, the casino manager or assistant manager on duty, then the security manager or senior security officer on duty.

PROCEDURES FOR THE SECURITY DEPARTMENT:

1. After notification from the telephone operator or another employee that a bomb threat has been received, the security dispatcher will notify his or her supervisor, who will then contact the manager on duty and the local police department. If a demand for ransom or other value item is accompanied by the bomb threat, the FBI will also be called. The dispatcher or supervisor must ensure that the person who received the call completes a bomb threat form or like-kind document, a copy of which will be made available to the local police department.

2. The security officer or dispatcher will consult with the security manager or security supervisor on duty, who will in turn consult with the general manager or next-highest-ranking manager on duty to determine if a bomb search is to be conducted.

3. If a search is to be conducted, the security manager or security supervisor on duty will establish a command post. This command post should be located in a pre-selected area that is easily accessible to employees and the police, yet is away from the view of casino guests and the general public.

4. At the request of the manager on duty or the security manager or representative, a systematic sweeping search of the building will be initiated. Specific assignments for searching certain areas should be given to key employees who have access to those areas and who are familiar with them. Each employee participating in the search should have the telephone number of the command post and should report the search results immediately. Participants in the search should not discuss their actions with guests or other nonparticipating employees.

5. A log of all pertinent activity should be maintained at the command post and should include entries such as:

   a. The time the police and the FBI were notified.

   b. The identity of the employees conducting the search and the searching areas assigned.

   c. The time of arrival of the law enforcement officers and/or firemen.

   d. The time the evacuation was ordered.

   e. The areas that were ordered to be evacuated.

   f. The time the explosive device was located.

   g. The place the explosive device was located.

SEARCHING PROCEDURES:

1. Employees who are most familiar with the area to be searched should be selected for the search team.

2. The areas to be searched should include ceiling areas, ventilation ducts, seldom used storage areas, telephone junction boxes, fan rooms, toilet water reservoir tanks, and elevator shafts; and special attention should be paid to washrooms, meeting rooms, and convention areas.

3. It is important to keep in mind that during the search, other than actual verbal communication, only telephone lines should be used to communicate. Hand-held radios can cause the detonation of an electric initiator.

4. Upon entering a room, search party members should move to various parts of the room, standing quietly at different intervals to listen for a clockwork or ticking device. While searching the room, they should also move systematically and check for items that look out of place and would not normally be found in the room being inspected.

5. If at all possible, search party members should not change the environment of the room prior to the search. They should use flashlights and in no circumstance should they turn on the lights. Thermostat settings should also remain untouched.

6. When conducting the search, logical areas should have priority. However, the search should still be conducted systematically and not at random. As an example, let's say that the threat-targeted group is using a meeting room, the meeting room should be searched first, followed by immediately adjacent areas.

7. Upon completion of the search, members of the search party should immediately report their findings to their supervisor.

8. If a strange or suspicious object is found while conducting the search, search party members must refrain from touching it. They should immediately report the location of the object to their supervisor.

9. It should be clearly understood that the removal of any strange or suspicious object must be left to the police, the fire department, or the military.

10. If the pertinent authorities have not yet arrived when the suspicious object is discovered, mattresses or like-kind materials may be placed around the object. However, it is important to note that objects made of metal would make a dangerous barrier and a poor choice for containment, and to cover the object would be a bad idea, also.

11. As a final protective measure, the search party members should open all the doors and windows in the immediate area where the object is found.

HANDLING THE MEDIA

1. Bomb threats received by casinos as well as explosions in public places such as hotels and casinos are of interest to the general public. When such an incident becomes public, there seems to be an immediate increase in similar incidents. To avoid such copycat occurrences, as well as to insure that the investigation of such instances isn't jeopardized by employee state-ments or comments, no statements or comments should be made by casino employees to the news media without prior consultation with law enforcement officials. Both security and casino management should ensure that this procedure is followed.

2. When an incident occurs that constitutes a violation of a federal, state, or local law, it is best to refer any news media inquiry to one of the law enforcement agencies involved in the investigation.

3. All inquiries by the news media must be referred to the general manager. Other employees, with the exception of those designated by the general manager, should not discuss the situation with anyone other than constituted authorities.

FIREARM POLICY

Firearm policies in casinos are similar to those in most other places. The discharge of a firearm can have a devastating effect and the consequences can be far-reaching. A firearm should only be discharged as a last resort when the security officer perceives that there is imminent danger of loss of life to self or to another person. Warning shots shouldn't be used at all, since that bullet has to come down and may land on somebody, or the deafening detonation may cause an innocent bystander who has a weak heart to have heart failure, and it will give casino guests a scare that will probably discourage them from returning to the casino again.

Security officers shouldn't be allowed to fire their weapons at vehicles, whether they're moving or standing still. Hollywood has glamorized this imagery, but in real life too many things can go wrong, and the casino's liability is always on the line. If it is poor judgment to fire at a car, firing at a fleeing person is totally out of the question. It should be further understood that because of the repercussions of using a firearm, a security officer should never draw a weapon unless he or she has no other choice but to use it. Drawing a firearm doesn't only cause panic among bystanders; it also allows for the possibility that it can be used against the officer.

Finally, it is important to note that most casinos and some states don't allow security officers to carry firearms. This policy in itself shows what a delicate issue this is. So in considering the use of firearms, casino operators should make it clear that with the authority to carry firearms comes an obligation and responsibility to show discipline, restraint, and good judgment in their use. The security officer must keep in mind that when firing a weapon, there's always danger to innocent people. Also, liability insurance rates where casinos use firearms are exorbitant.

The way in which firearms should be used by a security officer has been clarified, but there are measures that should be taken when security personnel are dispatched to answer a call where a weapon is involved.

First and foremost, security officers should notify the police department immediately for assistance. Second, security officers should be dispatched to the area of the incident to see what happened and to report their findings. After doing this, they should proceed to assist or question any victims or any witnesses to the incident. This should be done, preferably, away from the area of the incident. If the incident is still in progress, no action should be taken unless the life of the security officer or the lives of others are being threatened. Once the police arrive, security officers should immediately brief them on the situation and allow them to take any action deemed necessary to rectify the situation. Security officers will assist the police whenever possible.

PROCEDURES FOR HANDLING JACKPOTS AND FILLS

When inspecting jackpot payoffs, security officers should check to see that the winning combination shown on the payout line of the slot machine is the same as the winning combination written on the jackpot slip. They should also make sure that the proper amount of coins were inserted in the machine and that the amount of coins is expressed on the jackpot slip. Furthermore, they should check that the right pay line and the proper jackpot amount are written on the jackpot slip. If all these conditions exist, then the jackpot payoff may proceed.

In addition to the above, security officers must check to see that there's not a 50 code (door open) showing, which would invalidate the jackpot payoff. In an extremely rare occasion, a 50 code may show and it could still be a valid jackpot. If it does show, the security officer must call the slot shift supervisor and a technician for verification.

In no circumstance should security officers make any comments relating to the machine or its payoffs in front of casino guests, nor should they stand around in a posture that could be viewed as intimidating to a guest. Once security officers have made their verifications, they should then go about their normal activities as prescribed in security duties. Likewise, with all the work awaiting security officers, they should never have to wait at the booth while a jackpot slip is being processed. Once the slip is completed, the security officer can verify it, witness the count of the money, sign it, alert surveillance that the jackpot money is in transit, and then escort the custodian of the jackpot money until it is safely delivered to the lucky casino guest.

THE SURVEILLANCE DEPARTMENT

The surveillance department, also known as the *Eye in the Sky, Observation*, and *Big Brother*, has the task of monitoring all casino activities through video cameras and recorders. It is the preventive element that makes employees and guests alike think twice before breaking the law or company rules and regulations. It is such a powerful tool that a Mississippi casino has posted signs on Caribbean Stud games with high progressive jackpots that read: *The Caribbean Stud game is monitored by surveillance camera and any progressive jackpot winning hand will be reviewed before any payment is made.* How's that for deterrence? It sure is going to make people think twice about making a card switch to produce a winning combination and, in all likelihood, they will refrain from switching. Incidentally, the casino in question isn't bluffing. It will verify that the hand was legitimate before making payment to the winner.

So you see that the main function of the surveillance department is to prevent crime, not to detect it. But catching crime and violators of rules and regulations in a way that will leave no doubt as to the violator's guilt is also a major function of the surveillance department. There's probably nothing more incriminating than a video recording. By this means we are able to see, without a doubt, the facts as they unfold before our eyes.

The surveillance department is usually run by a director who has various supervisors to watch over the different shifts. There will also be one or two additional operators who will monitor the casino's different areas by using countless monitor screens. Some of these areas will be under videotape surveillance to provide a recourse of investigation if such should arise. These recordings are usually done in areas that are very vulnerable, such as the casino cage, the count rooms, high-limit table games and high-limit slot machines. They're also employed when requested by casino supervisors because of an existing situation such as high-limit play, suspect play, or suspect crime. The ideal situation would be to have all games on video recorder, from all different angles. But this is cost prohibitive, and it is also many times physically impossible due to space limitations, equipment limitations, and obstacles.

The next best thing is to have *adequate* coverage, which entails covering the most vulnerable games from as many angles as possible, hoping that if an unusual situation should arise, the supervisory staff will alert surveillance personnel, who can then cover the situation from different angles and with zoom shots as required. In this respect, surveillance personnel must be familiar with the use of sophisticated camera equipment. Areas of less security sensitivity can be monitored through *quads,* which are video recorders capable of recording off of four different cameras, although the images recorded are one-fourth the size; and, therefore, have very poor resolution when enlarged for closer inspection. They're handy for some situations, but inadequate for most. Multi-plexes are also available but the screens are even smaller and the time sequences at which they record leave gaps in the sequence of events.

The Director of Surveillance

The director of surveillance is responsible for the overall functioning and supervision of the surveillance department. This executive is entrusted with possibly the most important security function in the casino. Because of this responsibility, in most places surveillance responds directly to the general manager, and a clear-cut line is drawn between this department and the casino. In fact, in some establishments, only surveillance personnel are allowed inside the surveillance room. However, this cut-and-dry demarcation of boundaries doesn't foster a good working relationship between the surveillance department and the casino and many times serves to hinder the casino's security because of the conflict. There should be harmonious cooperation between the director of surveillance and the director of casino operations, and between the surveillance personnel and the casino executives. In this

way they can all work in unison to curtail and thwart the efforts of those who would do the casino harm.

Surveillance managers must determine what personnel requirements will be, depending upon the size and scope of the area to be observed. They will also have to establish what the performance standards will be for these employees and will have to plan and organize the procedures for surveillance of the property. A constant problem that plagues the surveillance department is obtaining and training qualified personnel. In this respect, surveillance managers have the unenviable task of finding people who have good knowledge of the games, some knowledge of the use of electronic equipment, common sense, a knack for discovery and investigation, *and . . .* are willing to work for less money than they would make while working on the casino floor, in most instances. It is easy to see why this would constitute a problem. The next best thing is to find individuals who are willing to be trained for the job. It will be the surveillance manager's task to plan and establish the job-training program, which in many instances requires that surveillance personnel take gaming courses in craps, roulette, and blackjack, to a minimum, with other games as required. The rest of the training will be in surveillance techniques and procedures.

Surveillance directors will also have to establish and maintain a good working relationship with local law enforcement agencies and investigators, as well as with the agents assigned to the gaming control board of the state. They will have under their supervision an in-house investigator who will help coordinate that function. Finally, in general, the surveillance director manages the department that discreetly observes the operation of the casino floor, the bars and lounges, the restaurants, and all the other money-handling operations of the casino.

The Surveillance Officer

The surveillance officer is assigned to the surveillance room to monitor all floor activities. This individual uses the surveillance equipment to identify and to record violations in procedures, rules, regulations, and laws. This officer observes all floor activities to detect errors on the games as well as irregularities and violations of established policies and procedures. He or she uses specialized equipment to verify possible abnormalities or suspicious behavior. These officers are also required to maintain complete written accounts of all the activities that were performed by them and any violations that may have been detected. All phone communication between surveillance and the pits or any department will be logged by the surveillance officer, and a permanent record of such will be kept. This will allow investigators to track incidents by the time of occurrence and pinpoint the individuals involved.

When casino executives wish to review tapes or monitor suspicious activities on the casino floor, they will contact the surveillance officer for assistance. That officer will then set up a location in the monitor room where casino executives will be able to view what they want. The surveillance officer will also assist the casino executive by performing such tasks as scanning, zooming, and setting up multiple screens. Some casinos have a separate room where surveillance personnel review tapes and monitors, while others provide a surveillance monitor for the casino manager, who can then personally monitor the casino floor.

Another function of the surveillance department is to interview suspects in a room that is usually adjacent to or within the surveillance room. They will employ the aid of video and audio recordings and have more than one person present. The interviews are preplanned by the director of the surveillance department or the in-house investigator and are usually conducted by one of those individuals. Questions can't be ambiguous, and all questions and answers should be clearly understood. If an answer is vague, it should be clarified until the answer is unequivocal.

As part of their job, surveillance operators keep in constant communication with other security personnel. This communication is mainly done through the use of radios. To do so, the surveillance operator becomes familiar with radio codes and communication. Surveillance officers also have to be familiar with the equipment they use. To assist in this respect, the director of surveillance will provide an operating manual and will train them to use it. The equipment mostly consists of light-sensitive cameras with zoom, scan, and tilt capability, and video units that have time and date insertion capability.

The Surveillance Supervisor

The surveillance supervisor performs many of the same duties the surveillance officer does, but also monitors the reports and observations that these officers have generated. Surveillance supervisors will also assign different tasks such as research viewing of tapes to look for specific incidents, setting up and participating in interviews, and scanning the casino floor in specific tasks.

Main Objectives of Surveillance

The main objectives of the surveillance department are to protect the company's assets, to ensure that company policies and procedures are followed, and to provide adequate surveillance of all areas of the establishment, placing special emphasis upon the gaming areas. The surveillance department will provide camera coverage for the most sensitive areas of gaming, will communicate with and advise department heads as to the best methods of protection within their departments from a surveillance viewpoint, will oversee and verify large payouts, marker issuance and cash outs, and will help observe and recognize possible cheaters and cheating actions, alerting casino supervisors and executives when they're in progress.

Surveillance Room Access

Access requirements to the surveillance room vary from operation to operation, but in general follow some specific rules. Most rules allowing access to the surveillance room by individuals other than security personnel usually require that everyone other than security personnel must be logged in on the surveillance room logs. Admission to the surveillance room must be for official business which has to do with the functions of surveillance. In some instances official business can be construed to include tours conducted at the request of high-ranking executives who can authorize such tours. These high-ranking officials are usually the general manager, the casino manager, and casino shift managers. In addition to these executives, members of the internal audit department and some government officials such as gaming control agents may also be admitted for official business.

In some operations, all persons allowed access to the surveillance room have to call prior to being granted access. The main reason for this is that an interview process can be in effect and would be interrupted by the person attempting to enter the surveillance room. However, in some casinos the manager and shift managers can access the room at any time.

We should point out here that the subject of access is sometimes a matter of conflict in some operations where surveillance personnel are highly protective of their domain, and this sometimes produces a rift between the casino department and the surveillance department. This unhealthy situation should be avoided whenever possible. Casino executives and surveillance personnel must be able to work in harmony in order to carry out their respective functions efficiently.

In these places where surveillance is very restrictive in its access, executives requiring access must call ahead and request permission to enter or schedule an appointment. When a taping of a situation has been requested by particular casino executives, and these individuals desire to view the tape and it is of an emergency nature, they're admitted to the surveillance room to review the tape, but usually in a separate section of the surveillance room that is set aside for this purpose.

It is important to point out that most surveillance departments will not allow patrons who are making claims or employees who are caught in procedural or monetary error violations access to the surveillance room to view their errors. The reasoning is that, by having access to the surveillance room, said individuals can assess the weaknesses of the surveillance operation and, more to the point, they have no business in there, anyway. In my opinion, this protectionism is unfounded. First of all, these individuals can be positioned where basically what they're watching pertains only to them. Second, even if they had access to the entire surveillance room, these individuals would have to do some detailed probing to determine the faults and weaknesses of the department, unless, of course, there's nobody in there and no equipment to speak of. The other side of that story is that sometimes the casino can avoid losing valued customers by showing the mistakes made if, of course, these customers are adamant about seeing proof. You not only preserve such customers by showing the evidence, you probably teach them to trust you the next time you tell them they're wrong. Not to show the mistake leaves the impression that we have something to hide—an impression that casino operators should always shy away from since some people, if not most, feel the casino is their enemy and is out to get their money.

In the case of the employee observing himself or herself in error, it is a learning experience not to be for-gotten. This insight runs counter to the concept that, if we aren't made aware of our errors, we don't commit them. But we all do. If we were to realize our errors as we deal a game, for example, we wouldn't commit the error in the first place. In keeping with the thinking that surveillance's primary function is a preventive one, then what better way to prevent errors and claims from occurring than to show the responsible people what they do?

I'm sure that many surveillance directors would object to my views on this matter and would rather maintain the mystique with which surveillance is associated, yet I hold firm to my belief that disclosure is the best policy.

PART V

GAMING-RELATED SUBJECTS

CHAPTER 17

CASINO MATHEMATICS

When I speak of casino mathematics, I speak mainly of arithmetic and statistical knowledge. With a fair knowledge of arithmetic, almost anyone can comprehend the statistics that are involved in casino mathematics. What is surprising, however, is the difficulty the University of Nevada Las Vegas has every year with the enrollment of its casino mathematics class. You would think that in a city that is highly dependant on gambling, people would be flocking to discover what makes the games that give this city life, a reason of being.

Lenny Fromm, a Las Vegas gaming analyst, showed extreme concern when he discovered that most casino managers, casino entrepreneurs, and casino personnel in general were totally oblivious to how the casino games statistically work and how to analyze them if they're not functioning properly. When trying to decide if an innovation or a new game would work, they were totally dependent on somebody else's expertise, a fact that made them vulnerable both in terms of game protection and in making unbiased projections and profitability comparisons. The scope of this book isn't to educate those people, or anyone else, for that matter, but to give an overview of what this understanding entails and a few examples of how this knowledge can be used.

Webster's Unabridged Dictionary defines probability as likelihood, a chance stronger than possibility but falling short of certainty. In mathematics, it is the ratio of the chances favoring a certain happening to all the chances for and against it. Although the mathematical definition is more applicable to the casino games, the general definition is more applicable to what is seen at the end of the gaming day when casino accounting is done, and it is found that some games won and some games lost.

When you ask casino supervisors what the casino advantage on the game of blackjack is, you will *probably* get different answers. Most of these answers will be based on something they read, something they heard, or what their experience has led them to believe. All their responses could be close to reality, but the truth is that the house advantage in blackjack is dependent on two factors, one of which can't be controlled and, therefore, will never be constant. The one factor that can be controlled is the factor that pertains to the rules of the game and the number of decks that are used on the game. These factors can be statistically analyzed to determine how their implementation affects the probability of a player's winning or losing. They can also be factored into a computer model to determine their effect on probability over the long run, usually based on millions of hands of play. Yet the factor that pertains to how people play the game and the decisions they make can only be guessed at. In fact, that factor will vary according to the geographical area of the casino and the gaming knowledge of the patrons of that area.

BLACKJACK ANALYSIS

Let's take a brief look at how mathematicians arrive at their statistical conclusions on this game. To begin with, the way a person plays a hand in blackjack is always going to determine the probable outcome. If an analyst is given any blackjack strategy, he can compare that strategy to what he determines to be perfect strategy. He can then come up with a probability disadvantage figure that will be a composite of perfect strategy with a differential for the errors in strategy which any given strategy incorporates. Perfect strategy always involves making a decision that has the most favorable outcome

for the player. This outcome can still be in the house's favor, yet the decision made is based on the best possible outcome, regardless of whether that outcome is going to be against the player most of the time.

Blackjack theory begins with probability. In a fifty-two card deck each card category has the same probability of occurring, i.e., 4/52, since there are four of each card in a deck. The lowest expression of that probability would be 1/13 since four fits thirteen times into fifty-two. So the chance of any card being the first card out of the deck is 1/13. However, if we wanted to be more specific, so as to express that card by its suit (three of clubs), since that card is unique, its probability at that time would be 1/52. Yet in blackjack, a ten, a jack, a queen, and a king all carry the same value and, therefore, for the purpose of blackjack strategy, they all count as the same card. That means that the ten value cards have a probability of 16/52 of being the first card out of the deck. Expressed at its lowest, it would be 4/13 or 30.77% probability (4 divided by 13) of occurring and 69.23% of not occurring.

So let's say we want to determine our chances of getting a blackjack at the commencement of play. Blackjack can occur one of two ways: either by getting an ace first and then matching it with a ten, or by getting a ten and then matching it with an ace. The probability of getting an ace is 4/52 and the probability of matching it with a ten is 16/51. Notice that after removing the ace from the deck there are now only fifty-one cards available. You could argue at this point that the dealer would have received one card and, therefore, there are actually only fifty cards remaining. And you would be right, except that at this time, the dealer's card is unknown and can't be accounted for. This takes us to the next probability, the probability of getting blackjack by first acquiring a ten. The ten, as I have said, occurs 16/52 and matching it with an ace would be 4/51. If we add those probabilities together, we would get the probability of getting a blackjack: (4/52 x 16/51 = 64/2652) + (16/52 x 4/51 = 64/2652) = 128/2652. If we divide this, we come out with a probability of .048 or one in 20.7. If the player has blackjack and the dealer does also, the player doesn't get paid; it's a push. So what is the probability of that? It would be the probability of getting an ace and a ten after withdrawing an ace and a ten. As expressed above, 3/50 x 15/49 + 15/50 x 3/49. So there's a .037 chance that the dealer will get blackjack after the player has gotten a blackjack. The probability of that event happening would be the probability of the player having blackjack times the probability of the dealer having blackjack since we are trying to predict both events consecutively and not separately. That probability would be .177% or one in 565.

As you can see, determining blackjack against a blackjack was involved enough, not complicated, but involving quite a few computations to explain just one event. The possible combinations in blackjack are numerous. But after adding card after card, it should become apparent that the results and counter results will be full of possibilities, to the point that it requires a computer to keep up with the computations of probability. Because of this physical limitation, I am going to concentrate more on how to use the computations already established by blackjack theorists.

When analyzing possible outcomes in blackjack, the many possible combinations and the fact that when drawing cards, these draws affect the subsequent probability of the draws of the dealer, it is too lengthy a process to hand-calculate all the possible outcomes. That is why mathematicians design models that are put into computers to do these lengthy computations. Yet the basis of all these models are the probable fifty-five hands of the player against ten different up-cards of the dealer. Add to these possibilities the variances for playing the hands on both sides and it is easy to see why, in this game, the aid of a computer is inevitable unless you desire to spend endless hours just to determine a few outcomes.

Fortunately, for those of us who don't have the computer technology available to make these computations nor the time and patience to figure them out by hand, this work has been done for us by reputable sources like Julian Braun, R.A. Epstein, Edward O. Thorpe, and Peter Griffin. The decision that we have to make as casino managers, aspiring managers, and administrators is how to use this fundamental knowledge in the analysis of different situations in our operations. One of the most prevalent situations that come to mind is the handling of card counters, computer cheats, card cheats, and card locators. There are also decisions regarding the rules of the game and how changing them will affect the revenue of the game if we decide to use rule changes as competitive moves or if we desire to introduce variations of the game.

One such variation we could consider would be an extra bet in blackjack where the customer wagers on whether or not the first two cards he recieves will be of the same suit. That probability would be expressed by multiplying the probability of getting any card as your first card 1/1 by the probability of matching the suit on the second one. We know that there are 13 cards of each suit in the deck, so if we subtract the one that we have to match (which is our first card), that leaves 12 additional cards of that same suit out of 51 cards to choose from. Therefore, the probability of getting two cards of the same suit as our first two cards would be 1/1 x 12/51 or 1 in 4.25. 3.25 to 1 odds.

If we decided to pay 3 to 1 odds on that bet, our advantage on the bet would be 5.88%. We take the difference between the true odds (3.25) and our payoff rate (3.00), which is .25, then we divide that difference by the occurrence of the event (4.25). If we decide to pay it at a rate of 2.5 to 1, the house advantage of the bet would be 17.6%. By the way, this bet is a component of the Royal Match Bet in blackjack.

The other part of the Royal Match Bet is the King and Queen of the same suit. That probability can be found by multiplying the probability of either a King or Queen on the first card (4/52 + 4/52 = 8/52) by the probability of matching it with one card—the matching King or Queen of the same suit (1/51). The resulting probability is 8/52 x 1/51 = 1/331.5. 330.5 to 1 odds.

Card Counting Analysis

Let's start by considering the decades-long debate about how to handle card counters. The official origin of card counting can be traced to a technical paper written in 1957 by Baldwin, Cantey, Maisel, and McDermott that was published in the *Journal of the American Statistical Association*. However, it wasn't until 1962 that Professor Edward O. Thorpe, in his book *Beat the Dealer*, revolutionized the game of blackjack.

Many card counting systems have been developed since Dr. Thorpe laid the statistical framework for blackjack strategy, most of which are so involved that they foster their own disuse. What system developers and counters alike have failed to realize is that the human brain can absorb only a certain amount of sensory information before it begins to filter and displace it. On the average, human beings retain 70% of the sensory information gathered in an hour's time. This limitation, added to the inappropriate environment of the casino, makes the counter's job one of extreme difficulty. Those of us familiar with the casino environment know that there are many distractions: the constant ringing and clinging of the slot machines, the chatter of fellow gamblers, the cocktail waitress with the extremely visible cleavage, and our own active minds. That's why counters can't count cards for long periods of time, four hours being about their tolerance limit.

Because of the limitations expressed above, the counter himself, realizes that he is going to make mistakes and that the system of his or her choice isn't going to be able to be optimized. And, of course, the more complicated the system, the greater the number of likely errors. Possibly the most powerful counting system available is Peter Griffin's Multi-parameter Hi-Opt I counting system with side counts of aces, deuces, sevens, eights, and nines. However, the mental gymnastics required to keep up with it makes it almost impossible to follow. Strategy has to deviate in accordance to each separate count. There may be a few individuals on this earth capable of doing this, but for the most part, it's wasted time, as are most advanced card counting systems for most of the population. Yet in order to better evaluate this, you must first understand the nature of card counting itself.

You must understand that blackjack is a game of depleting resources. The resources, which are the cards, are pulled out of a shoe or from a hand until the resources are almost depleted and the cut card shows up. Early blackjack didn't have a cut card and, therefore, the resource was totally depleted. As this resource is being depleted, the advantage of the house diminishes (if all other variables remain equal).I make this distinction because if more tens and aces have come out, the game would then be favorable to the house. The reverse is also true. If more small cards have come out (2-6), then the player would have an added advantage.

This depletion factor explains why it is to the player's advantage to play against a lessor number of decks, and to the house's advantage to have more. So even though this isn't a rule variation in itself, it is a factor to be considered as if it were a rule variation. The difference between increasing from one deck to two decks results in a player's disadvantage of .35%

from one to four of .51% and from one to six of .60%. This depletion factor is an advantage to all players, yet in the case of the card counter it's an opportunity to assess the composition of the remainder of the deck to his advantage. Although the chances of the dealer and the player making a two card hand are the same, the advantage of the counter in a *ten* rich game is that the counter not only has a better chance than usual of getting a good hand, but he can also avoid the *break* card and the dealer can't. Furthermore, under these favorable conditions, the player can increase his action by splitting and doubling.

Decisions on when to increase wagers and how much to increase the wager are based on the true count. The size of the bets are based on the counter's bankroll. Some counters are more aggressive than others, and opt for a riskier betting strategy that increases their element of ruin. For example, a player with a $10,000 bankroll who decides to bet between $1 and $10, has approximately a one in two thousand chance of losing his bankroll. In contrast, a player who opts to bet between $100 and $1000 has approximately a four in ten chance of losing all of his bankroll. The upside, of course, is that the second player will make a lot more money than the first player, approximately $300 to $400 an hour, in comparison to $3 to $4 an hour for the second player. Ken Uston's counting team used to use a 5% element of ruin which, according to him, gave them a nineteen in twenty chance of doubling their money and a one in twenty (5%) chance of losing their bankroll. A popular method of determining the size of wagers among card counters is the Kelly Criterion. It basically states that the player increases his bets in accordance to the advantage he has over the house. In other words, if the player has a 1% advantage over the house, he is to bet 1% of the bankroll. In the previous example, that would constitute $100.

There are various opinions as to what the counter's advantage is at the different stages of play under different true counts. Ken Uston rightfully acknowledges that the high advantage percentages that some systems claim are unrealistic since it is unavoidable that the counter is going to make mistakes and, therefore, perfect strategy play percentages are never going to be realized. With Las Vegas Strip rules, which are basically what we are using, Uston places the advanced counter's advantage according to the following table:

Notice that at true plus five, which is very rare, the most a counter could have on a casino using an eight deck shoe cutting off two decks would be 1.4%. That means that if he were to make that bet, at that given time, under those given conditions, one thousand times, he would lose that bet 493 times and win it 507 times. Since statistical probability isn't an exact science, the fluctuations of randomness could make life very miserable for this player, even though he would be at the peak of opportunity and just where he dreamed he could be. This is the sad truth that so many card counters have experienced. It is also the very reason why so many of them have become gamblers instead of counters. Contrary to the casino that curtails probability fluctuations by volume of play, the counter must live with the limitation of being one or a few individuals with limited time to spend on the tables. This limitation is the major flaw of card counting.

Although the above may seem a digression from the purpose of this section, it gives a clearer picture of how a simple mathematical analysis becomes part of a phenomenon which is a subject in itself. For us to arrive at the conclusions that we did, we had to take for granted that the mathematical conclusions that Ken Uston used derived from a valid computer study that he had performed. I didn't elaborate on much of the math because I deemed it to be self evident. But if you are wondering how I arrived at the 493 losing hands out of 1000, it was the product of taking 1.4% disad-vantage, subtracting it from 100% (98.6%) and dividing it by two (49.3%). That is the house's chance of winning in that particular situation as opposed to 50.7% which is the counter's (100 + 1.4/2). If you multiply those by ten, you find the nearest round number that avoids using a decimal, and from there, 493 losing hands for the card counter.

Card Counting and Shuffle Tracking Computers

Card counting computers and shuffle tracking computers present an altogether different problem. Since computer operators keep track of every single card, the computer is programmed to factor in the probability of every event and relays information that is far more accurate than any card counting system can devise. The advantage of the player is then increased tremendously, possibly up to 5% and, with the added advantage that mental fatigue doesn't set in as soon because the computer does all the calculations. The counter can then easily obtain an advantage without long and tedious sessions. There's only one deterrent to this situation and that is to observe the peculiar behavior and act against it.

Shuffle tracking, whether done by computer or by individuals, is claimed to be the strongest of all weapons against the casino. As a matter of fact, ace counters claim to have an advantage of between 12 to 25%. This is inconceivable mainly because all the possible

Uston Advanced Point Count Player's Edge

Number of Remaing Decks	Uston True Count Of:					
	0	1	2	3	4	5
1/2 Deck	0.800%	1.100%	1.400%	1.700%	2.100%	2.500%
1 Deck	0.000%	0.300%	0.700%	1.000%	1.400%	1.700%
2 Deck	-0.400%	0.000%	0.300%	0.700%	1.100%	1.400%
3 Deck	-0.400%	-0.100%	0.200%	0.600%	1.000%	1.300%
4 Deck	-0.500%	-0.200%	0.200%	0.500%	0.900%	1.300%

Note: This assumes Las Vegas Strip Rules. Also true counts are positive and it is assumed that the player is counting and making appropriate adjustments in the play of his or her hand.

circumstances that need to occur are virtually improbable. Yet card locators make a good mathematical case, and they base it on Peter Griffin's table of first card advantage which appears on the previous page.

Based on this table, if you knew that the next card out of the shoe was to be an ace, you would have an advantage of 52%. If you knew it was going to be either the first card or the second, you would have an advantage of 25.75% This is because you would have a .5% disadvantage on one hand (using basic strategy) and a 52% advantage on the second. If you add those together and divide them by two, you arrive at 25.75%. In the same way, if you knew that the ace was going to land on one of the first three spots, your advantage would be reduced to 17% (52-.5-.5/3). This is the type of manipulation that the card locator involves himself with. They record certain cards and play the game, usually with other contributors, in a manipulative way that allows them to trap the targeted cards and divert other unfavorable cards to the dealer. If they make minimum bets throughout the show and increase their bets when a manipulation situation arises, they definitely achieve a great advantage. You must also keep in mind that ten value cards are also targeted with these systems.

If an individual can achieve such a high percentage advantage under the above circumstances, then a shuffle tracking computer can do much better. The mathematical analysis here is simple and doesn't require much study. We don't want to allow this type of advantage, and we have to take measures to prevent it since we can't determine mathematically or otherwise if it is fact or fiction. I doubt sincerely that people would be paying these outrageous prices for these devices if there weren't something to their effectiveness. The research that I have conducted so far, which is purely based on second-hand information from reputable sources, tends to indicate that they're very effective.

CRAPS ANALYSIS

The game of craps has always challenged casino operators when they have tried to implement a rating system for its players that will take into account all the different ways in which a player can wager on the game. It has been particularly troubling when they have tried to determine the exact worth of premium players who try to hedge their bets by making bets that

seem to protect those that have been made. For example, let's consider a player who plays the don't pass for an amount that covers all the wagers that he will make on the place bets. In other words, the player makes a $137 bet on the don't pass and then plays $137 across. Or, he plays $100 on the don't pass and $100 on the point. In both situations, the player will make a profit when the number or numbers hit, and will lose nothing when the seven comes and wipes out the place bets. The only way that player will lose is on the come out roll, just as the player who plays the don't pass and pass line at the same time will only lose on the come out roll when a twelve hits, which will occur once every thirty-six come out rolls. I arrive at that conclusion because twelve can only be made one way on the throw of the dice (6 and 6). Since there are six sides to one die and only one of the sides is a six, the probability of a twelve occurring can be figured out by multiplying one in six by one in six ($1/6 \times 1/6$). Since there's a come out roll every 3.375 rolls, that player will lose one of his two bets in 121.5 rolls (36 x 3.375).

Determining Decisions Per Roll

How do we know that there's a come out roll every 3.375 rolls? If we take all the possible come out rolls and take them all to their respective decisions, we would come up with a frequency of decisions for each possible combination. This frequency would be expressed in fractions. The table on the following page shows the probabilities of occurrence for each decision and how these probabilities add up to show how often a decision will be made on the pass line. I include pass line decisions at this time since the pass line is the focal center of the game of craps. It is understood that every bet on the game of craps will have its own rate of decisions. One roll bets, of course, have decisions every roll.

The number category on Table I refers to the combination thrown; occurrence refers to the number of times that combination will be thrown in thirty-six hypothetical come out rolls; rolls refers to the number of rolls that will be necessary in order to have a decision with that combination; rolls x refers to the number of occurrences times the number of rolls necessary to have a decision on that combination; probability refers to the probability of occurrence of that particular combination; and, probability decisions refers to how often a decision will be made with that combination.

As you can see, probability decisions show fractions. Naturals result in an immediate decision, so there probability is one in one. A point numbers such as 4,5,6,8,9, or10, will result in a decision only after it has been repeated or a seven has come before it. That's why the probability of a decision on these numbers is represented by the probability of the number reoccurring in addition to the probability of a seven coming before it. The addition of these probabilities gives us the probability of a decision on that particular point. In the number four, for example, it takes four rolls to reach a decision, so the probability is one in four. Yet since the number has to be made before it can be repeated, the total number of rolls required for a decision in this case is five, as is shown in the rolls column. If we take the number of rolls necessary to reach a decision on a given point and we multiply that times the number of times that point would show up in thirty-six hypothetical rolls, we find the total number of rolls necessary to reach a decision as compared to the other combinations. That shows in the rolls x column. Now we can total the rolls x column and come up with the total number of rolls that would be necessary to compare all combinations to each other in terms of decisions. If we divide that total by the total number of probabilities in two dice (36), we come up with the number of rolls necessary to produce one decision, on the average—3.375. There's, therefore, a decision on the pass line every 3.375 rolls.

TABLE I

NUMBER OF PASS LINE DECISIONS PER ROLL

Number	Occurrence	Rolls	Rolls x	Probability	Probability Decisions
2	1	1	1	1/36	1/1
3	2	1	2	2/36	1/1
4	3	5	15	3/36	3/36 +6/36= 1/4
5	4	4.6	18.4	4/36	4/36 +6/36= 1/3.6
6	5	4.27	21.35	5/36	5/36 +6/36= 1/3.27
7	6	1	6	6/36	1/1
8	5	4.27	21.35	5/36	5/36 +6/36= 1/3.27
9	4	4.6	18.4	4/36	4/36 +6/36= 1/3.6
10	3	5	15	3/36	3/36 +6/36= 1/4
11	2	1	2	2/36	1/1
12	1	1	1	1/36	1/1
Total	36		121.5	36/36	1/3.375

Pass/Don't Pass System Analysis

Having arrived at this conclusion, we can now look at various betting systems and determine how good they are. We can also determine if systems that hedge their bets actually do that, or if it is all a myth. We could also answer the age-old debate about how much action, if any, a simultaneous pass and don't pass bettor gives the casino. Let's start out by analyzing precisely that situation by comparing it to a player who bets the exact amount of money on the pass line and takes double odds. Let's assume that one player is betting $100 on the pass line and $100 on the don't pass. The other player is betting $100 on the pass line and taking $100 odds. They're both betting $200, although both situations are debatable as to what the average bet for each bettor should be.

As I have said, a decision on the pass line occurs every 3.375 rolls. Every time there's a decision on the pass line, there's a decision on the don't pass except when the twelve rolls on the come out roll and the don't pass bet is void. For the purpose of this analysis, we are going to use 180 rolls per hour, with the understanding that variations will occur depending upon the activity on the game and the ability of the dealers involved. This means that we will have 53.33 decisions on the pass and don't pass in one hour (180/3.375). The pass line bet, as we will prove later on, has a disadvantage to the player of 1.414%. The don't pass bet has a disadvantage to the player of 1.402%. Odds bets have no disadvantage built into them since they're paid at a rate that is exact to their probability. In other words, a four occurs three times in thirty-six and a seven occurs six times in thirty-six so we pay the odds on the four 2 to 1 since that is the exact relationship between the seven with which it loses and the four with which it wins.

If we multiply 1.414% times 53.33, we find that the player will have lost 75.41% of his bet in one hour. If the bet was $100, that means that the player losses $75.41 in one hour. But how can that be, if he is making $100 bets? The loss, of course, is theoretical. The 1.414% disadvantage means that, on the average, a player betting the pass line is going to lose 1.414% of his bet each time that bet has action. And it is going to have action each time there is a decision on the pass line. So if we took the $100 bet and divided it into 1.414 portions, we would come up with 70.72 portions. Since we assumed 53.33 decisions in one hour, it would take this player one hour, nineteen minutes, and thirty four seconds to lose that bet.

TABLE II

PASS/DON'T PASS SYSTEM ANALYSIS

PASS/DON'T PASS

Time/Hrs	Rolls/Hr.	Rolls	Decisions	PC	Bet	Loss	Bettor
4	180	720	213.33	1.400%	100	$301.65	Pass Line
4	180	720	213.33	1.400%	100	$299.09	Don't Pass
Total						$600.75	Player

PASS/DOUBLE ODDS

Time/Hrs	Rolls/Hr.	Rolls	Decisions	PC	Bet	Loss	Bettor
4	180	720	213.33	1.400%	100	$301.65	Pass Line
4	180	720	213.33	0.000%	100	$0.00	Odds
Total						$301.65	Player
Difference						$299.09	

If we could visualize the above happening, what we would see would be one hand won, the other one lost, or two hands won, the other two lost, or three and three, or combinations of these, with the end result being that at the end of one hour, nineteen minutes, and thirty four seconds an additional unit would be lost that would never be recovered. This happens because 1.414% disadvantage means that the house has a 50.7% chance of winning the bet and the player has a 49.3% chance of winning it. It is almost a 50/50 chance. It is the long run that allows the casino to make the profit. So in a four hour playing session, the pass line bettor would lose $301.65 cents (53.3333 x 1.414% x 4 hrs.= 301.65%). A mathematical comparison between the two betting systems is shown in Table II.

Yet since some people have difficulty seeing it this way, let's look at it a different way, as in Table III:

As you can see from the following tables, the pass line bet will lose 3.00 times, the don't pass 2.91 times

and the odds bet will not lose since the odds payoff of 2 to 1, 3 to 2, and 6 to 5 will make up for the 26.72 bets that the odds bettor loses. So, if we compare the two betting strategies from this perspective, we find that the pass/don't pass bettor who thought that he was hedging his bets, in actuality loses $300 on the pass line (3.00 $100 bets) and $291 on the don't pass (2.91 $100 bets). The total loss for this player is $591. The total loss for the pass line with odds bettor is just $300, $291 less than the pass/don't pass bettor.

At this point someone is going to say, *"Wait a minute! The first table shows a loss of $299 for the don't pass bet, yet this table shows a loss of $291. Which one is correct, or are they both wrong?"* In his revised 1974 version of *Scarne's Guide to Casino Gambling*, Scarne refers to the fact that some analysts believe that the disadvantage to the player on the don't pass is 1.364% because they include tie trials on the don't pass. Since there's no decision on them, Scarne

TABLE III

SYSTEM ANALYSIS USING THEORETICAL TRIALS FOR PASS LINE

Combination	Probability	Rolls	Decisions	Winning Decisions	Losing Decisions	Difference
2	1/36	720	213.33	0	5.93	-5.93
3	2/36	720	213.33	0	11.85	-11.85
4	3/36	720	213.33	5.93	11.85	-5.93
5	4/36	720	213.33	9.48	14.22	-4.74
6	5/36	720	213.33	13.47	16.16	-2.69
7	6/36	720	213.33	35.56	0	35.56
8	5/36	720	213.33	13.47	16.16	-2.69
9	4/36	720	213.33	9.48	14.22	-4.74
10	3/36	720	213.33	5.93	11.85	-5.93
11	2/36	720	213.33	11.85	0	11.85
12	1/36	720	213.33	0	5.93	-5.93
Total	36/36	720	213.33	105.17	108.17	-3

TABLE IV

SYSTEM ANALYSIS USING THEORETICAL TRIALS DON'T PASS

Combination	Probability	Rolls	Decisions	Winning Decisions	Losing Decisions	Difference
2	1/36	720	213.33	5.93	0	5.93
3	2/36	720	213.33	11.85	0	11.85
4	3/36	720	213.33	11.85	5.93	5.93
5	4/36	720	213.33	14.22	9.48	4.74
6	5/36	720	213.33	16.16	13.47	2.69
7	6/36	720	213.33	0	35.56	-35.56
8	5/36	720	213.33	16.16	13.47	2.69
9	4/36	720	213.33	14.22	9.48	4.74
10	3/36	720	213.33	11.85	5.93	5.93
11	2/36	720	213.33	0	11.85	-11.85
12	1/36	720	213.33	0	0	0
Total	36/36	720	213.33	102.25	105.16	-2.91

TABLE V

SYSTEM ANALYSIS USING THEORETICAL TRIALS FOR PASS LINE ODDS

Combination	Probability	Rolls	Decisions	Winning Decisions	Losing Decisions	Difference	Odds Differential
2	1/36	720	213.33	0	0	0	0
3	2/36	720	213.33	0	0	0	0
4	3/36	720	213.33	5.93	11.85	-5.93	5.93
5	4/36	720	213.33	9.48	14.22	-4.74	4.74
6	5/36	720	213.33	13.47	16.16	-2.69	2.69
7	6/36	720	213.33	0	0	0	0
8	5/36	720	213.33	13.47	16.16	-2.69	2.69
9	4/36	720	213.33	9.48	14.22	-4.74	4.74
10	3/36	720	213.33	5.93	11.85	-5.93	5.93
11	2/36	720	213.33	0	0	0	0
12	1/36	720	213.33	0	0	0	0
Total	36/36	720	213.33	57.75	84.47	-26.72	26.72

believes that they should not be counted. That's why he sets the player's disadvantage at 1.402%. For the most part, and certainly for the last two decades, Scarne has remained the maximum authority on dice, and his 1.402% verdict has not been disproven. However, since the essence of gaming is how much money a player is going to lose given the conditions to which he must play, we have to agree with those analysts who concluded that the disadvantage was 1.364%. Only this way will the PC advantage agree with the amount of money the house makes on the bet. If we take the 213.33 decisions expressed in the first table and we multiply them by 1.364%, we find that the player loses 2.91 bets, just like in the last table.

The Don't Pass/Place Bet System

Having resolved, *hopefully,* the age-old debate of the pass and don't pass bettor, we can now proceed to analyze another controversial rating system, the player who hedges his don't pass bet (or vice versa), by playing place bets in the amount close or equal to the don't pass bet. So let's use as an example a player who bets $135 on the don't pass and $137 across, or something similar, once the point has been established.

One way of determining the disadvantage of an across bet is to first determine the frequency of each component bet and the individual disadvantages of each one of those components. The components of the across bet are the 4,5,6,8,9, and 10. To determine the disadvantage on the individual numbers, we compare the true payoff of the bet to the actual payoff. For example, the five and nine should be paid at odds of 7.5 to 5 yet we pay it off at 7 to 5. The difference between the true payoff (7.5 to 5) and the actual payoff (7 to 5) is .5. If we divide .5 (or 50 cents) by the sum total of the true payoff and the bet (7.5 + 5) we find that the player's disadvantage on the five and nine is 4%. It is 1.515% for the six and eight (6 to 5 compared to 7 to 6. The common denominator is 30, which makes the comparison 36 to 30 and 35 to 30. The difference between 36 and 35 is 1 which divided by 66 comes out to 1.515%). The four and ten, because they're buy bets, in this particular case, are paid at true odds and charged a commission. Normally the commission is 5%, but since casinos rarely carry twenty-five cent pieces on the crap games, casinos end up giving the patrons the advantage on the buy bets and only charge one dollar for the twenty-five dollar bet. In this instance, since the dollar brings the bet up to $26 and that dollar is what we make on the bet with no advantage on the play, the dollar is divided by the total amount of the bet to find what the house PC on the bet is. One divided by 26 is

TABLE VI

PLACE BET DISTRIBUTION AND ACROSS BET PC I

Number	Probability/36	PC	Total PC	Bet PC
4	3	4.762%	14.29	
5	4	4.000%	16.00	
6	5	1.515%	7.57	
8	5	1.515%	7.57	
9	4	4.000%	16.00	
10	3	4.762%	14.29	
Totals	24		75.72	3.155%

TABLE VII

PLACE BET DISTRIBUTION AND ACROSS BET PC II

Point	Place 4	Place 5	Place 6	Place 8	Place 9	Place 10	Totals
4	0	4.000%	1.515%	1.515%	4.000%	3.846%	
Probability		4	5	5	4	3	578
PC		400	227.25	227.25	400	299.99	2.689%

Point	Place 4	Place 5	Place 6	Place 8	Place 9	Place 10	Totals
5	3.800%	0	1.515%	1.515%	4.000%	3.846%	
Probability	3		5	5	4	3	556
PC	299.99		227.25	227.25	400	299.99	2.616%

Point	Place 4	Place 5	Place 6	Place 8	Place 9	Place 10	Totals
6	3.846%	4.000%	0.000%	1.515%	4.000%	3.846%	
Probability	3	4	0	5	4	3	506
PC	299.99	400	0	227.25	400	299.99	3.216%

Point	Place 4	Place 5	Place 6	Place 8	Place 9	Place 10	Totals
8	3.846%	4.000%	1.515%	0.000%	4.000%	3.846%	
Probability	3	4	5	0	4	3	506
PC	299.99	400	227.25	0	400	299.99	3.216%

Point	Place 4	Place 5	Place 6	Place 8	Place 9	Place 10	Totals
9	3.846%	4.000%	1.515%	1.515%	0.000%	3.846%	
Probability	3	4	5	5	0	3	556
PC	299.99	400	227.25	227.25	0	299.99	2.616%

Point	Place 4	Place 5	Place 6	Place 8	Place 9	Place 10	Totals
10	3.846%	4.000%	1.515%	1.515%	4.000%	0.000%	
Probability	3	4	5	5	4	0	578
PC	299.99	400	227.25	227.25	400	0	2.689%

3.846%. The following table shows the frequency of occurrence of each place bet number and the disadvantages distributed on the average:

If the across bet included all the numbers and, all the wagers were equal, 3.155% would be the disadvantage if we were buying the 4 & 10 paying full commission. If we were placing them, the disadvantage would be 3.63%. However, across bets are hardly ever made including all numbers and, in addition to that, wagers vary according to the point. Table VII shows that relationship.

As you can see, the house advantage on the across bet varies with the point that is established. You will also notice that where it says total PC the multiplication of the actual PC times its probability don't add up to the total. The reason for this discrepancy is that the total PC has been multiplied by the number of units that are normally bet on that number. Since the comparison we want to make is between a $135 don't pass bet and a $137 across bet, we have used twenty-five units for the five and nine which would be the wager on those bets, twenty-six units on the buy bets on the four and ten, and thirty units on the six and eight. The totals for all those probabilities times the number of the corresponding bets are added and totaled at the end of the probability row. This figure will be divided into the addtion of the total PCs to arrive at average at the end of the total PC row.

In order to determine what the house advantage for the across bet as a whole would be, we must use the conclusions arrived at in the previous table and use those percentages in conjunction with the probability of occurrence of those points. The table below shows that relationship.

It would seem that for all purposes the house advantage on the across bet where $25 is bet on the four and ten is 2.88%. However, a similar situation to that of the Scarne don't pass bet, and yet one even more complicated, occurs with the across bet. First of all, the across bet doesn't have action all at once and, therefore, numerous mathematical calculations must be done to determine how these variations are going to work to create one homogeneous bet. Second, the across bet doesn't have action on the come out so when comparing it to the pass line or the don't pass line bet, we immediately find that the number of decisions in the same amount of time is going to vary in favor of the pass line bet. This fact is going to narrow the gap between the across bet and the pass line bet. When doing an analysis for a computer program we must take this into consideration. And just like we saw with the Scarne don't pass bet previously, the actual house

TABLE VIII

ACROSS BET HOUSE ADVANTAGE

Point	Probability/36	Bet PC	Total PC	Across Bet PC
4	3	2.689%	8.07	
5	4	2.616%	10.46	
6	5	3.216%	16.08	
8	5	3.216%	16.08	
9	4	2.616%	10.46	
10	3	2.689%	8.07	
Totals	24		69.22	2.8843

TABLE IX

$25 ACROSS BET AVERAGE

Point	Probability/36	Across Bet PC	Total	Average
4 or 10	6	$136.33	817.98	
5 or 9	8	$137.60	1,100.8	
6 or 8	10	$132.55	1,325.5	
Totals	24		3,244.28	$135.18

advantage is going to diminish when we calculate the actual effect of the bet on the player's loss. For the other way of estimating the house advantage, which to my knowledge has never been considered before, I will use the base bet of craps, *the pass line*, as the main source of comparison, and the actual loss experienced as the indicator of house advantage.

Before I get into the steps and procedures for determining the actual loss in an across bet and how it compares to the pass and don't pass bet, let's go over a few facts that distinguish this bet and must be considered when determining house advantage. We know that place bets don't have action on the come out roll, so the come out roll can't be used in figuring out how much money will be lost by the player who makes the bet. That means that when we analyze the betting system that hedges the place bets or vice versa with the don't bet, we must deduct the come out roll when stripping percentages from the average bet. This would be the method to use if we already knew the house advantage on an across bet. But we don't know it, so we are trying to determine this by another means. Another thing we would have to do before taking any deductions from the bets would be to determine what the average bet on the across bet would be. To do so, again, we will have to apply the probability of occurrence of each across bet plus add to that the additional commissions that would be paid when the buy bets win. Let's look at how those individual across bets average

out to one definitive average. The table on the following page is a demonstration.

First you will notice that the across bet for the four and ten shows $136.33 instead of $136. The reason for this is that in the period of time that the across bet with a point of 4 or 10 will have action as a whole, again, *theoretically,* one four and ten bet will have action, and the $2 in extra commission divided by the 6 across bets will be applied to the $136 when trying to figure out what the average across bet will be. The same holds true for the other two across bets which are increased by 60 and 50 cents vigorish respectively. I realize that this concept can be a little difficult to comprehend, so instead of using algebraic formulas to prove it, I will demonstrate it by working out the progression of an across bet in a normal probability distribution. This will also serve to prove the mathematical veracity of the across bet PC. I will begin by presenting the assumptions and conclusions.

1. In thirty-six come out rolls, there will be twenty-four points and twelve naturals. Of those twenty-four points, three will be fours, three will be tens, four will be fives, four will be nines, five will be sixes, and five will be eights.

2. Of the six four and tens, four will lose and two will win or be repeated (3/36 for a four and ten, 6/36 for a seven which means that two thirds will lose and one third will win). Of the eight five and nines, 4.8 will lose and 3.2 will win (4/36 for the five and

nine, 6/36 for the seven which means that 3/5 will lose and 2/5 will win). Of the ten six and eights, 5.45 will lose and 4.55 will win (5/36 for the six and eight and 6/36 for the seven which means 6/11 will lose and 5/11 will win).

3. Since the probability of a four and ten occurring is 3/36 and the probability of a seven is 6/36, the addition of both probabilities would give us the rate at which there would be a decision on the four and ten. Nine thirty-sixes is equal to one in four which means that there will be a decision every four rolls on the point four and ten.

4. The five and nine occur 4/36 and the seven 6/36. That gives us 10/36 which is one in 3.6, one decision every 3.6 rolls.

5. The addition of the probability of either the six and eight and the seven is 11/36 which is one in 3.27, one decision every 3.27 rolls.

6. If we multiply the number of times that the four or ten will become a point out of the twenty-four point come out rolls (6) times the number of rolls necessary for a decision on the four and ten (4), we will find the number of rolls in which the across bet will have action when four and ten are the point (24).

7. If we multiply the number of times that the five or nine will become a point out of the twenty-four point come out rolls (8) times the number of rolls necessary for a decision on the five and nine (3.6), we will find the number of rolls in which the across bet will have action when five and nine are the point (28.8).

8. If we multiply the number of times that the six or eight will become a point out of the twenty-four point come out rolls (10) times the number of rolls necessary for a decision on the six and eight (3.27), we will find the number of rolls in which the across bet will have action when six and eight are the point (32.7).

9. On four as a point there will be twelve rolls (3 fours (3/24) times four rolls to a decision). Of those twelve rolls, one will be a ten (12/1 x 3/36) and one will be a four (12/1 x 3/36). The four will not affect the across bet since there's not a place bet on the point. The ten will win and pay $50 since the $25 buy bet on the ten pays 2 to 1. One dollar commission will be collected on this transaction.

10. Often as a point there will be twelve rolls (3 tens (3/24) times four rolls to a decision). Of those twelve rolls, one will be a four (12/1 x 3/36) and one

will be a ten (12/1 x 3/36). The ten will not affect the across bet since there's not a place bet on the point. The four will win and pay $50 since the $25 buy bet on the four pays 2 to 1. One dollar commission will be collected on this transaction.

11. Of the twenty-four rolls that have action on the across bet when four and ten are points there will be 5.33 fives and nines combined (24/1 x 8/36). There will also be 6.67 sixes and eights combined (24/1 x 10/36). The payoff for a $25 five or nine is $35. $35 times 5.33 is equal to $186.55. The payoff for a $30 six or eight is also $35. $35 times 6.67 is $233.45.

12. We can then conclude that the total amount of money won by an across bet when four and ten are the point is $520.

13. On five as a point there will be 14.4 rolls (4 fives (4/24) times 3.6 rolls to a decision). Of those 14.4 rolls, 1.6 will be a nine (14.4/1 x 4/36) and 1.6 will be a five (14.4/1 x 4/36). The five will not affect the across bet since there's not a place bet on the point. The nines will win and pay $56 since the $25 place bet on the nine pays 7 to 5 ($35 x 1.6).

14. On nine as a point there will be 14.4 rolls (4 nines (4/24) times 3.6 rolls to a decision). Of those 14.4 rolls, 1.6 will be a five (14.4/1 x 4/36) and 1.6 will be a nine (14.4/1 x 4/36). The nine will not affect the across bet since there's not a place bet on the point. The fives will win and pay $56 since the $25 place bet on the five pays 7 to 5 ($35 x 1.6).

15. Of the 28.8 rolls that have action on the across bet when five and nine are points there will be 4.8 fours and tens combined (28.8/1 x 6/36). There will also be eight sixes and eights combined (28.8/1 x 10/36). The payoff for a $25 buy bet four or ten is $50. $50 times 4.8 is equal to $240. The commission for these bets is going to be $4.80 ($1 for each bet). The payoff for a $30 six or eight is $35. $35 times eight is $280.

16. We can then conclude that the total amount of money won by an across bet when five and nine are the point is $632.

17. On six as a point there will be 16.35 rolls (5 sixes (5/24) times 3.27 rolls to a decision). Of those 16.35 rolls, 2.27 will be an eight (16.35/1 x 5/36) and 2.27 will be a six (16.35/1 x 5/36). The six will not affect the across bet since there's not a place bet on the point. The eights will win and pay $79.45 since the $30 place bet on the eight pays 7 to 6 ($35 x 2.27).

18. On eight as a point there will be 16.35 rolls (5 eights (5/24) times 3.27 rolls to a decision). Of those 16.35 rolls, 2.27 will be a six (16.35/1 x 5/36) and 2.27 will be an eight (16.35/1 x 5/36). The eight will not affect the across bet since there's not a place bet on the point. The sixes will win and pay $79.48 since the $30 place bet on the six pays 7 to 6 ($35 x 2.27).

19. Of the 32.7 rolls that have action on the across bet when six and eight are points there will be 5.45 fours and tens combined (32.7/1 x 6/36). There will also be 7.27 fives and nines combined (32.7 x 8/36). The payoff for a $25 buy bet on the four and ten is $50 times 5.45 is $272.50. The commission for these bets is going to be $5.45 ($1 for each bet). The payoff for a $25 place bet five or nine is $35. $35 times 7.27 is equal to $254.45.

20. We can then conclude that the total amount of money won by an across bet when six and eight are the point is $685.85

21. If we add all the money that these across bets won through all the twenty-four possible come out points, we find that the total amount won by the across bet was $1837.85.

22. If we consider the total of six four and ten come out points and their probability of losing and winning, we find that they will have lost four times (2 to 1). Since the across bet is $136 when four or ten is the point, four times $136 is $544 lost to the seven. In addition to this loss, we also have $2 in commissions from the two winning numbers which will not be recovered, increasing the total loss to $546.

23. As mentioned earlier, the points five and nine will lose 4.8 times out of the eight times that they will become a point. Since the across bet is $137 when the point is five or nine, the loss to the seven will be $137 times 4.8 or $657.60. Add to this the $4.80 in commissions paid when the buy bets on the four and ten hit, and the total loss becomes $662.40.

24. The points six and eight will lose 5.45 times out of the ten times they will become a point. Since the across bet is $132 when the point is six or eight, the lost to the seven out will be $719.40. Add to this $5.45 in commissions and the total loss becomes $724.85.

25. When we add all the losses together, we find that the total losses incurred by the across bets throughout all the points that they have action is $1,933.25.

Subtract from that the total winnings of the across bet, and we find that the house made a profit of $95.40.

26. If we notice, the $2 in commissions that we collected when the point was four and ten added to the total losses and divided by the 6 across bets gives us an average bet of $136.33. The $4.80 collected on the points five and nine added and divided the same way gives us an average bet of $137.60. The $5.45 collected on the points 6 and 8 added and divided the same way gives us an average bet of $132.55. This was the basis for the across bet average previously shown in TABLE IX.

27. Since we have established that the average across bet when betting $26 on the four and ten, $25 on the five and nine, and $30 on the six and eight is $135.18, this amount would constitute a 100% loss of the across bet.

28. In the loss distribution that we presented here, $95.40 was lost on the across bet. If we take $95.40 and divide it by the $135.18 average across bet, we find that the loss incurred is 70.57%.

29. To determine the amount of rolls it will take to incur these losses, we take the proportion of non point come out rolls and compare it to the proportion of point come out rolls. There's one non point come out roll [(two (2/36), three (3/36), seven (6/36) and twelve (1/36) = 12/36)] to every two point come out rolls [(four (3/36), five (4/36), six (5/36), eight (5/36), nine (4/36), ten (3/36) = 24//36)]. Assuming the first come out roll to be a natural, the next two will be points.

30. In order to achieve a decision on a point roll the point must be repeated or a seven must come out. That occurs every 3.5625 rolls as follows: 6 (3/36 + 3/36) x 4 rolls to a decision on the four and ten (3/36 + 6/36), 8 (4/36 + 4/36) x 3.6 rolls to a decision on the five and nine (4/36 + 6/36), and 10 (5/36 +5/36) x 3.27 rolls to a decision on the six and eight (5/36 + 6/36), divided by the twenty-four probable point occurrences [(24 + 28.8 + 32.7)/24)]. The result is 3.5625. Since the roll that establishes the point doesn't consitute a decision, it is added to 3.5625 to take us to the next come out roll (4.5625). If we add the first natural roll to 4.5625 for the one come out point and 4.5625 for the next come out point we find that the natural progression is 10.125 rolls to the next natural come out. Coincidentally, this agrees with the 3.375 rolls to a decision on the pass line (10.125/3).

TABLE X

ACROSS/DON'T PASS vs PASS LINE/ODDS
SYSTEMS ANALYSIS

ACROSS/DON'T PASS

Time/Hrs	Rolls/Hr.	Rolls	Decisions	PC	Bet	Loss	Bettor
4	180	720	145.04	2.883%	$135.18	$565.24	Across Bet*
4	180	720	213.33	1.364%	$135.00	$392.83	Don't Pass
Total						$958.06	Player

PASS LINE/ODDS

Time/Hrs	Rolls/Hr.	Rolls	Decisions	PC	Bet	Loss	Bettor
4	180	720	213.33	1.414%	$135.00	$407.23	Pass Line
4	180	720	213.33	0.000%	$135.00	$0.00	Odds
Total						$407.23	Player
Difference						$550.83	

INTEGRATION OF ACROSS/DON'T PASS

Time/Hrs	Rolls/Hr.	Rolls	Decisions	PC	PC x Dec	System PC	
4	180	720	213.33	1.960%	418.13		Across Bet
4	180	720	213.33	1.364%	290.98		Don't Pass
Total		1,440	426.66		709.11	1.662%	

*Since Across bets don't have action on the come out, the effective PC in comparison to the pass line would be 1.960%.

31. Since we are only concerned with point come out rolls at this time, we will again use the twenty-four point combinations in the roll of two dice to determine how many rolls will complete the across bet cycle. Twenty-four point come out rolls times 4.5625 to a decision gives us 109.5 rolls. Those rolls added to the inconsequential rolls (12 non point come out rolls) will give us the 121.5 rolls that complete the across bet cycle.

32. We already know that in the across bet cycle the $135.18 across bet losses $95.40. That, we have

established, is 70.57%. If 70.57% is achieved in 121.5 rolls, by dividing 70.57 into 121.5 and then multiplying it by one hundred, we find the amount of rolls it takes to completely lose the $135.18 across bet (172.17).

33. Now, if we wish to compare the across bet to the pass line bet, we have to use common ground. We know that there's a decision on the pass line bet every 3.375 rolls; we have already proven that. The across bet, however, presents us with a problem because the across bet doesn't have action as a whole. It is a combination

of 6 bets, one of which does not have action because it is the point. There can't be a decision on the across bet as a whole except when all the number lose with the seven. In order to determine the amount of rolls to a decision on the across bet, we have to find an alternative way. The way I have chosen is to take the 2.8834% average PC for the across bet (see Table VII) and divide 100% by it to arrive at the amount of decisions it would take to completely lose the $135.18 across bet. The resulting 34.6813 decisions is then divided into the 172.17 rolls that it takes to completely lose the across bet. That gives us 4.9643 rolls to a decision.

34. So to establish common ground, we will have to relate the decisions on the pass line with the decision on the across bet. Table X, on the previous page, does exactly that. Notice that we have used four hours of play for our comparison. The first part of the table shows how the across and don't pass system favors in comparison to the pass line with odds system by demonstrating theoretical play of 4 hours at the average bet of $135 which is the across bet average that I chose. If I had chosen $5 play, the percentage would have been slightly higher because of the percentage difference between the four and ten buy bets versus the four and ten place bets. The second part reduces the house advantage by adjusting the number of decisions to an equal amount to the pass line decisions. By doing this, the pass line bet and the across bet are brought to a level playing field where they can be effectively compared in terms of the amount of money the house will make from the players' wagers. If you notice, the resulting 418.13% that results from the multiplication of the 213.33 times the factored 1.960% PC for the across bet, when multiplied by the across bet ($135.18) results in the same loss as when the PC was 2.883 for the across bet (4.1813 x 135.18 = $565.23). Don't pay attention to the cents since they will vary with each percentage fraction that isn't considered. When considering the dollar worth of a player, these figures are rounded off anyway.

So we have now shown two different percentages of house advantage for the across bet. One was taken from the first table and the other was arrived at by comparing the across bet to the pass line bet. Since our objective was to analyze the system that hedges the across bet with the don't pass bet against the pass line bet, the final one works for us. Which one you, as an analyst, data processor, or marketer decide to use will depend upon your company's needs at the time, bearing in mind that if you decide to use the across bet as a stand-alone in a rating system, you will have to use the right number of decisions per hour and of wagers made per each component of the across bet. The style of play would determine in each individual case what the house advantage is going to be. I realize that this

Combinations	Decisions	Multiple	Additional Decisions	Winning Decisions	Losing Decisions
7	330	0	0	330	0
11	110	0	0	110	0
2,3,12	220	0	0	0	220
4 & 10	330	0	0	110	220
5 & 9	440	0	0	176	264
6 & 8	550	0	0	250	300
Total	1,980			976	1,004

Note: 976 winning decisions subtracted from 1004 losing decisions leaves the house with an advantage of 28 decisions. 28 divided by 1980 total decisions results in a house advantage of 1.414 % on the pass line.

doesn't make the analyst's job any easier, but I presented it to show the difficulties that can arise when establishing an effective rating system. And although it isn't in the scope of this book to design a rating system, I believe that I have laid the ground work for it.

I went through this lengthy process because I find that the system that uses the don't pass to hedge an across bet or vice versa falls way short of achieving that. If you notice, even though basically both players are betting the same amount of money, the don't pass/across bettor loses $958.09 to the pass/odds player's $407.23. This is a substantial difference that should erase the thought from any analyst's mind that there's such a thing as hedging a bet on a crap layout. Wherever you bet, you are going to pay the price.

MULTIPLE ODDS

Analysis on the game of craps would not be complete without some mention of the issue of multiple odds. This is a situation that all casino managers are confronted with when they have to decide whether or not to entice customers by extending the amount

Combinations	Decisions	Multiple	Additional Decisions	Winning Decisions	Losing Decisions
7	330	0	0	330	0
11	110	0	0	110	0
2,3,12	220	0	0	0	220
4 & 10	330	1	330	110	220
5 & 9	440	1	440	176	264
6 & 8	550	1	550	250	300
Total	1,980		1,320	976	1,004

Note: 976 winning decisions subtracted from 1004 losing decisions leaves the house with an advantage of 28 decisions. However, there are now 1320 additional decisions where the house doesn't win or lose. So 28 divided by 3300 (1980 + 1320) total decisions results in a house advantage of .848 % on the pass line with single odds.

Combinations	Decisions	Multiple	Additional Decisions	Winning Decisions	Losing Decisions
7	330	0	0	330	0
11	110	0	0	110	0
2,3,12	220	0	0	0	220
4 & 10	330	2	660	110	220
5 & 9	440	2	880	176	264
6 & 8	550	2	1,100	250	300
Total	1,980		2,640	976	1,004

Note: 976 winning decisions subtracted from 1004 losing decisions leaves the house with an advantage of 28 decisions. However, there are now 2640 additional decisions where the house doesn't win or lose. So 28 divided by 4620 (1980 + 2640) total decisions results in a house advantage of .606 % on the pass line with double odds.

Combinations	Decisions	Multiple	Additional Decisions	Winning Decisions	Losing Decisions
7	330	0	0	330	0
11	110	0	0	110	0
2,3,12	220	0	0	0	220
4 & 10	330	2	660	110	220
5 & 9	440	2.66	1,170	176	264
6 & 8	550	3.33	1,832	250	300
Total	1,980		3,662	976	1,004

Note: 976 winning decisions subtracted from 1004 losing decisions leaves the house with an advantage of 28 decisions. However, there are now 3661.9 additional decisions where the house doesn't win or lose. So 28 divided by 5642 (1980 + 3662) total decisions results in a house advantage of .496 % on the pass line with true double.

Combinations	Decisions	Multiple	Additional Decisions	Winning Decisions	Losing Decisions
7	330	0	0	330	0
11	110	0	0	110	0
2,3,12	220	0	0	0	220
4 & 10	330	3	990	110	220
5 & 9	440	3	1,320	176	264
6 & 8	550	3	1,650	250	300
Total	1,980		3,960	976	1,004

Note: 976 winning decisions subtracted from 1004 losing decisions leaves the house with an advantage of 28 decisions. However, there are now 3960 additional decisions where the house doesn't win or lose. So 28 divided by 5940 (1980 + 3960) total decisions results in a house advantage of .471 % on the pass line with triple odds.

Combinations	Decisions	Multiple	Additional Decisions	Winning Decisions	Losing Decisions
7	330	0	0	330	0
11	110	0	0	110	0
2,3,12	220	0	0	0	220
4 & 10	330	3	990	110	220
5 & 9	440	4	1,760	176	264
6 & 8	550	5	2,750	250	300
Total	1,980		5,500	976	1,004

Note: 976 winning decisions subtracted from 1004 losing decisions leaves the house with an advantage of 28 decisions. However, there are now 5500 additional decisions where the house doesn't win or lose. So 28 divided by 7480 (1980 + 5500) total decisions results in a house advantage of .374 % on the pass line with the 3-4-5 or 4.2 triple odds.

of odds that can be taken. It is always a controversial issue because increasing the odds that can be taken on the game of craps is going to have an obvious effect on the house advantage and, hopefully, on the volume of play. It is the hope of increasing the volume of play that, for the most part, induces casino operators to choose this dangerous alternative. The following report that was prepared for a Mississippi casino shows the effect of multiple odds on the casino operation.

Odds Analysis for Craps

OBJECTIVE: To determine how, if at all, increasing odds on a crap table affect the house hold percentage, the drop, and the win figures.

METHODOLOGY: First we will determine what exactly is the house advantage with the given odds bets by mathematical analysis of probabilities given the different scenarios. Second, we will determine how that house advantage will influence the percentage of all bets

FIVE DOLLAR FLAT BET 4.2 ODDS

Combinations	Decisions	Winning Decisions	Losing Decisions	Win	Loss	Win/Loss
7	6	6	0	30	0	30
11	2	2	0	10	0	10
2,3,12	4	0	4	0	20	-20
4 & 10	6	2	4	70	80	-10
5 & 9	8	3.2	4.8	112	120	-8
6 & 8	10	4.55	5.45	159.25	163.5	-4.25
Total	36	17.7	18.25	381.25	383.5	-2.25

Note: This computation assumes 36 decisions in one hour. The total win per hour per $5 flat bet with 4.2 odds would be $2.25.

TEN DOLLAR FLAT BET DOUBLE ODDS

Combinations	Decisions	Winning Decisions	Losing Decisions	Win	Loss	Win/Loss
7	6	6	0	60	0	60
11	2	2	0	20	0	20
2,3,12	4	0	4	0	40	-40
4 & 10	6	2	4	100	120	-20
5 & 9	8	3.2	4.8	128	144	-16
6 & 8	10	4.55	5.45	154.7	163.5	-8.8
Total	36	17.7	18.25	462.7	467.5	-4.8

Note: This computation assumes 36 decisions in one hour. The total win per hour per $10 flat bet with double odds would be $4.80.

that the house will retain assuming the circumstances that are currently in place at a Vicksburg, Mississippi casino. Third, once we arrive at a conclusion regarding the above, we will mathematically determine if the drop will be increased or decreased by any given policy, and how all of this will affect the win figures, if at all.

DETERMINING HOUSE ADVANTAGE: Instead of using algebraic formulas or complicated fractions, we will find a common denominator for the number of decisions necessary to determine house advantage in the game of craps. To the very least, craps personnel should understand that two dice with six numbers each result in 36 possible combinations (6 x 6). We multiply this by 55 to find the lowest possible common denominator to use whole numbers. This results in 1,980 decisions. The charts below will exemplify how these decisions are distributed according to probability.

THEORETICAL ASSUMPTIONS: For those of us who have had to deal with irate customers who claim to be cheated out of the averages that are supposedly, rightfully theirs, it is easy to understand and conclude that patrons look at flat bets and odds as one wager. If this is true, and I believe that it is, a customer's wager is going to be diluted by the number of odds that he intends to play. In other words, a customer first determines how much money he intends to risk out of his bankroll and then figures out how much of that amount will be allocated to flat bet and odds. If he feels that he should bet 10% of his bankroll at a time, a $300 buy-in player will allocate $30 per wager. If double odds are offered at the casino where this patron is wagering, he will allow $10 for a flat bet and $20 for odds. However, if the casino offers 4.2 odds, this customer will make a $5 wager so that he may be able to place the $25 additional wager that the most frequent six or eight point would require. This is the hypothesis that I will use to make the comparison between different odds bets.

Another assumption that I am forced to make because of the lack of empirical data is that the number of rolls per hour is going to be comparatively low. I base this assumption on the fact that our limited space forces us to have full tables with novice dealers who have trouble dealing with the action and, therefore, can't keep up with a normal pace. For simplicity, I am going to use 122 rolls per hour, which is well below the aver-

age, yet I sincerely doubt that this casino in Vicksburg is attaining these at this time. However, since there's a decision every 3.375 rolls of the dice, this number of rolls would give us the thirty-six decisions that equal the thirty-six combinations of the dice which will simplify the analysis for everyone's understanding.

WIN PER TABLE PER DAY: Since we have determined that the win per hour for the five dollar 4.2 odds bettor is going to be $2.25, we can multiply that by twenty-four to determine what one player at that rate would lose per day. The result is $54. This, times an almost full table with fourteen patrons on it, results in a table win of $756. If we also assume that they bet 10% of their bankroll, we find that the average buy-in is $300. Assuming an average play of two hours per customer, we find that we would have to multiply $300 times twelve two-hour sessions, then multiply that by fourteen customers to arrive at the total drop for that game. The result is $50,400 in drop. The hold percentage on this hypothetical game would be 1.5%. Fortunately, most players make other bets on the craps layout to offset this potentially disastrous situation.

The double odds players will lose $4.80 per hour times twenty-four is $115.20, times fourteen players is $1,612.80. With the same assumptions as above, the resulting PC is 3.2%. This is more than twice as good. However, since the 4.2 odds player gets to keep more of his bankroll per hour, he ends up playing longer than the double odds player. While the average bet for the double odds player will be $30, the average bet for the 4.2 odds player will be $26. At .606%, the $30 wager will be lost in 165 decisions as opposed to 267.38 for the $26 wager. This example demonstrates why the $26 bettor is going to be in action much longer than the $30 bettor and why, also, by virtue of the same condition there will be more money dropped in the double odds game of the $30 bettor. Single triple odds as currently proposed at the Isle of Capri would result in 212.31 decisions for the house to win one bet with odds. This would be fifty-five decisions less than the 4.2 odds or 20% faster.

GAMING COMPARISON: The difference between having single triple odds or having 4.2 odds is the same as adding conventional surrender to multiple deck blackjack and re-splitting aces. I'm sure that if we decided to add either one of these player advantageous rules to blackjack, many brows would raise. Yet the difference between single triple and 4.2 odds is equal to both these rules put together. Furthermore, if we compare a perfect basic strategy player's advantage at the Isle of Capri Vicksburg, we find that this tough customer has far less of an advantage at .53% than the 4.2 odds player at .37%.

The above analysis should give the analyst or manager a good idea of the effect of multiple odds on a casino operation and a working knowledge of how to estimate further permutations, up to and beyond the fifteen times odds offered by one of the Las Vegas casinos. It should also give him the data required to be put into a casino rating system to account for these variations.

Before concluding this chapter on mathematical analysis, I would like to mention an example of the dangers I speak of when I say that casino managers should be aware of the statistical makeup of their games when making decisions that affect them. In 1994, a casino in Mississippi and another one in Illinois put on a promotion which was copied from another competitor. However, to prevent it from being the same promotion and trying to outdo the other casino, the inexperienced casino managers threw the game of blackjack highly in favor of the player. The infamous promotion was dubbed *2 for 1 Tuesdays,* whereby players were paid 2 to 1 every time they had a blackjack on every shoe game from 2:00 p.m. until 1 a.m. every

Tuesday. It only lasted one and one-half Tuesdays before the promotion was canceled.

On the day the promotion began, many players circled the games waiting until 2:00 p.m. to sit down on the games and begin playing. Players came from all parts of the country including California, Washington, Colorado, Minnesota, Massachusetts, Nevada, Arizona, etc. It was as if an organization had been mobilized to take advantage of the promotion. This phenomenon is easy to understand. Suffice it to say that a card counter painstakingly struggles to achieve and advantage of about 1.5 percent over the house, and this promotion single-handedly gave the player an advantage of over 2 percent simply by playing basic strategy. It was blackjack player's heaven.

On the day the promotion began, that Mississippi casino saw action like it had never seen before. Almost every table in the house was swamped with players betting the table limit on the allowed three hands. The party didn't last too long, however, because as soon as the Assistant General Manager became aware of the invasion, all the out-of-state players were barred from playing and the promotion was modified to three hands at a $50 maximum. The following Tuesday the promotion was canceled.

The Mississippi casino was lucky. Although the casino had been losing a substantial amount of money

Combinations	Decisions	Multiple	Additional Decisions	Winning Decisions	Losing Decisions
7	330	0	0	330	0
11	110	0	0	110	0
2,3,12	220	0	0	0	220
4 & 10	330	10	3,300	110	220
5 & 9	440	10	4,400	176	264
6 & 8	550	10	5,500	250	300
Total	1,980		13,200	976	1,004
Total Dec	15,180				

Note: 976 winning decisions subtracted from 1004 losing decisions leaves the house with an advantage of 28 decisions. However, there are now 13,200 additional decisions where the house doesn't win or lose. So 28 divided by 15,180 (1980 + 13,200) total decisions results in a house advantage of .184 % on the pass line with 10 times odds.

at the beginning of the promotion, when the high-rollers were barred they were on a downswing and the casino was able to recover. Yet by the time the promotion was terminated, the casino was losing on the promotion. The Illinois casino wasn't as lucky. They waited until they were losing over $300,000 before they canceled it. *Smart thinking!*

Obviously these managers learned a costly lesson in management. Yet what is surprising is that, a few months later, the same casino manager embarked upon another risky promotion of which he had very little knowledge. Even though his casino was the leader in his area, he sought to attract a few players that had gravitated to another casino because of a 10 times odds promotion. The casino that enacted that promotion was desperate. They were doing very poorly and were close to bankruptcy. In essence, that casino was neither a threat to the leading casino nor had it managed to attract substantial play by the promotion for several months. Still, the leading casino took a chance on the promotion. It cost them over $200,000 when you consider the deficiency in win plus the expense of the promotion.

What is really baffling is that the month before this promotion the casino won almost half a million dollars in craps and held over 24 percent with triple odds. That statistic would have made many casino operators envious. How can anyone justify such a move?

The preceding table shows the house advantage with 10 times odds in craps. Notice that the house advantage is .184 percent, less than a fifth of a percent. That means that if the player makes a $5 pass line bet with $50 odds, it will take the casino over 10 hours to win that $55 bet. How many players stay in the casino that long? Very few. And this is exactly what you see when you offer 10 times odds. The player deflects his or her bankroll to the odds, reducing the pass line bet considerably.

It is not my intention to ridicule these managers. However, I do think it is important to alert future managers, and those with less experience, of the possible pitfalls that should be avoided.

The point is: *If you are a manager, you better know your business!*

CHAPTER 18

THE GAMING WORLD TODAY

GOVERNMENT REGULATION AND POLITICS

Gaming has always been a major political issue, yet for some time now it has probably been the major topic of conversation in political arenas everywhere in this country. It's no secret that politicians and government officials themselves participate in gaming activities, so they realize that the real issue of legislation isn't whether or not it's a moral one, but whether it is or isn't a campaign spoiler and what repercussions will follow their support or nonsupport of such an issue. And then again, there might be those who honestly see the gaming issue as immoral; however, they would have to be deaf and blind to be oblivious to what is happening in this country and around the world in terms of gaming expansion. Almost every state of the nation has approved some form of legalized gambling, and those who don't, have illegal gambling whether they like it or not. So the issue is no longer a moral one but one that pertains more to damage control and how to implement and take advantage of what is unavoidable.

That brings into focus the issue of regulation. Lotteries and horse racing were very common in the United States in the colonial period.

In fact, Jamestown was founded with money raised in England by lotteries. Just like today, state regulators saw in gambling a means to raise needed funds for public works, roads and hospitals. In order to do so effectively, governmental regulation of some kind was necessary. But the regulation process back then and until Nevada regulated state gaming in 1938 was always ineffective and many times corrupt. Nevada was the first state to truly regulate casino gaming, and, in spite of the constant attacks to its permissiveness, it certainly deserves credit for at least giving casino gaming some respectability and a sense of security to those who frequented Nevada casinos.

The philosophy in Nevada was and always has been one of friendship and cooperation to an industry that has made the state of Nevada what it is today—a state that's progressing in spite of being mostly a desert. The city of Las Vegas continues to be one of the most rapidly expanding cities in the nation and it is progressing at leaps and bounds. With its new emphasis in family recreation and in expansion of its infrastructure, Las Vegas and Nevada in general should continue to progress into cosmopolitan status into the twenty-first century. Sure they have growing pains, as all major growing areas have. But they're doing something about them. If I compare crime figures for the city of Las Vegas to other cities across the nation we may be surprised to see how well they actually fare. The 1990 census figures show that Las Vegas had 77 crime incidents per 1,000 population with a police force of 22.4 per 10,000. Los Angeles, California had 92.4 per 1,000 with a police force of 22.1 per 10,000. Albuquerque, New Mexico had 92.9 per 1,000 with a police force of 18 per 10,000. Houston, Texas had 89.3 per 1,000 with a police force of 25 per 10,000. New Orleans, Louisiana had 86.8 per 1,000 with a police force of 24.5 per 10,000. New York City had 83.7 per 1,000 with a police force of 36.3 per 10,000. And Boston, Massachusetts had 118.8! per 1,000 with a police force of 31.9 per 10,000. These are just a few examples to show how Las Vegas fares when crime figures are compared. I'm sure that many people are scratching their heads right now trying to figure that one out.

But there really isn't anything to figure out. No direct correlation between gambling and crime has been established. If we were to use the Las Vegas sta-

tistics we might even conclude that it is a deterrent. The truth is that it doesn't work either way because it has nothing to do with crime. Crime is an issue in and of itself that has its own contributors.

How states see the issue of regulation has much to do with their image and how they perceive themselves in the political arena both locally and nationally. As an example, let's look at the state of New Jersey. New Jersey gaming was passed by referendum in 1976 by a "Yes" vote of 56.5% after losing in 1974 with a "Yes" vote of 39.7%. The idea of gambling being linked to organized crime was prevalent at the time and, of course, New Jersey's reputation for organized crime was always an issue. So when the legislators got together to enact the law that would rule gaming, they did so under the premise that everyone coming into gaming was suspect of criminal behavior and regulations had to protect operators and patrons from these influences. It was in this spirit that the New Jersey Gaming Control Act was born. It was because of this philosophy that the New Jersey Gaming Control Act was so invasive, allowing the most sacred of all institutions, the home, to be violated. One of the conditions of receiving a New Jersey Gaming License was that the Division of Gaming Enforcement Agents could at anytime invade the privacy of your home and conduct searches and seizures. The gaming control act also allowed the Casino Control Commission to deny a license to whomever, if for whatever reason the Commission believed the applicant to be unsuitable. Even if a person were dismissed of wrong doing in a crime, if the Commission believed this person to be guilty of the crime, it had the right to deny licensing to that individual. The powers of the Casino Control Commission were and still are almost absolute.

I must admit, however, that the Casino Control Commission has come a long way from the initial position it assumed towards the industry. Earlier, everyone was guilty until proven innocent, instead of the other way around. Progressively it has relaxed many regulations and has allowed the casinos to compete more effectively in a market that continues to grow fast. This was a major concern in Atlantic City. I sincerely believe that the Casino Control Commission has realized the many mistakes it made in the beginning and is now in a better position to help Atlantic City's gaming grow and prosper as it should.

Although the focus of this book is casino gambling, sometimes, especially when I discuss the regulation of gaming, it is difficult for me to define what constitutes casino gaming and where and when I should use that term. If I look at the legislative process and referendums, I can see that since 1964, states have had referendums to approve state-operated lotteries. And I can certainly use the term *approve* here because every single one of these referendums has been successful in approving state lotteries. In 1964 it was the state of New Hampshire that initiated this process. Private lotteries had met with strict opposition and have been defeated both in Nevada and Colorado when placed on the ballot. Yet returning to the issue at hand, is a lottery much different than the game of Keno? And is Keno a casino game? Is limited gaming, casino gaming? And what exactly is limited gaming? Is horse racing a sport? Or is it gambling? If so, what kind of gambling is it? Is a sports book casino gambling? Or just a form a gambling that some casinos have? Should it be part of casino management theory? All these are the questions that make gaming regulation an interesting topic and a major source of debate for legislators and scholars alike.

Limited gaming, as the term is used today to define low limit forms of casino gaming, has its origin most probably in Montana where in 1972, 61.1% of the electorate voted "Yes" to gaming parlors. It later went on to establish itself more firmly in Deadwood, South Dakota where $5 maximum bet blackjack, poker, and slot machines were approved and became available in 1989. This isn't to say that similar types of gaming didn't exist elsewhere, but the problem of definition is always going to be present when dealing with gambling since it has been such an integral part of our culture. We must remember that there have been bingo referendums since 1957 in New York, charitable gambling referendums since 1975 in New York (not to mention unsanctioned charitable gambling), and off-track betting since 1963 in, where else, New York.

The idea behind limited gaming proponents was to infuse the economy with needed resources while maintaining damage control. But what these regulators quickly find out is that the gaming thirst isn't quenched with limited gaming and that by limiting gaming, states also limit the amount of the resources needed to solve the impending financial problems that they face which was the whole purpose of approving the legislation to begin with. Speculation quickly occurs, the costs of operation quickly escalates, and then the State finds itself with some other problems such as layoffs and bankruptcies it didn't think it would have to contend with. This has been a big problem that the state of Colorado.

The concept of limiting gaming isn't going to control damage to the population at large or, for that matter, the tourist population that may come to visit. If you gamble enough you can get hurt whether you bet five cent tokens in a slot machine or $200,000 a hand at a Las Vegas baccarat game. The amount of money a person can afford to lose is relative to the discretionary income that person has. A Japanese businessman who earns $3,000,000 a day can afford to lose $2,000,000 a day while a pensioned widower who lives off $500 a month can't afford to lose one cent. A person can lose a lot of money while gambling on a $1 limit slot machine in Colorado set at 10% in an eighteen hour period. That person could lose $3,888 if he were pulling that lever every five seconds and consecutively putting in $3 at a time. How many people in Colorado can afford to lose that kind of money a day? By comparison, a player in Las Vegas who's playing $500 on a Mirage double deck blackjack table for the same amount of time and who knows how to play would only lose approximately $1,600. Obviously, there's something definitely wrong with the thinking of limited gaming proponents.

As for the other side of the regulatory process in these low-limit states, basically the tendency has been to observe what the forerunners in Nevada and New Jersey have done. The Colorado licensing application is very similar to the New Jersey licensing application and so is the investigative process, for the most part. However, they've avoided the lengthy, drawn-out process that New Jersey regulators subjected so many applicants to in the beginning. There are individuals who had to wait more than a year to get a gaming license in New Jersey. This hasn't been the case in Colorado where the average is about three months. Yet even that is an unordinate time to wait for licensing. There's no reason why government should involve itself with tedious investigations of employees. The people who have most at stake regarding the individuals whom they hire are the casinos themselves. If they don't care to do exhaustive investigations and it is their money which is at risk, then why should the state concern itself with this process? How much can this individual cost the state?

The same holds true for gaming operators. Anyone who has the means should be allowed to invest capital and begin operations after a short investigation of police record and character. If it should turn out after a more exhaustive investigation or by coincidence that the applicant is unsuitable, the state can provide for an equitable transition of operations to another licensable concern. What is the risk? To the state or to anyone?

Legislation and regulation as well as any other life endeavor should follow a logical path. At the top of the logical path should be the goals the state desires to achieve, followed by the most effective ways to bring those goals about. These are the principals of logical reasoning as well as the *modus operandi* of most scientists. If it works for science and philosophy, why can't it work for legislators, government officials, and politicians?

An overview of regulation and highlights in the different gaming areas follows.

Las Vegas

Las Vegas will always be the gaming capital of the world, and it owes this distinction to the legislators and regulators who have looked out for the best interests of this colorful and radiant city. The flexibility and understanding of Nevada gaming officials have allowed this city to flourish and even become something that in a way is enviable. Nowhere in the world can one find a place filled with such recreation as Las Vegas is today. It used to be a playground for adults, where most first amendment rights were guaranteed to the point of being offensive to many. Yet today, Las Vegas sports attractions such as Wet and Wild, the Grand Slam Water Park with its super roller coaster and a replica of the Grand Canyon and rapids, Treasure Island's Caribbean Pirate Village where a live sea battle occurs every hour, the Mirage's volcano eruptions, tigers and dolphin habitat, or the Luxor's pyramid hotel where one can take a trip through the Nile in an ancient Egyptian boat, visit some simulated ruins and participate of entertainment facilities that attract adults, teenagers, and children alike. And then there's the MGM, the largest everything, the largest hotel in the world and the largest casino in the world. It has an amusement park that makes the experience in that hotel not only one for adults, but for the entire family. Las Vegas is no longer a resort for adults, it may have become the family entertainment center of the world. And it is not over.

Contrary to what many doom predictors believed, Las Vegas has made the best out of this expanding gaming world and will continue to do so. Yes, it is true that Las Vegas has enjoyed unfair competition because of its versatility and because of its enlightened and flexible legislators and regulators. Yes, it is true that Las Vegas has gotten away with such things as a very loose interpretation of the federal regulations that apply to currency transactions, and possibly some others. But as I see it, more power to them for having the insight to realize that something that's part of our culture and is unavoidable is best exploited in the most efficient way. Nevada may be lenient, but it is not unregulated. And because it knows what's best for the industry, it'll continue to be the leader of the industry and flourish in spite of the development of gaming in other areas. In actuality, gaming in other areas will end up benefiting Nevada since it'll introduce more people to the *wonderful* world of gaming which they'll want to come and see at its best. And that can only be done in one place—Las Vegas.

New Jersey

In recent years the Casino Control Commission, guided by its progressive Chairman Steven P. Perskie, has made considerable changes to regulations and has allowed the incorporation of new games to aid the Atlantic City gaming industry in its recovery. Casinos are now allowed to operate twenty-four hours, and some casino employees are permitted to gamble in other casinos. Casinos have been allowed to introduce more slot machines, and, incredibly, the casinos are allowed to reduce progressive jackpots in an effort to improve their bottom line. Most of these changes came about when the Legislature shifted authority to the Casino Control Commission in 1991 for many areas that could only be changed through legislative action. The Commission has used this flexibility to aid the industry, and it'll probably have to go further yet since competition in the gaming world is just beginning to heat up. In a Commission report titled *Years of Change:*

1990-1992, forty-six separate statutory, regulatory, and administrative changes are shown to have taken place between 1990 and 1992.

The new Atlantic City has broken away from the tradition that all casinos have to be uniform in their gaming operations. No longer does one casino have to offer the same games, odds, and so on, that the other ones do. Currently, casinos in Atlantic City can offer blackjack, craps, roulette, baccarat, mini baccarat, poker, red dog, sic bow, Caribbean stud, let it ride, and over and under bets in blackjack. Since the Commission now has the authority to allow any game, we'll probably see many others coming. The face of Atlantic City gaming is changing rapidly, and it'll be pressured to keep up with the competition. Will it survive? It has to. There's too much at stake in Atlantic City which can't be allowed to succumb. There'll be much more restructuring, and some if not all of the properties will encounter difficulties, but in the great scheme of things, I do believe Atlantic City will survive.

South Dakota

In November of 1989, Deadwood, South Dakota began low limit gaming operations. This possibly may have been the gaming movement that inspired Colorado gaming and later on Iowa's riverboats. It has been an unpretentious gaming movement that has its major thrust in the summer tourist months and then declines radically towards the cold winter. Like all small town gambling, it is characterized mainly by its rural look, limited spaces, and by the fact that it is recreational gambling.

Only blackjack, poker and slot machines are allowed. Bets are up to a $5 maximum. There are no restrictions on how much you can lose in one day.

Colorado

On November 6, 1990, the amendment that provided for limited gambling in the cities of Central City, Black Hawk, and Cripple Creek with a maximum bet of $5 on blackjack, poker and slot machines was passed with a "Yes" vote of 56 %. It became effective October 1, 1991. During 1991, the state of Colorado created a gaming commission and the necessary state mechanisms to license and regulate gaming. The insert on the following page shows the basics of the Colorado Gaming Law.

Colorado's government has made things difficult for the gaming industry. It began by imposing a gam-

ing tax that shot up to 12% after $1,200,000, which in gaming happens very quickly. Then it was later changed and raised to 20% after the $1,000,000 mark. Recently it again changed as casinos started to drop like dead flies. The most recent tax changes can be seen in insert on the following page.

The biggest problem in Colorado gaming, however, wasn't the anti-gambling government, but the government's failure to anticipate the problems associated with gaming expansion. The towns that were selected for gaming were small towns which lacked the necessary infrastructure to support gaming. The combined population of the three mining towns selected was less than 1,500 people. At this writing, water and sewer allocation continue to be a problem for new enterprises, the streets in these towns are still a mess, parking is very inconvenient, and the approval process through the Historical Preservation Society is extremely difficult, and sometimes illogical. In spite of all these difficulties, the gambling fever spread, to the point that at the end of 1994 there were fifty-nine casinos in Colorado, down from seventy-six in November of 1992. And of those fifty-nine, Cripple Creek, with one fourth the population base has twenty-three. It used to have thirty-three. In fact, in September of 1992, Cripple Creek owned 4,530 slot machines, which was almost 39% of the state total.

It is too late for Colorado to avoid unplanned, rapid expansion of gaming and, in a way, the people of Colorado have already expressed their views on further gaming expansion. It is basically implied by the way they voted in the November 1992 general election; they expressed their reluctance to expand gaming to any other city. Yet regardless of how the general population and the government may feel about gaming expansion, it is still too early to tell exactly how successful gaming in Colorado will be. From a financial point of view and compared to South Dakota, it can be considered a success. Gaming revenues for 1992 amounted to $180 million. The state collected $19.5 million in gaming taxes, without including device and licensing fees and many other indirect sources of governmental taxation influenced by gaming. However, if we compare those figures to the poorest state of the nation which, incidentally, started its gaming industry nine months after Colorado, we find that Mississippi gaming revenues for the first eight months amounted to $255.4 million. At 8%, gaming tax amounted to $20.4. So we see that success is a relative term and Colorado State legislators should take note. Especially since the population of the whole state of Mississippi is almost equal to that of Denver's metropolitan area, and tourism in Mississippi is a fraction of what Colorado's is. Denver receives 18,000,000 visitors a year while Colorado Springs receives 4,000,000.

Gaming revenues for 1994 have improved to $325.7 million; however, if the Colorado gaming industry is to survive, the government is going to have to take an active role in its preservation. Whether the government likes it or not, the people expressed their mandate by approving this industry. That means that the government has been charged with the responsibility for it, a responsibility that should not be seen any differently from any other state industry. If this industry fails, many state residents are going to lose a good source of income, become financially strapped, and become a burden to the state as well. It is, therefore, in the best interest of the state to take this industry seriously. The reason Mississippi gambling has shown the success it has so far is that the state has realized that in order for this business to really influence the state's economy it has to be given the chance to flourish, without choking restrictions. That's why they have not placed limits on gambling, and that's why their tax structure has been set at a rate that allows the casino operations to recover their extraordinary investments and to accumulate a steady stream of cash flow for future expansion. With

COLORADO'S LIMITED GAMING LAW

A. Limited gaming became lawful in Central City, Black Hawk and Cripple Creek, Colorado as of October 1, 1991.

B. Limited gaming includes slot machines, blackjack and poker, with a maximum of a $5 single bet.

C. Gaming will occur only in structures that have a Pre-World War I style and design and as otherwise conform to the individual cities own requirements.

D. No more than 35% of the square footage of any building may be used for gaming.

E. No more than 50% of any one floor of a building may be used for gaming.

F. No more than two non-contiguous gaming areas will be allowed per floor.

G. No gaming establishment shall be open from 2:00 am to 8:00 am.

H. Gaming Tax: 2% on the first $1 million of annual gross gaming revenues; 8% up to $2 million, 15% up to $3 million, and 18% for any amount thereafter.

a lower tax rate, Mississippi was able to accumulate more tax revenue in the first eight months than the state of Colorado did in all of 1992. In 1993, Mississippi brought in $790 million in gaming revenues. In 1994, gross gaming revenues were almost 1.5 billion.

Even with minor changes, the state of Colorado could infuse a needed stimulus into its gaming industry and its economy. Raising the limits would probably be the first place to start. Since legislators are skeptical of the impact of raised limits, a graduated experimental program could be a first phase. A better tax structure would definitely be another thing to be considered, together with incentives for development of needed hotels and infrastructure. The state should also take an active role in making the gaming areas more accessible and attractive.

As far as gaming rules are concerned, the state of Colorado allows liberal rules in blackjack which are similar to those in Atlantic City and Las Vegas. Blackjack rules are determined by the state but can be altered by the establishment if the changes are submitted to the state. A dealing shoe must be used. Poker has a 10% rake with, of course, a $5 maximum. Texas hold 'em, Five-card low draw poker, Five-card high draw poker, Five card high-low split draw poker, Five-card high stud poker, Seven-card high stud poker, Seven-card low stud poker, and Seven-card high-low split stud poker are allowed. Slot machines can be set up to an 80% pay-off, but are mostly set from 90% to 93%, which means that the house retains 7 to 10% on the average.

The licensing process in Colorado for operators is relatively quick and should be in place by the time the operation is completed. An operator's license is only $1,000 with an investigation fee that requires a $10,000 deposit for nonresidents and $5,000 for residents.

Iowa

What began as one of the nation's most interesting expansionist gaming moves in the heartland of the United States quickly ran out of steam in Iowa, mainly because of lack of vision. It was in Iowa that riverboat gaming was again brought back to life from its origins in the past century. It was actually a romantic idea that caught on so fast it left Iowa breathless and contemplating what to do after various operations abandoned them for greener pastures or deeper waters. Even as Illinois threatened to devastate the Iowa gaming industry by offering unlimited gambling across the river, the Iowa government refused to yield and allowed itself to lose valued tax dollars from fleeting ships that paddled their way down South. The Emerald Lady and the Diamond Lady were the first to abandon ship, turning a losing venture into a success story down in Mississippi. Today, Casino America, who owns the Emerald and Diamond Lady, has two successful gaming operations in Mississippi, the Isle of Capri in Biloxi and the Isle of Capri in Vicksburg. It has opened two more ventures in Louisiana in partnership with Louisiana Downs. The ascent in the gaming world has been a fast one for Casino America, after abandoning Iowa.

Recently, Iowa has changed its gambling laws to allow dockside gambling and unlimited wagers and losses in an effort to effectively compete against Illinois. The initial results are encouraging.

As it stands now, Iowa offers blackjack, craps, roulette, baccarat, slot machines and other games requested by operators after the approval process is completed. Slot machines are set around an average of 7.5 to 10% house advantage, or as industry people call it, 7.5 to 10% hold, which means that the house keeps 7.5 to 10% of all money wagered.

Mississippi

For many years Mississippi has had the unenviable distinction of being, if not the poorest, one of the poorest states of the nation. It is no surprise then that it had to find a way to work themselves out of the basement. And they're working themselves out of it brilliantly. Today Mississippi has one of the lowest unemployment rates in the nation and has brought in $210,703,633 in tax money up until November of 1994, two years after having implemented gambling. And that doesn't account for the tax money that the cities charge nor for the direct and indirect economic impact gaming has upon the areas it services.

If the Mississippi gaming law as a whole is looked at, one will see first of all that the state quickly attracted operators by establishing a tax rate that was fair and allowed operators to recover their investments. By doing so, operators were able to quickly expand and reinvest in Mississippi. What started out as two small riverboats from Iowa (the Emerald and Diamond Lady) is now a magnificent barge that sits on the Gulf Coast of Mississippi and is called the Isle of Capri. Casino

Magic and the Grand Casino are even more impressive and even show a hint of Vegas atmosphere. These are no longer riverboats; these are magnificent land-based structures which make contact with the water. And the 8% gaming tax has helped Mississippi have a surplus in their coffers.

As for gaming rules, the state of Mississippi has a well defined set of rules that allow operators sufficient flexibility to operate effectively. Almost any game is allowed in Mississippi as long as the casino makes a request in writing. Hand-held decks are allowed, and the limits are determined by the operator's internal controls, as are most of the rules that apply to the operation. Credit transactions are allowed as well as money plays and call bets. Regulation is pretty similar to Nevada, but not as liberal. There's no equivalent to regulation 6A where an individual can accumulate cash transactions up to $10,000 in five different areas without having to show identification and have a Currency Transaction Report filed.

Competition is already fierce in Mississippi which, up to now, has not restricted the issuance of licenses. Because of the favorable gaming conditions, there were many operators attempting to cash in on the gaming bonanza there. This, of course, can only lead to a saturated market that will leave some operators out in the cold. However, those that survive, like in Colorado, are doing very well.

In conclusion, Mississippi gaming is a good market and will be a solid industry after the smoke from the competition fire settles. There will be more casualties but there will also be some solid winners.

Illinois

The Illinois Riverboat Gaming Act was passed during the 1990 regular legislative session and provided for five licenses to be granted by January 1, 1991, and five licenses to be granted by March 1, 1992. The initial application fee for owners was $50,000 with a licensing fee of $25,000 for the first year and $5,000 thereafter. The restrictions were that an owner could operate no more than two boats, either of a nineteenth century Illinois riverboat replica design or of a casino cruise-ship design. However, contrary to Iowa, in the beginning Illinois operators weren't restricted to the amount of square footage allowable for gambling on the ship. If they want to use the whole boat for gaming, they can. Passengers on the vessel must pay a boarding fee of which the state taxes the operator per person. This tax will be levied whether or not the operator chooses to charge admission.

Other highlights of the Illinois gaming law include the absence of call bets and hand decks. But, the casino isn't limited on odds or wagers. One can issue markers to banks and can offer credit. One can also offer any game as long as it is submitted to the Commission. Other than that, game rules are pretty similar to general rules from Nevada and New Jersey. One significant rule that works against the gaming operation is that the boats must cruise.

Just like Louisiana and other states contemplating gambling, the state of Illinois has chosen to limit the amount of licenses granted, virtually guaranteeing monopoly to those applicants chosen. As I mentioned before, this condition assures that the large expense incurred by operators is quickly recovered, and therefore, the success of the operation is virtually guaranteed. This may change in the future as pressure mounts in favor of loosening this restriction which, in a way, makes it unfair to those who are excluded. It also limits the amount of revenue the state takes in. And although the state of Illinois does charge an exorbitant 20% gaming tax, it could make a lot more money if it allowed more competition.

In all, the gaming climate in Illinois is progressive and promises to be good, as it already has been to those who have invested in it. Gross gaming revenues 1994 were $979,551,638, and without a doubt, it will be much better for 1995.

If an operator can get in, Illinois is still a very good investment and will always be a steady market regardless of competition from other states. The state has a good population base of 11.5 million (1990) and a strong per capita income of $17,525. Disposable personal income is $15,150. The degree of success of the western side of the state will be dependent upon what the states of Iowa and Missouri do, yet by now they should have had enough time to recover their investments and it should be easy sailing from now on. The greatest success story in the state belongs to the Joliet Empress, whose 1994 earnings were over $202,771,210.

Missouri

Missouri was very slow in reacting to the pressure of casino gaming and took its time to decide how it wants to go about it. At the beginning of 1994, the gaming law was declared unconstitutional by the State Supreme Court. A subsequent vote failed to pass games of chance and gaming in Missouri was relegated at first to games that have been interpreted to be games of skill such as blackjack, poker, and craps. However, in November 1994, the electorate voted to include games of chance such as slot machines.

The highlights of the Missouri gaming law are: Unlimited licenses for St. Louis and Kansas City, one license for the other counties for the first three years of operation. Applicants must have an option on the proposed site, city approval, and a contract to build a boat or an option to buy one. Dockside gambling will be allowed if the operator can prove that cruising endangers the lives of the boat passengers. However, if the applicant's request for dockside gaming is denied, the applicant must then resubmit for cruising, which would raise some serious questions about the applicant's ethics.

A $500 wage loss limit has been imposed and it is certainly going to be a matter of controversy since the $200 wage loss limit in Iowa is one of the blames for the gaming problems they experienced. Applicants are required to post a nonrefundable $50,000 or $15,000 per key person application fee. It will be interesting to see how Missouri gaming develops, since it borders with two states that already have established gaming operations.

Louisiana

The first major obstacle to Louisiana gambling was the limitation of licenses. Out of forty-five applicants, only fifteen received preliminary approval to operate gaming in Louisiana. Appendix C shows the Louisiana gaming map and identifies those lucky candidates. Heavy hitters like Donald Trump, Hollywood Casino, President, Casino Magic, and many others were denied.

In November 1993, the first gaming ship in Louisiana paddled off into Lake Pontchartrain. This boat was the 265 foot by 78 foot Star Casino which houses 760 slot machines and 39 table games under 22,500 square feet of gaming space. The fierce lines that were evident in Mississippi were not present for this grand opening, possibly because New Orleans residents were accustomed to free access to the casinos in Gulfport and Biloxi and were expected to pay a $5 admission fee to get on the boat.

Louisiana gaming tax is 18.5%, and the license application fee for operators is a total of $80,000 between the Gaming Commission and the State Police. All vessels have to be of a paddle-wheel design and must cruise, except those that are being licensed in Bossier City and Shreveport, since the Red River isn't navigational. Most games are accepted in Louisiana but must be approved by the Gaming Commission. Credit, money plays, and call bets will be accepted but must be part of the Internal Controls of the operation.

Indian Gaming

Perhaps the most controversial issue of all, where gaming is concerned, is the issue of Indian Gaming. It is so because at stake is the sovereignty of the state and the Indian Nations. Sovereignty is a tricky concept. In practice, neither states nor Indian Nations are independent as far as the federal government is concerned. States were granted freedom of action subject to the mandate of the Constitution which rules this land, above all. In other words, they really aren't independent; they're allowed to pretend they are as long as they don't step out of bounds—then they find out who the real ruler is.

The situation of the Indian Nations is even more complicated because we have political and demographic division by race. I'm not going to discuss the merits of these divisions nor the right of the Indian Nations to be considered sovereign. That is for the United States government to determine and deal with. But the fact remains that state governments aren't happy with this arrangement since they see it as an infringement upon their sovereignty when Indian law is allowed to supersede state law which is guaranteed in the 10th Amendment of the Constitution.

Some things are certain though; it is true that the quality of life for certain tribes has improved enormously since the inception of Indian gaming. In many reservations, gaming dollars have provided for schools, hospitals, public works, many jobs, steady income, and so on. That was the main reason Indian gaming was allowed. However, on the other hand, Indian gaming has produced controversy within the tribes themselves. There has been widespread accusations of corruption, mob infiltration, and misuse of funds. There have been picketing and protests, all of the things that are going to accompany an unorganized money bonanza such as gaming. And that's one of the complaints of those who oppose unregulated Indian gaming.

The other reason for opposition to Indian gaming is the issue of unfair competition. While operators of regular gaming operations must be restricted to the areas where they can develop their operations, the way by which they operate, and the amount of funds they must disburse for their operations, Indian gaming operations, while *negotiated* with the states and approved by the NIGC, usually end up in very favorable situations since the courts have upheld their rights under the law, in most cases. While casino operators in some cases must pay up to 20% tax on gross revenues to states, the Indians don't, unless they negotiate a tax in order to get a compact. They do have to pay a small tax to the NIGC. While casino operators in some instances are obliged to set up costly operations which may include luxury hotels and costly entertainment, the Indians don't. While casino operators would love to have a monopoly of a gaming area close to a large metropolis, they can't, while Indians can if it is ratified by the state. If the state doesn't ratify it, they can then take it to the courts under the guise of *bad faith* negotiations of a compact. So the position of big business in this instance isn't totally unfounded. Atlantic City is especially vulnerable to the impact of Indian gaming.

The manner in which Indian gaming is approved through the various states varies tremendously. For example, the highly successful Foxwoods casino in Connecticut operates table games such as blackjack, craps, roulette, baccarat, mini baccarat, chuck-a-luck, red dog, pai gow poker, hickok poker, regular poker, multi-action blackjack, and big six. They also offer side bets such as over and under and super sevens, they offer keno, have a race book and high stakes bingo and, of course, they have slots machines which they pay $100 million a year to the state of Connecticut for the privileged. You can imagine what they're making on those tin treasures if they're willing to give the state that much for the privileged of having them. On the low side, we have the class II operations and the low limit gaming operations approved for states like Colorado. casinos offer only blackjack, poker and slots with a

maximum wager of $5. The tables on the following pages show the chronological development of Indian gaming and the states that had class II and III gaming as of June, 1993.

As can be seen, Indian gaming is pretty widespread throughout the United States and will continue to be in the years ahead. So in terms of Indian gaming, two things are certain: it is going to continue to grow rapidly in the future, and it is going to continue to be a heated issue. Since the main concern of this book is management and, to a certain degree, entrepreneurial considerations, let's briefly look at Indian gaming in that light.

In terms of management, Indian gaming produces many challenges both for the Indians as well as for the management companies that enter into managerial contracts with them. From the Indian's side there was, for the most part, total inexperience in the field, making them totally reliant on outside intervention. That has gradually changed, howeve. To protect them somewhat, the Indian Gaming Regulatory Act (IGRA) limits the number of years a management group can contract their services to the Indians to seven years. It also limits the amount of return management groups can take from the operations to 40%, and that percentage must first meet with the approval of the National Indian Gaming Association. The National Indian Gaming Commission (NIGC) didn't become operational until 1993. Until then, the Bureau of Indian Affairs was handling all contractual agreements between the tribes and management groups. Only under exceptional cases are 40-60% splits approved, and this is when the management groups have a substantial equity position in the operation. Most contracts today are for five years and a 30–70% split.

One other management problem the Indians have had to contend with is unscrupulous management groups who overcharge for services and equipment and use creative accounting methods that leave the tribe's share of profits relegated to handouts. The NIGA inow has a referral service available for the tribes so that better references can be available for those who intend to do business with the tribes. One problem in this respect, which is a problem also when dealing with the tribes in general, is the lack of trust the tribes exhibit towards themselves towards outsiders. This mistrust has an obvious historical background, and given recent

DEVELOPMENT OF INDIAN GAMING

1953: Public Law 83-280 conferring civil and criminal jurisdiction on five states over tribes in those states.

1976: The Supreme Court rules that states have criminal and civil jurisdiction but not regulatory jurisdiction over Indian Tribes.

1979: A Florida court uses the Supreme Court decision of 1976 to Florida's bingo laws. It decides that the state can't prohibit Indian bingo because it has no regulatory jurisdiction.

1987: The Supreme Court finds that the state of California can't apply its gaming laws to the Cabazon Band of Mission Indians since it doesn't have regulatory jurisdiction.

1988: The Indian Gaming Regulatory Act is enacted, providing regulation of gaming by Indian Tribes and three classifications of gaming.

1991: A Connecticut court determines that the state of Connecticut's failure to negotiate with Mashantucket Pequot Tribe as prescribed in the Indian Gaming Regulatory Act constituted *bad faith* (as opposed to negotiations in good faith as prescribed by IGRA). It also determined that casino gaming wasn't against public policy since it was allowed under certain circumstances. The Tribe was, therefore, allowed to go ahead with gaming operations.

1991: A Wisconsin court concludes that the state is required to negotiate with the Lac Du Flambeau Band of Lake Superior Chippewa to include in a compact any activity that includes prizes, chance and considerations that aren't expressly prohibited by the Wisconsin Constitution.

1991-92: The 11th Amendment defense is used by eight states against tribes claiming that the states were not negotiating in good faith.

1992: In Washington, DC. District Court, seven tribes bring suit against the National Indian Gaming Commission because of regulations regarding the use of technology in Class II gaming.

1993: The final rules defining the terms of the Indian Gaming Regulatory Act are issued by the National Indian Gaming Commission.

1993: The Mashantucket Pequot tribe agrees to pay the state of Connecticut $100 million annually in return for permission to operate slot machines and is granted permission to do so.

TRIBAL GAMING IN THE UNITED STATES

ALABAMA: Poarch Creek Indians, **Creek Bingo Palace**, Atmore, Alabama

ARIZONA: Ak-Chin Indian Community, Maricopa, Arizona*

Cocapah Tribe, **Cocapah Bingo & Casino**, Somerton, Arizona*

Fort McDowell Mohave-Apache Tribe, **Fort McDowell Gaming Center**, Scottsdale, AZ*

Papago Tribe, **Papago Bingo**, Tucson, Arizona

Tascua Yaqui Indians, **The Arizona Club and Yaqui Bingo,** Tucson, AZ

Tohono O'Odham Nation, Tucson, AZ--Bingo

White Mountain Apache Tribe, WhiteRiver, AZ

Yavapai-Prescott Tribe, Prescott, AZ*

CALIFORNIA: Barona Band of the Capitan Grande of Diegueno Mission Indians, **Barona Casino**, Lakeside, CA*

Paiyute-Shoshone Bishop Tribe, Bishop, CA

Cabazon Band of Cahuilla Mission Indians, **Indio Bingo Palace & Casino**, Indio, CA*

Cache Creek Indians, **Cache Creek Indian Bingo**, Brooks, CA

Cher-Ae Heights Community of the Trinidad Rancheria, **Cher-Ae Heights Bingo**, Trinidad, CA

Chichansi and Mono Tribes, **Table Mountain Rancheria Casino & Bingo**, Friant, CA

Chicken Ranch Rancheria Bank of Miwuk Indians, **Chicken Ranch Bingo**, Jamestown, CA

TRIBAL GAMING IN THE UNITED STATES

CALIFORNIA: Colusa Indian Community, **Colusa Indian Bingo**, Colusa, CA

Hoopa Tribe, Hoopa, CA

Pomo Indians, **Hopland Rancheria,** Hopland, CA

Kemeyaay Band of Mission Indians, **Sycuan Gaming Center**, El Cajon, CA

Miyuk Tribe, **Jackson Indian Bingo & Casino**, Jackson, CA

Morongo Band of Mission Indians, **Casino Morongo**, Cabazon, CA

Morongo Band of Mission Indians, Banning, CA

Robinson Rancheria, **Kabatin II Indian Bingo**, Nice, CA

San Manuel Band of Serrano Mission Indians, **San Manuel Indian Bingo**, Highland, CA*

Santa Rosa Rancheria, Lemoore, CA

Sycuan Band of Diegueno Mission Indians, El Cajon, CA*

Tachi Indian Tribe, **Palace Bingo**, Lemoore, CA

Viejas Group of Capitan Grande Band of Diegueno Mission Indians, Alpine, CA*

COLORADO: Southern Ute Indian Tribe, **Sky Ute Bingo**, Ignacio, CO*

Ute Mountain Tribe, **Ute Mountain Casino**, Towaoc, CO*

CONNECTICUT: Mashantucket Pequot Tribal Nation, **Foxwood High-Stakes Bingo & Casino**, Ledyard, CT

FLORIDA: Miccosukee Tribe, Miccosukee Indian Bingo, Miami, FL

Seminole Tribe of Florida, **Seminole Indian Bingo**, Hollywood, FL

Seminole Tribe of Florida, **Seminole Bingo of Tampa**, Tampa, FL

TRIBAL GAMING IN THE UNITED STATES

IDAHO: Coeur D'Alene Tribe, Plummer, ID*

Shoshone-Bannock Tribes, **Shoshone-Bannock Gaming Enterprises**, Fort Hall, ID

IOWA: Omaha Tribe of Nebraska, **Casino Omaha**, Onawa, IA*

Sac & Fox Tribe of Mississippi In Iowa, **Mesquaki Bingo**, Tama, Iowa*

Winnebago Tribe of Nebraska, **WinnaVegas Casino**, Sloan, IA*

KANSAS: Iowa Tribe of Kansas, White Cloud, KS

Prairie Band of Potawatomi, **Potawatomi Bingo**, Mayetta, KS

Sac and Fox Tribe of Missouri, Reserve, KS

Kikapoo Nation, Horton, KS

LOUISIANA: Chitmacha Tribe of Louisiana, **Chitmacha Bayouland Bingo**, Charenton, LA

Coushatta Tribe of Louisiana, Elton, LA*

Tunica-Biloxi Tribe of Louisiana, Mansura, LA*

MAINE: Penobscot Nation, **Penobscot Nation High Stakes Bingo**, Old Town, ME

MICHIGAN: Bay Mills Indian Community, **Bay Mills Indian Community Bingos**, Brimley, MI

The Grand Traverse Band of Ottawa & Chippewa Indians, **Leelanau Sands Casino & Grand Traverse Band Super Bingo Palace**, Sutton Bay, MI

TRIBAL GAMING IN THE UNITED STATES

MICHIGAN: Hannahville Tribe, **Hannahville Bingo & Chip-Inn Casino**, Harris, Michigan

Keweenaw Bay Indian Community, **Big Bucks Bingo**, Baraga, MI

Saginaw-Chippewa Indian Tribe, **Mt. Pleasant Indian Bingo**, Mt. Pleasant, MI

Sault Ste. Marie Tribe, **Vegas Kewadin Casino**, Sault Ste. Marie, Michigan

MINNESOTA: Bois Forte Band of Minnesota Chippewa (Nett Lake), **Fortune Bay Bingo Casino**, Nett Lake, MN*

Grand Portage Chippewa, **Grand Portage Lodge & Casino**, Duluth, MN*

Lake Superior Band of Chippewa, **Fond-Du-Luth Gaming Casino**, Duluth, MN

Leech Lake Band of Minnesota Chippewa, Cass Lake, MN*

Lower Sioux Medwakanton Sioux Tribe, **Jackpot Junction Casino**, Monton, MN*

Mille Lac Band of Ojibwe, **Grand Casino Mille Lacs**, Onamia, Minnesota*

Mille Lac Band of Minnesota Chippewa, **Star Route**, Onamia, MN*

Fond Du Lac Band of Minnesota Chippewa, **Fond Du Lac Big Bucks Casino & Bingo**, Cloquet, MN*

Prairie Island Community of the Minnesota Medwakanton Sioux, **Treasure Island Bingo & Casino**, Welch, MN*

TRIBAL GAMING IN THE UNITED STATES

MINNESOTA: Redlake Band of Chippewa, **Red Lake Tribal Bingo**, Redlake, Minnesota*

Shakopee Medwakanton Dakota, **Mystic Lake Boulevard**, Prior Lake, MN*

Upper Sioux Community, **Firefly Creek Casino**, Granite Falls, Minnesota*

White Earth Band of Minnesota Chippewa, White Earth, MN*

MISSISSIPPI: Mississippi Band of Choctaw Indians, Philadelphia, MS*

MISSOURI: Eastern Shawnee Tribe of Oklahoma, **Eastern Shawnee Tribal Bingo**, Seneca, MO

MONTANA: Assinibpoine & Sioux Tribes of the Fort Peck Reservation, Poplar, Montana*

Blackfeet, Browning, MT

Chippewa Cree, **Rocky Boys Agency**, Elder, MT

Fort Belknap Indian Community, **Fort Belknap Bingo Enterprise**, Harlem, MT

Northern Cheyenne Tribe, Lame Deer, MT*

NEBRASKA: Omaha Tribe of Nebraska, **Casino Omaha**, Macy, NE*

NEVADA: Fort Mohave Tribe, **Avi Casino**, Needles, CA (Nevada Border)*

NEW MEXICO: Acoma Pueblo, Acomita, NM

Mescalero Apache Tribe, **Inn of the Mountain Gods**, Mescalero, New Mexico

Isleta Pueblo, **Isleta Bingo Palace**, SE Albuquerque, NM

TRIBAL GAMING IN THE UNITED STATES

NEW MEXICO: Jicarilla Apache Tribe, **Jicarilla Inn Bingo**, Dulce, NM

Pojoaque Pueblo, Santa Fe, NM

Pueblo Sandia, **Sandia Indian Bingo**, Albuquerque, NM

San Juan Pueblo, San Juan Pueblo, NM

Tesuque Pueblo, Santa Fe, NM

NEW YORK: Oneida Indian Nation of New York, **Oneida Indian Nation Bingo**, Oneida, NY*

Seneca Nation of Indians, **Seneca Bingo**, Salamanca, NY

St. Regis Mohawk Tribe, **Mohawk Bingo Palace**, Hogansburg, New York

NORTH CAROLINA: Eastern Band of Cherokee Indians, Cherokee, NC

NORTH DAKOTA: Devils Lake Sioux Tribe, Fort Totten, ND*

Standing Rock Sioux Tribe, Fort Yates, ND*

Three Affiliated Tribes of Fort Berthold, New Town, ND*

Turtle Mountain Band of Chippewa Indians, **Turtle Mountain Casino**, Belcourt, ND*

OKLAHOMA: Apache, Anadarko, OK

Cherokee Nation, **Cherokee Nation's Bingo Outpost**, Roland, Oklahoma

Cheyenne & Arapaho Tribes, **Cheyenne & Arapaho Bingo**, Concho, OK

Chicasaw Nation, **Goldsby Gaming Center**, Norman, OK

TRIBAL GAMING IN THE UNITED STATES

OKLAHOMA: Choctaw Nation of Oklahoma, **Choctaw Indian Bingo Palace**, Durant, OK

Citizen Band Potawatomi Indian Tribe of Oklahoma, Shawnee, Oklahoma*

Comanche Tribe-Anadrako Agency, **Comanche Nation Games**, Lawton, OK

Creek Indians, **Bristow Indian Bingo**, Bristow, OK

Muscogee (Creek) Nation, **Creek Nation Okmulgee Bingo**, Okmulgee, OK

Delaware Tribe of Western Oklahoma, **Golden Nugget**, Anadarko, OK

Iowa Tribe of Oklahoma, **Cimarron Indian Bingo**, Perkins, Oklahoma

Kaw Nation, **Kaw Nation Bingo**, Newkirk, OK

Kiowa, Carnegie, OK

Osage Tribe, **Hominy Indian Village Bingo**, Pawhuska, OK

Otoe-Missouria, Red Rock, OK

Pawnee Tribe, Pawnee, OK

Ponca Tribe of Oklahoma, Ponca City, OK

Sac & Fox Nation, **Oklahoma Indian Country Bingo, Inc.**, Stoud, OK

Seneca-Cayuga, Miami, OK

TRIBAL GAMING IN THE UNITED STATES

OKLAHOMA: Shawnee Tribe of Oklahoma, **Thunderbird Entertainment Center**, Norman, OK

Tonkawa Tribe of Oklahoma, Tonkawa, OK

Thopthlocco Tribe, **Thopthlocco Tribal Bingo**, Wewoka, OK

United Keetoowah Band of Cherokees, **United Keetowah Bingo**, Tahlequah, OK

OREGON: Confederated Tribes of the Umatilla Indian, Pendleton, OR

Cow Creek Band of Umpqua Tribe, **Cow Creek Indian Bingo**, Canyonville, OR

Siletz Tribe, Siletz, OR

SOUTH DAKOTA: Cheyenne River Sioux, Eagle Butte, SD

Crow Creek Sioux Tribe, **Lode Star Casino**, Ft. Thompson, South Dakota*

Flandreau Santee Sioux Tribe, **Royal River Casino**, Flandreau, South Dakota*

Lower Brule Sioux Tribe, **Golden Buffalo Casino**, Lower Brule, SD*

Rosebud Sioux Tribe, Rosebud, SD*

Santee Sioux Tribe, **Royal River Casino**, Flandreau, SD

Sisseton-Wahpeton Sioux, **Dakota Sioux Casino**, Watertown, South Dakota*

Standing Rock Sioux Tribe, **Bear Soldier Jackpot Bingo**, Fort Yates, SD*

TRIBAL GAMING IN THE UNITED STATES

SOUTH DAKOTA: Yankton Sioux Tribe of South Dakota, **Fort Randall Casino**, Marty, SD*

WASHINGTON: Puyallup Tribe of Indians, **B.J.'s Bingo**, Tacoma, WA

Colville Confederated Tribes, Nespelem, WA

Confederated Tribes of the Chehalis Nation, Oakville, WA*

Jamestown S'Klallam Tribe of Washington, Sequim, WA*

Kalispel, Usk, WA

Shoalwater Bay Tribal Council, **Landry's Museum Bingo**, Tokeland, WA

Lower Elwha Klallam Tribe, Port Angeles, WA*

Makah, Neah Bay, WA

Microdome, Inc., **Microdome Bingo**, Milton, WA

Muckleshoot Indian Tribe, **Muckleshoot Indian Bingo**, Auburn, WA

Noonsack Indian Tribe of Washington, Deming, WA*

Spokane Tribe, **Spokane Indian Bingo Hall**, Wellpinit, WA

Swinomish Tribal Council, **Swinomish Indian Bingo**, Anacortes, WA*

Tulalip Tribe, **Tulalip Bingo & Casino**, Marysville, WA*

Upper Skagit Indian Tribe, Sedro Woolley, WA*

WISCONSIN: Bad River Band of Lake Superior Chippewa Indians, **Bad River Casino**, Odanah, WI*

Potawatomi Tribe, **Potawatomi Bingo**, Milwaukee, WI*

TRIBAL GAMING IN THE UNITED STATES

WISCONSIN: Lac Courte Oreilles Band of Lake Superior Chippewa, Hayward,

Wisconsin*

Lac Du Flambeau Band of Chippewa, **Lac Du Flambeau Band**

Bingo, Lac Du Flambeau, WI*

Menominee Indian Tribe of Wisconsin, Keshena, WI*

Oneida Tribe of Indians of Wisconsin, **Oneida Bingo & Casino**,

Oneida, WI*

Red Cliff Band of Lake Superior Chippewa, **Red Cliff**

Entertainment Center & Isle Vista Casino,

Bayfield, WI*

Sokogan Chippewa Community, Crandon, WI*

St. Croix Chippewa of Wisconsin, **St. Croix Casino**, Turtle Lake,

Wisconsin*

Stockbridge-Munsee Nation, **Mohican North Star Casino &**

Bingo, Bowler, WI*

* All asterisks in these tables and the previous ones represent Class III gaming operations.

developments in management contracts throughout the country, it is reasonable to think that it isn't unfounded. Yet this lack of trust and the racial distinctions that sometimes accompany perceptions and decisions make it difficult to deal with tribes in an ideal management sense.

So as I look at Indian gaming from a managerial or entrepreneurial point of view, I must caution that there are pitfalls that must be avoided and that opportunities must be well researched in advance so that the operator is very much aware of what to expect. There are still many good opportunities in Indian gaming, and they should be considered. Proformas should be done by reputable consultants or experts so that the operator and the tribe knows exactly what kind of a return will be received in terms of the investment. Considerations such as early termination of the contracts should be evaluated since contracts with Indian Nations are difficult to defend in regular court systems. Another fact to consider is that any improvements or edifications will be the property of the tribe once the contract has expired. However, the tribe usually pays for those out of revenues.

The positive side of investments in Indian gaming is that due to the factors we mentioned earlier regarding taxes, proximity to high populated urban areas, flexibility of regulation, and possible monopolies, they can be very lucrative. Also, Indian Nations have been so deprived in the past that by aiding them in getting these gaming operations off the ground, a socially beneficial function is being served. They're being helped to help themselves, and the burden that the federal and state governments have regarding this and other impoverished segments of the population is being reduced.

Puerto Rico

Puerto Rico had thirteen casinos as of 1995, most of which were based on the northern side of the island, in and around the capital city of San Juan. The Tourism Department of the Commonwealth of Puerto Rico oversees the gaming industry through their Division of Games of Chance. Puerto Rico, contrary to most gaming jurisdictions, has a representative of the government (the Gaming Inspector) in each casino to insure that the rules and regulations of the gaming law are followed without fault. They are also there to insure that

gaming patrons have someone to arbitrate in case of a dispute.

The Gaming Inspector in Puerto Rico also has the responsibility of inspecting all gaming equipment for its fairness. Other highlights of the Puerto Rican Gaming Law is that all must have a casino doorman who is charged with the responsibility of insuring the safety of all patrons and is also responsible for all underage patrons that come to the casino. No cameras, packages or briefcases are allowed on the casino floor.

Alcohol is also prohibited in Puerto Rico casinos, yet patrons are allowed to have snacks such as sandwiches at the gaming tables. All gaming rules are uniform in Puerto Rico where all casinos must use a variation of the London Deal in blackjack. In this variation the house does not keep splits and doubles if the dealer should have blackjack.

Table limits are capped by the government with the maximum bet allowed to be $2,000 on every game but baccarat, where $4,000 is allowed (it used to be $200). Credit play is allowed; however, the casino uses a separate set of chips for marker players so as to identify them when they cash out. Markers must be redeemed before any cash is disbursed.

The licensing program in Puerto Rico is very lenient for casino personnel where licenses can be obtained almost instantly after presenting a health certificate and a good conduct certificate from the police. For operators, licensing isn't difficult; however, the operation must have certain facilities, which include a hotel. As of November 1994, when the gaming law had its last revision, the taxation was based on a revenue scale and is extremely reasonable. Up to $25 million in revenues will pay $50,000, from $25 to $50 million in revenues will pay $100,000, from $40 million to $100,000 pays $150,000, and anything over $100 million will pay $200,000. However, the slot machines are owned and operated by the government, who in turn gives the casinos 40 percent of the revenue for housing the machines. The amount of slot machines that a casino can have is limited to the amount of gaming positions it has on the table games. No local advertising is permitted.

The many restrictions that the government has imposed on their gaming industry has been the major contributor to its slow growth and the main reason the major gaming companies have had no interest in this beautiful island. Also, since most of the gaming dollars are made in its short season (Thanksgiving to mid-March), operators become cautious. Yet recently, casino operators and legislators have had productive conversations, which are expected to promote legislation that would make Puerto Rico more competitive.

A view of the gaming statistics for each individual casino in Puerto Rico can been seen in Appendix B.

Gaming's Future:

Most gaming scholars or so called authorities are predicting a rapid decline and fallout from the tremendous expansion that gaming is enjoying at this moment and which it is agreed will continue for a few more years. Obviously, like anything else, a saturation point has to be reached. If this trend is viewed on a graphic, it would be noticed that an escalating line at one point levels off then begins to slowly decline. Since almost every state has some form of gaming within its frontiers, it isn't a great stretch to predict that within the next ten years there will be some form of casino gaming in every state. It will come as state economies struggle to meet budget requirements, and it will come as states realize the amount of tax money and income that they're losing to neighboring states and Indian Nations.

As the gaming proliferation continues, a few things are going to happen. Those operations that aren't well managed and have not been strategically planned are going to succumb to competition and to a market that is going to dwindle. Since most operations will be dependent mostly upon local support, revenues are going to drop considerably. The reason for that is obvious; at first there's always a gambling frenzy, but sooner or later people realize that they can't continue to invest so much of their discretionary income (and that which isn't discretionary) in the casino. The amount of their wagers and the frequency of their visits decrease, and so does the casino's revenue. In the meantime, the casino has to share its portion of the diminished revenues with more and more competitors that come in lured by past performances of successful operators. In conclusion, many operations will fail. The gaming industry, which as a whole, will survive and do well, will probably be seen as in crises because of the many bankruptcies and sellouts that are bound to occur.

There's really no gauge that can be used to determine how many gaming operations any certain area can

hold. Like any other business, this is a business that corrects itself by having the operators displace themselves. Displacement of operators occurs if the wrong location is chosen, if an over-investment is made, or if any of the mistakes that proper management should steer away from is made. This isn't any different from building a $1 million home in $100,000 neighborhood, or selling life jackets in the Sahara, or setting up a $100 million factory to sell $100,000 in products in one year. Freedom of enterprise and choice allows for all of these things to happen, and it isn't up to state governments to regulate this since it isn't done in any other business. Competition takes care of itself. For years, Nevada has operated under fierce competition, and although there has been many casualties, for the most part the state's gaming industry has been something to admire as far as business goes. It has sustained the state's economy, it has provided for education and many other public services, and continues to flourish to this day, now going on forty-six years.

How much is enough will never be settled and, I believe, it is a matter for those entrepreneurs who want to take a *chance* to settle. This is, after all, what the gaming business is all about. Gaming is going to flourish rapidly for the next few years, and there isn't anything anyone can do about it.

Conclusions and Recommendations:

Many adjustments in gaming regulations and laws will be necessary to assure the health of the gaming industry in many areas. These changes will invariably come about because they're part of the learning experience of inexperienced government bodies. Most gaming regulators start out with blindfolds and earplugs, but as they start to feel the heat, they begin to remove the obstacles that prevent them from making rational decisions. We have seen it in the evolution of the Gaming Board in Nevada, we saw it in the evolution of the gaming commission in New Jersey, and we've seen it happen in Puerto Rico where the wagering limits went from $200 to $4,000. It is, therefore, my recommendation to all gaming regulatory bodies that they save themselves and the people whom they serve a lot of grief and lost revenues by taking a long hard look at the regulations they impose and at the direction they believe their gaming future is heading.

GLOSSARY

The following words are used in the gaming business and in gaming related activities. Most of them apply mainly to casino gambling which is the major focus of this book. However, since sometimes street gambling terms enter into the regulated gaming arena, I have provided some of the terms that may be applicable.

ABOVE: The earnings of a gambling enterprise that are listed in their bookkeeping ledgers.

ACE: 1. The one spot on a die. 2. The highest ranking playing card in poker and most other card games.

ACES (CRAPS TWO): One die showing "one spot" up and the other die showing another "one spot" up.

ACE DEUCE (CRAPS THREE): One die showing "one spot" up and the other die showing "two spots" up.

ACE ADJUSTMENT: The adjustment for the proportion of aces remaining to be played in order to determine bet size.

ACE ADJUSTMENT FACTOR: The number specified by advanced card counting systems to be multiplied by the number of aces rich or aces poor in order to adjust the running count for betting purposes.

ACE POOR: A lower than average proportion of aces remaining to be played, favoring the house.

ACE RICH: A higher than average proportion of aces remaining to be played, favoring the player.

ACTION: 1. Gambling activity. 2. The total dollar amount bet by the player on all hands played.

ADJUSTED RUNNING COUNT: The value of the running count adjusted to reflect the number of aces rich or poor.

AGENT: 1. A person who solicits lottery bets. 2. A cheat who frequents casinos and works in collusion with casino dealers and employees. 3. A person who, for a profit, lures a player to a crooked gambling game.

ALL NIGHT BOARD BINGO: The card given to a player when he pays his admission, which is good for all games played during that session.

ALL OUT: Pushing the limit to win.

ANCHOR MAN: In blackjack, a player who sits to the dealer's extreme right and is the last player to play his hand.

ANGLE: 1. An idea. 2. A cheating method.

ANTE: In poker, chips or cash put into the pot before the deal. 2. In caribbean stud, a wager before getting the players first two cards.

APRON: 1. The outside part of the layout in front of the player past all designated betting areas. 2. A cloth shield a dealer must wear around his waistband to cover his pockets.

BP (BIG PLAYER): The member of a team who bets the money or makes the big bets.

BACK-TO-BACK STUD POKER: Two cards of the same denomination consisting of the hole card and the first upcard.

BACK COUNTING: A person counting down a deck or shoe without playing at the table while usually standing in back of the players. Also known as shadow counting.

BACKER: Someone behind the scenes who supplies gamblers with their bankrolls.

BACKING UP CARDS: 1. To prove a hand. 2. To move cards from one hand to another.

BACK LINE ODDS (TO LAY): A craps player who has a bet on the don't pass and lays the odds on the point number.

BAGGED: A term used to describe a cheat or crook who has been caught in the act of cheating or stealing.

BANK: 1. A gambling scheme's financier. 2. The bankroll. 3. Money used to operate a banking game or gambling establishment.

BANK CRAPS: A form of craps played on a layout in which players aren't permitted to bet among themselves, all bets are made against the house or bank.

BANKER: 1. An operator of a banking game. 2. A player who accepts bets from other players in a private banking game.

BANKING GAME: Any betting scheme that gives the operator or a player a percentage or odds advantage over his opponents: lotteries, casino games, numbers game, race and sports books, etc.

BANKROLL: 1. Casino money kept in a tray directly in front of the dealer. 2. Amount of cash set aside for gambling purposes.

BANKROLL MAN: The man who finances a gambling scheme.

BAR: 1. To permanently exclude a player from a casino to prevent him from causing problems or playing on a table game where he has proven above average skill, almost always in blackjack in regards to card counters. 2. In craps, the action of neglecting payment on a certain combination such as two sixes on the don't pass.

BARBER POLE: A stack of checks in which more than one denomination checks are included.

BARRING THE FIRST ROLL: A private craps hustler's bet in which a winning first roll for his opponent doesn't count but is a no decision or standoff.

BASIC STRATEGY: The optimum way for the blackjack player to play the hands if he isn't counting. These plays follow a prescribed set of house rules.

BASE: 1. In blackjack, a player's betting position at the table. First base is the position farthest to the dealer's left; second base is directly in the center; third base is the position furthest to the dealer's right. Second base is also called centerfield. 2. In craps this refers to the positions of the dealers. First base is the stickperson; second base is the dealer to the right of the boxperson; third base is the dealer to the left of the boxperson.

BASE DEALER: 1. A card mechanic who specializes in dealing off the bottom of the deck. 2. One of the dealers that deals from second or third base on a crap table.

BEAN SHOOTER: A simple holdout device worn on the arm.

BEARD: Someone who is used by the cheat to make bets for him because he is a known player.

BEAT: To cheat someone out of a sum of money in a gambling game. The same as trim.

BEEF: An argument or complaint over a play or call which delays the game.

BEEFER: A constant complainer.

THE BEST OF IT: Situation in which a player has a greater likelihood of winning than the other player due to a mathematical edge, a greater skill, or cheating.

BET: Any wager on the outcome of an event.

BET THE LIMIT: To bet the maximum amount permitted by the house or game rules.

BETTING RATIO: The mathematical ratio between the highest and the lowest bets placed by a player.

BETTING TRUE COUNT: The value of the true count adjusted to reflect the number of aces rich or poor.

BEVELS OR BEVELED SHAPES: Crooked dice having one or more sides slightly rounded rather than flat so that the dice tend to roll off the rounded surface more often than the flat.

THE BIG CON: Any elaborate con game stretching over several days, involving numerous con men as supporting players, and the use of a big establishment, as opposed to the short con.

BIG EIGHT: In craps, a space on a craps layout. A bet placed there indicates that the player is betting an eight will be thrown before a seven. It pays even money.

BIG SIX: In craps, the same as a big eight bet, except that a player is betting that a six will be thrown before a seven. Also pays even money.

BIRD DOG: An informant who provides hustlers with information on where they can find promising games or victims.

BLACK: One hundred dollar chips, generally black in color.

BLACKJACK: 1. A banking card game with the objective of reaching twenty-one. 2. An ace and ten valued card on the first two cards dealt; also called a natural or snapper.

BLACK LINE WORK: A technique of marking cards for low ball by making a small incision along the black line that borders each picture card on the face. The cheat feels the marks with his finger as he deals.

BLACKOUT BINGO: A winning setup in which a player must cover all twenty four numbers on his card.

BLANKET ROLL: In craps, a controlled two dice roll made on a soft surface, usually a blanket.

BLIND BET POKER: A bet made before the player looks at his cards.

BLISTER: A very minute bump placed on the back of a playing card so the cheat can identify it whenever it is on top of the deck by feeling it with the thumb of the hand holding the deck. This is usually used in conjunction with a second deal.

BLOCKOUT WORK: Cards which have been marked by blocking out a small portion of the back design with ink to match the color of the card back.

BLOOD MONEY: Hard-earned money that one has difficulty attaining.

BLOW: To lose.

BLOWOFF: Any technique for getting rid of a mark after he has been swindled in a con game.

BLUFF: In poker, to bet an inferior hand in such a way that the opponents will think it is a strong hand and retire from the pot.

BOARDS: The raised edge around a craps table against which the dice must be thrown. Also, the rail.

TO BOOK: 1. To supply the bankroll. 2. To finance a gambling scheme. 3. To accept a verbal wager on a casino game, especially in craps.

BOP: To jump from table to table as decks or shoes become favorable to the player. The favorable deck is signaled by a counter at each table.

BOTTOM DEALER: A card cheat who deals from the bottom of the deck while pretending to deal off the top. Also known as a base dealer, subway dealer.

BOWL: 1. Wooden bowl shaped recess which holds the roulette wheel. 2. In craps, the receptacle where the five dice are stored for selection.

BOX NUMBERS: 1. A betting space on a money craps layout, nearest to the dealer, where each of the possible point numbers 4, 5, 6, 8, 9 and 10 appear within a square or box. Players may bet each or all of these numbers at any time. 2. The same as place bets in bank craps, and off numbers in private craps.

BOX UP OR BOX THEM UP: In craps, to mix up a set of five dice so that a player may select a pair from the group.

BOXPERSON: A casino employee who is in charge of a craps table.

BREAK: 1. To win a player's bankroll. 2. In blackjack, to draw cards for a hard total of more than twenty-one.

BREAK DOWN: To cut chips into countable stacks.

BREAKS (THE): Good or bad luck, depending on the circumstances.

BREAKAGE: In craps, to allow more odds than what would actually be single, double, triple, etc. of the flat bet so as to avoid paying multiple colors and cheating the player out of the change.

BRICKS: Dice which have been misshapen so that two sides have more surface area than the other four sides. The same as flats.

BRUSH (THE): 1. A card cheating move in which the hustler exchanges one of the cards in his hand for one from his accomplice's hand in the act of pushing the other player's cards aside on the table. 2. A dice cheating move in which the hustler exchanges one pair of dice for another in the act of pushing the dice on the table.

BUBBLE PEEK: A method of peeking at the top card of the deck by which the cheat catches a glimpse of one of the indexes of the card by buckling the front end of the card with his thumb.

BUTTON: A small round chip used to designate action on certain bets during the course of the game. Referred to as "on" or "off" button.

BUG: 1. A steel gimmick placed in the mechanism of a slot machine which prevents certain combinations from hitting. 2. A clip which can be attached to the underside of a card table to hold cards secretly removed from the deck.

BUM MOVE: 1. A suspicious move. 2. A clumsy or obvious cheating move by a gambling crook. Bump or Raise: In poker, to bet an amount greater than that put into the pot by the last preceding bettor.

BUNDLE: A large bankroll.

BURN A CARD: In blackjack, after the cards have been shuffled and cut, the top card of the deck is burned by placing it face down in the discard rack. It is also done when a card is accidently exposed.

BURNED OUT: For a cheating method to become so well known among potential victims that it is no longer usable.

BURR DICE: Dice in which the edges of some spots have been left with burrs so those sides will tend to catch if the dice are rolled on a cloth covered surface.

BUST: In blackjack, a player busts when his total card count exceeds twenty one.

BUSTERS: In craps, a pair of tops (misspotted dice). Tops are made in various combinations which make only certain numbers and are called busters because they produce a one hundred percent chance of winning for whom uses them and a one hundred percent chance of losing for who bets against them. So they end up busting the opposition.

BUST IN: To switch in misspotted dice.

BUSTOUT JOINT: A gambling house that follows a policy of cheating the players.

BUSTOUT MAN: A dice mechanic whose specialty is switching crooked dice, usually busters, in and out of the game.

BUTTERFLY CUP: A dice cup that is gaffed so as to allow the cheat to switch dice in the process of shaking them in the cup prior to rolling them out.

BUY BETS: Wagers that are paid true correct odds but are handled like place bets. The players must pay five percent vigorish or commission on what they bet.

CACKLE THE DICE: To pretend to shake the dice by making them rattle when actually they're held by a special finger grip that prevents them from turning freely in the hand.

CAGE: Location of the chip bank where the casino cashier is.

CALL: In poker, to put into the pot an amount equal to the last preceding bet.

CALL BET: A bet made without money or chips usually allowed only to customers with casino credit, or with money on deposit in the cage. It is also allowed for well known players.

CALLER: In bingo, an employee who calls each bingo number as it is drawn. Also Tallyman.

CALL IN NUMBERS: Predetermined numbers representing the running count, adjusted for aces in counts which require a side count of aces and also used by the counter to summon a big player to his table.

CALL PLAYS: To count and signal a blackjack player how much to bet and how to play his hands.

CANADIAN BUILDUP: A short change sequence in which the hustler causes the cashier to hand over fifty dollars extra in the process of changing small bills for a large one.

CANOE: In roulette, a numbered or winning section of a roulette wheel in which the ball finally comes to rest after the spin.

CAPPED DICE: Dice that have certain sides made of a softer substance so as to give those sides more bounce and favor certain numbers.

CAPPING: Illegally adding chips to one's bet after the game is in progress. It is the same as pressing.

CAPPING THE DECK: Adding palmed cards to the top of the deck.

CARD EAT: To spread to multiple hands in order to cause more cards to be dealt, usually done with small bets in minus counts.

CARD MECHANIC: A person who manipulates cards for cheating purposes.

CARD MOB: Two or more card cheats working as a team.

CARRY A SLUG: To shuffle the deck without disturbing a particular group of cards, usually on the top or bottom which have been prearranged for cheating purposes.

CASE BET: A player's wager using all of the remaining monies in his possession. Usually a bet which is lower than the minimum required.

CASE CARD: 1. The one remaining card in the deck which will improve a player's hand. 2. The last card of a suit or denomination still in the deck. 3. The last one of anything, as in case note, one's last dollar.

CASE THE DECK: To remember many of the played and exposed cards during the play of a game.

CASING: Visually checking the layout to make sure all bets are properly placed and amounts of bets are correct. Also when a cheat surveys a gaming establisment or a game for its weaknesses.

CASINO HOST: A customer relations employee whose main consideration is the player. He is responsible for comping the player according to his play on the table games and the slot machines, as well as taking care of other needs.

CASH OUT: The act of redeeming the player's checks for cash or for larger value checks.

CASINO MANAGER: Person in charge of the casino operation.

CENTER BET: 1. In private craps, a wager between the shooter and the fader or faders which is placed in the center of the playing surface. 2. In bank or casino craps, another name for proposition bets.

CHANCE: The probability or possibility that a person has when making a bet.

CHASE: In stud poker, to play against a better hand which is exposed.

CHECK: A token which is commonly used, by law, for betting purposes on the layouts of the games instead of money. Each check or chip color has a different value.

CHECK CHANGE: Changing higher denomination checks for lower denomination.

CHECK COP: 1. An adhesive paste which a cheat places on his palm. When he puts his hand on a stack of checks or coins, the top one adheres to his palm, and he steals it. 2. Stealing chips out of a poker game.

CHIP: 1. A token used for betting purposes in place of money.

CHIP CUP: A gaff consisting of a simulated stack of chips, actually a hollow cup, used by a dealer and agent to steal chips from a casino.

CHISELER: 1. A gambler who tries to pick up another player's bet in a banking game. 2. A gambler who borrows money in a private game and doesn't repay it.

CHUNK: To bet large stacks of checks at one time.

CHUMP: An inexperienced gambler.

CINCH HAND: In poker, a hand which is sure to win the pot.

CLAIM: A player trying to get paid for a winning bet that he didn't wager on.

CLAIMER: 1. The participant in a slot cheating scam whose job is to actually claim the jackpot. 2. A person who claims to have a winning bet when he doesn't.

CLEAN: 1. Term used to describe a person who doesn't have a police record. 2. To win all the money from one or more opponents in a game. 3. Term used to describe any sleight of hand cheating move that is very deceptive and convincing.

CLEAN HAND: An empty hand which can be shown not to contain palmed cards or dice.

CLEAN MONEY: Checks taken from the dealers rack or tray for payment purposes.

CLOCK: To keep track of the amount of money won and lost during a game.

CLOCKER: One who clocks a banking game.

CLOSE TO THE BELLY OR VEST: A stud poker player who bets only on a wired pair or when he has the best hand showing is playing close to the belly.

COLD DECK: A deck of cards which has secretly been arranged by a card cheat in a certain order for the purpose of switching later with the deck in play.

COLD PLAYER: A player on a losing streak.

COLD TURKEY: When the two first cards that are dealt are face cards.

COLLECTOR: The participant in a slot cheating scam whose job is to actually claim the jackpot; the same as claimer.

COLOR CHANGE: Changing one color of checks for another color of higher denomination checks.

COLUMN BET: In roulette, a bet on twelve vertical numbers on the layout. The winning unit is paid off at two to one odds.

COME BET: In craps, a bet that the dice will pass the next roll which is considered to be a come out roll in the betting area.

COME OUT ROLL: The first throw of the dice or the first throw after a shooter's decision.

COME OUT BET: A bet made on a specific number or on a group of numbers that the number or one of the group will be thrown on the next roll of the dice.

COMING IN ONE HIGH: A method used by a casino dealer to short a player on the payoff by secretly transferring a chip from the player's bet to the payoff stack.

COMP: Complimentary privileges the casino offers .

CONSOLE: A flat top electrically powered slot machine which can be played by one or several players simultaneously.

CONTRACT BET: A bet which may not be removed or reduced once a point has been established. Pass line and come bets are contract bets.

CONVERSION FACTOR (CF): The number by which the running count is divided, sometimes multiplied, to derive the true count. It is generally equal either to the number of full decks or half decks that have not been put into play.

CONVERSION (PARTIAL): Paying a winning bet with a higher denomination check or checks and removing some of the players lower denomination checks to make the total payoff correct.

COOLER: A prestacked deck which is secretly switched for the deck in play, the same as a cold deck.

COOL OUT: To calm down a mark who has been swindled in order to keep him from making trouble.

COOLER MOVE: A sleight of hand technique for exchanging a prestacked deck for the one in play.

COP: 1. To win a bet. 2. To steal or palm something.

COUNT: 1. The value of a hand. 2. Usually used to refer to the running count, which is the cumulative value of all cards played at any given time, based on a set of preassigned values for each card denomination.

COUNTER: A player who uses a counting system to keep track of the type of cards played in order to determine whether the deck is favorable or unfavorable to the player.

COUNT ROOM: A room or office in which casino receipts are counted at the end of each gambling session.

COUNTER MAGNET: An electromagnet built under a bar or store counter on a craps table to control metallically loaded dice.

COUP: French word for "bet," used in the United States by baccarat and chemin de fer players.

COVER: 1. To accept a wager. 2. To place a bet on a gambling layout. 3. Measures used by counters to disguise from casino personnel that they're counting. 4. In bingo, to cover a drawn or called number on a card by placing a marker over the number.

COVER ALL: In bingo, a winning position on a card in which all twenty-four numbers have been called and covered.

COVER BET: A bet made by a counter to disguise from casino employees the fact that he is counting.

COVER PLAY: A play of the hand, usually a strategy error made by a counter to disguise from the casino employees the fact that he is counting.

COVERED SQUARE: In bingo, the center square in the N column of a bingo card. It has no number and is considered a free play.

CRAP: In craps, a losing throw by the shooter on his first come out roll of the dice.

CRAP OUT: In craps, to roll a two, three, or twelve on the first roll.

CRAPS: The most popular and biggest betting private and banking dice game in the world.

CRAPS CREW: Four dealers assigned to a single craps game.

CRAPS DEALER: A craps table employee who books, collects, and pays all winning and losing bets for the house.

CRAPS HUSTLER: A player who takes advantage of novices by placing craps bets at less than correct odds.

CREDIT SLIP: The slip that is returned to the table to account for the checks sent back to the cage.

CREDIT MANAGER: A casino employee who issues credit to customers after checking them with Central Credit or their banks.

CRIMP: A bend placed in the card to make it possible to identify or locate the card later.

CROSS (THE): A short con in which the victim is led to believe he is going to be partners with a cheat in swindling a card or dice game.

CROSS FIRING: Dealers talking to each other on a live game about things that aren't game related. This isn't permitted.

CROSSROADER: A card cheat who travels over the country seeking card games in which he can apply his trade. The term is now mainly applied to cheats who specialize in cheating casinos from the outside.

CROUPIER: 1. A casino employee who deals the game and collects and pays the winning and losing bets in a casino. 2. A French term for a dealer which some people use when referring to those that deal roulette, baccarat, chemin de fer and other games with French antecedents.

CUBES: Dice.

CULL: To sort particular cards out of the deck for use in cheating.

CUP: A leather receptacle used for shaking dice.

CUSHION: 1. Money in the bank. 2. Reserve bankroll.

CUT: 1. To divide the deck or decks of cards into two sections and then reassemble them in a single unit ready for dealing or to be placed into a shoe. 2. A house charge, taken by the dealer or croupier such as 2% or 5% of the money wagered by players at poker or baccarat.

CUT CARD: A card, usually a solid colored piece of plastic, which is inserted into the cards in a deck or shoe to determine when the deck or decks will be shuffled.

CUT EDGE DICE: Crooked dice with some edges cut at a sixty degree angle and others at a forty five degree angle. They tend to fall in the direction of the sixty degree cut more often than the forty five degree cut.

CUT IN: To switch in other dice for those in play.

CUT INTO: To match a stack of checks with the same denomination of checks, making them of equal height.

CUT A LINE: To divide the proceeds of a gambling scam equally between two or more people.

CUT OUT WORK: Cards that have been marked by extending a small part of the white part of the back design with an acid which removes the ink.

CUTTER: 1. In poker, a employee who takes a percentage of money out of the pot for supplying the gambling facilities. 2. In baccarat, the dealer takes a 5% cut from the banker's winning bet.

DAUB: A paste or fluid used in marking cards during play.

DEAD ACE: A die loaded to bring up the number one more often than it should.

DEAD CARD: A card which has already been played or one that can't be used in play.

DEAD NUMBER DICE: Dice loaded in such a way that one particular number comes up more often than it should. The most common type of dead number die is the dead ace.

DEALER: An employee of the casino who deals the cards, operates games, or makes payoffs, sees that the rules are followed at his table and plays the house cards or operates the game in accordance with a fixed specified set of instructions.

DEALING A BLISTER: To deal seconds in connection with a deck of cards in which certain cards have been tactually marked. The cheat can feel when a desirable card is on top of the deck and he holds it back for himself or a partner by second dealing.

DEUCE: 1. A die with two spots. 2. Any two spot card.

DEUCE DEALER: A dealer who specializes in dealing seconds.

DICE: Two six sided cubes with one to six spots on each face, giving thirty six possible combinations. All odds and probabilities are calculated from this figure. Opposite sides on each die will add up to seven (5/2, 4/3, 6/1).

DICE ARE OFF: Dice that aren't true.

DICE BOWL: The container on the craps game which holds dice that aren't in play but are available for use.

DIE: One cube out of a set of dice.

DIRTY MONEY: Losing bets picked up by the dealer.

DISCARD RACK OR HOLDER: The plastic box in which used cards are placed after a hand has been played.

DON'T COME BET: In craps, a bet that the dice don't pass, the next roll to be considered as a come out.

DON'T PASS LINE: A betting space on the craps layout. Money placed there is a bet that the dice will lose.

DOUBLE APRON: A kind of sub used by casino dealers to steal chips. The apron normally worn by dealers is made to create a pocket so that chips may be concealed inside.

DOUBLE DEAL: The process of dealing two cards together while pretending to deal only one.

DOUBLE DECK: A blackjack game played with two decks of cards.

DOUBLE DEUCE OR DEUCES: Altered dice that have two deuces (the number two). The extra deuce takes the place of a five.

DOUBLE DISCARD: A draw poker cheating ploy whereby the hustler actually discards twice.

DOUBLE DOWN: To make an additional bet of up to the amount of the original wager, usually on the initial two cards unless the point count is twenty one. When players double down, they receive only one additional card.

DOUBLE DUKE: A card mechanic who deals his victim a very good hand while dealing an even better one to himself or his partner.

DOUBLE NUMBER DICE: Dice that are misspotted so that one number appears twice, on opposite sides of the die while another number is left off entirely.

DOUBLE EXPOSURE: A blackjack game in which both of the dealer cards are shown to the player before the player plays his hand. Other rules are changed to restore to the house the overall edge.

DOUBLE FIVE OR FIVES: Altered dice that have two fives, the extra five spot taking the place of the two spot.

DOUBLING UP: To double the size of a previous bet on the next wager. Many betting systems are based on this principle.

DOUBLE STEER: A short con in which the victim is led to believe he is going to be partners with a cheat in swindling a card or dice game.

DOUBLE THE BANK: The goal of most card counters or teams to double the original playing stake.

DRAG DOWN: To reduce the size of a wager on the next bet.

DRAGGING: Illegally removing chips from the original bet after the game is in progress.

DRILLER: A slot machine cheat who specializes in drilling holes in the machines.

DRIVERS SEAT: In stud poker, to have the best hand showing or to have won most of the money in a game.

DROP: 1. The total amount of cash plus the value of markers drawn at a table game. 2. The total amount of cash and markers for the entire casino.

DROP BOX: A removable locked box located under all the casino games in which paper currency used by players for chips and all casino auditing documents are placed through a slot in the table top.

DROP SHOT: A sleight of hand technique for controlling the number on one of two dice thrown from the hand.

DRUNKEN MITT: A short con game built around a poker game in which the con man accidentally exposes his hand showing that he can't win.

DUKING IN: Involving a victim in a game by getting him to play for you or by making a bet for him.

DUMPING OFF: For a casino dealer to cheat so as to allow his agent to win money from the house by overpaying the bets.

DUMP SHOT: A sleight of hand technique for controlling the number on one of several dice rolled from a cup.

EAR: A bent corner put on a playing card to identify or locate it.

EARLY BIRD TICKET: A ticket to a bingo game sold at a special discount to induce players to come early.

EARLY SURRENDER: The player option of giving up half of the bet before the dealer checks to determine if he has a blackjack.

EARNEST MONEY: The money required of the victim in certain con games as a show of good faith.

EASY WAY CRAPS: To make a point number any way but the hardway.

EDGE: 1. The built in advantage characteristic of all casino games. 2. The sharp outer surface of the dice.

EDGE WORK OR MARKINGS: 1. A deck of cards marked with a slight bevel drawn on certain points of each card between the design and the edge of the card, usually marked high up indicates an ace and lower down a king. 2. Dice that have been altered on the edges (sanded or shaved).

EIGHTER FROM DECATUR: In craps, the point eight.

ELECTRIC DICE: Crooked dice loaded with steel slugs and used over an electric magnet hidden in or under a counter or dice table.

ELEMENT OF RUIN: The percentage probability that the player will lose his bet.

ELEVATOR: A method of performing the hop in which the two halves of the deck are transposed by the right hand as it places the deck into the left hand to start the deal.

EXTREME RIGHT MAN: The player who sits at the dealer's extreme right at the blackjack table. He is the last to act on his hand before the dealer.

ENGLISH: The simultaneous sliding and spinning action of the dice that is characteristic of most controlled shots.

EVEN SPLITTERS: Dice which are so misspotted as to make it possible for the shooter to roll any of the even point numbers 4, 6, 8, or 10.

EVEN UP OR EVEN UP PROPOSITION: 1. A bet or proposition that gives each player an equal chance to win. 2. A bet at correct odds. 3. A 50/50 bet.

EXIT: To get out of the game.

EXPECTED VALUE: The dollar amount that the player should win or lose, if encountering average luck, in exact accordance with the statistical advantage or disadvantage to the house.

FACE CARD: A king, queen, jack or ten in a deck of cards.

FADE CRAPS: To cover part or all of the shooter's center bet.

FADER CRAPS: A bettor who has made a fading bet.

FAIRBANK: 1. To make a cheating move in favor of the player to entice him to continue to play or to increase the size of his bet.

FALSE CUT: A cut which leaves the deck or part of the deck in its original position.

FAST COMPANY: Sophisticated players who are capable of spotting the cruder methods of cheating and are more difficult to swindle.

FAST COUNT: 1. Rapid counting for the purpose of concealing a miscount of one or more numbers. 2. Short changing a person.

FAST WORK: Playing cards that have been boldly marked so that they may be read more easily and quickly.

FIELD: In craps, a space on the layout containing a group of numbers, either 2, 3, 4, 9, 10, 11 and 12 or 2, 3, 5, 9, 10, 11 and 12.

FIELD BET: In bank craps, a bet that one of the group of seven numbers on the field will appear on the next roll.

FIELD SPLITTERS: A pair of misspotted dice, one of which bears only the numbers 1, 2, and 3 while the other bears only the numbers 4, 5, and 6. These are used by the house to beat the player who bets on the field in craps. The same as high low splitters.

FILL: Additional checks brought to the table to replenish the bankroll.

FILL SLIP: A casino form of paper signed by a casino supervisor to request that additional checks be brought from the cashier's cage to the gaming table to replenish the bankroll.

FINGER OR PUT THE FINGER ON: To point out a cheat or crook.

FINGER MAN: Someone who points out a cheat or illegal gambling game.

FIRST BASE: 1. The far left hand seat from where the dealer is standing on the blackjack table. 2. In craps, the stickman. 3. In baccarat, the dealer who calls the game, and so forth.

FIRST BASING: The technique of reading a blackjack dealer's hole card from the first base seat whenever he checks to see if he has a blackjack.

FIRST FLOP DICE: Loaded dice that have been so heavily weighted they're likely to come up on the favored number on the first roll.

FIVE CARD CHARLIE: A bonus popular in blackjack where a five card total equal to or less than twenty-one pays the player two to one.

FLASH: To show a dealer's hole card.

FLASHING: The practice of a casino blackjack dealer exposing the top card of the deck to an agent to help him win.

FLASH WORK: Cards that have been marked very lightly by shading the entire back of each card except for one small portion which is left white.

FLAT BET: To bet the same amount on each hand played usually done for cover purposes.

FLAT JOINT OR FLAT STORE: Any crooked gambling game.

FLAT PASSERS: Crooked dice which have the 6/1 sides cut down on one die and the 3/4 sides cut down on the other so that 4, 5, 9 and 10 appear more often.

FLATS: Crooked dice which have been shaved so that two sides have more surface area than the other four sides. Also called bricks.

FLICK: A small hidden mirror that allows the cheat to see the faces of the cards as he deals them.

FLOATING GAME: An illegal gambling game which is moved from place to place in order to avoid police raids.

FLOOR SUPERVISOR: 1. In table games, a lower level supervisor in the casino whose duties are to spot and correct irregularities. 2 In bingo, an employee who verifies the player's card aloud to the caller.

FLOPPING THE DECK: A method of cheating at blackjack whereby the dealer secretly turns the deck over so the used face up cards on the bottom are redealt. The same as rolling the deck.

FLUSH: In poker, a hand containing five cards of the same suit.

FLUSH SPOTTED DICE: Dice whose spots are flush with the surface rather than countersunk..

FOLD OR DROP: To retire from a poker hand or gambling game.

FOLDING MONEY: Paper money.

FOREIGN CHECKS: Checks from another casino.

FOUR EYED: Term used to describe a cheat who specializes in the use of a glim.

FOUR WAY PLAY BINGO: A game in which there are four winning positions. Also called round robin.

FREE BET: In bank craps, a bet which permits a player who has made a previous bet on the pass or don't pass line to lay or take the correct point odds equal to the amount he is playing on the line.

FREE DOUBLE ODDS BET: Same as free bet except that right or wrong bettors with line bets can take or lay double the amount riding on the line. Found in most legalized casinos.

FREE HAND: The hand in which the shoe isn't normally held while dealing.

FREE RIDE: Playing part of a poker hand without betting. A losing bet that goes unnoticed and plays again.

FREEZE OUT: To force a player out of a game.

FREEZE OUT PROPOSITION WAGER: A long series of bets between a hustler and a gambler in which the total sum to be wagered and the betting conditions are mutually agreed upon before the action begins.

FRETS: The metal partitions that separate each of the thirty eight numbered sections of a roulette wheel.

FRONT LINE: The pass line in craps.

FRONT LINE ODDS: Taking the odds on the point number.

FRONT LOADER: Blackjack dealer who unwittingly flashes his hole card to a player when he deals it to himself.

FRONT LOADING: Observing the value of the dealer's hole card as it is inadvertently exposed during the process of dealing by a careless dealer.

FRONT MAN: A player who is known and respected by the other players and who introduces a cheat into the game and vouches for his integrity in return for a share of the profits.

FRONT MONEY: Money placed on deposit in the casino cage from which a customer can draw markers.

FURNITURE MAN: A cheat who specializes in switching cards by means of a holdout machine.

GAFF: Any secret device or method that accomplishes or aids in cheating.

GAFFED: Any gambling device which has been illegally altered to favor the cheat.

GAFFED DICE: Doctored or crooked dice.

GATE: To stop the dice before they have finished rolling, usually when a roll appears suspicious.

GETS THE MONEY: Any cheating technique which is highly effective in winning the other players' money.

GLIM: A small hidden mirror that allows the cheat to see the faces of the cards as they're being dealt. Any shiny object used for this purpose.

GLIM WORKER: A card cheat who uses a small hidden mirror which allows him to see the faces of the cards as they're being dealt.

GO FOR THE MONEY: To cheat.

GORILLA: A non counting player who receives signals from a counter.

GO SOUTH WITH: To secretly palm cards, dice, money and take it out of action. Also a term used to describe the action of a player putting chips away.

GOOD MAN: 1. A player with a large amount of money. 2. A skilled cheater. 3. A good gambling scheme operator or employee.

GOULASH: Any business establishment such as a bar or restaurant that conducts card games on a regular basis in the back room.

GRAND: One thousand dollars.

GRAVEYARD SHIFT: The early morning shift usually two A.M to ten A.M. or four A.M. to twelve P.M.

GREEK DEAL: The technique of secretly dealing the second card from the bottom of the deck while pretending to deal off the top.

GREEK SHOT: A sleight of hand technique for controlling the number on one of two dice thrown against a wall or backboard.

GREEN: Twenty-five dollar chips, usually green in color.

GREEN HORN: An amateur gambler, one who is inexperienced.

GRIFT: All categories of theft in which the victim is robbed through trickery rather than force.

GRIFTER: Any kind of professional cheat or con man.

GRIFFIN AGENT: An employee of the Griffin Detective Agency who is hired by numerous casinos to detect slot and gaming cheats, dishonest employees, and card counters.

GRIND GAME: A low limit banking game which requires a good many players and good action in order to make a profit.

GRIND JOINT: A casino that relies on high volume low limit play for its profit.

HAND: One deal in a card game, or the cards held by a player.

HANDLE: The total amount of money that repeatedly changes hands before it is actually won or lost.

HANDLESLAMMING: A method of controlling the reel combination that comes upon a slot machine by first pulling the handle then slamming it back upward.

HAND MUCKER: A card cheat who specializes in palming cards.

HAND MUCKING: The practice of secretly switching cards one has been dealt for previously palmed cards.

HAND OFF: For a casino dealer to secretly hand chips to an accomplice who is posing as a player.

HAND SIGNAL: When a player uses his hand to inform the dealer whether or not he wants another card.

HANG THE FLAG: For a casino cheat to signal his partners that no cheating should take place at the moment because of heavy surveillance.

HARD COUNT ROOM: A room where all the coin is counted.

HARD HAND: A hand without an ace that can be counted as eleven.

HARD ROCK: 1. In poker, a tight player. 2. A gambler who refuses to lend money. 3. A player who is hard to beat.

HARDWAY BET: In craps, the numbers 4, 6, 8 or 10 thrown with two duplicate numbers such as two deuces, two threes, etc.

HAWKING THE DICE: Base dealer on one end of the table looking at the roll of the dice on the opposite end. This isn't permitted.

HEAD TO HEAD: Playing alone with the dealer as the only player at the table.

HEEL: When there's more than one check, you lean the entire stack off the bottom check. This is used on odds bets and in the placement of some proposition bets.

HEAT: Heavy surveillance which makes it more difficult to cheat successfully.

HEIST: A deck of cards doctored so that cards with high numerical values can be controlled.

HEAVY HAND: A hand of cards that secretly contains more cards than it is supposed to.

HEEL PEEK: A method of secretly glimpsing at the top card of the deck by lifting the inner corner of the card with the base of the thumb. Also used when dealing out of the shoe before exposing a card.

HIGH LOW PICKUP: A method of cheating at blackjack which involves picking up the discards in a high low alternating order.

HIGH LOW SPLITTERS: A pair of misspotted dice which has only the numbers 1, 2, and 3, while the other has only the numbers 4, 5, and 6. These are used by the house to beat the player who bets on the field at craps. The same as field splitters.

HIGH ROLLER: A player who bets large amounts of money.

HIPSTER: Someone who has a good knowledge of odds and percentages or of cheating and cheating devices.

HIT: To take additional cards in order to improve the hand count.

HITTING HAND: A two card hand with the value of eleven or less requiring an additional card or cards to complete the hand.

HIT IT: 1. In blackjack, to ask the dealer for another card. 2. In craps, to make the point or any desired number. 3. In stud poker, to call for a desired card.

HITS: Dice gaffed so as to favor the shooter.

HIT THE BOARDS: Craps term used by the stickperson when he requests the shooter to throw the dice against the back wall of the dice table.

HOLD: The ratio between the amount won by the house and the drop.

HOLE CARD: The dealer's bottom card, usually dealt face down and not exposed until after the players have played their hands.

HOLD OUT: To secretly keep certain cards out of play with the intention of later switching them for cards that one has been dealt.

HOLD OUT ARTIST: A gambler or cheat who, when calculating the score or dividing the amount of winnings with his partner or partners, says that his winnings are less so he can pocket the difference.

HOLD OUT MAN: A card cheat who specializes in palming cards to take them out of play and then reintroducing valuable cards into a game by means of palming.

HOLD OUT SHOE: A blackjack shoe that has been gaffed so as to allow the dealer to deal seconds whenever he wishes.

HOLD OUT TABLE: A card table that has been elaborately gaffed so as to conceal a card until the cheat wishes to retrieve it. Some of these tables can also secretly transfer cards from one player to another.

HOLE CARD: The dealer's bottom card that is dealt face down and not exposed until after the players have played their hands.

HOLE CARD PLAY: A blackjack play often involving more than one person which is based on the player having knowledge of the dealer's hole card.

HOP: A move that invisibly brings the cards back to their original order after they have been cut by another player.

HOP BET: A one roll bet that may be bet at any time on a specific combination of the dice. A hardway pays thirty to one and a two way combination pays fifteen to one. These are placed in front of the box-person.

HOT: A player on a winning streak.

HOT DECK: A deck or shoe favorable to the player.

HOT NUMBER: A number that has a better chance of being hit than any other number.

HOT PLAYER: A player on a winning streak.

HOT SEAT GAME: A card game in which every player is part of the cheating group except for one unsuspecting victim.

HOT SCORE: The profits of a gambling scam when accompanied by a beef or argument from the victim.

HOUSE: The operators of a casino or gambling games.

HUNCH PLAYERS: Players who know little or nothing about the game on which they're wagering and who bet on impulse.

HUSTLER: Any kind of gambling cheat.

HUSTLING: Hinting or asking a person for a tip or money. Also, the act of cheating.

HYPESTER: Someone who specializes in short-changing cashiers.

INDEX: The number in the upper left hand and lower right hand corner of a playing card which designates its denomination.

INSIDE (THE): The casino's side of the games inside the pit.

INSIDE MAN: 1. An employee in any gambling scheme.

INSIDE WORK: Any gaffs.

INSURANCE: An optional bet made by the players that the dealer has blackjack. It may be made only when the dealer's first card is an ace. Such a bet may not exceed one half of the player's original wager. The payoff is two to one.

INSURANCE COUNTER: A player who uses a special count, perfect for the insurance bet. He often signals the correct insurance play to another counter, who is playing a different system.

JACKPOT: 1. In poker, a form of betting in which each player antes a chip into the pot before the deal. 2.

In slots, the large money payoffs that are displayed on a machine.

JACKPOT LIGHT UP BOARD: An electric sign that hangs in a slot machine parlor or gambling establishment and is connected to the slot machines. It lights up and a chime rings whenever a jackpot is hit.

JOG: A card that sticks out slightly from the deck and acts as a marker. This is mostly used during crooked shuffles and cuts.

JOINT: Any gambling casino.

JOINT BANK: When two or more players join together their resources and play jointly sharing in the win or loss.

JOKER: An extra card furnished with each fifty two card deck, occasionally used as a wild card to represent any card desired.

JUICE DECK: Cards that have been marked by a method which makes the markings literally invisible to anyone who has not been taught how to see them. The cheat can easily read the marks from ten inches or ten feet away.

JUICE JOINT: A crooked dice or roulette game in which the cheating is done by concealed electromagnets in the table, and the roulette ball or the dice are gaffed with a steel slug.

JUNIOR JACKPOT TICKET BINGO: Tickets which pay off a smaller jackpot.

JUNKET REPRESENTATIVE: A person who brings in players from different areas to the casino and is paid according to these players' worth on the table games.

KICK BACK: 1. To return part or all of a score to a mark to avoid a beef. 2. To return a percentage of a player's losses as a marketing tool to secure future business. This practice is popular in Nevada casinos with super high rollers.

KILL (A NUMBER): To control a die during a roll so that a particular desired number comes up.

KITTY: 1. An amount taken out of the stakes of a private game to pay expenses. 2. A pool to which special bets are paid and from which royalties or special bonuses are collected.

KNOCK (A MARK): For an outsider to convince the potential victim of a gambling scam or con game that he is being swindled.

KNOCK OUT: A casino cheating term referring to a crooked dealer cleaning out a player.

LADDER MAN: A casino employee who sits on an elevated stand overlooking a craps, baccarat, or chemin de fer table and whose duty is to correct dealer's errors and to spot dice cheats.

LAMMERS: 1. The buttons used to space off the checks in the bankroll. 2. Buttons marked with different denominations that are placed on the game to let surveillance know the amount of a credit or a marker. Also used to mark the drop.

LARCENY: The inclination to take advantage of a dishonest opportunity when it comes along.

LAYDOWN: A wager or a bet.

LAY OR LAY IT: To bet a greater amount against a lesser amount.

LAYOUT: The felt on the gaming tables with spaces designated for different bets.

LAY THE ODDS: In craps, to bet that a point, box or place number 4, 5, 6, 8, 9, 10, will not be thrown before a seven.

LEAK: 1.The failure to completely hide a cheating move. 2. Revenues that are lost to cheating.

LEGAL TIE: 1. In blackjack, when a dealer's count is the same as the player's count. 2. In poker, when two players have the same ranking hand.

LEGIT GAME: An honest game.

LET IT RIDE: 1. To leave the original bet and the winnings of the previous bet on the gaming table and wager them again. 2. A poker based table game.

LEVELS: Any honest gaming equipment, particularly dice.

LIBERTY BELL: The first slot machine invented in San Francisco in 1895 by Charles Fey, a twenty-nine year old mechanic and the first slot machine operator in America.

LID: The cover that is placed over the tray or rack on a table game and is locked.

LIGHT: A small hidden mirror that allows the cheat to see the faces of the cards as the dealer deals them.

LIGHT WORK: Doctored cards marked with very fine lines.

LIMIT: The maximum amount a player may wager on a specific bet or event.

LIMITED STAKES GAMING: A type of gaming where as the maximum bet is five dollars on any gaming device. There are possible variations, so this definition may change.

LINE BET: 1. In roulette, a bet on six numbers in two

rows of three numbers each running across the layout. The payoff is five to one odds. 2. In craps, same as the pass line bet.

LINE WORK: Additional small markings on doctored cards added to the back design of playing cards so that they can be read from the back by the cheat.

LIVE CARD: A hidden card in an opponent's hand or in the remaining part of the undealt or unplayed part of the deck or shoe. A card that isn't dead because it has not yet been played.

LIVE ONE: A player with money.

LOAD: A weight placed within a die.

LOADS: Loaded dice.

LOADER OR FRONT LOADER: A careless dealer who exposes the hole card in the process of dealing.

LOCATION PLAY: Memorizing a group of cards in sequence so that when one of the cards appears during the game, the cheat will know that the valued ones are about to follow.

LOCK IT UP: Place chips in the tray.

LOOKOUT: A casino employee whose responsibility is to see that everything runs smoothly and is on the constant alert for dishonest players and casino personnel.

LOW BELLY STRIPPERS: A marked deck of cards in which the edges of the high cards are concave rather than straight, making it possible for the cheat to cut to a low or high card.

LUMINOUS READERS: Marked cards that can be read only through tinted glasses.

MACHINE: A secret device worn by a cheat which aids him in holding certain cards out of play.

MARK: The victim or intended victim of any con game or gambling scam.

MARKER: A special casino check or draft used by the gambler to draw chips against his credit or money on deposit in the casino cage.

MARKER PUCK: In craps, a large round puck approximately three inches across. It is black on one side where the word "OFF" is written and white on the side where the word "ON" is written.

MATCH UP: To locate or make a pair of gaffed dice which are identical in appearance to the dice in play.

MECHANIC: Any card or dice cheat who specializes in the use of sleight of hand.

MECHANIC'S GRIP: A method of holding a deck of cards, in either the left or right hand, with three fingers curled around the long edge of the deck and the index finger at the narrow upper edge away from the body.

MINUS COUNT: A cumulative negative count of the cards placed in play that tends to be to the disadvantage of the player.

MISS A PASS: Failure to make a point number in craps.

MISS OUT: A losing craps decision for the shooter and the other players who are betting with the shooter, on the come out roll when a crap is thrown, and after the come out roll when a seven is thrown instead of the shooter's point number.

MISSES: Dice so gaffed as to work against the shooter.

MISSPOTS: Misspotted dice which have certain numbers repeated on opposite sides while other numbers have been left off entirely.

MITT: A hand of cards.

MITT MAN: A card cheat who specializes in palming and switching the cards he has been dealt.

MITTING IN: To get a victim involved in playing in a game by getting him to play for you or by making a bet for him.

MONEY POKER: A guessing game played with dollar bills known as Liar Poker.

MONEY SWITCH: A dice switch performed under the cover of the bills the cheat holds in his hand for betting.

MONKEY: In baccarat, it refers to face cards or ten count valued cards.

MOVE: Any sleight of hand cheating technique.

MUCK: Any sleight of hand technique for switching one or all of the cards one has been dealt in a game for previously palmed cards.

MUCKER: 1. A card cheat who specializes in palming and switching the cards he has been dealt. 2. An extra dealer who helps the roulette dealer pick up the checks and sort them by color.

MULTIPLE DECKS: A blackjack game played with two or more decks of cards.

MULTIPLE SLOT MACHINES: Slot machines which accept from one to eight coins and pay off winners in multiple fashion.

NAIL: To catch someone cheating.

NAIL NICKING: Marking a card by means of a notch placed on the edge of the card with the thumbnail or fingernail.

NATURAL: 1. A blackjack consisting of an ace and a ten valued card. 2. In poker, a ranking hand without a wild card. 3. In craps, a winning decision on the first roll.

NECKTYING: The practice of tilting the front of the deck upward to hide a second deal.

NEGATIVE SWING: A period during which the player shows a loss.

NEW YORK CRAPS: A form of bank craps played mostly in the eastern states in which the player must pay a five percent commission for betting the box or off numbers.

NICKELS: Five dollar chips, usually red in color.

NINETY DAYS: In craps, the point nine.

NO DICE OR NO ROLL: A dice roll that doesn't count.

NUT: The operating costs a cheat incurs which must be deducted from his gross profits. The same refers to the establishment's bottom line.

ODDS: 1. Correct odds are the ratio of the unfavorable chances to the favorable chances. 2. In craps, a special bet which is paid without an advantage to the house and which accompanies a line bet, don't pass bet, come bet, or don't come bet.

ODD SPLITTERS: Dice which are so misspotted as to make it impossible for the shooter to roll either of the odd point numbers, five or nine.

OFF NUMBER BET: A bet made in craps with odds that the shooter will or will not throw a specified number other than his point before throwing a seven.

OFF NUMBERS: In private craps, all the numbers 4, 5, 6, 8, 9 and 10 except the point number the shooter is trying to make.

OFFICE (THE): Any kind of secret signal given by one cheat to another.

OFF THE TOP: At the beginning of a deck or shoe immediately after the shuffle.

ON THE RAIL: Observing a gambling game from behind the players but not playing.

ON THE SQUARE: Honest.

ONE ARMED BANDIT: A slot machine.

ONE NUMBER BET: In craps, betting that a certain number or group of numbers will or will not be thrown before another number.

ONE ROLL ACTION OR COME OUT BET: In craps, a bet that the shooter does or doesn't throw a certain number anyway or a certain number a certain way or one of a group of numbers on the next roll.

ONE ROLL BET: In craps, a bet which is decided on the next roll of the dice.

OPEN CRAPS: A banking dice game in which side bets among the players are permitted only on the point number.

OUTSIDE MAN: 1. A casino employee who observes from outside the pit. 2. Someone who is part of a cheating team.

OUTSIDE WORK: Anything done to gaff dice on their surfaces.

OVERBOARD (TO GO): To be unable to pay on gambling debts.

OVER LAY: In craps, this bet is made on the don't pass when a lay bet has been made to the maximum allowable. This an additional bet against the point that the player must pay a commission to make.

P.C.: 1. Percentage. 2. Mostly used as an abbreviation for the house hold percentage on casino games and the house advantage on various casino games. Example: Hold P.C. and game P.C.

PACKAGE: A prestacked deck which is secretly switched for the deck in play; the same as a cooler.

PADDLE: A plastic device used to push currency and pit documents down into the drop box.

PAD ROLL: A controlled dice shot in which the dice are thrown so they will roll like cartwheels without spinning. The move will work only on soft surfaces.

PAINT: A jack, queen, king or ten.

PAINTER: A card cheat who specializes in daubing the cards during play.

PAIR SPLITTING: Two cards of the same value or two ten valued cards.

PALETTE: A wooden palette with a long thin handle used by baccarat and chemin de fer dealers to move the cash and chips around.

PAPER: 1. Cards that have been marked on the backs prior to play. 2. A check or other negotiable document.

PAR: In slot machines, it refers to the expected hold of the machine.

PARLAY: To increase a wager by the total amount of the previous hand's winnings.

PASS: In craps, a winning decision for the craps shooter on the come out roll by throwing a seven or eleven or repeating the point before throwing a seven. 2. In poker, a declaration that the player doesn't wish to make a bet.

PASSERS: Dice that have been gaffed to favor the shooter.

PASS LINE: In craps, a space on the craps layout. Money placed in this space is a bet that the shooter will pass.

PAST POSTING: Secretly placing a bet in any game of chance after a decision has been reached.

PAT HAND: A hand in which the first two cards result in a high count and thus would not normally be hit. A hand that would break with a ten count card.

PAY LINE: The center line in the window of a slot machine on which the payoff symbols appear.

PAYOFF: The collection of a bet.

PAYOFF ODDS: The odds at which a bet is paid off, usually less than the correct odds.

PEEK: Any sleight of hand technique for secretly sighting the face of a card.

PEG: To mark cards so they can be identified by means of very minute bumps on the back known as blisters.

PERCENTAGE DICE: Gaffed dice that tilt the odds in the cheat's favor but don't guarantee a win.

PERCENTAGE TOPS AND BOTTOMS: A pair of gaffed dice, one of which is misspotted, and one number appears on the die twice.

PERFECTS: Dice that are true cubes to a tolerance of 2/10,000 of an inch.

PHILADELPHIA LAYOUT: The first bank craps layout to give the players an opportunity to bet the dice to win and lose.

PHONY: A crooked die.

PICKUP STACK: The technique of stacking certain cards in the process of picking up the cards lying face up from the previous round of play.

PINCHING: Illegally removing chips from one's bet after the game is in progress.

PIPS: The spots on a playing card that indicate the denomination of the card.

PIT BOSS: A casino employee who supervises the activities of a group of dealers and floor supervisors in an area consisting of several gaming tables.

PLACE BET: In bank craps, a right or wrong numbers bet, including 4,5,6,8,9 and 10.

PLAY BEST HAND: Two or more poker players to act in collusion, signaling each other's hands and having the strongest player stay in the pot while the others drop out.

PLAYER TRACKING SYSTEM: 1. In slots, computer software program that tracks all the coins put into the machines and the betting patterns they use. 2. A system in which the supervisors rate the player according to his action on the table games.

PLUG: The same as slug. A prearranged group of cards or a group of cards rich in low or high cards.

POINT: 1. Any number or total in a gambling game on which a wager can be placed. 2. In craps, the numbers 4, 5, 6, 8, 9 and 10 are possible point numbers.

POINT BET: In craps, a bet at odds that the shooter's point will or will not be made.

POT: 1. The aggregate of chips or money at stake in a betting scheme usually consisting of bets contributed by each contestant. 2. In poker, the total cash or chips bet on any single hand.

PREFERENTIAL SHUFFLING: The action by a dealer who shuffles up the decks that are favorable to the player and dealing decks that are unfavorable to the player.

PRESSING: 1. Illegally adding chips to the bet after the game is in progress. 2. Letting one's winnings ride on the next bet.

PRESS THE BET: To increase a wager for the same amount as the original bet after winning the bet.

PRIVATE GAME: Any game which has no houseman or banker and in which no charge is extracted for the privilege of playing.

PROGRESSIVE SLOT MACHINE: A slot machine in which a large jackpot increases in a predetermined ratio to the number of coins played into the machine.

PROP: 1. Any unusual type of wager that appears to favor both players equally. 2. In craps, short for proposition bets.

PROP HUSTLER: A grafter who specializes in luring victims into bets which they have little or no chance of winning.

PROPOSITION BET: 1. Any bet made at blackjack or any other game that isn't covered by the rules. 2. In craps, a center bet with high payoff odds which greatly favors the house.

PROPOSITION CHEAT: A crooked gambler whose policy is never to give his opponent a break.

PROPOSITION HUSTLER: A bettor who offers betting propositions which appear to be fair or to favor his opponent but actually gives the hustler a big advantage.

PROVE: To cut checks in a certain manner to verify accuracy.

PROVE A HAND: To reconstruct the hands just previously picked up in order to verify a decision.

PUCK: 1. A marker placed on a craps betting space to show what point the shooter is trying for.

PULL DOWN: To take down all or part of a wager just won.

PULL THROUGH: A sleight of hand move which appears to be a cut made just after a shuffle. It separates the two halves of the deck and replaces them as they were before the shuffle.

PULL UP: For a potential mark to lose interest in betting.

PULL UP A PLAY: To call off a play in the casino, usually a counting or hole card play by signaling another player.

PUNTER: In baccarat or chemin de fer, the player or shooter.

PUSH: A tie or stand off in which the player neither wins or loses.

PUT BET: A wager that may be made at any time on any of the numbers, 4, 5, 6, 8, 9, or 10 which shall win if the number on which the wager was placed is thrown before a seven appears and shall lose if a seven is thrown before that number. It may not be taken down after the next roll of the dice.

QUARTERS: Twenty-five dollar chips, usually green in color.

RACK: A container that holds chips or checks.

RAISE: In poker, to put more chips in a pot than any previous player.

RATS: Another name for dice.

READABLE DEALER: A dealer whose hole card can be spotted by a player or another person in the casino.

READERS: Marked cards.

READY UP: To get ready to make a cheating move.

REAL WORK (THE): Authentic, inside information on the correct way to perform a cheating move or scam.

RED: 1. Five dollar chips. 2. To owe money.

RELAY: A person who relays signals from one person to another.

REMBRANDT OR PICASSO: A card cheater who specializes in daubing the cards during play.

RENEGE: To refuse to pay a lost wager.

RESULT PLAYER: A gambler who tells you how you should have made your bet or play after the decision has been made.

RIDE (THE ACTION): For a victim to tolerate a hustler's cheating actions without complaining because he is unaware that anything dishonest is happening.

RIFFLE: The actual mixing together of two stacks of cards.

RIFFLE STACK: The process of stacking the cards while riffle shuffling the deck.

RIG: To gaff or make crooked.

RIGHT BETTOR: A player who bets the pass line or the come bets. A bet to win.

RING IN: To introduce crooked gaming equipment into a game.

RING IN ONE'S NOSE (TO HAVE A): To be losing heavily and betting high, hoping to get even.

RIP AND TEAR: To cheat freely and extensively without fear of repercussions.

RIP IN: In craps, to switch dice into a game.

ROAD HUSTLER: A card or dice cheat who travels around the country looking for games to cheat in.

ROAD MOB: A team of card or dice cheats who travel around the country looking for games to cheat in.

ROB: To cheat the players in a game of chance.

ROCK: 1. A player who won't lend any money. 2. In stud poker, a back to back player.

ROLL: To roll dice or a roulette ball.

ROLLING THE DECK: A method of cheating at blackjack whereby the dealer secretly turns the deck over so the used face up cards on the bottom are redealt.

ROPE: 1. To cheat or swindle. 2. To lure a victim into a crooked game.

ROUND: To cause someone to turn around to keep him from seeing a cheating move performed by one's partner.

RUBBER BAND: A system of assigning dealers to table games when the dealers aren't assigned to a specific table.

RUMBLE: To catch on to a gaffed mechanism or a sleight of hand move.

RUNDOWN: When a supervisor wants to know how much the table games are winning or losing.

RUNNER: A casino employee who carries cash outs, fill slips, and money between the cashier's cage and the pit.

RUNNING COUNT: The cumulative value of all cards played at any given time, based on a set of preassigned values for each card denomination.

RUNNING FLAT: For any gambling establishment to be operating crookedly.

RUN UP: To rearrange the cards while shuffling them so that a favorable hand will fall to one of the players..

SAND: 1.To edge mark cards with sandpaper. 2. To round off the edges of the dice.

SANDBAG POKER: A betting technique in which two players have a third sandwiched between them and keep raising without any consideration for the middle player.

SAND WORK: Cards marked by having a portion of the back pattern slightly scraped off with a piece of sandpaper.

SAW TOOTH EDGE WORK: Dice that have been gaffed by placing small cuts on certain edges to retard the roll of the dice when they roll over these edges and there by affecting the odds.

SCAM: A method for bilking a gambling opponent.

SCRATCH: To request another card from the dealer.

SCORE: The proceeds of any cheating scam or con game.

SCREEN OUT: To cover up or misdirect attention away from a crooked gambling move.

SECOND BASE: 1. In craps, the dealer to the boxperson's right. 2. In blackjack, the center position of the table.

SECONDS: A form of cheating by not dealing the top card from the deck.

SECOND DEALER: A dealer who deals the second card from the deck when he appears to be dealing the top card.

SEVEN OUT: In craps, a total of seven thrown by the shooter after his establishment of a pass line point.

SEVEN WINNER: In craps, a total of seven thrown by the shooter prior to his establishment of a pass line point.

SHADE: Any kind of cover or distraction for a cheating move.

SHADING: A method of marking the backs of cards by delicately shading them with a dilute solution of marking ink which is the same color as the ink already printed on the backs.

SHAPES: Dice whose shapes have been altered in some way so that they're no longer perfect cubes.

SHARK: A cheater.

SHIFT THE CUT: To return secretly the halves of a cut deck to their original position.

SHILL: A casino employee who plays to generate business for a casino game. In baccarat they're called a starter.

SHIMMY: Chemin de fer.

SHIMMY TABLE: A table at which chemin de fer is played.

SHINER: A small mirror which reflects the face of the top card of the deck as it is dealt.

SHOE: A container used to hold undealt cards when four or more decks are used and from where the dealer pulls out cards to be dealt in blackjack and baccarat.

SHOOTER: In craps, the player who throws the dice.

SHORT SHOE: A blackjack dealing shoe from which certain cards have been secretly removed prior to the start of play so as to affect the odds.

SHORTCAKE: When a crooked gambler short changes his partners in cutting up the score by underreporting the amount won.

SHOT: Any cheating move made by a player in a casino. Also, a claim.

SHUFFLE: The process of handling and mixing the cards from the completion of one shoe to the beginning of the next shoe or, in hand decks, when the cut card comes out.

SHY: A bet that lacks the necessary amount to comply with procedure.

SILVER: Silver dollar gaming tokens.

SINGLE ACTION NUMBERS BET: A bet on one digit.

SINGLE DECK: A blackjack game played with one deck almost always hand held by the dealer.

SINGLE 0 (ZERO): A bet on the roulette game.

SINGLE O: For a cheat to work without any partners.

SIX ACE FLATS: Dice that have been shaved so that the ace side and the opposite side of the six will have more surface area and therefore come up more often.

SIX DECK: A blackjack game played with six decks and dealt from a shoe.

SIXES: In craps, a craps twelve which is both die showing six spots up.

SIZE: The numerical value of a card, disregarding the suit. This term is primarily used in regard to marked cards.

SKIMMING: Secretly taking money from the gross revenues of a casino or other gambling operation to avoid taxes.

SKY: An area above the main casino where play is observed through one way mirrors by a surveillance team.

SLEEPER: Money or a bet left on a gaming table which belongs to a player who has forgotten about it.

SLICK CUP: A dice cup that has had its inner surface polished for use in combination with gaffed dice.

SLIDE SHOT: A sleight of hand technique for controlling one or both dice thrown from the hand.

SLOT: A slot machine.

SLOUGH THE JOINT: To close down a gambling game or gambling house.

SLUG: 1. Any group of cards within the deck which has been prearranged for cheating purposes and which therefore must not be disturbed during the shuffles. It could also be rich in either low or high cards. 2. A metallic substitution for a coin or token in a slot machine.

SMACK (THE): A gambling short con built around a game of matching coins.

SNAPPER: A blackjack or natural.

SNAKE EYES: In craps, a one spot showing on both dice.

SNEAK POCKET: A hidden pocket within the lining of the pants along the fly used by a dice cheat to store dice.

SNOWBALLS: Misspotted dice which bear only the numbers 4, 5, and 6.

SOFT ACTION OR SOFT GAME: A game composed of players with limited gambling knowledge who are therefore particularly easy to cheat.

SOFT COUNT ROOM: A room where all the bills are counted.

SOFT HAND: In blackjack, any hand consisting of an ace and another card.

SPELL: A series of winning or losing decisions.

SPILL: For a dice mechanic to accidentally drop one or both palmed dice so that more than two dice are in evidence at one time.

SPLASH MOVE: The process of going through the motions of performing a cheating move without actually doing it in order to see if it will arouse suspicion.

SPLIT: An option allowing the player to make two cards of identical value into two hands, betting an amount equal to the original wager on the second card.

SPLIT BET: In roulette, a bet on two adjacent numbers each paying seventeen to one odds.

SPOOK: The member of the team in a spooking operation whose job it is to spot the dealer's hole card and signal it to the player.

SPOOKING: Spotting the dealer's hole card from the rear when the dealer checks to see if he has a blackjack and then signals that information to a player at the dealer's table.

SPOONING: Cheating a slot machine by inserting a spoon shaped tool up through the payout tray to cause the machine to discharge its coins.

SPOT: To detect an irregularity.

SPOT CARD: Any card ranked from ace to ten.

SPREAD: 1. A cheating move whereby a palmed card is secretly added to an accomplice's hand in the act of spreading his cards out on the table. 2. To play more than one hand.

SQUARE BET: In roulette, a bet on four corners of the layout each paying off at eight to one odds.

SQUARES: Any honest gambling equipment, particularly dice.

SQUEEZE: The control that operates an electrically operated cheating device.

SQUEEZE PLAY: A method of playing a slot machine without depositing a coin by squeezing the handle inward as it is pulled down so that it goes around the locking mechanism which is normally released only when a coin is inserted.

STACKED DECK: A prearranged sequence of cards used to cheat players.

STAND: To decide not to take additional cards.

STANDOFF: 1. No decision, a tie, or cancellation of a bet. 2. In blackjack, when a player and a dealer have the same count. 3. In craps, a two ace standoff means that the wrong bettor doesn't win when two aces appear on the first roll. The same happens with two sixes on the Don't Pass.

STAY: 1. In poker, to remain in the pot without raising. 2. In blackjack, to not take any additional cards.

STEAM: Heavy surveillance which makes it more difficult to cheat successfully. Also used to refer to a player making heavy wagers.

STEAMING: Betting higher and higher usually after a series of losing hands.

STEER: To lure a victim into a swindle.

STEERER: A con man or hustler whose job it is to lure victims into a scam.

STEER JOINT: A crooked gambling house to which players are taken for the express purpose of being swindled.

STICK: In craps, a stick used by the stickperson to push the dice around the table to the player.

STICKPERSON: In craps, it's the dealer who calls the game and who moves the dice.

STIFF: 1. A hard hand which consists of a total of twelve to sixteen and can break if another card is drawn. 2. A player who doesn't tip the dealer after he wins.

STRAIGHT: In poker, a hand of five cards in sequence, not of the same suit.

STRAIGHT BET: In roulette, a bet on one number paying off thirty five to one odds.

STREAK: A run of good or bad luck.

STREET BET: In roulette, a bet on three numbers running across the layout paying off eleven to one odds.

STRIKE (THE): A second dealing technique in which the top card is pushed over slightly so as to expose the outer corner of the second card which is then dealt out by the thumb.

STRIKE NUMBER: The plus or minus count in a counting system at which the size of the bet or the play of the hand is varied.

STRINGING: Cheating a slot machine by putting a coin on a string which is inserted into the machine, then pulled back up. Also called a yo-yo.

STRIPPERS: Cards that have been gaffed by shaving them along the edges so that certain cards can be located by feel.

STRONG: 1. Any cheating move that is particularly effective. 2. A cheat who is very proficient.

STRONG WORK: Crooked cards marked with heavy lines.

STUCK: Money the player has lost.

STUD: Form of poker in which three or more cards are dealt face up.

SUB: A secret pocket in the clothing of a casino dealer used to hide stolen chips.

SUCKER: Anyone who isn't a member of the hustling subculture.

SUCKER BET: A bet that supplies the operator or hustler with a high percentage.

SUCKER WORD: Any cheating term that is used only by non cheats or amateurs.

SUCKER WORK: Ineffective gaffs sold to amateurs who don't know any better.

SWEATER: 1. Someone who watches a gambling game without taking part. 2. A casino employee who worries excessively about winning or losing.

SWEETEN A BET: Legally adding checks to a wager before the cards have been dealt.

SWINGING: The process of stealing chips by a casino employee.

SWITCH: To secretly exchange one object for another.

SWITCHING: 1. The process of transferring the mark's interest from the come on proposition to the deal that actually constitutes the con. 2. The process of transferring the mark's confidence from the outside man to the inside man in a big con.

TABLE STAKES: In poker, a method of placing a maximum betting limit on wagers.

TAKE: 1. The receipts of a banking game or gambling scheme. 2. To accept a bribe. 3. To cheat.

TAKE AN EDGE: To give oneself any kind of dishonest advantage in a game of chance.

TAKE A BATH: To lose heavily or to go broke.

TAKE IT OFF FROM THE INSIDE: The act of stealing from the house by casino personnel.

TAKE OFF: To cheat someone in a gambling game.

TAKE OFF MAN: The player, usually in a spooking or cheating operation, who bets the big money.

TAKE THE ODDS: To take odds on an event that has a lower probability of occurring. By doing so, one ends up paying more than even odds. The same as laying odds.

TAPPED OUT: To lose one's total bankroll.

THE TAT: 1. A gambling scam built around a game employing a single die. 2. The misspotted die, bearing only the numbers five and six, used in the scam.

TEAR UP (THE): The cheat pretends not to accept the mark's gambling loss and tears up the check when actually he switches in a dummy check and destroys it, then cashes the original check before the mark can stop payment.

TEES: Misspotted dice which have certain numbers repeated on opposite sides while other numbers have been left off entirely.

TELEGRAPH: To unwittingly alert the other players

to the fact that you are about to make a cheating move through nervousness or because of some clumsy preparatory action.

TELL: Any unconscious signal or discrepancy which may be spotted by a knowledgeable observer as evidence that a cheating move has taken place.

TELL THE TALE: For a con man, usually the inside man, to explain to the mark the deal by which he is supposed to profit.

TEN STOP MACHINE: A gaffed slot machine that has twenty symbols on each of its reels but is gaffed so that only ten of them can appear on its pay line.

THERE'S WORK DOWN: There are crooked dice or cards in play.

THIRD BASE: The far left hand seat on the blackjack table from a player's perspective.

TIE UP: For the outside man in a con game to keep the mark involved in the scam until the sting in which his money is taken.

TIGHT: 1. Term used to describe any cheating technique that is very little known even among professional cheats. 2. Term used to describe any hustler who can be relied on to keep confidential any cheating secrets that are passed on to him.

TIP: 1. To reveal cheating secrets. 2. A gratuity.

T.I.S. OR TABLE INVENTORY SLIP: The accounting document that records the monetary amount of checks that are in each table game rack at the end of each shift or when a game is closed.

TOKE: A tip to a casino employee.

TOOLS: The gaffed dice that a dice cheat employs in his work.

TOP: The gross handle of a game or gambling scheme.

TOPPING THE DECK: Palming cards off the top of the deck.

TOPS: Misspotted dice which have certain numbers repeated on opposite sides while other numbers have been left off entirely.

TOPS AND BOTTOMS: Gaffed dice which bear only three different numbers on each die.

TRAY: The device attached to the table that contains the bankroll. Also called a float.

TRIMS: Crooked cards gaffed by trimming some cards one way and the others another way.

TRIP WORK: Dice gaffed by extending certain of the edges slightly to discourage the dice from rolling over those edges.

TRUE COUNT: The running count adjusted for the number of cards or decks remaining to be played.

TWENTY-ONE: 1. The game of blackjack. 2. The highest hand at blackjack.

TWINKLE: A small hidden mirror that allows the cheat to see the faces of the cards as he deals them.

TWO CARD PUSH OFF: A second dealing technique in which the top two cards are slid over together in alignment then the second card pulled out as the top card is drawn back onto the deck.

TWO NUMBER BET: In craps, a bet that one of two specified numbers will or will not be thrown before a seven.

TWO ROLL BET: In craps, a bet which is decided within the next two rolls.

UNDER THE GUN: 1. In draw or stud poker, a situation in which a player must pass, bet or check before other players do so. 2. The first player to the dealer's left.

UNPAID SHILL: A casino operator's term for describing a consistent small money bettor or a player who likes to play by him and opens dead games.

UPCARD: The card that the dealer turns up for the players to see before they start to play their hands.

VIGORISH OR VIG: The percentage taken by the casino in some of the casino table games.

WASHING THE CARDS: A mixing of the cards face down in a circular motion with both hands prior to the shuffle when opening the game and using brand new cards.

WAVE: To bend the edge of a card during play for identification purposes.

WEED: To secretly palm or remove bills while handling or counting money.

WEIGHT: Loaded dice.

WELCHER: One who doesn't honor a gambling debt.

WHEEL ROLLER: In roulette, the dealer who spins the wheel and deals the game.

WHIP CUP: A dice cup that has had its inner surface polished for use in combination with gaffed dice.

WHIP SHOT: A controlled dice shot in which the two dice are spun from the hand and strike the table surface with a flat spinning motion so that the controlled numbers are on top when the dice stop.

WHITE ON WHITE: Cards that have been marked by means of small white markings on the white border. The cheat can spot the marks because they don't have the glaze finish which the rest of the border has.

WINDOW: 1. The space, usually between the left side of the dealer's body and his left upper arm, through which the value of his hole card is seen when he checks to see if he has a blackjack. 2. The opening in the face of the dealing shoe where the dealer pulls the card from.

WIRE: 1. A signal used between two gamblers or cheats. 2. In stud poker, a player who has a pair back to back is said to be wired. 3. To have a good hand.

WIRED: A player who is wearing a concealed microcomputer to aid in beating the casino at blackjack or roulette.

WIREMAN: A slot machine cheat who inserts a wire into a drilled hole in the machine in order to manipulate the mechanism.

WORK: 1. Any kind of crimp or nick placed onto a card for identification purposes. 2. Any kind of gaffed dice. 3. Any kind of secret technical information on the correct working of a cheating move or scam.

WORKING STACK: In craps, stacks of checks directly in front of a base dealer used for making payoffs.

WRONG BETTOR OR WRONG PLAYER: In craps, a player who bets the dice to lose.

YARD: A hundred dollars.

GAMING STATISTICS AND GRAPHICS

NOTE: WIN FIGURES MAY SHOW MINOR DIFFERENCES DUE TO ROUNDING

UNITED STATES GAMING STATISTICS 1993

STATE	Colorado	Iowa	Illinois	Mississippi	Nevada	New Jersey	Puerto Rico	S. Dakota	Totals
Table Games	312	65	391	758	5,128	1,288	282	61	8,285
Table Game Win	29,972,568	6,001,058	234,129,563	300,086,000	1,948,998,000	1,086,673,000	88,987,379	3,334,123	3,698,181,691
Table Win Per Day/Unit	283	253	2,217	2,486	1,041	2,507	865	172	1,223
Table Game Win %	37.01		21.78		15.71	15.76	18.25	19.87	21.4
Slot Machines	12,685	1,200	5,518	13,616	147,174	24,561	2,042	2,009	208,805
Slot Machine Win	285,996,468	35,559,944	371,554,919	489,618,000	3,944,041,000	2,203,595,900	94,625,978	38,294,201	7,463,286,410
Slot Machine Win Per Day	68	81	244	225	73	253	127	53	98
Slot Machine Win %	8.32		7.65		5.77			9.64	7.85
Gross Win	315,969,036	41,561,002	605,684,482	789,704,000	6,247,509,000	3,135,662,900	183,613,357	43,342,153	11,363,045,930

UNITED STATES GAMING STATISTICS 1992

STATE	Colorado	Iowa	Illinois	Mississippi	Nevada	New Jersey	Puerto Rico	S. Dakota	Totals
Table Games	258	84	156		4,963	1,144	225	91	6,921
Table Game Win	18,511,850	123,310,505	81,375,462		1,860,162,000	1,101,342,000	81,022,759	4,856,709	3,270,581,285
Table Win Per Day/Unit	314	300	2,127		1,027	2,517	987	176	1,295
Table Game Win %	39		23.53		15.76	15.7	17		22.2
Slot Machines	11,723	1,619	2,225		136,145	22,774	1,842	1,910	178,238
Slot Machine Win	181,000,813	764,504,545	117,274,026		2,479,339,237	2,118,517,000	59,463,794	34,859,500	5,754,958,915
Slot Machine Win Per Day	72	98	212		50	259	88	50	88
Slot Machine Win %	10.28		8.5		5.93	9.72			8.61
Gross Win	199,512,663	887,815,050	198,649,487		4,626,783,237	3,215,969,000	140,486,553	39,716,209	9,308,932,199

UNITED STATES GAMING STATISTICS 1994

STATE	Colorado	Iowa	Illinois	Nevada	New Jersey	S. Dakota	Totals
Table Games	253	92	429	5,834	1,341	77	8,026
Table Game Win	26,874,539	24,047,000	334,304,446	2,699,860,000	1,122,269,000	4,891,835	4,212,246,820
Table Win Per Day/Unit	298	662	2,137	1,268	2,287	174	1,438
Table Game Win %		28.49	19.77	14.64	16.06	19.59	16.43
Slot Machines	10,767	1,550	6,716	156,837	25,891	2,117	203,878
Slot Machine Win	298,811,102	76,270,000	645,247,192	4,307,726,000	2,297,481,000	40,995,041	7,666,530,335
Slot Machine Win Per Day	73	134	264	75	243	53	103
Slot Machine Win %		8.34	6.68	5.74	8.82	9.51	9.77
Gross Win	325,685,641	100,317,000	979,551,638	7,007,586,000	3,419,750,000	45,886,876	11,878,777,155

GAMING STATISTICS AND GRAPHICS

COLORADO

COLORADO GAMING STATISTICS FOR 1993

BLACKHAWK	JAN	FEB	MAR	APR	MAY	JUN	JUL	AUG	SEP	OCT	NOV	DEC	AVG
Casinos	19	20	20	22	22	20	21	21	21	21	21	23	21
Days	31	27.70	31	30	29.45	30	31	31	30	31	30	28.83	30
Nickel Slots	427	453	440	528	530	497	580	588	581	589	584	703	542
Nickel Win Per Day	39	39	42	37	41	42	42	45	47	41	33	33	40
Dime Slots	0	0	0	0	0	0	0	0	20	0	0	46	6
Dime Win Per Day	0	0	0	0	0	0	0	0	24	0	0	22	4
Quarter Slots	1,947	2,000	2,035	2,177	2,153	1,992	2,216	2,294	2,177	2,125	2,104	2,724	2,162
Quarter Win Per Day	59	64	64	59	67	65	70	68	76	75	60	60	66
Fifty Cent Slots	9	9	9	9	9	9	20	28	32	33	33	33	19
Fifty Cent Win Per Day	50	61	60	60	64	56	32	47	65	58	38	39	53
Dollar Slots	708	711	712	771	754	732	890	821	818	815	831	1,092	805
Dollar Win Per Day	109	126	127	122	143	136	122	139	147	146	129	115	130
Five Dollar Slots	14	15	15	21	25	25	32	31	31	38	40	61	29
Five Dollar Win Per Day	274	487	555	577	542	395	420	429	511	495	417	266	447
Total Slots	3,105	3,188	3,211	3,506	3,471	3,255	3,738	3,762	3,659	3,600	3,592	4,659	3,562
Win Per Day Per Slot	69	76	77	73	83	80	81	83	91	90	75	71	79
Blackjack Tables	57	69	72	79	77	74	80	80	73	73	73	95	75
Blackjack Win Per Day	235	234	249	202	247	220	264	258	274	314	224	244	247
Poker Tables	11	19	18	15	15	17	20	20	19	19	16	25	18
Poker Win Per Day	824	516	571	657	683	580	576	598	642	601	670	514	619
Table Games	68	88	90	94	92	91	100	100	92	92	89	120	93
Table Win Per Day	330	295	313	275	318	287	326	326	350	373	304	300	317
Total Gross Revenues	7,344,966	7,430,020	8,550,119	8,428,818	9,363,589	8,641,793	10,402,227	10,531,289	10,895,272	11,082,925	8,942,475	10,553,929	9,347,285
Total Annual Gross													112,167,422

COLORADO GAMING STATISTICS FOR 1993

CENTRAL CITY	JAN	FEB	MAR	APR	MAY	JUN	JUL	AUG	SEP	OCT	NOV	DEC	AVG
Casinos	19	20	20	22	22	20	21	21	21	21	21	23	21
Days	31	28	31	30	29	30	31	31	30	31	30	29	30
Nickel Slots	427	453	440	528	530	497	580	588	581	589	584	703	542
Nickel Win Per Day	39	39	42	37	41	42	42	45	47	41	33	33	40
Dime Slots	0	0	0	0	0	0	0	0	0	0	0	0	0
Dime Win Per Day	0	0	0	0	0	0	0	0	0	0	0	0	0
Quarter Slots	1,947	2,000	2,035	2,177	2,153	1,992	2,216	2,224	2,177	2,125	2,104	2,724	2,156
Quarter Win Per Day	59	64	64	59	67	65	70	68	76	75	60	60	66
Fifty Cent Slots	9	9	9	9	9	9	20	28	32	33	33	33	19
Fifty Cent Win Per Day	50	61	60	70	64	56	32	47	65	58	38	39	53
Dollar Slots	708	711	712	771	754	732	890	821	818	816	831	1,092	805
Dollar Win Per Day	109	126	127	122	143	136	122	139	147	146	129	115	130
Five Dollar Slots	14	15	15	21	25	26	32	31	31	38	40	61	29
Five Dollar Win Per Day	274	487	555	577	542	395	420	429	511	495	417	266	447
Total Slots	3,105	3,188	3,211	3,506	3,471	3,256	3,738	3,692	3,639	3,601	3,592	4,613	3,551
Win Per Day Per Slot	67	74	75	69	79	77	77	80	87	85	71	68	76
Blackjack Tables	67	69	72	79	77	74	80	80	73	73	73	95	76
Blackjack Win Per Day	235	234	249	202	247	220	264	258	274	314	224	244	247
Poker Tables	11	19	18	15	15	17	20	20	19	19	16	25	18
Poker Win Per Day	824	516	571	657	683	580	576	598	642	601	670	514	619
Total Tables	78	88	90	94	92	91	100	100	92	92	89	120	94
Win Per Table Per Day	318	295	313	274	318	287	326	326	350	373	304	300	315
Total Gross Revenues	5,897,979	5,338,512	6,503,351	6,643,211	7,606,504	7,150,305	8,257,518	7,540,309	6,741,561	6,638,751	5,002,005	5,643,801	6,580,317
Total Annual Gross													78,963,807

COLORADO GAMING STATISTICS FOR 1993

CRIPPLE CREEK	JAN	FEB	MAR	APR	MAY	JUN	JUL	AUG	SEP	OCT	NOV	DEC	AVG
Casinos	26	26	26	26	26	29	28	28	27	27	27	26	27
Days	30.73	27.62	31	30	30.57	29.90	31	31	30	31	30	31	30
Nickel Slots	600	616	682	675	803	830	818	853	850	775	811	816	761
Nickel Win Per Day	27	34	31	32	35	34	42	41	37	38	24	23	33
Dime Slots	9	9	9	9	9	9	9	9	9	9	9	9	9
Dime Win Per Day	30	30	28	23	27	26	32	38	30	34	18	22	28
Quarter Slots	1,950	1,803	1,777	1,846	2,118	2,188	2,172	2,166	2,102	2,007	1,938	1,938	2,000
Quarter Win Per Day	33	41	43	44	46	47	58	56	58	52	33	34	45
Fifty Cent Slots	6	6	6	6	26	32	30	25	25	25	25	29	20
Fifty Cent Win Per Day	74	74	70	47	30	40	48	51	50	47	29	34	50
Dollar Slots	670	589	589	589	681	707	697	707	667	608	614	592	643
Dollar Win Per Day	60	74	87	81	77	74	94	85	96	97	68	68	80
Five Dollar Slots	11	11	11	14	20	19	19	22	22	22	24	29	19
Five Dollar Win Per Day	164	217	281	186	185	114	233	235	239	260	150	146	201
Total Slots	3,246	3,034	3,074	3,139	3,657	3,785	3,745	3,782	3,675	3,446	3,421	3,413	3,451
Win Per Day Per Slot	38	47	50	49	50	49	62	59	61	58	38	38	50
Blackjack Tables	52	53	52	57	65	68	64	61	59	54	54	54	58
Blackjack Win Per Day	148	146	166	148	168	187	208	234	191	196	161	145	175
Poker Tables	20	17	18	21	23	20	19	19	19	16	16	18	19
Poker Win Per Day	239	279	286	247	267	274	340	325	298	342	267	229	283
Table Games	72	70	70	78	88	88	83	80	78	70	70	72	77
Table Win Per Day	173	178	197	175	194	207	238	256	217	229	185	166	201
Total Gross Revenues	4,116,066	4,252,049	5,089,498	5,009,123	6,145,770	6,155,487	7,802,939	7,569,501	7,226,781	6,692,792	4,250,143	4,426,305	5,728,038
Total Annual Gross													68,736,454

COLORADO GAMING STATISTICS FOR 1993

COLORADO	JAN	FEB	MAR	APR	MAY	JUN	JUL	AUG	SEP	OCT	NOV	DEC	AVG
Casinos	64	66	66	70	70	69	70	70	69	69	69	72	69
Days	92.73	83.32	93	90	89.02	89.9	93	93	90	93	90	88.83	90
Nickel Slots	1,454	1,522	1,562	1,731	1,863	1,824	1,978	2,029	2,012	1,953	1,979	2,222	1,844
Nickel Win Per Day	34	37	37	35	38	38	42	43	43	40	29	29	37
Dime Slots	9	9	9	9	9	9	9	9	29	9	9	55	15
Dime Win Per Day	30	30	28	23	27	26	32	38	26	34	18	22	19
Quarter Slots	5,844	5,803	5,847	6,200	6,424	6,172	6,604	6,684	6,456	6,257	6,146	7,386	6,319
Quarter Win Per Day	50	57	58	55	60	59	66	64	70	68	51	53	59
Fifty Cent Slots	24	24	24	24	44	50	70	81	89	91	91	95	59
Fifty Cent Win Per Day	56	64	63	61	44	46	39	48	61	55	36	37	52
Dollar Slots	2,086	2,011	2,013	2,131	2,189	2,171	2,477	2,349	2,303	2,239	2,276	2,776	2,252
Dollar Win Per Day	93	111	115	111	122	116	114	123	132	133	113	105	116
Five Dollar Slots	39	41	41	56	70	70	83	84	84	98	104	151	77
Five Dollar Win Per Day	243	415	481	479	440	319	377	378	440	442	355	243	387
Total Slots	9,456	9,410	9,496	10,151	10,599	10,296	11,221	11,236	10,973	10,647	10,605	12,685	10,565
Win Per Day Per Slot	58	66	67	64	70	68	73	74	79	78	62	61	68
Blackjack Tables	176	191	196	215	219	216	224	221	205	200	200	244	209
Blackjack Win Per Day	209	210	227	188	224	210	248	251	250	282	207	222	227
Poker Tables	42	55	54	51	53	54	59	59	57	54	48	68	55
Poker Win Per Day	545	443	476	488	502	467	500	510	527	524	536	439	503
Table Games	218	246	250	266	272	270	283	280	262	254	248	312	263
Table Win Per Day	274	262	281	245	278	261	300	306	310	334	271	269	283
Total Gross Revenues	17,359,011	17,020,581	20,142,968	20,081,152	23,115,863	21,947,585	26,462,684	25,641,099	24,863,614	24,414,468	18,194,623	20,624,035	21,655,640
Total Annual Gross													259,867,683
Table Game Gross	1,814,816	1,711,470	2,050,307	1,884,736	2,185,436	2,099,756	2,459,927	2,372,210	2,085,460	2,196,444	1,724,162	1,958,530	24,543,254
Slot Gross	15,544,195	15,309,111	18,092,661	18,196,416	20,930,427	19,847,829	24,002,757	23,268,889	22,778,154	22,218,024	16,470,461	18,665,505	235,324,429
Slot Percent of Revenues	89.55	89.94	89.82	90.61	90.55	90.43	90.70	90.75	91.61	91.00	90.52	90.50	90.56

COLORADO GAMING STATISTICS FOR 1994

BLACKHAWK	JAN	FEB	MAR	APR	MAY	JUN	JUL	AUG	SEP	OCT	NOV	DEC	AVG/TOT
Casinos	22	21	20	20	20	21	20	20	20	20	19	19	20
Days	31	27	30	29	31	30	31	31	30	31	30	31	30
Nickel Slots	669	693	669	656	686	701	698	699	720	721	642	648	684
Nickel Win Per Day	41	42	44	44	44	44	51	47	48	47	42	38	44
Dime Slots	0	0	0	0	0	0	3	3	4	4	4	4	4
Dime Win Per Day	0	0	0	0	0	0	2	36	47	35	34	35	32
Quarter Slots	2,674	2,648	2,568	2,591	2,602	2,675	2,558	2,591	2,538	2,485	2,406	2,387	2,560
Quarter Win Per Day	69	75	76	79	77	76	95	88	92	88	80	75	81
Fifty Cent Slots	18	18	11	10	11	11	14	14	19	19	31	33	17
Fifty Cent Win Per Day	47	54	87	100	80	52	60	68	82	46	37	43	63
Dollar Slots	1,081	1,090	1,070	1,063	1,127	1,157	1,156	1,146	1,138	1,137	1,094	1,073	1,111
Dollar Win Per Day	129	145	143	161	142	144	167	170	169	168	158	157	154
Five Dollar Slots	65	65	64	73	82	82	82	84	84	86	86	86	78
Five Dollar Win Per Day	370	327	305	336	339	315	430	335	408	347	311	301	344
Total Slots	4,507	4,514	4,382	4,393	4,508	4,626	4,511	4,537	4,503	4,452	4,263	4,231	4,452
Win Per Day Per Slot	83	90	91	98	93	92	113	107	110	107	99	94	98
Blackjack Tables	92	91	87	89	90	91	87	87	87	80	73	78	86
Blackjack Win Per Day	269	293	294	284	268	252	305	301	287	304	322	279	288
Poker Tables	25	26	26	26	27	21	23	23	23	27	27	25	25
Poker Win Per Day	625	644	698	697	584	738	777	744	742	656	647	631	682
Table Games	117	117	113	115	117	112	110	110	110	107	100	103	111
Table Win Per Day	345	371	387	377	341	343	404	394	382	393	410	364	376
Total Gross Revenues	12,962,682	12,420,076	13,373,707	13,673,961	14,244,985	13,996,093	17,139,506	16,401,773	16,183,348	16,987,477	13,830,045	13,515,609	14,560,772
Total Annual Gross													174,729,262

COLORADO GAMING STATISTICS FOR 1994

CENTRAL CITY	JAN	FEB	MAR	APR	MAY	JUN	JUL	AUG	SEP	OCT	NOV	DEC	AVG/TOT
Casinos	15	15	15	15	16	16	16	15	15	16	16	17	16
Days	31	28	31	30	29.5	30	30.19	31	30	30.25	30	29.65	30
Nickel Slots	543	537	555	564	594	591	619	586	600	655	644	751	603
Nickel Win Per Day	35	37	36	34	35	35	41	38	39	33	29	33	35
Dime Slots	0	0	0	0	0	0	0	0	0	0	0	0	0
Dime Win Per Day	0	0	0	0	0	0	0	0	0	0	0	0	0
Quarter Slots	1,787	1,787	1,791	1,689	1,729	1,727	1,760	1,735	1,741	1,890	1,834	2,417	1,824
Quarter Win Per Day	48	52	47	51	50	48	64	55	56	48	43	53	51
Fifty Cent Slots	10	10	10	5	1	0	0	0	0	0	0	0	3
Fifty Cent Win Per Day	36	21	30	96	12	0	0	0	0	0	0	0	16
Dollar Slots	670	700	728	724	757	757	773	790	770	806	794	1,072	778
Dollar Win Per Day	80	79	79	79	72	67	85	72	75	71	58	69	74
Five Dollar Slots	36	37	38	43	43	43	43	42	42	46	46	71	44
Five Dollar Win Per Day	153	125	114	157	139	97	183	114	48	149	144	193	135
Total Slots	3,046	3,071	3,122	3,025	3,124	3,118	3,195	3,153	3,153	3,397	3,318	4,311	3,253
Win Per Day Per Slot	52	55	52	54	52	50	64	56	57	50	44	53	53
Blackjack Tables	50	50	50	50	49	49	49	44	47	53	55	77	52
Blackjack Win Per Day	259	259	243	215	229	205	275	284	228	201	172	231	233
Poker Tables	13	13	13	11	11	11	9	8	8	8	8	15	11
Poker Win Per Day	293	317	271	291	271	195	336	328	337	248	223	402	293
Total Tables	63	63	63	61	60	60	58	52	55	61	63	92	63
Win Per Table Per Day	266	271	249	229	236	203	284	291	244	211	178	260	244
Total Gross Revenues	5,586,753	5,299,593	5,657,726	5,499,222	5,396,101	5,107,978	6,896,069	6,029,826	5,791,618	5,727,224	4,852,596	7,856,999	5,808,475
Total Annual Gross													69,701,705

COLORADO GAMING STATISTICS FOR 1994

CRIPPLE CREEK	JAN	FEB	MAR	APR	MAY	JUN	JUL	AUG	SEP	OCT	NOV	DEC	AVG/TOT
Casinos	26	23	23	24	24	24	26	26	25	22	23	23	24
Days	31	28	31	29.08	31	30	30.18	31	29.88	31	29.91	31	30
Nickel Slots	771	774	787	820	843	842	891	896	873	798	818	838	829
Nickel Win Per Day	31	31	31	31	35	38	45	41	42	39	28	28	35
Dime Slots	9	9	9	9	9	9	9	9	9	9	0	0	8
Dime Win Per Day	30	22	24	27	28	30	43	37	37	-6	0	0	23
Quarter Slots	1,816	1,823	1,833	1,907	1,936	1,926	2,033	2,048	2,004	1,884	1,936	1,952	1,925
Quarter Win Per Day	46	48	47	49	53	58	72	63	68	58	49	44	55
Fifty Cent Slots	29	29	30	26	26	30	35	35	35	35	35	33	32
Fifty Cent Win Per Day	46	57	43	61	69	53	86	75	77	73	43	57	62
Dollar Slots	545	562	567	604	610	617	660	668	643	629	664	677	621
Dollar Win Per Day	94	98	96	96	107	103	128	117	123	120	89	101	106
Five Dollar Slots	44	32	31	32	38	41	45	46	46	45	45	45	41
Five Dollar Win Per Day	137	249	206	197	204	177	200	189	127	200	163	152	183
Total Slots	3,214	3,229	3,257	3,398	3,462	3,465	3,673	3,702	3,610	3,400	3,498	3,545	3,454
Win Per Day Per Slot	52	55	53	54	60	62	77	69	72	67	53	53	61
Blackjack Tables	53	53	53	55	56	58	56	60	58	58	56	57	56
Blackjack Win Per Day	189	185	183	174	194	192	271	236	226	196	172	174	199
Poker Tables	20	20	19	20	22	21	20	20	21	21	20	20	20
Poker Win Per Day	248	273	270	283	269	314	401	363	345	322	290	300	307
Table Games	73	73	72	75	78	79	76	80	79	79	76	77	76
Table Win Per Day	205	209	206	203	215	224	305	268	258	229	203	207	228
Total Gross Revenues	5,593,186	5,359,320	5,779,978	6,797,698	6,933,942	7,038,915	9,215,516	8,604,326	8,372,419	7,600,758	5,709,171	6,274,440	6,939,972
Total Annual Gross													83,279,669

COLORADO GAMING STATISTICS FOR 1994

COLORADO	JAN	FEB	MAR	APR	MAY	JUN	JUL	AUG	SEP	OCT	NOV	DEC	AVG/TOT
Casinos	63	59	58	59	60	61	62	61	60	58	58	59	60
Days	31	27	30	29	31	30	31	31	30	31	30	31	30
Nickel Slots	1,983	2,004	2,011	2,040	2,123	2,134	2,208	2,181	2,193	2,174	2,104	2,237	2,116
Nickel Win Per Day	35	36	37	36	38	39	46	42	43	40	33	33	38
Dime Slots	9	9	9	9	9	9	12	12	13	13	4	4	9
Dime Win Per Day	30	22	24	27	28	30	33	37	40	7	34	35	29
Quarter Slots	6,277	6,258	6,192	6,187	6,267	6,328	6,351	6,374	6,283	6,259	6,176	6,756	6,309
Quarter Win Per Day	56	61	59	62	62	63	79	71	74	67	59	58	64
Fifty Cent Slots	57	57	51	41	38	41	49	49	54	54	66	66	52
Fifty Cent Win Per Day	45	50	50	75	71	53	79	73	79	64	40	50	61
Dollar Slots	2,296	2,352	2,365	2,391	2,494	2,531	2,589	2,604	2,551	2,572	2,552	2,822	2,510
Dollar Win Per Day	106	114	112	120	112	111	133	127	129	126	109	110	117
Five Dollar Slots	145	134	133	148	163	166	170	172	172	177	177	202	163
Five Dollar Win Per Day	245	253	227	254	255	224	307	242	245	258	230	230	248
Total Slots	10,767	10,814	10,761	10,816	11,094	11,209	11,379	11,392	11,266	11,249	11,079	12,087	11,159
Win Per Day Per Slot	65	70	68	72	71	71	87	80	83	78	68	67	73
Blackjack Tables	195	194	190	194	195	198	192	191	192	191	184	212	194
Blackjack Win Per Day	245	255	250	235	237	223	287	277	254	243	232	233	247
Poker Tables	58	59	58	57	60	53	52	51	52	56	55	60	56
Poker Win Per Day	421	446	462	473	411	457	556	529	519	472	456	463	472
Table Games	253	253	248	251	255	251	244	242	244	247	239	272	250
Table Win Per Day	285	299	299	289	278	272	345	330	311	296	283	284	298
Total Gross Revenues	24,142,622	23,078,989	24,811,412	24,970,882	26,576,029	26,142,988	33,245,092	31,035,920	30,347,386	29,295,460	24,391,813	27,647,048	27,140,470
Total Annual Gross													325,685,641
Table Game Gross	2,200,721	2,097,182	2,268,774	2,114,257	2,174,155	2,049,364	2,573,460	2,477,126	2,272,134	2,254,609	2,027,220	2,365,537	26,874,539
Slot Gross	21,941,901	20,981,807	22,542,638	22,856,625	24,401,874	24,093,624	30,671,632	28,558,794	28,075,252	27,040,851	22,364,593	25,281,511	298,811,102
Slot Percent of Revenues	90.88	90.91	90.86	91.53	91.82	92.16	92.26	92.02	92.51	92.30	91.69	91.44	91.75%

TABLE & SLOT WIN COMPARISON COLORADO

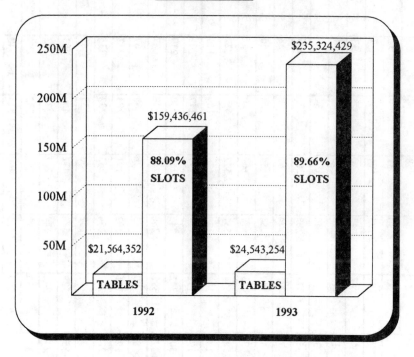

TABLE & SLOT WIN COMPARISON COLORADO

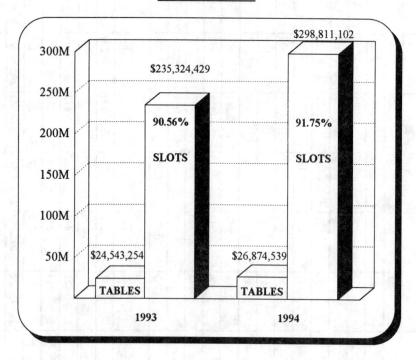

ILLINOIS

ILLINOIS GAMING STATISTICS FOR 1993

RIVERBOATS	JAN	FEB	MAR	APR	MAY	JUN	JUL	AUG	SEP	OCT	NOV	DEC	AVG/TOT
Days	31	28	31	30	31	30	31	31	30	31	30	31	
ALTON BELLE													
Table Games	21	21	21	21	25	36	36	36	36	41	41	41	31
Table Game Win	1,738,078	1,444,487	1,555,223	1,871,518	2,083,298	2,680,558	1,629,319	1,398,241	1,650,898	1,694,806	1,929,900	2,003,618	21,679,944
Table Win Per Day/Unit	2,670	2,457	2,389	2,971	2,688	2,482	1,460	1,253	1,529	1,333	1,569	1,576	2,031
Table Game Win %	22.65	20.89	19.16	24.24	24.99	23.23	23.62	26.01	25.27	24.48	22.96	20.44	23.16%
Slot Machines	287	287	287	287	308	649	649	649	649	649	632	632	497
Slot Machine Win	2,435,884	2,317,665	2,747,487	2,683,903	3,089,888	4,706,789	2,928,050	3,164,941	3,298,967	3,436,296	3,676,689	3,935,581	38,422,140
Slot Machine Win Per Day	274	288	309	312	324	242	146	157	169	171	194	201	232
Slot Machine Win %	10.43	10.21	10.66	10.52	10.02	10.82	10.49	10.78	9.80	8.36	8.62	8.20	9.91%
Gross Win	4,173,961	3,762,152	4,302,709	4,555,421	5,173,186	7,387,347	4,557,369	4,563,182	4,949,864	5,131,103	5,606,589	5,939,199	60,102,082
PAR-A-DICE													
Table Games	42	40	41	42	41	43	41	41	41	41	41	40	41
Table Game Win	1,872,775	1,796,005	2,032,580	1,826,285	1,673,045	1,298,892	2,005,891	2,110,331	1,877,862	1,931,821	1,590,924	2,115,997	22,132,408
Table Win Per Day/Unit	1,438	1,604	1,599	1,449	1,316	1,007	1,578	1,660	1,527	1,520	1,293	1,706	1,475
Table Game Win %	28.22	29.07	28.62	26.29	24.33	20.23	22.94	24.49	23.64	22.99	17.53	21.89	24.19%
Slot Machines	480	486	486	486	486	486	486	486	486	486	486	530	489
Slot Machine Win	2,664,258	2,591,297	3,247,036	3,475,157	3,438,655	3,497,706	4,449,242	4,155,350	3,699,819	4,007,561	3,781,442	3,388,939	42,396,462
Slot Machine Win Per Day	179	190	216	238	228	240	295	276	254	266	259	206	237
Slot Machine Win %	9.42	9.39	9.88	9.92	9.56	10.21	10.43	10.38	9.73	9.71	9.17	9.08	9.74%
Gross Win	4,537,033	4,387,302	5,279,616	5,272,849	5,111,700	4,796,598	6,455,133	6,265,681	5,577,681	5,939,382	5,372,366	5,504,936	64,500,277
ROCK ISLAND													
Table Games	23	23	23	23	23	23	23	23	23	23	23	23	23
Table Game Win	1,297,504	1,032,257	1,345,728	1,300,295	1,108,261	1,270,410	1,300,287	1,102,867	1,213,385	1,253,218	1,076,814	1,363,711	14,664,737
Table Win Per Day/Unit	1,820	1,603	1,887	1,884	1,554	1,841	1,824	1,547	1,759	1,758	1,561	1,913	1,746
Table Game Win %	23.48	19.74	22.36	22.01	20.55	26.03	21.23	19.37	20.82	22.36	18.78	22.24	21.58%
Slot Machines	371	371	371	371	371	371	371	371	364	428	402	402	380
Slot Machine Win	1,788,113	1,687,417	2,187,295	2,158,094	2,097,244	2,055,032	2,529,535	2,186,151	2,079,380	2,117,056	1,872,640	1,682,006	24,439,963
Slot Machine Win Per Day	155	162	190	194	182	185	220	190	190	160	155	135	177
Slot Machine Win %	9.53	9.46	9.61	9.36	8.68	8.78	9.5	9.14	8.95	9.14	9.15	8.36	9.14%
Gross Win	3,085,617	2,719,674	3,533,023	3,458,389	3,205,505	3,325,442	3,829,822	3,289,018	3,292,765	3,370,274	2,949,454	3,045,717	39,104,700

ILLINOIS GAMING STATISTICS FOR 1993

RIVERBOATS	JAN	FEB	MAR	APR	MAY	JUN	JUL	AUG	SEP	OCT	NOV	DEC	AVG/TOT
Days	31	28	31	30	31	30	31	31	30	31	30	31	30.42
CITY LIGHTS I & II													
Table Games						62	63	63	63	63	63	63	62.86
Table Game Win						1,303,742	4,148,119	5,245,928	5,140,818	5,777,891	6,231,551	6,262,512	34,110,561
Table Win Per Day/Unit						1,502	2,124	2,686	2,720	2,958	3,297	3,207	2,642
Table Game Win %						20.83	18.06	19.98	19.76	19.93	19.83	20.01	19.77%
Slot Machines						614	614	614	614	638	638	688	631
Slot Machine Win						1,250,460	4,142,175	4,728,880	4,556,279	5,137,877	5,367,915	4,845,474	30,029,060
Slot Machine Win Per Day						145	218	248	247	260	280	227	232
Slot Machine Win %						7.43	7.02	7.85	7.51	7.04	7.33	7.09	7.32%
Gross Win						2,554,201	8,290,294	9,974,807	9,697,096	10,915,768	11,599,466	11,107,986	64,139,618
PLAYER'S CASINO													
Table Games		35	35	35	38	38	38	38	38	38	38	38	37
Table Game Win		235,617	1,888,082	2,039,994	1,841,899	1,817,117	2,135,086	1,839,070	2,104,464	1,811,575	1,612,229	2,117,593	19,442,726
Table Win Per Day/Unit		1,122	1,740	1,943	1,564	1,594	1,812	1,561	1,846	1,538	1,414	1,798	1,630
Table Game Win %		30.84	26.09	25.88	25.54	25.50	23.96	22.62	25.19	24.10	21.38	28.3	25.4
Slot Machines		634	634	634	634	634	634	634	634	634	634	634	634
Slot Machine Win		227,953	2,253,827	3,030,483	3,461,628	3,517,975	4,171,817	4,038,797	3,918,562	3,871,775	3,296,281	3,170,629	34,959,727
Slot Machine Win Per Day		60	115	159	176	185	212	205	206	197	173	161	168
Slot Machine Win %		7.73	7.66	8.76	9.37	9.45	9.43	9.72	9.51	9.15	9.27	8.61	8.97%
Gross Win		463,570	4,141,909	5,070,476	5,303,528	5,335,092	6,306,903	5,877,867	6,023,026	5,683,349	4,908,510	5,288,222	54,402,452
CASINO QUEEN													
Table Games						50	58	58	58	58	58	62	57
Table Game Win						432,988	2,657,584	3,743,553	3,244,188	3,914,483	4,285,106	4,181,965	22,459,867
Table Win Per Day/Unit						1,082	1,478	2,082	1,864	2,177	2,463	2,176	1,903
Table Game Win %						14.28	20.22	22.97	20.39	23.78	25.29	22.55	21.35%
Slot Machines						853	853	852	852	852	852	870	855
Slot Machine Win						998,335	3,331,540	4,044,436	4,576,169	5,091,420	5,535,626	5,503,883	29,081,409
Slot Machine Win Per Day						146	126	153	179	193	217	204	194
Slot Machine Win %						7.78	5.79	6.67	6.36	6.33	6.20	6.12	6.46%
Gross Win						1,431,323	5,989,214	7,787,989	7,820,357	9,005,903	9,820,732	9,685,848	51,541,366

ILLINOIS GAMING STATISTICS FOR 1993

RIVERBOATS	JAN	FEB	MAR	APR	MAY	JUN	JUL	AUG	SEP	OCT	NOV	DEC	AVG/TOT
Days	31	28	31	30	31	30	31	31	30	31	30	31	
SILVER EAGLE													
Table Games	25	25	25	25	25	25	25	25	25	25	25	25	25
Table Game Win	830,104	737,222	893,393	862,324	874,159	846,739	893,044	746,224	846,734	967,152	661,331	786,210	9,944,636
Table Win Per Day/Unit	1,071	1,053	1,153	1,150	1,128	1,129	1,152	963	1,129	1,248	882	1,014	1,089
Table Game Win %	26.72	24.14	26.51	26.29	22.68	25.58	23.85	21.38	25.81	28.5	23.24	25.35	25.00%
Slot Machines	468	468	468	468	468	468	468	468	468	468	468	468	468
Slot Machine Win	1,337,913	1,404,934	1,833,310	1,748,967	2,032,095	2,140,935	2,397,060	2,100,069	2,106,437	2,277,636	1,648,092	1,558,171	22,585,619
Slot Machine Win Per Day	92	107	126	125	140	152	165	145	150	157	117	107	132
Slot Machine Win %	9.10	8.56	8.39	8.19	14.65	8.39	8.08	8.18	8.49	8.61	8.17	8.29	8.92%
Gross Win	2,168,017	2,142,456	2,726,703	2,611,291	2,906,253	2,987,673	3,290,104	2,846,293	2,953,171	3,244,788	2,309,423	2,344,381	32,530,553
EMPRESS CASINO													
Table Games	46	46	46	46	46	46	46	46	46	46	46	46	46
Table Game Win	6,056,718	5,615,110	6,499,556	5,725,756	4,712,230	5,445,133	5,940,292	5,029,795	4,816,913	4,455,967	4,985,341	4,931,742	64,214,553
Table Win Per Day/Unit	4,247	4,360	4,558	4,149	3,305	3,946	4,166	3,527	3,491	3,125	3,613	3,247	3,811
Table Game Win %	22.54	21.93	22.47	21.18	18.75	22.1	20.63	19.81	21.86	18.68	19.55	17.79	20.61%
Slot Machines	611	611	611	611	623	623	623	623	623	623	623	688	624
Slot Machine Win	7,828,737	7,908,272	9,027,579	9,001,102	9,378,565	8,693,913	9,894,517	10,069,849	8,993,050	9,828,415	8,781,566	9,239,515	108,645,080
Slot Machine Win Per Day	413	462	477	491	486	465	512	521	481	509	470	433	477
Slot Machine Win %	6.19	6.33	6.21	6.77	6.25	6.33	6.21	6.42	6.21	6.36	6.07	6.17	6.29%
Gross Win	13,885,455	13,523,382	15,527,135	14,726,858	14,090,795	14,139,045	15,834,809	15,099,643	13,809,962	14,284,382	13,766,907	14,171,257	172,859,630
HARRAH'S N. STAR													
Table Games					43	43	43	44	44	44	43	50	30
Table Game Win					1,541,056	2,760,031	2,966,147	3,106,697	3,339,357	3,754,212	3,965,266	4,047,371	25,480,137
Table Win Per Day/Unit					1,279.95	0.02	0.04	0.05	0.05	0.05	0.05	0.04	162.06
Table Game Win %					16.97	21.72	17.80	18.01	19.65	19.06	18.56	17.79	12.46%
Slot Machines					571	571	571	571	595	571	606	606	389
Slot Machine Win					3,233,906	3,941,205	5,212,012	5,285,025	5,367,499	5,960,242	6,118,241	5,905,927	41,024,057
Slot Machine Win Per Day					183	230	294	299	301	337	337	314	287
Slot Machine Win %					7.95	7.87	7.9	8.00	7.75	7.72	7.22	7.18	5.13%
Gross Win					4,774,962	6,701,237	8,178,160	8,391,722	8,706,856	9,714,453	10,083,507	9,953,298	66,504,195

ILLINOIS GAMING STATISTICS FOR 1993

ILLINOIS	JAN	FEB	MAR	APR	MAY	JUN	JUL	AUG	SEP	OCT	NOV	DEC	AVG
	31	28	31	30	31	30	31	31	30	31	30	31	30.42
Table Games	157	190	191	192	241	366	373	374	374	379	378	391	301
Table Win	11,795,178	10,860,697	14,214,561	13,626,172	13,833,948	17,855,610	23,675,769	24,322,705	24,234,617	25,561,125	26,338,462	27,810,719	234,129,563
Table Win Per Day	2,424	2,405	2,413	2,366	1,884	2,009	2,048	2,098	2,160	2,176	2,323	2,294	2,217
Table Win Percent	23.68	22.75	23.39	23.18	21.00	22.34	20.49	20.95	21.57	21.15	20.44	20.37	21.78%
Slots	2,217	2,857	2,857	2,857	3,461	5,269	5,269	5,268	5,285	5,349	5,341	5,518	4,296
Slot Win	16,054,904	16,137,538	21,296,535	22,069,113	26,731,980	30,802,349	39,055,948	39,773,498	38,596,161	41,728,276	40,078,492	39,230,125	371,554,919
Slot Win Per Day	234	247	240	257	253	238	239	244	243	252	250	229	244
Slot Win Percent	7.59	7.60	7.66	8.11	7.80	8.09	7.61	7.89	7.60	7.46	7.26	7.11	7.65%
Admissions	417,891	417,359	574,904	562,399	684,377	848,513	1,163,390	1,172,804	1,132,185	1,212,397	1,218,987	1,274,284	10,679,490
Win Per Admission	67	65	62	63	59	57	54	55	55	56	54	53	58
Gross Win	27,850,082	26,998,236	35,511,095	35,695,284	40,565,929	48,657,959	62,731,717	64,096,203	62,830,778	67,289,401	66,416,954	67,040,844	605,684,482

RIVERBOATS	Alton Belle	Par-A-Dice	Rock Island	Joliet Empress	Silver Eagle	Metropolis Players	Harrah's N. Star	Aurora Hollywood	Casino Queen	Win %	Totals
Table Win	21,679,944	22,132,408	14,664,737	64,214,550	9,944,633	19,442,727	25,480,138	34,110,560	22,459,867	38.66%	234,129,564
Slot Win	38,422,139	42,367,869	24,439,963	108,645,079	22,585,619	34,959,725	41,024,057	30,029,059	29,081,409	62.34%	371,554,919
Gross Win	60,102,083	64,500,277	39,104,700	172,859,629	32,530,252	54,402,452	66,504,195	64,139,618	51,541,276	100.00%	605,684,483

ILLINOIS GAMING STATISTICS FOR 1994

RIVERBOATS	JAN	FEB	MAR	APR	MAY	JUN	JUL	AUG	SEP	OCT	NOV	DEC	AVG/TOT
	31	28	31	30	31	30	31	31	30	31	30	31	45
ALTON BELLE													
Table Games	41	41	41	41	41	41	55	55	55	41	41	41	45
Table Game Win	2,147,016	2,274,249	2,364,144	2,339,237	2,433,551	1,645,050	1,841,943	1,746,496	1,520,962	1,633,192	1,474,349	1,418,322	22,838,511
Table Win Per Day/Unit	1,689	1,981	1,860	1,902	1,915	1,337	1,080	1,024	922	1,285	1,199	1,116	1,442
Table Game Win %	22.58	20.83	22.16	21.13	23.3	23.74	23.32	23.84	21.1	22.61	20.59	17.65	21.90%
Slot Machines	635	652	652	633	651	653	940	939	939	653	636	636	718
Slot Machine Win	4,416,682	4,604,350	5,238,195	5,687,982	5,544,361	5,497,834	6,192,957	6,080,806	5,615,899	6,094,394	5,927,273	5,334,676	66,235,409
Slot Machine Win Per Day	224	252	259	300	275	281	213	209	199	301	311	271	258
Slot Machine Win %	8.05	6.84	6.75	6.98	6.82	7.14	6.36	6.32	5.85	6.20	6.29	6.14	6.65%
Gross Win	6,563,698	6,878,599	7,602,339	8,027,219	7,977,912	7,142,884	8,034,900	7,827,302	7,136,861	7,727,586	7,401,622	6,752,998	89,073,920
PAR-A-DICE													
Table Games	40	40	40	40	41	41	41	41	41	41	44	44	41
Table Game Win	2,470,849	1,683,793	2,074,195	1,700,462	2,154,625	1,859,164	2,279,803	1,969,668	1,773,122	2,157,321	1,936,210	2,419,384	24,478,596
Table Win Per Day/Unit	1,993	1,503	1,673	1,417	1,695	1,512	1,794	1,550	1,442	1,697	1,467	1,774	1,626
Table Game Win %	27.13	18.96	22.02	17.91	23.96	20.4	22.52	21.86	19.24	22.57	20.1	24.63	21.78%
Slot Machines	530	530	530	531	779	779	779	779	779	779	779	793	697
Slot Machine Win	2,792,956	3,715,709	4,465,293	4,046,911	4,529,427	5,353,786	6,587,097	6,249,270	5,721,578	5,759,726	5,631,658	5,015,228	59,868,639
Slot Machine Win Per Day	170	250	272	254	188	229	273	259	245	239	241	204	235
Slot Machine Win %	8.05	14.81	9.31	8.93	8.35	7.93	7.78	8.04	7.81	7.65	7.78	7.65	8.67%
Gross Win	5,263,805	5,399,502	6,539,488	5,747,373	6,684,052	7,212,950	8,866,900	8,218,938	7,494,700	7,917,047	7,567,868	7,434,612	84,347,235
CASINO ROCK ISLAND													
Table Games	23	23	23	23	23	22	24	24	24	24	25	26	24
Table Game Win	1,139,948	1,328,075	1,403,079	1,117,688	937,685	627,941	430,645	658,384	519,822	556,310	615,685	484,641	9,819,903
Table Win Per Day/Unit	1,599	2,062	1,968	1,620	1,315	951	579	885	722	748	821	601	1,156
Table Game Win %	20.59	24.78	23.05	20.65	21.35	23.31	14.88	22.7	22.5	22.77	26.74	24.52	22.32%
Slot Machines	402	402	402	402	402	395	395	393	393	393	393	393	397
Slot Machine Win	1,580,194	1,823,526	2,092,721	2,048,628	1,810,456	1,485,251	1,749,010	1,735,537	1,533,140	1,624,426	1,378,322	1,129,593	19,990,804
Slot Machine Win Per Day	127	162	168	170	145	125	143	142	130	133	117	93	138
Slot Machine Win %	7.85	8.36	7.57	7.68	7.51	7.57	7.59	8.09	7.76	7.79	7.76	7.61	7.76%
Gross Win	2,720,142	3,151,601	3,495,800	3,166,316	2,748,141	2,113,192	2,179,655	2,393,921	2,052,962	2,180,736	1,994,007	1,614,234	29,810,707

ILLINOIS GAMING STATISTICS FOR 1994

RIVERBOATS	JAN	FEB	MAR	APR	MAY	JUN	JUL	AUG	SEP	OCT	NOV	DEC	AVG/TOT
	31	28	31	30	31	30	31	31	30	31	30	31	
CITY LIGHTS I & II													
Table Games	62	62	62	62	62	62	62	60	60	60	60	60	61
Table Game Win	5,288,501	5,342,165	6,427,078	5,161,320	5,953,367	5,857,665	5,269,791	5,235,751	5,477,831	5,507,587	5,066,480	4,304,407	64,891,943
Table Win Per Day/Unit	2,752	3,077	3,344	2,775	3,097	3,149	2,742	2,815	3,043	2,961	2,815	2,314	5,392
Table Game Win %	17.25	19.59	19.41	16.17	20.15	19.56	16.31	15.91	17.85	19.39	19.14	16.54	18.11%
Slot Machines	688	688	688	710	710	710	710	710	710	712	712	712	705
Slot Machine Win	4,725,451	4,786,273	5,632,130	6,561,397	6,328,043	6,065,023	7,368,790	7,568,302	7,090,659	6,638,648	6,095,768	5,963,879	74,824,363
Slot Machine Win Per Day	222	248	264	308	288	285	335	344	333	301	285	270	538
Slot Machine Win %	6.93	6.24	5.81	6.35	5.79	6.13	6.23	6.53	6.61	6.77	6.35	6.38	6.34%
Gross Win	10,013,952	10,128,438	12,059,208	11,722,717	12,281,410	11,922,688	12,638,581	12,804,053	12,568,490	12,146,235	11,162,248	10,268,286	139,716,306
PLAYER'S CASINO													
Table Games	38	38	38	38	38	39	39	39	39	39	39	43	39
Table Game Win	1,752,069	1,890,897	2,106,437	1,892,855	1,898,814	1,899,342	2,354,173	1,823,399	2,069,048	2,143,372	1,844,061	2,403,117	24,077,584
Table Win Per Day/Unit	1,487	1,777	1,788	1,660	1,612	1,623	1,947	1,508	1,768	1,773	1,576	1,803	1,990
Table Game Win %	28.44	24.57	25.54	24.34	23.83	25.30	27.20	23.07	27.23	27.43	22.62	26.28	25.49%
Slot Machines	634	634	634	632	632	660	660	672	672	672	672	660	653
Slot Machine Win	2,480,002	3,406,101	3,703,896	3,973,427	3,813,006	3,801,906	4,916,622	4,329,513	4,283,872	4,280,332	3,805,688	3,737,271	46,531,636
Slot Machine Win Per Day	126	192	188	210	195	192	240	208	212	205	189	183	229
Slot Machine Win %	9.17	9.39	9.00	9.25	9.23	9.69	9.46	9.43	9.64	9.21	9.13	8.89	9.29%
Gross Win	4,232,071	5,296,998	5,810,333	5,866,282	5,711,820	5,701,248	7,270,795	6,152,912	6,352,920	6,423,704	5,649,749	6,140,388	70,609,220
CASINO QUEEN													
Table Games	62	62	62	62	62	62	62	62	62	62	62	64	62
Table Game Win	4,239,761	4,080,355	4,208,927	4,179,135	3,794,311	3,124,543	3,588,214	3,248,729	3,259,302	3,030,025	3,198,219	2,972,068	42,923,589
Table Win Per Day/Unit	2,206	2,350	2,190	2,247	1,974	1,680	1,867	1,690	1,752	1,576	1,719	1,498	3,629
Table Game Win %	24.64	24.83	21.04	21.73	19.85	21.01	21.86	20.58	22.50	21.38	21.60	20.66	21.81%
Slot Machines	876	870	870	886	939	916	916	916	916	916	922	922	905
Slot Machine Win	5,739,654	6,360,449	6,657,634	6,560,950	6,597,167	7,507,040	8,303,626	8,249,952	7,936,753	7,988,292	7,939,119	7,021,222	86,861,858
Slot Machine Win Per Day	211	261	247	247	227	273	292	291	289	281	287	246	503
Slot Machine Win %	6.21	6.18	6.03	5.97	5.79	6.02	5.67	5.68	5.48	5.58	5.70	5.55	5.82%
Gross Win	9,979,415	10,440,804	10,866,561	10,740,085	10,391,478	10,631,583	11,891,840	11,498,681	11,196,055	11,018,317	11,137,338	9,993,290	129,785,447

ILLINOIS GAMING STATISTICS FOR 1994

RIVERBOATS	JAN	FEB	MAR	APR	MAY	JUN	JUL	AUG	SEP	OCT	NOV	DEC	AVG/TOT
	31	28	31	30	31	30	31	31	30	31	30	31	
SILVER EAGLE CASINO													
Table Games	25	25	25	25	25	25	25	25	25	25	25	25	25
Table Game Win	718,828	776,913	899,043	883,282	768,819	514,892	728,530	667,837	546,273	478,473	416,313	502,758	7,901,961
Table Win Per Day/Unit	928	1,110	1,160	1,178	992	687	940	862	728	617	555	649	867
Table Game Win %	25.65	25.85	26.79	26.71	24.42	20.86	24.11	23.36	19.6	17.14	19.83	23.98	23.19%
Slot Machines	468	468	468	468	468	468	468	468	468	468	468	468	468
Slot Machine Win	1,548,123	1,787,741	2,222,426	2,097,370	1,894,415	1,659,917	2,128,643	1,966,376	1,862,959	1,866,160	1,318,768	1,152,767	21,505,665
Slot Machine Win Per Day	107	136	153	149	131	118	147	136	133	129	94	79	126
Slot Machine Win %	7.96	8.16	7.96	8.33	7.99	8.84	8.49	8.51	8.29	8.49	8.23	8.45	8.31%
Gross Win	2,266,951	2,564,654	3,121,469	2,980,652	2,663,234	2,174,809	2,857,173	2,634,213	2,409,232	2,344,633	1,735,081	1,655,525	29,407,626
EMPRESS CASINO													
Table Games	60	60	60	60	60	60	59	59	59	62	61	59	60
Table Game Win	5,704,058	5,447,780	5,566,190	5,887,127	5,788,455	5,122,259	5,849,841	5,747,322	6,089,979	5,555,115	5,996,322	5,465,454	68,219,902
Table Win Per Day/Unit	3,067	3,243	2,993	3,271	3,112	2,846	3,198	3,142	3,441	2,890	3,277	2,988	3,122
Table Game Win %	19.76	18.97	16.86	18.74	19.49	17.46	17.68	17.09	19.19	18.02	20.01	17.30	18.38%
Slot Machines	951	951	951	951	951	951	960	960	960	969	969	964	957
Slot Machine Win	9,112,768	9,822,751	11,778,883	11,453,442	11,398,826	11,485,820	13,355,877	12,403,984	11,558,363	11,303,163	10,864,837	10,012,594	134,551,308
Slot Machine Win Per Day	309	369	400	401	387	403	449	417	401	376	374	335	385
Slot Machine Win %	5.85	6.14	6.17	6.16	5.94	6.22	6.29	6.07	5.88	5.88	6.16	5.97	6.06%
Gross Win	14,816,826	15,270,531	17,345,073	17,340,569	17,187,281	16,608,079	19,205,718	18,151,306	17,648,342	16,858,278	16,861,159	15,478,048	202,771,210
HARRAH'S N. STAR													
Table Games	58	62	62	62	62	62	62	62	62	62	62	59	61
Table Game Win	3,929,208	4,275,487	4,880,759	4,871,422	4,450,753	4,961,911	4,879,412	5,353,019	4,421,687	4,799,778	4,744,041	4,797,026	56,364,503
Table Win Per Day/Unit	2,419	2,463	2,812	2,806	2,564	2,668	2,539	2,785	2,377	2,497	2,551	2,623	3,937
Table Game Win %	20.85	20.55	19.75	19.84	16.95	20.86	18.29	19.4	16.38	17.16	17.12	16.74	18.66%
Slot Machines	814	929	938	938	938	938	938	930	938	938	938	958	928
Slot Machine Win	5,674,877	7,546,561	8,923,585	8,989,311	9,194,530	8,849,397	10,747,563	10,378,460	10,498,087	10,103,820	9,807,966	10,405,577	111,119,734
Slot Machine Win Per Day	249	290	340	342	350	314	370	360	373	347	349	350	511
Slot Machine Win %	6.71	7.32	7.25	7.12	7.32	7.23	6.78	6.41	6.59	6.36	6.16	6.13	6.78%
Gross Win	9,604,085	11,822,048	13,804,344	13,860,733	13,645,283	13,811,308	15,626,975	15,731,479	14,919,774	14,903,598	14,552,007	15,202,603	167,484,237

ILLINOIS GAMING STATISTICS FOR 1994

RIVERBOATS	JAN	FEB	MAR	APR	MAY	JUN	JUL	AUG	SEP	OCT	NOV	DEC	AVG/TOT
	31	28	31	30	31	30	31	31	30	31	30	31	
ELGIN GRAND													
Table Games										44	44	48	45
Table Win										3,031,011	4,635,961	5,120,989	12,787,961
Table Win Per Day										2,222	3,512	3,442	3,059
Table Win Percent										16.23	18.93	19.4	18.22
Slots										1,055	1,055	1,017	1,039.78
Slot Win										7,396,878	8,257,789	8,103,111	23,757,778
Slot Win Per Day										226	261	257	249
Slot Win Percent										6.64	6.17	5.94	6.25
Gross Win										10,427,889	12,893,750	13,224,100	36,545,739
ILLINOIS													
Table Games	409	413	413	413	414	414	429	427	427	460	463	469	429
Table Win	27,390,237	27,099,714	29,929,851	28,032,528	28,180,380	25,612,766	27,222,351	26,450,606	25,678,025	28,892,183	29,927,641	29,888,164	334,304,446
Table Win Per Day	2,160	2,343	2,338	2,263	2,196	2,062	2,047	1,998	2,005	2,026	2,155	2,056	2,137
Table Win Percent	21.29	20.99	20.14	19.44	20.19	20.22	19.30	18.90	19.30	19.28	19.59	18.90	19.80
Slots	5,998	6,124	6,133	6,151	6,470	6,470	6,766	6,767	6,775	7,555	7,544	7,523	6,689.67
Slot Win	38,070,706	43,853,462	50,714,765	51,419,417	51,110,230	51,705,976	61,350,185	58,962,201	56,101,308	63,055,839	61,027,188	57,875,915	645,247,192
Slot Win Per Day	205	256	267	279	255	266	293	281	276	269	270	248	264
Slot Win Percent	6.83	7.13	6.82	6.88	6.68	6.87	6.68	6.61	6.49	6.52	6.45	6.31	6.69
Admissions	1,253,207	1,363,150	1,571,666	1,528,138	1,544,689	1,640,296	2,035,999	1,920,967	1,755,455	1,973,718	1,940,607	1,839,227	20,367,119
Win Per Admission	52	52	51	52	51	47	44	44	47	47	47	48	48
Gross Win	65,460,943	70,953,176	80,644,616	79,451,945	79,290,610	77,318,742	88,572,536	85,412,807	81,779,333	91,948,022	90,954,829	87,764,079	979,551,638

RIVERBOATS	Alton Belle	Par-A-Dice	Rock Island	Joliet Empress	Silver Eagle	Metropolis Players	Harrah's N. Star	Aurora Hollywood	Casino Queen	Elgin Grand	Win %	Totals
Table Win	22,838,511	24,478,596	9,819,903	68,219,902	7,901,961	24,077,584	56,364,503	64,891,943	42,923,589	12,787,961	34.13%	334,304,453
Slot Win	66,235,409	59,868,639	19,990,804	134,551,308	21,505,665	46,531,636	111,119,734	74,824,363	86,861,858	23,757,778	65.87%	645,247,194
Gross Win	89,073,920	84,347,235	29,810,707	202,771,210	29,407,626	70,609,220	167,484,237	139,716,306	129,785,447	36,545,739	100.00%	979,551,647

GAME STATISTICS FOR ILLINOIS 1994

GAMES	JAN	FEB	MAR	APR	MAY	JUN	JUL	AUG	SEP	OCT	NOV	DEC	AVG/TOT
DAYS	31	28	31	30	31	30	31	31	30	31	30	31	319
BLACKJACK	311	311	311	311	311	310	323	322	322	337	327	328	319
Gross Win	16,691,707	16,621,807	17,699,053	16,336,645	16,443,698	14,834,402	16,298,677	15,038,479	14,495,444	16,000,053	15,823,526	15,459,371	15,978,572
Win Per Unit	1,731	1,909	1,836	1,751	1,706	1,595	1,628	1,507	1,501	1,532	1,613	1,520	1,652
MULTI-ACTION	0	1	1	1	1	1	1	1	1	1	1	1	1
Gross Win	0	28,851	78,808	20,375	46,728	79,253	62,939	54,985	64,231	41,587	60,900	40,269	48,244
Win Per Unit	0	1,030	2,542	679	1,507	2,642	2,030	1,774	2,141	1,342	2,030	1,299	1,585
CRAPS	54	55	55	55	56	56	57	57	57	61	61	62	57
Gross Win	7,368,408	7,224,103	8,632,179	8,038,810	8,442,708	7,310,033	7,306,033	7,786,714	7,502,848	8,257,247	8,171,348	8,373,123	7,867,796
Win Per Unit	4,402	4,691	5,063	4,872	4,863	4,351	4,135	4,407	4,388	4,367	4,465	4,356	4,530
ROULETTE	32	33	32	32	32	33	34	34	34	38	38	39	34
Gross Win	2,600,055	2,394,978	2,655,479	2,523,117	2,558,727	2,607,443	2,774,910	2,663,223	2,619,168	3,144,980	3,351,878	3,059,956	2,746,160
Win Per Unit	2,621	2,592	2,677	2,628	2,579	2,634	2,633	2,527	2,568	2,670	2,940	2,531	2,633
CARIBBEAN STUD	0	0	0	0	0	0	0	0	0	10	22	25	19
Gross Win	0	0	0	0	0	0	0	0	0	599,373	1,590,852	2,080,358	1,423,528
Win Per Unit	0	0	0	0	0	0	0	0	0	1,933	2,410	2,684	2,343
BACCARAT	2	2	2	2	2	2	2	2	2	0	0	0	2
Gross Win	182,297	275,778	231,109	329,998	202,246	124,176	200,374	184,471	388,324	0	0	0	235,419
Win Per Unit	2,940	4,925	3,728	5,500	3,262	2,070	3,232	2,975	6,472	0	0	0	3,900
MINI-BACCARAT	7	8	8	8	8	9	9	8	8	10	10	10	9
Gross Win	482,713	442,705	514,753	649,161	370,451	571,287	470,305	624,530	522,897	758,890	831,288	756,442	582,952
Win Per Unit	2,224	1,976	2,076	2,705	1,494	2,116	1,686	2,518	2,179	2,448	2,771	2,440	2,219
BIG SIX	3	3	4	4	4	3	3	3	3	3	4	4	3
Gross Win	65,058	111,493	118,470	134,424	115,822	86,172	109,112	98,204	85,113	90,053	97,848	118,645	102,535
Win Per Unit	700	1,327	955	1,120	934	957	1,173	1,056	946	968	815	957	992
TOTAL GAMES	409	413	413	413	414	414	429	427	427	460	463	469	429
TOTAL REVENUES	27,390,238	27,099,715	29,929,851	28,032,530	28,180,380	25,612,766	27,222,350	26,450,606	25,678,025	28,892,183	29,927,640	29,888,164	334,304,448

GAME STATISTICS FOR ILLINOIS 1994

SLOTS	JAN	FEB	MAR	APR	MAY	JUN	JUL	AUG	SEP	OCT	NOV	DEC	AVG/TOT
DAYS	31	28	31	30	31	30	31	31	30	31	30	31	
05 CENT	21	37	47	47	68	68	67	67	67	67	67	67	58
Gross Win	47,710	89,205	124,729	130,601	162,734	196,667	234,725	239,836	212,287	221,662	202,131	176,677	169,914
Win Per Unit	73	86	86	93	77	96	113	115	106	107	101	85	95
25 CENT	3,468	3,490	3,524	3,547	3,706	3,692	3,910	3,920	3,920	4,359	4,362	4,349	3,854
Gross Win	15,798,203	18,379,403	21,653,790	21,580,321	21,545,365	21,865,472	26,353,488	24,675,407	23,064,524	26,786,341	25,092,290	22,785,601	22,465,017
Win Per Unit	147	188	198	203	188	197	217	203	196	198	192	169	191
50 CENT	247	267	230	230	230	230	230	223	230	278	278	282	246
Gross Win	1,621,935	1,932,881	2,027,483	2,048,316	2,103,922	1,979,098	2,443,486	2,506,124	2,328,366	2,640,736	2,569,103	2,624,118	2,235,464
Win Per Unit	212	259	284	297	295	287	343	363	337	306	308	300	299
01 DOLLAR	1,986	2,034	2,042	2,041	2,187	2,196	2,283	2,274	2,275	2,518	2,519	2,509	2,239
Gross Win	16,561,404	18,841,155	21,919,892	22,040,938	21,861,028	21,303,712	25,867,155	24,824,878	24,099,826	26,475,247	26,223,968	25,460,814	22,956,668
Win Per Unit	269	331	346	360	322	323	365	352	353	339	347	327	336
05 DOLLAR	243	263	260	258	250	255	246	253	253	299	285	283	262
Gross Win	3,858,704	4,367,328	4,936,561	5,381,331	5,155,725	5,943,826	6,066,898	6,379,515	5,840,935	6,458,051	6,401,065	6,460,784	5,604,227
Win Per Unit	512	593	612	695	665	777	796	813	770	697	749	736	701
25 DOLLAR	24	24	21	19	21	22	23	23	23	28	27	27	24
Gross Win	162,399	182,470	142,450	201,000	245,035	387,431	356,353	389,841	475,291	415,701	554,030	336,871	320,739
Win Per Unit	218	272	219	353	376	587	500	547	689	479	684	402	444
100 DOLLAR	9	9	9	9	8	7	7	7	7	6	6	6	8
Gross Win	20,350	61,020	-90,140	36,910	36,422	29,770	28,080	-53,400	80,080	58,100	-15,400	31,050	18,570
Win Per Unit	73	242	-323	137	147	142	129	-246	381	312	-86	167	90
TOTAL GAMES	5,998	6,124	6,133	6,151	6,470	6,470	6,766	6,767	6,775	7,555	7,544	7,523	6,690
TOTAL REVENUES	38,070,705	43,853,462	50,714,765	51,419,417	51,110,231	51,705,976	61,350,185	58,962,201	56,101,309	63,055,838	61,027,187	57,875,915	645,247,191

TABLE & SLOT WIN COMPARISON ILLINOIS

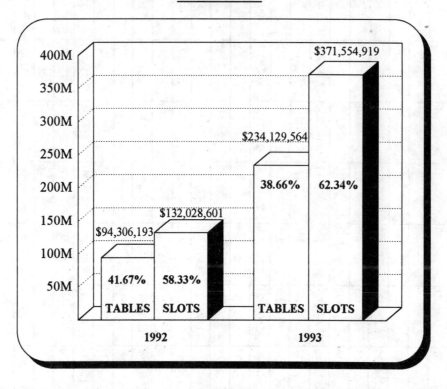

TABLE & SLOT WIN COMPARISON ILLINOIS

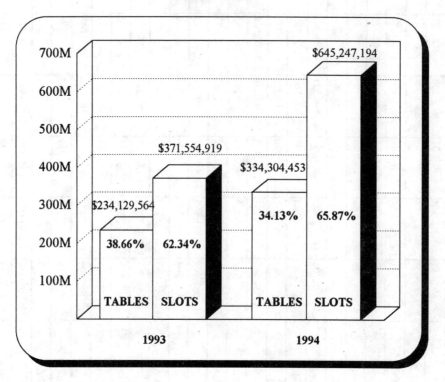

GROSS ANNUAL WIN PER BOAT FOR 1994
ILLINOIS

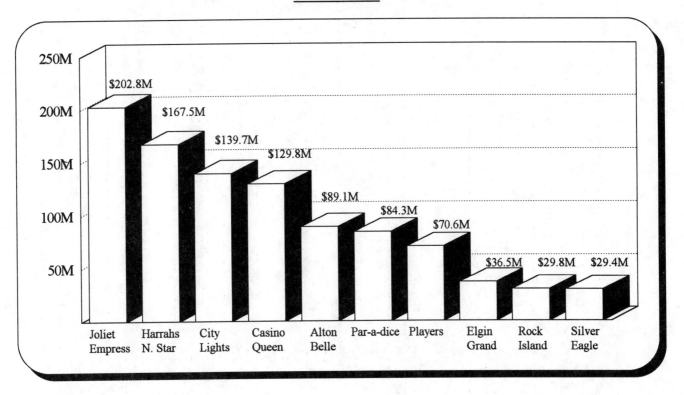

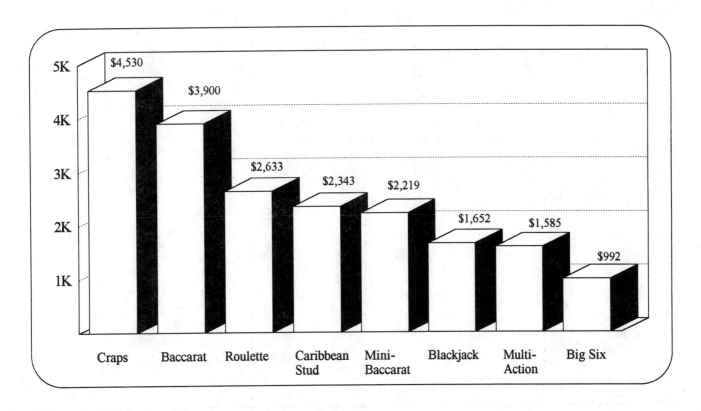

IOWA

IOWA RIVERBOAT GAMING STATISTICS FOR 1993

PRESIDENT	JAN	FEB	MAR	APR	MAY	JUN	JUL	AUG	SEP	OCT	NOV	DEC	AVG/TOT
Days	31	28	31	30	31	30	31	31	30	31	30	31	
Month Table Drop	1,061,860	862,445	1,003,286	764,832	1,159,542	863,202	578,495	847,991	879,977	1,102,484	1,017,600	834,741	10,976,455
Month Table Win	398,579	318,862	359,285	246,360	382,904	323,418	174,649	294,065	323,436	396,398	372,658	302,300	3,892,914
Table Win Per Day	357	316	322	228	343	299	156	263	299	355	345	271	296
Table Hold Percent	37.54	36.97	35.81	32.21	33.02	37.47	30.19	34.68	36.76	35.95	36.62	36.21	35.29
Month Slot Coin In	26,820,589	26,298,356	29,810,307	22,363,738	36,180,351	26,343,268	15,271,011	23,749,602	25,303,202	30,885,641	26,381,006	21,000,243	310,407,314
Month Slot Win	2,339,818	1,973,988	2,422,574	1,920,131	2,920,915	2,219,185	1,271,418	1,909,319	2,081,517	2,533,745	2,061,590	1,696,584	25,350,784
Slot Win Per Day	108	101	112	91	135	106	59	88	99	117	98	78	99
Slot Hold Percent	8.72	7.51	8.13	8.59	8.07	8.42	8.33	8.04	8.23	8.2	7.81	8.08	8.18

MISS. BELLE II	JAN	FEB	MAR	APR	MAY	JUN	JUL	AUG	SEP	OCT	NOV	DEC	AVG/TOT
Month Table Drop	266,513	228,316	240,701	405,748	301,753	216,395	360,850	217,279	215,538	240,635	218,955	223,475	3,136,158
Month Table Win	116,033	96,768	92,435	245,302	112,312	71,568	135,313	78,497	83,860	102,837	88,414	88,008	1,311,347
Table Win Per Day	250	230	199	545	242	159	291	169	186	221	196	189	240
Table Hold Percent	43.54	42.38	38.4	60.46	37.22	33.07	37.5	36.13	38.91	42.74	40.38	39.38	40.84
Month Slot Coin In	7,559,323	6,096,428	7,164,212	7,097,963	8,948,033	6,300,290	10,062,715	6,634,252	7,406,743	8,037,292	6,803,779	6,266,742	88,377,772
Month Slot Win	631,531	523,665	622,929	487,041	809,908	557,460	875,142	612,491	619,468	707,206	565,578	509,942	7,522,361
Slot Win Per Day	78	72	77	62	100	71	109	76	79	88	73	63	79
Slot Hold Percent	8.35	8.59	8.7	6.86	9.05	8.85	8.7	9.23	8.36	8.8	8.31	8.14	8.49

SIOUX CITY SUE	JAN	FEB	MAR	APR	MAY	JUN	JUL	AUG	SEP	OCT	NOV	DEC	AVG/TOT
Month Table Drop	23,352	299,878	292,489	283,794	290,874	158,640	177,640	121,952	120,427	112,610	119,972	106,796	2,108,424
Month Table Win	8,885	87,532	94,814	100,246	114,661	62,509	79,400	55,648	47,221	51,201	45,997	48,683	796,797
Table Win Per Day	20	223	218	239	264	149	183	128	112	118	110	112	156
Table Hold Percent	38.05	29.19	32.42	35.32	39.42	39.4	44.7	45.63	39.21	45.47	38.34	45.58	39.39
Month Slot Coin In	583,054	4,129,879	2,924,343	3,433,914	3,680,247	2,221,675	2,497,486	2,127,665	2,066,260	2,093,314	1,582,878	1,634,449	28,975,164
Month Slot Win	60,644	388,457	287,523	312,428	323,192	205,095	234,488	197,025	196,853	194,951	139,887	146,256	2,686,799
Slot Win Per Day	8	58	39	43	43	28	32	26	27	26	19	20	30.76
Slot Hold Percent	10.4	9.41	9.83	9.1	8.78	9.23	9.39	9.26	9.53	9.31	8.84	8.95	9.34

STATE OF IOWA	JAN	FEB	MAR	APR	MAY	JUN	JUL	AUG	SEP	OCT	NOV	DEC	AVG/TOT
Month Table Drop	1,351,725	1,390,639	1,536,476	1,454,374	1,752,169	1,238,237	1,116,985	1,187,222	1,215,942	1,455,729	1,356,527	1,165,012	16,221,037
Month Table Win	523,497	503,162	546,534	591,908	609,877	457,495	389,362	428,210	454,517	550,436	507,069	438,991	6,001,058
Table Win Per Day	260	276	271	304	303	235	193	213	233	273	260	218	253
Table Hold Percent	38.73	36.18	35.57	40.7	34.81	36.95	34.86	36.07	37.38	37.81	37.38	37.68	37.01
Month Slot Coin In	34,962,966	36,524,663	39,898,862	32,895,615	48,808,631	34,865,233	27,831,212	32,511,519	34,776,205	41,016,247	34,767,663	28,901,434	427,760,250
Month Slot Win	3,031,993	2,886,110	3,333,026	2,719,600	4,054,015	2,981,740	2,381,048	2,718,835	2,897,838	3,435,902	2,767,055	2,352,782	35,559,944
Slot Win Per Day	82	86	90	76	109	83	64	73	80	92	77	63	81
Slot Hold Percent	8.67	7.9	8.35	8.27	8.31	8.55	8.56	8.36	8.33	8.38	7.96	8.14	8.32

IOWA RIVERBOAT GAMING STATISTICS FOR 1994

	JAN	FEB	MAR	APR	MAY	JUN	JUL	AUG	SEP	OCT	NOV	DEC	AVG/TOT
Days	31	28	31	30	31	30	31	31	30	31	30	31	
PRESIDENT													
Number of Tables	36	36	36	36	36	36	52	52	52	52	52	52	44
Month Table Drop	1,160,000	970,000	1,010,000	1,420,000	2,410,000	6,300,000	8,700,000	6,720,000	8,450,000	6,700,000	7,200,000	8,200,000	59,240,000
Month Table Win	430,000	360,000	360,000	490,000	560,000	1,400,000	2,010,000	1,570,000	1,890,000	1,390,000	1,800,000	1,880,000	14,140,000
Table Win Per Day	385	357	323	454	502	1,296	1,247	974	1,212	862	1,154	1,166	828
Table Hold Percent	36.80	37.30	36.00	34.50	23.10	21.60	22.90	23.30	22.40	20.80	25.01	22.90	27.22
Number of Slots	691	691	691	691	691	720	776	776	776	776	776	776	736
Month Slot Coin In	29,430,000	26,280,000	30,980,000	44,080,000	39,060,000	48,250,000	62,490,000	56,510,000	75,240,000	56,940,000	58,140,000	69,440,000	596,840,000
Month Slot Win	2,430,000	2,180,000	2,610,000	3,530,000	3,360,000	3,940,000	5,520,000	4,580,000	5,920,000	4,370,000	4,320,000	4,900,000	47,660,000
Slot Win Per Day	112	111	120	168	155	188	254	211	282	201	206	226	186
Slot Hold Percent	8.30	8.30	8.40	8.00	8.60	8.20	8.80	8.10	7.90	7.70	7.40	7.10	8.07
MISS. BELLE II													
Number of Tables	15	15	15	15	15	15	15	15	15	15	25	26	17
Month Table Drop	280,000	220,000	280,000	360,000	530,000	810,000	1,170,000	910,000	1,180,000	940,000	1,140,000	2,040,000	9,860,000
Month Table Win	120,000	80,000	90,000	130,000	190,000	210,000	360,000	280,000	340,000	220,000	310,000	550,000	2,880,000
Table Win Per Day	258	190	194	289	409	467	774	602	756	473	689	1,183	524
Table Hold Percent	41.60	38.20	35.70	37.10	35.60	26.40	30.50	30.30	28.90	23.80	22.10	26.90	31.43
Number of Slots	260	260	260	260	260	260	260	260	260	260	444	440	290
Month Slot Coin In	8,030,000	7,090,000	8,230,000	10,850,000	9,350,000	9,370,000	13,980,000	11,530,000	14,360,000	12,050,000	19,170,000	23,270,000	147,280,000
Month Slot Win	680,000	630,000	740,000	970,000	830,000	860,000	1,230,000	1,030,000	1,290,000	1,060,000	1,460,000	1,780,000	12,560,000
Slot Win Per Day	84	87	92	124	103	110	153	128	165	132	187	221	132
Slot Hold Percent	8.50	8.90	8.90	8.90	8.90	9.20	8.80	8.90	9.00	8.80	7.60	7.70	8.67
SIOUX CITY SUE													
Number of Tables	14	14	14	14	14	14	14	14	14	31	31	29	18
Month Table Drop	170,000	170,000	190,000	230,000	280,000	720,000	1,150,000	1,100,000	1,360,000	1,920,000	1,890,000	2,260,000	11,440,000
Month Table Win	60,000	70,000	80,000	97,000	130,000	200,000	280,000	290,000	350,000	510,000	430,000	560,000	3,057,000
Table Win Per Day	138	179	184	231	300	476	645	668	833	1,175	1,024	1,290	595
Table Hold Percent	36.20	42.30	41.90	41.70	44.50	27.70	24.70	26.00	26.70	26.50	22.80	24.80	32.15
Number of Slots	240	240	240	240	240	240	240	240	240	441	441	441	290
Month Slot Coin In	2,240,000	2,390,000	2,630,000	3,390,000	2,770,000	2,910,000	4,450,000	4,640,000	7,290,000	10,990,000	11,060,000	10,290,000	65,050,000
Month Slot Win	190,000	160,000	290,000	360,000	290,000	340,000	520,000	490,000	810,000	1,090,000	1,090,000	1,000,000	6,630,000
Slot Win Per Day	26	24	39	50	39	47	70	66	113	147	151	134	75
Slot Hold Percent	8.50	6.70	11.30	10.70	10.40	11.70	11.60	10.60	11.10	10.00	9.90	9.70	10.18

IOWA RIVERBOAT GAMING STATISTICS FOR 1994

MONTH	JAN	FEB	MAR	APR	MAY	JUN	JUL	AUG	SEP	OCT	NOV	DEC	AVG/TOT
Days	31	28	31	30	31	30	31	31	30	31	30	31	

DUBUQUE JO

MONTH	JAN	FEB	MAR	APR	MAY	JUN	JUL	AUG	SEP	OCT	NOV	DEC	AVG/TOT
Number of Tables								17	17	17	17	17	17
Month Table Drop								2,260,000	2,940,000	2,510,000	2,010,000	2,580,000	12,300,000
Month Table Win								560,000	590,000	580,000	660,000	600,000	2,990,000
Table Win Per Day								1,063	1,157	1,101	1,294	1,139	1,151
Table Hold Percent								24.60	20.20	23.30	29.40	23.20	24.14
Number of Slots								332	332	332	332	332	332
Month Slot Coin In								17,400,000	23,140,000	18,210,000	17,620,000	20,070,000	96,440,000
Month Slot Win								1,390,000	1,880,000	1,470,000	1,350,000	1,430,000	7,520,000
Slot Win Per Day								135	189	143	136	139	148
Slot Hold Percent								8.00	8.10	8.10	7.70	7.20	7.82

CATFISH BEND

MONTH	JAN	FEB	MAR	APR	MAY	JUN	JUL	AUG	SEP	OCT	NOV	DEC	AVG/TOT
Number of Tables											20	20	20
Month Table Drop											630,000	2,170,000	2,800,000
Month Table Win											190,000	690,000	880,000
Table Win Per Day											317	1,113	715
Table Hold Percent											29.30	31.70	30.50
Number of Slots											260	260	260
Month Slot Coin In											3,830,000	8,140,000	11,970,000
Month Slot Win											300,000	910,000	1,210,000
Slot Win Per Day											500	1,468	984
Slot Hold Percent											8.00	11.10	9.55

MISS MARQUET

MONTH	JAN	FEB	MAR	APR	MAY	JUN	JUL	AUG	SEP	OCT	NOV	DEC	AVG/TOT
Number of Tables												31	31
Month Table Drop												660,000	660,000
Month Table Win												100,000	100,000
Table Win Per Day												454	454
Table Hold Percent												14.90	14.90
Number of Slots												620	620
Month Slot Coin In												6,730,000	6,730,000
Month Slot Win												690,000	690,000
Slot Win Per Day												36	36
Slot Hold Percent												10.30	10.30

IOWA RIVERBOAT GAMING STATISTICS FOR 1994

MONTH	JAN	FEB	MAR	APR	MAY	JUN	JUL	AUG	SEP	OCT	NOV	DEC	AVG/TOT
Days	31	28	31	30	31	30	31	31	30	31	30	31	
STATE OF IOWA													
Number of Tables	65	65	65	65	65	65	81	98	98	115	145	175	92
Month Table Drop	1,610,000	1,360,000	1,480,000	2,010,000	3,220,000	7,830,000	11,020,000	10,990,000	13,930,000	12,070,000	12,870,000	17,910,000	96,300,000
Month Table Win	610,000	510,000	530,000	717,000	880,000	1,810,000	2,650,000	2,700,000	3,170,000	2,700,000	3,390,000	4,380,000	24,047,000
Table Win Per Day	303	280	263	368	437	928	1,055	889	1,078	757	779	807	662
Table Hold Percent	37.89	37.50	35.81	35.67	27.33	23.12	24.05	24.57	22.76	22.37	26.34	24.46	28.49
Number of Slots	1,191	1,191	1,191	1,191	1,191	1,220	1,276	1,608	1,608	1,809	2,253	2,869	1,550
Month Slot Coin In	39,700,000	35,760,000	41,840,000	58,320,000	51,180,000	60,530,000	80,920,000	90,080,000	120,030,000	98,190,000	109,820,000	137,940,000	924,310,000
Month Slot Win	3,300,000	2,970,000	3,640,000	4,860,000	4,480,000	5,140,000	7,270,000	7,490,000	9,900,000	7,990,000	8,520,000	10,710,000	76,270,000
Slot Win Per Day	89	89	99	136	121	140	184	150	205	142	126	120	134
Slot Hold Percent	8.31	8.31	8.70	8.33	8.75	8.49	8.98	8.31	8.25	8.14	7.76	7.76	8.34
Gross Revenues	3,910,000	3,480,000	4,170,000	5,577,000	5,360,000	6,950,000	9,920,000	10,190,000	13,070,000	10,690,000	11,910,000	15,090,000	8,359,750
Total Gross Revenues													100,317,000
Slot Percent of Gross	84.40	85.34	87.29	87.14	83.58	73.96	73.29	73.50	75.75	74.74	71.54	70.97	76.03

TABLE & SLOTS WIN COMPARISON
IOWA

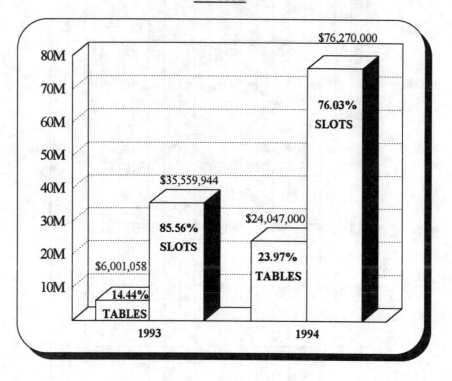

1994 MONTHLY GROSS REVENUES

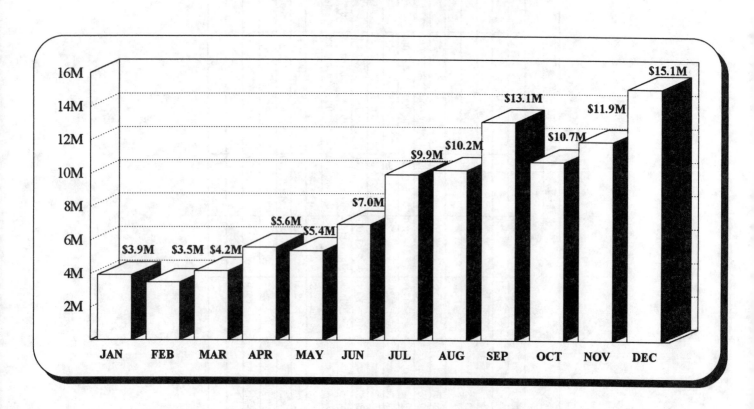

MISSISSIPPI

MISSISSIPPI RIVERBOAT GAMING STATISTICS FOR 1993

ESTIMATED TOTAL GAMING REVENUE

CASINOS	JAN	FEB	MAR	APR	MAY	JUN	JUL	AUG	SEP	OCT	NOV	DEC	TOTAL
	31	28	31	30	31	30	31	31	30	31	30	31	
Isle of Capri-Biloxi	5,300,000	6,100,000	6,700,000	6,800,000	7,100,000	5,800,000	8,000,000	8,000,000	7,400,000	7,200,000	7,500,000	6,500,000	82,400,000
Biloxi Belle-Biloxi	4,500,000	5,100,000	6,700,000	5,700,000	4,900,000	3,400,000	5,700,000	5,800,000	5,400,000	4,500,000	4,500,000	4,000,000	60,200,000
President-Biloxi	7,500,000	7,400,000	7,500,000	8,500,000	7,600,000	5,100,000	6,400,000	5,600,000	4,200,000	4,900,000	5,300,000	4,400,000	74,400,000
Casino Magic-B-StL	11,000,000	11,600,000	12,200,000	12,900,000	13,500,000	13,900,000	14,300,000	16,000,000	14,500,000	13,700,000	13,500,000	12,300,000	159,400,000
Splash-Tunica	11,800,000	12,200,000	12,700,000	12,800,000	13,000,000	13,100,000	14,400,000	14,000,000	11,800,000	10,000,000	11,000,000	8,000,000	144,800,000
Lady Luck-Natchez		200,000	5,400,000	5,700,000	5,800,000	5,400,000	6,400,000	5,400,000	4,800,000	4,600,000	4,200,000	3,500,000	51,400,000
Grand Casino-Gulf					6,900,000	11,700,000	13,900,000	13,200,000	13,100,000	13,300,000	13,400,000	11,700,000	97,200,000
Casino Magic-Biloxi						3,000,000	5,600,000	4,700,000	4,600,000	5,000,000	5,800,000	5,000,000	33,700,000
Isle of Capri-Vicksbg								5,300,000	7,400,000	8,300,000	7,400,000	7,100,000	35,500,000
Copa Casino-Gulf									1,100,000	2,000,000	2,200,000	2,200,000	7,500,000
Lady Luck-Tunica									2,700,000	7,000,000	6,500,000	6,700,000	22,900,000
Harrahs-Vicksburg											1,500,000	3,500,000	5,000,000
Harrahs-Tunica												4,700,000	4,700,000
Bally-Tunica												4,200,000	4,200,000
President-Tunica												2,300,000	2,300,000
Cotton Club-Greenville												2,100,000	2,100,000
Lady Luck-Biloxi												2,000,000	2,000,000
Total	40,100,000	42,600,000	51,200,000	52,400,000	58,800,000	61,400,000	74,700,000	78,000,000	77,000,000	80,500,000	82,800,000	90,200,000	789,700,000

ESTIMATED WIN PER DAY

CASINOS	JAN	FEB	MAR	APR	MAY	JUN	JUL	AUG	SEP	OCT	NOV	DEC	TOTAL
Isle of Capri-Biloxi	170,968	217,857	216,129	226,667	229,032	193,333	258,065	258,065	246,667	232,258	250,000	209,677	225,753
Biloxi Belle-Biloxi	145,161	182,143	216,129	190,000	158,065	113,333	183,871	187,097	180,000	145,161	150,000	129,032	164,932
President-Biloxi	241,935	264,286	241,935	283,333	245,161	170,000	206,452	180,645	140,000	158,065	176,667	141,935	203,836
Casino Magic-B-StL	354,839	414,286	393,548	430,000	435,484	463,333	461,290	516,129	483,333	441,935	450,000	396,774	436,712
Splash-Tunica	380,645	435,714	409,677	426,667	419,355	436,667	464,516	451,613	393,333	322,581	366,667	258,065	396,712
Lady Luck-Natchez		200,000	174,194	190,000	187,097	180,000	206,452	174,194	160,000	148,387	140,000	112,903	140,822
Grand Casino-Gulf					431,250	390,000	448,387	425,806	436,667	429,032	446,667	377,419	424,454
Casino Magic-Biloxi						125,000	180,645	151,613	153,333	161,290	193,333	161,290	157,477
Isle of Capri-Vicksbg								252,381	246,667	267,742	246,667	229,032	232,026
Copa Casino-Gulf									57,895	64,516	73,333	70,968	71,429
Lady Luck-Tunica									245,455	225,806	216,667	216,129	222,330
Harrahs-Vicksburg											107,143	112,903	111,111
Harrhs-Tunica												151,613	151,613
Bally-Tunica												155,556	155,556
President-Tunica												95,833	95,833
Cotton Club-Greenville												123,529	123,529
Lady Luck-Biloxi												117,647	117,647
Mississippi	258,710	285,714	275,269	291,111	300,778	258,958	301,210	288,616	249,395	236,070	234,762	180,018	263,384

MISSISSIPPI RIVERBOAT GAMING STATISTICS FOR 1993

ESTIMATED WIN PER DAY PER UNIT

CASINOS	JAN	FEB	MAR	APR	MAY	JUN	JUL	AUG	SEP	OCT	NOV	DEC	AVG
Isle of Capri-Biloxi	147	188	186	195	197	167	177	177	169	159	171	144	173
Biloxi Belle-Biloxi	227	285	338	297	247	177	287	292	281	227	234	202	258
President-Biloxi	416	454	416	487	421	292	355	310	241	272	304	244	350
Casino Magic-B-StL	299	350	332	363	367	391	389	436	408	373	380	335	369
Splash-Tunica	635	727	684	712	700	729	775	754	657	539	612	431	662
Lady Luck-Natchez		452	394	430	423	407	467	394	362	336	317	255	319
Grand Casino-Gulf					275	248	286	271	278	273	285	240	270
Casino Magic-Biloxi						169	244	205	207	218	261	218	213
Isle of Capri-Vicksbg								466	455	494	364	338	423
Copa Casino-Gulf									78	87	98	95	96
Lady Luck-Tunica									347	319	306	305	314
Harrahs-Vicksburg											166	175	173
Harrahs-Tunica												121	121
Bally-Tunica												128	128
President-Tunica												169	169
Cotton Club-Greenville												190	190
Lady Luck-Biloxi												170	170
Mississippi	345	409	392	414	376	323	373	367	317	300	292	221	259

ESTIMATED WIN PER DAY PER TABLE GAME

CASINOS	JAN	FEB	MAR	APR	MAY	JUN	JUL	AUG	SEP	OCT	NOV	DEC	AVG
Isle of Capri-Biloxi	1,083	1,380	1,369	1,436	1,451	1,224	1,634	1,634	1,562	1,471	1,583	1,328	1,430
Biloxi Belle-Biloxi	1,379	1,154	1,369	1,203	1,001	718	1,165	1,185	1,140	919	950	817	1,045
President-Biloxi	2,189	2,391	2,189	2,563	2,218	1,538	1,868	1,634	1,267	1,430	1,598	1,284	1,844
Casino Magic-B-StL	2,175	2,539	2,412	2,635	2,669	2,840	2,827	3,163	2,962	2,709	2,758	2,432	2,677
Splash-Tunica	5,563	6,368	5,988	6,236	6,129	6,382	6,789	6,600	5,749	4,715	5,359	3,772	5,798
Lady Luck-Natchez		3,619	3,152	3,438	3,386	3,257	3,736	3,152	2,895	2,685	2,533	2,043	2,548
Grand Casino-Gulf					2,341	2,117	2,434	2,312	2,370	2,329	2,425	2,049	2,304
Casino Magic-Biloxi						1,188	1,716	1,440	1,457	1,532	1,837	1,532	1,496
Isle of Capri-Vicksbg								3,425	3,348	3,634	2,467	2,290	3,033
Copa Casino-Gulf									489	545	619	599	603
Lady Luck-Tunica									2,120	1,950	1,871	1,867	1,920
Harrahs-Vicksburg											925	975	960
Harrahs-Tunica												1,048	1,048
Bally-Tunica												909	909
President-Tunica												888	888
Cotton Club-Greenville												1,739	1,739
Lady Luck-Biloxi												1,176	1,176
Mississippi	2,478	2,909	2,747	2,919	2,742	2,408	2,771	2,727	2,305	2,174	2,077	1,573	2,486

MISSISSIPPI RIVERBOAT GAMING STATISTICS FOR 1993

ESTIMATED WIN PER DAY PER SLOT MACHINE

CASINOS	JAN	FEB	MAR	APR	MAY	JUN	JUL	AUG	SEP	OCT	NOV	DEC	TOTAL
Isle of Capri-Biloxi	96	123	122	128	129	109	114	114	109	103	111	93	113
Biloxi Belle-Biloxi	150	188	223	196	163	117	190	193	186	150	155	133	170
President-Biloxi	278	303	278	325	281	195	237	207	161	181	203	163	234
Casino Magic-B-StL	196	229	217	237	240	256	255	285	267	244	248	219	241
Splash-Tunica	412	471	443	462	454	472	503	489	426	349	397	279	429
Lady Luck-Natchez		295	257	280	276	265	304	257	236	219	206	166	207
Grand Casino-Gulf					178	161	185	176	180	177	185	156	175
Casino Magic-Biloxi						111	160	134	136	143	171	143	139
Isle of Capri-Vicksbg								304	298	323	239	222	269
Copa Casino-Gulf									51	57	65	63	63
Lady Luck-Tunica									229	211	202	202	208
Harrahs-Vicksburg											111	117	115
Harrahs-Tunica												78	78
Bally-Tunica												84	84
President-Tunica												113	113
Cotton Club-Greenville												123	123
Lady Luck-Biloxi												111	111
Mississippi	226	268	257	271	246	211	244	240	207	196	191	145	225

RIVERBOAT SPECIFICATIONS

	LOCATION	DIMENSIONS	CASINO SIZE (Sq. Ft.)	GAMING POSITIONS	NUMBER OF SLOTS	NUMBER OF TABLES	START DATE
Isle of Capri	Biloxi		65,000	1,580	1,400	60	08-01-92
Biloxi Belle	Biloxi	217' x 44'	18,000	800	600	40	08-28-92
President-Biloxi	Biloxi	287' x 65'	20,000	750	540	42	08-13-92
Casino Magic	Bay St. Louis	300' x 74'	41,000	1,433	1,123	62	09-30-92
Splash	Tunica	250' x 50'	16,000	723	573	26	10-19-92
Lady Luck	Natchez	302' x 66'	9,400	526	421	21	02-27-93
Grand Casino	Gulfport	600' x 110'	90,000	1,850	1,500	70	05-14-93
Casino Magic	Biloxi	300' x 110'	31,000	900	700	40	06-05-93
Isle of Capri	Vicksburg		20,000	785	640	38	08-09-93
Copa Casino	Gulfport	505' x 90'	25,000	970	700	45	09-10-93
Lady Luck	Tunica	300' x 75'	25,000	928	664	44	09-18-93
Harrahs	Vicksburg	297' x 90'	20,000	864	600	44	11-15-93
Harrahs	Tunica	300' x 100'	32,000	1,530	1,200	55	11-29-93
Bally	Tunica	300' x 75'	40,000	1,540	1,150	65	12-03-93
President	Tunica	297' x 65'	25,000	771	525	41	12-06-93
Cotton Club	Greenville	246' x 58'	27,632	786	624	27	12-13-93
Lady Luck	Biloxi	300' 75'	21,000	884	656	38	12-13-93
Mississippi			526,032	17,620	13,616	758	

MISSISSIPPI GAMING STATISTICS FOR 1994

MONTH	GULF COAST	MISSISSIPPI RIVER	TOTALS
JANUARY	53,322,303	46,644,365	99,966,668
FEBRUARY	58,170,877	48,207,481	106,378,358
MARCH	60,329,743	59,840,790	120,170,533
APRIL	64,221,627	56,862,106	121,083,733
MAY	66,784,833	58,015,782	124,800,615
JUNE	62,332,692	57,532,709	119,865,401
JULY	72,102,662	69,809,172	141,911,834
AUGUST	63,719,238	68,631,095	132,350,333
SEPTEMBER	61,470,651	66,869,528	128,340,179
OCTOBER	58,208,055	68,520,808	126,728,864
NOVEMBER	56,449,035	67,216,709	123,665,744
DECEMBER	53,426,653	68,910,422	122,337,075
GROSS REVENUES	730,538,368	737,060,967	1,467,599,335

GAMING STATISTICS AND GRAPHICS

NEVADA

NEVADA GAME STATISTICS FOR 1993

TABLES	# Units	Annual Win	Win/Unit	Per Day	Win %
Blackjack	3,402	912,404,000	268,196	735	14.45%
Craps	422	362,016,000	857,858	2,350	13.67%
Roulette	335	142,283,000	424,725	1,164	22.21%
Baccarat	65	345,431,000	5,314,323	14,560	15.08%
Big Six	61	10,817,000	177,328	486	44.04%
Mini Baccarat	50	29,161,000	583,220	1,598	13.46%
Pai Gow	37	27,546,000	744,486	2,040	21.07%
Sic-Bo	3	858,000	286,000	784	41.08%
Pai Gow Poker	160	44,878,000	280,488	768	20.63%
Red Dog	22	2,790,000	126,818	347	30.89%
Poker	571	70,814,000	124,018	340	*
Total Tables	5,128	1,948,998,000	380,070	1,041	15.71%

GAMES	# Units	Annual Win	Win/Unit	Per Day	Win %
Keno	160	133,435,000	833,969	2,285	26.92%
Bingo	30	-17,000	-567	-2	-0.02%
Race Book	62	83,099,000	1,340,306	3,672	16.19%
Sports Book	112	75,035,000	669,955	1,835	3.74%
Other Games	233	62,918,000	270,034	740	25.11%
Total Games	597	354,470,000	593,752	1,627	9.60%
Total Tables/Games	5,725	2,303,468,000	402,352	1,102	15.00%

SLOT MACHINES	# Units	Annual Win	Win/Unit	Per Day	Win %
01 Cent	161	1,201,000	7,460	20	11.23%
05 Cent	32,272	471,600,000	14,613	40	8.60%
10 Cent	952	14,728,000	15,471	42	8.24%
25 Cent	78,980	1,874,615,000	23,735	65	5.15%
50 Cent	1,230	32,075,000	26,077	71	4.23%
01 Dollar	30,032	1,283,963,000	42,753	117	4.36%
01 Dollar Megabucks	777	63,717,000	82,004	225	10.94%
05 Dollar	2,206	163,447,000	74,092	203	3.55%
25 Dollar	280	20,093,000	71,761	197	3.30%
100 Dollar	94	9,667,000	102,840	282	2.80%
Other	190	8,935,000	47,026	129	N/A
Total Slots	147,174	3,944,041,000	26,798	73	5.77%
Grand Totals	152,899	6,247,509,000	40,860	112	6.14%

*Poker rakes can be based on a fixed percentage or on a charge per hand or per hour. Therefore no hold percentage is given.

LAS VEGAS STRIP GAME STATISTICS FOR 1993

TABLES	# Units	Annual Win	Win/Unit	Per Day	Win %
Blackjack	1,295	507,626,000	391,989	1,074	14.13%
Craps	178	209,204,000	1,175,303	3,220	13.46%
Roulette	144	95,245,000	661,424	1,812	22.71%
Baccarat	50	329,045,000	6,580,900	18,030	15.71%
Big Six	34	7,753,000	228,029	625	45.81%
Mini Baccarat	36	23,980,000	666,111	1,825	12.96%
Pai Gow	21	22,558,000	1,074,190	2,943	21.23%
Sic-Bo	0	0	0	0	0.00%
Pai Gow Poker	76	28,217,000	371,276	1,017	20.70%
Red Dog	10	1,776,000	177,600	487	28.88%
Poker	244	35,821,000	146,807	402	*
Total Tables	**2,088**	**1,261,225,000**	**604,035**	**1,655**	**15.77%**

GAMES	# Units	Annual Win	Win/Unit	Per Day	Win %
Keno	45	42,406,000	942,356	2,582	26.47%
Bingo	6	-401,000	-66,833	-183	-1.26%
Race Book	24	54,540,000	2,272,500	6,226	15.84%
Sports Book	27	39,436,000	1,460,593	4,002	3.13%
Other Games	92	36,229,000	393,793	1,079	24.52%
Total Games	**194**	**172,210,000**	**887,680**	**2,432**	**8.50%**
Total Tables/Games	**2,282**	**1,433,435,000**	**628,149**	**1,721**	**15.08%**

SLOT MACHINES	# Units	Annual Win	Win/Unit	Per Day	Win %
05 Cent	7,522	119,869,000	15,936	44	10.69%
10 Cent	178	3,050,000	17,135	47	13.03%
25 Cent	28,210	678,045,000	24,036	66	5.88%
50 Cent	384	11,581,000	30,159	83	4.82%
01 Dollar	11,560	519,453,000	44,935	123	4.73%
01 Dollar Megabucks	298	27,446,000	92,101	252	10.16%
05 Dollar	1,011	75,984,000	75,157	206	3.99%
25 Dollar	172	13,467,000	78,297	215	3.62%
100 Dollar	64	6,051,000	94,547	259	2.93%
Other	152	7,161,000	47,112	129	5.67%
Total Slots	**49,551**	**1,462,107,000**	**29,507**	**81**	**6.33%**
Grand Totals	**51,833**	**2,895,542,000**	**55,863**	**153**	**6.75%**

*Poker rakes can be based on a fixed percentage or on a charge per hand or per hour. Therefore no hold percentage is given.

DOWNTOWN LAS VEGAS GAME STATS FOR 1993

TABLES	# Units	Annual Win	Win/Unit	Per Day	Win %
Blackjack	329	76,543,000	232,653	637	10.93%
Craps	63	54,140,000	859,365	2,354	10.30%
Roulette	33	7,305,000	221,364	606	11.59%
Big Six	6	1,084,000	180,667	495	35.59%
Mini Baccarat	5	977,000	195,400	535	12.81%
Pai Gow Poker	17	4,687,000	275,706	755	19.37%
Red Dog	0	0	0	0	0.00%
Poker	89	11,609,000	130,438	357	*
Total Tables	542	156,345,000	288,459	790	11.55%

GAMES	# Units	Annual Win	Win/Unit	Per Day	Win %
Keno	18	17,854,000	991,889	2,718	25.58%
Bingo	3	61,000	20,333	56	0.25%
Race Book	7	7,735,000	1,105,000	3,027	14.19%
Sports Book	8	8,112,000	1,014,000	2,778	2.75%
Other Games	42	17,437,000	415,167	1,137	19.85%
Total Games	78	51,199,000	656,397	1,798	7.47%
Total Tables/Games	620	207,544,000	334,748	917	10.95%

SLOT MACHINES	# Units	Annual Win	Win/Unit	Per Day	Win %
01 Cent	126	1,083,000	8,595	24	11.78%
05 Cent	4,054	62,227,000	15,350	42	8.71%
10 Cent	91	1,264,000	13,890	38	12.40%
25 Cent	10,012	235,809,000	23,553	65	4.30%
50 Cent	204	6,001,000	29,417	81	2.86%
01 Dollar	3,034	145,852,000	48,073	132	4.46%
01 Dollar Megabucks	79	7,284,000	92,203	253	11.98%
05 Dollar	189	18,689,000	98,884	271	3.69%
25 Dollar	18	1,509,000	83,833	230	3.82%
Other	9	133,000	14,778	40	1.57%
Total Slots	17,816	479,851,000	26,934	74	5.43%
Grand Totals	18,436	687,395,000	37,285	102	5.65%

*Poker rakes can be based on a fixed percentage or on a charge per hand or per hour. Therefore no hold percentage is given.

LAUGHLIN GAME STATISTICS FOR 1993

TABLES	# Units	Annual Win	Win/Unit	Per Day	Win %
Blackjack	235	40,815,000	173,681	476	14.50%
Craps	25	17,516,000	700,640	1,920	16.48%
Roulette	24	7,546,000	314,417	861	24.46%
Big Six	4	294,000	73,500	201	41.85%
Pai Gow Poker	9	1,635,000	181,667	498	21.67%
Poker	47	6,085,000	129,468	355	*
Total Tables	344	73,891,000	214,799	588	16.06%

GAMES	# Units	Annual Win	Win/Unit	Per Day	Win %
Keno	11	9,742,000	885,636	2,426	26.15%
Race Book	6	4,533,000	755,500	2,070	19.87%
Sports Book	8	1,819,000	227,375	623	4.98%
Other Games	27	7,538,000	279,185	765	26.64%
Total Games	52	23,632,000	454,462	1,245	22.42%
Total Tables/Games	396	97,523,000	246,270	675	17.01%

SLOT MACHINES	# Units	Annual Win	Win/Unit	Per Day	Win %
05 Cent	2,495	55,284,000	22,158	61	11.70%
10 Cent	78	2,530,000	32,436	89	11.52%
25 Cent	6,503	229,110,000	35,231	97	5.44%
50 Cent	81	23,296,000	287,605	788	5.15%
01 Dollar	2,618	134,233,000	51,273	140	4.13%
01 Dollar Megabucks	62	4,124,000	66,516	182	10.06%
05 Dollar	228	14,219,000	62,364	171	3.42%
25 Dollar	24	1,046,000	43,583	119	2.27%
Other	10	142,000	14,200	39	1.11%
Total Slots	12,099	463,984,000	38,349	105	6.46%
Grand Totals	12,495	561,507,000	44,939	123	6.82%

*Poker rakes can be based on a fixed percentage or on a charge per hand or per hour. Therefore no hold percentage is given.

SOUTH LAKE TAHOE GAME STATISTICS FOR 1993

TABLES	# Units	Annual Win	Win/Unit	Per Day	Win %
Blackjack	288	76,390,000	265,243	727	15.93%
Craps	29	23,558,000	812,345	2,226	16.01%
Roulette	24	9,953,000	414,708	1,136	25.59%
Baccarat	5	3,682,000	736,400	2,018	3.32%
Big Six	5	628,000	125,600	344	40.70%
Mini Baccarat	5	3,942,000	788,400	2,160	17.69%
Pai Gow	0	0	0	0	0.00%
Pai Gow Poker	13	2,755,000	211,923	581	21.91%
Total Tables	369	120,908,000	327,664	898	16.96%

GAMES	# Units	Annual Win	Win/Unit	Per Day	Win %
Keno	8	6,923,000	865,375	2,371	29.74%
Race Book	3	4,197,000	1,399,000	3,833	17.58%
Sports Book	4	4,109,000	1,027,250	2,814	5.84%
Other Games	24	6,117,000	254,875	698	26.64%
Total Games	39	21,346,000	547,333	1,500	24.45%
Total Tables/Games	408	142,254,000	348,662	955	17.68%

SLOT MACHINES	# Units	Annual Win	Win/Unit	Per Day	Win %
05 Cent	1,088	16,018,000	14,722	40	9.62%
10 Cent	0	0	0	0	0.00%
25 Cent	3,718	82,022,000	22,061	60	6.65%
50 Cent	92	1,747,000	18,989	52	7.37%
01 Dollar	1,730	63,078,000	36,461	100	4.44%
01 Dollar Megabucks	43	3,583,000	83,326	228	11.56%
05 Dollar	199	13,208,000	66,372	182	2.92%
25 Dollar	28	2,015,000	71,964	197	2.64%
100 Dollar	17	2,941,000	173,000	474	2.52%
Other	99	3,799,000	38,374	105	5.75%
Total Slots	7,014	188,411,000	26,862	74	6.46%
Grand Totals	7,422	330,665,000	44,552	122	7.08%

*Poker rakes can be based on a fixed percentage or on a charge per hand or per hour. Therefore no hold percentage is given.

RENO GAME STATISTICS FOR 1993

TABLES	# Units	Annual Win	Win/Unit	Per Day	Win %
Blackjack	499	108,427,000	217,289	595	16.77%
Craps	49	29,405,000	600,102	1,644	17.18%
Roulette	42	11,340,000	270,000	740	24.95%
Baccarat	7	4,272,000	610,286	1,672	12.18%
Big Six	6	739,000	123,167	337	45.36%
Pai Gow	8	2,355,000	294,375	807	18.78%
Pai Gow Poker	33	8,002,000	242,485	664	20.90%
Red Dog	0	0	0	0	0.00%
Poker	59	5,848,000	99,119	272	*
Total Tables	703	170,388,000	242,373	664	17.79%

GAMES	# Units	Annual Win	Win/Unit	Per Day	Win %
Keno	29	28,768,000	992,000	2,718	27.44%
Bingo	0	0	0	0	0.00%
Race Book	7	6,950,000	992,857	2,720	17.52%
Sports Book	7	6,509,000	929,857	2,548	5.32%
Other Games	37	6,274,000	169,568	465	24.39%
Total Games	80	48,501,000	606,263	1,661	23.23%
Total Tables/Games	783	218,889,000	279,552	766	18.39%

SLOT MACHINES	# Units	Annual Win	Win/Unit	Per Day	Win %
01 Cent	13	82,000	6,308	17	15.60%
05 Cent	4,651	55,142,000	11,856	32	8.06%
10 Cent	179	2,079,000	11,615	32	9.63%
25 Cent	8,869	198,781,000	22,413	61	6.23%
50 Cent	217	4,072,000	18,765	51	4.62%
01 Dollar	4,318	169,119,000	39,166	107	4.08%
01 Dollar Megabucks	118	9,549,000	80,924	222	12.00%
05 Dollar	208	19,480,000	93,654	257	3.08%
25 Dollar	24	1,442,000	60,083	165	3.19%
Other	14	523,000	37,357	102	2.44%
Total Slots	18,611	460,269,000	24,731	68	6.20%
Grand Totals	19,394	679,158,000	35,019	96	6.72%

*Poker rakes can be based on a fixed percentage or on a charge per hand or per hour. Therefore no hold percentage is given.

NEVADA GAME STATISTICS FOR 1994

TABLES	# Units	Annual Win	Win/Unit	Per Day	Win %
Blackjack	3,387	955,210,000	282,022	773	14.15%
Craps	423	386,197,000	912,995	2,501	14.13%
Roulette	352	190,315,000	540,668	1,481	22.54%
Baccarat	67	491,244,000	7,332,000	20,088	15.19%
Big Six	59	12,686,000	215,017	589	44.94%
Mini Baccarat	56	44,512,000	794,857	2,178	14.01%
Pai Gow	28	35,709,000	1,275,321	3,494	23.10%
Pai Gow Poker	156	51,487,000	330,045	904	20.80%
Red Dog	11	1,613,000	146,636	402	32.01%
Poker	586	71,667,000	122,299	335	*
Total Tables	**5,125**	**2,240,640,000**	**437,198**	**1,198**	**15.54%**

GAMES	# Units	Annual Win	Win/Unit	Per Day	Win %
Keno	166	136,139,000	820,114	2,247	27.44%
Bingo	38	544,000	14,316	39	0.50%
Race Book	66	86,864,000	1,316,121	3,606	16.53%
Sports Book	112	122,450,000	1,093,304	2,995	5.73%
Other Games	327	113,223,000	346,248	949	25.07%
Total Games	**709**	**459,220,000**	**647,701**	**1,775**	**8.90%**
Total Tables/Games	**5,834**	**2,699,860,000**	**462,780**	**1,268**	**14.64%**

SLOT MACHINES	# Units	Annual Win	Win/Unit	Per Day	Win %
01 Cent	169	1,565,000	9,260	25	10.81%
05 Cent	34,573	501,568,000	14,508	40	8.45%
10 Cent	877	13,855,000	15,798	43	7.90%
25 Cent	85,146	2,076,409,000	24,386	67	5.19%
50 Cent	1,304	36,237,000	27,789	76	4.28%
01 Dollar	30,998	1,393,611,000	44,958	123	4.33%
01 Dollar Megabucks	803	46,760,000	58,232	160	9.44%
05 Dollar	2,452	195,791,000	79,850	219	3.53%
25 Dollar	291	22,566,000	77,546	212	2.81%
100 Dollar	97	12,419,000	128,031	351	2.78%
Other	127	6,945,000	54,685	150	N/A
Total Slots	**156,837**	**4,307,726,000**	**27,466**	**75**	**5.74%**
Grand Totals	**162,671**	**7,007,586,000**	**43,078**	**118**	**6.08%**

*Poker rakes can be based on a fixed percentage or on a charge per hand or per hour. Therefore no hold percentage is given.

LAS VEGAS STRIP GAME STATISTICS FOR 1994

TABLES	# Units	Annual Win	Win/Unit	Per Day	Win %
Blackjack	1,210	553,067,000	457,080	1,252	13.73%
Craps	176	231,546,000	1,315,602	3,604	13.77%
Roulette	151	141,549,000	937,411	2,568	23.09%
Baccarat	52	449,682,000	8,647,731	23,692	14.70%
Big Six	33	9,484,000	287,394	787	45.93%
Mini Baccarat	37	40,378,000	1,091,297	2,990	14.13%
Pai Gow	15	31,911,000	2,127,400	5,828	23.59%
Pai Gow Poker	74	34,901,000	471,635	1,292	20.94%
Red Dog	7	937,000	133,857	367	31.22%
Poker	229	38,054,000	166,175	455	*
Total Tables	1,984	1,531,509,000	771,930	2,115	15.64%

GAMES	# Units	Annual Win	Win/Unit	Per Day	Win %
Keno	45	47,808,000	1,062,400	2,911	28.71%
Bingo	6	612,000	102,000	279	2.04%
Race Book	23	57,137,000	2,484,217	6,806	16.08%
Sports Book	32	68,859,000	2,151,844	5,895	4.90%
Other Games	122	60,176,000	493,246	1,351	24.85%
Total Games	228	234,592,000	1,028,912	2,819	8.03%
Total Tables/Games	2,212	1,766,101,000	798,418	2,187	14.77%

SLOT MACHINES	# Units	Annual Win	Win/Unit	Per Day	Win %
05 Cent	7,471	134,720,000	18,032	49	10.69%
10 Cent	171	3,264,000	19,088	52	11.32%
25 Cent	28,767	811,572,000	28,212	77	6.11%
50 Cent	418	14,918,000	35,689	98	5.55%
01 Dollar	11,212	605,706,000	54,023	148	4.75%
01 Dollar Megabucks	306	22,247,000	72,703	199	9.23%
05 Dollar	1,061	95,808,000	90,300	247	3.89%
25 Dollar	173	15,839,000	91,555	251	3.05%
100 Dollar	63	10,532,000	167,175	458	3.09%
Other	62	4,591,000	74,048	203	2.92%
Total Slots	49,704	1,719,197,000	34,589	95	6.46%
Grand Totals	51,916	3,485,298,000	67,133	184	6.84%

*Poker rakes can be based on a fixed percentage or on a charge per hand or per hour. Therefore no hold percentage is given.

DOWNTOWN LAS VEGAS GAME STATS FOR 1994

TABLES	# Units	Annual Win	Win/Unit	Per Day	Win %
Blackjack	313	73,332,000	234,288	642	10.99%
Craps	61	50,083,000	821,033	2,249	10.93%
Roulette	32	5,591,000	174,719	479	9.39%
Big Six	6	882,000	147,000	403	37.15%
Mini Baccarat	7	1,603,000	229,000	627	15.03%
Pai Gow Poker	16	3,670,000	229,375	628	17.99%
Poker	101	10,108,000	100,079	274	*
Total Tables	536	145,269,000	271,024	743	11.55%

GAMES	# Units	Annual Win	Win/Unit	Per Day	Win %
Keno	18	17,502,000	972,333	2,664	26.49%
Bingo	3	482,000	160,667	440	1.90%
Race Book	9	7,469,000	829,889	2,274	16.06%
Sports Book	11	13,890,000	1,262,727	3,460	4.24%
Other Games	46	25,632,000	557,217	1,527	28.24%
Total Games	87	64,975,000	746,839	2,046	7.74%
Total Tables/Games	623	210,244,000	337,470	925	10.92%

SLOT MACHINES	# Units	Annual Win	Win/Unit	Per Day	Win %
01 Cent	131	1,409,000	10,756	29	10.53%
05 Cent	4,010	60,638,000	15,122	41	8.48%
10 Cent	84	978,000	11,643	32	11.37%
25 Cent	10,083	234,670,000	23,274	64	4.38%
50 Cent	207	6,309,000	30,478	84	3.16%
01 Dollar	3,028	143,798,000	47,489	130	4.48%
01 Dollar Megabucks	83	4,696,000	56,578	155	10.02%
05 Dollar	193	18,670,000	96,736	265	3.47%
25 Dollar	17	1,683,000	99,000	271	3.27%
Other	8	172,000	21,500	59	1.20%
Total Slots	17,844	473,023,000	26,509	73	5.40%
Grand Totals	18,467	683,267,000	36,999	101	5.61%

*Poker rakes can be based on a fixed percentage or on a charge per hand or per hour. Therefore no hold percentage is given.

LAUGHLIN GAME STATISTICS FOR 1994

TABLES	# Units	Annual Win	Win/Unit	Per Day	Win %
Blackjack	242	38,871,000	160,624	440	14.57%
Craps	25	16,614,000	664,560	1,821	16.66%
Roulette	25	7,895,000	315,800	865	25.38%
Big Six	6	396,000	66,000	181	39.87%
Pai Gow Poker	10	1,817,000	181,700	498	21.31%
Poker	45	5,908,000	131,289	360	*
Total Tables	353	71,501,000	202,552	555	16.33%

GAMES	# Units	Annual Win	Win/Unit	Per Day	Win %
Keno	12	9,347,000	778,917	2,134	26.63%
Race Book	6	4,326,000	721,000	1,975	19.05%
Sports Book	8	3,113,000	389,125	1,066	9.13%
Other Games	40	10,464,000	261,600	717	23.63%
Total Games	66	27,250,000	412,879	1,131	22.00%
Total Tables/Games	419	98,751,000	235,683	646	17.33%

SLOT MACHINES	# Units	Annual Win	Win/Unit	Per Day	Win %
05 Cent	2,675	54,063,000	20,210	55	11.82%
10 Cent	81	2,270,000	28,025	77	11.30%
25 Cent	6,991	229,141,000	32,777	90	5.41%
50 Cent	93	2,629,000	28,269	77	5.94%
01 Dollar	2,646	127,760,000	48,284	132	4.08%
01 Dollar Megabucks	63	3,229,000	51,254	140	10.13%
05 Dollar	256	15,635,000	61,074	167	3.45%
25 Dollar	27	1,221,000	45,222	124	2.78%
Other	14	294,000	21,000	58	1.58%
Total Slots	12,846	436,242,000	33,959	93	6.49%
Grand Totals	13,265	534,993,000	40,331	110	6.85%

*Poker rakes can be based on a fixed percentage or on a charge per hand or per hour. Therefore no hold percentage is given.

SOUTH LAKE TAHOE GAME STATISTICS FOR 1994

TABLES	# Units	Annual Win	Win/Unit	Per Day	Win %
Blackjack	269	71,010,000	263,978	723	15.71%
Craps	27	24,692,000	914,519	2,506	17.21%
Roulette	23	9,992,000	434,435	1,190	24.84%
Baccarat	4	26,485,000	6,621,250	18,140	22.98%
Big Six	4	708,000	177,000	485	44.91%
Mini Baccarat	4	2,048,000	512,000	1,403	11.36%
Pai Gow Poker	9	2,992,000	332,444	911	23.83%
Total Tables	340	137,927,000	405,668	1,111	17.04%

GAMES	# Units	Annual Win	Win/Unit	Per Day	Win %
Keno	8	6,330,000	791,250	2,168	28.33%
Race Book	4	4,265,000	1,066,250	2,921	18.97%
Sports Book	5	8,698,000	1,739,600	4,766	10.14%
Other Games	24	8,802,000	366,750	1,005	26.01%
Total Games	41	28,095,000	685,244	1,877	23.84%
Total Tables/Games	381	166,022,000	435,753	1,194	17.77%

SLOT MACHINES	# Units	Annual Win	Win/Unit	Per Day	Win %
05 Cent	987	14,354,000	14,543	40	9.49%
10 Cent	0	0	0	0	0.00%
25 Cent	3,621	81,295,000	22,451	62	6.67%
50 Cent	56	1,111,000	19,839	54	3.43%
01 Dollar	1,783	62,937,000	35,298	97	4.43%
01 Dollar Megabucks	40	2,268,000	56,700	155	9.22%
05 Dollar	226	12,735,000	56,350	154	2.83%
25 Dollar	27	1,532,000	56,741	155	1.89%
100 Dollar	20	1,044,000	52,200	143	1.31%
Other	98	3,070,000	31,327	86	3.33%
Total Slots	6,858	180,346,000	26,297	72	6.27%
Grand Totals	7,239	346,368,000	47,847	131	6.88%

*Poker rakes can be based on a fixed percentage or on a charge per hand or per hour. Therefore no hold percentage is given.

RENO GAME STATISTICS FOR 1994

TABLES	# Units	Annual Win	Win/Unit	Per Day	Win %
Blackjack	501	107,848,000	215,265	590	16.74%
Craps	48	29,998,000	624,958	1,712	16.25%
Roulette	40	11,839,000	295,975	811	25.55%
Baccarat	7	4,495,000	642,143	1,759	13.90%
Big Six	4	694,000	173,500	475	44.32%
Pai Gow	8	2,203,000	275,375	754	19.95%
Pai Gow Poker	32	6,231,000	194,719	533	21.02%
Red Dog	0	0	0	0	0.00%
Poker	60	5,640,000	94,000	258	*
Total Tables	700	168,948,000	241,354	661	17.65%

GAMES	# Units	Annual Win	Win/Unit	Per Day	Win %
Keno	30	27,138,000	904,600	2,478	26.48%
Bingo	0	0	0	0	0.00%
Race Book	8	6,829,000	853,625	2,339	17.37%
Sports Book	12	12,922,000	1,076,833	2,950	9.93%
Other Games	48	12,073,000	251,521	689	26.47%
Total Games	98	58,962,000	601,653	1,648	23.70%
Total Tables/Games	798	227,910,000	285,602	782	18.45%

SLOT MACHINES	# Units	Annual Win	Win/Unit	Per Day	Win %
01 Cent	12	70,000	5,833	16	15.83%
05 Cent	4,707	54,651,000	11,611	32	7.72%
10 Cent	151	1,782,000	11,801	32	10.18%
25 Cent	9,282	196,780,000	21,200	58	6.00%
50 Cent	166	3,596,000	21,663	59	4.33%
01 Dollar	4,332	174,415,000	40,262	110	4.12%
01 Dollar Megabucks	119	5,547,000	46,613	128	9.52%
05 Dollar	282	24,641,000	87,379	239	3.32%
25 Dollar	26	1,524,000	58,615	161	1.98%
Other	14	639,000	45,643	125	2.34%
Total Slots	19,091	463,645,000	24,286	67	6.00%
Grand Totals	19,889	691,555,000	34,771	95	6.52%

*Poker rakes can be based on a fixed percentage or on a charge per hand or per hour. Therefore no hold percentage is given.

TABLE GAMES & SLOT WIN COMPARISON
NEVADA

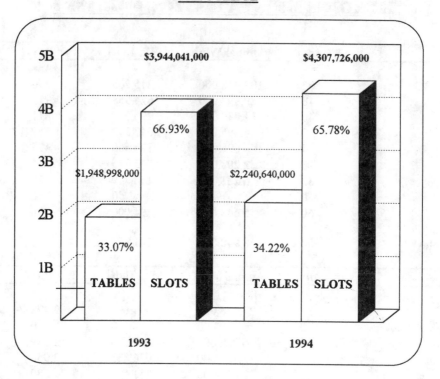

TABLE GAMES & SLOT WIN COMPARISON
LAS VEGAS STRIP

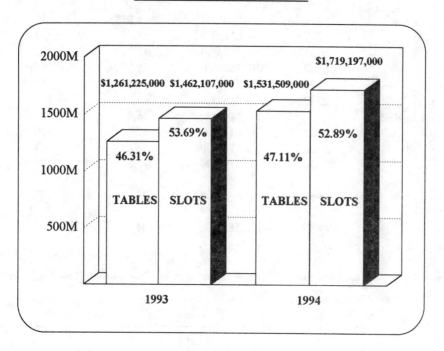

A1

WIN PER DAY PER UNIT FOR 1994
NEVADA

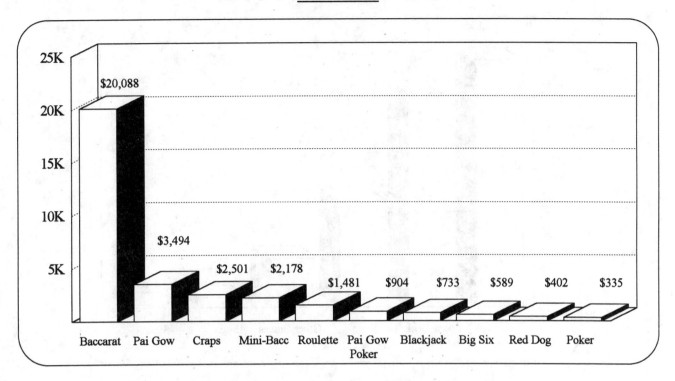

WIN PER DAY PER UNIT FOR 1994
LAS VEGAS STRIP

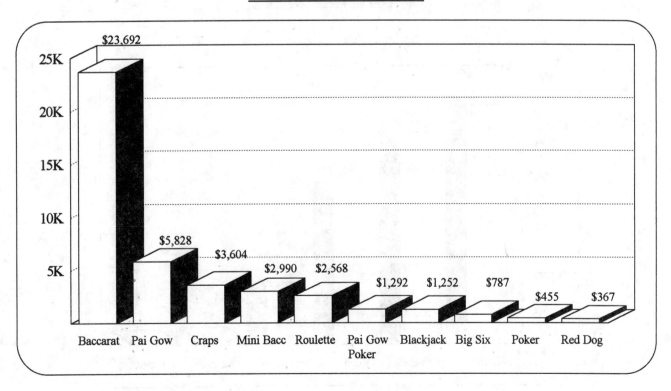

WIN PER DAY PER UNIT OTHER DEPARTMENTS LAS VEGAS STRIP 1994

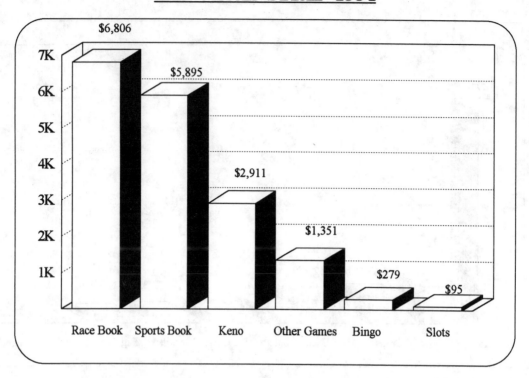

WIN PER DAY PER UNIT OTHER DEPARTMENTS NEVADA 1994

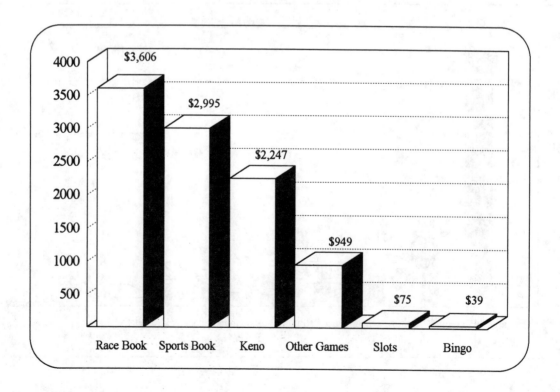

NEW JERSEY

ATLANTIC CITY GAMING STATISTICS FOR 1993

CASINOS	JAN	FEB	MAR	APR	MAY	JUN	JUL	AUG	SEP	OCT	NOV	DEC	AVG	TOTAL
	31	28	31	30	31	30	31	31	30	31	30	31		
BALLY'S GRAND														
Number of Tables	89	88	88	88	88	88	88	87	88	88	88	87	88	
Table Win	7,745,000	6,625,000	6,210,000	6,121,000	6,534,000	5,715,000	8,717,000	8,810,000	7,513,000	8,423,000	7,621,000	7,107,000	7,261,750	87,141,000
Table Win Per Day	2,807	2,689	2,276	2,319	2,395	2,165	3,195	3,267	2,846	3,088	2,887	2,635	2,714	
Table Win Percent	18.90	20.80	18.10	16.20	15.30	13.70	16.00	15.40	15.40	16.60	15.50	15.90	16.48	
Number of Slots	1,449	1,449	1,448	1,448	1,454	1,455	1,447	1,488	1,488	1,488	1,487	1,477	1,465	
Slot Win	10,089,000	8,955,000	9,925,000	11,306,000	12,490,000	10,535,000	13,248,000	13,108,000	11,903,000	11,451,000	9,632,000	7,778,000	10,868,333	130,420,000
Slot Win Per Day	225	221	221	260	277	241	295	284	267	248	216	170	244	
Slot Win Percent	10.10	9.80	9.60	10.00	9.70	9.30	9.40	9.20	9.30	9.50	9.20	8.70	9.48	
Gross Win	17,834,000	15,580,000	16,135,000	17,427,000	19,024,000	16,250,000	21,965,000	21,918,000	19,416,000	19,874,000	17,253,000	14,885,000	18,130,083	217,561,000
BALLY'S PP														
Number of Tables	97	97	97	96	95	95	110	115	115	115	115	115	105	
Table Win	7,383,000	5,989,000	6,104,000	7,331,000	7,795,000	6,712,000	8,746,000	10,013,000	7,630,000	7,607,000	8,612,000	8,937,000	7,738,250	92,859,000
Table Win Per Day	2,455	2,205	2,030	2,545	2,647	2,355	2,565	2,809	2,212	2,134	2,496	2,507	2,413	
Table Win Percent	16.20	16.00	16.30	17.30	16.20	15.60	15.40	17.70	15.30	15.40	17.80	18.50	16.48	
Number of Slots	1,897	1,896	1,897	1,907	1,923	1,933	1,924	1,996	2,000	2,000	2,000	2,009	1,948.5	
Slot Win	16,096,000	15,373,000	14,431,000	17,807,000	18,477,000	17,597,000	20,649,000	20,096,000	17,901,000	18,204,000	16,185,000	12,920,000	17,144,667	205,736,000
Slot Win Per Day	274	290	245	311	310	303	346	325	298	294	270	207	289	
Slot Win Percent	9.60	9.90	9.80	9.90	9.70	9.70	8.50	9.70	9.50	9.30	9.40	9.00	9.50	
Gross Win	23,479,000	21,362,000	20,535,000	25,138,000	26,272,000	24,309,000	29,395,000	30,109,000	25,531,000	25,811,000	24,797,000	21,857,000	24,882,917	298,595,000
CAESARS														
Number of Tables	95	95	95	95	95	86	86	86	86	123	123	123	99	
Table Win	12,068,000	9,180,000	8,656,000	10,364,000	11,565,000	9,193,000	12,158,000	13,612,000	11,329,000	9,863,000	9,938,000	8,019,000	10,495,417	125,945,000
Table Win Per Day	4,098	3,451	2,939	3,636	3,927	3,563	4,560	5,106	4,391	2,587	2,693	2,103	3,588	
Table Win Percent	16.80	16.50	14.80	17.60	15.60	13.50	16.70	19.20	17.90	15.70	17.20	13.30	16.23	
Number of Slots	1,805	1,845	1,845	1,845	1,845	1,979	1,979	1,979	1,979	2,075	2,076	2,073	1,944	
Slot Win	13,759,000	13,981,000	13,575,000	15,474,000	17,020,000	16,554,000	20,387,000	19,469,000	16,107,000	16,487,000	15,105,000	12,546,000	15,872,000	190,464,000
Slot Win Per Day	246	271	237	280	298	279	332	317	271	256	243	195	269	
Slot Win Percent	9.10	9.90	9.50	9.60	9.60	9.40	9.80	9.80	9.70	9.30	9.50	9.20	9.53	
Gross Win	25,827,000	23,161,000	22,231,000	25,838,000	28,585,000	25,747,000	32,545,000	33,081,000	27,436,000	26,350,000	25,043,000	20,565,000	26,367,417	316,409,000
CLARIDGE														
Number of Tables	67	67	67	67	67	67	67	67	67	67	67	67	67	
Table Win	3,799,000	2,708,000	3,018,000	3,348,000	3,920,000	3,526,000	3,943,000	4,072,000	3,344,000	3,188,000	3,196,000	2,893,000	3,412,917	40,955,000
Table Win Per Day	1,829	1,443	1,453	1,666	1,887	1,754	1,898	1,961	1,664	1,535	1,590	1,393	1,673	
Table Win Percent	16.20	13.70	14.80	14.60	15.20	14.30	14.00	15.10	14.80	13.80	15.20	14.40	14.68	
Number of Slots	1,332	1,332	1,343	1,350	1,350	1,350	1,350	1,350	1,356	1,361	1,368	1,368	1,351	
Slot Win	8,415,000	8,050,000	8,617,000	10,401,000	10,801,000	10,627,000	11,295,000	10,966,000	9,473,000	10,127,000	8,215,000	6,664,000	9,470,917	113,651,000
Slot Win Per Day	204	216	207	257	258	262	270	262	233	240	200	157	230	
Slot Win Percent	11.10	11.10	10.90	11.00	10.90	10.90	10.60	10.70	10.90	10.60	10.10	10.00	10.73	
Gross Win	12,214,000	10,758,000	11,635,000	13,749,000	14,721,000	14,153,000	15,238,000	15,038,000	12,817,000	13,315,000	11,411,000	9,557,000	12,883,834	154,606,000

ATLANTIC CITY GAMING STATISTICS FOR 1993

CASINOS	JAN	FEB	MAR	APR	MAY	JUN	JUL	AUG	SEP	OCT	NOV	DEC	AVG	TOTAL
	31	28	31	30	31	30	31	31	30	31	30	31		
HARRAH'S														
Number of Tables	95	93	93	93	93	93	93	93	93	80	89	89	91	
Table Win	6,244,000	6,018,000	5,900,000	6,887,000	6,414,000	5,850,000	7,581,000	6,311,000	5,868,000	6,041,000	5,120,000	4,905,000	6,094,917	73,139,000
Table Win Per Day	2,120	2,311	2,046	2,468	2,225	2,097	2,630	2,189	2,103	2,436	1,918	1,778	2,193	
Table Win Percent	14.90	16.40	16.90	17.20	15.20	15.30	15.50	14.00	16.60	16.70	14.80	16.30	15.82	
Number of Slots	1,921	1,904	1,906	1,801	1,906	1,913	1,913	1,913	1,917	1,874	1,891	1,891	1,896	
Slot Win	17,233,000	15,232,000	1,504,900	18,024,000	18,631,000	18,020,000	21,459,000	20,702,000	18,350,000	18,533,000	16,567,000	14,429,000	16,557,075	198,684,900
Slot Win Per Day	289	286	25	334	315	314	362	349	319	319	292	246	288	
Slot Win Percent	8.80	9.00	8.80	8.90	8.80	8.00	8.90	8.40	8.20	7.20	8.30	7.20	8.38	
Gross Win	23,477,000	21,250,000	7,404,900	24,911,000	25,045,000	23,870,000	29,040,000	27,013,000	24,218,000	24,574,000	21,687,000	19,334,000	22,651,992	271,823,900
RESORTS														
Number of Tables	87	87	87	76	75	80	107	106	106	106	106	106	94	
Table Win	6,703,000	7,236,000	6,135,000	4,792,000	7,955,000	6,006,000	8,926,000	8,600,000	6,674,000	6,760,000	5,920,000	5,429,000	6,761,333	81,136,000
Table Win Per Day	2,485	2,970	2,275	2,102	3,422	2,503	2,691	2,617	2,099	2,057	1,862	1,652	2,395	
Table Win Percent	13.70	18.30	15.10	11.10	16.30	13.70	14.80	14.10	13.30	14.10	13.30	12.90	14.23	
Number of Slots	1,790	1,794	1,792	1,691	1,763	1,856	1,859	1,859	1,857	1,858	1,830	1,916	1,822	
Slot Win	12,343,000	11,176,000	12,062,000	13,798,000	14,774,000	14,123,000	17,471,000	15,929,000	14,761,000	14,492,000	13,310,000	9,895,000	13,677,833	164,134,000
Slot Win Per Day	222	222	217	272	270	254	303	276	265	252	242	167	247	
Slot Win Percent	9.70	9.40	10.10	9.70	9.10	9.30	9.70	9.50	9.30	9.00	8.90	8.50	9.35	
Gross Win	19,046,000	18,412,000	18,197,000	18,590,000	22,729,000	20,129,000	26,397,000	24,529,000	21,435,000	21,252,000	19,230,000	15,324,000	20,439,167	245,270,000
SANDS														
Number of Tables	85	85	85	85	85	89	119	115	114	112	112	113	100	
Table Win	8,893,000	6,432,000	6,831,000	8,087,000	7,819,000	8,190,000	10,630,000	9,258,000	7,235,000	6,666,000	6,931,000	8,550,000	7,960,167	95,522,000
Table Win Per Day	3,375	2,703	2,592	3,171	2,967	3,067	2,882	2,597	2,116	1,920	2,063	2,441	2,658	
Table Win Percent	16.90	15.90	15.20	14.60	14.40	15.30	16.70	15.10	15.20	12.30	14.60	18.30	15.38	
Number of Slots	1,553	1,553	1,524	1,556	1,578	1,586	1,662	1,662	1,662	1,662	1,662	1,627	1,607	
Slot Win	10,987,000	9,705,000	10,605,000	12,881,000	13,714,000	12,638,000	14,923,000	15,283,000	13,707,000	13,476,000	12,026,000	9,527,000	12,456,000	149,472,000
Slot Win Per Day	228	223	224	276	280	266	290	297	275	262	241	189	254	
Slot Win Percent	9.30	9.40	8.90	9.30	9.60	9.10	8.90	9.30	9.40	9.00	9.30	9.00	9.86	
Gross Win	19,880,000	16,137,000	17,436,000	20,968,000	21,533,000	20,828,000	25,553,000	24,541,000	20,942,000	20,142,000	18,957,000	18,077,000	20,416,167	244,994,000
SHOWBOAT														
Number of Tables	70	70	69	69	69	93	98	98	98	98	98	98	86	
Table Win	6,322,000	4,360,000	4,332,000	6,216,000	6,193,000	5,942,000	7,666,000	7,006,000	5,697,000	6,077,000	5,678,000	4,337,000	5,818,833	69,826,000
Table Win Per Day	2,913	2,224	2,025	3,003	2,895	2,130	2,523	2,306	1,938	2,000	1,931	1,428	2,276	
Table Win Percent	16.30	14.20	14.50	18.30	15.60	14.70	14.40	14.80	15.00	16.80	15.40	13.10	15.26	
Number of Slots	2,067	2,071	2,102	2,123	2,078	2,390	2,411	2,411	2,422	2,405	2,409	2,379	2,272	
Slot Win	18,219,000	14,129,000	14,478,000	15,181,000	15,781,000	16,861,000	20,773,000	21,193,000	18,284,000	18,011,000	16,550,000	12,901,000	16,863,417	202,361,000
Slot Win Per Day	284	244	222	238	245	235	278	284	252	242	229	175	244	
Slot Win Percent	9.50	9.30	9.50	9.40	9.40	9.50	9.60	9.10	9.00	8.90	8.80	8.50	9.21	
Gross Win	24,541,000	18,489,000	18,810,000	21,397,000	21,974,000	22,803,000	28,439,000	28,199,000	23,981,000	24,088,000	22,228,000	17,238,000	22,682,250	272,187,000

ATLANTIC CITY GAMING STATISTICS FOR 1993

CASINOS	JAN	FEB	MAR	APR	MAY	JUN	JUL	AUG	SEP	OCT	NOV	DEC	AVG	TOTAL
	31	28	31	30	31	30	31	31	30	31	30	31		
TROPWORLD														
Number of Tables	111	99	99	83	83	85	85	85	85	85	87	89	90	
Table Win	6,247,000	5,461,000	5,782,000	6,408,000	5,940,000	5,524,000	6,686,000	6,826,000	5,885,000	5,286,000	6,613,000	5,580,000	6,019,833	72,238,000
Table Win Per Day	1,815	1,970	1,884	2,573	2,309	2,166	2,537	2,591	2,308	2,006	2,534	2,022	2,226	
Table Win Percent	14.90	15.60	17.50	17.50	15.10	15.30	14.90	16.20	16.60	15.00	17.90	15.40	15.99	
Number of Slots	2,560	2,496	2,506	2,551	2,683	2,711	2,735	2,737	2,740	2,736	2,732	2,731	2,659.83	
Slot Win	19,869,000	17,445,000	17,604,000	20,331,000	21,179,000	21,871,000	25,208,000	23,792,000	20,891,000	18,240,000	16,650,000	14,892,000	19,831,000	237,972,000
Slot Win Per Day	250	250	227	266	255	269	297	280	254	215	203	176	245	
Slot Win Percent	8.20	8.50	8.30	8.70	8.10	8.10	8.10	8.00	8.30	8.00	7.90	8.10	8.19	
Gross Win	26,116,000	22,906,000	23,386,000	26,739,000	27,119,000	27,395,000	31,894,000	30,618,000	26,776,000	23,526,000	23,263,000	20,472,000	25,850,833	310,210,000
TRUMP CASTLE														
Number of Tables	91	91	91	91	91	93	92	92	92	92	93	94	92	
Table Win	5,948,000	5,680,000	5,402,000	5,509,000	6,258,000	5,648,000	6,827,000	7,725,000	5,687,000	5,551,000	7,881,000	5,265,000	6,115,083	73,381,000
Table Win Per Day	2,108	2,229	1,915	2,018	2,218	2,024	2,394	2,709	2,061	1,946	2,825	1,807	2,188	
Table Win Percent	13.90	15.40	14.60	14.00	14.70	14.80	13.00	16.30	13.50	12.90	19.50	12.30	14.58	
Number of Slots	1,841	1,843	1,850	1,851	1,834	1,862	2,110	2,110	2,110	2,102	2,098	2,098	1,975.75	
Slot Win	13,639,000	12,479,000	13,097,000	14,248,000	14,744,000	14,051,000	17,445,000	17,151,000	15,266,000	15,376,000	13,974,000	11,522,000	14,416,000	172,992,000
Slot Win Per Day	239	242	228	257	259	252	267	262	241	236	222	177	240	
Slot Win Percent	9.20	9.40	9.40	9.30	9.20	9.30	9.40	9.50	9.50	9.40	9.40	9.00	9.33	
Gross Win	19,587,000	18,159,000	18,499,000	19,757,000	21,002,000	19,699,000	24,272,000	24,876,000	20,953,000	20,927,000	21,855,000	16,787,000	20,531,083	246,373,000
TRUMP PLAZA														
Number of Tables	97	97	90	85	83	83	83	83	83	83	85	86	87	
Table Win	8,874,000	7,020,000	7,296,000	7,041,000	8,446,000	8,664,000	7,932,000	8,871,000	7,852,000	7,238,000	7,168,000	7,188,000	7,799,167	93,590,000
Table Win Per Day	2,951	2,585	2,615	2,761	3,283	3,480	3,083	3,448	3,153	2,813	2,811	2,696	2,973	
Table Win Percent	16.10	15.90	15.00	15.00	16.00	15.10	12.50	14.80	15.70	13.90	13.90	16.00	14.99	
Number of Slots	1,736	1,761	1,760	1,830	1,829	1,831	1,831	1,831	1,830	1,830	1,839	1,834	1,811.83	
Slot Win	13,276,000	11,947,000	13,049,000	14,536,000	16,359,000	14,912,000	18,324,000	17,538,000	15,124,000	15,367,000	12,425,000	10,353,000	14,434,167	173,210,000
Slot Win Per Day	247	242	239	265	289	271	323	309	275	271	225	182	262	
Slot Win Percent	8.70	9.10	9.30	9.20	9.60	9.40	9.60	9.80	9.80	9.40	9.60	9.40	9.41	
Gross Win	22,150,000	18,967,000	20,345,000	21,577,000	24,805,000	23,576,000	26,256,000	26,409,000	22,976,000	22,605,000	19,593,000	17,541,000	22,233,333	266,800,000
TRUMP TAJ														
Number of Tables	164	164	158	162	161	166	221	222	220	220	219	221	192	
Table Win	15,158,000	12,146,000	13,711,000	13,424,000	17,385,000	12,817,000	17,684,000	17,439,000	15,131,000	15,070,000	14,816,000	16,160,000	15,078,417	180,941,000
Table Win Per Day	2,982	2,645	2,799	2,762	3,483	2,574	2,581	2,534	2,293	2,210	2,255	2,359	2,623	
Table Win Percent	17.50	16.40	16.50	15.60	19.00	15.50	15.30	16.50	15.40	16.10	15.10	17.10	16.33	
Number of Slots	2,914	3,016	3,110	3,157	3,158	3,158	3,153	3,148	3,158	3,158	3,158	3,158	3,120.5	
Slot Win	20,646,000	18,304,000	19,269,000	22,415,000	23,661,000	22,101,000	27,101,000	26,347,000	22,810,000	22,777,000	20,692,000	18,376,000	22,041,583	264,499,000
Slot Win Per Day	229	217	200	237	242	233	277	270	241	233	218	188	232	
Slot Win Percent	9.30	9.40	9.60	9.40	9.30	9.10	9.40	9.30	9.30	9.20	8.90	8.80	9.25	
Gross Win	35,804,000	30,450,000	32,980,000	35,839,000	41,046,000	34,918,000	44,785,000	43,786,000	37,941,000	37,847,000	35,508,000	34,536,000	37,120,000	445,440,000

ATLANTIC CITY GAMING STATISTICS FOR 1993

	JAN	FEB	MAR	APR	MAY	JUN	JUL	AUG	SEP	OCT	NOV	DEC	AVG	TOTAL
	31	28	31	30	31	30	31	31	30	31	30	31		
NEW JERSEY														
Number of Tables	1,148	1,133	1,119	1,090	1,085	1,118	1,249	1,249	1,247	1,269	1,282	1,288	1,190	
Table Win	95,384,000	78,855,000	79,377,000	85,528,000	96,224,000	83,787,000	107,496,000	108,543,000	89,845,000	87,770,000	89,494,000	84,370,000	90,556,083	1,086,673,000
Table Win Per Day	2,680	2,486	2,288	2,616	2,861	2,498	2,776	2,803	2,402	2,231	2,327	2,113	2,507	
Table Win Percent	16.27	16.50	15.87	15.96	16.11	14.79	15.14	16.07	15.55	15.16	15.97	15.79	15.76	
Number of Slots	22,865	22,960	23,083	23,110	23,401	24,024	24,374	24,484	24,519	24,549	24,550	24,561	23,873	
Slot Win	174,571,000	156,776,000	148,216,900	186,402,000	197,631,000	189,890,000	228,283,000	221,574,000	194,577,000	192,541,000	171,331,000	141,803,000	183,632,992	2,203,595,900
Slot Win Per Day	246	244	207	269	272	263	302	292	265	253	233	186	253	
Slot Win Percent	9.27	9.41	9.46	9.46	9.33	9.16	9.25	9.27	9.25	8.98	9.03	8.69	9.26	
Gross Win	269,955,000	235,631,000	227,593,900	271,930,000	293,855,000	273,677,000	335,779,000	330,117,000	284,422,000	280,311,000	260,825,000	226,173,000	274,189,075	3,290,268,900

ATLANTIC CITY GAMING STATISTICS FOR 1994

	JAN	FEB	MAR	APR	MAY	JUN	JUL	AUG	SEP	OCT	NOV	DEC	AVG	TOTAL
	31	28	31	30	31	30	31	31	30	31	30	31		
BALLY'S GRAND														
Number of Tables	88	88	88	88	88	88	88	88	88	88	88	88	88	
Table Win	6,812,000	5,096,000	7,142,000	8,513,000	8,462,000	6,880,000	9,737,000	7,966,000	7,351,000	8,549,000	7,647,000	9,678,000	7,819,417	93,833,000
Table Win Per Day	2,497	2,068	2,618	3,225	3,102	2,606	3,569	2,920	2,784	3,134	2,897	3,548	2,914	
Table Win Percent	15.62	12.90	15.80	18.70	17.50	15.00	16.80	15.50	15.20	17.60	17.40	21.50	16.63	
Number of Slots	1,487	1,507	1,507	1,507	1,389	1,404	1,404	1,404	1,404	1,408	1,408	1,407	1,436	
Slot Win	7,703,000	8,784,000	10,307,000	11,393,000	10,973,000	11,850,000	13,969,000	13,371,000	14,123,000	12,287,000	11,405,000	8,890,000	11,254,583	135,055,000
Slot Win Per Day	167	208	221	252	255	281	321	307	335	282	270	204	259	
Slot Win Percent	9.20	9.10	9.00	9.00	8.70	8.70	8.40	8.40	8.90	8.30	8.60	7.70	8.67	
Gross Win	14,515,000	13,880,000	17,449,000	19,906,000	19,435,000	18,730,000	23,706,000	21,337,000	21,474,000	20,836,000	19,052,000	18,568,000	19,074,000	228,888,000
BALLY'S PP														
Number of Tables	115	115	115	115	115	123	125	125	125	125	125	125	121	
Table Win	7,670,000	6,637,000	7,837,000	8,633,000	8,004,000	7,729,000	10,836,000	9,814,000	8,475,000	8,695,000	8,612,000	8,787,000	8,477,417	101,729,000
Table Win Per Day	2,151	2,061	2,198	2,502	2,245	2,095	2,796	2,533	2,260	2,244	2,297	2,268	2,304	
Table Win Percent	18.03	16.20	17.00	17.50	15.60	17.30	17.30	17.20	17.00	17.70	17.60	17.80	17.19	
Number of Slots	2,000	2,065	2,113	2,138	2,138	2,136	2,286	2,266	2,265	2,265	2,264	2,232	2,181	
Slot Win	12,663,000	14,358,000	17,379,000	18,639,000	19,102,000	19,036,000	22,710,000	22,447,000	20,971,000	20,774,000	18,877,000	14,609,000	18,463,750	221,565,000
Slot Win Per Day	204	248	265	291	288	297	320	320	309	296	278	211	277	
Slot Win Percent	9.10	9.00	9.00	9.20	9.10	9.00	8.90	9.10	8.80	8.80	9.00	8.30	8.94	
Gross Win	20,333,000	20,995,000	25,216,000	27,272,000	27,106,000	26,765,000	33,546,000	32,261,000	29,446,000	29,469,000	27,489,000	23,396,000	26,941,167	323,294,000
CAESARS														
Number of Tables	123	123	121	121	107	117	118	118	118	118	118	118	118	
Table Win	11,909,000	6,886,000	9,052,000	8,597,000	10,323,000	10,588,000	14,152,000	14,387,000	8,951,000	13,318,000	10,097,000	8,503,000	10,563,583	126,763,000
Table Win Per Day	3,123	1,999	2,413	2,368	3,112	3,017	3,869	3,933	2,529	3,641	2,852	2,324	2,932	
Table Win Percent	19.50	12.60	14.70	13.20	14.90	14.80	16.70	17.80	13.10	17.20	14.80	12.70	15.17	
Number of Slots	2,073	2,076	2,093	2,103	2,120	2,153	2,155	2,155	1,917	2,035	2,039	2,039	2,080	
Slot Win	11,563,000	14,136,000	16,289,000	18,418,000	18,310,000	17,851,000	21,520,000	21,604,000	19,785,000	19,070,000	17,888,000	16,083,000	17,709,750	212,517,000
Slot Win Per Day	180	243	251	292	279	276	322	323	344	302	292	254	280	
Slot Win Percent	9.00	9.40	9.60	9.60	9.20	9.10	8.90	8.70	9.30	8.40	8.50	7.70	8.95	
Gross Win	23,472,000	21,022,000	25,341,000	27,015,000	28,633,000	28,439,000	35,672,000	35,991,000	28,736,000	32,388,000	27,985,000	24,586,000	28,273,333	339,280,000
CLARIDGE														
Number of Tables	67	67	67	67	63	79	81	80	80	82	82	82	75	
Table Win	2,678,000	2,625,000	3,256,000	3,241,000	3,078,000	3,390,000	4,294,000	4,247,000	2,891,000	3,293,000	3,150,000	2,912,000	3,254,583	39,055,000
Table Win Per Day	1,289	1,399	1,568	1,612	1,576	1,430	1,710	1,713	1,205	1,295	1,280	1,146	1,435	
Table Win Percent	14.80	14.10	15.50	14.60	13.30	14.20	13.90	14.90	11.70	14.00	14.30	14.00	14.11	
Number of Slots	1,368	1,377	1,393	1,377	1,374	1,312	1,896	1,896	1,896	1,896	1,887	1,887	1,630	
Slot Win	5,908,000	7,042,000	8,603,000	9,602,000	10,132,000	9,946,000	12,981,000	12,130,000	11,066,000	11,558,000	10,204,000	7,738,000	9,742,500	116,910,000
Slot Win Per Day	139	183	199	232	238	253	221	206	195	197	180	132	198	
Slot Win Percent	9.90	10.20	10.20	10.30	10.40	10.50	10.20	9.70	9.70	9.60	9.60	9.20	9.96	
Gross Win	8,586,000	9,667,000	11,859,000	12,843,000	13,210,000	13,336,000	17,275,000	16,377,000	13,957,000	14,851,000	13,354,000	10,650,000	12,997,083	155,965,000

ATLANTIC CITY GAMING STATISTICS FOR 1994

	JAN	FEB	MAR	APR	MAY	JUN	JUL	AUG	SEP	OCT	NOV	DEC	AVG	TOTAL
	31	28	31	30	31	30	31	31	30	31	30	31		
HARRAH'S														
Number of Tables	80	84	88	88	88	89	97	97	97	97	96	97	92	
Table Win	4,628,000	4,273,000	5,184,000	5,061,000	5,478,000	4,456,000	6,368,000	6,685,000	5,355,000	5,506,000	5,828,000	6,249,000	5,422,583	65,071,000
Table Win Per Day	1,866	1,817	1,900	1,917	2,008	1,669	2,118	2,223	1,840	1,831	2,024	2,078	1,941	
Table Win Percent	15.40	14.30	15.20	15.30	15.80	13.00	14.60	15.80	14.90	15.00	17.40	20.10	15.57	
Number of Slots	1,696	1,676	1,679	1,850	1,848	1,849	1,858	1,873	1,887	1,900	1,900	1,962	1,832	
Slot Win	14,150,000	15,440,000	17,222,000	18,381,000	19,120,000	19,291,000	22,884,000	22,316,000	20,963,000	21,606,000	18,587,000	16,743,000	18,891,916.67	226,703,000
Slot Win Per Day	269	329	331	331	334	348	397	384	370	367	326	275	338	
Slot Win Percent	7.80	7.50	8.40	8.20	7.80	8.40	8.30	8.20	8.10	8.10	8.00	7.80	8.05	
Gross Win	18,778,000	19,713,000	22,406,000	23,442,000	24,598,000	23,747,000	29,252,000	29,001,000	26,318,000	27,112,000	24,415,000	22,992,000	24,314,500	291,774,000
RESORTS														
Number of Tables	106	106	106	106	106	112	113	113	113	113	104	103	108	
Table Win	6,120,000	5,079,000	5,908,000	6,979,000	5,893,000	6,398,000	6,474,000	7,753,000	6,103,000	5,876,000	6,194,000	7,016,000	6,316,083	75,793,000
Table Win Per Day	1,862	1,711	1,798	2,195	1,793	1,904	1,848	2,213	1,800	1,677	1,985	2,197	1,915	
Table Win Percent	14.90	12.50	12.20	15.20	12.80	17.50	12.40	16.20	14.10	13.30	14.80	16.90	14.40	
Number of Slots	1,944	1,954	1,959	1,958	1,957	1,957	1,955	1,947	1,956	1,964	1,949	1,944	1,954	
Slot Win	10,001,000	11,566,000	14,895,000	15,475,000	15,295,000	14,761,000	16,759,000	16,873,000	15,521,000	15,883,000	14,177,000	12,778,000	14,498,667	173,984,000
Slot Win Per Day	166	211	245	263	252	251	277	280	265	261	242	212	244	
Slot Win Percent	8.40	8.80	9.10	9.20	9.50	9.50	9.30	9.50	9.20	9.30	9.30	9.10	9.18	
Gross Win	16,121,000	16,645,000	20,803,000	22,454,000	21,188,000	21,159,000	23,233,000	24,626,000	21,624,000	21,759,000	20,371,000	19,794,000	20,814,750	249,777,000
SANDS														
Number of Tables	113	112	112	113	108	94	128	130	128	128	128	128	119	
Table Win	7,424,000	6,879,000	8,487,000	6,275,000	7,722,000	8,059,000	11,418,000	11,987,000	7,656,000	7,494,000	7,305,000	8,578,000	8,273,667	99,284,000
Table Win Per Day	2,119	2,194	2,444	1,851	2,306	2,858	2,878	2,974	1,994	1,889	1,902	2,162	2,298	
Table Win Percent	17.50	18.10	18.80	13.40	14.30	15.90	16.20	18.70	14.20	13.70	13.40	17.60	15.98	
Number of Slots	1,652	1,635	1,630	1,627	1,627	1,616	1,972	1,992	1,996	2,013	2,016	2,016	1,816	
Slot Win	8,550,000	10,449,000	12,345,000	12,928,000	12,823,000	12,453,000	17,605,000	15,903,000	14,619,000	14,021,000	13,062,000	10,894,000	12,971,000	155,652,000
Slot Win Per Day	167	228	244	265	254	257	288	258	244	225	216	174	235	
Slot Win Percent	8.40	9.10	9.10	8.80	9.00	9.00	9.10	8.70	9.00	8.80	8.60	8.40	9.86	
Gross Win	15,974,000	17,328,000	20,832,000	19,203,000	20,545,000	20,512,000	29,023,000	27,890,000	22,275,000	21,515,000	20,367,000	19,472,000	21,244,667	254,936,000
SHOWBOAT														
Number of Tables	102	102	102	103	116	117	121	121	121	121	120	122	114	
Table Win	5,389,000	4,587,000	5,936,000	5,554,000	6,689,000	5,860,000	7,417,000	7,410,000	5,804,000	6,715,000	6,112,000	7,211,000	6,223,667	74,684,000
Table Win Per Day	1,704	1,606	1,877	1,797	1,860	1,670	1,977	1,975	1,599	1,790	1,698	1,907	1,788	
Table Win Percent	16.30	13.40	16.20	13.70	16.80	16.20	15.60	16.10	13.60	16.30	14.90	17.30	15.53	
Number of Slots	2,418	2,382	2,390	2,389	2,497	2,933	3,018	3,024	3,026	3,026	3,024	3,025	2,762.67	
Slot Win	13,305,000	14,921,000	16,871,000	18,128,000	18,753,000	19,432,000	22,847,000	21,708,000	20,330,000	20,008,000	18,355,000	15,004,000	18,305,167	219,662,000
Slot Win Per Day	177	224	228	253	242	221	244	232	224	213	202	160	218	
Slot Win Percent	8.70	8.80	8.60	8.70	8.60	8.90	8.70	8.50	8.50	8.50	8.40	7.80	8.56	
Gross Win	18,694,000	19,508,000	22,807,000	23,682,000	25,442,000	25,292,000	30,264,000	29,118,000	26,134,000	26,723,000	24,467,000	22,215,000	24,528,833	294,346,000

ATLANTIC CITY GAMING STATISTICS FOR 1994

	JAN	FEB	MAR	APR	MAY	JUN	JUL	AUG	SEP	OCT	NOV	DEC	AVG	TOTAL
	31	28	31	30	31	30	31	31	30	31	30	31		
TROPWORLD														
Number of Tables	92	95	93	93	93	101	101	101	101	101	99	99	97	
Table Win	5,767,000	5,871,000	6,078,000	6,061,000	5,413,000	5,363,000	7,509,000	7,194,000	5,434,000	4,975,000	6,289,000	5,519,000	5,956,083	71,473,000
Table Win Per Day	2,022	2,207	2,108	2,172	1,878	1,770	2,398	2,298	1,793	1,589	2,118	1,798	2,013	
Table Win Percent	17.40	17.50	16.90	16.00	14.20	14.70	15.20	15.90	13.90	12.30	16.70	14.60	15.44	
Number of Slots	2,717	2,722	2,773	2,800	2,799	2,791	2,783	2,800	2,797	2,800	2,800	2,797	2,782	
Slot Win	14,908,000	15,418,000	17,823,000	19,050,000	18,324,000	20,026,000	22,730,000	22,925,000	20,623,000	19,913,000	19,140,000	17,755,000	19,052,917	228,635,000
Slot Win Per Day	177	202	207	227	211	239	263	264	246	229	228	205	225	
Slot Win Percent	7.80	7.90	8.10	8.00	7.50	8.30	7.70	7.90	7.60	7.70	7.50	7.40	7.78	
Gross Win	20,675,000	21,289,000	23,901,000	25,111,000	23,737,000	25,389,000	30,239,000	30,119,000	26,057,000	24,888,000	25,429,000	23,274,000	25,009,000	300,108,000
TRUMP CASTLE														
Number of Tables	94	94	94	94	94	94	94	94	103	100	100	100	96	
Table Win	12,078,000	5,140,000	5,714,000	7,527,000	6,383,000	5,321,000	8,787,000	7,370,000	5,962,000	6,660,000	3,836,000	5,820,000	6,716,500	80,598,000
Table Win Per Day	4,145	1,953	1,961	2,669	2,190	1,887	3,015	2,529	1,929	2,148	1,279	1,877	2,299	
Table Win Percent	28.60	14.90	15.20	18.80	15.70	14.90	15.10	16.20	15.00	15.80	9.50	17.60	16.44	
Number of Slots	2,078	2,053	1,961	1,957	1,900	2,123	2,123	2,115	2,114	2,113	2,121	2,122	2,065	
Slot Win	12,190,000	12,026,000	14,672,000	15,506,000	15,655,000	15,319,000	18,332,000	16,759,000	15,440,000	14,801,000	13,968,000	12,701,000	14,780,750	177,369,000
Slot Win Per Day	189	209	241	264	266	241	279	256	243	226	220	193	236	
Slot Win Percent	9.00	9.10	9.20	9.20	9.30	9.00	9.10	8.90	9.10	9.00	8.90	8.70	9.04	
Gross Win	24,268,000	17,166,000	20,386,000	23,033,000	22,038,000	20,640,000	27,119,000	24,129,000	21,402,000	21,461,000	17,804,000	18,521,000	21,497,250	257,967,000
TRUMP PLAZA														
Number of Tables	86	88	89	89	89	89	89	89	88	88	89	91	89	
Table Win	7,272,000	5,447,000	8,088,000	8,074,000	6,462,000	8,215,000	9,217,000	9,026,000	7,483,000	8,253,000	7,991,000	7,242,000	7,730,833	92,770,000
Table Win Per Day	2,728	2,211	2,932	3,024	2,342	3,077	3,341	3,271	2,834	3,025	2,993	2,567	2,862	
Table Win Percent	15.50	14.00	17.80	16.80	13.50	15.90	14.90	15.40	14.60	15.40	17.10	14.80	15.48	
Number of Slots	1,830	1,833	1,807	2,016	2,187	2,188	2,188	2,187	2,188	2,184	2,116	2,189	2,076	
Slot Win	10,022,000	11,201,000	12,522,000	14,601,000	15,676,000	14,958,000	17,746,000	17,331,000	15,313,000	14,925,000	14,347,000	11,674,000	14,193,000	170,316,000
Slot Win Per Day	177	218	224	241	231	228	262	256	233	220	226	172	224	
Slot Win Percent	9.20	9.00	8.70	9.20	9.40	9.40	9.10	9.10	8.90	9.00	9.00	8.50	9.04	
Gross Win	17,294,000	16,648,000	20,610,000	22,675,000	22,138,000	23,173,000	26,963,000	26,357,000	22,796,000	23,178,000	22,338,000	18,916,000	21,923,833	263,086,000
TRUMP TAJ														
Number of Tables	212	213	215	214	210	206	241	241	240	237	233	227	224	
Table Win	15,536,000	12,894,000	14,482,000	14,555,000	16,090,000	13,941,000	18,950,000	18,778,000	18,683,000	17,826,000	14,653,000	24,828,000	16,768,000	201,216,000
Table Win Per Day	2,364	2,162	2,173	2,267	2,472	2,256	2,536	2,513	2,595	2,426	2,096	3,528	2,449	
Table Win Percent	17.30	15.00	15.70	14.10	15.80	14.90	15.50	16.70	17.40	17.50	15.30	21.50	16.39	
Number of Slots	3,158	3,158	3,135	3,126	3,189	3,256	3,348	3,398	3,400	3,382	3,323	3,421	3,275	
Slot Win	17,040,000	18,181,000	21,896,000	22,292,000	23,316,000	21,645,000	26,779,000	25,916,000	23,149,000	22,707,000	18,567,000	17,625,000	21,592,750	259,113,000
Slot Win Per Day	174	206	225	238	236	222	258	246	227	217	186	166	217	
Slot Win Percent	8.70	8.90	9.10	8.90	9.20	8.70	8.60	8.80	8.80	8.90	8.60	8.60	8.82	
Gross Win	32,576,000	31,075,000	36,378,000	36,847,000	39,406,000	35,586,000	45,729,000	44,694,000	41,832,000	40,533,000	33,220,000	42,453,000	38,360,750	460,329,000

ATLANTIC CITY GAMING STATISTICS FOR 1994

	JAN	FEB	MAR	APR	MAY	JUN	JUL	AUG	SEP	OCT	NOV	DEC	AVG	TOTAL
	31	28	31	30	31	30	31	31	30	31	30	31		
NEW JERSEY														
Number of Tables	1,278	1,287	1,290	1,291	1,277	1,309	1,396	1,397	1,402	1,398	1,382	1,380	1,341	
Table Win	93,283,000	71,414,000	87,164,000	89,070,000	89,997,000	86,200,000	115,159,000	112,617,000	90,148,000	97,160,000	87,714,000	102,343,000	93,522,417	1,122,269,000
Table Win Per Day	2,355	1,982	2,180	2,300	2,273	2,195	2,661	2,600	2,143	2,242	2,116	2,392	2,287	
Table Win Percent	18.48	14.8	16.03	15.65	15.23	15.44	15.62	16.63	15.08	16.03	15.54	18.15	16.06	
Number of Slots	24,421	24,438	24,440	24,848	25,025	25,718	26,986	27,057	26,846	26,986	26,847	27,041	25,888	
Slot Win	138,003,000	153,522,000	180,824,000	194,413,000	197,479,000	196,568,000	236,862,000	229,283,000	211,903,000	207,553,000	188,577,000	162,494,000	191,456,750	2,297,481,000
Slot Win Per Day	182	224	239	261	255	255	283	273	263	248	234	194	243	
Slot Win Percent	8.67	8.80	8.95	8.96	8.91	8.96	8.79	8.74	8.76	8.47	8.60	8.20	8.82	
Gross Win	231,286,000	224,936,000	267,988,000	283,483,000	287,476,000	282,768,000	352,021,000	341,900,000	302,051,000	304,713,000	276,291,000	264,837,000	284,979,167	3,419,750,000

TABLE GAMES AND SLOT WIN COMPARISON 1993-1994

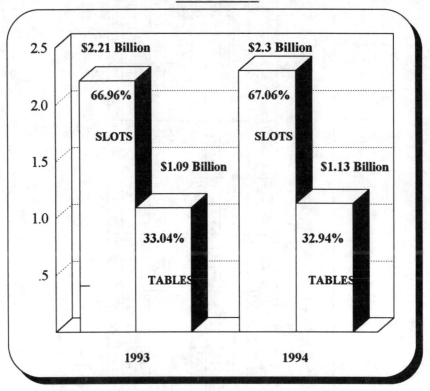

TOTAL WIN COMPARISON FOR 1994

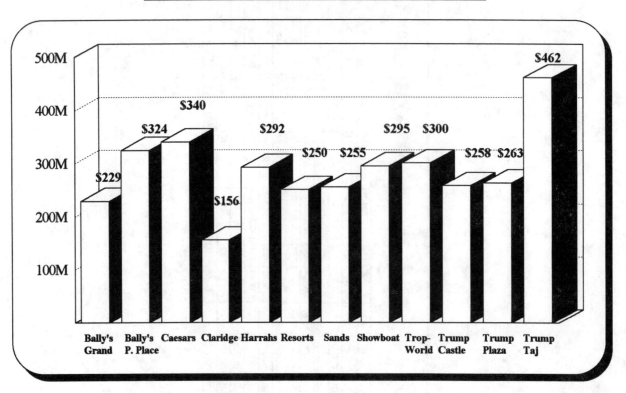

GAMING STATISTICS AND GRAPHICS

SOUTH DAKOTA

SOUTH DAKOTA GAMING STATISTICS FOR 1993

DEADWOOD	JAN	FEB	MAR	APR	MAY	JUN	JUL	AUG	SEP	OCT	NOV	DEC	AVG/TOT
Days	31	28	31	30	31	30	31	31	30	31	30	31	61
Blackjack Tables	58	75	55	59	62	62	62	62	64	59	58	59	61
Blackjack Win	221,883	236,525	230,680	227,581	256,194	306,470	432,836	436,977	316,569	288,334	175,253	204,821	3,334,123
Win Per Day/Unit	123	113	135	129	133	165	225	227	160	158	101	112	148
Win Percent	20.86	21.11	19.95	20.11	18.97	18.64	19.2	19.82	19.05	21.17	18.91	20.62	19.87
Poker Tables	21	19	15	21	20	20	19	18	19	19	19	20	19
Poker Win	151,944	127,037	99,149	143,397	145,265	149,886	182,094	190,684	155,773	138,112	118,076	112,412	1,713,829
Win Per Day/Unit	233	239	213	228	234	250	309	342	264	234	207	181	245
Win Percent													
Number of Tables	79	94	70	80	82	82	81	80	83	78	77	79	80
Table Win	373,827	363,562	329,829	370,978	401,459	456,356	614,930	627,661	472,342	426,446	293,329	317,233	5,047,952
Win Per Day/Unit	153	138	152	155	158	186	245	253	190	176	127	130	172
Table Win Percent	20.86	21.11	19.95	20.11	18.97	18.64	19.2	19.82	19.05	21.17	18.91	20.62	19.87
Number of Slots	1,959	1,947	1,954	1,957	1,944	1,957	1,960	2,019	2,035	1,983	1,993	2,009	1,976
Slot Win	2,112,941	2,374,020	2,981,110	2,755,748	3,129,298	3,801,830	4,753,959	4,475,612	4,487,361	3,294,515	2,142,082	1,985,725	38,294,201
Slot Win Per Day/Unit	35	44	49	47	52	65	78	72	71	54	36	32	53
Slot Win Percent	9.80	9.76	9.59	9.94	9.51	9.07	9.35	9.76	9.90	9.79	9.41	9.74	9.64
Gross Win	2,486,768	2,737,582	3,310,939	3,126,726	3,530,757	4,258,186	5,368,889	5,103,273	4,959,703	3,720,961	2,435,411	2,302,958	43,342,153

SOUTH DAKOTA GAMING STATISTICS FOR 1994

DEADWOOD	JAN	FEB	MAR	APR	MAY	JUN	JUL	AUG	SEP	OCT	NOV	DEC	AVG/TOT
Days	31	28	31	30	31	30	31	31	30	31	30	31	
Blackjack Tables	59	59	61	59	59	61	59	58	58	58	58	57	59
Blackjack Win	230,009	253,973	258,812	222,453	253,194	270,333	386,304	425,388	297,513	295,817	208,111	209,671	3,311,578
Win Per Day/Unit	126	139	137	126	138	148	211	237	165	165	120	119	153
Win Percent	20.8	21.71	20.59	18.67	18.79	17.62	18.02	18.97	18.34	20.86	19.91	20.74	19.59
Poker Tables	20	20	17	20	20	18	17	17	17	17	19	17	18
Poker Win	126,095	122,823	115,577	127,769	117,669	121,215	169,262	177,285	138,890	134,707	115,449	113,516	1,580,257
Win Per Day/Unit	203	198	219	213	190	224	321	336	264	256	203	215	237
Number of Tables	79	79	78	79	79	79	76	75	75	75	77	74	77
Table Win	356,104	376,796	374,389	350,222	370,863	391,548	555,566	602,673	436,403	430,524	323,560	323,187	4,891,835
Win Per Day/Unit	145	170	155	148	151	165	236	259	194	185	140	141	174
Table Win Percent	20.8	21.71	20.59	18.67	18.79	17.62	18.02	18.97	18.34	20.86	19.91	20.74	19.59
Number of Slots	1,984	1,994	2,034	2,027	2,025	2,098	2,226	2,194	2,198	2,170	2,197	2,255	2,117
Slot Win	2,228,124	2,137,365	2,994,817	2,814,295	3,278,205	3,931,609	4,960,827	5,030,355	4,888,835	3,841,760	2,646,438	2,242,411	40,995,041
Slot Win Per Day	36	38	48	46	52	62	72	74	74	57	40	32	53
Slot Win Percent	9.88	8.60	10.08	9.85	9.86	9.79	9.61	9.98	9.30	9.48	8.70	8.98	9.51
Gross Win	2,584,228	2,514,161	3,369,206	3,164,517	3,649,068	4,323,157	5,516,393	5,633,028	5,325,238	4,272,284	2,969,998	2,565,598	45,886,876

TABLE & SLOT WIN COMPARISON
SOUTH DAKOTA

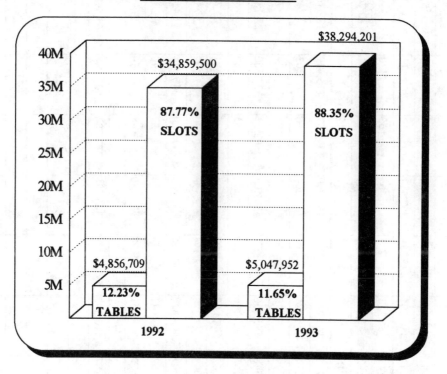

$34,859,500

$38,294,201

87.77%
SLOTS

88.35%
SLOTS

$4,856,709

$5,047,952

12.23%
TABLES

11.65%
TABLES

1992

1993

40M
35M
30M
25M
20M
15M
10M
5M

TABLE & SLOT WIN COMPARISON
SOUTH DAKOTA

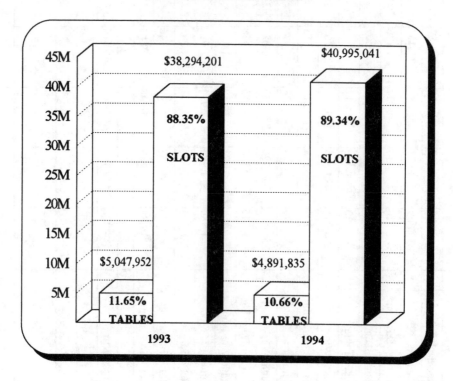

$38,294,201

$40,995,041

88.35%

89.34%

SLOTS

SLOTS

$5,047,952

$4,891,835

11.65%
TABLES

10.66%
TABLES

1993

1994

45M
40M
35M
30M
25M
20M
15M
10M
5M

OTHER GAMING AREAS

OTHER GAMING AREAS FOR 1994
Gaming Statistics

CASINO	JAN 31	FEB 28	MAR 31	APR 30	MAY 31	JUN 30	JUL 31	AUG 31	SEP 30	OCT 31	NOV 30	DEC 31	AVG/TOT
Foxwoods													
Number of Slots								3,850	3,854	3,854	3,864	3,864	3,857
Slot Handle								581,082,265	514,049,767	556,042,419	518,385,922	461,187,385	2,630,747,758
Slot Win								48,747,246	44,585,109	45,908,493	41,585,458	35,320,609	216,146,915
Slot Win %								8.40	8.70	8.30	8.00	7.90	8.26
Windsor													
Number of Tables								65	65	66	68	68	66
Number of Slots								1,703	1,703	1,715	1,706	1,712	1,708
Gross Revenue								45,000,000	43,600,000	47,600,000	43,500,000	41,700,000	221,400,000
Louisiana													
Isle of Capri								13,500,000	12,900,000	12,800,000	12,200,000	13,090,000	64,490,000
Harrah's								8,300,000	8,300,000	8,400,000	8,200,000	7,320,000	40,520,000
Horseshoe								9,900,000	12,500,000	10,900,000	10,200,000	10,620,000	54,120,000
Players								10,900,000	13,100,000	12,000,000	12,400,000	12,730,000	61,130,000
Star								8,500,000	6,900,000	6,700,000	6,500,000	5,910,000	34,510,000
Hilton Queen								6,300,000	6,300,000	5,800,000	7,100,000	6,750,000	32,250,000
Boomtown								6,300,000	6,400,000	6,100,000	6,500,000	5,680,000	30,980,000
Belle of Baton Rouge									180,000	6,800,000	6,600,000	6,450,000	20,030,000
Treasure Chest									7,600,000	9,000,000	9,000,000	9,020,000	34,620,000
Casino Rouge												470,000	470,000
Gross Revenues								63,700,000	74,180,000	78,500,000	78,700,000	78,040,000	373,120,000
Missouri													
Argosy							4,386,948	5,366,862	5,579,796	4,340,064	4,018,056	5,072,085	24,376,863
St. Charles							2,915,132	2,532,013	2,952,462	3,544,576	4,015,546	7,180,926	20,225,523
St. Joseph							1,072,459	1,351,236	1,305,770	1,239,298	1,038,139	1,682,394	6,616,837
Admiral							2,949,879	2,831,571	3,217,222	3,284,482	3,109,366	6,722,010	19,164,651
Harrahs									1,126,040	5,388,329	6,480,150	8,151,617	21,146,136
Gross Revenues							11,324,418	12,081,682	14,181,290	17,796,749	18,661,257	28,809,032	91,530,010

TABLE WIN & SLOT DROP COMPARISON PUERTO RICO

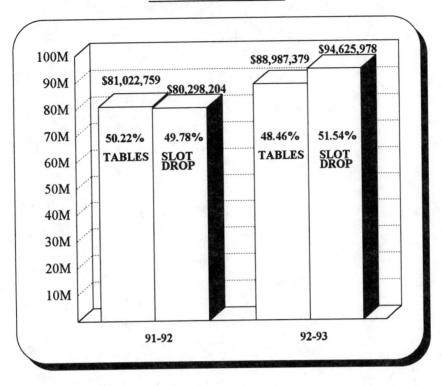

TABLE & SLOT WIN COMPARISON PUERTO RICO 1991-92

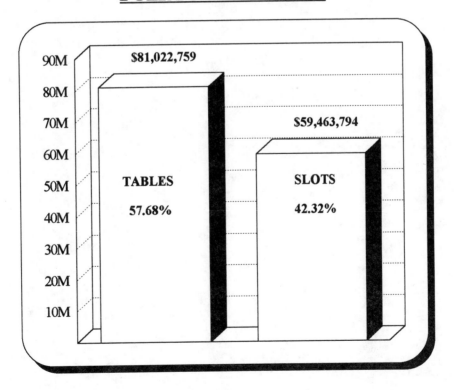

CASINO GAMING FORMS

TABLE GAMES

IRREGULARITY NOTIFICATION SLIP

LOGO

CASINO EMPLOYEE:

AMOUNT: | **LOCATION:**

FORM TYPE: | **NUMBER:**

| DATE | TIME | SHIFT |
| | | D   S   G |

SUPERVISOR:

EXPLANATION:

TABLE REQUEST

LOGO

FILL

DATE	TIME	SHIFT		
		D	S	G

GAME	PIT	TABLE	DENOM.	AMOUNT
BACCARAT			$5,000.00	
BIG SIX			$1,000.00	
BLACKJACK			$500.00	
CARIB STUD			$100.00	
CRAPS			$25.00	
MINI-BACC			$5.00	
PAI GOW PK			$2.50	
RED DOG			$1.00	
ROULETTE			$1 TOKENS	
SIC BO			$0.50	
OTHER			$0.25	
			TOTAL >	

CASINO SUPERVISOR	LIC. NO.
SECURITY	LIC. NO.

1. CAGE   2. DROP BOX

TABLE REQUEST

LOGO

CREDIT

DATE	TIME	SHIFT		
		D	S	G

GAME	PIT	TABLE	DENOM.	AMOUNT
BACCARAT			$5,000.00	
BIG SIX			$1,000.00	
BLACKJACK			$500.00	
CARIB STUD			$100.00	
CRAPS			$25.00	
MINI-BACC			$5.00	
PAI GOW PK			$2.50	
RED DOG			$1.00	
ROULETTE			$1 TOKENS	
SIC BO			$0.50	
OTHER			$0.25	
			TOTAL >	

CASINO SUPERVISOR	LIC. NO.
SECURITY	LIC. NO.
DEALER	LIC. NO.

1. CAGE   2. DROP BOX

TABLE INVENTORY

LOGO

SHIFT		DATE	
GAME		GAME NO.	

DESCRIPTION	AMOUNT					
$5,000.00						
$1,000.00						
$500.00						
$100.00						
$25.00						
$5.00						
$2.50						
$1.00						
TOKENS $1.00						
$0.25						
TOTAL $						

SIGNATURES

OUTGOING   ON COMING

_____   _____
Dealer/Boxperson   Dealer/Boxperson

_____   _____
Dealer/Boxperson   Dealer/Boxperson

WHITE - CLOSER   **YELLOW - OPENER**

CARIBBEAN STUD POKER

LOGO   LOGO

HARD COUNT
METER READING

SHIFT: D   S   G

HARD COUNT: _____

METER READING: _____

_____

SUPERVISOR SIGNATURE

1. DROP BOX   2. ACCOUNTING

CARIBBEAN STUD POKER

REQUEST FOR JACKPOT

DATE	SHIFT	TIME	PIT/TABLE

AM0UNT PAID ON GAME $ _____

AMOUNT PAID FROM CAGE $ _____

DEALER SIGNATURE	LIC. NO

SUPERVISOR SIGNATURE	LIC. NO

SHIFT MANAGER SIGNATURE	LIC. NO

LOGO

SUPERVISOR WORKSHEET

DATE	SHIFT D S G	SUPERVISOR

TABLE	$500	$100	$25	FILLS	CREDITS	MARKER	DROP
OPENER							
							TOTAL DROP
OPENER							
							TOTAL DROP
OPENER							
							TOTAL DROP
OPENER							
							TOTAL DROP

PLAYER RATING FORM

LOGO

LAST NAME		FIRST NAME		M.I

DATE	DATE OF BIRTH	ACCOUNT NUMBER

CREDIT LINE	CREDIT USED	CREDIT AVAILABLE

PIT/GAME/TABLE	POSITION	SHIFT			TIME IN		TIME OUT		SPEED			PLAYER TYPE	AVERAGE BET
		D	S	G	A	P	A	P	S	M	F		
CASH		MONEY PLAY		CHECKS		MARKERS						1	
												2	
												3	
												4	
												CHECKS OUT	WIN LOSS
TOTAL BUY													

CLERK SIGNATURE	LIC. NO.

SUPERVISOR SIGNATURE	LIC. NO.

PIT BOSS SIGNATURE	LIC. NO.

GAME CODES & PLAYER TYPES

		1 ADVANCED 0 MISTAKES	2 GOOD 1-2 MISTAKES	3 AVERAGE 3-4 MISTAKES	4 POOR 5+ MISTAKES
J	BLACKJACK				
R	ROULETTE	1 INSIDE	2 OUTSIDE		
P	POKER				
CS	CARIBBEAN STUD POKER				
B	BACCARAT				
C	CRAPS	1 PASS/DON'T PASS LINE COME/DON'T COME PLACE 6 & 8	2 ACROSS BETS, INSIDE, OUTSIDE, BUY, LAY, PLACE BETS	3 PROPOSITION BETS, HARDWAYS, FIELD BETS	
	GAME SPEED	S SLOW	M MEDIUM OR AVERAGE	F FAST	

NAME

STREET ADDRESS

CITY   STATE   ZIP CODE

TELEPHONE   SOCIAL SEC. NUM.   DATE OF BIRTH

COMMENTS

PLAYER RATING FORM

LOGO

LAST NAME   FIRST NAME   M.I.

DATE   DATE OF BIRTH   ACCOUNT NUMBER

CREDIT LINE   CREDIT USED   CREDIT AVAILABLE

PIT GAME	S H I F T	TIME IN	TIME OUT	BUY-IN CASH	CHIPS	CREDIT	S P E E D	P T	AVG. BET	CHECKS OUT	WIN/ LOSS	SUPERVISOR INITIAL & LICENSE
TABLE NO.												PIT BOSS INITIAL & LICENSE
D							S					
S	A	P					M					
G	A	P					F					
D							S					
S	A	P					M					
G	A	P					F					
D							S					
S	A	P					M					
G	A	P					F					
D							S					
S	A	P					M					
G	A	P					F					
D							S					
S	A	P					M					
G	A	P					F					
D							S					
S	A	P					M					
G	A	P					F					
D							S					
S	A	P					M					
G	A	P					F					

STREET ADDRESS

PLAYER ACTIVITY SHEET

SUPERVISOR	SHIFT			PIT				DATE
	D	S	G	A	B	C	D	

NAME	GAME TABLE	PLAY TIME	AVG BET	CASH BUY	CR	CHIP BUY	WIN	LOSS	COMMENTS

CUSTOMER NAME   TO   _____   A.B..A. | MARKER NUMBER |
_____   BANK

DATE _____ TIME _____   BRANCH   ACCOUNT NUMBER   DATE _____

GAME _____ SHIFT _____   CITY   STATE

TABLE _____   PAY TO THE
                                             ORDER OF $ _____
PIT _____
                                                                                                   U.S. DOLLARS

                                             I REPRESENT THAT I HAVE RECEIVED CASH FOR THE ABOVE AMOUNT AND THAT SAID AMOUNT IS ON DEPOSIT IN SAID FINANCIAL ENTITY
                                             IN MY NAME, IS FREE FROM CLAIMS AND IS SUBJECT TO THIS CHECK AND IS HEREBY ASSIGNED TO PAYEE AND GUARANTEE PAYMENT
SUPERVISOR   WITH EXCHANGE AND COSTS IN COLLECTING
_____

LOGO   ADDRESS _____   SIGNATURE _____

                                             CITY _____ STATE _____ ZIP CODE _____   PRINT NAME _____

LOGO		NUMBER OPTIONAL

COMPLIMENTARY SLIP

DATE: _____

NAME: _____

NO. in PARTY: _____

BUSINESS PURPOSE: _____

_____

AUTHORIZED SIGNATURE: _____

_____

NAME OF AUTHORIZER: _____

DEPARTMENT: _____

SPECIAL INSTRUCTIONS: _____

_____

_____

_____

_____

GRATUITIES NOT INCLUDED

CARD AND DICE PICKUP

LOGO   LOGO

SHIFT			PIT				DATE	
D	S	G	A	B	C	D		

BLACKJACK CARDS		POKER CARDS	
TABLE NUMBER	**DECKS**	**TABLE NUMBER**	**DECKS**

CARIBBEAN STUD CARDS		DICE	
TABLE NUMBER	**DECKS**	**TABLE NUMBER**	**SETS**

TOTALS	BLACKJACK	POKER	CS POKER	DICE

SECURITY		LIC. NO	
SUPERVISOR		LIC. NO	

1. SECURITY   2. CASINO   3. ACCOUNTING

CARD AND DICE DESTRUCTION

LOGO

LOGO

COLLECTION AUDIT			
BLACKJACK CARDS		**POKER CARDS**	
TOTAL ISSUED		TOTAL ISSUED	
TOTAL RETURNED		TOTAL RETURNED	
NET ISSUED		NET ISSUED	
TOTAL COLLECTED		TOTAL COLLECTED	
VARIANCE		VARIANCE	
CARIBBEAN STUD CARDS		**DICE SETS**	
TOTAL ISSUED		TOTAL ISSUED	
TOTAL RETURNED		TOTAL RETURNED	
NET ISSUED		NET ISSUED	
TOTAL COLLECTED		TOTAL COLLECTED	
VARIANCE		VARIANCE	

DESTRUCTION

TOTAL BJ DECKS		TOTAL POKER DECKS	
TOTAL CS POKER DECKS		TOTAL DICE SETS	

CERTIFIED BY:

1. SECURITY   2. CASINO   3. ACCOUNTING

ESTIMATED TABLE GAME WIN REPORT

LOGO   LOGO

SUPERVISOR:	DAY:	DATE:		

DAY SHIFT	CASH DROP	MARKERS	TOTAL DROP	WIN/LOSS	WIN %
BACCARAT					
BIG SIX					
BLACKJACK					
CARIB STUD					
CRAPS					
MINI-BACC					
PAI GOW PK					
POKER					
RED DOG					
ROULETTE					
SIC BO					
SUB TOTAL					
SWING SHIFT	CASH DROP	MARKERS	TOTAL DROP	WIN/LOSS	WIN %
BACCARAT					
BIG SIX					
BLACKJACK					
CARIB STUD					
CRAPS					
MINI-BACC					
PAI GOW PK					
POKER					
RED DOG					
ROULETTE					
SIC BO					
SUB TOTAL					
GRAVE SHIFT	CASH DROP	MARKERS	TOTAL DROP	WIN/LOSS	WIN %
BACCARAT					
BIG SIX					
BLACKJACK					
CARIB STUD					
CRAPS					
MINI-BACC					
PAI GOW PK					
POKER					
RED DOG					
ROULETTE					
SIC BO					
SUB TOTAL					
TOTAL					

PIT ACCOUNTING SHEET

SUPERVISOR	SHIFT			PIT				DATE
	D	S	G	A	B	C	D	

OPENER		OPENER		OPENER		OPENER		OPENER		OPENER	
FILLS	CREDITS	FILLS	CREDITS	FILLS	CREDITS	FILLS	CREDITS	FILLS	CREDITS	FILLS	CREDITS
CLOSER		CLOSER		CLOSER		CLOSER		CLOSER		CLOSER	

OPENER		OPENER		OPENER		OPENER		OPENER		OPENER	
FILLS	CREDITS	FILLS	CREDITS	FILLS	CREDITS	FILLS	CREDITS	FILLS	CREDITS	FILLS	CREDITS
CLOSER		CLOSER		CLOSER		CLOSER		CLOSER		CLOSER	

BACCARAT		BIG SIX		BLACKJACK		CARIBBEAN STUD		CRAPS		MINI-BACC	
OPENER		OPENER		OPENER		OPENER		OPENER		OPENER	
FILLS		FILLS		FILLS		FILLS		FILLS		FILLS	
CREDITS		CREDITS		CREDITS		CREDITS		CREDITS		CREDITS	
TOTAL		TOTAL		TOTAL		TOTAL		TOTAL		TOTAL	
CLOSER		CLOSER		CLOSER		CLOSER		CLOSER		CLOSER	
NEED		NEED		NEED		NEED		NEED		NEED	
CASH		CASH		CASH		CASH		CASH		CASH	
MARKERS		MARKERS		MARKERS		MARKERS		MARKERS		MARKERS	
T. DROP		T. DROP		T. DROP		T. DROP		T. DROP		T. DROP	
WIN		WIN		WIN		WIN		WIN		WIN	

ROULETTE										TOTAL	
OPENER		OPENER		OPENER		OPENER		OPENER		OPENER	
FILLS		FILLS		FILLS		FILLS		FILLS		FILLS	
CREDITS		CREDITS		CREDITS		CREDITS		CREDITS		CREDITS	
TOTAL		TOTAL		TOTAL		TOTAL		TOTAL		TOTAL	
CLOSER		CLOSER		CLOSER		CLOSER		CLOSER		CLOSER	
NEED		NEED		NEED		NEED		NEED		NEED	
CASH		CASH		CASH		CASH		CASH		CASH	
MARKERS		MARKERS		MARKERS		MARKERS		MARKERS		MARKERS	
T. DROP		T. DROP		T. DROP		T. DROP		T. DROP		T. DROP	
WIN		WIN		WIN		WIN		WIN		WIN	

PIT INVENTORY SHEET

LOGO   LOGO

SUPERVISOR		SHIFT			PIT				DATE
		D	S	G	A	B	C	D	

TABLE NUM.		TABLE NUM.		TABLE NUM.		TABLE NUM.	
$5,000.00		$5,000.00		$5,000.00		$5,000.00	
$1,000.00		$1,000.00		$1,000.00		$1,000.00	
$500.00		$500.00		$500.00		$500.00	
$100.00		$100.00		$100.00		$100.00	
$25.00		$25.00		$25.00		$25.00	
$5.00		$5.00		$5.00		$5.00	
$1.00		$1.00		$1.00		$1.00	
TOKENS $1		TOKENS $1		TOKENS $1		TOKENS $1	
TOTAL		TOTAL		TOTAL		TOTAL	

TABLE NUM.		TABLE NUM.		TABLE NUM.		TABLE NUM.	
$5,000.00		$5,000.00		$5,000.00		$5,000.00	
$1,000.00		$1,000.00		$1,000.00		$1,000.00	
$500.00		$500.00		$500.00		$500.00	
$100.00		$100.00		$100.00		$100.00	
$25.00		$25.00		$25.00		$25.00	
$5.00		$5.00		$5.00		$5.00	
$1.00		$1.00		$1.00		$1.00	
TOKENS $1		TOKENS $1		TOKENS $1		TOKENS $1	
TOTAL		TOTAL		TOTAL		TOTAL	

TABLE NUM.		TABLE NUM.		TABLE NUM.		TABLE NUM.	
$5,000.00		$5,000.00		$5,000.00		$5,000.00	
$1,000.00		$1,000.00		$1,000.00		$1,000.00	
$500.00		$500.00		$500.00		$500.00	
$100.00		$100.00		$100.00		$100.00	
$25.00		$25.00		$25.00		$25.00	
$5.00		$5.00		$5.00		$5.00	
$1.00		$1.00		$1.00		$1.00	
TOKENS $1		TOKENS $1		TOKENS $1		TOKENS $1	
TOTAL		TOTAL		TOTAL		TOTAL	

MULTIPLE TRANSACTION LOG

LOGO		PAGE NO.	OF

NAME		DATE

PIT/TABLE NO.	CAGE/WINDOW NO.	DATE

DESCRIPTION OF PATRON

SEX	RACE	HAIR	AGE	BUILD	HEIGHT	TRANS TYPE

TIME	EMPLOYEE SIGNATURE	AMOUNT	BALANCE FOWARD

APPROVAL NAME	AVERAGE BET

ADDITIONAL COMMENTS:

	CTR	YES	NO

RACE	HAIR	AGE	BUILD	HEIGHT
C--CAUCASIAN	1--BLACK	1 21-35	H--HEAVY	1--UNDER 5'6"
B--BLACK	2--BROWN	2 36-50	M--MEDIUM	2--5'6" TO 6'
O--ORIENTAL	3--BLOND	3 51-60	T--THIN	3--OVER 6'
H--HAWAIIAN	4--GRAY	4 65+		
S--SPANISH	5--RED			
I--INDIAN	6--THIN			
	7--BALD			

TRANSACTION TYPE		
1. CASH BUY-IN	5. MARKER REDEMPTION	9. CAGE MARKER
2. CHIP/TOKEN CASHOUT	6. TOKEN PURCHASE	10. MARKER ACTIVITY
3. DEPOSIT	7. COMCHECK	11. OTHER (SPECIFY IN COMMENTS SECTION)
4. WITHDRAWAL	8. OTHER CHECK CASHED	

1. ACCOUNTING   2. CAGE

CURRENCY TRANSACTION REPORT

LOGO

		CCTV NOTIFIED
PART I	**INDIVIDUAL FOR WHOM THIS TRANSACTION WAS COMPLETED**	☐ YES ☐ NO

LAST NAME	FIRST NAME	MIDDLE INITIAL	DATE	TIME

SOCIAL SECURITY NUMBER	CASINO ACCOUNT NUMBER		

ADDRESS (STREET)	CITY	STATE	ZIP CODE

TYPE OF IDENTIFICATION	IDENTIFIACTION NUMBER	BUSINESS/OCCUPATION

PART II	**AGENT CONDUCTING THE TRANSACTION FOR THE PERSON LIST IN PART I**

LAST NAME	FIRST NAME	MIDDLE INITIAL	DATE	TIME

SOCIAL SECURITY NUMBER	CASINO ACCOUNT NUMBER		

ADDRESS (STREET)	CITY	STATE	ZIP CODE

TYPE OF IDENTIFICATION	IDENTIFICATION NUMBER	BUSINESS/OCCUPATION

PART III	**PATRON'S ACCOUNT OR RECEIPT NUMBER**

ACCOUNT NUMBER	DEPOSIT RECEIPT NUMBER

PART IV	**TRANSACTION DESCRIPTION**

☐ CASH OUT	☐ BUY-IN	☐ DEPOSIT	☐ WITHDRAWAL	☐ OTHER	
PIT/TABLE NO.		BUY-IN AMOUNT		NUMBER OF $100'S	
CASINO CAGE		DOLLAR AMOUNT $		NUMBER OF $100'S	

OTHER CASH TRANSACTIONS

☐ CHECK TRANSACTION	☐ OTHER CASH (DESCRIBE BELOW)	☐ OTHER CASHOUT (DESCRIBE BELOW)

IF A CHECK WAS INVOLVED IN THIS TRANSACTION PLEASE FURNISH THE FOLLOWING INFORMATION:

DATE OF CHECK	AMOUNT OF CHECK $	PAYEE OF CHECK
MAKER OF CHECK		DRAWEE BANK AND CITY

DESCRIPTION/COMMENTS:

PART V	**CASINO REPORTING THE FINANCIAL TRANSACTION**

NAME	IDENTIFYING NUMBER (EIN)	

NUMBER AND STREET	CITY	STATE	ZIP CODE

	(Casino Employee Who Handled The Transaction)	TITLE	DATE
SIGN HERE	(Casino Official Reviewing And Approving The Form Number _____)	TITLE	DATE

1. ACCOUNTING   2. ORIGINATING DEPARTMENT   3. MISCELLANEOUS

CURRENCY TRANSACTION REFUSAL FORM

CCTV NOTIFIED
☐ YES ☐ NO

NAME	ACCOUNT NUMBER	DATE	TIME	PIT

On this date, I approached the above-named patron and asked for his/her social security number, driver's license, and/or other identification.

The patron refused to give this information. So, at that time, I informed the patron that he/she was not permitted to play until we received the required identification information.

DESCRIPTION OF PATRON

SEX	RACE	HAIR	AGE	BUILD	HEIGHT	TRANS TYPE

RACE	HAIR	AGE	BUILD	HEIGHT	TRANSACTION TYPE
C--CAUCASIAN	1--BLACK	1 21-35	H--HEAVY	1--UNDER 5'6"	1--BUY-IN
B--BLACK	2--BROWN	2 36-50	M--MEDIUM	2--5'6"-6'	2--CASHOUT
O--ORIENTAL	3--BLOND	3 51-60	T--THIN	3--OVER 6'	3--OTHER (DESCRIBE BELOW)
H--HAWAIIAN	4--GRAY	4 65+			
S--SPANISH	5--RED				
I--INDIAN	6--THIN				
	7--BALD				

TRANSACTION DESCRIPTION

☐ CASH OUT ☐ BUY-IN ☐ DEPOSIT ☐ WITHDRAWAL ☐ OTHER

PIT/TABLE NO.	BUY-IN ACCOUNT $	NUMBER OF HUNDREDS
CASINO CAGE	DOLLAR AMOUNT $	NUMBER OF HUNDREDS

OTHER TRANSACTIONS

☐ CHECK TRANSACTION   ☐ OTHER CASH-IN (DESCRIBE BELOW)   ☐ OTHER CASH-OUT (DESCRIBE BELOW)

IF A CHECK WAS INVOLVED IN THIS TRANSACTION, PLEASE FURNISH THE FOLLOWING INFORMATION:

DATE OF CHECK	AMOUNT OF CHECK $	PAYEE OF CHECK
MAKER OF CHECK		DRAWEE BANK AND CITY

COMMENTS/ADDITIONAL DESCRIPTION: (ATTACH CCTV PHOTO)

NAME (PLEASE PRINT) _____

POSITION _____

SIGNATURE _____

LOGO

1. ACCOUNTING   2. ORIGINATING DEPARTMENT   3. MISCELLANEOUS

SLOT DEPARTMENT

SLOT MACHINE CHANGE FORM

LOGO

THESE CHANGES MUST BE SENT TO THE COMPUTER OPERATOR PRIOR TO THE COMPLETION OF THE CHANGES

* NEW MACHINE PLACED IN SERVICE -- COMPLETE THE INFORMATION BELOW

* MACHINE BEING MOVED TO NEW LOCATION

* MACHINE BEING REMOVED FROM THE CASINO FLOOR

* DENOMINATION CHANGE (Treat original machine number as having been removed from the floor as above. Two forms will be required.)

INFORMATION CATEGORY	DATA	INFORMATION AND COMMENTS
1. SLOT NUMBER		
2. DENOMINATION		
3. TYPE NUMBER		
4. DIVERTER		
5. DCU NUMBER		
6. BOX NUMBER		
7. SECTION		
8. ROW		
9. LOCATION		
10. HOLD PERCENTAGE		
11. HOPPER MAXIMUM		
12. FILL OK		
13. SERIAL NUMBER		
14. ON FLOOR DATE		
15. OFF FLOOR DATE		
16. IN METER		
17. OUT METER		
18. DROP METER		

DATE:	PREPARED BY:
	APPROVED BY:
	(SLOT MANAGER)

MALFUNCTION LOG

LOGO

DATE	TIME	LOCATION NUMBER	ASSET NUMBER	DESCRIPTION OF PROBLEM	ATTENDANT'S SIGNATURE/LICENSE	TECHNICIAN'S SIGNATURE/LICENSE

LOGO DENOMINATION CHANGE FORM

LOCATION	OLD DENOMINATION
ASSET	NEW DENOMINATION

CHECKLIST	X
TAKE SNAP OF EDT METERS AND RECORD	
CHANGE COIN HEAD	
ADJUST COIN ASSEMBLY, MOVE ACCEPTOR CLIPS, SHIFT LEFT OR RIGHT, CHANGE ENCODER INSERT	
CHANGE HOPPER PIN WHEEL, SHELF WHEEL, KNIFE, PROBE LEVEL	
CHANGE PROGRAM CHIPS	
CHANGE DIP SWITCHES	
SET MACHINE PAY, PARTIAL PAY, DENOMINATION IN SOFTWARE	
IGB KOBOTRON RESEAL CHIPS & BOARD	
CHANGE ALL DENOMINATION, MAX PAY AND PARTIAL PAY SIGNAGE	
CHANGE TOWER LIGHT COLOR	
MAKE CHANGES IN EDT SYSTEM	
E DENOMINATION	
D TYPE CODE	
T PERCENTAGE OF HOLD	
COIN TEST	

LOGO

EDT ADDRESSES CHANGING FORM

LOCATION		OLD DENOMINATION	
ASSET		NEW DENOMINATION	
DCU		BOX	
DCU		BOX	

CHECKLIST		X
DISCONNECT FOUR WIRE DATA CONNECTORS ON PT		
SET NEW ADDRESS ON DIP SWITCHES USING (N-1) LOGIC. (SET SWITCHES TO THE NUMBER YOU WANT MINUS ONE)		
SHORT RESET PINS TOGETHER TO REINITIALIZE PT		
MAKE CHANGES IN THE EDT SYSTEM, FEC, SECURITY STATIONS, AND BANK STATION MUST BE TAKEN TO LOGO AND BROUGHT BACK UP FOR CHANGES TO TAKE EFFECT		
CONNECT FOUR WIRE DATA CONNECTORS		
USING LAPTOP VERIFY THAT METERS ARE UNCHANGED. IF THEY HAVE CHANGED, DUMP OLD VALUES BACK INTO PT		
TAKE EDT METER READINGS AND RECORD		
E	COIN-IN	
D	COIN-OUT	
T	DROP	

MACHINE SWITCH FORM

LOGO

LOCATION			OLD ASSET		NEW ASSET		NEW MODEL	
ADDRESS	DCU		BOX		METERS	COIN-IN	COIN-OUT	DROP

PROCEDURE	INITIAL	DATE	TIME
SNAP (LAPTOP)			
EMPTY HOPPER			
REMOVE DROP FLOOR			
UNBOLT AND LIFT WIRING UP			
REMOVE PT-95 AND HARNESS			
REMOVE LOCKS			
REMOVE MACHINE			
POSITION & BOLT NEW MACHINE			
RUN NEW WIRING			
DROP FLOOR IN (TAPE, TIE, AND GLUE)			
ATTACH MACHINE TO WALL			
INSTALL LOCKS (DOORS AND CPU)			
SET PT-95 ADDRESS			
LOCATION AND ASSET NUMBERS			
DROP BUCKET NUMBERS			
DUMP METERS (LAPTOP)			
FILL HOPPER			
IGB KOBOTRON EPROMS			
IGB SEAL BOARD			
CHANGE EDT (COMPUTER SYSTEM)			
COIN TEST			

REQUEST FOR JACKPOT OR HOPPER FILL

LOGO

☐ HOPPER FILL   ☐ CREDIT METER   ☐ DOUBLE JACKPOT PAYOUT   ☐ JACKPOT PAYOUT

DATE	TIME	SHIFT
		D S G

LOCATION	MACHINE NUMBER

DENOMINATION							
0.05	0.25	0.5	$1	$5	$25	$50	$100

NUMBER OF COINS PLAYED

NUMBER OF LINES PLAYED

COMBINATION

TOTAL PAID BY MACHINE

TOTAL JACKPOT

TOTAL PAID BY ATTENDANT

CREDIT METER PAY

PREPARED BY:	LIC. NO.

1. CAGE   2. SLOT DEPARTMENT   3. ACCOUNTING

LOGO

JACKPOT & HOPPER SLIP

DATE	TIME	DENOMINATION
SLOT MACHINE NUMBER	ASSET NUMBER	COINS PLAYED

JACKPOT

PAYOFF LINE	1ST		2ND		3RD		4TH		5TH		6TH	

COMBINATION

AMOUNT PAID	PRINT DOLLAR AMOUNT HERE
$	$ DOLLARS

PRINT AMOUNT

$5,000 & ABOVE		APPROVAL TO PAY		WITHHOLD PAY

HOPPER FILL

AMOUNT FILLED	PRINT DOLLAR AMOUNT HERE
$	$ DOLLARS

PRINT AMOUNT

- ☐ $50 IN NICKELS
- ☐ $200 IN QUARTERS
- ☐ $300 IN 50 CENTS
- ☐ $300 IN DOLLARS
- ☐ $1000 IN $5 TOKENS
- ☐ $2500 IN $25 TOKENS
- ☐ $5000 IN $50 TOKENS
- ☐ $5000 IN $100 TOKENS

CASHIER	LIC. NO.
SLOT ATTENDANT	LIC. NO.
SLOT SHIFT MANAGER	LIC. NO.
SECURITY	LIC. NO

1. CASHIER   2. SECURITY   3. ACCOUNTING

CASINO CAGE FORMS

COUNT SHEET SUPPLEMENT

LOGO

DATE		SHIFT		TIME		LOCATION	
		D S G					

CURRENCY

	BUNDLED	STRAPPED	CLIPPED	LOOSE	TOTAL
$100					
$50					
$20					
$10					
$5					
$2					
$1					
TOTAL					

US COIN

	BOXED	RACKED	BAGGED	LOOSE	TOTAL
0.50					
0.25					
0.10					
0.05					
0.01					
TOTAL					

TOKENS

	BOXED	RACKED	BAGGED	LOOSE	TOTAL
$100					
$25					
$5					
$1					
$.25					
TOTAL					

CHIPS

	RESERVE	FULL	LOOSE	NON VALUE	TOTAL
$5000					
$1000					
$500					
$100					
$25					
$5					
$2.50					
$1					
TOTAL					

COUNT SHEET

LOGO

DATE	SHIFT			TIME	LOCATION
	D	S	G		

CURRENCY		
	$100.00	$
	$50.00	$
	$20.00	$
	$10.00	$
	$5.00	$
	$2.00	$
	$1.00	$
US COIN	0.50	$
	0.25	$
	0.10	$
	0.05	$
	0.01	$

CHIPS	
$500.00	$
$100.00	$
$25.00	$
$5.00	$
$2.50	$
$1.00	$

TOKENS	
$100.00	$
$25.00	$
$5.00	$
$1.00	$
0.50	$
0.25	$

MISCELLANEOUS	
	$
	$
DEPOSIT TOTAL	$
TOTAL	$
OPENING INVENTORY	$
OVERAGE/SHORTAGE	$

SIGNATURE/LIC NO	SIGNATURE/LIC NO
1. LOCATION	2. SUPERVISOR

TRANSFER SLIP

LOGO

FROM: TO:

DATE	SHIFT			TIME
	D	S	G	

CURRENCY
- $100
- $50
- $20
- $10
- $5
- $1
- CHANGE

CHIPS
- $5000.00
- $1000.00
- $500.00
- $100.00
- $25.00
- $5.00
- $2.50
- $1.00

TOKENS
- $100.00
- $25.00
- $5.00
- $1.00
- $.50
- $.25

TOTAL >

EMPLOYEE ISSUING

EMPLOYEE RECEIVING

VERIFICATION

1. ISSUING 2. RECEIVING 3. ISSUING

MARKER TRANSFER SLIP

LOGO

SHIFT	DATE	GAME	PIT TABLE

CUSTOMER NAME

MARKER NUMBER

MARKER AMOUNT (NUMERIC)

MARKER AMOUNT (PRINTED)

CASHIER SIGNATURE — LIC. NO.

SECURITY SIGNATURE — LIC. NO.

DEALER SIGNATURE — LIC. NO.

SUPERVISOR SIGNATURE — LIC. NO.

MT-000000

1. CASHIER 2. DROP BOX 3. ACCOUNTING 4. MARKER BANK

LOGO	OVER/SHORT SLIP	DATE		
		SHIFT		
			D S G	

CASHIER	$
WINDOW/LOCKER	
CASHIER SIGNATURE	
SUPERVISOR SIGNATURE	

WHITE - ACCOUNTING   YELLOW - CAGE   PINK - CASHIER

LOGO	CAGE PAID OUT	DATE
		NUMBER
		PO – 00000

PAID OUT TO: _____ $ _____

_____ DOLLARS

REASON _____   AUTHORIZED BY _____

_____

_____   PAID BY _____

_____

MAIN BANK SETTLEMENT SHEET

LOGO

DATE		SHIFT			
			D	S	G

OUTGOING	INCOMING
PREPARED BY	**SHIFT MANAGER**

ACCOUNTABILITY

#								
1	OPENING BALANCE							

ADDITIONS

#								
2	CASH FROM GEN CASHIER							
3	COIN FROM HARD COUNT							
4	LOCKER TRANS ISSUED							
5	TABLE CREDITS							
6	EMPLOYEE GRATUITY							
7	W2G WITHHOLDING							
8	JACKPOT CHECKS							
9	FOUND MONEY							
10	POKER JACKPOT-STUD							
11	POKER							
12	OTHER							
13	TRANS FROM MARKER BK							
14								
15								
16								
17								
18								
19								
20								
21								

SUBTRACTIONS

#								
22	DEPOSITS TO G. CASHIER							
23	DEPOSITS TO H. COUNT							
24	CHANGE DEPOSITS							
25	CAGE PAID OUTS							
26	TABLE FILLS							
27	JACKPOTS							
28	HOPPER FILLS							
29	WINDOW VARIANCES							
30	LOCKER TRANS FILLED							
31	OTHER							
32	TRANS TO MARKER BANK							
	TOTAL ACCOUNTABILITY							

INVENTORY

#								
33	CURRENCY							
34	FOREIGN CURRENCY							
35	US COIN							
36	TOKENS							
37	CHIPS							
38	CHECKS							
39	JET SORT							
40	OTHER							
41	COIN ROOM							
42	BANK 1/WINDOW 1							
43	BANK 1/WINDOW 2							
44	BANK 1/WINDOW 3							
45	BANK 1/RELIEF							
46	BANK 2/WINDOW 1							
47	BANK 2/WINDOW 2							
48	BANK 2/WINDOW 3							
49	BANK 2/RELIEF							
50	BANK 3/WINDOW 1							
51	BANK 3/WINDOW 2							
52	BANK 3/WINDOW 3							
53	BANK 3/RELIEF							
54	CHANGE BOOTH 1							
55	CHANGE BOOTH 2							
56	CHANGE BOOTH 3							
57	CHANGE BOOTH 4							
58	CHANGE PEOPLE OUT							
59	LOCKERS							
	TOTAL CASH INVENTORY							
	LESS: ACCOUNTABILITY							
	CASH OVER (SHORT)							

1. INCOME AUDIT   2. CAGE COPY